toward

a

democracy

**A BRIEF INTRODUCTION
TO AMERICAN GOVERNMENT**

toward

a

democracy

A BRIEF INTRODUCTION
TO AMERICAN GOVERNMENT

LOUIS W. KOENIG
NEW YORK UNIVERSITY

HARCOURT BRACE JOVANOVICH, INC.
NEW YORK   CHICAGO   SAN FRANCISCO   ATLANTA

ISBN: 0–15–592183–5

Library of Congress Catalog Card Number: 72–94551

Printed in the United States of America

Cover: Paper sculpture by Benedict Umy

Illustration credits

TABLES AND FIGURES

p. 8: Table reprinted from "The Modes of Democratic Participation: A Cross-National Comparison," by Sidney Verba, Norman H. Nie, and Jae-on Kim, Sage Professional Papers in Comparative Politics, Volume 2, Number 01-013, p. 20, by permission of the Publisher, Sage Publications, Inc., and the senior author. **33, 47:** From *Public Opinion and American Democracy,* by V. O. Key, Jr. Copyright © 1961 by V. O. Key, Jr. Reprinted by permission of Alfred A. Knopf, Inc. **161:** © The Washington Post. **201, 406:** © 1971–72 by The New York Times Company. Reprinted by permission. **279:** From *The Legislative Process in the United States,* by Malcolm E. Jewell and Samuel C. Patterson. Copyright © 1966 by Random House, Inc. Reprinted by permission of the publisher. **417:** From Ralph M. Kramer, *Participation of the Poor: Comparative Community Case Studies in the War on Poverty* © 1969. Reprinted by permission of Prentice-Hall, Inc., Englewood Cliffs, New Jersey. **462:** Table adapted from *The Politics of Consumer Protection* by Mark V. Nadel, copyright © 1971, by the Bobbs-Merrill Company, Inc., used by permission of the publisher.

PHOTO CREDITS

p. 2, Alan E. Cober; **10,** Charles Gatewood from Magnum; **14,** Charles Gatewood, **23,** United Press International; **35,** Charles Gatewood; **38, 39,** Wide World; **46,** Charles Gatewood; **52,** United Press International; **64,** Worcester Art Museum; **65,** Library of Congress; **68,** The Metropolitan Museum of Art, The Michael Friedsan Collection 1931; Culver Pictures; **69,** Culver Pictures; **76,** two by Culver pictures; two by Library of Congress; **101,** Medical Committee for Human Rights; **102, 104,** United Press International; **119,** Joel Gordon; **131,** AFL-CIO; **132,** The New York Times; **134,** United Press International; **135,** AFL-CIO; **139,** United Press International; **152,** Charles Gatewood; **157,** United Press International; **160,** Wide World; **170,** Virginia Hamilton; **176,** The New York Times; **182,** Charles Gatewood; **185,** United Press International; **190, 191,** The New York Times; **197, 208,** Library of Congress; **217,** Wide World; **218,** White House Photo; **219,** United Press International; **227, 229, 234,** White House Photo; **241,** © 1972 by The New York Times Company; reprinted by permission; **253,** Wide World; **259,** White House Photo; **262,** United Press International; **292,** Cornell Capa from Magnum; **294,** White House Photo; **296,** Wide World; **310, 316,** United Press International; **323,** Joel Gordon; **328,** Photo Trends; **330,** The New York Post; **337,** Wide World; **345, 350,** United Press International; **353,** Wide World; **359,** United Press International; **360,** Bruce Davidson from Magnum; **363,** Wide World; **384,** Courtesy of Hill, Holliday, Connors, Cosmopulos, Inc.; **387, 395, 397,** United Press International; **425,** White House Photo; **429,** United Nations; **444,** J. P. Laffont from Gamma; **446,** Philip Jones Griffiths from Magnum; **456,** Joel Gordon; **463,** New York State Department of Health; **467,** Tony Spina from the Detroit Free Press; **471,** Long Island Press.

preface

Democracy is being seriously questioned in many quarters of American society, particularly among the young. There is a steady pall of pessimism. American democracy seems to respond only inadequately to the demands on it. Instead of a good society of peace and general well-being, there is lengthy or recurrent war, the threat of curtailed civil liberties, and the confinement of far too many people to a shabby life that contrasts sharply with the nation's resources and potential. Inevitably, the quality of our political institutions and their ability to do good works become suspect.

Although these matters are the central concern of this book, its mood and direction are not pessimistic. Nor is it a call to revolution. Rather, it assumes that the processes and institutions of American democracy can be made to function better, if we seek to understand them and the causes of their flawed performance. Further, we can weigh proposals, which are in good supply, to make the democratic system function more effectively, to promote the general welfare in the most literal sense.

These objectives provide both the framework and the approach of this book. The institutions and processes of American government are examined in the light of their democratic ideals. Then they are examined in terms of how short they fall of their ideals. Specific proposals are addressed to these weaknesses.

As is appropriate for democracy, which values every individual, this book is not confined to observing elite decision-makers, but devotes considerable attention to nonelites, such as blacks, women, the young, and how they can improve their political effectiveness. The book is also attentive to contemporary issues and political movements that can do much to shape future American society. Prominent among these are the environmental and consumer movements, minority civil rights movements, and the major transformations taking place within the parties of the seventies.

I found that the most serviceable approach to this very practical task of understanding and improving American democracy combines traditional political science analysis with some behavioral analysis. Consequently, the discussion draws on psychological and sociological findings at points where they can enlarge understanding of American political processes. At no point, however, is the discussion subordinated to the demands of an exclusively behavioral approach. Since the emphasis is on the contemporary American political system, historical references are made only when clearly necessary.

This book attempts to present American government within a brief compass. It examines the essentials of the political system, conveyed through basic concepts, legal framework, key problems, and illustrative situations, with the expectation that the student who is interested will move on to more specialized studies that examine particular aspects of the system more fully.

Some of these further studies and the nature of their usefulness are suggested at the close of each chapter.

It is a pleasure to acknowledge the valuable contribution of many scholars who read portions of the manuscript and made suggestions. These include: Joel D. Aberbach, University of Michigan; Charles R. Adrian, University of California, Riverside; James David Barber, Duke University; Lewis Coser, State University of New York, Stony Brook; Thomas E. Cronin, The Brookings Institution; John T. Elliff, Barnard College; Sheldon Goldman, University of Massachusetts; Stanley Greenberg, Yale University; Fred I. Greenstein, Wesleyan University; John D. Montgomery, Harvard University; Gary Orfield, Princeton University; Benjamin I. Page, Dartmouth College; Frances Fox Piven, Columbia University School of Social Work; Randall B. Ripley, Ohio State University; Robert Salisbury, Washington University; Allan P. Sindler, University of California, Berkeley; Alan F. Westin, Columbia University; Peter Woll, Brandeis University. Chapter 1 was presented to a colloquium of the Department of Politics at New York University, and I benefited from the fruitful suggestions of my colleagues. To all these reviewers I am most grateful, while also acknowledging that responsibility for judgments expressed in these pages and for whatever shortcomings may remain rest with me.

Finally, this book has been fortunate in having many friends at Harcourt Brace Jovanovich who contributed their skills to its development. Whether as a book or as a vision of American society, each advance *Toward A Democracy* requires many good hands.

LOUIS W. KOENIG

contents

1

democratic

man

In his utopian novel, *Walden Two,*[1] psychologist B. F. Skinner depicts how the controlled environment of a society can enhance its well-being. "Behavioral engineering," or the application of reason and science to all activity, including the achievement of society's purposes, would eliminate fatiguing, uninteresting work and would release energies for the arts, science, play, the satisfaction of curiosity, the conquest of nature, the conquest of self (never of others). In *Walden,* society does not make or exploit war, personal jealousy is "almost unknown," and unnecessary possessions are avoided, although an exceptionally high living standard is enjoyed. Destructive, wasteful emotions —sorrow, hate, anger, fear, rage—being "out of proportion with the needs of modern life," are "trained out." No one is necessary to anyone else, no one is imposed on.

Is democratic man
obsolete?

In *Walden,* planning ("behavioral engineering") is the key to societal bliss. Democracy and freedom, as we know them, do not exist. Government is monopolized by a "Board of Planners" whose policies are put into operation by "Managers." Members of the community have no voice in affairs, nor do they wish to have. Everyone *feels* free because he is doing what he wants to do, and not what he is forced to do, a happy state induced by control of the inclination to behave—motives, desires, wishes—rather than the final behavior. Through the manipulation of psychological techniques, behavioral engineering conditions man for harmonious group living and achieves a universally observed code of behavior, guaranteeing the community's success.

The enemy of this utopia of controlled behavior is democracy's hero—autonomous man. He is the individual who derives his freedom from nature and therefore possesses an innate dignity that transcends society's regulation of his behavior. He has his own life to live and must not let others live it for him, nor let them manipulate it. He is capable of making his own decisions, is responsible, and assumes duties and obligations, including the defense of

[1] B. F. Skinner, *Walden Two* (New York: Macmillan, 1948).

1

*B. F. Skinner depicted in a
"controlled environment."*

his freedom. Much of his behavior is self-regulated or regulated by non-governmental sources—conscience, folkways, customs. The concept of democratic man embraces all human beings, regardless of education, social status, and economic level.

Democratic man restricts government to a demarcated sphere and enumerates and protects his freedoms in an effective constitution. He participates in the governmental process; he, better than anyone, can evaluate governmental activities because he lives with them. In the view of this autonomous democratic man, government is not a fit monopoly for experts and specialists, including *Walden's* behavioral manipulators. The democratic rationale affirms that broad issues are at the heart of government and that to them every man and woman, no matter how "ordinary" in knowledge and background, can contribute a precious "common sense" or sound judgment, often more readily than it is found in the dispensations of the experts.[2]

In his 1971 study, *Beyond Freedom and Dignity,* Skinner remains unimpressed by autonomous man and his democratic justification. "His abolition has long been overdue," he writes. "He has been constructed from our ignorance, and as our understanding increases, the very stuff of which he is

[2] A. D. Lindsay, *The Modern Democratic State* (London: Oxford University Press, 1943), Vol. 1, 267–69.

composed vanishes." [3] Skinner persists in his proposal to strip away the functions assigned to autonomous man and transfer them to the controllers of the environment. He attributes man's historic struggle for freedom not to a will to be free, but to behavioral processes characteristic of the human organism that have the goal of avoidance or escape from "aversive" (unpleasant, hurtful) features of the environment. A self is therefore a repertoire of behavior appropriate to a given set of contingencies. Man's dignity, prized in democratic theory, would be provided for in the controlled environment by "positive reinforcers," rewards or expressions of approval, such as the "bravo" or "encore" that we shout at a performing artist. The manipulators of man's environment, whom democracy would darkly regard as dangerous, potential tyrants, Skinner confidently views as safely controllable by contingencies. Unfortunately, a glance about the world does not confirm Skinner's view that tyrants and despots are with us any less than when the older literature of democracy warned against them.

Other assessments consign autonomous, democratic man to doom. Society's most potent trends, it is contended, move against him. Power in society is subject increasingly to specialization of function, and leadership and decision-making belong less to prudence and common sense than to expertise. Man is likened to a pebble on a beach in a mass society denoted by megalopolitan areas, intricate technology, mass media, and gigantic industries.

Even so, many remain optimistic about the future of autonomous, democratic man. Technology is not an unmitigated burden. It has expanded the range of his choices and enhanced his mobility on the social ladder and between occupations. If large organizations become threatening, he can structure them in smaller units, with greater allotments of independence. Instead of throwing up his arms in abject surrender to experts and environmental controllers, autonomous man, as David Riesman has suggested,[4] can improve himself in quality and effectiveness: he can use education to develop the skills he wants to acquire; he can become more highly motivated concerning self-selected goals, more capable of enlarging his life experiences in a rich culture providing a multiplicity of choices. Autonomous man is alive and well, and he will flourish even more through increases of real freedom—through enlargement of his capabilities and concrete opportunities.

The nature of democratic man

Who is this allegedly anachronistic figure, democratic man? For one thing, he was not created at some single moment in time. Over long centuries many persons and institutions have contributed thought and practice toward his

---

[3] B. F. Skinner, *Beyond Freedom and Dignity* (New York: Knopf, 1971), 200.
[4] David Riesman, *The Lonely Crowd* (New York: Doubleday, Anchor Books, 1953), 346–50.

development. One of the earliest contributors was the small city-state of Athens where citizens themselves, or a large portion of them, made decisions directly. "Our constitution," said Pericles, "is named a democracy, because it is in the hands not of the few but of the many." Aristotle justified the arrangement in contending that many heads are wiser than one, that the majority is more likely to be right. (Later, he viewed democracy less admiringly when the majority included "men of low birth, no property, and vulgar employments.") Rome contributed a key element to democracy, the gift of universalist thinking, expressed in a concept of citizenship that embraced all as equal under the law, regardless of individual power and wealth. Western religions provided an even greater universality: "There is neither Greek nor Jew, . . . Barbarian, Scythian, bond nor free" (Col. 3:11).

In America, democracy is deeply rooted in the Anglo-Saxon tradition of Protestantism in religion and parliamentarianism in politics, both of which value liberty, freedom of choice, and human diversity—in ideas, aspirations, and talents. Doubtless, the most influential of English political writers on American practice was John Locke, whose work inspired Thomas Jefferson in composing the Declaration of Independence. Locke discerned the superiority of "natural rights" over arbitrary government. These rights, with which everyone is born, include the rights to life, liberty, and property. They are primordial rights, existing before the creation of government, and "unalienable," as Jefferson stated in the Declaration of Independence, since they are part of the laws of the universe.

A lengthy parade of American political thinkers and practitioners have contributed to democracy. James Madison previsioned present-day democracy in his ideal of a political system contested for by many economic and social groups and perpetuated through restraint and balance in the contest. Andrew Jackson brought the word "democratic" into respectable usage—"Let the people rule" became his motto. In *Democracy in America* (1835) the French nobleman Alexis de Tocqueville praised the American experiment in promoting the people's identification with their government as a masterstroke for gaining political stability. In his *Democratic Vistas,* Walt Whitman hailed democracy as embracing "the highest forms of interaction between men," and for serving as a training ground "for making first-class men." [5]

Liberty and equality. If one were forced to utter a single word most descriptive of democracy, that word, most likely, would be "freedom" or "liberty." Liberty has been defined as "the absence of restraint" and "free choice, each individual's own decision concerning his course of action." [6] Democracy acknowledges and safeguards liberty.

There are many kinds of liberties, not all of equal importance. A central ideal of democracy—the assertion of popular control over government— requires certain political liberties: the freedom to speak, assemble, petition, vote, and run for office. Such freedoms interlock. Voting cannot be effective

[5] Saul K. Padover, *The Meaning of Democracy* (New York: Praeger, 1963), 20–27.
[6] Massimo Salvadori, *Liberal Democracy* (New York: Doubleday, 1957), 21.

without free choice. There cannot be free choice without the freedom to organize and express opposing opinions, including the promotion of candidates and their party's platform. Generally, economic liberties are more fit for regulation and restraint than political liberties. Economic liberties have become relative because of society's complex economic interdependence, which necessitates the regulation of individuals and organizations.

The closest to absolute liberties are liberties of the mind, for these, unlike others, are not intrinsically hampered by the exercise of the same kinds of liberties by other persons. Furthermore, liberties of the mind and their external expression (freedom of speech) are functionally necessary for attaining truth. That purpose, rather than to give vent to whatever fulminations spring from the larynx, is the justification for freedom of speech. "The ability to raise searching difficulties on both sides of a subject," wrote Aristotle, "will make us detect more easily the truth and error about the several points that arise." But freedom of speech, although more protected than economic liberties, is not an absolute liberty. There can be no right, as Justice Oliver Wendell Holmes asserted, to falsely cry "fire" in a crowded theater.[7]

Is equality necessary for democracy? Our answer differs, depending on whether we are talking in political, economic, or social terms. Democracy affirms the principle of political equality and institutionalizes it in voting. Equal political rights, however, do not mean equality of political power. Some persons in a democracy enjoy superior impact, skill, and resources. Democracy does not aspire to the impossible by indulging in the fantasy of making all men equal in skill, intelligence, position, or authority. Nor is equality necessarily prized for itself. If all men were equally poor or ill, nothing meaningful would be gained. But democracy, as it matures, will promote equality of opportunity, and it may foster social equality in setting minimum standards of health care, housing, nutrition, and the like—in effect, levels below which no citizen will be allowed to sink.[8]

Principles and institutions. Democracy consists of a body of principles that have been institutionalized; that is, they have been given an enduring character in law and practice and, therefore, a measure of protection from any hostile whim of the moment. The following are the chief of these principles:

• Democracy is "rule by the people." The "people" is an inclusive entity, well expressed by the concept of universal suffrage. In a sizable state, "rule" does not mean that the people "govern." Instead, they determine who shall govern and, broadly, to what ends. "Rule," in that case, refers to popular control of policy-makers, asserted through periodic elections. Popular influence over policies is asserted continuously through a variety of means, including the pressure groups that abound in the United States.

• Popular control gains effectiveness from various political freedoms.

[7] Robert M. MacIver, *The Ramparts We Guard* (New York: Macmillan, 1950), 19–20; Walter Lippmann, *The Public Philosophy* (Boston: Little, Brown, 1955), 125. Concerning Holmes, see *Schenck v. United States,* 249 U.S. 47 (1919).

[8] MacIver, 14; Yves R. Simon, *Philosophy of Democratic Government* (Chicago: University of Chicago Press, 1951), 197.

Ideally, the voter makes a free choice, untrammeled by fraud and intimidation, between rival candidates who come forward freely. Popular control requires a variety of other freedoms—speech, press, assembly, petition, and association. While the elected representatives govern, political opposition is tolerated and accepted, and minorities are free to criticize and agitate.

• When representatives are divided, the will of the majority prevails. Presumably, the representatives have been chosen by a majority of the voters; hence determinations by the legislature are as legitimate as those made by a majority of the voters. Majorities, whether of citizens or representatives, act within the framework of political freedoms. Opponents may be compelled to obey the law, but not silenced or deprived of their political liberties. The minority of representatives and their adherents may work to win further converts to their views, to become a majority eventually and replace the incumbent policy-makers.[9]

• Modern liberal democracy stresses "fraternity." We treat others not simply as persons with rights equal to ours, but with concern for their welfare —what John Stuart Mill spoke of as "benevolence" and the "social feelings of mankind." The older or classical democratic theory is atomistic, stressing rights to the neglect of duties and obligation, individual indulgence at the expense of society, competition at the expense of cooperation.[10]

• Democracy is not a creed—a fixed, detailed body of beliefs and purposes. Essentially, democracy is a method, a way of arriving at political decisions, to which all goals are subordinated. The dominance of methods over goals goes far to assure that changes in office-holders and the structure of power will be accomplished peacefully.[11]

Environmental conditions. Democracy is a fragile plant. Historically, it has seemed to thrive only in propitious environments where certain conditions exist, but these conditions do not have such precision or common incidence that we can predict with assurance whether or when democracy will blossom in a given society. One nourishing condition is universal education, to which American democracy has long been committed. The general availability of education is a way to economic opportunity, social mobility, and a more competent electorate.

Democratic man functions better if he lives in a thriving, productive economy, rather than in harsh poverty. In a study of many societies, sociologist Seymour Martin Lipset found that average wealth and degree of industrialization are much higher for the more democratic countries than for the less democratic and the nondemocratic. Historian David Potter and others place great weight on America's extraordinary expansion in the nineteenth

---

[9] These principles are adapted from Henry B. Mayo, *An Introduction to Democratic Theory* (New York: Oxford University Press, 1960), 61–69.

[10] J. Roland Pennock, *Liberal Democracy* (New York: Holt, Rinehart and Winston, 1950), 16.

[11] Mayo, 277; Charles Frankel, *The Democratic Prospect* (New York: Harper & Row, 1962), 167.

century, which produced a higher living standard and renewed faith in "progress," leading, in turn, to a broadened franchise and strengthened political liberties. A mark of democratic industrial societies, and especially of the United States, is social mobility—the free access to the upper classes. The stratified structure of poorer societies resembles a pyramid with a large lower class base; the United States class structure resembles a diamond because of its substantial middle class. A valued component of democracy, the middle class moderates conflict and blunts extremist pressures.[12]

The political life of democratic man

Participation. The Declaration of Independence assumes that "all men" will be political participants. Despite the disparagement of participation that is sometimes fashionable, it is clear that in the United States today and in certain other countries, participation has soared to new levels of effectiveness. A larger proportion of society than ever before can influence and shape their immediate environments. More pressure groups are better organized and more effective, and the news coverage of television provides an access for the protesting individual, the group, the neighborhood, those with grievances and little power, to a degree unknown for other media. "Participatory democracy" has become a slogan and a rallying cry in the civil rights movement in the 1960s, in the war on poverty, and in student politics. When exercise of the traditional democratic liberties appeared to be inadequate, participatory democracy emerged, entrusting the power to make decisions to the people whom public programs were supposed to help. In this manner the poverty program has involved poor people and their neighborhoods in decision-making, on the theory that they could better represent their needs and preferences than the middle-class-oriented civil service.

The numbers of people who vote, give speeches, participate in political parties, serve on juries are far beyond anything contemplated by the early champions of democracy. Equally important, research discloses that such participation may embrace constellations of activities rather than a solitary act. It is true that some activities, such as voting, are both more general in the population and more solitary, but less frequent activities are more intertwined. For example, a study of two North Carolina counties revealed that if a person helps campaign in an election he is almost certain to attend party meetings. If he does attend, he is almost certain to be in touch with public officers and other political leaders. A person who makes such contacts is almost certain to be a member of some politically oriented association, such as a farm cooperative or the Chamber of Commerce.[13]

[12] Seymour Martin Lipset, *Political Man* (New York: Doubleday, Anchor Books, 1963), 32–33, 51; David Potter, *People of Plenty* (Chicago: University of Chicago Press, 1954).
[13] Robert E. Lane, *Political Life* (New York: Free Press, 1959), 93.

Participation in political activities in the United States

	Percent active
Campaign Activities	
Persuaded others how to vote	28
Ever worked for a party	26
Attended political rallies	19
Contributed money to a political campaign	13
Member of a political club or organization	8
Voting	
Voted in 1964 presidential election	72
Voted in 1960 presidential election	71
Votes regularly in local elections	47
Cooperative Activities	
Worked through local group	30
Helped form local group	14
Active member of organization in commu-	
nity activities	32
Contact with Officials	
Contacted local officials	20
Contacted extralocal officials	18

Source: Sidney Verba, Norman H. Nie, and Jae-on Kim, "The Modes of Democratic Participation: A Cross-National Comparison," *Sage Professional Papers in Comparative Politics* (Beverly Hills, Calif.: Sage Publications, 1971), Vol. 2, No. 01-013, p. 20.

Generally, those who participate most in political life have fared far better in the distribution of value benefits than those who participate least. Both nonvoters and nonparticipants are apt to have lower education, income, and occupational status than voters and participants. Repeatedly, research has shown that lower status groups harbor the most intolerance and ignorance of political issues and background information.

The political life of democratic man cannot be understood or assessed if it is seen as separate and removed from his social life. His social conduct contributes to the enlargement and reduction of political problems; his social behavior can serve or inhibit democracy. In this time of difficult race relations in American society, a modest social endeavor in California called Counterpart makes a creative contribution to the political realm. One day Mrs. Josephine Jackson, a seventy-year-old white widow, was astonished when eight young black men appeared to paint her house without charge. The men were hired and paid by Counterpart, an interracial community service organization. Counterpart consists of two teams, one black and one white, that devise and carry out community improvement projects in two mostly black suburban communities. Participating whites gain insights into black community problems, and the many executives and businessmen among them provide access to money and skills. "We say to the white counterparts," noted Kemp

Miller, the black director of the organization, that "we want your help, but not your patronage or a crutch. It takes a very Christian man to subordinate himself to that." Counterpart's projects include the purchase and renovation of a run-down shopping center and the operation of a civic center and community service complex, a teen-agers' center, and a Paint-Up–Clean-Up program, resulting in the painting of homes, repairing of fences, and cleaning of yards of hundreds of homes like Mrs. Jackson's.[14]

Forms of participation. In the United States, as in other democratic nations, the most structured and normally the most consequential act of participation is voting. In all democratic countries for which data are available, the incidence of participation among population sectors follows identical patterns. Men vote more than women, the better educated more than the less educated, urban residents more than rural, those between thirty-five and fifty-five more than younger and older voters, higher-status persons more than lower, married more than unmarried, members of organizations more than nonmembers.[15] But trends that narrow some of these contrasts, particularly in the categories of sex and age, suggest that future democratic man may become a better political man.

Most of the contrasts in voting patterns persist in other forms of participation. Face-to-face petitioning of public officials occurs most frequently among those of higher status, whose position in the social hierarchy provides access to officials and the sense of freedom and confidence to write and see them. Officials deal more responsively with petitioners who can "make trouble" and conceivably influence groups of voters than with citizens who lack these means. Petitioning by letter-writing is more widely dispersed among status ranks. Those willing to write to their congressman range from half to almost three-fourths of the adult population, although one study found that those who had ever actually written or telegraphed totaled only about a seventh, or 14 percent. Professional and business people and those with college education write more than those in other categories, and Jews more than Catholics or Protestants. The rate of letter-writing is more sensitive to events than is voting turnout.[16]

Americans are indefatigable joiners of organizations, from bowling leagues to political clubs. The organizations differ widely in political content. One national study found that in a given year only 2 percent belonged to a political club or organization, 31 percent to organizations that sometimes took a stand on public issues, while 64 percent belonged to organizations without a discernible link to politics. Since the political club may serve social as well as political purposes, the joining of such clubs may not be motivated by political concerns. Lower and middle income individuals join political clubs

---

[14] *New York Times,* September 6, 1972.
[15] Lipset, 187.
[16] Lane, *Political Life,* 65–76.

to satisfy social needs in decidedly greater proportions than those of high income.[17]

It is a sign of the vigor of democracy that participation takes many forms and is engaged in with high degrees of personal intensity. A 1972 "prisoners' march for peace" revealed a high degree of commitment. Protesting the Vietnam war and the imprisonment of those who had refused induction into the armed forces, the participants marched from Danbury, Connecticut, to New York City while simultaneously conducting an eight-day fast. Handcuffed together in pairs, the marchers carried signs that said, "In times like these, only criminals remain silent." Several of the marchers had themselves already served jail sentences for refusing induction. Some dropped out of the pilgrimage for medical reasons, but others resolved to persist in the "sacrificial act" of fasting until "Americans [looked] at the war not just from the standpoint of our own boys but with decency toward humanity." [18]

Virtually every individual also participates in comments exchanged with small groups and friends—in the home, community, and office. These expressions, often denoted by genuineness and particularity, are valued by politicians eager to sense what public opinion really is on some issue or policy. It is an opinion that is informed and shaped daily by the news media, especially television.

[17] *Ibid.*
[18] *New York Times,* September 6, 1972.

Inducing the individual to act. Many people in democracy are indifferent to politics and are absorbed in their own affairs. This is to be expected, but on occasion political indifference may have unpleasant consequences for democracy—when, for example, stay-at-home voters forfeit an election to an active minority. The question therefore sometimes becomes critical: What induces citizens to invest their energies in political activity as opposed to absorption in their private concerns?

James David Barber contends that the individual's motives, opportunities, and resources are prime determinants of his activity. The sense of an "obligation to participate" may be derived from upbringing and education, and shared beliefs may ignite action. Information about politics is presumably necessary for rational action, and here the findings of studies are not heartening. Typically, less than half the people know who their congressman is and only a bare majority can name one of their senators. On issues, the information picture is even bleaker. If anything, Americans suffer from an excess of opportunities to acquire information. From the news media flows a daily avalanche of information, but the citizen's special difficulty is his inability to organize the information into a coherent whole. Rising education levels are an antidote to these failings, as is the awareness that political knowledge and understanding can have valuable payoffs, such as establishing policies and programs that one believes in or gaining a benefit for one's neighborhood.[19]

Fortunately, scattered among the general body of citizens are "stimulators," who wield an energizing effect on their less politically kinetic fellow citizens. At every status level, there are those who are more interested, better informed, and more active, who are more likely to have their minds made up on issues. Their enthusiasm and commitment bestir other citizens. A frequent pattern is the tandem of adviser-and-dependent, where one looking for help turns to someone near his own status level, but somewhat higher. That person is apt to be a steady newspaper reader and better educated; nearly half of the college educated who are exposed to several media try to influence others how to vote.[20] Families, interest group leaders, and arresting political candidates and leaders can also arouse latent citizen interest.

The *withdrawal* of participation may have a significant democratic effect. A resignation of protest, like Robert Cahn's from the Council of Environmental Quality, may direct attention to official lapses and public need. Established by environmental legislation, the Council was a "watchdog," advising the President on policy and scrutinizing the environmental implications of federal activities. Cahn, a former journalist, was to develop a system under which federal agencies by law must report to the Council assessments of environmental impact before they begin any new project. To his distress, Cahn found that agencies like the Department of Transportation were agile in sidestepping the requirement "by snowing us under with mountains of paper on every six-block paving project in the country." Soon Cahn resigned, both as an act of

[19] James David Barber, *Citizen Politics* (Chicago: Markham, 1969), 17–25.
[20] *Ibid.,* 139.

protest and as the result of a judgment that he could better advance his environmental goals by returning to journalism.[21]

Democratic politics. Democratic man functions in a particular kind of politics. In democracy, no individual gets his own way or imposes his will on others absolutely and continuously. He may act independently or through pressure groups, but what he wants must be adjusted to what others want. Only when many democratic men accommodate to one another can majorities be fashioned. Politicians and elected representatives manage the processes of adjustment or the invention of compromises that produce a majority consensus. Presumably, the wider and more diversified are the interests of democratic man, the more readily there will be compromise—democracy thrives on divided loyalties.

The view that politics in democracy should offer choice and be competitive is widely held among citizens. In fact, this view allowed George McGovern to advance his political career. When McGovern seriously entered state politics in South Dakota, the Democratic party there was in collapse. Some felt this condition was well deserved, but nevertheless it disturbed many South Dakotans. When McGovern warned against one-party rule, barely suggesting that it was antidemocratic, he hit home, and the results were evident in the 1954 elections. Although Democratic registration did not increase appreciably, Democratic representation in the state legislature expanded from almost nothing to 25 seats.[22]

Democratic politics is constructive: in dealing with society's cleavages it contributes to society's integration. Like other successful democracies, American democracy has found stability in regulating tensions and holding them to moderate levels. Generally, moderation has prevailed through the political system's capacity to resolve or render innocuous important dividing issues before new ones arise. There are serious exceptions—relations between the races, between the central cities and the suburbs, between the well-to-do and the poor. But in its ideal form, democratic man's management of conflict is a product of democratic feelings. He rejects a society that is divided into exploiters and exploited, pursues the ideal of enabling each individual to develop into his full being, and treats his fellow citizens with the consideration and respect that equals accord equals.

The making of democratic man

Political socialization. Except for his innate liberties, democratic man is made; he is not born. He is a product of *political socialization*—of acquired attitudes,

[21] *New York Times,* September 6, 1972.
[22] In Robert Sam Anson, *McGovern* (New York: Holt, Rinehart and Winston, 1972), 73.

Political information among children

	Percent giving "reasonably accurate" response				
			School grade		
Information asked	4th	5th	6th	7th	8th
President's name	96%	97%	90%	99%	100%
Mayor's name	90	97	89	99	97
President's duties	23	33	44	65	66
Mayor's duties	35	42	50	66	67
Governor's duties	8	12	23	36	43
Role of state legislature	5	5	9	24	37

Source: Fred I. Greenstein, "The Benevolent Leader: Children's Images of Political Authority." *American Political Science Review*, LIV (December 1960), p. 937, Table 2.

beliefs, and values relating to the political system and his role as citizen. The individual internalizes this body of norms, thus facilitating his future conduct congruent with them. Socialization can make the individual better informed about politics and more highly motivated toward public affairs.

Individuals are exposed to several common agents of socialization before they are adults. The family influences attitudes toward authority, rules, and compliance. It may also transmit preference for a political party and related political attitudes, such as feelings of pleasure or distress over electoral results. There appears to be a relationship between family attitudes and the child's interest in the political system. Children who view their fathers as powerful tend to be better informed and more interested, while children who see their mothers as dominant are less interested and acquire political attitudes in later years. The political learning of the preschool child usually begins when he discovers that the public and private sectors of life differ, that a higher authority exists outside the family, to which even the all-powerful parents respond and whose rules they must obey regardless of preference.[23]

While the family helps build basic loyalty to the country, the school provides the young child with content, information, and concepts about the functioning political system (see table). Instruction is by no means heavily democracy-oriented. Teachers are prone to stress compliance with law, authority, and school regulations and to underemphasize the rights and obligations of the citizen to participate in politics, the ways the citizen can influence government, and the issues of partisanship and political conflict.[24]

[23] David Easton and Robert D. Hess, "The Child's Political World," *Midwest Journal of Political Science,* 6 (No. 3, 1962), 229–46; reprinted in Norman Adler and Charles Harrington, *The Learning of Political Behavior* (Glenview: Scott, Foresman, 1970), 37–47.

[24] Robert D. Hess and Judith V. Torney, *The Development of Political Attitudes in Children* (Chicago: Aldine, 1967), 212–25; reprinted in Edward S. Greenberg, ed., *Political Socialization* (New York: Atherton Press, 1970), 64–82.

Socialization of ghetto children concerning drugs.

Despite democracy's sparse pedagogical diet, socialization is not unpromising at the school-child level. In his study of school children, aged nine to thirteen, in New Haven, Connecticut, Fred I. Greenstein found that children have far more positive political orientations than adults, who commonly express political cynicism and distrust. Greenstein and others suggest that the child's benevolent image of political authority may be traced to his feelings toward his parents.[25]

For the future democratic man, the adolescent years (eleven through eighteen) are usually most important. A study of school children in Ann Arbor, Michigan, probed attitudes toward conflicts between community demands and individual freedom. The results disclosed a clear transition from the young child's personalized approach, which sees politics in terms of visible figures (the President, the policeman), often referred to in terms of "likes" and "dislikes" ("I like Kennedy," "I like the President"), to the sociocentric perspective of the older school child, a more abstract view of institutions and increasing concern for individual liberties. The shift was especially noticeable in the period between eleven and thirteen years. The fifteen-year-old shows an assured grasp of formal thought, and the eighteen-

[25] Fred I. Greenstein, "The Benevolent Leader: Children's Images of Political Authority," *American Political Science Review,* LIV (December 1960), 934–43.

year-old even more so: he is knowledgeable, facile, and can elaborate ideas fluently.[26]

As the individual grows away from exclusive attachment to parents, he takes on the political complexion of other groups—friends, teachers, husbands or wives, co-workers. Ordinarily, the views of these new agents do not conflict with those of the parents. Frequently, these groups hold a common political orientation, and the individual deliberately selects them with a view to avoiding conflict. Studies disclose that most children do not manifest rebellion against parents by adopting an opposing view of politics.[27]

Class also fortifies stability. A study was made of three American communities of differing socioeconomic characteristics and levels of political activity. In the working class community, where there was little political activity, it was found that civic education deemphasized the importance of political participation and conveyed a largely passive, harmonious view of politics. In the lower middle class community, where political life was moderately active, education in democratic government stressed citizenship responsibilities, but not the dynamics of public decision-making. Only in the upper middle class community were insights into political processes and functions passed on to those who in the future would most likely be involved in them.[28] Here is a cogent argument for school busing—only a scholastic class mix will allow the functional upper middle class view of democratic politics to be imparted more widely.

Senator McGovern was once asked by an historian: "George, what makes you tick?" The explanation was in terms of socialization: "My father's philosophy," McGovern replied. And he delineated it with a quotation from St. Matthew (16:25): "Whosoever shall save his life shall lose it, and whosoever shall lose his life for my sake shall find it." [29] Like many other politicians, McGovern's preparation for politics has been shaped by religion. And the religious thread in his life, if it is followed, reveals that socialization is a lifetime process, dynamic and varying as the individual's experience proceeds, but never altogether free from past influences.[30]

The political culture. Many varieties of democratic man make up the political culture, which includes the basic attitudes and skills that determine how politics is conducted. There are those who are well informed and highly active— the rationality-activist model. Advocates of that type look askance at the passive citizen, the nonvoter, the poorly informed, and the apathetic. Research findings are clear, however, that the great body of citizens do not live up to

[26] Joseph Adelson and Robert P. O'Neil, "Growth of Political Ideas in Adolescence," *Journal of Personality and Social Psychology,* 4 (No. 3, 1960), 295–306.
[27] Herbert H. Hyman, *Political Socialization* (New York: Free Press, 1969), 89–90.
[28] Edgar Litt, "Education, Community Norms, and Political Institutions," *American Sociological Review,* 28 (February 1963), 69–75.
[29] In Anson, 63.
[30] Charles P. Henderson, Jr., "McGovern's Gospel," *New York Times,* September 5, 1972.

the rationality-activist model. Gabriel Almond and Sidney Verba have suggested that the reality of American and other democracies might better be captured if the active participant's role is put in perspective with two other roles, the subject and the parochial.

In this scheme, the participant role is "activist," and the participant type makes evaluations of the parts of the political system ranging from acceptance to rejection. The subject role is oriented toward the output or administrative aspects of the political system, but orientations toward input objects and toward the self as an active participant approach zero. The subject type has attitudes toward government as a whole, taking pride in it or disliking it, and evaluating it as legitimate or not. The parochial type expects a minimum of change initiated by the political system; the agencies of government seldom touch the consciousness of the parochial citizen. Over time, a single individual may manifest all these orientations and fluctuate in his degree of commitment to them. Others may be deeply engrossed in a particular orientation and infrequently relinquish it.[31]

The subject and parochial orientations, Almond and Verba argue, are important to any political culture, including a democratic culture. Both orientations can usefully modify the intensity of the individual's political involvement and help produce a set of social attitudes enabling democratic man to make a balanced response to the demands of private and public life. The balance among these orientations profits democracy itself, which requires a foundation of support in both the political and social systems. Most citizens have career and family responsibilities. Clearly, no society could accomplish its necessary tasks, if day after day each citizen was committed around-the-clock to the activist model. For both the individual and society, participation has outer limits of desirability.[32]

The stress on balance does not help us with the perennial democratic problem of an undersupply of informed, rational participants. If society is to change and improve through democratic means, their numbers and social variety must be increased. A candidate in the 1972 New Hampshire presidential primary declared that it does not matter "whether you are a Democrat or Republican, but whether you are active or passive, whether we can be a catalyst to motivate people to go on the offensive in the war against racism and despair." [33]

But the activist norm cannot be translated into reality unless the individual *perceives* that he is able act, to vote, to speak, to petition. The individual needs a sense of civic competence. A citizen who believes he has influence is more likely to use it. The sooner that citizens of the deprived classes view themselves as competent, the sooner will society's weaknesses be reduced.

Sometimes, paradoxically, the participants may be too confident and the

---

[31] Gabriel Almond and Sidney Verba, *The Civic Culture* (Princeton: Princeton University Press, 1963), 17–21.

[32] *Ibid.*, 474–76.

[33] Edward Coll, quoted in *New York Times,* February 11, 1972.

political system, in some ways, overresponsive. The present environmental movement, for example, has been flooded with organizations—in the San Francisco Bay area, according to one count, there were more than 200—with politically skillful leaderships and memberships ranging from conservatives to the Students for a Democratic Society. Confronted with such widespread grass-roots outpourings, Democrats, Republicans, liberals, and conservatives jostled one another for places in the vanguard of the environmental crusade. Governor Ronald Reagan pledged "an all-out war against the debauching of the environment," and his liberal rivals for the governorship responded with expressions of deep commitment. A bill barring any new off-shore oil drilling was delayed while Democrats and Republicans squabbled over who would get credit for it. What appeared to be a highly responsive political system prompted Phillip Berry, president of the Sierra Club, to declare, "Politicians paying lipservice, industrialists laying down public relations smokescreens, and anarchists voicing legitimate concerns about the environment for the ulterior purpose of attacking democratic institutions are all suspect." [34]

The inner life of democratic man

Democratic theory, which is denoted by emphasis on the individual, regards him confidently. John Locke perceived man as "good," in the sense that he accords others the same rights and privileges and attributes to them the same needs that he himself has. Some advocates of democracy see him as a creature of reason, capable of discovering and applying rational solutions to political problems. But other opinion disputes these claims and beholds man as selfish, mediocre, factional, passionate, and unequal by biological heritage.

If the more favorable image of democratic man is to prevail, much depends, in particular cases, on the man within. The freedom to speak is meaningful only if a person is capable of thoughts of his own. Freedom from external authority and restraint is valuable only if one's inner psychological conditions are such that he is able to establish his own individuality, or achieve individuation. The effective democratic man achieves it by discarding his original ties to the world around him and becoming aware of himself as a separate entity while also feeling part of his surroundings. Individuation entails the growth of self-strength, of self-awareness, which includes knowledge of one's goals and values, reflection on one's inner conflicts—in a word, a capacity for introspection. Individuation helps the person develop a political belief system that responds better to his inner needs and improves his prospects for democratic survival by making him less pliable to external manipulators (a Hitler) than the unaware person, with his immature belief system.

Although we cannot reliably predict who among us will function as a participating democratic man, the brighter prospects seem to be those with ego

[34] *New York Times,* February 24, 1970.

strength—those who can stand up against the political environment, make decisions, order their life rationally. Such people view themselves as active or assertive rather than passive and feel confident toward government power, even if they may politically oppose it. (Passive individuals are prone to be fearful of government power, even if they support it.) Robert E. Lane speculates that confidence is prompted by a sense of a capacity to "fight back" against governmental intrusion into one's private sphere, and by the feeling that governmental power can be "used" for one's own purposes.[35] Persons of such ego strength are apt to believe that their votes are important, politicians respect their views, and elections are therefore meaningful. Studies illuminate the distribution of these attitudes of political effectiveness: men are more likely to possess them than women, those better educated more than those less educated, those with higher income and status more than those with less.[36]

Some of the personal ingredients necessary for effective participation in democratic politics are suggested by the person and career of Denis Allen Hayes, who at twenty-five became national coordinator of Earth Day, a nationwide observance of the environment. Hayes fondly recalled a childhood in the Cascade Range of Washington state, a world of dense forests, rushing streams, and lonely foothills. His father worked at the Crown Zellerbach Corporation's paper mill as did many others in his hometown. For years, the mill had befouled the Columbia River and filled the air with acrid chemicals. After hitchhiking around the world and viewing in many places the human capacity to damage the environment, Hayes became even more aware that "Washington state is deteriorating. . . . I feel a genuine sense of anger that those who are responsible are buffered from the results of their decisions." [37]

Hayes had the capacity to act, intellectually and politically. Educated at leading universities, he had been president of the student body at Stanford. Having been "uptight about the war," he became versed in the ways of opposition to that venture. An omnivorous reader (about thirty books a week), he impressed others as extremely well-versed in the complexities of environmental problems. He could render statistics, arguments, and examples in an eloquent rush of words, a useful capacity for a confident political participant.

Democratic man is also a composite of human needs, some of which can be served by politics. Psychologists M. Brewster Smith, Jerome Bruner, and Robert White contend that individuals take in political information and develop political opinions to meet several general needs: to understand the world and to control events, to get along well with others, to vent psychic tensions.[38] In a more extensive listing of needs, Lane noted that individuals seek through

---

[35] Robert E. Lane, *Political Thinking and Consciousness: The Private Life of the Political Mind* (Chicago: Markham, 1969), 85–86.
[36] Lane, *Political Life,* 147–49.
[37] *New York Times,* April 23, 1972.
[38] M. Brewster Smith, Jerome Bruner, and Robert White, *Opinions and Personality* (New York: Wiley, 1941), 41.

political expression to advance their economic or material well-being, to relieve tensions arising from aggressive impulses, to gain power over others chiefly to satisfy doubts about themselves, and generally to protect and improve their self-esteem.[39] Other needs abound: the need to take a moral stand, which some may achieve by taking sides on public issues; cognitive needs of learning, curiosity, and understanding—the range is enormous. Democracy ministers to even the most self-serving of these needs and often directs them into channels that make them more public-serving.

Typically, man seeks to satisfy identity needs through a search for ideas, including political ideas. "Identity and ideology," Erik Erikson contends, "are two aspects of the same process": ideas help identify the self.[40] The person therefore searches the environment for ideas and selects from among the bountiful supply that he discovers. The process, so critical both for the individual and democratic politics, is one about which we know little. At least we are aware that it is guided by features of the individual's *personality*—his identity, self-awareness, self-esteem, and "objective self" (intelligence, energy, emotional balance). Guidance also comes from the engaged elements of his *philosophical and operational belief system,* including his concepts of reality, morality, and other values; from his *learning strategies,* such as his curiosity and his tolerance of ambiguity and dissent; from his *references to groups and persons,* serving as models, audiences, and antagonists, and his characteristic modes of interaction with them. In addition, he is guided by his *definitions of situations,* especially his interpretation of what is expected of him and what motives, values, and goals are at stake. All these elements nourish the individual's political and social belief systems.[41] Democracy and its values and methods can be accepted or rejected or earn a shrug of indifference in these mental processes.

Many bridges connect the self and politics. Particularly important to democracy are personal political doctrines, derived from general political philosophy, that stress equality, freedom, justice, the distribution of power, war and peace, alienation and allegiance. For most persons, these doctrines exist in varying degrees of particularity; some of their elements can be gleaned from a reporter's interviews with Americans, from various walks of life, across the country in 1970: [42]

> "To me patriotism means that no matter which way you voted, you go and support the man who is elected as the majority of the people wanted."

> "I'd like to see us put all the attorneys right out in the middle of a big field and just march around and around them all day protesting

[39] Lane, *Political Life,* 101–02.

[40] In Maurice R. Stein, Arthur J. Vidich, and David M. White, eds., *Identity and Anxiety* (New York: Free Press, 1960), 81.

[41] Lane, *Political Thinking and Consciousness,* 48–49.

[42] In Bill Moyers, *Listening to America* (New York: Harper's Magazine Press, 1971), 28, 129, 152, 183.

and demonstrating and raising the devil with them for all the trouble they've caused."

"Out there on the playing field if you're really equal you prove it, and winner take all."

"I'm worried about this country. There's so much discord. Everybody puts everybody else in a strait jacket. How do you break out of a stereotype once you're in it?"

A local administrator of unemployment compensation: "We get hippies who don't wear shirts or shoes or socks. But they're eligible as long as they're laid off from work. People come over to me and say, 'Why are you giving *them* benefits?' I say it's the state law."

Political beliefs are linked to the individual's underlying motives, which they serve. Motives are more or less characteristic of the individual in many situations; they spring from needs—indeed they reflect chronic needs or needs that are latent but easily stimulated. Thus in an interview conducted by Robert E. Lane, a student whose parents had risen from lower middle class status said he dreamed of owning a manor in Scarsdale; he disposed of questions of party choice by associating Republicans with policies that will allow his dreams of wealth to materialize. He also displayed a degree of partisanship appropriate to the status level to which he aspired. Here was a person who was aware of his own motives. The capacity to examine and tolerate the less attractive side of one's own personality is related to hospitability to doubt and ambiguity in politics, a stance that can be highly valuable to democracy's functioning. It makes one less prone to reject others, more open to compromise that responds to the needs and views of others, and less susceptible to the naive suggestion that there are "right" or "perfect" solutions to society's problems.[43]

Escapes from freedom

Escape from self. A hazard to which democracy may succumb is that its autonomous man may find freedom a taxing anxiety, an intolerable burden. Freedom then becomes something to escape from, as millions of Germans did in embracing Hitler's totalitarian regime. Given societies at particular stages in their experience are vulnerable to some variant of such shattering transformations. In a society that is rapidly changing, whose traditional authorities are weakening, the individual develops feelings of isolation and powerlessness, especially in a context of big organizations—industries, cities, and bureaucracies. He becomes prey to conversion from a free human being into an instrument of ponderous forces, including the state.

[43] Lane, *Political Thinking and Consciousness,* 56–61.

As a prelude to its complete breakdown, freedom deteriorates into hollowness, or as Erich Fromm particularizes it, man fails to unite himself with the world "in the spontaneity of love and productive work." The relationship of one individual to another loses its direct, human quality; in social and personal relations the rugged, unfeeling laws of the marketplace govern. Competitors fulfill their assigned economic function by fighting and possibly destroying one another. The relationship is instrumental; each uses the other to pursue his economic interests. This dispiriting plight poses a central problem for autonomous, democratic man. Only by connecting himself adequately with the world while maintaining his individuality can he avoid the aloneness and anxiety to which he is susceptible and that can destroy his democratic functioning.[44]

But the faltering democratic man may become alienated from his own self. Even this seemingly internal relationship is subject to corrosive instrumentality. The "feeling of self," a manifestation of which is self-confidence, is substantially a product of what others think of the person. He alone cannot convince himself of his value, but depends on power, prestige, property, the attachments of family and friends. He must test his popularity and sell his skills in the marketplace. If he is sought after, his services hired, he is somebody; if he is ignored, his offer rejected, he is nobody. These brutally clear reactions determine his self-esteem and, critical for democracy, whether or not he lapses into feelings of inferiority. At its worst, alienation from self leads to authoritarianism, for the weakened person may seek a higher power outside himself, to which he does nothing but submit.

More common than escape into authoritarianism is the drift into apathy, the withdrawal or turning away from politics as something unimportant or futile. The politically apathetic individual may be fettered by any one of several attitudes. He feels that he has no influence and therefore need not participate. He perceives and resents that government is not run in his interest, that policy-makers are indifferent, and therefore it is not his government, but the happy hunting-ground of privileged influentials. He does not approve of the way decisions are made and therefore disdains the rules of the game as unfair.[45]

A casualty of mass society. Democratic man, as sociologist William Kornhauser has suggested, may become a casualty in the politics of mass society. Various social phenomena feed into the swollen stream of mass society. Sprawling cities, giant industries, and layered bureaucracies deprive people of the social bases of their involvement and control in the social order. The "organization man," who participates wholeheartedly in large organizations, eventually loses his identity. Serious discontinuities in society, such as war and depression, are other unsettling factors. Worst of all, perhaps, as the

[44] Erich Fromm, *Escape From Freedom* (New York: Holt, Rinehart and Winston, 1941), 22–23.
[45] Barber, 87.

Great Silent Majority

era of McCarthyism in the 1950s and the May Day arrests in Washington in 1971 suggest, mass politics may countenance activity outside of the established rules of democratic society and trample on the constitutional order and civil liberties. Ironically, democracy lays itself open to the assault by encouraging the participation of the mass of people, regardless of their current or transitory mood.

Mass society's politics is a web of distortions. It focuses attention not on matters close to personal experience and daily life—the stuff of democracy— but on national and international events and issues and abstract symbols —"the Communists," "the enemy"—known only through the media. Mass politics weakens intermediate relations of the political system—the local community and pressure groups, which often act in behalf of the individual and his concerns with the national government. In mass society, the individual becomes self-estranged. The cities, the industries, the bureaucracies deprive him of control of the social order. The loss of control diminishes the individual's sense of purpose, and for some it leads easily to alienation. Individuals "who feel alienated from the social order," writes Kornhauser, "tend to feel alienated from themselves." [46]

Edward Coll, a candidate in the 1972 New Hampshire presidential primary, hardly more visible politically than he was physically, was in essence campaigning against a mass society and its politics, although he generally got lost in the dust of the campaign stampede of well-known national figures. Impressed that urban problems were being ignored and misunderstood, that society was becoming hardened to their devastation, Coll had quit his job as a junior insurance executive to organize the Revitalization Corps, an urban storefront venture that offered community services to bring blacks and whites to-

[46] William Kornhauser, *The Politics of Mass Society* (New York: Free Press, 1959), 108.

In a televised debate during the 1972 New Hampshire primary, Edward Coll holds up a rubber rat as a symbol of the urban crisis today.

gether. His purpose in entering the campaign, he said, was to get people to think about problems that a mass society easily ignores.[47] He was fearful that the nation would become "more and more pessimistic and hopeless about our political leadership," and he wanted to bring "the issues of racism, of poverty, of urban decay into the campaign. I just want to force the others to talk about these things."

Radicalization. Some who despair of the ability of orthodox democracy to get things done take up the radical life, which may evoke behavior antithetical to democracy. Hate, certainly an undemocratic feeling, may become a ruling passion. The radical means to impose his will on society, whereas in democracy no one imposes his will or gets his way regardless of the wishes of others, least of all the majority. The radical scorns existing democratic processes as too slow, too piecemeal. Revolution is the answer, but precisely what happens after the revolution, when injustice is to be eradicated, is vague, although it is euphorically contemplated.

Consider, for example, Cathlyn P. Wilkerson—slender, pretty, and described by associates as totally committed to the necessity of revolution. She participated in the "four days of rage" during the 1968 national Democratic convention in Chicago, where she was accused of attacking a policeman with a four-foot club. In 1970, when she was twenty-five years old, Miss Wilkerson disappeared with another member of the Weatherman faction of the Students for a Democratic Society soon after dynamite explosions shattered her father's town house in Greenwich Village in New York City. Like other radical young

[47] *New York Times,* February 11, 1972.

women of that era, she came from an upper class background, was educated at a prestigious college, and took the religious values of her upbringing seriously—"a violent Quaker," an SDS colleague called her. "Gradually I became alienated from the suburban middle class life style and the values it offered," she once explained, so she adopted the life of a radical organizer. "All organizers are underfed, underpaid, underslept," she acknowledged, "but to me, it's the only liberating thing to do. . . . The struggle to be human is primary." The goals of the struggle, as she defined them, were "to change the system and give power to the 90 percent of the people who have no economic or political control now." But beyond this general aspiration, Miss Wilkerson provided no further details, in an extended interview, of what future society would be like after a successful struggle.[48]

Important to democracy are the steps by which the radical leaves its fold. In his study of young radicals, Kenneth Keniston found that none of his subjects deliberately set out to be radicals.[49] Rather, they realized eventually that because of their activities they had become radicals. Through interviews with members of Vietnam Summer, a New Left movement, Keniston discovered no clear patterns of the relative weight of emotion and intellect in radicalization. Some ascribed their involvement to such feelings as indignation, idealism, frustration, and anger, the product of situations to which they had a "gut reaction" that triggered the development of more articulated intellectual positions. But others felt that their radicalization was the result of intellectual awareness of and conscious reflection on the discrepancy between what America is and what they believed it should be. Radicalization was sometimes a response to personal needs—the problem of "what to do with my life" and the need to "find out more about myself."

Keniston was impressed with the strong continuity in the lives of radicals he interviewed—the lack of fundamental change in their core values. The radicals' core values were often congruent with those of their parents. For some individuals, radicalization did not mean acquiring new values, but instead represented unsparing effort to realize their families' values. Other radicals revealed continuity with religious values learned at home and in church. What denotes the radical is that he takes these values seriously, to the point of viewing them as absolutes, and is driven to implement them immediately. As radicalization sets in, these feelings are transvalued into a positive sense of enlightened rightness, special belonging, participation in a distinctive movement comprising a small minority.

"Commitment" comes after the individual joins the organization and finds himself more and more involved in radical activities. Some who come from affluent backgrounds suffer shock at their initial confrontation with social injustice, with poverty and political and institutional dishonesty. Disillusioned with working "within the System," they commence a radical re-

---

[48] *New York Times,* March 16, 1970.
[49] Kenneth Keniston, *Young Radicals* (New York: Harcourt Brace Jovanovich, 1968), 106–46.

interpretation of the social and political world. Typically, they perceive society to be run by a "power elite" of industrial, corporate, and military interests that are oblivious to implementing society's creedal values. Progressive estrangement from the mainstream follows, although commitment to the creedal values remains intact. The radical comes to feel personally responsible for effecting change, but many of the radicals that Keniston studied had little faith in the historic inevitability of their revolutionary efforts. Instead, they alternated between hopes of effectiveness in the very long run and the view that the intrinsic rightness of their task made the issue of ultimate success irrelevant. Paradoxically, they did not accord the same tolerance and charitableness of judgment to democracy's gropings and fumblings.

Proposals

Democracy's future depends on the quality of autonomous man, on the improvement of a type of man that some social scientists consider an anachronism fit only for the discard heap. If democracy's task is to save—if not rehabilitate—autonomous man, what can be done?

1. David Riesman believes that in the present state of social science learning we are limited to a "few paltry" suggestions and that we badly need a vastly greater stream of creative, utopian thinking before we can see more clearly the goal dimly suggested by the word "autonomy." Despite forbidding economic and technological changes, which threaten to overwhelm autonomous man, Riesman is confident that ideas will be generated and will catch on. Any assistance given to bolster autonomous man must recognize, Riesman insists, his differentiation from his fellow human beings. "The idea that men are created free and equal," he writes, is "both true and misleading: men are created different; they lose their social freedom and their individual autonomy in seeking to become like each other." [50]

2. Political socialization can be employed more deliberately than it has been to help create the kind of citizenry democracy requires. Assume that we follow the prescriptions of Almond and Verba and seek a mix of citizens with parochial, subject, and participant orientations in proportions suitable for democracy. Education can develop the cognitive skills required for participation, but it is less likely to impart the underlying social attitudes that are an important part of the political culture—social trust and confidence, for example. Channels of political socialization outside of formal education can do this. Thus, the family, the work place, and voluntary associations (such as churches and clubs) constitute important socializing agencies, with untapped potential for training the individual in attitudes and skills that will allow each of his orientations to operate, especially the participant. [51]

3. The quality of citizen participation must be of continuous concern to

[50] Riesman, 346–49.
[51] Almond and Verba, 502.

any democracy. Some suggest, however, the desirability of divorcing obligatory participation from concepts of civic duty. Thus if those who vote or follow public affairs through the news media are a small proportion of the population, there should be no cause for alarm. For the self-selection that has taken place will best assure that the interested, the informed, and those with political responsibilities will perform democracy's necessary civic duties at suitable levels of quality. Nevertheless, as Robert Lane suggests, moralizing and urging such acts of participation can induce action by dutiful, responsive, and humane citizens who might not otherwise participate and whose noninvolvement would forfeit public affairs to those with special interests, a condition unpropitious for democracy.[52]

Empirical findings suggest the surest paths to higher levels of participation. Some of the highest participation rates prevail in the Eastern suburbs, places with greater education, income, and occupational status. If we want still higher rates of participation, we could seek to make these social factors more widespread in the population and increase cultural pressure to participate by manipulating the moral content of civic norms. But cultural pressure has limited promise since its most effective appeal is to the middle class, while the lowest participation rates occur in the working class.

To strengthen democracy, we can encourage the search for political understanding. Enlightenment is a hallowed concept of democracy, and its use through more informative political discussion in the media and in electoral campaigns might enhance popular understanding of politics and public policy. Improved enlightenment may be nothing more than semienlightenment, if community harmony becomes even more jarred than it now is. Nevertheless, we can increase the general level of education, which is indeed transpiring. Education, particularly college education, is clearly associated with active participation.

If autonomous man, however well educated, is simply the embodiment of atomized individualism, of extreme self-centeredness to the point that he is incapable of relating and adjusting his purposes to those of others, he will move away from political involvement. In the United States we depend heavily on group identifications to reverse this possibility. But here again a dilemma awaits. If the individual sees himself primarily as a manager or worker, Catholic or Protestant, Northerner or Southerner, we are in danger of losing more than we gain. The intransigence of status identification is much less easily loosened than party or issue preference. Clearly the creation of social patterns and conditions of personality growth that will nurture a democratic and humane political life is a task of many parts.

In this book, we shall be concerned with democracy as an ideal, as a means of enhancing human happiness, realizing the individual's potential, and best reconciling the need for government, the need for order, with the need for individual freedom, the need to live one's own life. We shall also be con-

[52] Lane, *Political Life,* 349.

cerned with democracy as a reality—and how American democracy falls short of the ideal (as other democracies also do) in its institutions and practices. The democratic ideal for the courts, the legislature, parties, and other institutions will be suggested—how they were conceived to best serve democracy— and the imperfect reality will be explored, for both its nature and causes. Each chapter will examine proposals to reduce the gap between the ideal and reality, on the assumption that the political system can be improved and is indeed worth improving. To begin, these same steps shall be taken as we look at several basic processes a democratic system must cope with, the processes of conflict, consensus-building, and change.

Suggested Reading

Almond, Gabriel A., and Verba, Sidney, *The Civic Culture* * (Princeton University Press, 1963). The standard work concerning the attitudes and behavior that support democratic political life. This cross-national study treats the United States and four other countries.

Barber, James David, *Citizen Politics* * (Markham, 1969). An imaginative study of participation by the private individual in democratic processes. Barber analyzes the forms of participation, the forces that make the individual act, and the factors that limit him.

Fromm, Erich, *Escape From Freedom* * (Holt, Rinehart and Winston, 1941). A study of what induces individuals and societies to surrender democratic freedoms. Fromm stresses the fragility of the individual as well as his capacity to resist external pressures that can push him into abandoning democracy.

Greenberg, Edward S., *Political Socialization* * (Atherton Press, 1970). A useful compilation of readings on political socialization. The selections deal with major contributors to socialization (such as the family, education, religion), with alienation and radicalization, and with resocialization.

Hyman, Herbert H., *Political Socialization* * (Free Press, 1969). A revision of a pioneering work that emphasizes such elements as learning, the formation of political attitudes, the influence of age, peers, family, and class in political socialization.

Lane, Robert E., *Political Life* * (Free Press, 1969). Interprets and integrates a large body of research on popular participation and factors that influence democracy, such as the individual's needs, economic conditions, social mobility, leadership, and class. Lane also examines the principal methods of participation and their gains and costs.

Lane, Robert E., *Political Thinking and Consciousness* * (Markham, 1969). Based on a study of twenty-four persons, this book explores the relation of needs, values, and other aspects of the self to political thinking. While not explicit in democratic terms, Lane's analysis can be readily applied to a democratic political system.

Lindsay, A. D., *The Modern Democratic State,* * 2 volumes (Oxford University Press, 1943). A classic treatment of the nature of democracy by the British political scientist and historian. Lindsay discusses some key concepts of democracy, their historic roots, and the dangers of modern industrial life to democracy.

Lipset, Seymour Martin, *Political Man* * (Doubleday, 1963). A wide-ranging work analyzing forces and conditions that affect democracy, such as equality, cleavage, apathy, the economy, class, and the distribution of political skills.

MacIver, Robert M., *The Ramparts We Guard* (Macmillan, 1950). A cogent analysis, by a distinguished sociologist and political theorist, of such concepts as equality, popular control, minority rights, and class. MacIver traces the impact on democracy of forces such as anomie and war.

Mayo, Henry B., *An Introduction to Democratic Theory* * (Oxford University Press, 1960). The leading work on the nature of democracy, its theory, historic components, and key concepts. Mayo also includes Marxist and other critiques of democracy.

Padover, Saul K., *The Meaning of Democracy* (Praeger, 1963). A convenient, brief treatment of the problem of defining democracy and of the historic contributors to that task—early and modern European and American writers and public figures, religion, and social movements. Particularly useful is the author's assessment of democracy's links to utopian and moralistic thinking.

Simon, Yves R., *Philosophy of Democratic Government* * (University of Chicago Press, 1951). A keen analysis of democratic concepts like equality, "the people," and the majority-minority relationships, and of the influence on democracy of such forces as humanism, technology, urbanism, and large organizations.

Skinner, B. F., *Beyond Freedom and Dignity* * (Knopf, 1971). An eminent psychologist, in assessing the possibilities of behavioral engineering, rejects democracy as scientifically invalid.

* Available in paperback edition

consensus,

conflict,

change

Shortly before the 1972 Democratic National Convention, a National Conference on Strip Mining met at Middleboro, Kentucky, in the scenic Cumberland Gap, and delegates reported on how strip mining defaced hillsides in many areas of the country, how coal company lawyers employed divisive tactics, how government officials responded cautiously, and how giant earth-moving machines threatened life styles in growing numbers of states. Strip miners, declared the president of the conservation group "Save Our Kentucky," are "just a bunch of primitives running around profit-crazy on a bulldozer." The delegates adopted a resolution urging the abolition of strip mining and laid plans to push for its incorporation into the national Democratic platform.

As they deliberated, the delegates' fervor was somewhat modulated by the presence of more than one hundred strip miners from nearby counties who wore their work clothes and hard hats pasted with stickers that said "Coal Puts Bread on My Table." A spokesman for small mining companies addressed the conference and defended "responsible" surface mining as preferable to more perilous underground mining. Afterward, he said of the delegates, "These people have the emotions of idealism, which is fine, but my men have the emotions of their livelihood, which is a lot stronger." Although the miners booed most of the speakers, many engaged in earnest discussion with conservationists outside the meeting, and, according to a reporter, "some participants expressed hope of reaching deeper understanding." [1]

The two faces
of democracy

The episode at Middleboro illuminates the two faces of democratic society. Democracy requires a process of conflict to permit challenges to established policy and those in authority, leading possibly to the replacement of both.

[1] George Vecsey, "Parley Concerned Over Increased Use of Strip Mining," *New York Times,* June 19, 1972.

Democracy also requires a consensus-structure that permits the peaceful play of power—the effective right of both sides of the mining question to speak at the conference and at the Democratic National Convention and, by their exchange, to promote "deeper understanding." Indulgence in conflict and in explorations for consensus is predicated on the widely held value of the right of each side of the question to be heard. Consensus and conflict both contribute to the integration of society, and in Kentucky they were complementary and mutually supporting.

Powerful forces in American society feed the chances of conflict. Clashes of interest between economic groupings, especially between industrial workers and their employers, are frequent. Fluctuating economic conditions sometimes bring severe unemployment, a powerful seed of conflict. The luxury and conspicuous consumption of the wealthy contradict the equalitarian ideals of a culture that rejects privilege for any special group or class. Relatively high levels of aspiration prevail at nearly all levels of income-power hierarchies. But the continuous upward pressures thereby generated cause strain because opportunities are not bountiful or available enough for the actual success of each. The people are polarized into camps of "haves" and "have nots," and conflict in the moral framework erupts when the criteria of equal opportunity and personal achievement clash head-on, particularly in the embittering experiences of ethnic and racial minorities restricted by discrimination.[2]

Nevertheless, America is often hailed as a society that is remarkably free of conflict, with a high order of consensus and integration. The image is fostered by the high level of real income and its relatively wide distribution, by the strong reality of upward mobility and its steady reinforcement of the hope of "getting ahead," by the existence and the spurting growth in the last decades of a huge middle-income, middle-prestige group, by the widespread enhancement of equal legal rights for minorities, and by the persistence of an elaborate body of beliefs and values that impart legitimacy to the political and social system. Friction is held to a low point by the vagueness and flexibility of status discriminations, the prevalence of "democratic manners." And the fact that the composition of the various classes is not homogeneous diminishes the likelihood of class-structured collective action, particularly in labor organization and political activity.

Consensus gains from America's attempt to actualize its ideal of equal opportunity through mass education. No other society commits so much time and resources to formal schooling, nor makes it more widely available. Consensus also draws strength from the ability of various religious groups— Protestants, Catholics, Jews—to live together harmoniously in the same society, thanks to the diminished intensity of their traditional religious values and the sharing of a substantial body of nonreligious goals. Society's unity needs are well served by a body of common symbols that, because they have a minimum of specific ideological content, create a common allegiance by being all things to all people. The Constitution, the Supreme Court, and George

[2] Robin M. Williams, Jr., *American Society* (New York: Knopf, 1952), 12–14, 124–26.

Washington embody national virtues, a set of referents useful for a wide range of citizen orientations.[3]

The two faces of democratic politics—conflict and consensus—are mirrored in the behavior of its politicians. Not a few gain popularity by cultivating combative images, in the manner of a former mayor of Jersey City who blocked workmen from cutting trees on a public road and who told a group of businessmen seemingly lacking in civic spirit that their anthem should be, "O say can you see what's in it for me."[4] Most politicians, however, are masters of a consensus style—mild in discourse, adept at appeal to the better side of obstinate interests, and capable of smoothing and patting their way through erupting trouble.

Examination of the tenure of virtually any political officeholder discloses striking moments of both consensus-building and conflict. Within a matter of mere days President Nixon consorted with the leaders of Communist China and the Soviet Union, exchanging toasts of lofty sentiment and concluding momentous agreements, while almost simultaneously he imposed a blockade on North Vietnam's ports to cut off the vast inflow of armaments from those giant Communist powers, thereby endangering their vessels and risking episodes that have in the past led to war.

Bruce Mazlish, in his *In Search of Nixon: A Psychohistorical Inquiry,*[5] reveals that the ambivalence of democratic society is duplicated in President Nixon's own make-up. On the one hand, as Mazlish recounts, there is a competitive, fighting "Tricky Dick," enamored of strength, who contrasts weak, self-indulgent students with the brave soldiers who "stand tall" in Vietnam. On the other hand, there is the Nixon who has an "obsession" (his own word) for peace, who visualized that the "major role" of his Presidency was "to attempt to make a contribution toward building world peace, with freedom for all people." In Freudian fashion, Mazlish traced the roots of Nixon's ambivalence to the mixed peaceful and combative nature of his parents—to a mother who was a devout Quaker committed to peace and to a competitive father, dreaded for his irritability and temper.

The basic consensus

Doesn't democracy require a basic consensus? Without an agreement on fundamentals, including the values on which democracy itself is predicated, effective government would be impossible. A basic consensus softens the animosities of conflict and permits divisive issues, which might otherwise rip society apart, to be coped with.

If we seek to identify the basic consensus, we would start by assuming that

[3] *Ibid.,* 128–32, 529–30.
[4] "Hard-Hitting Mayor: Thomas Joseph Whelan," *New York Times,* February 14, 1970.
[5] Bruce Mazlish, *In Search of Nixon: A Psychohistorical Inquiry* (New York: Basic Books, 1972).

people hold certain beliefs and attitudes widely. Measured by attitude scales, these would appear as strong unimodal distributions, which, when plotted, would most likely form a J-curve or a double J-curve (see figure). Presumably this basic consensus would include components like freedom of speech, the representative legislature, the courts, and their methods and roles. These generally held attitudes would be articulated to such a degree that they limit and guide government on specific matters.

Some sociologists contend that consensus is found less in commonly held beliefs than in a functional framework—the interdependence of groups and individuals regulates their conflicts. The division of labor among groups establishes their interdependence and·restrains extreme behavior against the system. Most labor unions, for example, are restrained to some degree by the recognition of their dependence on the continued survival of business. Such feelings of dependence underlie conflict situations generally—the legislature versus the executive, church versus state, family versus school—where, in each case, there are separate but interdependent functions. But interdependence is also a fulcrum of conflict since the withholding of cooperation provides one social entity with pressure against the other.[6]

Some assert that a basic consensus is revealed in the characteristic attitudes, beliefs, and behavioral patterns of the American people—in essence, their national character. Historians have turned out books sufficient to fill a sizable library delineating the components of the American character. The result is something like a warehouse inventory. The items also tend to cancel each other out. Compiling a list of American qualities from commentaries published at home and abroad, Lee Coleman found that every trait, good and bad, has been cited. Americans are generous and niggardly, sympathetic and unfeeling, idealistic and cynical. They are as bewilderingly human as any other people.[7]

Still other writers find the essence of the basic consensus in society's core values. Sociologist Seymour Martin Lipset argues that America's most continuing and dominant values have been equality and achievement.[8] Emphasis on work and success was long a tenet of the Protestant ethic, which early European immigrants brought to America. Equality or equalitarianism was part of the revolt against Old World traditions, but its chief impact has been in the political rather than in the economic order. The nation's wealth has never been as equally distributed as its political franchise because the ideal of achievement has tended to produce some persons who succeed more than others. But the uneven distribution of society's benefits has been checked to some degree by recurrent triumphs of equality's forces in the political order. These two dominant values are not always contradictory. Much discussion of

---

[6] Emile Durkheim, *Division of Labor in Society* (New York: Free Press, 1947), 129; Wilbert E. Moore, *Industrial Relations and the Social Order* (New York: Macmillan, 1951), 338–39.

[7] In Michael McGiffert, ed., *The Character of Americans* (Homewood, Ill.: Dorsey Press, 1970), 14–16.

[8] *Ibid.*, 269 ff.

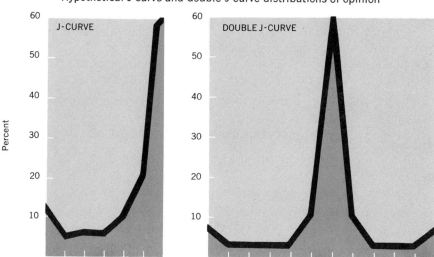

Hypothetical J-curve and double J-curve distributions of opinion

Source: Adapted from V. O. Key, Jr., *Public Opinion and American Democracy* (New York: Knopf, 1965), 29.

equality has centered on equality of opportunity, which affirms that achievement and success should be the goal of all, regardless of class, color, or other differences.

The continuity of the core values has been questioned. Lipset argues that these values have persisted, but that changing conditions sometimes fortify one at the expense of the other or alter the internal content of each. Equality has recently been advanced by rising education levels and liberal social programs, and nowadays achievement is scored less by swashbuckling entrepreneurs than through striving in bureaucratic elites. Lipset interprets the thesis of David Riesman's *The Lonely Crowd*—that America is moving from its historic inner-directed character to being other-directed—as essentially manifesting institutional adjustment to social changes. Other-directedness stems from the rise of urban and bureaucratic life requiring the enlargement of an already existing equalitarian disposition to be concerned with the opinions of others and to stress social mobility.[9]

A basic consensus should not only have substance; it should be widely held. But a study by political scientist Herbert McClosky of the extent to which beliefs are shared on such components of a basic consensus as freedom of speech, equality of opportunity, majority rule, and minority rights, revealed that the consensus holders may be limited in number.[10] On the basis of national surveys carried out on two separate samples, one consisting of "political

[9] David Riesman, Nathan Glazer, and Reuel Denney, *The Lonely Crowd* (New York: Doubleday, Anchor Books, 1953), 269–89.
[10] Herbert McClosky, "Consensus and Ideology in American Politics," *American Political Science Review,* LVIII (June 1964), 361–74.

actives" or "influentials" or "leaders," and the other a representative selection of adults in the general population, McClosky found that political influentials (government officials, elected office-holders, active party members, publicists, opinion-makers, and interest group leaders) have a more developed sense of the basic consensus and a firmer grasp of its essentials than has the general electorate. This superiority is evident in the influentials' stronger approval of democratic ideas, higher regard for fair procedures and citizen rights, and more affirmative attitudes toward the democratic system in general. In contrast, large portions of the electorate have failed to grasp many underlying democratic ideas and principles. The influentials rather than the public are major repositories of the basic consensus, and responsibility for its perpetuation falls heavily on them.

Do these findings reveal a major flaw in the fabric of basic consensus? As McClosky notes, his survey may exaggerate the role of intellectual factors and ideas in the operation of democracy, and the high order of rationality in the system. Although many people cannot articulate the basic consensus, it is nevertheless a part of their lives. Also, the electorate is improving. Higher education, rapid social mobility, urbanization, and the media should produce a more numerous class of influentials schooled in the basics of democracy.[11]

Building and maintaining consensus

Consensus is built and maintained by institutions, public and private. Among the more important public institutions are the major political parties, which are accustomed to making broad appeals to all strata. The practice of electing legislative representatives from territorial—and therefore heterogeneous—constituencies forces parties to foster concern for many viewpoints and tolerate compromise. Bureaucracy is one of the most assured means of building consensus, since it tends to draw into its own processes the conflicts exploding in the political arena. By stressing objectivity in coping with these conflicts, bureaucracy plays mediating, and therefore consensus-building, roles.

The role of community. The possibilities of building political consensus depend heavily on how well what sociologist Robert Nisbet calls "the quest for community" is proceeding. Community is a complex of healthy social conditions concerning integration, status, membership, norms, identification, groups.[12] Contemporary democracy is hampered in seeking consensus by the weakening of historic forces that have been beneficial to community. For example, the transformation of the United States from an agricultural to an urban-industrial society has diminished the significance of the family, the

---

[11] *Ibid.*, 379.
[12] Robert A. Nisbet, *The Quest for Community* (New York: Oxford University Press, 1953), 23.

Consensus: "Sweep-in" in Spanish Harlem, 1968. Volunteers from suburbs surrounding New York City organized a clean-up campaign in a ghetto neighborhood.

small local community, and other traditional relationships that have mediated between the individual and society. Those institutions nurture the principal types of identification—affection, friendship, prestige, and recognition—and the incentives of work and devotion to freedom and order.

The contemporary weakening of consensus and its collapse into alienation for many citizens is aggravated in the industrial-urban culture by inadequate interpersonal relations. Feelings of moral estrangement, of the world's hostility, of irrational aggressiveness, of helplessness in the face of problems stem in no small degree from the individual's sense of the unavailability of fruitful primary (face-to-face) relationships. Their denial is contrived by the hidden decision-makers where he works whose rulings hurt his advancement, the remote union chief, the faceless bureaucracy that disposes of his rights. The solution to this woe? Nisbet looks to the restoration of meaningful interpersonal relations through strengthening the family, the local community, the small informal groups that spring up around common interests and social needs. As well, he proposes the personalization of the larger social associations —the churches, businesses, labor unions, universities, and the professions, "the real sources of liberal democracy." [13]

In consensus politics, the squeaking wheel gets the grease. Consensus

[13] *Ibid.*, 49–51, 268.

politics tends to count silence as acquiescence and therefore to overlook the unarticulated need, the unspoken resentment. Consider, for example, the plight of the white suburban "invisible poor," as they have been called by one victim, who also described her poverty as "quiet," "hidden," and "voiceless." Often the victims of economic recession, white suburban poor typically live dispersed in their community in neat, although aging and crumbling, working class homes. They are much less obvious than the nonwhite poor who are generally restricted to segregated housing. Most antipoverty programs are concentrated in nonwhite areas, but the white poor are reluctant to participate anyway. "People treat you differently if they find you're poor or on welfare," a poor white suburban woman said, "I have friends who never tell. Some landlords will evict you if they find out." The black and Puerto Rican officials of suburban antipoverty agencies will make only the most cursory effort to involve their white clients. They contend that whites can pull themselves out of poverty since they do not suffer from racial discrimination. "A white man's got no business being poor in America" is a common expression among black antipoverty officials.[14]

Political integration. According to the logic of consensus, democratic citizens should aspire to the integration of political communities. Integration is marked by strong cohesiveness within a social group. It encompasses a variety of mutual ties that heighten for the individual and the groups to which he belongs feelings of identity and self-awareness. Political integration, which any political entity, whether the local community, state, or nation, may aspire to, can reduce the isolation of the individual or distance between the races.[15]

Integrative influences include geographic proximity, transactions or interactions among persons or groups, mutual knowledge, shared functional interests, governmental effectiveness, the particular system of power and decision-making, and previous integrative experiences. Transactions include communications or the interchange of messages (mail, telephone, television), trade, and the mobility of persons or frequency of personal contact. Mutual knowledge is more than just a product of propinquity; it must rise to the level of understanding.

There are several theories and models to enhance the progress of political integration. A "spillover" theory, for example, holds that agreements between communities beget more agreements; for example, local neighborhoods or governments that agree to mutual use of libraries are more likely to move on to mutual use of police facilities than communities lacking such agreements. A "payoffs" model for political cooperation attributes the incidence and increase of cooperative acts between individuals and communities to rational calculation by each side of payoffs and rewards. Thus if the white businessman

---

[14] *New York Times,* August 2, 1971.
[15] Philip E. Jacob and James V. Toscano, *The Integration of Political Communities* (Philadelphia: J. B. Lippincott, 1964), 3–4.

is confronted with losses for continuing discriminatory practices, he may be motivated to change his habits and welcome black customers.[16]

There is such a thing as excessive consensus or integration. An investigative study of the United States Forest Service, for example, was highly critical of the organization's tendency to overrespond to pressures from exploitative interests, particularly from mining and grazing representatives, to the neglect of other responsibilities, such as conservation and recreation. A prime exhibit in the study was a comparison of the Forest Service's budget adjustments. Over an eight-year period, from 1962 to 1970, outlays for timber-sale administration and management were trimmed only 5 percent, while those for recreation fell by 55 percent.[17]

Anatomy of conflict

Conflict, democracy's other face, involves struggle over values and claims to scarce status, power, and resources, in which the opponents seek to neutralize, injure, or eliminate one another. Conflict is the typical process by which candidates are elected and public policy is produced in democracy. The passage of any important law is the product of a series of conflicts. Typically, American democracy is the scene of multiple conflicts, as the daily newspaper and television all too amply testify. But the number of conflicts may not be a reliable clue to the seriousness of the phenomenon. As sociologist Edward A. Ross observed: "A society . . . which is ridden by a dozen oppositions running in every direction may actually be in less danger of being torn with violence or falling to pieces than one split just along one line." [18]

The individual's conflict behavior has psychological contours. It may erupt when, frustrated or blocked from attaining some goal, he responds with aggression. His spring into conflict may be prodded by his perceptions, or how he sees his environment, a motivation that is highly vulnerable to error, subjectivity, and distortion. A very selective perception maintains differential images of reality, in the sense of portraying "our" group as virtuous and deserving and "their" group as bad and treacherous. Recall also may be selective, favoring one point of view and forgetting contradictory evidence. Individuals may indulge in displacement, or the transfer of their hostility to a person or object not involved in the original frustration, and in projection, which exaggerates in other persons a characteristic one does not wish to recognize in himself. Conflict may be triggered by threat and anxiety, or by what in reality is tension. This also induces polarization, an exaggeration of attributes that would otherwise appear only slightly good or bad.[19]

[16] *Ibid.,* 259–62.
[17] *New York Times,* June 6, 1970.
[18] Edward A. Ross, *The Principles of Sociology* (New York: The Century Company, 1920), 164–65.
[19] Elton B. McNeil, ed., *The Nature of Human Conflict* (Englewood Cliffs, N.J.: Prentice-Hall, 1965), 46–62.

Conflict: Antiwar demonstrators vs. Washington police . . .

Types of conflict

What differentiations can we make among the many kinds of conflicts raging in the daily turmoil of politics? To begin with, sociologists distinguish between *realistic* and *nonrealistic* conflict. Nonrealistic conflict, typified by the rioting in the black urban ghettos in the late 1960s, does not calculate the chances for success or gain, and it may be undertaken when neither is possible. It is occasioned by the need of one or more of the interacting persons or groups to release aggressive tensions arising from deprivations and frustrations and from the conversion of originally realistic antagonism that was not allowed expression.

Realistic conflict evolves from rational assessments concerning means and needs, and is exemplified by the marches led by Martin Luther King, Jr., to protest some defined evil and exert pressure for its abolition. Realistic conflict will cease if the actor can find equally satisfying alternative ways to achieve his purpose. Alternative ways other than conflict are ordinarily available, but they may not be as satisfactory. Realistic conflict is apt to arise from competing claims to scarce status, power, and resources, from assertion of opposing values, from the frustration of demands, and from expectation of gains.[20]

[20] Lewis A. Coser, *The Functions of Social Conflict* (New York: Free Press, 1956), 50–54.

. . . And hardhats vs. antiwar demonstrators.

Political conflict is often *communications* conflict. Political words and acts convey cues and signals of combative intentions and resolves. A confrontation between the Nixon administration and the Union Carbide Corporation over the adequacy of the company's plans to diminish air pollution at its Marietta, Ohio, ferro-alloy plant was watched as a likely indicator of the strength of the administration's determination to curb pollution. The company proposed to cut sulphur dioxide emissions by 12.5 percent, but the administration, rising to its test, insisted on a 40 percent reduction. Ralph Nader and his associates had contributed to making it a test case by giving attention to the depredations of the offending Marietta plant and by publicizing calls on government to act.[21]

In politics, conflicts also have *symbolic* functions. Political leaders, for example, sometimes eagerly seek out new enemies in order to maintain or improve group cohesion or to deflect blame for the failure of a program or policy. Franklin Roosevelt inveighed against "economic royalists," vaguely identified business interests that, he declared, were obstructing his own good works. In Roosevelt's eyes, a function of his conflict with this business scapegoat was to move labor more solidly into the ranks of his supporters.

Politics is ridden with *value* conflicts. Values embrace ideals, goals, norms, and standards, and are objects of individual or collective striving. Value

[21] *New York Times,* December 24, 1970.

conflicts may involve costs, in the sense that if the goal of one contestant is fulfilled it will be at the cost of the other. In politics, value conflicts often derive from formulations calling on government to "do more" or "do less." Illustrative of this type of conflict is the departure in 1970 of Dr. Stanley F. Yolles as chief mental health officer of the Department of Health, Education, and Welfare. Dr. Yolles charged the Nixon administration with "abandonment of the mentally ill," "sharp curtailment" of research support, and "substitution of rhetoric for monetary support in Federal drug abuse and alcohol control programs." "Because of the money shortage," Dr. Yolles noted, no new Community Health Centers were to be started. After these prickly observations, Dr. Yolles did not remain long in his post. Press reports attributed his departure to "pressure from presidential aides," and administration spokesmen were soon citing his "complete unwillingness to cooperate . . . for more effective mental health programs." [22]

Conflict may be a *power struggle* for dominance over decision-making that determines the allocation of governmental resources and benefits. The Model Cities program, a federal-local attack on urban problems, has long been the scene of conflict between organizations of residents of model neighborhoods and city hall over control of the money to be spent. Originally, the Johnson administration called for citizen control, but in the Nixon administration control was shifted to city hall. The struggle moved into the courts when a citizens' board sued the principal federal agency involved, the Department of Housing and Urban Development, but the suit was dismissed. In further actions the administration induced several cities to revise ordinances that gave the neighborhood boards a veto over city hall. It was argued that only regularly elected officials and not special organizations can ultimately be held accountable for funds. Power conflicts, too, require rationalization. [23]

Conflict-generating situations

Several kinds of situations, experience amply demonstrates, are especially apt to generate conflict. One is the discovery of problems that insist on public policy response. In the late 1960s and in the 1970s, congressional hearings and White House conferences brought to light the widespread incidence of malnutrition in the United States, a problem long ignored and sometimes blatantly denied. One of the more startling revelations emerged in the testimony of a medical expert before a Senate committee recounting gross malnutrition among children of migrant workers, to the point of serious protein and calorie deficiencies. Accompanying the testimony were slides showing a bloated, spindly-limbed baby suffering from marasmus, scurvy, rickets, and pneumonia. The child, it was said, had "no detectable vitamin C in his blood."

[22] *New York Times,* June 3, 1970.
[23] *New York Times,* December 15, 1969.

Nov.4,1972 **THE** Price 50 cents

NEW YORKER

Further testimony disclosed widespread incidence of migrant-worker babies with graying hair, and children with distended mouths and disorders of the skin, eye, tongue, nose, ear, ribs, and liver.

To officials in power, a particularly unwelcome aspect of these startling findings was their implied criticism of existing policies, a judgment that other witnesses candidly articulated. A churchwoman attacked "the stifling bureaucracy, at all levels of government." Others blamed the absence of effective moral leadership from the President, and still others pointed out that existing programs were hobbled by administration foot-dragging, prompted not by any excessive scope of its program but because of "underfunding of practically every program." And others criticized impending nutrition surveys "which will provide interesting data for the health professions but will not bring any benefits to the participants or the people examined." [24]

Another source of conflict is the newcomer, a ready object of suspicion and rejection, particularly if he is beheld as a threat to established power. The potency of the newcomer to arouse conflict is evident in the experiences of the body of new young voters created by the Twenty-Sixth Amendment, which lowered the voting age for all elections to eighteen. By this innovation quantities of college students were transformed into potential voters in local elections. State attorneys general and courts had to rule on whether students could vote in their college community, claimed as their place of residence,

[24] *New York Times,* February 24, 1971.

even though they dwelt in dormitories and were financially dependent on their parents. In Massachusetts, the Attorney General ruled that they could choose their college community as their place of residence, for voting purposes. Suddenly, the electorate in some of the state's college towns consisted of a brand new majority—students—often to the dread of noncollege townfolk and their leaders. The real test, said one selectman, is the town meeting, normally attended by 10 percent of the voters in his community, but "if the students come out in force they could flood the town meeting and put through anything they want without having the interest of the town at heart." [25] Other pronouncements from the established power centers were even less hospitable to the newcomers.

A fertile situation promoting conflict is the possibility of gain or loss for some interest, particularly if the interest is of the bread-and-butter variety. Phases 1 and 2 of the Nixon administration's wage-price controls provide ample evidence. The AFL-CIO, several of whose officers originally were members of the federal Pay Board, received a jolting blow when the Board voted to set a 5.5 percent standard for wage increases. All five labor members dissented but were outvoted, and the flames of conflict crackled when George Meany, the AFL-CIO president, declared that unions "will not stand still and see our contracts abrogated, our work standards destroyed, and our earnings diminished while all around us other sections of the community are doing business as usual." [26] The conflict escalated to the point that all labor members, except one, withdrew from the Pay Board.

Conflict is also to be expected when public policy moves to shift the established balance of power between classes and groups, particularly if the redress favors the less propertied. The California Rural Legal Assistance project, which drew financial support from both the federal Office of Economic Opportunity and the state of California, provides legal aid to the state's poor. Governor Ronald Reagan's rising displeasure with the project and its work resulted in his veto of refunding by his state and the issuance, over his signature, of a 283-page document of charges against the project. Among other things, these statements declared that the project had fomented violence in penal institutions, unlawfully represented labor unions, forced clients to initiate class action suits, and participated in the case of Angela Davis. In a counterthrust, the OEO appointed a panel of justices whose report absolved the project of wrongdoing and criticized the Reagan administration for making the accusations. [27]

Conflict regulation

One cannot imagine a successfully functioning democracy where conflict rages furiously and continuously and its waging becomes a general preoccupation.

[25] *New York Times,* July 25, 1971.
[26] *New York Times,* November 11, 1971.
[27] *New York Times,* July 1, 1971.

In democracy, conflict requires at least a modicum of regulation, whose purpose is not to eliminate conflict, but to restrict, control, redirect, and sometimes even to encourage it.

The culture is a major source of regulation; it stresses cooperation, patience, self-control, and other conflict modifiers. Any culture is concerned with curbing hostility and aggression. Early socialization contributes to conflict regulation. Children learn that if they engage in too much conflict, they lose parental approval and affection. Political society provides rules governing conflict that protect the contestants' freedom and safety and bar such acts as slander and conspiracy. Much of the federal Constitution, with its Bill of Rights, regulates conflicts, including those in which government itself is a contestant.

The social system provides for ways to regulate conflict. The moral consensus embracing commitments to justice and equity enables conflicts to be settled by appeals to those norms. Another mode is physical coercion, by which legitimate agencies of enforcement impose settlements in conflict situations according to their own operational code, subject in some instances to constitutional review. A further mode, facilitated by society but enforced by the contestants themselves, is a bargaining process, by which each side calculates the pros and cons of the solutions available and then chooses the most rationally gainful one. Political society also provides incentives for conflict settlement—the approval of the public and of political leaders, the allocation of extra benefits, and the withholding of penalties. In effect, it is a reward and punishment system, with the rewards bestowed only on those who display certain kinds of defined behavior or become a specific kind of person.

The uses of conflict

In the prevailing stereotype, conflict is abhorred as disruptive and divisive, a threat to democratic functioning and stability. But conflict can also serve democracy. Some of its more constructive possibilities are suggested by the experience of the black civil rights movement.

The movement can be interpreted as employing "realistic conflict" to achieve its purposes. This model views race relations as power relations and race prejudice as "a sense of group position." Within the guidelines of realistic conflict, the movement employs rational assessments concerning both means and ends, overt action directed toward specific social goals, and collective sanctions to enforce black demands. The realistic conflict model excludes such elements as spontaneous outbursts and nonrationalized violent behavior.[28] In implementing the realistic conflict approach, the black civil rights movement of the 1950s and 1960s used legal redress or court action; political action

[28] Joseph S. Himes, "The Functions of Racial Conflict," *Social Forces,* 45 (September 1966), 1–10. Also in Edward S. Greenberg, Neal Milner, and David J. Olson, *Black Politics* (New York: Holt, Rinehart and Winston, 1971), 325–39.

through individual voting, bloc voting, and lobbying; and nonviolent mass action applying overt pressure and public relations techniques to enforce specific demands.

What gains did blacks achieve through realistic conflict according to democratic criteria? Mobilized black social power reduced differences in power between blacks and whites and altered the direction of social interaction. It diminished superficiality and digressiveness in racial issues, and the fact of conflict itself was rewarding, since it redefined previously unequal adversaries as status equals. Through realistic conflict many blacks gained a substantial measure of identity within the social system (although for many others, it must be conceded, realistic conflict has so far been grossly insufficient).

Martin Luther King, Jr., described the function of realistic conflict this way: "Nonviolent direct action seeks to create such a crisis and foster such a tension that a community which has constantly refused to negotiate is forced to confront the issue. It seeks so to dramatize the issue that it can no longer be ignored." [29] Through voter registration campaigns, boycotts, and sit-ins blacks assumed status equality and rejected traditional, nonequalitarian poses of supplication and condescension. The ultimate aim of realistic conflict is to institutionalize these equalitarian gains into the larger social system—to desegregate education and eliminate discrimination in employment, housing, recreation, and other social endeavor.

If, as may be argued, justice can be won in democracy chiefly by mobilizing group strength, realistic conflict contributes significantly to that purpose. Rather than destroying group unity, realistic conflict increases it by strengthening group awareness, maintaining group boundaries, and making more definite the group's identity in the political-social system. Realistic conflict helps stabilize the social system by engaging groups in interaction that clears the air through free expression. Otherwise, in the contrived atmosphere of general consensus, groups may become disaffected to the point of alienation and withdrawal.

Conflict is, then, a safety valve for the social system. It enables hostile and aggressive sentiments to be released, instead of being bottled up and ultimately exploding. Realistic conflict enlarges the scope of those involved in democratic politics. The drama of conflict and the emergence of charismatic leaders have focused public attention on the racial issue. The mass media have reported the controversies and events, and millions of otherwise uninformed and indifferent persons have become attentive to the conflict.

Realistic conflict, as typified by the black civil rights movement, can serve to affirm the core values of American democracy. One of these values— equality and its corollary, justice—initiated both creed and action in the conflict, and the demonstrators' opponents—the burly sheriffs with their police dogs, the local vigilantes, and cross-burners—have been left in the posture of attacking the national ethos. Conflict can reaffirm the basic values of society,

[29] Greenberg, Milner, and Olson, 329–30.

and the consensus into which they are woven, and endow them with fresh concern and understanding.[30]

Public opinion

An underlying ingredient of both consensus and conflict is public opinion. The question to what extent either mood prevails at any moment in democracy depends on the state of that amorphous entity, public opinion—on how satisfied the giant public is with affairs or how much dissent and conflict rumble within its ranks.

What is this extraordinary phenomenon, public opinion? V. O. Key, Jr., defined it as encompassing "those opinions held by private persons whose governments find it prudent to heed. Many or few people may share this opinion, governments may feel compelled to act or not to act, and they may attempt to alter, divert, or pacify it." [31] So unevenly is public opinion distributed that distinction is made between an attentive and inattentive public. The attentive public is watchful and informed on public affairs, but on most issues it probably numbers no more than a quarter of the electorate. It is regrettable for democracy that no informed majority exists.

Some typologies of the inattentive public subdivide its membership. One survey taken in the late 1940s estimated that 30 percent of the population were "unaware" of any given event in foreign affairs. Another 45 percent were estimated to be "aware but uninformed," in the sense that they might have heard of the Marshall Plan (operating then) but were uninformed of its purpose. The rest were classed as "informed" in that they could tolerably explain the Marshall Plan's purposes. Generally, public opinion shows a more favorable distribution on broad questions than on specific laws or actions of which there is no wide awareness.[32]

Who are the attentive public? Unfortunately, surveys are lacking to afford a very precise idea. Among the most prominently identified are those with a direct concern in particular policies or public actions, such as veterans and Parent-Teacher Associations. Professional groups are habitually alert, and others who believe that their exertions affect what government does. Many are psychologically involved, with a particular care or taste for political life. But the composition of the attentive public fluctuates on different issues and occasions.

The general public expresses itself with greatest clarity in elections, when it disapproves of past policy and official performance, although it cannot specify with particularity what it disapproves and what it wants changed. A

[30] *Ibid.,* 336; Coser, 8.
[31] V. O. Key, Jr., *Public Opinion and American Democracy* (New York: Knopf, 1965), 14.
[32] Martin Kriesberg, "Dark Areas of Ignorance," in Lester Markel, ed., *Public Opinion and Foreign Policy* (New York: Harper & Row, 1949), 51.

An attentive public gives its opinion.

common frustration of electorates is the phenomenon of noncongruent majorities, such as may transpire when two or more issues divide voter opinion along different planes. If a majority on one issue prevails, the majority on the other may be defeated. Thus those who were both isolationist and liberal or internationalist and conservative could not, during the 1960s, adjust easily to the alternatives offered by the major parties.

The view of popular democracy as interaction between public opinion and government assumes a two-way flow of communications between citizens and officials. Political leaders may use communications persuasively to induce citizens to consent to policy. As a defense, the citizen can obtain information and interpretations concerning governmental actions from sources independent of government. As critical communications stemming from the public come to outweigh favorable ones, governmental policy may change to synchronize better with public opinion. Key has likened public opinion to a system of dikes that channel public action or delimit a range within which government may act. Key does not conceive of public opinion as some mysterious kind of referendum on every issue that instructs government how to act. Rather, he contended, a rough parallelism exists between action and opinion that is imprecise in detail and prevails for broad purposes.[33]

[33] Key, 552–53.

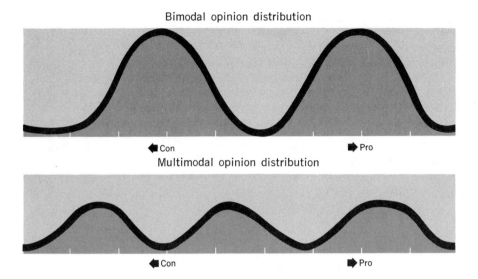

Source: Adapted from V. O. Key, Jr., *Public Opinion and American Democracy* (New York: Knopf, 1965), 55.

Consensus and conflict are largely matters of opinion. When much of the population is involved in conflict, as it has been over school busing or ending the Vietnam war, the distribution of opinion takes either a bimodal form, with two clusters of opinion, or a multimodal form, with clusters of opinion concentrated at three or more points along a scale (see figure). For the multimodal pattern to occur, three or more solutions to a problem, or viewpoints about it, must command sizable public support. Its distribution is especially common among political elites and highly informed and interested publics. In the general public, the bimodal pattern is far more common. Often the stirrings of reconciliation may lurk in opinions arrayed in a firm conflict pattern. The outcome of a conflict may depend on the direction in which those citizens shift who occupy the central position or on their ability to pull to a central position those situated at the extremes.

What bearing do conflict and consensus patterns in public opinion have on the governmental apparatus? The most marked political consensus—the unity of public opinion after the attack on Pearl Harbor, for example—can prompt congressional action without delay and with absolute clarity. On the other hand, data indicate that a fairly small minority (such as the gun lobby) can also support a formidable outcry in Congress.

In the interaction between leaderships and the public, bipolarized clusters of opinion form foundations of support for opposing leadership cliques. In turn, the leaders' divisive oratory and aggressive maneuvers maintain cleavages within the public. But if a contending leadership viewpoint loses public support, it will most likely be weakened, and even destroyed, should it tarry

too long over a declining conflict. The wind-down of conflict and its displacement by consensus involves crucial interactions between leaderships and
masses of the public. Controversial policies such as Medicare, once established, may in time gain approval, and hostile leaderships and public opinion
clusters may lapse into passivity or even acquiescence. At other times, reconciliation may transpire first at the level of political leadership, after which
clusters of opposing public opinion may subside because of the lack of encouragement from leaders.

Party identification can be a powerful force in conflict distribution. For
many persons, parties are all-embracing reference symbols around which
loyalties, attitudes, beliefs, and opinions of the most diverse content may be
concentrated. For such persons, the parties form bimodal distributions, which
sometimes coincide with distributions of opinions about substantive issues.

The ordeal of change

Conflict and consensus are not terminal processes; they are often stepping-
stones to a further, equally important process—change. Like any other approach to the tasks of government and society, democracy is buffeted by alterations in the environment and the need for change they engender.
Accordingly, democracy is often the scene of conflict between those who profit
from established habits, on the one hand, and those, on the other, who wish to
transform responses to environmental alterations into new values and new
structures of allegiance.

At any moment, conflict over change may rage virtually anywhere—in
the family, at the work place, in the legislature, in professional meetings. The
conflict may be within a social system (a family or a community), but change
often encompasses conflict among institutions as well. Since each institution
constitutes a complex of functions and meanings in the lives of individuals
and demands their loyalties, a change in one institution—the loss or addition
of functions and meanings—must often react on the structure of some other
institution and thus ignite conflict.[34]

But change may be regulated, contained within well-defined parameters,
by consensus. Consensus politics is incremental politics—that is, bargaining
produces new policies that are only slightly different from the old. This procedure fosters stability, tolerates what at most is modest change, and forces
debate about change to center on means more than ends. Sets of complex operating procedures in the legislature, the political parties, and the selection of
the President all assure the ascendance of the bargaining-incremental approach
to change.

Conflicts that are less regulated by consensus and can therefore be broader

[34] Nisbet, 87–88.

and more intensive are valued by some sociologists for their capacity to produce major change. Such conflict, in their view, keeps the political and social system from ossification.[35] Two predominant forces are in a state of relative and almost continuous tension over change: those that seek to promote change and those that mean to keep the status quo. Since a tendency to change is fundamental in any culture, the forces favoring change eventually have their day of triumph, but the degree of their ascendance and the tempo at which it comes are uneven. Change often catches individuals and institutions unprepared, and "every radical adjustment," as Eric Hoffer put it, "is a crisis in self-esteem." [36] To change is to acknowledge the inadequacy both of existing policies and of the decision-makers who provided them, and drastic change reveals failure in its starkest outline.

Social group change. The worst problems of American democracy are those for which change is too slow or too drastically resisted. The readiest illustration is the plight of American blacks. Despite changes in laws and social attitudes, blacks remain the most deprived social group in America. Basically the problem is one of enabling a distinct subgroup, with little power, to gain the resources of power. The quest is not power for blacks over others, but a position in society permitting as much power over one's own life and over community and national actions as other citizens have—in short, full democratic citizenship. To suggest that change to achieve that end is possible is to assume that individuals and societies can alter their environment by force of will, that social change is not something the individual must stand helplessly by and await, but that he can control and direct.

In applying the concept of directed change to blacks, James S. Coleman has suggested the optimum state to strive for is "equality of opportunity." [37] He has also catalogued the several kinds of resources necessary to achieve it. These include private economic resources and public resources such as community services, political power, and the freedom of action implied by civil rights and civil liberties. Some resources can produce other resources that are deemed desirable. For example, Coleman cites data showing that freedom of social action, which includes work opportunities, affects other resources such as income. Economic power, in turn, is both a resource desirable in itself and a source of other resources—social position and political strength.

Coleman developed a system of social accounts, listing both assets and liabilities for such factors as black community and ethnic solidarity, family and personal resources, and political power. Among the liabilities are attributes of the larger community with adverse effects, such as white prejudice and the discriminatory job structure. Assets include the expanding wealth of the

---

[35] McNeil, 104.
[36] Eric Hoffer, *The Ordeal of Change* (New York: Harper & Row, 1952), 1.
[37] James S. Coleman, *Resources for Social Change: Race in the United States* (New York: Wiley-Interscience, 1971), *passim.*

nation (in which everybody gains) and sharp increases in black political power. A better life for blacks requires social change directed at reducing liabilities, enhancing assets, and converting assets of one type into assets of another. The timing and priorities of actions are crucial, since effects are interactive. As managers of social accounts, decision-makers would manipulate the many factors to produce change and improvement for a social group in the shortest possible time. Democracy, in these senses, is a matter of investment and profit.

Program change. Program change is a product of the interplay of environment and institutions, as illustrated by the Model Cities program, initiated in the Johnson administration and continued in altered form in the Nixon administration. In its original conception, the Model Cities program was to enable slum dwellers to fight back and rise out of urban squalor rather than resignedly subside into it. Enacted in 1966, the program was first called "Demonstration Cities," a name that understandably was changed following a summer of urban riots. The Model Cities program was distinctive for its many-pronged attack on social, economic, and physical problems of blighted city neighborhoods. Cities could not be improved simply by rebuilding them: education, health, transportation, and other facts of urban living must also be coped with. The Johnson administration stressed citizen participation in planning and implementing the program, while protecting and assuring the established local government's role.

The advent of the Nixon administration became a source of change for the Model Cities program. Presidential discourse quietly declined, presumably because the program was strongly identified with its Great Society origins. Some changes of administrative theme were also soon evident. For example, the program began to deemphasize citizen participation and enhance the role of the mayor and the local government. The highly inflated promises of results conveyed by the Johnson administration's rhetoric were curtailed and stress was put on the need for "more unified administration" at all levels. In other shifts, the Nixon administration reduced its budgetary support, and the radical impact that the program was originally envisioned to have on society has been deemphasized to the point of extinction. In the Nixon era, the program is chiefly used to regulate inter- and intragovernmental relations, rather than to manipulate city conditions in order to redistribute resources in favor of the ghetto poor, once a dream of Model Cities administrators in the Johnson era.[38]

Congress also produced changes in the program, although not as a result of party change, as in the Presidency. Members of Congress, some in key committee positions, forced the Johnson administration to modify its plans. In accordance with tradition, Congress was enthusiastic about local subsidy, but the administration was forced to include small cities and to drop its plan to

[38] Randall B. Ripley, *The Politics of Economic and Human Resource Development* (Indianapolis: Bobbs-Merrill, 1972), 138–39, 146–49.

use the program to further racial integration. In the Nixon era, Congress rejected some proposed administration modifications of the program. And while the Nixon administration has rendered dwindling support, Congress has gradually increased funding of the program.[39]

Change, as this experience indicates, is a product of interbranch and interparty rivalry, a ready source of issues, and an instrument in the quest of a Presidency for identity. Throughout the Model Cities experience, conflict raged between those who wanted more change and those who wanted less, and neither branch—Congress or the executive—continuously held a monopoly of either role, although each continuously asserted one or the other.

Institutional change. More resistant to change is an institution such as bureaucracy. For one thing, to a significant degree it is insulated from the effects of direct electoral action, a leading source of political change. The tendency of bureaus to routinize their work and to cherish an existing consensus for prevailing policy also makes the bureaucracy a mighty rock for resisting the forces of change. The problems and the possibilities are suggested by a 1971 reorganization of the Indian Affairs Bureau of the Interior Department after a prolonged struggle between young, activist "red power" Indians and old-line officials, most of them white.

After making striking gains during the tenure of Walter J. Hickel as Secretary of the Interior, the activists lost ground under his successor, Rogers C. B. Morton. The bureau's top official, Commissioner Louis Rooks Bruce, Jr., an Indian and pro-activist, found his power diluted when Secretary Morton appointed an old-line official, John O. Crow, a Cherokee, as deputy commissioner. Given sole power to redelegate authority, including that reserved for Commissioner Bruce, Crow quickly transferred the activists out of influential positions and forced others to resign. Tribal leaders who had once hoped for policy reforms now characterized the situation as "much thunder, but little rain."

The tempo of conflict stepped up when a group of tribal chiefs came to Washington and requested that the Indian Bureau be removed from the Interior Department and be placed in the White House. Simultaneously, a band of young militants invaded the bureau and attempted a citizens' arrest of Deputy Commissioner Crow who, to his own good fortune, was not in. The dual events sparked a quick reaction from President Nixon, who felt strongly that Indians should run their own affairs. The President summoned a high-level conference between Interior officials and the White House staff and admonished Secretary Morton concerning the Indian Bureau bureaucracy to "shake it up, shake it up good." A new day dawned for the activists. Commissioner Bruce was restored to full power, and activists refilled the key posts in the top echelon.

The reallocation of bureaucratic power was not the only prize of the conflict. At stake was a change in key policies. In the White House discussions

[39] *Ibid.,* 144–45.

Indians occupying the Bureau of Indian Affairs, November 1972.

President Nixon had called for a "new and coherent strategy." Commissioner Bruce soon announced that the bureau would push for a "total reservation economy," a main plank in the activist platform. The new policy, said Bruce, meant something more "than bringing to the reservation industries seeking cheap labor." Rather, Indian services would be developed on the reservation so that the Indian payroll will be spent among Indians rather than in the white satellite towns off the reservation. The change looked to the eventual possibility of Indian plumbers, Indian electricians, and Indian bankers. Instead of shipping young reservation Indians to job training centers in distant cities, they would henceforth be centered on the reservation for development of a local labor force.

But a year later the Indians felt these promising developments had not gone far enough, and they marched on Washington again in a protest of "broken treaties." After occupying the Bureau of Indian Affairs building for six days about 500 Indians agreed to evacuate on the basis of a peace pact worked out with presidential aides. It was agreed that on June 1, 1973, a federal study group would make recommendations to President Nixon that would take into consideration "the adequacy of governmental structures to coordinate programs and services for Indians" and "issues concerning fairness in institutions and practices for Indian self-government." A bureaucratic power conflict gave hope of producing policy changes that responded to constituency needs.[40]

Proposals

A high percentage of responses in surveys show the citizen to be ignorant of democratic values and uninformed in the basic knowledge of everyday politics. The citizen is not entirely at fault for these dreary showings. Blame can also be laid at government's doorstep. If it seems remote and indifferent to the citizen, more a source of burdens and obligations than of help, it is not surprising that he turns away.

If this diagnosis has merit, it can at least be hypothesized that citizen interest in politics will increase when government becomes more attentive and constructive toward the individual's needs and aspirations. By providing greater payoffs for the citizen's heightened interest and concern, a more responsive government would serve to enhance the quality of his performance as petitioner and participant. In time, this kind of citizen would come to value government and would become sophisticated in the ways of successful action. The display of petitioner-participant skills, it is submitted, is at least as valid a test of democratic performance as the surveys that ask respondents to recall the Bill of Rights and explain its key concepts. Fortunately, developments are stirring that better link the citizen and his needs with an attentive government.

1. A valuable trend that should be encouraged and extended is represented by two innovations of the federal government in New York City. Rather than wait for slum dwellers to come to them, federal officers are going into the slums themselves to seek out consumer complaints. Law students from the office of the United States Attorney for the New York district began by visiting housing projects in Harlem and the Lower East Side, querying families on their experiences with stores, door-to-door salesmen, bill collectors, and health clinics. In a second initiative, the Federal Trade Commission (FTC) is giving courses on consumer fraud to welfare clients.

In both ventures, the objective is to make low-income consumers, who usually are those most exploited by unconscionable merchants, aware of their rights and of the governmental agencies available to protect those rights. Slum residents "don't know where to turn or whom to turn to," remarked an Assistant United States Attorney and head of the consumer fraud unit. "Our survey is really educating them to the fact that we're here." An important ingredient in the development is the dependence of both the United States Attorney and the FTC on citizen response before they themselves can act. "We're absolutely powerless unless people in the community tell us about merchants who cheat them," the FTC regional director said. "We don't have all the answers, but we have the tools." The initial surveys turned up a substantial

[40] *New York Times,* November 18, 1971; January 9, 1972; November 8, 1972.

volume of matters to be investigated: neighborhood groceries that raise prices the day welfare checks arrive, door-to-door salesmen who take deposits on merchandise that is never delivered, butchers who sell rotten meat, credit agencies that use unlawful methods to collect debts, furniture dealers whose goods fall apart several weeks after they are bought.[41]

2. The consensus pattern of pluralism and incrementalism is, as we have seen, criticized for retarding change and for responding to it with inhibiting qualifications and limitations that leave public policy time and again out-stripped by technological change, economic fluctuations, and social trans-formations. Because of governmental inadequacy, the citizen is left to flounder and suffer with overwhelming problems ensuing from change—unemployment, the need to learn new job skills, catastrophic illness, and bureaucratic mysti-fications that affect his rights and that no one will clarify.

Louis Gawthrop has proposed that government make wider use of "the change agent." This is a type not often found in the bureaucracy. His major function would be to assist in improving the problem-solving ability of the private individual in relationship to his environment. Change agents are dis-tinguishable from "transfer agents," whose chief concern is the movement of material resources from government to individuals and communities.

The change agent, among other duties, would acquire information con-cerning the environment to guide decision-making by top executive officials. The agent must link centralized planning and programming with decentralized administration, where general policy is transformed into solutions of problems in a specific environment. Inventiveness will need to be a key trait of the change agent, together with a capacity to break away from orthodox ad-ministrative behavior. Finally, and most important, the agent must be a buffer between the citizen and his idiosyncrasies on the one hand and the im-personalized action-arm of democratic government, the bureaucracy, on the other hand.

This proposal assumes that democratic politics can help the individual de-velop skills to cope with change and to become, as much as possible, the master of his own destiny, the fulfillment of the ideal of democratic man— sovereign, capable, and responsible for making meaningful choices. The change agent would assist the individual in realizing that a life built around choices is far preferable to one without choice.[42]

Suggested Reading

Coleman, James S., *Resources for Social Change: Race in the United States* (Wiley-Inter-science, 1971). A cogent analysis of how blacks might achieve gainful social change, with an exploration of the kinds of resources that are necessary, the available assets,

---

[41] *New York Times,* August 8, 1971.
[42] Louis C. Gawthrop, *Administrative Politics and Social Change* (New York: St. Martin's Press, 1971), 99–102.

and their conversion into resources. The discussion focuses on major theories of social change.

Coser, Lewis A., *The Functions of Social Conflict* * (Free Press, 1956). A sociologist's pioneering study of social conflict, its sources and uses, and the means and strategies of waging it. Coser also explores the relationship of conflict to social consensus.

Foster, George M., *Traditional Cultures and the Impact of Technological Change* (Harper & Row, 1962). As a participant-observer in foreign aid programs in the newer nations, Foster writes from experience and offers many arresting insights concerning the role of culture in change, the cycle of change, barriers to change and strategies for dealing with them, and the motivations for change.

Greenberg, Edward S., Milner, Neal, and Olson, David J., *Black Politics* * (Holt, Rinehart and Winston, 1971). A wide-ranging collection of readings with valuable material on social consensus and conflict and their uses, from the vantage point of black politics. Particularly valuable is the presentation of the views of Martin Luther King, Jr., and his successors in the civil rights movement.

Hoffer, Eric, *The Ordeal of Change* * (Harper & Row, 1963). Penetrating philosophical insights into the nature of change and its functions by the former longshoreman and California agricultural worker.

Jacob, Philip E., and Toscano, James V., *The Integration of Political Communities* (Lippincott, 1964). A leading interpretive work of the motives, attitudes, and activities that promote political integration. The authors develop models and explore theories concerning their subject.

Key, V. O., Jr., *Public Opinion and American Democracy* (Knopf, 1965). The best work on the subject by an eminent political scientist. Key explores the nature of consensus and conflict, chiefly in terms of public opinion and the forces that influence it. He stresses the contributions of political parties, leaders, and interest groups.

McGiffert, Michael, *The Character of Americans* * (Dorsey Press, 1970). A valuable collection of readings concerning national characteristics, core values, value conflicts, and continuity and change in American values.

McNeil, Elton B., ed., *The Nature of Human Conflict* (Prentice-Hall, 1965). A comprehensive anthology dealing with the psychology of conflict, goals and methods of conflict management, and the uses of strategic and game-theory analysis.

Mills, C. Wright, *White Collar* * (Oxford University Press, 1951). Analysis of the impact of economic change on the middle class, the emergence of a new middle class, and its possibilities. The author, a distinguished sociologist, skillfully argues his thesis that politics and change are based on economics.

Nisbet, Robert A., *The Quest for Community* * (Oxford University Press, 1953). One of the best explorations of the nature of consensus, its contemporary weaknesses, and ways of strengthening it. Nisbet's analysis is developed within a framework of popular democracy.

Williams, Robin M., Jr., *American Society: A Sociological Interpretation,* 3rd edition (Knopf, 1970). A useful analysis of forces in American society that contribute to consensus, conflict, and change. Particularly valuable are White's analyses of the factors that contribute to social cohesiveness and those that make for anomie.

* Available in paperback edition

3

---

the

constitution:

origins

and

change

In 1970, Rexford Tugwell of the Center for the Study of Democratic Institutions in Santa Barbara, California, published his model for a new constitution for the United States.[1] The effort produced outcries from conservatives, who, as Felix Belair of the *New York Times* observed, viewed Tugwell's exercise as akin to redecorating a cathedral. It also displeased New Left radicals, who disdain any effort at constitutional reform as diversionary, a tactic to coopt the revolutionary drive for systemic change.

Tugwell, a former Roosevelt "Brain Truster" of the 1930s, argues that the present Constitution provides for "atomized government" and an approach to free enterprise that promotes "deliberate divisiveness, competition, the pursuit of self-interest, the exploitation of other individuals, and the private appropriation of natural materials and forces." During his public career and in constructing his model, Tugwell aspired to a constitutional order that would stress opposite qualities—"cooperation, integration, loyalty to the whole, and guidance by a concept of public rather than private interest."

In Tugwell's eyes, the existing Constitution suffers from serious omissions. It was a product of "battles now almost forgotten." Many important public activities are not contemplated by its provisions—education, Social Security, the system of national highways, the massive regulatory structure. The Constitution does not provide for public planning or for political parties; and while it speaks of the obligations of government to the citizen, little or nothing is said of the citizen's obligations to government. Its vague provisions, its excessive dispersal of power among three branches, and between the states and nation, and the difficulties of changing the Constitution, particularly by amendment, result, Tugwell finds, in a governmental system that favors the

---

[1] Rexford Guy Tugwell, *Model for a New Constitution* (Santa Barbara: Center for the Study of Democratic Institutions, 1970). This publication included both Tugwell's explanatory comments and his constitution.

well-to-do. Consequently, tax "reform" caters to wealthy donors to the congressman's election campaign. Farmers who need them least get the most subsidies. Where a national highway is routed depends on local interests; consumers are protected reluctantly and in ways not too burdensome to business; banking laws help the banks and only nominally their customers. Tugwell's model constitution is designed to overcome, or at least to reduce, these and other distortions. Its underlying principles are "equality of opportunity; substantial justice; liberty to act and to undertake enterprises provided they do no harm; fair sharing of our affluence; decent respect for the rights and feelings of others."

Does American democracy need a new constitution? Must a constitution be rewritten for each new era or age, or can it embody principles of democratic government with enduring validity and utility, adaptable to any time and to any change? If a new constitution is adopted periodically, do we risk the impairment of key values—like civil liberties—that are incorporated in the existing constitution? In order to weigh these questions, we must look into the Constitution—its background and beginnings, its objectives, its underlying principles and methods, its means for adapting to a changing environment, and, above all, its usefulness for democracy, both in terms of what has been accomplished or left undone, and what might be further gained.

The English heritage

When the United States Constitution was drafted, nine generations of colonists had dwelt in North America since the landings at Jamestown and Plymouth. But their ties with England were intact. The colonists had prospered in trade with England and its other colonies; they read English literary works, followed English religious and educational practices, and cherished English political values.

The Constitution benefited from a long-building English heritage, one that prized political liberty. In 1100 Henry I granted a charter of liberties to his subjects, and in 1215 John I assented to Magna Carta and its stipulations that various feudal rights, chiefly those of barons, would not be infringed. The subsequent Petition of Right (1628) and the Bill of Rights (1689), which listed certain rights that were "true, ancient, and indubitable rights and liberties of the people," provided England with elements of a written constitution, limited as their application may have been at first.

England's movement toward democracy was assisted by Parliament, which emerged as an institution capable of checking the monarch's excesses. Gradually, a concept of legislative or parliamentary power materialized; by the seventeenth century, laws—and above all, tax laws—were enacted with Parliament's advice and sanction. In Parliament's emerging status was the outline of a theory that the burdens of government should not be imposed without the consent of the governed. Parliament was also acquiring characteristics of representation. At first it represented only the upper classes, but the membership of the House of Commons was continually enlarged until eventually the House became the prototype of the representative assembly acting for popular constituencies.

England was also the home of the common law, which originated in customs of the people and in time developed through judicial reasoning into a substantial body of law. The English revered the rule of law in lieu of the rule of men. Accordingly, the individual entrusted with governmental power was not to indulge in self-interested aggrandizement of his power. He was expected to act not according to whim, but according to procedures and purposes delimited in acts of Parliament and the Constitution.

Generally, these English developments were grounded in pessimism concerning human nature and in a historical perspective that viewed mankind's experience as a discouraging record of human weakness. But the English did not resign themselves to cynicism: they harnessed human weakness and strength to produce constructive results by dividing and balancing power among a monarch, a House of Lords, and a House of Commons. Each component could check the others and encourage them to remain within their assigned spheres. English reform was confined to political matters. Left untouched were the realms of social and economic reform and therefore left largely intact was a tightly defined class structure with harsh discriminations and gross imbalances in the distribution of wealth.

The colonial experience

America's social revolution, if it has ever had one, occurred in its early decades, and it lacked the crashing turbulence of the later French and Russian revolutions that ruined thousands of lives. The American social revolution was an emancipation from European ways: from the church and its enforced orthodoxy, from the state and its imperious authority, and from the gradations of society. Restrictive European practices faded when exposed to America's rough, open frontier. The poorest immigrant could hope to improve his condition. The indentured servant, the apprentice, the common laborer could expect eventually to become independent and to move upward, economically and socially. The only flaw, and it was a most serious one, was that the black bondsman was barred from such betterment.

Although it was far removed from the fixed stratifications of European feudal society, colonial society was by no means free of rank and status. With passing years, families with fortunes won on land or sea were admitted to a kind of colonial aristocracy. The South resembled the English landed gentry, since in its predominately rural society, ambitious men could accumulate vast acres for tilling by a servile class. Josiah Quincy, Jr., whose Massachusetts knew little of such distinctions, was impressed on a visit to South Carolina in

1773 that "the inhabitants may well be divided into opulent and lordly planters, poor and spiritless whites and vile slaves." [2]

Distinctions existed not only between the sections, North and South, but within each colony. Wealth and political power tended to concentrate along the coast, in the hands of planters in the South and of merchants in the North. With few exceptions, colonial governments were controlled by economic upper classes. Toward the western frontiers of the colonies, the inhabitants tended to become debtor in character, although the towns in coastal areas also had their quota of the propertyless and poor.

In pursuing freedom, several colonies incorporated into their political systems unique arrangements significant for the future American democracy. The Pilgrims subscribed to the Mayflower Compact, which asserted that government derives from social contract, or that political power stems from the consent of the governed. Puritanism perceived consent largely in terms of local autonomy, for Puritan theology valued independent congregational control of ecclesiastical matters. In effect, the Pilgrims were saying that they could fashion their own political institutions, an idea that became basic in the New World and ultimately shattered the traditions of the Old.

But Puritanism had many authoritarian aspects. One enterprising member of the sect who was displeased by these aspects withdrew in 1636 to found his own colony in what became Rhode Island. Imbued with creative notions about how the community is best organized, Roger Williams developed the first colony whose governance approached the modern democratic model. The intolerance he witnessed in the Puritan government of Massachusetts convinced him that civil officers must be distinguished from clergy to reflect a necessary separation between church and state. Each should function in a distinguishable domain. No single religious doctrine was required for the safety of the state or even to save men's souls. And paraphernalia of the state such as "stocks, whips, prisons, swords, gibbets, stakes, etc." transgressed the teachings of the Prince of Peace. [3]

In fashioning his new political state, Williams beheld government as the mere creature of the sovereign people, established by their consent expressed in contract. The social contract was a basic working instrument through which the people could control the government they created and alter it as they willed. Political participation reflected Williams's conviction that all those subject to government should share in it. Elections were to be frequent and local autonomy real. A majority of towns could reject measures of the General Court, the colony's legislature, and the governor possessed no veto over measures enacted by the towns and General Court. Elected magistrates could be recalled or removed from office. Williams's inventive agrarian democracy endured in Rhode Island long after it became a state.

In some colonies the governor, the Crown's representative, was a powerful

---

[2] From Arthur M. Schlesinger, *The Birth of the Nation* (New York: Knopf, 1968), 131.
[3] From Alpheus T. Mason and Richard H. Leach, *In Quest of Freedom: American Political Thought and Practice* (Englewood Cliffs, N.J.: Prentice-Hall, 1959), 35.

figure; in others he was an absentee or a bumbling dullard. Because governors depended on the legislatures for their pay, they were most attentive to legislative opinion in conducting their duties and wielding their power. The colonial assembly soon displayed great ingenuity in circumventing the Crown's restrictions asserted by the governor. Each colony had a two-house legislature, one chamber of which was chosen by the local electorate and the other either appointed by the governor or elected. Royal governors often lamented their legislatures' stubborn inclination to ignore orders from the mother country. Generally, the colonies managed their own internal affairs, subject to the occasional intrusion of royal instructions and disallowance of colonial acts. The Crown handled external affairs, and acts of Parliament dealt with foreign commerce; these were more or less obeyed. Certain decisions made in Britain could be appealed from colonial courts, but the procedure was expensive, slow, and complex, and therefore seldom used. The functions of government tended to be held to a minimum and taxation was light. In 1749, the governor of New Jersey boasted that " 'Tis seventeen years since any Tax was raised on the people," and in 1755 the governor of Pennsylvania declared with pride that we "are not only out of Debt, but have . . . Fifteen Thousand in Bank." [4]

The makings of revolution

The overlay of well-being and consensus in colonial society was disarrayed by the advent of the Seven Years' War or French and Indian War (1756–63) between France and Britain for supremacy in North America. It was more than a struggle between two nation states; it was a contest between opposing conceptions of political society. One, the French, represented absolute monarchy, religious intolerance, commercial monopoly, and arbitrary colonial rule. The other, the English, fostered democratic political, economic, and religious institutions and practices. Britain's triumph over France cast the American political culture in an Anglo-Saxon rather than a Gallic mold, a result as consequential as the political conflict smoldering in the ashes of the war.

Burdened with a huge war debt, the British felt that the Americans should help pay for the Empire's military forces stationed in their midst, purportedly to guard against future danger and war. In 1765 Parliament passed a Stamp Act imposing a tax on some fifty items, such as customs papers, playing cards, and marriage licenses, all of which were to use stamped paper or be affixed with stamps. Although they had long paid local taxes enacted by their assemblies, and indirect taxes, such as customs duties imposed by Parliament, Americans were distressed that the Stamp Act was a direct tax on the Amer-

[4] Schlesinger, 12.

ican consumer, not for regulation but for revenue. The rates could reach 200 percent, and such opinion-makers as lawyers, merchants, and editors were irate. The Americans coped with the unwanted law by ingeniously evading it. Cargoes lacking stamped papers were cleared without duties, many courts suspended proceedings against violators, and colleges awarded degrees by letter rather than by stamped diplomas. The colonists also took counter-measures. Nonimportation agreements against British goods spread through seaboard communities, and homespun garments became a badge of defiance. The conflict instilled a sense of unity among the colonists. In 1765, delegates from nine colonies gathered in New York City to draw up a statement of their rights and grievances and request repeal of the hated law.

The American side of the conflict required a theory to justify it, which was supplied by the cry, "Taxation without representation is tyranny." Under-lying this slogan was the contention that English constitutional practice re-quired that taxes be imposed only by the consent of those on whom they were levied, expressed through their representatives in Parliament. Englishmen in America were as protected by this principle as Englishmen in the mother country. Since Americans were unrepresented in Parliament, Parliament lacked jurisdiction to tax them. Only Americans, through their colonial leg-islatures, could tax Americans. Unfortunately, the colonists had not applied the principle conveyed by the rallying slogan to their own domestic politics with pure regularity. For American religious dissenters, small farmers, and back-country pioneers, taxation without representation had long been an un-pleasant fact of their existence. In addition, the direct representation clamored for in Parliament was more symbolic of the colonists' chafing than a real change in their status, for if it was conferred, American representatives would comprise a minority of Parliament, and they would be outvoted as further taxes were imposed.

Parliament repealed the Stamp Act, thus raising the colonists' confidence in their prowess at waging political conflict. But Parliament continued to im-pose other taxes, which colonists protested, resisted, and evaded. In 1770, blood was spilled in the Boston Massacre, when eleven townspeople were killed by British soldiers who fired a volley apparently without orders and under extreme provocation. The apparatus of colonial resistance continued to evolve. In Massachusetts, Samuel Adams, a writer and orator brilliantly gifted at stirring discontent, organized local committees among colonial towns to keep opposition to British policy alive: they spread propaganda and informa-tion by establishing a communication network, and soon this enterprise was intercolonial in scale, with each colony establishing a central Committee of Correspondence.

The conflict with Britain was maintained by an array of vigorous, expert controversialists. Many were lawyers who employed their courtroom oratory skills in the political arena. The press was a busy tool of the patriots' cause, prompting one Tory, as British sympathizers were known, to complain that "the Press is to them what the Pulpit was in times of Popery." No weapon was more powerful than pamphleteering. Pamphleteers thrived in a society that, thanks to its growing system of widely available education, contained one of the biggest concentrations of literate people in the world. The pamphlets were used for reasoned arguments and conveyed scorn and indignation but rarely hate or fear. They aimed to convince their opponents, not to annihilate them.[5]

The rising conflict inspired broadening conceptions of local rights articulated by the pamphleteers. James Otis of Massachusetts demonstrated that the colonists were entitled to the same rights as their brothers in Britain since they were "the common children of the same Creator." After contending that taxation could not be imposed without representation, Otis asserted that Parliament is obligated "to declare what is for the good of the whole," and its failure to do so violated both the constitution and "a higher authority, viz. GOD." A transgressive act of Parliament, he said, was to be considered void. Years later, John Adams saw in this reasoning "the child Independence." Otis himself did not aspire to independence, and neither did John Dickinson, whose *Letters from a Farmer in Pennsylvania* appeared in 1767 and 1768. Seeking to join the colonists together in a moderate, nonviolent stand, Dickinson meant to confine the conflict to the rights of Americans under the British Constitution. Under that constitution, Parliament, he contended, stood in the same relation to colonial legislatures in fiscal matters that the King did to Parliament. While Parliament might regulate the external affairs of America, such as trade with the mother country, it lacked authority to impose internal American taxes.

The conflict escalated sharply with the Boston Tea Party and Parliament's retaliatory "Intolerable Acts" that revoked many rights of the Massachusetts charter. Town meetings were curbed. Fighting erupted at Lexington and Concord between colonial "Minutemen" and a detachment of British troops sent by their commander in Boston; war was at hand. For all the severity of the crisis, Americans were confused about their purpose. Were they fighting Parliament only and not their King; or was it both? Were they fighting to restore a happier status quo; or had the hour of separation come? The day's supreme pamphleteer, Tom Paine, provided the catalytic answers in *Common Sense* (1776). He exhorted Americans not only to resist Parliament but to sever their ties with the King. Monarchy, Paine argued, contradicted the equality of all men. Any present king derived from a first king who was "nothing better than the principal ruffian of some restless gang, whose savage manners, or preeminence in subtlety obtained him the title of chief among plunderers." The time for reconciliation was past; "A government of our own is our natural right," Paine held. " 'TIS TIME TO PART." [6]

---

[5] Bernard Bailyn, *The Ideological Origins of the American Revolution* (Cambridge: Harvard University Press, 1967), 18–19.

[6] Quotations are from Mason and Leach, 51–52; Schlesinger, 176; and Alan P. Grimes, *American Political Thought* (New York: Holt, Rinehart and Winston, 1955), 87–88.

The Declaration
of Independence

The conflict of ideas had become a conflict of arms. War spread along the seaboard. As all revolutions are, the American Revolution was promoted by an energetic, politically skillful minority. But it was a "soft" or limited revolution in that it was essentially a political struggle centering on constitutional issues framed in ideological terms. The enterprise promised to cause only minimum disturbance to the existing order because it was not primarily a struggle between social groups and classes to force social and economic changes. Except for some who opposed the Revolution, property rights and their attendant economic privileges were not disturbed; no questions of consequence were raised about the most inhumanely exploitative of economic enterprises, the plantation system and its field labor force of slaves. As Bernard Bailyn suggests, the orators and pamphleteers of the prerevolutionary crisis conceptualized, to the point of radical idealization, the experience and developing political principles of the previous century and a half, and it was the close relationship between revolutionary thought and the political (but not economic) realities of life in eighteenth-century America that infused the Revolution with special force and made it a transforming event.[7]

By no means did all Americans follow the revolutionary philosophers and activists. Many reviled what one loyalist called "the ill-shapen, diminutive brat, *Independency,*" and years after the war, John Adams estimated that one-third of the people opposed separation from the mother country. Despite their numbers, the loyalists were handicapped by ineffective leadership and organization, and they were prey to economic disruption—to seizures of their property and the loss of their employment.

The revolutionaries, in contrast, were led by the most remarkable combination of public men in the history of the United States and possibly of any other nation. From a country of little more than two million inhabitants emerged such giants as Washington, Franklin, John and Samuel Adams, Jefferson, Hamilton, and Madison, and close behind came James Monroe, George Mason, James Wilson, George Wythe, Robert and Gouverneur Morris, Richard Henry Lee, and others of equal distinction. They lived in conditions highly propitious for the participation of talented men in political affairs: the fertile economic opportunities of the new country gave them wherewithal to afford leisure for political activity; a widely diffused system of education made them familiar with classical writings on government and liberty as well as the self-government of their own colonial era. The fluidity of social classes increased their numbers.

Sentiment in society was rapidly growing for independence, and in June of 1776 the Second Continental Congress approved a resolution by Richard

[7] Bailyn, vi–vii, 19–20.

Thomas Jefferson

Henry Lee declaring the colonies independent. A committee was deputed to prepare a suitable declaration. The task of drafting the document fell on Jefferson who had a "peculiar felicity of expression."

Jefferson's task was to convince the world that the colonies had a moral and legal right to separate from Britain. His philosophical argument is based on "self-evident truths," or statements that stand on their own merits. One of these articulated a natural rights philosophy that had been developing in England and the colonies for over a century. Holding that "all men are created equal," the Declaration voiced belief in man's original equality as an endowment of God. By right of birth all men are equal, not in condition or ability, but in basic inalienable rights—life, liberty, and the pursuit of happiness. Men established government to preserve these rights. Being inalienable, the rights cannot be bargained away, nor can any government legitimately usurp them. Governments exist only at the pleasure of those subject to them, and if they persist without the approval of the governed, they violate the rights of man. Since man's rights are the foundation of government, its failure to uphold them justifies its overthrow. According to the Declaration, a long list of abuses had been suffered by the colonies, and it climactically pronounced them to be "free and independent states."

Under Jefferson's formulation, the American Revolution was one of carefully limited aims—it meant only to sever "all political connection" with Britain, and its justifying statement in the Declaration of Independence borrowed

Original draft of the Declaration of Independence by Thomas Jefferson.

heavily from John Locke's *Second Treatise on Civil Government* (1690). Locke's book, widely read in America, argued the case for England's Glorious Revolution of 1688–89, which was also confined to political purposes and did not aspire to social and economic change.

A glaring contradiction existed between what the colonists asked for themselves and what they imposed on others. While they sought freedom, from British rule, black slaves lived among them in misery and degradation. But slavery was an agitated question sometime before the Declaration of Independence. Several colonies voted to abolish the slave trade, and in 1774 the Continental Congress resolved to discontinue the trade everywhere. But when independence came, slavery still flourished, even in the North.

White over black

For what would become American democracy's most scarring and enduring problem, slavery began quietly and virtually unheeded. The first blacks landed in Virginia in 1619, but little is known of their status over the next two decades. Between 1640 and 1660 evidence of enslavement appears, and after 1660 it is firmly implanted on the statute books of Virginia, Maryland, and other colonies. By 1700 the black was caught in chattel slavery, a condition and a legal status created by Englishmen in America but that ran counter to law in the English homeland.

Initially slavery was one of several labor systems in the colonies. There were, in addition, wage labor, based on contract and monetary payment, and indentured servitude, which was a temporary bondage for a term of years as repayment for one's ocean passage. Indentured servitude disappeared, but after an early vagueness and elasticity, slavery became established enough to become an institution. Slavery meant the loss of all freedom, a perpetual condition of lifetime labor that was hereditary. With some Englishmen, the slave lost more than his freedom; he lost his humanity as well. Unlike other servitude, slavery entailed captivity and prejudice.

Political and legal recognition of slavery mirrored economic and social realities. Tobacco-growing, first in Virginia and Maryland and then in other Southern states, required labor that was permanent rather than transitory, tireless more than skilled—the enforced qualities of the slave. Most colonial churches came to regard the black as a "heathen," because of his African origins, and therefore susceptible to treatment that was decidedly inferior to what Christians accorded Christians. As slavery burgeoned in the eighteenth century, it remained a largely unexamined fact of life.

The movement toward the Revolution quickened American self-awareness, a proneness to question practices instituted under English rule, a growing hospitality to the concept of the fundamental equality of black and white men, and consciousness of white "prejudices." Among religious sects, the Quakers, concentrated in Pennsylvania, were becoming the national conscience, attesting to the inward sin that degradation of blacks represented and the erosion of humane judgment. Benjamin Franklin expounded on the logical absurdities underlying all racial categorizations: "If an *Indian* injures me, does it follow that I may revenge that Injury on all *Indians?*" A leading orator of the impending revolution, James Otis, denied the dependence of rights on the accident of color: "The Colonists are by the law of nature free born, as indeed all men are, white or black." [8]

The Revolution was somewhat ameliorative for the blacks. Many won freedom by fighting on the American side. During the Revolution, the belief spread that someday the institution of slavery, that English invention foisted on the colonies, must be demolished. Although antislavery pronouncements on this scale were absent in the South, no important Southern figure openly endorsed slavery during the Revolution. When the Revolution neared its end, slavery had a decidedly sectional pattern of distribution, with heavy concentrations in the states south of Pennsylvania. Within the South there was variation: states of the Upper South, such as Virginia, in contrast to states of the Lower South, such as South Carolina, had been driven by agricultural changes to harbor a diminished proportion of blacks, to regard slavery as less profitable, and to give stronger voice to the abolition sentiment. [9]

[8] Winthrop D. Jordan, *White Over Black: American Attitudes Toward the Negro, 1550–1812* (Chapel Hill: University of North Carolina Press, 1968), 44–278.
[9] *Ibid.*, 316.

The new state constitutions

The Declaration of Independence necessitated the creation of a new governmental structure, a task that was already under way when the document appeared. The Second Continental Congress, which gathered in 1775, was pressed by events to assume wide-ranging functions. It organized an army, established a postal system, issued currency, supervised control of foreign trade and Indian relations, and directed the colonies to establish popularly elected governments. Successfully, although not always gloriously, the Congress managed the Revolution, whose fighting extended from 1776 to 1781 and whose major battles crossed the sprawling American terrain, north, south, and west.

During the Revolution, most of the states drafted and adopted new constitutions. Their efforts sparked renewed discussion of the ideal nature of government, an examination of principles of politics, and a weighing of institutions and practices. Many of these exchanges directly continued the discussions that had preceded Independence; they were original, intense and both idealistic and pragmatic. Among other things, American writers and constitution-makers were engrossed in a question that was at the heart of the Declaration of Independence and the new state constitutions: the relation of power to liberty. To them, power meant the dominion of some men over others, the human control of human life, and ultimately force and compulsion. The writers were concerned with the aggressiveness of power and the fact that its natural victim was liberty, law, or right. On the other hand, power was necessary: those who govern could not do without it. But power could be transformed into an evil force, a scourge, not by its own nature, but by the nature of men who wielded it. Man and his institutions were susceptible to corruption and to his unceasing appetite for self-aggrandizement. Obsessed with power, man could best be checked by a constitution, or the confinement of social and political powers within specified, limited spheres. Power was most subject to abuse if it was concentrated and most likely to be benign and constructive if it was dispersed.

The new state constitutions reflected these theories. Power was divided among executive, legislative, and judicial branches. Since the colonial legislature, most particularly, the lower house or assembly, had been the foremost organ of local and popular assertion, the new constitutions concentrated power there. Since the power of the King or Chief Executive was so denigrated in the propaganda of the Revolution, the Chief Executive in the new constitutions fared poorly in the allocations of power. The courts did little better. Jefferson attributed these imbalances to the inexperience of many makers of the new constitutions. Eight states adopted bills of rights, a logical corollary of limited government, and together they protected the rights of the people as a whole as well as those of individual human beings.

The Articles
of Confederation

The Declaration of Independence had freed Americans of all central government, and the successful Revolution made the thirteen colonies independent of Great Britain and of one another. A crucial question emerged: Could the former colonies achieve a sufficient consensus to sustain a central government adequate to the demands of war, peace, and growth? This test of consensus politics centered on the willingness of the individual states to surrender power, and possibly even sovereignty, to a central government.

Fortunately, there was substantial agreement that a central organization was necessary to handle such matters of general concern as war and peace, the army and navy, and Indian affairs. Likewise it was readily agreed that the states should manage matters of local interest. In 1776, the Second Continental Congress approved a proposal by Richard Henry Lee of Virginia and directed the preparation of what was to become the Articles of Confederation. John Dickinson of Delaware wrote the first draft, and Congress, after some disagreement and delay, approved the Articles in 1777. Twelve states soon ratified it, but Maryland, because of a western land claims dispute, withheld its approval until 1781. The central controversy involved in the adoption of the Articles flared over the allotment of the great body of other affairs to "local" or "general" concern. The issue was contested by two strong blocs of opinion.

One was the republican faction, which looked askance at central government and preferred a maximum role for the states. It had two wings. One, based in New England, was led by John and Samuel Adams, John Hancock, and Elbridge Gerry; the other was Southern and embraced such personalities as Thomas Jefferson, Patrick Henry, George Wythe, and Richard Henry Lee. Republicans, north and south, were given to rectitude and self-righteousness; they believed in and practiced simplicity. Children of the Age of Reason, they were confident of the power of systematic thought and fervent in devotion to

American public men: Benjamin Franklin, Richard Henry Lee, and John Adams

the natural rights of man. Republicans tended to be born and educated in British North America and their attachments were local. With feeling Jefferson once said, "Virginia, Sir, is my country." [10]

The rival bloc, the nationalists, inhabited three major sites of power. They flourished in Pennsylvania, where they were led by Benjamin Franklin, John Dickinson, Robert Morris, and James Wilson; in New York, led by John Jay and Robert Livingston; and in the South Carolina low country, led by Edward Rutledge. To the nationalists, nationhood was inconceivable without strong central government. They believed that government ought not to rely on man's reason or goodness, but, as Hamilton put it, rely on "men's interest." Believing that men were ruled by ambition and avarice, the nationalists were distrustful of reason and considered men, as Hamilton wrote, to be "governed more by passion and prejudice than by an enlightened sense of their interests." Dickinson added, "Experience must be our only guide. Reason may mislead us." Nearly all leading nationalists were born or educated abroad. While republicans were predominantly farmers and planters, nationalists were typically occupied with intercolonial and international business.[11] In 1777, the republicans rather than the nationalists were the dominant political force.

Some issues cut across the two camps. Regardless of their disposition toward nationalism and republicanism, the large and small states quarreled, during the preparation of the Articles of Confederation, over the basis of representation in Congress. The large states pressed for representation based on population; the small states called for representation of the states and not the people. After a bitter wrangle, a compromise emerged. Congress would represent the states but on certain important matters the votes of nine states would be necessary, which was deemed a concession to the large states.

Another conflict raged over taxation. The nationalists proposed that each state pay in proportion to the total number of its inhabitants, but states with

[10] From Forrest McDonald, *E Pluribus Unum: The Formation of the American Republic* (Boston: Houghton Mifflin, 1965), 1.

[11] *Ibid.,* 1–6.

large slave populations, which would feel a tax on number of inhabitants most, pressed for taxation based on land values. Each side won, in the sense that the central government under the Articles was not empowered to tax. The worst controversy centered on the control of the western lands. States like Virginia, with charter claims to lands reaching to the Mississippi River, finally yielded to "landless" states, which insisted that Congress control the western lands.

The issue that overrode all others was the location of ultimate political authority, the problem of sovereignty. The nationalists pressed for Congress to possess a "superintending" power over the states and individual citizens. Indignant republicans deemed the issue of centralized power at the very heart of the struggle with Britain; in their eyes union was an evil tolerable only to the degree necessary to assure the independence of the states. In most decisions about the Articles, the republicans prevailed. They had the votes.

In its final form, the Articles of Confederation vested all power of the central government, or confederation, in a single body, Congress. Congress was granted only delegated powers, including the important powers to control war and foreign affairs. Congress also was given control of the postal service and the regulation of weights and measures, and it was a court of last appeal in disputes between the states. It could regulate the value of coinage but had no control over paper money issued by the states. Republicans ingeniously hobbled Congress by making its functioning tentative and cumbersome. No one could be a member of Congress for more than three of any six years, nor could anyone be president of Congress for more than one year out of three. State governments could recall their delegates to Congress at any time. Such provisions plainly militated against the emergence of national political personalities and the maturing of national political loyalties. Few restrictions were placed on the states, and they existed as equals. Congress was barred from encroaching on them and in most matters was subordinate to them. No important power of the central government, such as the appointment of a commander in chief, entering into treaties and alliances, or coining money, could be exercised, the Articles specified, without a two-thirds vote of the states in Congress. Even then, that government lacked power to compel compliance by the states.

The central government had no executive beyond committees of Congress and a few military and diplomatic appointees. Courts were tightly limited in jurisdiction. Lacking the power to tax, Congress depended on contributions from the states, which proved to be fitfully forthcoming. Congress also lacked power over commerce, which soon became a thicket of self-interested regulation by the states. Nor could Congress deal with the individual citizen except through the states. Currency and credit became a tangle of ineffectuality as the states pressed for self-advantage to the point of irresponsibility.

Nevertheless, at first the Articles of Confederation provided better government than might be expected. The Confederation concluded a successful war and administered a workable peace. It managed its credit despite heavy burdens of debt, fielded an admirable team of diplomats (Franklin, Jefferson,

Jay, and others), founded a national domestic bureaucracy, and helped people redistribute their loyalties from states to nation. But the Articles eventually showed strain. In the late 1780s economic depression blanketed many ports and rural areas. Hard money was scarce, paper money too abundant, and public debts were rising beyond management by prevailing tax structures. The back country was distressed by lack of currency, and merchants worried over the steady imbalances of trade running against the United States. In their foreign relations, Americans suffered pangs of inadequacy. "There is something . . . diminutive and contemptible," wrote Hamilton, "in the prospect of a number of petty states, with the appearance only of union, jarring, jealous and perverse . . . in the eyes of other nations." [12]

Men of property nervously questioned the capacity of government to preserve order. Their doubts soared when an armed mob moved on the New Hampshire legislature and what became known as Shays' Rebellion erupted in Massachusetts, an uprising in 1786 of hard-pressed rural debtors who resisted payments of taxes, prevented county courts from sitting, assaulted the Springfield arsenal, and demanded revision of the state constitution. Many distressed public men concluded that the time had come to "look to our national character."

The Constitutional Convention of 1787

The fatal flaw for the Articles was their loss of political support. Dominant political power, once enjoyed by the republicans, had passed to the nationalists. The difficulties of the Confederation and especially Shays' uprising played into their hands and redoubled their purpose to establish their own conceptions of government. Meanwhile the republicans had lapsed into disorganization and inattention.

The nationalists quickly moved to convert their advantage into profit. In 1786, Virginia issued a call for a convention at Annapolis to unravel the tangled conditions of commerce. Five states participated at Annapolis, where Alexander Hamilton brilliantly steered through a resolution requesting Congress to summon a convention of delegates from the various states to meet in Philadelphia the next year to overhaul the Articles. Congress, understandably reluctant to dig its own grave, issued—in guarded language—the call for a convention "for the sole and express purpose of revising" the Articles of Confederation.

The nationalists' domination was apparent from a glance at the fifty-five delegates from twelve states who convened at Philadelphia on May 25, 1787. (The thirteenth state, Rhode Island, refused to attend because it opposed the

---

[12] Quotations are from Clinton Rossiter, *1787 The Grand Convention* (New York: Macmillan, 1966), 43–45.

creation of a stronger national government at the expense of the states' power.) Such prominent republicans as Samuel Adams and John Hancock failed to be elected delegates in Massachusetts. Patrick Henry, a leading orator of the states' rights school, declined to serve as Virginia's delegate, perceiving in the awaiting enterprise only mischief to his principles. Republicanism's leading philosopher, Thomas Jefferson, was on diplomatic duty in France.

The delegates as a whole were well-to-do and property-connected—for the most part, lawyers, merchants, moneylenders, and land speculators. The common person of town and backwoods and of the debtor class was unrepresented. But the Founding Fathers, as John Roche reminds us, were gifted democratic politicians, practiced at keeping their ear to the ground to heed the opinions of constituent groups. Accustomed to working in a framework of public approval, they intended for their work to evoke general acceptance.[13]

James Madison, rightfully remembered as "The Father of the Constitution," had a plan by which the nationalists could gain their objectives. In letters to Washington, Jefferson, and Edmund Randolph, he specified matters on which the convention might focus. His thinking was reflected in the Virginia Plan, which his state adopted in a preconvention caucus. When the convention began at Philadelphia, Virginia was prepared to supply proposals that shaped the subsequent discussion. Governor Edmund Randolph, recognized by a nod from the convention's President, George Washington, presented the Virginia Plan. Calling in effect for a new constitution, as Madison intended, the plan envisaged a scheme of representation based on "the numbers of free inhabitants," thus favoring the large states. The national legislature would be bicameral, with the first chamber elected by the people and the second by the state legislatures. The national legislature could pass laws "in all cases to which the separate states are incompetent," and it could veto state laws violating the new charter. An executive, of unspecified number, would be elected by the legislature. The executive would have general authority to execute the laws, but would be ineligible for reelection. A judiciary of both supreme and inferior tribunals, chosen by the new legislature, would exercise national jurisdiction.

The Virginia Plan assured the large states' dominance of the new government. The small states, acting through William Paterson of New Jersey, introduced a rival plan. The New Jersey Plan provided for equal representation in Congress of the states, regardless of size and population, which was the method of the Articles of Confederation. In a series of amendments to the Articles, Paterson proposed that Congress be empowered to regulate commerce, raise additional revenues, and compel delinquent states to honor requisitions. Congress would elect a plural executive, which would appoint a supreme court.

---

[13] John P. Roche, "The Founding Fathers: A Reform Caucus in Action," *The American Political Science Review*, LV (December 1961), 799–800.

The rival plans constituted a head-on clash between nationalists in the large and small states. After several days of debate, the Virginia Plan bested the New Jersey Plan. Madison believed that if the "affair of representation . . . could be adjusted," all other difficulties "would be surmountable." Several circumstances contributed to consensus. Most delegates were governed by a sense of mission: they sensed that what they did would affect all humanity for generations to come. They were united by the hard work involved in meeting for lengthy periods of time, six days a week. The delegates faithfully abided by the rule to keep convention deliberations secret. Disagreements were not flaunted and exacerbated in the press. In the success or failure of the convention—in their ability to resolve their conflicts internally—the reputation of each delegate was at stake.

Much of the search for agreement was conducted off the convention floor in caucuses of state delegations and of the competing camps. Intense negotiations took place at tea at the home of wealthy Robert Morris, and in the tavern of the Indian Queen Inn, the convention's unofficial headquarters. Out of the turmoil of conversations, debates, and committee studies, and a fortunate break in the muggy weather that served to cool tempers, what became known as the Great Compromise at last emerged. It stood virtually at midpoint between the large and small state positions. The large states were granted representation by population in the House of Representatives. The small states were satisfied by equal representation in the Senate; each state, regardless of size, would have two senators. The large states, restive under the prospect of bearing the heavy share of taxation, were somewhat appeased by a provision that every tax or revenue measure must originate in the House. The Great Compromise tolerably satisfied both those bent on preserving the states as substantial political communities and those eager for union and nationhood well beyond the capacity of the Articles. One political society, the union, would coexist with many political societies, the states.

After the Great Compromise, the convention moved on to the resolution of other issues. From lengthy wrangling came the decision to elect the President indirectly through the electoral college rather than by direct popular vote. North and South disagreed over the inclusion of slaves in the population count for representation. A grotesque compromise resulted, by which a slave was counted as three-fifths of a man. Most states wanted to shut off the slave trade completely, but a compromise permitted its continuation until 1807, when Congress was to stop it. Plainly the framers accorded higher priority to national unity than to dealing seriously with the problem of slavery.

Frequent pressures for compromise and consensus were exerted by delegates who threatened to leave the convention without approving the completed Constitution. At the end of the convention's seventeen weeks, only forty-two of the original fifty-five delegates remained to sign the document and three of those abstained. The delegates built an enduring constitution by facing and resolving deep conflicts or by redefining them in ways that made them manageable. They overcame the spectres of deadlock and disruption by processes of reason. Politically mature and disciplined, they could engage in sharp clashes without ferocity or malevolence.[14]

The United States
Constitution

In its final form, the Constitution embodied a strong national government with separate legislative, executive, and judicial branches, whose powers were derived from the people and the states, yet with power over them. A legal hierarchy was created in which the national Constitution, laws, and treaties were superior to state constitutions and laws. The lower house of the legislature was endowed with a national popular character, while the Senate and the electoral college represented the states. In their work, the framers borrowed key concepts, such as the ideal of balanced government in the distribution of power among the branches, from classical writers like Locke, Montesquieu, Harrington, Blackstone, and others in whose works they were well read.

The framers were concerned that a balance be preserved against the pressures of "factions and interests" rife in society, ceaselessly competing for wealth and power.[15] The appetite of factions for self-aggrandizement could lead to the degeneration of government into the oppressions of tyranny, oligarchy, and mob rule. The framers sought constitutional arrangements by which no faction could dominate and manipulate all or particular institutions of government, but would conduct conflicts within each institution and "blend" with competing factions into a general consensus. To achieve these ends, the framers relied on separation of powers, or the distribution of powers among several branches of government—the legislative, executive, and judiciary— and checks and balances, which John Adams described as "a multitude of curious and ingenious inventions to balance . . . all those powers [legislative, executive, and judicial], to check the passions peculiar to them, and to control them from rushing into the exorbitancies to which they are most addicted." [16] By dividing governmental power among three branches, and by equipping each to check the encroachment of the others, the framers meant to ensure that factions would be restrained and disciplined for the sake of the commonwealth and other men's liberties.

The draft Constitution contained no bill of rights. Believing that such rights were clearly implied in the Constitution, many framers considered an

---

[14] Rossiter, 181–83; Conyers Read, ed., *The Constitution Reconsidered* (New York: Columbia University Press, 1938), 121–25.

[15] From "Federalist No. 10," in Edward Mead Earle, ed., *The Federalist* (New York: Random House, Modern Library ed., n.d.), 55.

[16] Adams is quoted in Charles C. Thach, *The Creation of the Presidency, Johns Hopkins University Studies in Historical and Political Science,* Ser. 40, No. 4 (Baltimore: Johns Hopkins University Press, 1922), 22.

explicit bill of rights unnecessary. The Preamble acknowledged that a fundamental purpose of the Constitution was "to secure the blessings of liberty to
ourselves and our posterity." And Section 9 of Article I enumerated eight
prohibitions on the national government, from which stem some of the most
important civil liberties.

By the decisions reached at Philadelphia, the national government was to
function within the powers delegated to it, and limitations were imposed on
the states. The conflict over the respective powers of states and nation was
displaced, at least for the time being, with a consensus creating a federal
system of government, or dual structures, the nation and the states, each
endowed with striking but limited powers. The framers struck blows for
democratic man at Philadelphia by creating governmental machinery whose
motive force was reason and that institutionalized processes to convert conflict into compromise and consensus.

In forging the Constitution, the Founding Fathers made notable innovations in the craft of constitution-making. They broke away from the older
political writers whose classical delineations of constitutional structures displayed little awareness of the shifting possibilities of political life, and who
explored the forms of government but not their institutions. The framers
appreciated that the institutions a constitution created were not abstract
categories. Rather, institutions were the arenas of "interests" that, when
organized for political action, became factions and parties. These factions were
the sources of conflicts within and between institutions and the means by
which men organized themselves in the quest for wealth, prestige, and power.
The framers perceived that politics had a social basis, which marked a new
turn toward realism in political and constitutional thought.[17]

Ratification

The Constitution provided that it would become effective when ratified by the
conventions of nine states. Ratification was an intense political contest in five
states, including the three largest states, Virginia, Massachusetts, and New
York, without whose approval the new government would be ineffective. The
most dependable line that can be drawn between those for and against the
Constitution is geographic. Repeatedly the supporters of ratification tended to
be concentrated in ports, market towns, and settled areas, and along the more
traveled rivers and roads, where trade flourished. Opponents were clustered in
less developed, more isolated areas. Where farming was for subsistence, life
was rugged, and the outer world was remote, the mood toward the Constitution tended to be rejection or apathy. Typically, the small farmer was in
debt and regarded the Constitution as favoring creditors or the propertied
class at the expense of the debtors. The new national government would become the instrument of the well-to-do, such as eastern merchants, and would

[17] Bailyn, 299–300.

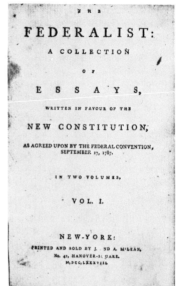

James Madison, John Jay, and Alexander Hamilton—authors of The
Federalist *papers.*

eventually replace the states, which were more tolerant of debtors. The omis-
sion of a bill of rights from the Constitution increased their fears that the
national government would rapidly become dominant.

Thus at least two key issues dominated the conflict over ratification—
the lack of a bill of rights protective of civil liberty and the fear that the
national government might in the future impair the authority of the states.
The lines on these issues divided debtor and creditor interests, east and west,
north and south.

The first complaint was coupled with a proposal calling for a second
constitutional convention to draw up a bill of rights. Madison and other
nationalist framers, however, feared that such a gathering would be disastrous
for their program. They halted the clamor simply by agreeing to add nine
amendments to the Constitution comprising a bill of rights. A tenth amendment responded to the criticism of inadequate protection of the states by
safeguarding their authority in broad, resolute language.

The nationalist forces working for ratification, or the Federalists, as they
became known, possessed a leadership elite that was continental in outlook
and formidable in influence and skill. Largely above the battle was the heroic,
reassuring figure of Washington, while participating in the struggle were such
mighty gladiators as Madison, Hamilton, James Wilson, John Langdon, John
Rutledge, John Jay, and Edmund Randolph. The opposition could not command anything approaching an equal roster, nor the network of contacts that
gave the Federalists a national organization. They made effective use of

campaign literature supporting the Constitution in *The Federalist,* a series of articles published originally in the New York press by Hamilton, Madison, and Jay. They provided a persuasive and classic exposition of principles underlying the Constitution.

On June 21, 1788, the ninth state (New Hampshire) ratified, and on May 29, 1790, Rhode Island became the last of the thirteen states to approve.

A question
of motives

Were the framers pure in motive, as well as eminently practical in method? A long-prevailing judgment rated the framers as praiseworthy on both counts until the historian Charles A. Beard challenged the first part of the judgment. Beard, writing in 1913, characterized the constitution-making in 1787 as a self-serving enterprise to enhance the property interests of a corps of shrewd activists.

Beard argued in his famous book, *An Economic Interpretation of the Constitution,*[18] that the constitution produced at Philadelphia was a conservative economic document, the handiwork of an unrepresentative minority with "personalty interests," that is, holdings in public securities that had been bountifully issued, particularly by the states, to finance the Revolution; investments in lands for speculation; money loaned at interest; investments in mercantile, manufacturing, and shipping concerns; and holdings of slaves. An overwhelming majority of the men at Philadelphia, "at least five-sixths," held one or more of these forms of personalty. Another economic interest, realty or land, Beard noted, was underrepresented. Most delegates came from towns on or near the coast, where personalty was concentrated, and "not one member" represented "the small farming or mechanic classes."

According to Beard, the Constitution was tailored to fit the personalty interests of the framers in two chief ways. A positive feature vested four great powers in the new national government—those of war, taxation, commerce, and control of western lands. Accordingly, the national government could protect business from foreign competitors and from the internal unrest of disgruntled debtors of the Shays genre, and with its broadly authorized revenues it could pay off the public creditors. A negative, protective feature of the Constitution restricted those economic powers of the states that might jeopardize the personalty interests. For example, states were barred from impairing the obligations of contracts. As for the Constitution's ratification, Beard considered that process an extension of the Constitutional Convention's pattern. The same self-interested individuals also controlled the ratifying conventions and overwhelmed the opposition of small farmers and debtors.

For many years, Beard's interpretation enjoyed wide acceptance until

[18] Charles A. Beard, *An Economic Interpretation of the Constitution* (New York: Macmillan, 1913).

some historians raised challenges. In *The Making of the Constitution,*[19] Charles Warren suggested that the Constitutional Convention exemplified the dictum of Justice Oliver Wendell Holmes that high-mindedness is not impossible in human beings: "I don't readily give up the belief," said Holmes, "that Washington and the rest had for their dominant motive a patriotic desire to see a powerful nation take the place of squabbling states." [20]

One distinguished historian, Robert E. Brown, termed Beard's scholarship "unmitigated rot." In his study, *Charles Beard and the Constitution,*[21] Brown argued that the Constitution was democratically framed and ratified, although he went on to make the untenable claim that it was framed for an ongoing democratic society. In *We the People: The Economic Origins of the Constitution,*[22] Forrest McDonald did not, like Brown, reject the primacy of economic forces, but he did consider Beard's particular economic interpretation simplistic. According to McDonald, complex, pluralistic economic factors swayed the framers. Thus, a delegate might have been both a farmer and a large holder of public securities or a merchant who was also deeply in debt. McDonald discovered that realty rather than personalty was the dominant form of wealth represented, and a thorough analysis of convention voting behavior showed that generally no significant property differences divided opposing sides. The most conspicuous alignment was that of the extreme northern states with the extreme southern states (New Hampshire, Massachusetts, North Carolina, South Carolina, and Georgia). And no discernible factor aligned these states. McDonald also found that holders of public securities were almost as numerous among opponents of the Constitution as among its framers and advocates.

The historians' debate has persisted. McDonald's analysis of the delegates' personal economics has been attacked as obscuring the fact that over two dozen of the sixty-five elected delegates and more than half of those who signed the Constitution were "rich" and others were well-to-do.[23] That opponents of the Constitution also owned public securities is rejected as proving little, since popular parties tend to bestow their leadership on individuals of substantial property. In a more recent interpretation,[24] Stanley M. Elkins and Eric McKitrick argue that the framers have been prey to misinterpretation because of their dual "father" (Founding Fathers) and "conservative" images.

[19] Charles Warren, *The Making of the Constitution* (Cambridge: Harvard University Press, 1928).

[20] In Leonard W. Levy, ed., *Essays on the Making of the Constitution* (New York: Oxford University Press, 1969), 34. Excerpts from all the writers cited in this section are available in Levy's volume.

[21] Robert E. Brown, *Charles Beard and the Constitution: A Critical Analysis of an Economic Interpretation of the Constitution* (Princeton, N.J.: Princeton University Press, 1956).

[22] Forrest McDonald, *We the People: The Economic Origins of the Constitution* (Chicago: University of Chicago Press, 1958).

[23] Levy, 153.

[24] Stanley M. Elkins and Eric McKitrick, "The Founding Fathers: Young Men of the Revolution," *Political Science Quarterly,* LXXVI (June 1961), 181–216.

Actually, the framers were young men, favored with the energy of their years, which makes the constitutional enterprise explicable in terms of an "energy principle." By determination and youthful drive, such nationalist leaders as Hamilton, Madison, Jay, Knox, and the Morrises brought down the Confederation and substituted a new government mirroring their national ideals. On the average, Federalists were ten to twelve years younger than the Anti-Federalists, were no more or no less conservative than the Anti-Federalists (who suffered the frustrations of noninvolvement in state politics), were distressed by the Confederation's inadequacies, and being talented and energetic, resolved to do something about it. Outwitting and outworking the Anti-Federalists, they made *their* vision of the new nation prevail.

The first new nation

The real significance of the events that have been examined, sociologist Seymour Martin Lipset asserts, is that they provide the foundation of a distinction of the United States as "the first new nation," the first major colony to break away successfully from colonial rule through revolution. Unlike most of the Spanish colonies of Central and South America, which became independent in ensuing decades, the United States exemplifies the new nation that has moved on to develop a stable democratic polity, an industrial economy, and a relatively integrated social structure, with the large exception of racial cleavages.[25]

Any new political system, such as that of the first new nation, requires legitimacy. Lacking, for the most part, the tradition that endows an established state, a new state depends on the two alternatives identified by sociologist Max Weber as legal domination and charismatic authority. The newness of the Constitution and the habituation of the states to their own authority precluded any immediate development of the former. But charismatic authority responds effectively to the needs of a new nation since it requires neither time nor a well-established set of rational rules, and it is flexible. In all particulars, George Washington fulfilled the requirements of charisma—magnificent in character and achievement, idolized and venerated, to the extent that Ezra Stiles of Yale was inspired to exclaim in a sermon in 1783, "O Washington! How do I love thy name! How have I often adored and blessed thy God, for creating and forming thee the great ornament of human kind!" Among those who thought the Washington cult went too far was John Adams, for whom the last straw was the suggestion that God had denied Washington children of his own so that he might assume paternity for the whole nation. But Adams managed to bear such pious insipidities, aided by the conviction that Washington's virtues were America's virtues, rather than vice versa.[26]

[25] Seymour Martin Lipset, *The First New Nation* (New York: Basic Books, 1963), *passim*.
[26] *Ibid.,* 19.

Like other new nations, the United States faced the problem of creating and maintaining a national unity and a basic consensus among its diversity of peoples and sections. The sense of identity with the new nation had to be developed, the pull toward parochialism resisted, and movement speeded toward compatibility of values. But national unity had many a horrendous hour in the first decade of national existence, as both Northern and Southern states threatened to secede. Beyond lay the War of 1812, with its menacing prospect of the secession of the New England states, and the long struggle for the abolition of slavery and its cataclysmic conclusion in the Civil War.

The launching of the first new nation had other ingredients. The development of "rules of the game" permitting freedom of speech to the opposition did not come easily, as occasional suppressions of civil liberties testify. The preservation of national unity also had to pass a pragmatic test: it had to provide sufficient payoffs to its people to hold their loyalty. The new national government did prove effective in the economic sphere. In both the production and distribution of economic benefits, the United States has surpassed other new nations. But the performance has had wide fluctuations, including economic depressions, with severe unemployment and hardship. The political payoffs have also been mixed; the unfavorable side, by democratic standards, has included devitalization by political machines of popular participation and the magnification of executive power in the national security domain, but the latter has been a relatively recent failing.

Changing
the Constitution

The amending process. In the tradition of constitutions, the United States Constitution provides formal means for its own change. Article V specifies that amendments may be proposed either by a two-thirds vote of both houses of Congress, or by a constitutional convention called on petition from two-thirds of the state legislatures. No amendment has been proposed by the latter method. An even greater majority, or consensus, is required for ratification of amendments: approval of three-fourths of the states is necessary, either by their legislatures or by conventions. States may select either method unless Congress specifies which should be followed.

Because of the enormous consensus required, the amending process enjoys only minor importance for resolving the conflicts of American democracy. The first ten amendments, or Bill of Rights, are virtually a part of the original Constitution since they were adopted with its ratification. The next two amendments aimed to alter unsatisfactory workings of the Constitution: the Eleventh Amendment took jurisdiction of suits brought against states by private persons away from federal courts; the Twelfth moved to eliminate the possibility of a tie in electoral votes for President, which happened in the 1800 election. Several other amendments have altered governmental institutions and processes. The Twentieth eliminated "lame duck" Congresses by advancing the date when congressmen (elected in November) might take their seats, from March to January. The Twenty-Second Amendment limits the terms one can serve as President, and the Twenty-Fifth provides for filling a vacancy in the Vice-Presidency and for the Vice-President to be acting President during presidential disability. The Twenty-Sixth Amendment extended the right to vote to all U.S. citizens who are eighteen years or older.

Pairs and clusters of amendments have appeared at certain periods, sometimes as the product of a sustained consensus. The Civil War amendments (Thirteenth, Fourteenth, and Fifteenth) guaranteed to the blacks the rights won from the abolition of slavery. The Progressive movement early in this century, which aimed at advancing democracy and social reform, resulted in amendments Sixteen, permitting the federal income tax; Seventeen, the direct election of senators (formerly elected by state legislatures); Nineteen, women's suffrage; and Eighteen, prohibiting the sale of intoxicating liquors. Later, when the consensus for it dissolved, prohibition was repealed by the Twenty-First Amendment. The modern civil rights movement produced the Twenty-Fourth Amendment, abolishing payment of state poll taxes (which poor voters, both black and white, usually were not able to raise) as a voting qualification in federal elections, and the Twenty-Third, which enables residents of the District of Columbia to participate in presidential elections.

Judicial interpretation. Far more important for adjusting the Constitution to change than amending has been the process of judicial interpretation. Since the Constitution is not self-explanatory, it sometimes requires interpretation, a function that falls on the judiciary, a clarifier of the meaning of laws. "We are under the Constitution," wrote Chief Justice Charles Evans Hughes, "but the Constitution is what the judges say it is." The general words and phrases of the Constitution make much of it wide open to judicial interpretation, and therefore to change. After devotion to an interpretation in one era, the Supreme Court may change it in another. In the 1950s and 1960s, for example, the so-called Warren Court (under Chief Justice Earl Warren) interpreted certain constitutional provisions with marked liberality in favor of criminal defendants. But the "Nixon Court," whose core is four justices appointed by the President (Warren Burger, Harry Blackmun, Lewis Powell, and William Rehnquist), addressing itself to the same issues, shows promises of living up to the contentions of a fund-raising leaflet circulated by the Finance Committee for the Reelection of the President in the 1972 campaign. According to the leaflet, the Nixon-appointed justices "can be expected to give a strict interpretation of the Constitution and protect the interests of the average, law-abiding American." The Nixon-appointed justices formed the main nucleus of a majority that accepted two novel assertions by prosecutors—that convictions should be allowed by less-than-unanimous jury verdicts in state courts, and that witnesses compelled to testify before grand juries should not be given immunity against prosecution for crimes they were forced to disclose, if independent evidence could be uncovered.[27] In dissenting opinions, the four Nixon nominees also opposed the abolition of capital punishment. And in contributing to majority opinions they upheld the federal government against the claims of constitutional privilege made by *New York Times* reporter Earl Caldwell and Senator Mike Gravel (D., Alaska), both of whom refused to disclose the sources of information they released to the public.

Sometimes judicial interpretation may invoke new social policy before the other governmental branches have taken it up. In 1954, in *Brown v. Board of Education of Topeka*,[28] the Court found that the Constitution required racial integration of public schools. At that time neither Congress nor the President had as yet identified themselves with that policy.

Other interpreters. Congress makes its own interpretations of its delegated constitutional powers. The Constitution says little about the executive departments, but those that Congress has created—Defense, State, Health, Education, and Welfare, and others—have been the chief means for the nation to act as a superpower in the Nuclear Age and to grapple with severe urban problems, preoccupations plainly unanticipated by the framers. By broadly interpreting its delegated powers, Congress in the twentieth century has brought the federal government solidly into such activities as education, insurance, health care and research, old-age pensions, producing and selling electrical power, and placing man on the moon.

Presidents have interpreted the Constitution expansively. Despite his doubts about the legality of his action, Jefferson completed the Louisiana Purchase and tripled American territory. While others disagreed, Lincoln ruled that the seceded Southern states had never been out of the Union and thus spared them a more severe retribution. Unable to move civil rights legislation through Congress, Kennedy freely interpreted the general language describing the President's powers so he could curb racial discrimination in housing, integrate public schools and universities, and induce the Interstate Commerce Commission to designate for purposes of desegregation those facilities used in interstate bus travel. For the Southeast Asian war, all the Presidents involved have liberally interpreted their powers.

Federalism, a basic, structural principle of the Constitution, has markedly altered since 1789. The states have undertaken functions in education, health, and welfare far beyond any prediction of the Founding Fathers. Even more unimagined is the enormous relative growth of the federal government, which began in an age when the states overshadowed the central government. Custom and usage too have altered the Constitution's workings. Political parties, unforeseen by the Fathers, developed into key institutions after the nationalists and republicans of the convention underwent some regrouping and elaboration of organization to become the Federalist and Anti-Federalist parties. The electoral college, originally beheld as an awesome invention of

[27] Fred P. Graham, "Profile of the 'Nixon Court,'" *New York Times,* May 24, 1972.
[28] 347 U.S. 483 (1954).

the Fathers, languished into a minor device. The Cabinet and legislative committees, unmentioned in the Constitution, were soon created out of need to carry out the functions of the executive and legislative branches.

Itself only the bare bones of government, and little touched by formal amendment, the Constitution has been fleshed out by interpretation to become a "living" document. In nearly two centuries of existence, it survived the transformation of the United States from a simple agricultural society to a complex industrial technological one, from an isolated frontier land to a world superpower. The Constitution has survived civil war and has moved from a restricted electoral base to remarkably expanded participation.

A new constitution?

John Adams defined a constitution as "a frame, a scheme, a system, a combination of powers for a certain end, namely—the good of the whole community." [29] How well does the Constitution fit Adams' description? Are its shortcomings great enough to warrant adoption of a new constitution, on the order of Tugwell's model? Some critics have suggested that political rights and civil liberties, which are treated quite fully in the Constitution, are not enough for democracy. Contemporary life also requires a Bill of Economic Rights and a Bill of Social Rights to cover such essentials as the right to employment, health care, and access to a level of education suitable for a technological society. In Tugwell's model, these matters would be cared for by a Planning Branch of the government, whose work would require active citizen participation. Tugwell considers planning an inherently democratic process: it develops objectives and alternatives, estimates their costs and benefits to affected individuals, and lends itself to being done sufficiently far ahead to permit the development of a majority consensus. [30]

The tendency of the existing Constitution to utilize general language facilitates its adjustment to the changing circumstances of different times. But Tugwell rejects this in favor of a more precise constitution. He argues that the more general technique allows the Supreme Court and the legislature to overuse interpretation to fill the vacuum of silent areas, and the results may be helpful or harmful. Democracy is better served, he feels, by the assurance of precise constitutional provisions. But precision too would have drawbacks. If times and needs change, a detailed constitution cannot adjust until a new constitutional consensus is established; meanwhile, government is hobbled with outmoded detail.

Tugwell argues that the present difficult amending process should be replaced by one that would make amendment easier and more responsive to changing circumstance. The arduous amending process has served to limit

[29] Charles Francis Adams, ed., *The Works of John Adams* (Boston, 1850–56), Vol. III, 478–79.
[30] Tugwell, 52–54.

most amendments to minor matters. But there are also questions about Tugwell's freer amending procedure. Would it not make the Constitution and its key democratic elements, particularly protection of civil liberties, unduly susceptible to attack by a hostile, although momentary, popular mood? In the 1950s, for example, Senator Joseph McCarthy held sway with his anti-Communist crusade and severely damaged civil liberties. It is arguable that the damage would have been even greater if the Constitution's civil liberties provisions had been open to easy amendment. The advantage of rigidity is that it assures an enduring standard to which a people and their political system can readily return when reason is restored, as fortunately it was in the McCarthy era.

Social justice, in Tugwell's view, is best provided for by precise prescription in a constitution. Generalized provisions about regulating commerce and levying taxes open the door to favoritism and abuse. But would not the more precise language of Tugwell's constitution be written by those who are well-off and directed toward serving their interests? And could there be any escape from their dominance, as there is under the existing Constitution, through interpretation by the judiciary and the other branches? In Tugwell's order of things, the battle for justice would be concentrated in a single arena, the constitution. The present Constitution permits the battle to be fought in many arenas—the branches of government—and if there is defeat in one, the struggle can be continued in the others.

Suggested Reading

Bailyn, Bernard, *The Ideological Origins of the American Revolution* * (Harvard University Press, 1967). An insightful analysis of British and early American ideas that shaped the ideological justification of the American Revolution and provided the basis for the emerging state constitutions and the subsequent federal constitution.

Beard, Charles A., *An Economic Interpretation of the Constitution of the United States* * (Macmillan, 1913). A classic argument that the framers of the Constitution were influenced by economic considerations. The thesis is still being debated.

Earle, Edward Meade, ed., *The Federalist* (Random House, Modern Library). The series of essays written by Alexander Hamilton, James Madison, and John Jay in support of the Constitution during the struggle over its ratification. Originally published in the press, they comprise an authoritative exposition of the Constitution and the governmental system it created.

Farrand, Max, *The Framing of the Constitution of the United States* * (Yale University Press, 1926). An able account of the proceedings and issues of the constitutional convention. The book draws on the author's four-volume compilation of documentary sources on the convention.

Jensen, Merrill, *The New Nation: A History of the United States During the Confederation 1781–1789* * (Knopf, 1950). An astute interpretation of the American experience under the Articles of Confederation. The author views the Articles favorably and offers a challenging explanation of their demise.

Jordan, Winthrop D., *White Over Black: American Attitudes Toward the Negro, 1550–1812* * (University of North Carolina Press, 1968). An invaluable work that explores the experience of blacks in the United States from its beginnings through the early decades following the adoption of the Constitution. The book traces the origins of slavery and its place in the Revolution and in the formation of the Constitution.

Kelley, Alfred H., and Harbison, Winfred A., *The American Constitution: Its Origins and Development,* 3rd edition (Norton, 1963). A general history of American constitutional development, commencing with the colonial period.

Levy, Leonard W., ed., *Essays on the Making of the Constitution* * (Oxford University Press, 1969). A convenient collection of essays drawn from the extended debate over the motivations of the framers in drafting the Constitution. Beginning with Charles A. Beard, the collection includes the principal scholars who have challenged, modified, or extended his analysis.

Lipset, Seymour Martin, *The First New Nation* * (Basic Books, 1963). A sociologist traces the relationship between the values of a nation and the development of effective political institutions. America's early experience is compared with that of contemporary emerging nations.

McDonald, Forrest, *E Pluribus Unum: The Formation of the American Republic 1776–1798* * (Houghton Mifflin, 1965). An explanation of the origins of the Constitution in terms of advocates and opponents—their interests, their strategies, and the issues that divided them.

Rossiter, Clinton, *Seedtime of the Republic* * (Harcourt Brace Jovanovich, 1953). An astute examination of the colonial and revolutionary eras. The study focuses on the political ideas that influenced the formation of the American nation, including the colonists' concern for political liberty.

Rossiter, Clinton, *1787: The Grand Convention* * (Macmillan, 1966). A highly readable treatment of the emergence of the Constitution at the convention and in the struggle for ratification. The personalities of leading Founding Fathers are vividly presented, as are their strategies and tactics.

Schlesinger, Arthur M., *The Birth of the Nation* (Knopf, 1968). A useful account of colonial social structure and political ideas, and their impact on the governmental system. The analysis extends to the Declaration of Independence and the Constitution.

* Available in paperback edition

4

the

powerful

In his farewell address on leaving the Presidency in 1961, Dwight D. Eisenhower warned against the "military-industrial complex," against its gaining "unwarranted influence, whether sought or unsought." [1] Repeatedly in the sixties and seventies, this military-industrial complex (MIC) has been under attack for its huge size, massive influence, and questionable methods, for its prolongation of an unwanted war and its siphoning off of support from critical, underfinanced domestic programs.

The MIC is overwhelming in its vastness. It employs one of every ten working Americans, either in the armed forces or in the service of thousands of industrial suppliers. Its products range from ammunition, aircraft, ships, and nuclear warheads, to furniture and musical instruments. The glue that holds the MIC together is money. MIC money flows into every state of the Union and into at least 363 of the 435 congressional districts. Entire communities depend on the largess of the MIC. Sunnyvale, California, has largely forsaken the industry that once made it known as "the prune capital of the world" to concentrate on the design and production of Polaris and Poseidon missiles and the Agena rocket. "Death is our favorite industry," a local planner has said.

Like any business whose well-being depends on public expenditure, defense firms seek to influence the amount and allocation of military spending. That task is not difficult. The congressional power centers most concerned with the MIC—the armed services and appropriations committees of each house—are chaired and staffed, with few exceptions, by members with large defense establishments in their constituencies (which, according to a Washington adage, "would sink if they got another defense installation"). [2] Between the firms and the armed services, the ties of mutual interests are strong. The shipbuilding and aircraft industries are relentless boosters of an ever larger navy and air force. Their private status and financial resources permit them to generate local political support and freely engage in public relations and propagandizing activities. "The aircraft industry," Senator Barry Goldwater has noted, "has probably done more to promote the Air Force than the Air

---

[1] In Dwight D. Eisenhower, *The White House Years: Waging Peace, 1956–1961* (New York: Doubleday, 1965), 616.

[2] Samuel P. Huntington, "Interservice Competition and the Political Roles of the Armed Services," *American Political Science Review,* LV (March 1961), 40–52; "The Military-Industrial Complex," *Newsweek* (June 9, 1969), 74–84.

Force has done itself." What appears to be interservice rivalry is often industrial rivalry in the scramble for public outlays.

Propagandizing is a major activity for the armed forces as well. By one count, the armed services maintain a force of some six thousand public relations officers around the world and over three hundred "legislative liaison" lobbyists on Capitol Hill to promote their interests. Each service has "backstop" private organizations like the Navy League, the Air Force Association, and the Association of the U.S. Army, which articulate service interests and programs. Since political power is dispersed in the American federal system, the services have promoted local advisory committees that consist of leading community figures in business, religion, education, the communications media, and civil organizations—people with grassroots power. The structures of the military reserve and the National Guard also facilitate access to local opinion.

The MIC is a microcosm of how power is distributed and wielded in the United States. The alliance of interest groups, the tactics of lobbying, the uses of grassroots pressure, the maneuvers of a power elite—that is what this chapter is about. But we shall also see what elements in our democratic structure can withstand some of these pressures.

The pyramid of power:
the power elite

When Walter Lippmann in an interview with Soviet Premier Nikita Khrushchev asserted that foreign policy decisions would be made by President Kennedy, Khrushchev insisted that forces behind Kennedy would determine his policy. When Lippmann asked what these forces were, Khrushchev uttered a single word: "Rockefeller." Likewise, Khrushchev contended that Kennedy could not accelerate American economic growth, again "because of Rockefeller" and, he added, "Du Pont. They will not let him." [3]

Constructors of elitist theory perceive society as a vast pyramid of power,

with the hierarchies of economic or corporate wealth in control, running the state and directing the military. The sociologist C. Wright Mills has labeled those in control "the power elite." The power elite are not solitary rulers; in wielding their power, they enjoy the support of auxiliaries—advisers and consultants, spokesmen and opinion-makers, politicians, small businessmen. According to elitist theory these assorted lesser subalterns receive orders from the largely hidden economic elite and operate the control mechanisms of society. Still lower are the local leaders and opinion-makers

[3] In Arnold M. Rose, *The Power Structure* (New York: Oxford University Press, 1967), 1.

with grassroots followings, who comply more or less automatically with the will of the higher-ups. Institutions such as the family, churches, and schools adapt easily to the way of life decreed by the elite and remain off to the side of power. At the bottom of the pyramid are the mass of people, inert, unconcerned, and faithfully serving the interests of society's top command.

According to Mills, the elite are extraordinarily integrated. "They accept one another, understand one another, marry one another, and tend to work and to think if not together, at least alike." [4] Mills claims that "insofar as national events are decided, the power elite are those who decide them." [5] Elitist theory allots the masses an ignominious status. Incompetent and passive, they do not count. With little knowledge of public affairs and less interest, they yield easily to their elitist superiors. To man in the mass, politics is a sideshow little noticed in his absorption in gaining a livelihood, in evenings spent with his family, mired in the insipidity of television. This elitist theory holds that for most citizens, distracted and apathetic, politics is remote and secondary.

But all is not lost. These two worlds of slumbering masses and kinetic elites have been joined, even integrated, by an elitist theory of democracy. Either directly or through talented subordinates, the elite also function as political entrepreneurs. There is at least limited competition among members of the elite for the official positions of leadership in a democracy. Elitist thought defines democracy as essentially a method for making decisions, a complex of procedures that produces competent policy and yet requires the governing elite to be somewhat responsive to popular opinion. Despite his limitations, the ordinary citizen possesses a measure of political effectiveness through his right to vote, exercised in regular, prescribed elections. To win at the polls, elitist leaders shape policies responsively to citizen desires.[6]

The elitist theory of democracy holds that the capacity of the elite to absorb democratic values and to observe appropriate rules of the political game protects democracy. Values and rules are woven into an elite consensus, which spurs the elite to safeguard democracy against demagoguery, to which the masses, if sufficiently aroused, might succumb. Meanwhile, the elite, held accountable by democratic processes of discussion and elections, will normally govern on the basis of service to the interests of the people. Advocates of elitist democracy maintain that outputs of security and services benefit the people, and the less the ordinary individual, with all his limitations, has to participate on the "input" or demand side, the better off he and the political system will be.

Elitist theory thus scorns the classical theory of democracy, which visualizes the masses of citizenry as wholly capable of participating in public affairs. But the elitist portrayal of the citizen as wallowing in indifference and lassitude

[4] C. Wright Mills, *The Power Elite* (New York: Oxford University Press, 1956), 11.
[5] *Ibid.*, 3–4.
[6] See Joseph Schumpeter, *Capitalism, Socialism and Democracy* (New York: Harper & Row, 1942), Part IV.

and yet satisfied with how the elite is running the system is utterly at odds with some overpowering evidence from every side today: the protest demonstrations now common in urban life, marches against the Vietnam war, suburban voters pouring out to the polls to defeat the school budget, the high rates of strikes and crime.[7]

In the eyes of elite theorists, democracy's prime goals are stability and efficiency, but this excessively constraining formulation leaves the political system uncommitted to social justice and major improvement of the quality of life, and indifferent to utopian visions of what a good life for all might be. Finally, by beholding democracy as *political* method, elite thinkers subscribe to the view that democratic method is properly limited to the political realm and is therefore inapplicable to elite decision-making processes in corporations and other large private organizations. Corporate leaders continuously make decisions affecting social values that are answerable, almost entirely, only to themselves.

The plural elite
model

In contrast to the power elite is the plural elite model, in which power is more widely shared among leadership groups. In this model, elites are more competitive and politics has greater play. The individual counts for more, particularly as he associates with other individuals. Politics is less subordinate to economic power, to the point that a major political party, usually the Democratic, sometimes thwarts the special interests of the economic elite. With its multiple centers of power, democracy functions as a system of social pluralism.

The plural or multiple-power influence has been formulated in various ways. John Kenneth Galbraith has advanced the thesis of countervailing power: "Private economic power is held in check by the countervailing power of those who are subject to it. The first begets the second." [8] Concentrated economic power stimulates other business interests likely to suffer from its arbitrary dispensations to organize and thwart them. To counter big suppliers, big commercial purchasers may combine and bargain from strength, seek other suppliers, or buy alternative products; to stay the heavy hand of the great corporation, working men form unions. If private means of countervailing power are inadequate, as is sometimes the case, Galbraith calls for government to create and support organizations capable of containing overweening power. Consequently, and fortunately for democracy's safety, power tends toward an equilibrium, with a watchful government ready to set aright deviations and

[7] See Peter Bachrach, *The Theory of Democratic Elitism* (Boston: Little, Brown, 1967), 97; Jack L. Walker, "A Critique of the Elitist Theory of Democracy," *American Political Science Review*, LX (June 1966), 285–95.
[8] John Kenneth Galbraith, *American Capitalism* (Boston: Houghton Mifflin, 1952), 118.

disarray. In this view, democracy remains secure because the powerful can never become too powerful.

In comparable vein, Robert A. Dahl and Charles E. Lindblom perceive American democracy as a polyarchy, with a diversity of social organizations, each possessing impressive autonomy and power.[9] Key economic processes buttress this pluralist social structure and regulate the powerful. Thus the price system superintends the hierarchy of economic power by decentralizing decision and power (unless government intervenes and centrally determines prices). Through the price system, consumers control the businessman, because they pay him for producing only what they want, and they can buy someone else's products rather than submit to his high prices. Through the price system, the businessman also regulates consumers by setting prices at levels to assure that they will not consume more production than is available. If disequilibrium jars the world of social pluralism, government can intervene to shore up the bargaining strength of the faltering.

Sociologist Arnold Rose gives still further dimensions to social factors in his multi-influence hypothesis.[10] While acknowledging the importance of economic forces, Rose contends that semi-independent forces of social change latent in technology, cultural contact and conflict, and concrete social movements also shape the pluralist world. Vested interests of economic power resist social changes, manipulate law to that end, and draw support from custom and the social structure generally. But impersonal forces of social change set controlling limits on the power of any elite to determine the nature and course of society. For example, medical technology has been able to reduce deaths through acute illness strikingly but it has left increasing numbers of elderly people prey to chronic illnesses and heavy medical expense, which makes the choice between life and death sometimes a choice between bankruptcy and solvency. To meet their needs, social movements vied with political and medical elites to establish a federal program of medical care. The Medicare program that was eventually adopted reflected changes in medical technology and the social changes it engendered. According to the multi-influence hypothesis, social change occurs in a matrix of social forces, resistances, and conflicts, only some of which are susceptible to elite manipulation and control.

Not only do some writers contend that power is pluralistic, or divided among groups, but they see that power as largely confined to its particular sphere. The different spheres of life—the family, religious values and institutions, the artistic and educational realms—do not interpenetrate in a democracy as they do in a totalitarian system, where political values permeate all other spheres. In the United States and in other democratic countries, virtually every person has differentiated roles and values for each of the many spheres of life; therefore, power does not significantly cross the boundaries of its own sphere. Sociologist Robert Merton writes: "Men with power to affect the

[9] Robert A. Dahl and Charles E. Lindblom, *Politics, Economics and Welfare* (New York: Harper & Row, 1953).

[10] Rose, 7–9.

economic life-chances of a large group may exert little interpersonal influence in other spheres: the power to withhold jobs from people may not result in directly influencing their political or associational or religious behavior." [11]

Nevertheless, all is not well within particular hierarchies of power. The pluralist interpretation of American democracy has come under fire for its inclusion, if not tacit approval, of processes and structures that are blatantly undemocratic. Organizations of hierarchical power such as General Motors and the American Medical Association speak with a single voice, even though they include significant multiple-interest constituencies. What appears to be forced unanimity implies that big private power is a poor protector of the rights of the individual. Ironically, while the Constitution fragments political power to safeguard individual rights, the technological system consolidates it and opens the gates to arbitrariness. In a further mockery of democracy, private organizations can often use public agencies such as the courts to support their control of the work, consumption, and leisure of the individual.[12]

The big private organizations—particularly the great corporations—are actually oligarchies, in which decisions are made by the few. They hold a disproportionate share of assets and resources and produce disproportionate shares of necessary commodities. Endowed with vast power, the corporation sets its own goals, decrees those of its employees, and those of outsiders as well—the consumers who are lulled by advertising into consumption habits that engender even more production. The general public is locked into an attitude of approval, which brings them to assume that their interests are identical with the corporations' interests. Unaware of their real interests, the general public is easily fooled and diverted by a power elite whose game they cannot see through and therefore cannot influence.

Labor unions too are oligarchic. Their leaders absorb potential dissidents into their administrations and press a mold of harmony on simmering conflicts. Technology can also stifle pluralism. Power units cannot genuinely compete when entrenched leaders monopolize television and other opinion-manipulating tools. If conflicting articulations of interest in large organizations occasionally bubble to the surface, it is only because the leadership, secure in tenure and certain of survival, can afford the luxury of momentary free expression.

Organized power:
voluntary associations
and interest groups

Another model of power rejects the conception of elite power. Despite the awesome presence of big business and big labor, proponents of this model see power as highly dispersed, thanks to the large realm of private decision-

---

[11] In *ibid.*, 33.
[12] Henry M. Kariel, *The Decline of American Pluralism* (Stanford, Calif.: Stanford University Press, 1961).

making, the elaborate diversity of the economy, the variety of the nation's peoples and regions, the sheer breadth of Americans' interests—their hobbies, clubs, and causes. In keeping with the variety of its life, the United States is dotted with group organizations, easy to initiate and extraordinary in variety. Public policy, or the output of political power, is determined by these groups; for major policy, combinations of groups are necessary.

A large class of organization is the voluntary association, typified by continuing relationship among its members, formal structure, and specialization in one or only a few interests. The voluntary association provides a forum for discussion sometimes leading to social action. The associations may spring from tangent relations, like those between the parents and teachers of a child: the widespread incidence of this pattern and the desire to regularize it led to the formation of the Parent-Teacher Association. The American Farm Bureau Federation, the League of Women Voters, the American Legion, and the American Civil Liberties Union—these organizations suggest the associations' enormous range of interests.

Voluntary associations distribute power. Until recent decades, the upper class and ethnic groups of Western European origin maintained their preeminent power in society, at least partly, by ascendance in these organizations. But the associations' power picture has changed somewhat with the organization of increasing proportions of the lower classes into labor unions and the tendency of the middle classes to assume leadership in associations with social influence. Ethnic minorities are organizing their own social-influence groups and directing their activity toward politics and economics. Broader participation in voluntary associations is distributing power more widely.

The associations perform other functions beneficial to democracy. They help rescue the ordinary citizen from the sterile fate of being a mere spectator of society, manipulated by the power-holders. Associations enable the citizen to act. Thus an individual who is distressed by industry's onslaughts on the environment can join any of a number of associations dedicated to curbing the devastation, and he can contribute his time and ability to the extent that he wishes. His participation increases his knowledge and sophistication about the operation and abuses of the power structure, and how it might be influenced in behalf of his causes. Voluntary associations help bring about social change—a higher minimum wage, Social Security, Medicare. They develop cohesion among members whose interests may otherwise differ, and they impart to the individual a sense of identification in a mass society of big organizations.

The voluntary associations become interest groups or pressure groups when they resort to politics to get what they want in public policy. According to David Truman, interest groups are characterized by shared attitudes and may be organized or "potential," that is, brought into being by events that activate the latent attitudes of their members—as with a proposed highway routed through the living rooms of a residential neighborhood.[13]

[13] David B. Truman, *The Governmental Process* (New York: Knopf, 1951), Chapter 2.

Robert H. Salisbury has distinguished between two major categories of interest groups. Material benefit groups, represented by farm, business, and labor groups, are characterized by leaderships of long tenure that are seldom challenged. Expressive groups, the other type, are inexpensive to organize, are easily established, and just as easily disappear. Frequently this type is racked by schisms and its leadership topples.[14] Interest groups also may be private or public. An example of the latter is a government bureau that is pressing legislators to enlarge its programs. Some interest groups promote their own selfish or material gain, while others advocate some public good, such as the preservation of historic landmarks. Often these lines are blurred.

Interest groups may be seen as communications systems of varying complexity and sophistication, with transmitters, receivers, relay stations, filters. Their messages influence opinion and link policy-makers and political parties to the individual. Interest groups may also be seen as brokers, pressing members' demands and bargaining, often in competition with other groups, with policy-makers. In the American political system, according to Truman, interest group politics remains vital and healthy because of the ease of access to the governmental process and because of government's ready response to those who achieve access. Access denotes influence whose reward is governmental programs, maintained or enlarged.[14]

Pervasive and powerful, interest groups have spurred the fashioning of bold theories. In a classic work, *The Process of Government,* Arthur F. Bentley equated groups with action; through groups, masses of individuals achieve political, economic, and social satisfaction. The individual, beheld as a social unit, "is a fiction." Truman, who extended Bentley's theories, contends that interest groups emerge to satisfy the needs of society, and as society grows in complexity and specialization, more groups will appear. Likewise, the onset of disturbances causing suffering and dislocation will almost invariably induce organized political pressure. In a further broad formulation, Earl Latham holds that "the chief social values cherished by individuals in modern society are realized through groups." [16]

The political interest group, then, serves democracy in its ability to achieve action in behalf of individuals. But the coin has another side: interest groups pose certain handicaps for democracy. They tend toward oligarchy, with self-indulgent leaderships and submissive, uninformed memberships. Many interest groups, operating in tight secrecy, have low public visibility and little public accountability. Their dedication to the "Me First" rule of life submerges the public interest and subjects the weak and the unorganized to gross, if not cruel, injustices in the distribution of social values. They are fertile sources of unethical practices in politics—cheating, falsifying, bribing, deceiving in a society-be-damned drive to obtain their selfish objectives. Tactics

[14] Robert H. Salisbury, *Interest Group Politics in America* (New York: Harper & Row, 1970), 48–53.
[15] Truman, 264–68.
[16] These views are collected in H. R. Mahood, *Pressure Groups in American Politics* (New York: Scribner's, 1967), 17–23.

that confuse the public with unbridled propaganda and badger officials with self-interested claims are hardly akin to the democratic spirit.

Some pressure groups
visited

Business. Though the operating heads of six or seven hundred corporations dispose of most of the nongovernmental economic power, they are not organized as a tight-knit elite. No one of them accepts orders or instructions from another. No single corporate manager or coterie of managers has attained permanent national-scale power. Instead of constituting an elite model of pyramided power, the big corporations are more accurately depicted as members of a polyarchic system of power. Paradoxically, although the great corporations and financial institutions have grown enormously since the Second World War, their relative power has eroded. Governmental activities have dramatically expanded at all levels to the point that they now account for between 20 and 25 percent of all economic activity, compared with 8 percent in 1929. Social service expenditures and government regulation have multiplied, even to the point that the Republican Nixon administration, long a friend to the businessman, imposed wage and price controls.

The power of the great corporations is still awesome, however. They can impose "administered prices," by which they maintain automobile prices, for example, over long intervals despite fluctuations of demand. They have a formidable power to accumulate capital, aggregating in a single year into billions of dollars, which they are free to invest. They abuse the environment, flood the country with costly, inane advertising, market products that are shoddy or unsafe, subject the worker and the consumer to dehumanizing processes, and engage in malpractices sufficient to engross indefinitely whole legions of Nader's Raiders. An Alabama business concern runs a paper mill whose stench reaches twenty miles to the state capitol building, forcing Governor George Wallace to rationalize, "That's the smell of money." A mill owner who unabashedly pollutes the Savannah River has replied to environmentalists with fine imperiousness, "it probably won't hurt mankind a whole hell of a lot in the long run if the whooping crane doesn't quite make it." [17] But the corporation's most serious affront to democracy is its tight internal autonomy. Its managers, making their far-reaching decisions, are not seriously answerable to any constituency, not to stockholders, consumers, or the ordinary employee.

When a business wishes to influence public policy, it can utilize its own resources or entrust its cause to a trade association like the National Association of Manufacturers. What does the business pressure group strive to extract from government? All businesses thirst for tax reductions, although

[17] From Leonard Ross, "Who Regulates the Regulator? The Regulated," *New York Times Book Review* (August 8, 1971), 1.

different businesses clash over exactly which taxes to cut. Business cherishes government subsidies and services for itself, but strenuously opposes their dispensation to other sectors of the population. And business struggles to avoid public regulation, a battleground on which it suffers many defeats. Governmental controls are mounting to the point that present-day enterprise is no longer recognizable in the mirror of free-enterprise theorists like William Graham Sumner and Adam Smith.

But business too responds to pressure. General Motors may have a ponderous record of foot-dragging on proposals to improve auto safety and to reduce pollution, yet it did elect a black to its board of directors—the Reverend Leon Sullivan, a Philadelphia clergyman. As a board member, Sullivan has pushed for more black GM dealerships and for the movement of more blacks into middle management positions. Between 1965 and 1971, GM's black workers rose from 11 percent to 15.3 percent of GM's workforce. In addition, GM has deposited $5 million in thirty-five minority-owned banks in twenty-five cities, has invested in low-cost housing projects sponsored by civil rights groups, and has provided low-cost loans to minority-owned businesses. "I will keep on talking, walking, and working," said the Reverend Sullivan, "until the walls come down."

What business needs, economist Henry Wallich has said, is an "economic justification of what it already wants to do." Traditional profit and growth drives restrain business from being more responsive to public needs. Possibly there is both incentive and rationalization in Wallich's view that corporate shareholders have a financial stake in improving the total society, and management might legitimately use some of their profits on social projects.[18]

A sturdy bridge between business and the politician is money, which the former has lots of and the latter needs in quantity for expensive electoral campaigns. In 1970, Senator Vance Hartke (D., Ind.) won a hairsbreadth victory over his Republican opponent, Richard L. Roudebush. Hartke's campaign was aided by an $80,000 send-off derived from a fund-raising dinner attended by the presidents of nine railroads and leaders of the trucking industry. By interesting coincidence, Hartke was chairman of the Senate subcommittee handling rail and truck laws. Hartke also received help from other industries—steel, drugs, Wall Street finance, and mail order concerns. The latter possibly derived incentive from the fact that Hartke was a member of a Senate committee that at the time dealt with postal rates.[19]

One of the saltier controversies stemming from business relations with government transpired in the International Telephone and Telegraph Corporation (ITT) affair of 1972, which came to light when the name of Acting Attorney General Richard G. Kleindienst was before the Senate for confirmation as Attorney General. Syndicated newspaper columnist Jack Anderson accused Kleindienst of lying about his role in settling out of court a milestone antitrust case against the conglomerate ITT. Some suggested,

[18] In "The American Corporation Under Fire," *Newsweek* (May 24, 1971), 74–84.
[19] *New York Times,* April 12, 1971.

Drawing by Joseph Farris; © 1972 The New Yorker Magazine, Inc.

"This country has been good to me."

furthermore, that the settlement was made in return for a $400,000 pledge by ITT to underwrite the coming Republican national convention, then scheduled to be held in San Diego. The disclosures were based on a confidential memorandum by an ITT lobbyist that said, "Certainly the President has told (Attorney General) Mitchell to see that things are worked out fairly. . . . Mitchell is definitely helping us, but cannot let it be known."

Defenders of the Nixon administration maintained that out-of-court settlements were common in antitrust suits and the settlement with ITT was a tough one. But the real issue, many felt, was what should be the boundary lines of propriety in relations between government and business. Economist

John Kenneth Galbraith pointed out that the impact on the national economy of a corporate empire such as ITT can be so great that government regulators may be forced to consider that what is bad for ITT is bad for the country. "The ITT thing," observed Congressman Paul McCloskey (R., Calif.), who briefly challenged President Nixon's renomination, "is just the tip of the iceberg with [the Administration] and the worst thing is that they don't even realize that what they've done is wrong. They've turned areas of government which should be immune from political influence into political tools. . . . And they don't even see that it's indecent." [20]

Labor. Signs of weakness are apparent in that bastion of elitist power known as organized labor. Union membership reached a peak in 1956; since then employment has continued to grow, but union membership has declined. In an economy that John Kenneth Galbraith has called the technostructure, the element that makes up most of the labor force—the great homogeneous blue-collar proletariat—is sharply in decline.[21] Advanced technology has reduced the need for blue-collar workers, both skilled and unskilled. Union memberships, in addition to being in decline, are not well distributed around the nation: 55 percent are located in three Middle Atlantic states (New York, Pennsylvania, and New Jersey) and five East North Central states (Illinois, Ohio, Michigan, Wisconsin, and Indiana). Union memberships are disproportionately male, with men outnumbering women by six to one, although their proportion is three to one in the labor force.[22]

Yet, despite these and other soft spots, labor unions today are at their height of power. Adolf Berle compares the present power of union leaders to that of the captains of industry at the turn of the century. Those financiers could dominate American life by withholding capital just as union leaders today can wreak hardship and untold expense by withholding the labor of workers.[23]

Internally, unions, like corporations, are a nest of practices antithetical to democracy. Though many unions affirm the right of free speech and the secret ballot, these count little when leadership controls administrative resources— the union administrative and field staffs, the union newspaper, expense accounts—and there is no counterpropaganda structure for waging dissent. Challenges to incumbent leaders in the more monolithic organizations usually have to assume the form of revolution.

Unions curtail the worker's freedom of choice in establishing formal wage structures, seniority rosters, work schedules, the pace of output, the pattern of occupational opportunities, and by determining whether he shall strike or not. The ties of some unions to racketeering and their indulgence in fraudulent

[20] "The ITT Affair: Politics and Justice," *Newsweek* (March 20, 1972), 24–28.
[21] Galbraith, *The New Industrial State,* 233–38.
[22] W. Lloyd Warner, D. B. Unwalla, and John H. Trimm, *The Emergent American Society,* Vol. 1, *Large-Scale Organizations* (New Haven: Yale University Press, 1967), 373.
[23] Berle, 223–24.

elections are further blots on labor's democratic escutcheon. These incidents persist despite the Landrum-Griffin Act of 1959, which is meant to regulate union conduct.

Organized labor's chief spokesman is the AFL-CIO (American Federation of Labor and the Congress of Industrial Organizations), a confederation of craft, or skilled worker, unions (AFL) and industrial unions (CIO) embracing both skilled and unskilled industrial workers. In exerting political pressures, the AFL-CIO utilizes a Committee on Political Education (COPE), which promotes a national legislative program and informs workers about election issues and candidates. Although professing to be nonpartisan, organized labor commits its political money almost wholly to the needs of the Democratic party. Estimates of the number of votes labor contributes to the Democrats range from one to about three million. Unions thus are far from a voting monolith, for great numbers of union members vote contrary to the public endorsements made by their leadership.[24]

Union lobbying activity concentrates on bread-and-butter measures shaping the mode of union operations and improving the condition of workers. Labor leaders and conventions have supported the Vietnam war and civil rights laws and have expressed opinions on innumerable other matters from education to postal reform. The AFL-CIO day-to-day lobbying activities on Capitol Hill are run by Andrew Biemiller, a former congressman from Milwaukee, and his staff of five. On major drives, such as the campaign to defeat the Supreme Court nominations of Clement Haynsworth, Jr., and G. Harrold Carswell, Biemiller can draw on the AFL-CIO affiliated unions for help and pull together an army of over eighty lobbyists. And on hard-fought issues, George Meany himself, the blunt and crotchety leader of the AFL-CIO, talks with key congressmen.

Much of the AFL-CIO's pressure capacity is at the grassroots, where efficient organizations and sheer numbers have impressive force. The AFL-CIO can have enormous impact in support of favored presidential and congressional candidates, who are nearly always Democrats. In the 1968 campaign, Theodore White credited labor with the ultimate registration of 4.6 million voters, with printing and distributing 55 million pamphlets and leaflets out of Washington and 60 million more from local unions, with operating telephone banks in 638 communities, and with providing 94,457 volunteers as car-poolers, distributors, baby sitters, poll-watchers, and telephoners. Concerning this formidable power, a Democratic senator has said, "When I get a call from the AFL-CIO boss back home, I listen. I may not go along, but believe me, I listen. After all, whom do I depend on most when the next campaign comes along?"[25]

Agriculture. The agricultural community clearly wields disproportionate political power. Despite a drastically declining farm population—from 20 million

[24] Mahood, 129, 147.
[25] "George Meany: Fight over the Freeze," *Newsweek* (September 6, 1971), 48.

twenty years ago to 10 million—governmental appropriations for agriculture and the size of the Department of Agriculture have consistently increased. The greater part of the Agriculture Department expenditures are allotted to farm subsidies, paid to those who agree to limit their crop acreage and help relieve pressure on prices by controlling "surpluses." Subsidies annually exceed outlays for such national problems as housing, urban transportation, air and water pollution, and hunger.

The bulk of government expenditure goes not to the millions of rural poor, nor to the small farmer, but to the big producer. National farm policy is dedicated to making the rural rich richer. A farmer whose thriving acreage in the San Joaquin Valley in California is so vast that he can view its full expanse in a single day only by swinging his little red and white monoplane over it, received nearly $1.7 million in subsidies in 1971. Meanwhile a farmer with sixty-seven sandy acres and a sagging house on a muddy road in South Carolina, received a subsidy of about $300.

Some of these distortions in the allocation of public largess are attributable to agriculture's power infrastructure—to the major farm organizations, their leaders, the heads of large-scale agricultural enterprises, and the principal members of the congressional agriculture committees. Largest and most powerful of the farm pressure groups, with enormous influence in Congress and the Department of Agriculture, is the American Farm Bureau Federation, which speaks principally for the corn and cotton farmers. It is the only truly national farm organization, although its membership is concentrated in the Midwest and South. It generally takes a middle-of-the-road stance. The far smaller Grange, despite a stormy, illustrious past, now avoids controversial economic or political issues. The National Farmers' Union embodies old-fashioned militant radicalism, evidenced by its stress on cooperatives as the most democratic farming enterprise. Its strength centers in the North Central and Great Plains states.

Powerful men in Congress harmonize with Farm Bureau opinion, marred by partiality to the relatively prosperous farmers from areas with sufficient rainfall to reduce the hazard of farming. The Bureau opposes rural social programs and favors the channeling of public expenditure to the substantial commercial farmer. One congressional power center is the House Appropriations Subcommittee on Agriculture and its chairman, Jamie L. Whitten (D., Miss.). A top Agriculture Department aide has said: "Jamie just can't see agriculture as a Department of Rural Affairs. He's a traditionalist. He's concerned with farmers, crops, and commodities." Another power-wielder in the agricultural firmament is W. R. Poage (D., Texas), chairman of the House Agriculture Committee. With his bulldog manner and rasping voice, Poage allowed as how many of the poor are merely shiftless: "I am ready to help all those who need help. But I definitely am not ready to pass out free food or food stamps to those who can but won't work." The circle of power of interest groups and congressional committees is completed by sympathetic officials in the Agriculture Department. In the Nixon administration, several top aides are substantial landowners, drawing large federal subsidy payments in addition to their salaries.[26]

A profession: the American Medical Association. The American Medical Association illustrates that the members of an organization may not always function within the elitist mold—supine and acquiescent to dominating leadership. Across the country chapters of the Medical Committee for Human Rights are sprouting, a militant organization of about seven thousand doctors who consider the AMA "a menace to enlightened medical care," an organization that "has opposed everything without offering viable alternatives." Younger practitioners are declining to join the Association to the point that the AMA—long the most powerful medical interest group—for the first time in over half a century faces the prospect of having less than half of the country's active physicians in its fold. Conservative doctors too are dissatisfied. The issue of national health insurance deeply divides the members: conservative doctors view the AMA's Medicredit proposal as a socialist sellout, while liberals term it a weak palliative.

The AMA leadership is an elite under stress, a condition that enhances the power of members and potential members. Their choices, and thereby their power, include joining rival organizations, continuing as members and working for change from within, pressing the leadership to admit into its ranks younger liberal doctors, or setting up still other organizations, as some conservative members are doing.[27]

The public interest groups. Any roll call of the powerful must include the public interest groups, encompassing Ralph Nader and his Raiders, John Gardner's Common Cause, and a host of environmental groups. These groups support causes that evoke or can be made to evoke widespread concern. Often little material gain accrues to champions of these causes. Instead, they may be rewarded with aggrandizement of personal power and the realization of ideals. Frequently the public interest causes have their own charismatic leader, like Ralph Nader.

In the 1960s, Nader emerged as a hero of the consumer movement after disclosures that General Motors had hired a detective to probe his life, presumably for unsavory details that might compromise him. Nader's sudden martyrdom brought him national fame and enormous influence. Aided by talented young people, and in summer months by students of law, medicine, and the social sciences, Nader and his associates have published books on the auto industry, medicine and health, pollution, and on federal agencies such as the Interstate Commerce Commission and the Federal Trade Commission. He has been a major force in the passage of auto safety, antipollution, and meat inspection laws.

What, besides martyrdom, are the sources of Nader's power? He is a

[26] *New York Times,* April 5, 1970.
[27] *New York Times,* September 4, 1971.

magnet of information (and for Nader information is power) from citizens with complaints about faulty products or services, from personnel within industry who secretly communicate corporate lapses, from federal bureaucrats who cavil at seeing potentially explosive information suppressed or defused by inertia. Nader and his associates gain further information through their own widespread research into government agencies and business practice. Nader then disseminates his information through the press, his books and articles, and testimony at congressional hearings.[28]

Information is power only because Nader communicates it in ways that create new opinion. Thus he jolted prevailing public opinion that felt all meat was reasonably safe, and he induced a new view that some meat was dangerous. That belief enabled the Wholesome Meat Act of 1967 to come into effect. Nader can be seen at work in the development of that act. From a little known Department of Agriculture report on meatpacking plants beyond federal control, he plucked sentences such as: "A man was wrapping pork shoulders. He dropped one in the sawdust, picked it up, wiped it off with a dirty, sour rag. . . . Beef was being broken on an open dock by a dirt road, in 95-degree weather. There were flies on the meat." Nader sent off a series of letters bearing this kind of evidence to influential congressmen and released them to the press. He also ventured forth on a coast-to-coast ten-city tour to detail the meat story in lectures and interviews. The White House was flooded with letters that, according to Betty Furness, President Johnson's consumer adviser, demanded "tough action." When the House of Representatives passed a weak bill, despite his testimony, Nader helped to surface a story during Senate hearings that Western meat packers were threatening to withhold

[28] Mark V. Nadel, *The Politics of Consumer Protection* (Indianapolis: Bobbs-Merrill, 1971), 182–83.

Ralph Nader addressing law students from the University of Maine in an attempt to take his consumer crusade to the grassroots.

campaign contributions from certain congressmen who voted for a tough bill. The crusader also concentrated on putting grassroots pressure on the White House. Eventually the Johnson administration bowed to this pressure and pushed through a tough bill.[29]

Like others with imposing power, Nader is an object of criticism. To some, he is abrasive and intolerant. A GM lobbyist, who knew him well, has said: "He is an important and effective social and political force, but he'd be more effective if he were more charitable of the motives and integrity of the people he attacks." [30] Others criticize the stress on "witchhunts," on exposing skeletons in closets, and the lack of a coherent program. The Nader forces do not hesitate to cite chapter and verse of the lapses of the Food and Drug Administration and industry evils, but they are shy in offering substantial proposals with analysis and documentation.[31]

Another people's organizational phenomenon is the public interest law firm. It consists typically of young, socially conscious lawyers who serve people with significant complaints but without means to pay legal fees. One of the more successful of these enterprises is the Citizens Communications Center in Washington, which is supported by several foundations. The Center specializes in keeping watch over the Federal Communications Commission. It forced the purchaser of television and radio stations in Philadelphia, New Haven, and Fresno (the largest transfer in communications history) to arrange with community groups to provide a million dollars of minority programming,

[29] "Meet Ralph Nader," *Newsweek* (January 22, 1968), 70.
[30] *Ibid.*
[31] Ross, 1.

a trailblazing achievement. The Center has also aided citizen groups that challenge the renewal of media licenses in cities where programming does not serve all elements of the community. And the Center participated in the successful legal fight that induced the FCC to rule that the networks must provide equal time for opposing viewpoints when the President speaks on his war policies.

According to these and many other instances, the people do count; they do have power and impact. Marching, demonstrating, pressuring, suing are their ways of forceful political expression that command results when those in formal positions of power are indifferent or negative. And sometimes the people also throw such types out of office.[32]

Lobbying

In 1971, what was described as "an orchestrated team" of Nixon administration officials, executives of the nearly bankrupt Lockheed Aircraft Corporation, and representatives of its subcontractors, bankers, and union members fanned out through the halls of Congress to call on legislators. Lockheed was seeking a government loan to stave off its imminent financial collapse. Lockheed officials and representatives spoke with virtually every member of Congress once and some of them several times. "They were softsell and professional—very impressive," said a Texas congressman who was long undecided about how to vote. A wholehearted supporter of Lockheed was the National Association of Machinists and Aerospace Workers. That union contributed $50,000 to the effort of persuading Congress, and, according to one spokesman, generated half a million pieces of mail to Washington on the subject. "For us and for Lockheed," a union official said, "it was a 'bread-and-butter issue.' Our jobs were on the line." Despite fierce opposition within Congress, the Lockheed bill was eventually adopted by a margin of 1 vote in the Senate and 3 in the House.[33]

This is lobbying, the exerting of pressure on decision-makers in order to protect or enhance special interests. It is a common pursuit of organized power.

Lobbyists represent all sorts of causes, work at all levels of government, and deal with both legislators and administrators. Many lobbyists are lawyers who devote a part of their practice to lobbying. The executives of trade associations whose headquarters are located in Washington are usually lobbyists. Most lobbyists are envoys for organizations with headquarters in another city; as the sole representative, or as a member of a small staff, the lobbyist is commonly "jack-of-all-trades" in his activity.

In his study, *The Washington Lobbyists,* Lester Milbrath found that nearly

32 Robert Sherrill, *Why They Call It Politics* (New York: Harcourt Brace Jovanovich, 1972), 268–86.
33 *New York Times,* August 8, 1971.

A coalition of twenty-four bankers testifying before the House Banking
Committee in support of the Lockheed loan.

all lobbyists call on members of Congress and other decision-makers; most of
them also prepare written comment, testify before committees, contact constituents, and entertain. A growing trend stresses communication with decision-
makers through intermediation of people at the grassroots level (as Lockheed
did). Lobbyists stationed in Washington stimulate communications from
constituents back home (known as "farming the membership").[34]

An important member of the Washington lobbying community is the
public relations firm. Hill and Knowlton is typical; according to its brochure
it offers "counsel on congressional hearings, legislation, and developments;
intelligence concerning government activities, policies, and decisions, and
representation of clients in these areas; Washington press relations—counsel
and operations." [35]

According to a *Congressional Quarterly* study, business spends more on
lobbying than any other source, more than twice as much as its closest com-
petitor, labor unions and employee associations. A Brookings Institution
study of business representatives revealed that many lobbyists complained
of difficulty in interesting their companies in Washington affairs.[36] But when
business really wants something it usually gets it—the 27½ percent oil depletion allowance and scores of other tax loopholes and advantages, a Du

[34] Lester W. Milbrath, *The Washington Lobbyists* (Chicago: Rand McNally, 1963),
7–8, 116.
[35] In James Deakin, *The Lobbyists* (Washington: Public Affairs Press, 1966), 33.
[36] *Ibid.,* 119–20.

Pont-General Motors stock bill, and the Telstar bill for American Telephone and Telegraph Company.

Lobbying is not altogether democracy's friend. In recent decades the most prodigal expenditures of money and influence have been directed *against* proposals to advance the general welfare, to relieve the distress of the cities, to expand educational and economic opportunities for the deprived, and to allocate the nation's material wealth more equitably. Lobbyists have toiled unstintingly to prevent regulation of interstate traffic in firearms and to block legislation to protect the consumer from hidden credit charges and misleading packaging. Lobbyists delayed legislation to protect the public from dangerous drugs and to help the elderly meet the soaring costs of hospital and medical care. The intensity of these efforts is suggested by the lavishness of their expenditure. The American Medical Association is estimated to have spent between $7 and $12 million in a single year to kill Medicare, and the petroleum industry $25 million to exempt natural gas producers from federal regulation.[37]

Lobbying is unhampered by serious regulation. A 1946 Lobbying Act defines a lobbyist as one whose "principal purpose" is to influence the passage or defeat of legislation and requires him to register with the Clerk of the House and the Secretary of the Senate and to report the amount and sources of his income and the expenditure on lobbying. The "principal purpose" clause has caused perpetual confusion over who should register. It has allowed trade associations and Washington law firms, which do important lobbying but also perform quantities of other services, to escape from registering. The act also leaves untouched the executive agencies—a busy terrain of lobbying —and its general enforcement has always been sparse. Disaster was piled on confusion when the Supreme Court ruled in 1954 that the act applied only to direct communication with members of Congress. All indirect lobbying, including grassroots pressure, where money is lavished, is free of public control.

Fortunately, there are impressive sources of counterpower to check the lobbyists. Legislators can make decisions without consulting or depending on anyone else except the voters. It is the legislator who admits the lobbyist into his trust and confidence, and not vice versa; the lobbyist must follow the legislator's ground rules to retain his privilege. In any case, legislators may be generally skeptical of the traditional methods of interest articulation. A study of 112 city councilmen in twenty-two cities of the San Francisco Bay area found that most councilmen did not consider interest group activities indispensable to the political system.[38] Only one-fourth of the respondents were receptive and accommodating to interest groups. The balance were either neutral or hostile toward group activities. Unless groups are both salient and valued, the local legislator does little to modify his behavior in their behalf.

---

[37] Deakin, 22–23.

[38] Betty H. Zisk, Heinz Eulau, and Kenneth Prewitt, "City Councilmen and the Group Struggle: A Typology of Role Orientations," *Journal of Politics,* 27 (August 1965), 618–46.

These findings question the adequacy of the "group struggle" explanation of politics.

Policy is influenced more by elections and public opinion than by lobbying, as is testified to by the increasing attention of interest groups to grassroots campaigns. The public interest groups, in particular, utilize tactics of massive letter-writing to impress the legislator that his constituents are aroused and to bring him to consider his vote more carefully.

The 1960s and 70s are witnessing the development of another kind of lobby to challenge the practiced, well-financed, and organized power groups. These are people's lobbies—*ad hoc* organizations of the people. Across the country, they have been springing up for all kinds of causes—to protest jet ports, strip mining, pollution of waterways. The success of Earth Day in 1970 attested that citizens can organize and demonstrate simultaneously in scores of communities on a national scale and prompt all manner of politicians to support their cause.

Some people's lobbies are more than *ad hoc*—they bear the trappings of other power groups. And like Ralph Nader's organization, some are national in scope. Common Cause, for example, founded by John Gardner, former Secretary of Health, Education and Welfare, has both national and local organizations and a membership of around a quarter of a million in 1972. Common Cause publishes a cogent newsletter on public issues and reforms, lobbies on such issues as the SST in Congress, and has sued the major parties for election law violations. Common Cause has followed the principle put by Gardner, "To make the system work, you've got to be a little outside, on the sidelines."

Who is powerful?

The view of America as ruled by a power elite, united and purposeful, was tested in a study of foreign trade legislation, beginning with the renewal of the Reciprocal Trade Act in 1953 and ending with the passage of the Trade Expansion Act of 1962.[39] The study focused on attitudes, communications, and attitude change among relevant elements of the business community. Since legislation was at stake, Congress was the ultimate decision-maker, and the study particularly spotlighted business communications to Congress. It embraced varieties of elitist business organizations—Du Pont, giants of the automobile industry, and Wall Street banking firms. To what extent, according to the elitist model, were these centers of power united in common cause?

Certainly the findings did not bear out the hypothesis of one commentator expressed at the study's inception: "Tell me what a businessman manufactures, and I will tell you where he stands on foreign trade." Consider Du Pont, whose place in the economy of Delaware has been likened to that of an

[39] Raymond A. Bauer, Ithiel de Sola Pool, and Lewis Anthony Dexter, *American Business and Public Policy* (New York: Atherton Press, 1968).

elephant among chickens. On trade questions, as it turned out, Du Pont was no monolith; the family members most influential in the company were of divided opinions. Nor were Du Pont's true interests easily definable—the company had so many irons in the fire. Eventually, Du Pont took no stand and played no discernible part in congressional action on the tariff.

Even supposing Du Pont had strong opinions it is doubtful that the congressmen and senators from Delaware would have been impressed. According to elitist theory, we might expect Delaware's representatives to fall quickly into line with whatever stand Du Pont takes on legislation. But Delaware's legislators are noted for their uncommon care to avoid the impression that they are in Du Pont's pocket, a plight regarded as a sure ticket to political oblivion.

A matchless symbol of the power elite is Wall Street, traditional object of politicians' thunder against concentrated power. According to the common stereotype, Wall Street is puppeteer of the American economy, pulling the strings and making things go as it wishes. But in the reciprocal trade controversy, the study found that Wall Street "played a small part because it was afraid to use the power that it had. The banking community was conspicuously silent." Business was divided on the tariff, and because Wall Street bankers regard themselves "as the servants of business, of *all* business," they could not take sides for fear of offending one client or another. In the trade debate of 1962, Wall Street bankers remained subdued and only a few were involved. They had the power to act and influence others to act, but they chose not to. Is unused power elite power? Is it power at all?

Even if the powerful are aroused and mobilized, they can be defeated, as many an encounter proves. One of the more arresting dramas of the 1971 Congress fits the plural elite model—the vote on the supersonic transport (SST), a government-subsidized venture prodigiously lobbied for by the aerospace industry, organized labor, an array of businesses and associations of the military-industrial complex, and the President of the United States. But the SST's opponents, led by John Gardner's Common Cause organization and other citizens' and environmental groups, countered with massive letter-writing campaigns and expert witnesses. Soundings revealed that the new under-twenty-one voters were intensely concerned with the environmental issue. Ultimately, Congress voted to defeat the SST.[40]

The elitist model can be objected to, or qualified, on other grounds. That approach risks making oversimplified, if not fallacious, explanations of complex events. It has been used to suggest that the military-industrial complex is a conspiracy of iron-and-blood generals and greedy contractors plotting future wars. Few would support this contention, which overlooks that popularly elected civilian decision-makers in the United States have always determined questions of war and peace. Moreover, several legislators that one would presume to be committed to the MIC have not behaved appropriately. Congressman Otis Pike, whose New York district embraces Grumman

40 *New York Times*, March 25, 1971.

Aircraft and several military bases, has followed a highly independent course, often critical of the military, as did former Senator Stephen Young of Ohio, a lieutenant colonel in the reserves.

In beholding the mass of citizens as apathetic, the elitists undervalue the contribution of social movements in American policy-making. The civil rights movement is redefining the role of blacks in society; the Wagner Act, passed in 1935 amidst severe mass unemployment, endowed labor with vast new powers to organize, bargain, and strike; the distress of Western farmers near the turn of the century produced Populism as a mass social movement, which broke ground for the later innovative economic regulations of Theodore Roosevelt and Woodrow Wilson. The elitist conception of the political leader as a limited innovator regulated by the elitist framework of public order is excessively narrow.

If the elite model is not altogether satisfactory, neither is the interpretation of American politics as a process of group politics. (Indeed, given the complexities of our politics, it would be extraordinary if a single hypothesis could explain everything.) One drawback of interest groups is their narrow scope. There is a lopsided concentration among business organizations, not surprising since the business community is by far the most organized sector of society. The pressure system bears an upper class bias: businessmen and college graduates are far more apt to belong to voluntary associations than are people of lower status.[41]

Pressure politics, as E. E. Schattschneider has suggested, is essentially the politics of small groups, with the majority of the people excluded from the system. Consequently, pressure groups have performed poorly as mobilizers of the interests of large numbers of people. The group approach makes no adequate acknowledgment of party politics and its correlative, majoritarian politics.[42]

Power in the world of groups is different from power in the world of parties. Among groups, power and conflict are largely private and center on such things as economic competition, withholding of goods and services, struggles for corporate and union control, private negotiations and bargaining, all conceivably accomplished outside the political process. In group politics, numbers may count for very little. In party politics, numbers are power—the schoolteacher and the president of the Chamber of Commerce are equally powerful, for each counts as one vote. Since numbers are the basis of its power, no American political party can afford to work in simply the group or the elitist mold. No party can wholly espouse the cause of the few against the many and expect to gain power. Neither major party can afford to be completely pro-segregation, anti-immigrant, or committed to the abolition of the

[41] Charles R. Wright and Herbert H. Hyman, "Voluntary Association Membership of American Adults: Evidence from National Sample Surveys," *American Sociological Review*, 23 (June 1958), 284–94.

[42] E. E. Schattschneider, *The Semi-Sovereign People* (New York: Holt, Rinehart and Winston, 1960), 35–36.

income tax or the Social Security system, all of which have much to do with shaping the nature of society.

Proposals

When we study power, we study both the distortions of democracy and its effectuation. Power, one group of scholars tells us, is held in many hands, and the more numerous and varied they are, the better will democracy be approximated. Fortunately, the voluntary association and the interest groups, on which dispersal of power heavily depends, thrive in the United States. But, according to other scholars, power is concentrated in an elite whose competence towers above the ineptitude of unknowing masses. In their view, democracy exists only by grace of a beneficent elite. Not a pleasant picture for those who believe in the centrality of the individual and his capacity to live his own life, whatever his talents and foibles, and not have others live it for him.

1. We need clear, well-defined alternatives to the democratic elitist interpretation. Peter Bachrach has proposed that contemporary formulations of democracy concentrate on the self-development of the individual. As reconstituted, democratic theory would claim that most individuals grow and gain in self-esteem by participating more actively in society's decisions. Consequently, the people would have a dual interest in politics—in the policies determined and in the process of participation.

2. For this conception to advance, we must redefine democratic political power to embrace many large areas now reserved to oligarchic private power. We must throw them open to wide, democratic sharing in decision-making. Since General Electric and General Motors authoritatively allocate values for society, they should be considered a part of the political sector in which democratic norms apply. Quite possibly, the issues that affect the individual in the factory, office, or enterprise, would arouse his concern more than the relatively remote present politics. Democracy is most blatantly denied in the oligarchic work situation. As Bachrach contends, "The fundamental issue no longer relates to the problem of production or distribution but to the problem of power." [43] Responses are stirring. Cooperative enterprises are appearing in more fields of production and distribution and accord power to broadly defined memberships. Profit sharing in some enterprises contributes a new sense of power to the worker, as do efforts to reduce the monotony of the assembly line and to give more variety and autonomy to the worker in his duties.

The democratization of the corporate realm might be approached through interest group management, or the presence of workers, consumers, and public interest representatives on the boards of directors of private enterprises. The step would be consistent with the sturdy place of interest groups in the American ethos and political culture as representatives and negotiators of conflict-

[43] Bachrach, 99–106.

ing views in the movement toward policy. In a sense, the structuring of Phase II of the Nixon administration's price and wage controls to include business, labor, and public participants in decision-making is a step toward this principle. Nevertheless, as Phase II illustrates, the approach has serious limitations. No convenient unit is available for selecting consumer representatives and holding them accountable: the more powerful, better organized groups and professional associations would dominate the process; and, because the federal government would probably play a central part in selecting the delegates, its needs would be paramount. For all interests, the resulting system would rest on a structure of rather remote delegated authority. And, as Robert Dahl notes, the arrangement would do little to reduce the powerlessness of the individual worker.[44]

3. Another approach might be to specifically and carefully articulate the obligations of members of organizations to democratic society. Those who have studied large organizations have long been intrigued by the possibility that professionals serving within the ranks might resist potentially destructive decisions of top leadership. In effect, the professional is asked to heed his conscience when it conflicts with the oligarchy's edicts. Ralph Nader has suggested that the professional has the duty to reveal irregularities of his organization's leadership to higher authority, the public, and to any other useful source that will listen. With his superior knowledge, the professional is better situated than anyone to know the likely consequences of such transgressions as the dumping of mercury into lakes, defectively designed automobiles, the undisclosed adverse effects of certain drugs. If, as Alfred North Whitehead observed, "Duty arises from our potential control over the course of events," the professional, silent in the face of incipient wrongdoing, both violates his professional code of ethics and acquiesces to affronts to democracy's welfare. The professionals are also the first to perceive the technical means to prevent existing product hazards or to stop pollution damage. Alas, in spite of the growing cause of environmentalism, professionals are all too frequently the last to speak out, and rarely do they refuse to participate in corporate collusion against society. Take the example of the 1973 Ford cars, which failed to pass safety standards. Some participants in the episode suggest that the Ford engineers, putting their sense of professional commitment aside, cut corners on safety standards in order to produce a car that met the specifications of the profit-minded Ford leadership.

A clear obstacle to the professional's behaving in a more democracy-serving fashion is his dependence on his employer's approval for career advancement. To reduce this restraint, Ralph Nader has called for national legislation to protect the professional against arbitrary treatment and for improved readiness by professional societies to defend colleagues from such treatment. Most professional societies have never challenged corporate or government abuse of their members.[45]

[44] Robert A. Dahl, "Citizens of the Corporation," *New York Times,* March 17, 1971, 45.
[45] Ralph Nader, "A Code for Professional Integrity," *New York Times,* June 6, 1971.

4. The national lobbying act and comparable state legislation badly need strengthening. The late George Galloway suggested that the guiding principle of a better law must be "full disclosure by all persons and groups whose purpose and substantial effort is to influence legislation." [46] He and others have urged that grassroots lobbying be brought within the legislation's scope by its inclusion in a broad definition of the term "to influence legislation," a step that admittedly would be like walking on eggshells since the First Amendment must not be violated. Anything in the law that restricted freedom of speech or of petition (which might be found to occur if the act's provisions were vague or imposed even the semblance of censorship) would invite hostile court rulings.

Which is well and good. For history amply teaches that the regulator and guardian, too, can misuse power. Or, as theologian Reinhold Niebuhr has warned, "Goodness, armed with power, is corrupted." [47]

Suggested Reading

Bachrach, Peter, *The Theory of Democratic Elitism: A Critique* * (Little, Brown, 1967). A penetrating analysis of the relationship of democracy and elitism, and the nature and functions of elites. The author draws on a wide array of sources in offering a new theory of democracy.

Bauer, Raymond A., Pool, Ithiel de Sola, and Dexter, Lewis Anthony, *American Business and Public Policy* (Atherton Press, 1968). An important study of the behavior of different business organizations and groups concerning foreign aid legislation. The conclusions challenge some of the clichés that link economic interest with political behavior.

Berle, Adolf A., *Power* (Harcourt Brace Jovanovich, 1967). A perceptive analysis of power that concentrates on economic and political power and their interplay. The author's intimate knowledge of the great corporations is used to full advantage.

Galbraith, John Kenneth, *The New Industrial State* (Houghton Mifflin, 1967). Asserts that a close fusion exists between the industrial system and the state and predicts that the line between the two will disappear. Contends that corporations, as beneficiaries of a technological revolution, shape society's goals and reduce the individual to the status of servant of a structure that was designed to serve him.

Key, V. O., Jr., *Politics, Parties, and Pressure Groups,* 5th edition (Crowell, 1964). A useful source for a discussion of the nature and behavior of the more powerful interest groups.

Mahood, H. R., *Pressure Groups in American Politics* * (Scribner's, 1967). A wide-ranging collection of essays on interest groups, with contributions by leading scholars on the subject.

Milbrath, Lester W., *The Washington Lobbyists* (Rand McNally, 1963). An empirical study of the role of lobbying and lobbyists utilizing interviews with lobbyists and those whom they seek to influence.

Mills, C. Wright, *The Power Elite* * (Oxford University Press, 1956). The most widely discussed of the works that contend that the United States is run by an integrated elite

[46] Deakin, 261.
[47] Reinhold Niebuhr, *Beyond Tragedy* (New York: Scribner's, 1937).

of corporate, governmental, and military leaders. Political and social institutions support the elite's decisions, which are based on their wealth, prestige, and power.

Olson, Mancur, Jr., *The Logic of Collective Action: Public Goods and the Theory of Groups* * (Harvard University Press, 1965). Analyzes the important role of groups in the political and economic system.

Rose, Arnold M., *The Power Structure: Political Process in American Society* (Oxford University Press, 1967). A sociologist cogently examines a multi-influence hypothesis in connection with American economic and political decision-making.

Salisbury, Robert H., *Interest Group Politics in America* * (Harper & Row, 1970). An able discussion of the nature of pressure groups and the leading theories concerning them. The treatment of business, labor, and agricultural groups is particularly useful.

Schattschneider, E. E., *The Semisovereign People* * (Holt, Rinehart and Winston, 1960). A cogent analysis of the interest group system in American politics, with particular illumination of the relationships of business groups with politics. The author sees governmental power as a balance to business power.

Truman, David B., *The Governmental Process* (Knopf, 1951). Applies a general theory of groups to American politics.

Warner, W. Lloyd, Unwalla, D. B., and Trimm, John H., *The Emergent American Society;* vol. 1: *Large-Scale Organizations* (Yale University Press, 1967). Sociologists examine the nature of large-scale business and labor organizations, their structures and distributions of power, and their relationships with society and politics. Valuable for both its analysis and data.

Zisk, Betty H., *American Political Interest Groups* * (Wadsworth, 1969). A useful compilation of readings that present major theories concerning interest groups and analyses of their behavior and connections with social and political processes.

* Available in paperback edition

the

deprived

People on welfare, democracy's children, are speaking:

> "I can remember the last time they turned off the lights. It was the winter they killed Kennedy. My mother was so cold she started to cry. Then we all started to cry because it was so dark. We had to eat cold food out of tin cans."

> "I tell you it gets pretty boring with no money and nothing to do."

> "I pity the young ones. They still want things."

> "Worst of all, though, is when you got kids They need gym shoes. You got to go to Welfare. . . . If you spend the money for food to buy your girl shoes . . . the next thing you know the man wants to know why you ain't got no money."

> "You want to know how they close a case? I'll tell you. They know the mail is always late for people like us. If the investigator writes a letter to come for an appointment the day after tomorrow and he mails it tomorrow, you will not get the letter on time to come for the appointment. Then he closes the case just like that." [1]

Who are the deprived?

People on welfare are but one grouping of a vast aggregation of the deprived. Just as there are those in society who are excessively powerful, there are others who are excessively powerless, and a society with serious democratic pretensions must struggle to cope with both distortions. Everyone lacks some kinds of power, but the deprived suffer gross shortages of highly consequential kinds of power that do much to determine the quality of life and the genuineness of democratic freedoms and rights—economic power, political power, and social power. By definition, the deprived are shortchanged in the distri-

[1] In Richard Elman, *The Poorhouse State* (New York: Pantheon Books, 1966).

Family income and poverty, 1970

	Whites	Blacks
Average family income	$10,326	$6,279
Percentage gain over 1965 [1]	40%	60%
Percentage of families earning more than $10,000	52%	28%
Percentage gain in number of families earning $10,000 or over, 1965 to 1970 [1]	33%	100%
Percentage of families below poverty level [2]	8%	29%

[1] Percentages computed by The Conference Board based on Census data. Constant 1970 dollars used in computation.

[2] Using the 1970 official poverty level established for a nonfarm family of four of $3,968. The poverty line varies by family size, sex and age of family head, number of children, and farm—nonfarm residence. It is updated annually to reflect changes in the Consumer Price Index.

Source: U.S. Bureau of the Census, cited in "The Economic Status of Black Americans," The Conference Board *Record,* August 1972.

bution of society's benefits, in the use of its freedoms and access to its opportunities, and in influence on its decisions.

There are many types of deprived groups—the poor, the blacks, women, the elderly—which suffer in varying degrees and ways for varying reasons. Most visible certainly are those who fare badly in the distribution of basic economic values and benefits. Income and employment are tickets of admission to a wide array of the elements of life and its basic necessities—to adequate nutrition levels, education, health care, aspirations for one's children. The "poor" or "poor people" are a vast, diversified aggregate of deprived human beings in American society. People on welfare constitute a large category, but one that is far exceeded by poor people who are not on welfare. "The poor" encompass all races and ages and both those who are employed and unemployed. Since the inception of the national poverty program in 1965, the federal government has defined the poor as those who fall below a certain poverty income level. For 1971, the official poverty level was $4,137 for a family of four, and, according to a 1972 Census Bureau report, that meant 3.8 million families were living in poverty. The whites are the most numerous of the poor, but a far greater proportion of the black population lives in poverty.[2] Economic deprivation, therefore, has stark racial contours, with high incidence among blacks, Puerto Ricans, and Chicanos.

Unlike the poor, the general body of American women do not suffer acute deprivation of life's necessities, nor do they lack the means to improve their status. Nevertheless, women suffer their own brand of economic and political

[2] St. Clair Drake, "The Social and Economic Status of the Negro in the United States," *Daedalus,* 94 (Fall 1965), 771–814, reprinted in Edward S. Greenberg, Neal Milner, and David J. Olson, *Black Politics* (New York: Holt, Rinehart and Winston, 1971), 48. For poverty income level, see *New York Times,* July 13, 1972.

deprivation. The contemporary movement for equal rights for women, for example, stresses that women are discriminated against in selection for high level employment and in equal payment for the same jobs men hold, and that a wealth of federal, state, and local laws require or sanction discrimination based on sex. State abortion laws restrict a woman's right to decide whether or not she will have a child. Some state laws require a woman to quit her job at a certain point in pregnancy, regardless of her desire to continue working or her doctor's opinion that she could do so without harm. And a study by the Citizens' Advisory Council on the Status of Women concluded that child support payments "generally are less than enough to furnish half of the support of the children" and that "even these small payments are frequently not adhered to." [3]

The elderly may have enjoyed at least a passable fulfillment of economic needs through most of their lives, only to find that in forced retirement, with reduced income and inflated costs, they must pass their remaining years in economic helplessness should they fall victim to catastrophic illness, to which they are especially vulnerable. Still other categories of deprived people may lack political rather than economic power. Historically, the young have been badly deprived of political power. Although society's most oppressive burden —military service—has been forced on them at age eighteen, they have lacked the power to hold office, to influence public decision-makers, and, until recently, to vote. Some redress has been won by the Twenty-Sixth Amendment, which reduces the voting age to eighteen, and by the improved representation of the young at the 1972 Democratic convention. But the force of these gains, particularly their impact on policy, remains to be seen.

Despite their variety, the deprived share certain general characteristics. Usually they are numerous. They are generally unorganized or only partially organized. And typically even when the deprived are organized they are ineffective in that they have little money, few lobbies, and exert pressure that is in no way commensurate with their numbers.

Stripped of power, the deprived also lack access to those who have it and whose dispensations might reduce their suffering. Indeed, the accustomed estate of many deprived groups is to be scorned and discounted by the powerful. Floyd Hunter's study of Atlanta found that community power there was pyramided and the local black leadership had little voice in the important policy decisions of the larger community. Black leaders could only make their views known to the city's political leaders, a group that was subordinate to the industrial, financial, and social elites. [4]

The deprived also fare badly in the workings of the pluralist model. Not all abused, suffering, discontented people are able to organize and assert political pressure, behavior that pluralist society expects from its members. Officials tend to recognize established groups as the only legitimate spokes-

---

[3] *New York Times,* March 20, 1972.
[4] Floyd Hunter, *Community Power Structure* (Chapel Hill: University of North Carolina Press, 1953, 1968), 100.

men. In bargaining, a key process of pluralist politics, the deprived all too often come out with empty hands, having had nothing to offer. The stark evidence of their suffering makes clear that conventional politics alone does not always work for the deprived; to improve themselves, they must look for alternative modes of political assertion.

The deprived are people who are victimized. That is, because they are poor or powerless, rejected by an economy that will not employ them, society withholds its benefits and rewards to a degree well beyond any reasonable penalty, if any at all is justified, for whatever faults or lapses may be attributed to them. Moreover, their deprivation feeds on itself—lacking certain kinds of power they are denied or deprived of other kinds of power. For example, the poor person's lack of education means lack of a job, lack of money, lack of access to decision-makers; in this way a basic deprivation induces other deprivations. It is a cycle of defeat.

The deprived are also afflicted by indirect victimization, or the consequences emanating from their powerlessness. Thus a black living in a ghetto not only suffers deprivations in education, employment, and income power, but the circumscribed social structure in which he lives also decreases his "life chances"—subjecting his deprived group to high morbidity and mortality rates, severe incidence of psychopathology, and perpetuation of personality traits and attitudes that impose crippling handicaps in society's rugged competition.

The plight
of the poor

One of the larger categories of the deprived are the poor, who are also by far the most victimized. Except for the poverty-level income previously noted, there is little in the way of defined criteria identifying the poor. Only now are traditional concepts concerning the poor's plight undergoing challenge and reconsideration. For example, a common condition of deprivation is "unemployment." The federal government periodically reports the rate of unemployment in the national economy, a figure that is often a focus of political controversy. But the official unemployment figure, as more sophisticated research reveals, is only the tip of an iceberg, for it is unrealistically limited to those who seek jobs they cannot find.

The publicly announced figure omits three other groups: (1) those who have become so discouraged at not finding work that they have dropped out of the active labor market; (2) those who work part time but want to work full time; (3) those with full-time jobs whose earnings put them below the official poverty level—the "subemployed." Low wage scales in marginal employment and racial discrimination in craft enterprises imprison these workers in the ranks of the poor. In mid-1972, when 6 percent were officially counted as unemployed, the inclusion of these three categories would have

Average annual unemployment rates

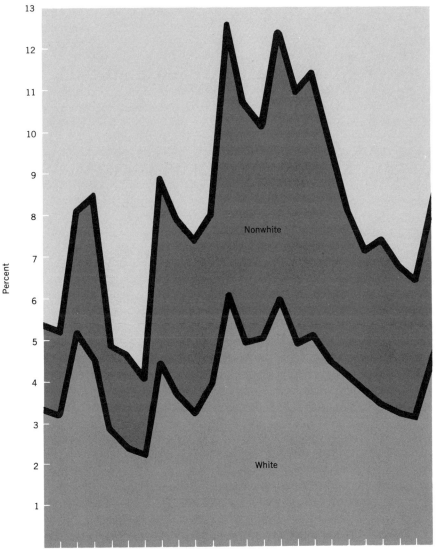

Source: U.S. Bureau of the Census.

trebled that figure to a total of fifteen million workers, or better than one out of every six persons in the national labor force.[5]

The idea for a special unemployment census originated with Secretary of Labor W. Willard Wirtz of the Johnson administration, who checked ten urban ghettos in 1966. Appalled by his findings, Wirtz warned in a confidential memorandum to the President, "If a third of the people in the nation

[5] The principal source for these kinds of data is a sixty-eight-volume special survey of forty-five major cities made by the U.S. Bureau of the Census in 1970.

couldn't make a living, there would be a revolution. This is the situation—and the prospect unless action is taken in that nation-within-a-nation, the slums and ghettos." The following summer witnessed the first series of urban riots, the first of the "long, hot summers." [6]

The American culture holds a special place for those who strive and achieve in its presumed open and competitive economic system; those who fail—the poor—are beheld as morally or personally defective. Where possible, society separates the poor physically and psychologically from the rest of the nation. They cluster in the urban ghettos, places of dilapidation, dirt, and ugliness, of deteriorated schools and housing. It is a landscape cluttered with the symptoms of lower class society—family instability, poor education, low aspiration, unemployment, crime, drug addiction, alcoholism, illegitimacy, illness, and early death. Incapable of supporting its population, the ghetto is not a viable community. The streets are crowded with people and debris. There are few, if any, museums, art galleries, and libraries, but an infinity of bars, hundreds of churches, and scores of fortune tellers. The community is overlayered with signs of fantasy, abandonment, and defeat—the air is heavy with the sense of inadequacy.[7] There is also an enormous world of rural poverty, the dimensions of which we are just now beginning to learn.

The welfare poor. A substantial part of the poor are those on welfare or public assistance. To be eligible for welfare, one must be impoverished, in absolute need, and with no other recourse, a state of abject desperation that drove one recipient to exclaim: "Some people say when you're on welfare you're in the gutter and no use trying to pull yourself out." [8] The welfare poor forfeit control over their lives and destinies in exchange for demeaning "benefits." The poor person is perceived not as an individual, a human being, but as a social problem whose malfunctioning is to be corrected with minimal handouts each month. In the early 1970s, fifteen million people, or about 7 percent of the population, were on welfare. The welfare system embraces substantial percentages of city populations—15 percent of New York City's and 25 percent of Newark's—and massive, soaring expenditures: national outlays rose from an average of $.325 billion a month in 1965 to an average of $1.6 billion a month in 1972.[9]

In welfare programs generally, the federal government provides most of the money and the states set most of the policy. Thus the public assistance system is a collection of fifty different welfare programs fashioned by the individual states from a patchwork of federal laws and programs for special needs. State practices vary widely concerning the crucial factors of eligibility and benefits. In 1969, Mississippi allotted a family of four with no income $69 a month, while comparable New Jersey families received $347.

[6] *New York Times,* June 25, 1972.
[7] Kenneth B. Clark, *Dark Ghetto* (New York: Harper & Row, 1965).
[8] In James Graham, *The Enemies of the Poor* (New York: Random House, 1970), 15.
[9] *New York Times,* July 30, 1972.

Local governments and local welfare centers also set policy. In New York City, for example, the rejection rate of welfare applicants varies strikingly among neighborhoods. According to one study, two welfare centers in East Harlem have consistently low rejection rates, averaging about 14 percent, while a center in the borough of Queens rejects up to 40 percent of the applicants. Psychological factors seem to have contributed to the differences in rates. Some social workers in the East Harlem centers, where poor people are concentrated, acknowledged the numbing effect of seeing endless streams of poorly clothed, undernourished mothers and children pour into the dismal reception rooms, a scene that makes the decision-makers more sympathetic toward the poor and less strict in interpreting the rules.[10] Such decisions are also directed by "practical political considerations." For instance, in the 1960s the Johnson administration thought it was necessary to give blacks something to help solidify their allegiance to the national Democratic party, and to quiet them. Giving welfare is cheaper, at least in the short run, and quicker than other conceivable actions, such as building housing.

The largest, fastest growing, most controversial welfare program is Aid to Families with Dependent Children (AFDC), a feature of the national Social Security Act that provides payments to dependent children and their guardians in homes where the breadwinner has deserted the family or died.

[10] *New York Times,* April 25, 1971; Frances Fox Piven and Richard A. Cloward, *Regulating the Poor* (New York: Pantheon Books, 1971), Chapter X.

Almost half of AFDC recipients are white; nearly 45 percent are black, a high proportion since blacks comprise only about 10 percent of the population.[11] Far less controversial welfare programs provided by Social Security include aid to the blind and the disabled.

To receive his relief handout, the applicant must submit to degrees of humiliation and degradation. This is especially true of an AFDC mother. Poverty alone is not enough for eligibility. She must prove to the satisfaction of her interviewer or caseworker that no man lurks in the background willing or able to feed her children. The AFDC applicant must have nothing to hide, must acquiesce to whatever search of her premises is asked, and to intrusion into her emotional privacy. As a condition of continuing aid, she must accept the caseworker's services designed to straighten out her presumably personal flaws and assure that she can maintain "a suitable home."

A favorite object of taxpayer scorn is the stereotype of a black welfare mother, her hair in curlers, with a cluster of children tugging at her torn dress, the progeny of sinful living. Outlandish ways have been contrived to keep these women off welfare, including the bringing of criminal charges of "fornication" against mothers of illegitimate children who apply for assistance. In New Jersey, one welfare mother was not only convicted and imprisoned, but she was forced to name the father, who suffered the same fate.[12]

Typically, the men in the lives of welfare women are shadowy figures who hover in the background and seldom partake directly of welfare benefits. The poverty of the welfare women stems largely from the economic distress of their men. According to the Kerner Commission (U.S. Commission on Civil Disorders), "the single most important source of poverty among Negroes" is the concentration of unemployment among black males. The economic and psychological harm that society inflicts on them for their unemployment falls indirectly on welfare women.

The world of welfare abounds in regulations. A New Jersey Manual of Administration contains five close-printed pages of instructions on how to deduct the 1968 increase in Social Security payments from a welfare recipient's relief. A 1971 New York State law requires recipients classified as employable to pick up their checks at state employment offices. In the second month of the rule, 22.1 percent of the checks were not picked up, to the delight of budget-pinched administrators. The rule persisted despite federal warnings of illegal harassment and criticism that clients were forced to divert their food and clothing allowances to pay for travel to the state centers and job interviews.[13]

The budget allotted to a welfare recipient accentuates deprivation. Some states set budget ceilings that penalize large families by not varying by a single penny the payments for families with two or with seven children. In other states, food budgets are supposed to increase with the advancing age

---

[11] Herbert J. Gans, "Three Ways to Solve the Welfare Problem," *New York Times Magazine* (March 7, 1971), 7.

[12] Piven and Cloward, 128.

[13] *New York Times,* September 8 and 15, 1971.

Recipients of public assistance, 1950 to 1970
(in thousands)

	1950	1955	1960	1965	1967	1968	1969	1970
Old age assistance	2,786	2,538	2,305	2,087	2,073	2,027	2,074	2,081
AFDC	2,233	2,238	3,073	4,396	5,309	6,086	7,313	9,657
Aid to blind	97	104	107	85	83	81	81	81
Aid to disabled	69	241	369	557	649	702	803	933
General assistance	413	314	431	310	352	391	426	549

Source: U.S. Bureau of the Census, *Statistical Abstract of the United States, 1971* (Washington, D.C.: U.S. Government Printing Office), p. 291, Table 463.

of children, but the adjustment often fails to be made, leaving thousands of families to live on smaller budgets than the regulations prescribe. Miserly allowances make welfare families regard fresh milk, butter, fresh eggs, fruits, and vegetables as luxuries and drive them to substitute peanut butter for chicken.

Welfare administrative practice tends to be more restrictive and severe than the statutes and formal regulations themselves are. The welfare applicant is a puttylike object of bureaucratic manipulation. A black from South Carolina strove for three years to establish his eligibility in New York City, despite an incessant bureaucratic runaround. "Seems like all I ever got was that slip of paper," he said. "You go to Fifth Street, they tell you 'case closed.' They send you uptown to Twenty-eighth Street. They tell you to go to Fifth Street. It's a real runaround. . . . That's the hardest two dollars you'll ever earn." [14]

If the client is assertive or disruptive, he jeopardizes his benefits. When he comes to recognize this harsh reality he lapses into the controlled acquiescence that bureaucracies prefer. Since benefits are not a matter of unambiguous right, they can be easily wielded as threats and rewards. The bureaucracy has another manipulative opportunity in the information it chooses to release to the client about its procedures and the kinds of benefits he is eligible for. The client has no independent knowledge of his own.

Welfare offices are often described as bare and drab. Many do not provide special facilities for women and children waiting to apply for assistance. When offices are jammed, harassed caseworkers lock the door and clients unfortunate enough to be left outside must return another time. On a particular day in a major city, welfare applicants began gathering outside one welfare center at 7 A.M., hoping to be at the head of the line when business began at 8:45. Just before the doors opened, a shock force of young men, many presumably addicts, muscled into the head of the line, squeezing women, children, and elderly to the rear. Later in the morning, when the doors were

[14] Elman, 151.

locked, welfare clients trying to force their way inside shattered the glass. The scene suggested the storming of the Bastille.[15]

The plight of
the aged and women

Many of the aged face poverty, although from causes different from those afflicting the nonelderly poor. In contemporary society, the aged must live on retirement income, which is sharply reduced from the income of their employment years, on savings, if they are fortunate, on welfare, or on some otherwise scratched-together income. But they are battered by soaring prices, by rising taxes and rents and medical costs, which chew up their fixed income and force the reduction of an already sparse expenditure for food. Many elderly who live alone, often without cooking facilities, are harried by the high cost of restaurant meals and transportation. Two of their worst afflictions are noneconomic— loneliness and boredom. Although local governments maintain programs to assist the elderly, they fail to keep up with the inflationary spiral. Their economic deprivation and dependence, coupled with the disdain of a dynamic, youthful society, underscores the observation of one specialist on problems of the elderly: "Needs change with age, but the need for self-respect never changes." [16]

The plight of women as a deprived group, as depicted by some writers and activists of the contemporary women's liberation movement, is stated in terms of victimization by a patriarchal society, in which every avenue of power is in male hands. Their sexual role seems to limit women rather than open to them the broader human possibilities available to men. Careers in the elite professions are largely closed to her; while she is given every opportunity to become a secretary, teacher, or nurse, she is not expected to become a doctor, lawyer, or executive. And even when she does, she earns less than men and has fewer prospects for promotion, no matter how superior she may be. In a capitalist state, her assigned role is that of principal consumer; the makers and sellers of products pamper her with goods and attention that only reinforce a distorted sexual image. A commercially oriented society treats cooking, children, clothes, beauty, housekeeping as compulsive activities, in which "the anxiety quotient," Germaine Greer notes, "has long replaced the pleasure or achievement quotient." [17]

Politics too is a tightly restricted arena for women, as a 1972 conference of women legislators of twenty-six states revealed. Women legislators, who consider themselves generally more industrious, more informed, and more ethical than male legislators, seldom attain leadership positions. A woman legislator, the conference disclosed, hurts her standing with her male colleagues when she

[15] *New York Times,* December 14, 1971.
[16] *New York Times,* February 21, 1971.
[17] Germaine Greer, *The Female Eunuch* (New York: McGraw-Hill, 1970), 324.

champions such "women's issues" as abortion, divorce law reform, or ratification of the proposed amendment for equal rights for men and women. Voter bias opposes a woman running for office if she has children and a husband, whom, voters feel, she should stay home and take care of.[18] For all the discussion of women's rights, women achieved no significant electoral successes in 1972. The number of women in Congress, for example, did not change.

Causation

With the suffering of the deprived widespread, severe, and continuous, the question inevitably arises: Who or what is to blame? The answers tend to vary, depending on their sources. Each purports to assert the "facts," to state that something which exists or is true prompts something else to happen. Concerning facts, sociologist Louis Wirth has spoken a wise caution: "Since every assertion of a 'fact' about the social world touches the interests of some individual or group, one cannot even call attention to the existence of certain 'facts' without courting the objections of those whose very *raison d'être* in society rests upon a divergent interpretation of the 'factual situation.' " [19]

Those with stakes in the problem of poverty and its causation include civil rights organizations, governmental agencies that deal with the deprived, politicians responsive to their plight, and other politicians representing voters who are resentful of poverty expenditures and receptive to suggestions that the cause of their plight lies within the poor themselves. These various participants are spurred to formulate causes, for if they are reticent or fail to champion their explanations, they become politically vulnerable or morally implicated, since others might exploit their passivity in order to buttress injustice or slow the movement toward corrective action. Because the several actors or interests impute differential meaning to the "facts" of a public policy issue, social science, at least in such a highly motivated context, cannot be entirely objective; social science becomes in actuality "political" science, or just politics. The findings of social science are politically useful. They can also be politically costly when they offend or are "disproven" or embarrass those with whose cause the social science researcher feels identified.

The play of these interests and forces is evident in the saga of what became known as the "Moynihan Report," entitled more formally, "The Negro Family: The Case for National Action." [20] Completed in 1965 by Assistant Secretary of Labor Daniel Patrick Moynihan and two members of his staff, the report argued that established civil rights policies removing legal barriers to the black would not alone gain for him a place in society comparable to that of whites. Blacks, the report contended, are hampered by "the deterioration of the Negro

---

[18] *New York Times,* May 22, 1972.
[19] In Lee Rainwater and William L. Yancey, *The Moynihan Report and the Politics of Controversy* (Cambridge, Mass.: M.I.T. Press, 1967), 1.
[20] The text of the report is in Rainwater and Yancey, 39–124.

family." The report cited data that nearly a quarter of urban black marriages are dissolved, that nearly a quarter of black families are headed by females, that nearly a quarter of black births are illegitimate, and that black family breakdown has led to startling increases in welfare dependency. The report concluded that the root of the trouble was the economic system, which denied black men a stable place and consequently made them unable to function as strong husbands and fathers.

Social scientists generally considered the report to contain nothing new, for it reflected themes developed earlier by the black sociologist E. Franklin Frazier, and mirrored the findings of black psychologist Kenneth B. Clark, whose book *Dark Ghetto* was published shortly before the Moynihan Report appeared. But public interest in the Moynihan Report was aroused when its findings infiltrated the text of President Johnson's 1965 address at Howard University, which was widely regarded as heralding a change of course in civil rights policies. Moynihan's work and its explanation of causation then met with clamorous disapproval. Women thundered against the assumption that men should necessarily be the heads of American households. Representatives of the civil rights movement feared that the emphasis on the black family might be exploited to blame blacks for their own problems and divert governmental action into miserly, futile self-help programs. Sociologist Herbert Gans was apprehensive that the report would trigger a wave of social work and psychiatric solutions intended to transform the black female-based family into a middle class entity, a course perpetuating the paternalistic manipulation of the black poor by welfare policy. Murmurings circulated that Moynihan was anti-Negro, a subtle racist, an apologist for the white power structure—his personal background and previous writings provided the makings of an emerging villain of the civil rights movement, the "white liberal." [21]

The permanent bureaucracy was also aroused. Bureaucratic personnel who had stakes in existing administrative programs vigilantly scrutinized the report for contentions and recommendations that might jeopardize their interests. Alarmed by their findings, they mobilized to combat the report. They developed staff papers, solidly anchored in the social sciences, which disputed or amended Moynihan's findings. They rallied professionals outside the government, who could criticize with greater freedom and impunity, and activated a communications network linking their fellow professionals inside and outside government. Through this network messages discrediting the report were passed to places where the effects would be most telling. But the report also had potential bureaucratic allies who might profit from its findings. For example, bureaucrats eager to expand their modest population control program as a remedial policy perused the Moynihan Report for ways to justify their own program's future enlargement.

Some who controverted the Moynihan Report advanced their own explanations of the black's plight, and those which attained the greatest impact offered more careful grounding in social science analysis than Moynihan's.

[21] Reactions to the report are from Rainwater and Yancey, 172–95.

One study attacked an implicit assumption of the report that the absolute increase in female-headed households was as large as the absolute increase in AFDC cases. Instead, it was found that even if all the new female-headed families in the interval from 1959 to 1966 had received AFDC assistance, they would constitute only about 10 percent of the AFDC increase. Social scientists Frances Piven and Richard Cloward argued that a wholly different cause spurred the growth of welfare rolls. The expansion was a response to spreading civil disorders in the cities, sparked by severely dislocating economic change, chiefly the modernization of Southern agriculture. The forced migration of blacks from the farms to Northern cities altered the geography of black poverty and simultaneously created a measure of black power. In the 1960s the black urban poor emerged as a political force, both in elections and in the streets, and an expanded welfare system was essentially a response to that force.[22]

The politics of hope

In a democratic society, misery need not be accepted with resignation. Succor can come from leaders and decision-makers who are able to direct governmental programs toward the relief of the deprived. Or the deprived can fight back and strive to escape their hardships by organizing and exerting pressure. These two possibilities of help from others and political self-help are the foundations of a particular kind of politics for deprived people, the politics of hope.

The search for solutions. As with the discovery of causes, the framing of solutions involves diverse actors, whose handiwork is shaped by their particular perspectives, skills, and interests. Generally, they offer solutions in the rhetoric of confidence and hope, with bold claims that the problem at hand will diminish and vanish and the lot of the deprived will be transformed.

Solutions and their development follow different patterns. A common type of solution is the *expert-complex,* posed by specialists and professionals inside and outside the bureaucracies and founded on social science research. In the late 1960s hunger began to be recognized as a serious general problem of the poor; Charles Murphy, an assistant to President Johnson and a former Under Secretary of Agriculture, recruited a team of experts and developed a plan to combat the problem. So that "every American" might be enabled to avoid hunger, a $2 billion food stamp program was proposed that would operate like a negative income tax, with the Internal Revenue Service distributing the stamps. Both the justification and the nature of the program were developed in a report by Dr. Arnold Schaefer, an HEW veteran of studies of malnutrition in countries served by the foreign aid program. In a "National Nutrition Survey of the United States," Schaefer found, among other things, that poverty children lagged from six months to two-and-a-half years behind their peers in physical development; 34 percent were badly anemic, 33 percent suffered

[22] Piven and Cloward, 195–97.

severe shortage of Vitamin A, and 16 percent lacked adequate amounts of Vitamin C. The hunger program that was proposed addressed itself systematically to these lackings.[23] The proposal promised substantially more help for the poor than the existing food stamp program, which was dominated by the Agriculture Department and tailored more to the needs of farm interests than those of the poor.

Another kind of solution now emerged, the *politician-simple,* which went not to the heart of the problem, but only to its edges. This is the solution of politicians who value the appearance of action as much, if not more, than the reality cherished by the experts. In a 1969 message to Congress, President Nixon called for more food stamps at less cost, national uniform standards of eligibility, establishment of a Food and Nutrition Service, and careful discussion of the hunger problem in a White House Conference on Food and Nutrition.[24] In such modest formulations, stressing reorganization and further study and geared to the President's own value preferences and political needs, the more elaborate or costly proposals of the experts were reduced, condensed, or ignored.

The typology of solutions includes that of *stages-plateaus,* the advance by stages to a succession of plateaus, each representing a new kind or level of solution. Movement to a new plateau may be spurred by the success of present solutions, warranting higher levels of future aspirations. Or experience with these solutions may reveal inadequacy, necessitating their amendment. The modern civil rights movement can be analyzed in terms of stages and plateaus. Initially, in the 1950s, the movement took a highly legalistic focus, selecting for its targets discrimination and segregation embedded in laws and elaborately developed practices, for which the court case was an appropriate weapon. In the early and middle 1960s, the movement entered a new stage: it sought positive political power to attack deep social need. The march to a new plateau paid off with the passage of voting rights legislation in 1965. Again need persisted, and the movement for racial justice is now in a stage of reaching for a new plateau of public and private action to advance social and economic integration in employment, housing, health, and other services.

Social movements. In seeking escape from their plight, particular categories of deprived people may organize as a social movement. The advent of that phenomenon is not a common historical occurrence since it ordinarily requires a blend of several crucial elements: a crisis of hardship perceived and defined; leadership, preferably charismatic; explanations of causation; shared values to which thousands if not millions of deprived citizens can subscribe; a plan or solution simple enough to be widely understood and complex enough for serious problems; and symbols connoting organizational solidarity, such as songs, badges, salutes, and flags.

[23] Nick Kotz, *Let Them Eat Promises: The Politics of Hunger in America* (Englewood Cliffs, N.J.: Prentice-Hall, 1969), 195–96.
[24] *Ibid.,* 228–29.

One of the most extraordinary social and political movements is the modern civil rights movement, a melange of demonstrations, court cases, new laws, diverse leaders and philosophies, whose accumulated impact on social policy has exceeded that of any other force in its time, including the Presidents in whose administrations it has thrived. The movement converted the weakness of individuals into the power of numbers, and a magic element in that accomplishment was the politics of hope.

Originally, the movement drew strength from the rising political power of blacks in the 1930s and 1940s—their share in the broadly beneficial social programs of Roosevelt's New Deal, the decisions of a liberal Supreme Court that outlawed the white primary and committed itself to a collision course with segregation, the massive emigration of blacks to Northern cities, their decisive contribution to Truman's surprise victory in 1948. The movement's early strategies were based on the assumption, which proved valid, that the courts and the executive could be looked to for help.

Like other social movements, the civil rights movement was shaped by the subculture from which it derived. The Southern wing of the movement relied heavily on established power—the churches, fraternal organizations, and a hierarchy of local middle class black leadership that was unable to enter the white world in the South. Cumulatively, these sources of established power had a cautionary effect on the movement. In the Northern wing of the movement, these contributing forces were either much diminished or totally absent. Moreover, each wing focused on different problems—the South on overturning legal segregation and the North on de facto segregation and ghetto poverty. Any national social movement must link organizations with regional differences, a formidable task that bedeviled the civil rights movement.

The civil rights movement is a mix of national and regional organizations: the National Association for the Advancement of Colored People (NAACP), the Southern Christian Leadership Conference (SCLC), the Northern-based Congress of Racial Equality (CORE), the Student Nonviolent Coordinating Committee (SNCC), and the Urban League, each with its own theory of the movement's proper direction and the surest paths to its goals. Equally, if not more, important have been the local organizations, the churches and clubs that became centers for immediate action and levers for lifting the cause to regional levels. The larger organizations acted as catalysts, style-setters, and providers of services—workers, literature, and training.[25]

A social movement like civil rights seeks to amend, even reconstruct, communications between the deprived and the powerful. As an essential first step, the movement worked to enhance the black's self-perception. Many participants in the marches and clubs found a confidence that they had never known before in their lives. The movement enabled blacks to achieve substantial identity within the social system. As a further step, the movement sought to project the new image into communications between the races. The

[25] Pat Watters and Reese Cleghorn, *Climbing Jacob's Ladder: The Arrival of Negroes in Southern Politics* (New York: Harcourt Brace Jovanovich, 1967), 311.

movement therefore had to dismantle the traditional stance of the black as inferior and supplicant in black-white communications. The civil rights movement stirred whites, formerly oblivious to blacks, to perceive them as fellow citizens with problems and aspirations. For whites, the civil rights movement destroyed what Gunnar Myrdal called the "convenience of ignorance." [26]

The task of reconstructing interracial communications was eased by the civil rights movement's stress on society's ultimate values, on the Bible and the Constitution. The movement contended that the major transformations it insisted on in race relations were ordained by both documents. The Bible imparted spiritual overtones to the movement, sanctioned invocations of religious guilt, stressed forgiveness and salvation for an errant society, and prescribed courage and love in the face of violence from the movement's oppressors. The Constitution set forth goals of equality and promised the protection of its provisions.

Political and social movements are highly dependent on leadership in order to grow and attain national stature. Particularly in their earlier stages, these movements thrive on charismatic leaders like Martin Luther King, Jr. With an eloquence embellished with Biblical texts, King preached a gospel of hope, his "dream" of equitable race relations, achieved through nonviolence and civil disobedience and pursued with dignity and "love of the oppressor." Critics within the movement contended that King's philosophy was better suited to the Southern blacks' religious orientation than to dealing with the subtle forms of segregation and discrimination in the North. Other leaders and philosophies began to emerge, particularly after King's murder in 1968.

A contemporary Northern-based philosophy, black nationalism, perceives American society as programmed to cause blacks suffering and accordingly chooses to remain out of politics. Instead, black nationalists keep themselves separate from general society, stress black individuality, work to strengthen ties between black Americans and Africans, and revere the culture, languages, and customs of Africa. Even more moderate black organizations are revising their goals and strategies in that direction. CORE, for example, used to be integration-oriented. Integration is now seen as contributing to the "short-changing" of blacks and as the ideological preserve of "the Afro-European, the mixed blood." CORE's newer strategy of self-determination is intended to attract the Afro-African, or the blacker black.

The National Urban League is stressing "the economic empowerment of black people" and a fair share of jobs, income, opportunities, and political representation. Vernon E. Jordan, Jr., National Urban League Director, has pointed out that whereas the issue in the sixties was whether blacks would be allowed to ride the buses and where they would sit, the issue in the seventies is whether black people will be allowed to drive that bus. "We have found," Jordan added, "that it does not mean much to have the right to sleep at the Hilton if you don't have the money to pay the rent." [27]

[26] Gunnar Myrdal, *An American Dilemma* (New York: Harper & Row, 1944), 40–42.
[27] Vernon E. Jordan, "Just What Do Black People Want?" *Newsday,* January 31, 1972.

The Reverend Jesse Jackson, a present-day disciple of Martin Luther King, also stresses economic themes. "The black liberation movement is moving into its final phase and that's economic," he has said, adding that blacks are no longer interested in the "rhetoric of civil rights." To speed the economic development of black communities, Jackson urges massive assistance from government and industry on the scale that the United States provided for the postwar economies of Japan, Germany, and Israel, and programs that were not considered "welfare or handouts." "We have the potential and desire to be a productive people," Jackson said, and "do not desire a welfare state." [28]

In its definition of economic objectives, the NAACP has stressed that black survival and prosperity depend on the blacks' ability to move from the inner cities to the suburbs, which is where the jobs are according to 1970 Census Bureau figures. Vital services such as education are also seen in inner-city/suburban contrasts since they are financed largely by local revenues and the inner-city poor cannot produce sufficient financial support. One NAACP official said: "It is like taxing the rich to provide for the rich and taxing the poor to take care of the poor." [29]

Like other social movements with choices between varied goals and strategies, the presence of many organizations reflecting them, and a variety of charismatic leaders, the black rights movement has grappled seriously and often futilely with the attainment of unity and its anticipated gains of strength. Some of the problems surfaced at the first National Black Political Convention in 1972. The delegates adopted a National Black Political Agenda calling for an "independent black political movement," but it left largely unsaid what specifically was to be done. This was hardly surprising in light of the conflicting positions of the nationalists, with their separationist orientation, and the NAACP, which opposes that position. Eventually, the NAACP withdrew from the convention "because of a difference in ideology." [30]

Conventional politics

In its workings, the politics of hope often links political and social movements to conventional political organizations. In this way much of the substance of the early civil rights movement came to be represented in the national platform of the Democratic party. President Kennedy incorporated many of the movement's goals into his legislative program, and President Johnson transformed the movement's goal to remove racial barriers to voting into the Voting Rights Act of 1965. And he borrowed from the movement the slogan "We Shall Overcome" to characterize the civil rights policies of his own administration.

But the responses of conventional politics may be more shadow than substance, more rhetorical and symbolic than concrete. In spite of the Kennedy-

[28] *New York Times,* September 30 and October 10, 1971.
[29] *New York Times,* July 11, 1971.
[30] *New York Times,* May 17, 1972.

Johnson commitment, the relative position of blacks in the economy and society has remained unchanged. In 1971, one-third of the nation's blacks lived below the official poverty level, compared with 10 percent of the white population. Although black families increased their average income by 60 percent from 1965 to 1970 while white families increased theirs by only 40 percent, by 1970 black family incomes were still only three-fifths that of whites. In 1970 black unemployment remained significantly higher than that among whites—8.2 percent to 4.5 percent. In the 1960s education of blacks, stressed in governmental programs, contributed little to equalizing black and white incomes. Blacks who completed college received an income only 70 percent as high as white college graduates, which was nearly the same percentage gap prevailing between blacks and whites who had fewer than eight years of school.[31]

Conventional politics also may slickly co-opt a social movement by adopting a portion of its program and effectively defusing the remainder. In the 1930s the old age pension movement suffered this fate. The Social Security Act legislated then provided old age assistance at a miserly rate compared with the aspirations of the movement, but at a level sufficient to weaken the movement, grievously and irretrievably. In resorting to conventional politics, deprived groups venture on an uncertain terrain where power is diffused and politicians' ambitions and necessities hold sway, potential booby traps for programs born of the politics of hope. Yet these same elements may also respond to the deprived and produce Medicare and Medicaid, school lunch programs, Head Start, the Job Corps, the Neighborhood Youth Corps.

Several major groups of current society, it should be noted, rely heavily on conventional politics and the established political system. The twenty million elderly, sixty-five years and over, show little militancy, but increasingly they are resorting to club activities, social and political. The Washington-based National Council of Senior Citizens claims a membership of two million, including allied local and state clubs. Politically oriented organizations flourish at the state level; for example, in California, where 1 of every 4¼ votes is cast by a resident over sixty-five, a statewide senior citizens organization is pushing for a national pension equivalent to the federal minimum wage computed on a monthly basis. In Florida, where senior citizens are also concentrated, a veteran Republican county chairman has said that every statewide candidate "must take a stand on the matters of vital interest to the older people [or] lose at the polls." A strong bastion of "senior power" is the suburb, where the solidarity of the elderly has defeated swimming pool referenda, school budgets, and other calls for major appropriations.

Among the elderly conflict grows over the extent to which their activity should be limited to conventional politics or assume greater militancy. Not surprisingly, more established organizations prefer the conventional route. Occasional picketing and such demonstrations as deluging the office of a Connecticut governor with tea bags to protest a proposed sales tax increase are the most militant activities yet undertaken—"We're not going out to break win-

[31] *New York Times,* July 27, 1971 and July 13, 1972.

Delegates to the convention of the National Council of Senior Citizens
petition Congress to get out of the horse-and-buggy era by increasing
Social Security benefits.

dows," one leader of the elderly has said. But not a few organizers criticize the elderly for not being more belligerent.[32]

The number of rival women's organizations gives women's liberationists a choice between conventional and unconventional politics. Adhering for the most part to conventional politics is the National Organization for Women (NOW). Reformist in approach, NOW attacks job inequalities and other injustices through court action and legislative lobbying and election of more women to public office. Occasionally NOW engages in demonstrations; for example, it has picketed a traditional men-only lunch place in Chicago. Needless to say, the established political system is not always appreciative and responsive. The lunch-place episode eventually reached court, where, according to the local chapter president of NOW, "the prosecutor laughed and the judge, who happened to be a black man, laughed and threw the case out." [33]

[32] *New York Times,* March 1, 1970 and February 21, 1971.
[33] *Newsweek,* "Women's Lib: The War on 'Sexism'" (March 23, 1970), 73–74.

Elizabeth Holtzman and supporters celebrating her victory over veteran congressman Emanuel Celler in the New York State Democratic primary, June 1972.

The increasing political emphasis of the women's movement has enhanced the importance of the National Women's Political Caucus, formed in 1971 by Congresswoman Bella Abzug (D., N.Y.), Congresswoman Shirley Chisholm (D., N.Y.), Gloria Steinem, and Betty Friedan to "awaken, organize and assert the vast political power represented by women." In preparation for the 1972 national party conventions, the Caucus held seminars around the country to teach women how to become convention delegates. The most visible breakthroughs in the women's rights movement have been political—passage of the Equal Rights Amendment in Congress and occasional repeals of state abortion laws. But in terms of political power, the women's movement has many miles to go. "We got this far only because of our nuisance value," Gloria Steinem has said, "You've got to get to the state where your legislators say, 'Call your people off.' "

The more radical wing of the feminist movement has declined in influence after much division over ideological issues. The names of the early radical groups—Red Stockings, WITCH, Bread and Roses—are now seldom heard. Some organizations that tried to function without leaders have fallen by the wayside—the approach did not work. While NOW seeks equality by working within the system, the radical wing means to change the system, an objective that includes not only capitalism, but patriarchy.[34]

Political strategies

The powerful resist the assertions of the deprived. To win power, to gain the benefits of value allocations, to transform hope into actuality, the deprived must engage successfully in the processes and contests of the political system. Their representatives and those likely to befriend their cause must win elections, promote legislation, influence party platforms and bureaucratic functioning. Lacking power, the deprived may be driven to resort to a wide range of strategies, conventional and unconventional.

The success of the civil rights movement. Limited access to regular political channels may compel the deprived to employ less conventional means of political assertion. In the South, the civil rights movement faced that necessity in its early stages, when it pursued a *strategy of direct action*. This strategy called for the controlled resort to the streets (chiefly marches and demonstrations) and pressures (sit-ins and boycotts) on economic institutions like buses and dime stores that depended on black patronage but were sources of the indignities of segregation. Eventually, demonstrations were aimed at entire towns and cities to force general community action, and the more than 700 demonstrations across the South in 1963 were a mighty force in moving the nation toward enactment of the 1964 Civil Rights Act, a turning point in the civil rights movement.

During the 1965 march on Selma, Alabama, television captured the brutal attack on the participants—black men, women, and children were shown being tear-gassed, beaten, and trampled by state troopers on horseback. These scenes helped assure the passage of the most important of civil rights laws, the Voting Rights Act of 1965. Despite their apparent political productivity, demonstrations also have limitations. They are subject to what Kenneth B. Clark has termed a psychological law of diminishing returns. As repeated experiences, however dramatic and intense, they decrease in sensitivity to both actors and audiences. They lose value when they become diffuse and unrelated to specific goals, and they are susceptible to being used as instruments to prop up the egos and ambitions of local and would-be civil rights leaders.[35]

Another major civil rights weapon was the *strategy of voting*. Voting was beheld as the key to other political rights and to social and economic services

[34] *Ibid.*; *New York Times,* August 22, 1972.
[35] Clark, 206–07.

Sit-ins—a strategy used by blacks in the civil rights movement.

and opportunities. Massive registration drives and passage of the Voting Rights Act of 1965 paid off with a marked expansion of the active Southern black electorate. More radical factions, such as SNCC, deprecated voting as a perpetuation of inadequate gradualism. But voting registration projects joined the disparate civil rights organizations in common cause, and they were a bridge to cooperation between the organizations and the Justice Department. Eventually, they led to the election of blacks to Southern public offices. By the 1970s, the election of blacks to mayoralties, county offices, and the U.S. House of Representatives had become commonplace. "If blacks use their votes intelligently," declared Walter Fauntroy, a black political leader in Washington, D.C., "they can affect the outcome of every election from city council to the Presidency." [36]

Older civil rights organizations espouse the *strategy of law and maneuver.* The NAACP and the National Urban League, working within the system of constitutional politics and private capitalism, press white political and economic power-holders to support innovative civil rights policies and to improve hiring practices and career opportunities of blacks. These established or-

[36] In *Newsweek* (June 7, 1971), 30.

Boycotting—a strategy used in behalf of the Chicano movement, led by Cesar Chavez (shown here).

ganizations are derided by younger, militant leaders impatient with the slow pace of their progress.

CORE and SNCC leaders prefer the *strategy of direct encounter*—sit-ins, boycotts, and picketing. This approach represents a return to direct action, but in a more hardnosed fashion. It directly involves committed individuals, dramatizes flagrant injustices, and mobilizes social forces and institutions to affect change. The strategy looks askance at charismatic leaders. As Saul Alinsky, activist and organizer, has noted: "Che Guevara—what . . . did he do except get himself shot?" [37]

There is also the *strategy of alienation* advocated by the Black Muslims and black nationalists. For them, the function of politics is to gain for blacks community control, from which a "black nation" will emerge—a series of black islands in the cities, permitting cultural identity, a consciousness of being black, and continuity with the past. Alienation comes in many doctrinal packages. The Black Panthers call for integration and liberation, with or without the aid of whites, as the paths of black development. They have adopted a self-defense principle, derived from the view that blacks are an oppressed colony and the police are the armed forces of the oppressor. As a defensive organization, the Panthers shadow the police in the black community to see that the rights of black citizens are not abused.

The failure of the poor. In contrast to the substantial political achievements of the civil rights movement is the powerlessness of other sectors of deprived people, most notably the poor. The ghetto is a monument to this powerlessness, proof of the inability of the poor to exert sufficient political force to alter a wretched status quo.

The poor's political ineffectuality forfeits the shaping of welfare policy to

[37] In *New York Times,* January 5, 1971.

the more powerful elements of society. Sociologist George Simmel has written that "public assistance is perhaps the only branch of administration in which the interested parties have no participation." [38] The low position that public assistance occupies in the federal hierarchy is another symptom of the poor's lack of influence. Welfare administrators are under steady pressure to apply rules strictly against their clients, who are incapable of exerting counter-pressure. Administrators live in fear of the type of investigation mounted by Senator Robert C. Byrd (D., W. Va.) in the early 1960s, a spectacular exposé of lapses in the District of Columbia's welfare administration. Byrd so frightened the administrators into applying eligibility standards with a new tough-minded stringency that he soon could boast that the District's welfare rolls had been reduced by half.[39]

The poor's inability to generate their own political power makes them excessively dependent on succor from other political quarters. Recent Presidents have been responsive—Johnson with his war on poverty and Nixon with his welfare reform plan. To Presidents, the poor represent potential votes, great masses of them concentrated in the cities of states with large electoral votes. The geography of misery has its political blessings.

Borrowing from the civil rights strategy, the poor are resorting increasingly to the courts, chiefly through the Office of Economic Opportunity's neighborhood legal services program. That program is reaping a harvest of landmark cases, including one declaring a state's relief residency requirements unconstitutional. Other cases have struck at arbitrary administrative procedures, man-in-the-house rules, and discrimination against black mothers.

In the late 1960s, the poor at last took a giant step when they fielded a substantial pressure group, the National Welfare Rights Organization (NWRO). Composed mostly of black women, NWRO is strongest in Northern cities, where local units have demonstrated against welfare restrictions. Among other activities, NWRO has staged a "Mother's Day" march in the riot-torn section of Washington, pushed for a floor of $6,500 rather than the $2,400 of Nixon's welfare reform plan, and protested the Vietnam war for having diverted attention and funds from their needs. But the most potent weapon of the poor has been the threat of rioting, which, coupled with recollections of its devastation in the 1960s, has imposed real outer limits on the efforts of the foes of welfare to reduce its rolls and restrict its benefits.

Violence

Can deprived people properly resort to violence? Ought blacks, for example, having failed to win redress of old grievances after 300 years in American society, be permitted to take up violence? Violence has been a continuing issue of the modern civil rights movement—abhorred by Martin Luther King,

[38] In Elman, 210.
[39] Piven and Cloward, 150.

Jr., and advocated by some black leaders and by New Left figures in the 1960s and after.

Violence has been defined as "the most direct form of power in the physical sense." [40] Hannah Arendt provides an important caveat: "Power is indeed of the essence of all government, but violence is not. Violence by nature is instrumental; like all means, it always stands in need of guidance and justification through the end it pursues. And what needs justification by something else cannot be the essence of anything." [41]

Those who value violence as an instrument of the deprived contend that it serves as a warning signal to the powerful of the community who fail to perceive or are insensitive to social failings. Those with power may then be moved to improve on the oppressive conditions. The sharp expansion in welfare roles in the mid-sixties and after is largely credited to the effect of waves of violent urban demonstrations. Welfare benefits had long been restricted in their distribution until the rioting in the black ghettos helped political decision-makers to realize that one way to reduce urban upheaval was to make welfare substantially more available. Violence can also be a catalyst. The violence used by Southern sheriffs and law enforcement officers against blacks engaged in protest activities aroused public opinion and spurred the advance of federal civil rights legislation. But sociologist Lewis Coser argues that whereas the danger signal and catalytic functions of violence allow the political system to "adjust" and "adapt," they do not themselves effect a redistribution of power allocations.[42]

Violence is arbitrary. It thrusts the results of men's actions beyond their control. In no other pursuit does luck or chance play a more fateful role. Worst of all, violence denies one's common humanity. To speak of "the black man" vs. "the white man" is to speak in abstractions and to look past the specific black youth whose hopeless poverty trajects him into a life of drugs, or the faithful white Head Start volunteer who is classified merely with "the system" and "the guilty." On the other hand, as Walter Reuther, late president of the United Auto Workers, warned, "it is not enough to say we have got to stop violence," but, rather, it must be appreciated that unless there can be "peaceful social change, then we are inevitably going to get violent social change." [43] Those who reject violence have an obligation to make the existing political system more responsive to its underdogs.

Finally, and fortunately, the technique of nonviolent protest, as practiced by Gandhi and King, is far from dead. In the 1970s, it is achieving quiet gains, both in the black rights movement and among alienated youths of all races. University courses and research in nonviolent methods have increased sharply; most student protests, contrary to general belief, are nonviolent;

[40] H. L. Nieburg, "Violence, Law, and the Social Process," in Greenberg, 354.

[41] Hannah Arendt, *On Violence* (New York: Harcourt Brace Jovanovich, 1969, 1970), 51.

[42] Lewis A. Coser, *Continuities in the Study of Social Conflict* (New York: Free Press, 1967), 76.

[43] *New York Times,* April 21, 1970.

and minority movements have continued to resort successfully to nonviolence in specific instances.

The fulfillment gap

When government does act for the deprived, its efforts are susceptible to what might be called a fulfillment gap. (Some would term it a credibility gap.) What is promised is not delivered. The 1949 Housing Act, for example, pledged "a decent home in a suitable living environment for every American family," but more than two decades later only a small fraction of the original six-year authorization for 800,000 public housing units had been built, and the need had meanwhile expanded to 6 million units. Early in his term, President Kennedy issued an executive order "to expand and improve the program of food distribution throughout the United States," but more than a decade later food assistance for the poor remains grossly inadequate.

Launching his war on poverty, President Johnson announced that "the days of the dole in our country are numbered." To emphasize his commitment, the President spoke not in the regal comfort of the White House, but from the crumbling front porch of Tom Fletcher's shack in Appalachian Kentucky. Five years later Tom Fletcher still sat on the same front porch, barely subsisting and untouched by the war on poverty.[44]

The fulfillment gap afflicts the deprived more severely than any other population sector. Even when gains are being enjoyed by a general group, those most deprived—the lower class—share least in those gains. Thus the U.S. National Advisory Commission on Civil Disorders found that in 1966 the percentage of black families with incomes of $7,000 or more was 1.6 times the proportion of blacks receiving comparable incomes in 1960, and 4 times greater than the proportion receiving such incomes in 1947. But for blacks in the lowest income categories, the picture was quite different. The Commission found that about two-thirds of the lowest income group made no significant gains.[45]

The kinds of deprivation vary in tenacity. Some contribute to the fulfillment gap more persistently than others. For many groups it is easier to cast off the political shackles of deprivation than the social or economic. It is one thing for blacks to obtain the vote and related political rights and quite another to penetrate labor unions and suburban neighborhoods. In effect, this is to say that while the political spirit may be willing, the economic and social flesh may remain weak. The economic and the social encompass private, personal interests, which fortunately situated whites guard jealously, while politics and its decisions are more remote, less valued, and therefore more readily accepted. A National Opinion Research Center study found a steady rise of white ac-

[44] Kotz, 226.
[45] U.S. National Advisory Commission on Civil Disorders, *Report of the National Advisory Commission on Civil Disorders* (New York: Bantam Books, 1968), 251–52.

President Johnson announced his war on poverty from the front porch of Tom Fletcher's Appalachian shack.

ceptance of legislated integration in the 1960s: on issues of integrated public transportation, parks, restaurants, hotels, and schools more than 70 percent of the nation's whites expressed "integrationist responses." But the more personal issues of neighborhood integration and mixed marriages still divided white Americans about equally.[46]

A major cause of the fulfillment gap, then, is the limited ability of the political system to command social and economic results and its considerable ability to make symbolic concessions. As a common condition, the political rhetoric of electoral campaigns and high-level pronouncements is inflated, while subsequent program commitments and accomplishments are considerably less. The so-called war on poverty, heralded with extravagant rhetoric, was fought with a poor man's budget. Problems of ghetto living, hunger, and neglected health needs are massive, of the magnitude, as some have suggested, of a "domestic Marshall Plan." But nothing on that scale is in the offing, and these enormous problems are left to patchwork palliatives and feeble appropriations. A fulfillment gap, the distance between the problem and the available remedy, is preordained. In addition, governmental programs for the deprived are vulnerable to shifts in presidential priorities. After proclaiming the war on poverty, President Johnson was distracted by another war—in Vietnam.

Because programs for the deprived are spending or money programs, they depend on annual appropriations, which, experience shows, may fluctuate from year to year. Even when Congress responds generously, the President may

[46] *New York Times,* December 8, 1971.

impound appropriations or spend only a portion of them, a fate often accorded domestic social programs in the Nixon administration. Finally, programs for the deprived are easily thwarted in a political system of dispersed power: committee bottlenecks on Capitol Hill, hostile state legislatures and administrations, the well-financed, assured lobbying by the powerful—business, labor unions, and agriculture. Given these malfunctions of the political system, he who is deprived is indeed fortunate if he can lift himself by his own bootstraps—or, more accurately, if he can perform that miracle without boots or straps.

Proposals

In a country as favored as the United States, one might contend that the deprived ought not exist, that all should have access to life's amenities and opportunities, that the spectacle of millions living in hunger and destitution testifies that the political system is underproductive and underachieving. If the lot of the deprived is to be improved, a task any genuine democracy ought to undertake, what might be done?

1. The general possibilities of conventional politics must again and again be explored and tried, for they have been the historic escape routes to power of the formerly deprived, most notably the industrial worker and the waves of European immigrants in the nineteenth and twentieth centuries who initially were consigned mainly to urban slums.

Occasionally Presidents, such as Lincoln, the Roosevelts, Kennedy, and Johnson, have taken up the causes of the deprived. Candidates for executive and legislative posts whose value commitments accord a high priority to the needs of the deprived need to be found and supported. Increasing the number of advocates of the deprived in party councils and conventions will enhance the prospects of the search. At the 1972 Democratic National Convention the sharp gains of blacks, women, and the young among the delegates enabled them to control the presidential nomination and the platform and to defeat the "power-brokers"—the union chiefs and city bosses—who ordinarily dominate such decisions.

Deprived groups fare better in politics when they are transformed into pressure groups. The National Labor Relations Act of 1935 transformed much of the labor force, then unorganized and suffering severe unemployment, into unions that soon gained imposing economic and political power. In one perspective, the Economic Opportunity Act of 1965 was designed to do the same for the poor—to give them political cohesiveness and power and thereby the competence to extract a better life from the social system. The effort did not succeed largely because the Vietnam war foreclosed a fair test of it. In view of its potential benefits, the effort deserves to be made again.

2. The life of the deprived can be improved through better governmental

programs. Piven and Cloward have suggested that if economic policy is adopted which will lead to full employment at decent wages, poor men could resume breadwinner roles at wages sufficient to support women and children. Fewer women would need to ask for assistance for lack of male support. As well, if adequately paying jobs existed on a large scale, AFDC mothers could take them and thereby shrink relief rolls.

In the absence of full employment, Piven and Cloward advocate further expansion or "explosion" of relief rolls, mindful that hundreds of thousands of impoverished families now eligible for assistance receive none at all. They oppose work-enforcing policies for those on welfare; experience shows they are a forerunner of the eventual expulsion of great numbers of people from the rolls, leaving them to forage on a labor market with little work and subject to low-wage exploitation.[47] Gilbert Y. Steiner argues that cash assistance is more efficient and less imposing on the poor than "in-kind" assistance, such as food stamps.[48]

To improve the prospects of the poor for employment, government can provide training to prepare the unskilled unemployed person for future skilled work. A feature of the war on poverty, job training, has unfortunately been far from a glorious success. Effective training techniques for the unskilled are lacking, and it is difficult to persuade uncertain, insecure trainees to stick with the program and employers and co-workers to be patient with them. On-the-job training seems preferable to training off the job, for a job can be more easily guaranteed at the end of the course. But guarantees become difficult to honor when business falters, unemployment sets in, and federal program grants diminish.

A simpler alternative is to create jobs that the unskilled unemployed can fill. Governmental policies could encourage such jobs in private industry, and government could also function as an employer of last resort, hiring the unskilled for public works programs. The unskilled would do hauling and sweeping and other support work for the skilled. A drawback is that these tend to be dead-end jobs, but that stigma might be reduced if the worker were adequately paid.

Still another possibility for governmental aid is the guaranteed annual income. The Nixon administration's Family Assistance Plan would guarantee a minimum income of $2,400 a year for two parents and two children. Many have criticized the sum as unrealistically low, but the lack of political leverage on the part of the poor does not promise a significantly higher figure. Herbert Gans has proposed that a low annual income guarantee be supplemented by multiple-income grants, such as family or children allowances, not only to the poor but also to the moderate-income category. A single-income grant focuses only on the poor; diversified grants might enhance the program's political

[47] Piven and Cloward, 345–48.
[48] Gilbert Y. Steiner, *The State of Welfare* (Washington, D.C.: The Brookings Institution, 1971).

support by enlarging its potential beneficiaries and linking the powerless with those who have a modicum of power.[49]

3. Many sources in the private sector can help the poor toward a better life. A common problem among the poor is the violation of their rights, the denial of benefits to which they are entitled. Law students, working under an attorney's supervision, might help the poor in dealing with government administrators, who often shortchange them. They could make phone calls, write letters, and appear at welfare centers and hearings. Later, when these lawyers gain full professional status and come into positions of power, they would have knowledge of, and possibly sympathy for, deprived people.[50]

4. For women, politics is a fruitful avenue that is yet to be fully utilized. The battles against the abortion laws will have to be fought out in the legislatures and courts. Political leverage will also be important in the fight for equality in employment waged against management and labor unions. For the elderly, conventional politics is also the main hope; greater organization and more pressure are necessary for better payoffs. And for blacks who are deprived of rights, the whole array of strategies and organizations that promote them need to be weighed for greatest effectiveness. Fortunately, strategic thinking in the black civil rights movement has been creative and resourceful, as it must be for any social movement for deprived people to have significant impact.

Suggested Reading

Arendt, Hannah, *On Violence* * (Harcourt Brace Jovanovich, 1970). A penetrating essay on violence and its implications.

Clark, Kenneth B., *Dark Ghetto* * (Harper & Row, 1965). A black psychologist's astute analysis of life in the black ghetto, and strategies for dealing with its problems.

Graham, Hugh Davis, and Gurr, Ted Robert, *Violence in America: Historical and Comparative Perspectives* * (Bantam Books, 1969). A study group of the National Commission on the Causes and Prevention of Violence places violence in contemporary America in historical perspective. Comparison is made with other countries.

Greenberg, Edward S., Milner, Neal, and Olson, David J., *Black Politics* * (Holt, Rinehart and Winston, 1971). An extremely useful collection of readings on various aspects of the black experience in American society. Considers the role of violence in black conflicts.

Greer, Germaine, *The Female Eunuch* * (McGraw-Hill, 1970). A spirited, well-written examination of woman's roles in society, with proposals for her escape from the more oppressive of them.

Hofstadter, Richard, *The Age of Reform* * (Knopf, 1956). An analysis of Populism and Progressivism as reform movements. An invaluable background essay for evaluating the possibilities of contemporary reform movements in behalf of deprived people.

Kotz, Nick, *Let Them Eat Promises: The Politics of Hunger in America* * (Prentice-Hall, 1969). A journalist's vividly written, insightful account of hunger as a major affliction

[49] Gans, 27.
[50] Graham, 101–02.

of contemporary American society. The roles of the national executive and legislative branches, the civil rights movement, and other parts of the political system are ably explored.

Lowi, Theodore J., *The Politics of Disorder* (Basic Books, 1971). Thoughtful essays on social movements, including their encounters with institutions and their vulnerabilities.

Millett, Kate, *Sexual Politics* * (Doubleday, 1970). A pioneering work by a political scientist on woman's subordination in the social system, with an assessment of possible means of her liberation.

Piven, Francis Fox, and Cloward, Richard A., *Regulating the Poor* * (Pantheon Books, 1971). A leading work on the poor, presented in historical perspective. Excellent treatment of the welfare system, its operations, and the forces affecting it. The authors also present and assess proposals for improving the condition of the American poor.

Rainwater, Lee, and Yancey, William L., *The Moynihan Report and the Politics of Controversy* * (MIT Press, 1967). An excellent account of the origins of the Johnson Administration's poverty program and its shifting political fortunes. The causes of the program's decline are explored.

Steiner, Gilbert Y., *The State of Welfare* * (The Brookings Institution, 1971). An able analysis of the welfare system by a leading authority. Concentrates on the political maneuvers of the legislatures and bureaucracies in the development of welfare policies. The author assesses the Johnson and Nixon policies and the potential for future welfare crises.

Watters, Pat, and Cleghorn, Reese, *Climbing Jacob's Ladder: The Arrival of Negroes in Southern Politics* * (Harcourt Brace Jovanovich, 1967). A vivid and skillful analytical account of the black civil rights movement in the 1950s and 60s. The authors focus on strategies, black organization, and ideologies.

* Available in paperback edition

6

responsible
parties:
instruments
of
mass
democracy

As college students, Mark and Linda Bernstein organized the McCarthy campaign in Annapolis, Maryland, in 1968, and as law students they worked for McGovern in 1972. "When McCarthy didn't get nominated, we really sat it out," said Linda. "I don't really know why, but we're not quitters. You can't run away from the problems. We were saying all along that there was no difference between Nixon and Humphrey. Well, it turns out there was a difference. Most people who think there was no difference aren't involved in politics any more, but those who think there was a difference are still fighting. That difference is important." But Paul Roeder, another young McGovern worker, was less certain about the value of party politics. "I have real difficulty saying that one politician is different from any other. Johnson and Nixon promised to end the war, too. I find myself with an integrity problem." [1]

Implicit in these remarks and in the experiences of the speakers is the assumption that democracy requires responsible parties. If democracy entails the making of significant choices, the policies, programs, and candidates of the parties must offer the voter, and the party worker, real alternatives. The experience of the Bernsteins and Roeder also suggests that responsible parties need workers whose perspectives are not wholly regulated by appetite for material gain or career advancement, but by commitment to conceptions of public interest and to the specific programs and policies that give them content. Some policies offer little material gain, and all policies derive strength from the commitment and zeal of their champions. Beyond these factors there are still other criteria of the "responsible party," which this chapter will seek to identify.

[1] *New York Times*, March 8, 1972.

How well do American major parties respond to the Bernsteins and Roeder? Are parties instruments of significant choice? Probably the oldest, most deeply felt complaint about the parties is that despite their skill at mobilizing vast majorities to elect candidates to office, through lavish expenditure of money and effort, they cannot convert electoral victory into responsible policy-making. Parties do not have the power to assure that the men they elect will transform campaign platforms into public policy. The parties of European democracies excel at this function, but it has generally eluded American parties. The failure allows problems to drift and tips the political scales in favor of the status quo and its hard injustices. We need new political parties that will embrace policy and program as ideology, respond to the needs of the aggrieved, and be capable of bold assaults on public problems.

American parties have their defenders. For them parties offer significant differences on important national issues. They point out that in Congress, the parties more usually than not hold their ranks on votes, including those stirring major controversy, with sufficient solidarity to enable the voters to perceive a Republican and a Democratic point of view. Thus, when Senator Robert Taft (R., Ohio) offered amendments in 1971 to delete from the Emergency Public Service Employment Act requirements that the federal minimum wage be paid for public work by the unemployed and that the prevailing wage for similar occupations be observed, the vote had party contours. The amendments were rejected 50 votes to 27 in the Senate. Twenty-four Republicans supported Taft's amendments and 11 opposed, while 3 Democrats supported them and 39 opposed. When the House voted to authorize $4.3 billion through fiscal 1973 for expenditure under the work relief act, the vote again followed party lines, as it was adopted 245–141. Fifty-two Republicans voted for the authorization and 113 opposed, while 193 Democrats voted for it and 28 opposed.[2]

Defenders of American parties also hail them for measuring up to the concept of the responsible party that requires them to be resilient and supple in adjusting to severe and sweeping change. Except for the Civil War, when they were the last bond of union to snap, parties have tended to moderate conflict and narrow cleavages in society, and have produced governments humane in policy and forceful in crisis.

Democracy needs parties

Whatever their faults, parties are rightly hailed as major contributors to the development of modern democracy. Merely proclaiming man's right to share in government does not effectuate it—an individual requires institutions through which to exercise his right. Ideally parties in a democracy ought to

[2] *1971 Congressional Quarterly Almanac* (Washington, D.C.: Congressional Quarterly, 1972), 6S.

excel at recruiting popular leaders, promoting the competition of political preferences, and mobilizing vast majorities. They should play a central part in helping people to control the actions of their leaders. When people assert themselves most forcefully—throwing incumbents out of office and substituting a new corps of elected officials—the parties provide the candidates, debate the issues, and spur the electorate to vote.

According to the democratic ideal, parties link organized bodies of majority and minority opinion with the responsible conduct of government. Parties allot defined roles to each of these bodies. Majority opinion organizes and rules, and minority opinion persists in competition by watching and criticizing the majority's conduct of government. By increasing its adherents, the minority can transform itself into a new majority. A cardinal feature of democracy is choice, and parties, to the extent that they express majority and minority opinion, can institutionalize alternatives.

The presence of the minority party is a crucial and difficult part of the democratic formula. The minority party can make the concept of the "loyal opposition" work; that is, it allows one to criticize and oppose the incumbent government without being automatically viewed as treasonous, seditious, or conspiratorial. The legitimacy of opposition is established in the Constitution, particularly in the guarantees of civil liberties. In effect, these are limitations on the means used by the government, or the majority, to counter the opposition. But an opposition works within clear constraints. While it can attack policies and illuminate the flaws of incumbents, it does not direct its thunder against the constitutional regime itself. Instead, the majority and minority are united in an agreement that accepts the governmental order set forth in the basic law.

Ideally, the opposition, or minority, must also be responsible, conducting itself as a potential alternative government and criticizing present policies and formulating new ones—not in wild, improbable shapes—but within the tolerances of the historic constitutional and social framework. The norm of optimally functioning parties requires that the opposition must also be effective. It should be capable within a reasonable time of winning office through an ample organization, an agenda of promised policies, and a roster of attractive candidates. This difficult, shifting balance between majority and minority is, according to James Madison, embedded in human psychology. Men are driven by the impulse to differ, and "the latent causes" of party, Madison noted, are "sown in the nature of man." Since tyranny alone can suppress these differences, the American philosopher Francis Lieber rightly insisted in 1838 that "without well-understood opposition liberty cannot coexist with peace and order." [3]

Parties are expected to perform other services for democracy. They serve as intermediaries between the people and the formal, remote governmental institutions. They assist in transposing popular interests and needs into legis-

---

[3] In Richard Hofstadter, *The Idea of a Party System* (Berkeley: University of California Press, 1969), 259.

lative and administrative policies. By dealing in numbers of votes, parties can give weight to the less fortunate in society and counter the influence of the wealthy, the educated, and the expert. Parties can link political "leaders" and "followers." The serious aspirant for office must be attentive to varied groupings to win their support.

Democracy may need parties, but parties also need democracy. An optimally responsible party must practice internal democracy. Party policy must not be the preserve of an oligarchy, or of the deliberations of a smoke-filled room. "Followers" and "workers" must have a meaningful part in the development of party decisions. Here the performance of American parties is creditable. As American major parties have developed, they have become increasingly democratic internally. Unlike parties in other advanced industrial nations, they have shunned the concentration of organization and decision-making authority, elaborate bureaucracies, an oligarchy of elites, and class representation. Rather, American parties have remained open, voter-oriented, and permeable from top to bottom. A recent impressive example was the 1972 Democratic convention. Many delegates, particularly the young and blacks, had been poorly represented in the 1968 convention at Chicago, and some even had participated in the street upheavals there. A leader of that episode, Abbie Hoffman, played an opposite role in 1972 at Miami, gracing the convention floor and worrying that the tossing of a pumpkin pie at a city councilman by a member of the Zippies (a splinter group of Hoffman's Yippies) would play into the hands of President Nixon and the Republicans.

But it will be seen in this chapter that American parties do not always function credibly, much less ideally. Some functions are performed better than others. The American experience shows that the mere presence of parties is no assurance of the exercise of man's right to share in government.

Nature of the American
party system

The American party system is the oldest among the nations. In the lengthy American experience, parties have undergone several stages of development. The first, 1789–1820, was preoccupied with experimentation. The Federalists, led by Hamilton, and the Republicans, by Jefferson, functioned in a new political system that also was pragmatic and experimental. These parties were more centralized than our later parties, less dependent on state structures, and offered contrasting approaches to foreign and domestic policy.

The second stage, 1828–60, established enduring forms and processes. The underlying tendency of the Democrats (the former Republicans) and the Whigs was to build national popularity by courting a majority of the popular vote in contests for the Presidency, embracing nearly all the states. The enlarged suffrage, the national nominating convention, perfected techniques of popular appeal (songs, marches, a partisan press and literature), the growth

The development of American major parties

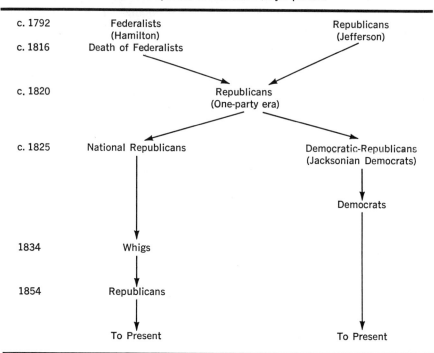

Source: Adapted from Thomas A. Bailey, *Democrats vs. Republicans: The Continuing Clash* (New York: Meredith Press, 1968), p. 36.

of state and local organizations that contributed vitally to national party nominations and campaigning, all fed into the development of national popular parties.

The third era, 1865 to the present, has extended earlier forms and adapted them to a changing political and social environment. Not essentially creative, the changes have been largely incremental. The urban boss and machine maximized earlier tendencies to loyalty and discipline. The Populist and Progressive political movements, 1896–1932, aimed to perfect the parties as the people's institutions by widely establishing the direct primary for nominating candidates. In the New Deal era and beyond, previously neglected groups —labor, blacks, the young and old—became objects of party solicitude. The advent of television enlarged the merchandising aspect of campaigning, elevated the public relations expert and the pollster, and downgraded the traditional party worker.[4]

Except for one interval, the United States has had a national competitive

---

[4] William Nisbet Chambers and Walter Dean Burnham, eds., *The American Party Systems: Stages of Political Development* (New York: Oxford University Press, 1967), 8–15.

two-party system. (From approximately 1816 to 1825, the Jefferson-founded Republicans were the sole national party.) The nature of key political institutions works powerfully to reinforce the two-party system. To win the Presidency, governorship, or mayoralty, it has proven better to have no more than two parties, because victory cannot be gained without a mighty concentration of forces. Unlike a multiparty cabinet, the Presidency cannot be parceled out among the parties. Groups obsessed with beliefs that are parochial, divisive, and irreconcilable are a common feature of multiparty countries. The impotence of such groups here has restricted minor parties to a modest role in the American system.

The major parties are elaborately decentralized, their power dispersed. From the national to local levels, they parallel the segments of the governmental system, and present, therefore, a federated rather than a hierarchical structure. Thus state parties do not legally control or remove incumbents of lower level party positions; their destiny is determined locally.

Party functions

As a central institution of both the political and social orders, the responsible party must perform a variety of functions vital to the daily life of a complex society. Some are "manifest" functions, tasks like electoral campaigning that the party consciously performs and on which its immediate success or failure depends. Simultaneously, the party provides "latent" or more indirect functions, byproducts of its manifest functions. In selecting candidates from its workers, for example, the party serves as a training school for future political leaders, certainly a serious function of a responsible party. In another perspective, the parties' functions are both political and nonpolitical. Their most distinctive political task, of course, is mobilizing voters behind candidates for election. But parties also respond to social need: the party club of the city and suburb nourishes the yearnings for gregarious endeavor.[5] It is a mark of the responsible party that it serves various social needs, promoting social integration and personal fulfillment.

If parties are to perform their functions responsibly, they must do so in a highly competitive environment, vying with one another, with minor parties, and with interest groups and other private organizations for citizen approval and support. Parties compete to mobilize money, skills, citizen concern, and manpower, all scarce commodities but imperative if they are to win the votes necessary for advancing their goals. There is, however, a dilemma for the responsible party. If it collects needed funds from oil millionaires, the heirs of automobile fortunes, and other moneyed people, or if the Rockefeller family spends nearly $4 million to reelect Nelson Rockefeller governor of New York, must not the party trim and bend its policies to the preferences

---

[5] Frank J. Sorauf, *Political Parties in the American System* (Boston: Little, Brown, 1964), 4.

of its financial angels? And to that degree is not a basic responsibility eroded—the framing and execution of party policy in accord with the will and aspirations of the mass of its supporters?

Managing social conflict. Responsible parties in a democracy contribute to maintaining orderly social processes in a mass society of peoples of different backgrounds, ways, and goals. Since they must seek broad support to obtain the majorities necessary to win the most prized offices, parties tend to shun extremists and polarizing acts. In outlook, party leaders are pragmatic, and their most common mood in conflict is restraint.

Thus the 1972 presidential candidacy of George McGovern faced the task, as American society itself did, of joining in common purpose a number of antagonistic groups. The strongest of tensions prevailed between organized labor and the middle class youth and minority coalition. Typically, labor prefers a meat-and-potatoes approach to politics; labor leaders seek candidates of dependable loyalty on legislative issues affecting labor interests, candidates who put domestic economic and social welfare questions ahead of "abstract" causes of civil rights, foreign affairs, and institutional reform. Therefore, many union chieftains viewed with disdain the causes of various groupings in the McGovern coalition—peace, amnesty, abortion, women's liberation. The chieftains prefer machine politicians whose behavior is more predictable and habituated to the processes of bargaining. The Democratic party regulars in the Northern states and cities share these perspectives. Likewise, the Democratic party's traditional ethnic base of Irish, Italians, Jews, and less numerous European ethnic groups incorporates socially conservative attitudes that are less than accepting of youths with long hair or of the newer styles of expressing love of country.

Despite these gaps of understanding and acceptance, the party had healing and binding resources. The disparate elements could be held together by the presidential candidate's skill in defining the issues, evoking broad commitment, and focusing the attack on the Nixon administration. The older ethnic groups might hold to the party as a symbol, an object of loyalty for one's lifetime. And there are the implicit rewards of electoral victory—the prospect of gaining desired programs and policies, jobs and power.[6] To the extent that the Democratic party failed at reconciliation, the Republican party awaited with blandishments for the disaffected to come into its camp, and it was prepared with formulas for the political integration of the newcomers with the older followers. Thus the 1972 Republican platform contained a labor plank, projecting a calculated appeal to organized labor; with Nixon's strong support, its toleration was forced on conservative elements of the party.[7]

But parties, within the limits of broad national consensus, perpetuate conflicts as well as subdue them. Such enduring issues of American politics as centralism versus federalism, private action and enterprise versus public

---

[6] William Shannon, "How New a Party?" *New York Times,* July 11, 1972.
[7] *New York Times,* August 18, 1972.

action, paternalism versus individualism, have been diligently cultivated by the parties over the decades, even the centuries. Parties and candidates are also watchful for issues that will provide the most promising agenda for debate or conflict for the next election. Witness the sudden emergence of the school busing issue in the 1972 elections and its emphasis in the primaries and platforms after a period of quiescence.

Even while exploiting their points of difference, parties manage to build and maintain consensus on public policies and methods, and they accept the broad terms of the capitalistic system. If party debate is viewed over a long period, a cycle is often apparent whereby one party proposes an innovative policy, and the other party resists; but in time it accepts, and the issue is muted by reconciliation. For example, much of Franklin Roosevelt's New Deal program met bitter Republican resistance, and in 1936 the party's presidential nominee, Alf M. Landon, even attacked the recently passed Social Security Act. In the 1940s and 1950s Republicans moved toward acceptance of most New Deal measures; a proud accomplishment of the Eisenhower Administration was the largest extension of Social Security coverage since the act's passage. Indeed, Eisenhower fell into the bad graces of the John Birch Society primarily because of his failure to repudiate any major part of the Democratic party's legislation enacted between 1932 and 1952.

Mobilizing the electorate. Democracy, with its stress on citizen involvement and participation and its dependence on a continuous supply of qualified candidates for office-holding, must rely on responsible parties in the electing function. Their near-monopoly of it is sanctioned by state laws, which define the parties almost entirely in terms of their electoral responsibilities. American parties concentrate on the electing function far more than most other parties in the world. The scheduling of party activities—conventions, committee meetings, delegate selection, and the like—is dominated by the election-year timetable.

The electing function is directed at fulfilling the democratic principle of governments based on the consent of the governed. This implies an opportunity for people to displace those governing them and substitute new rulers. Competitive parties are the chief instrument to give reality to the principle.

The parties take great pains in simplifying the electorate's choices. They winnow out the candidates for office and reduce the options of the voter to two, three, or a few choices, on a scale and in terms the average voter can understand. Ordinarily, the party's framing of choices is not arbitrary or imposed. Since the great bulk of voters have stable party preferences, politicians develop clear perceptions of the groups supporting them. By anticipating and meeting their needs, politicians seek to consolidate the support of core constituents of different purposes and interests. Since neither party can feel assurance about winning national elections, they are both equally attentive to groups whose loyalties seem to fluctuate or whose commitment to the opposing party is weak.

Democratic party workers "mobilize the electorate" for the McGovern campaign in 1972.

Elections can be won at all levels of government only by popular majorities. Parties can deliver majorities by curbing excessive divisions and uniting disparate elements in tenable partisan combinations. Nixon's appeal in 1972 was addressed to the suburbs, the South, noncollege youth, Jews, Italians, Poles, organized labor—a combination never before known to the Republican party, but whose common needs and interests were suddenly being defined with concern and commitment by Republican orators.

Constituting the government. The party that wins the election fills the offices of government. Partisan office-holders, legislative and executive, serve in a dual capacity, in public and party roles. Thus the President is both the leader of the nation and the head of his party; members of Congress function in the making of party policy as well as representing their constituents in making public legislation.

A traditional responsibility of parties is to staff the appointive offices of administration. In the nineteenth century, patronage (or spoils) was a flourishing party activity. One of the more persuasive inducements for a faithful party worker was the reward of appointment to an administrative or clerical post, sanctioned by the battle cry, "To the victor belong the spoils!" Although the rise of the merit personnel system has reduced federal spoils to a shadow of its former self, it still flourishes in many state and local governments. At all levels of contemporary politics, the party sees to it that faithful partisans garner many rewards and preferments from the administration's daily operations. The award of lucrative contracts, special treatment for party donors and workers, winking at illicit activity, favoritism in enforcing the law—these are commonplace means by which administration comes under the sway of party largess. Here the party, if it aspires to be responsible, is trapped in a dilemma. In the democratic formulation, the responsible party must reflect the will and aspirations of the great mass of people. But if it is to be in a position to meet this objective, the party needs money and workers, neither of which it can attract without incentives. In turn, the incentives may cramp the party's ability to represent mass opinion adequately.

At all levels of government, parties are recruiters for judicial posts. Twentieth-century Presidents have appointed between 80 and 95 percent of the judges they nominate from the ranks of their own party. Among those rewarded are former office-holders, valiant but unsuccessful candidates, hardy local supporters of the President, and the eagerly promoted favorite of a senator. (The Senate's advice and consent is necessary for judicial appointments.)

A historic responsibility of American parties is the defense of the federal system, which in late decades has been buffeted by strong trends toward centralization. Parties themselves are federal in structure, so they have a self-interested claim to arrange national programs along federal lines. Time and again, good party men in Congress will insist on large roles for state and local governments in the administration of new laws. State and local party organizations are built around state and local patronage, which, to be well preserved, requires recognition in national programs. To watchful party leaders, the state boundary is the largest optimal unit; all else beyond is ephemeral and unpredictable. President Eisenhower was right in observing that in the United States there are no national parties.

Providing program and policy. In the eyes of their critics, American parties fall shortest of the ideal of responsible organizations in their poor capacity to provide program and policy. Some critics attribute the parties' low policy output to the nature of the electoral process. Typically, the parties present few issues to the voters as referenda; instead, they deal in what has been called, "the behavior of numbers." [8] Astute party candidates appeal to clusters of opinion around a variety of issues and contrive "an artificial majority" necessary for victory. But it is only a numerical majority; it rarely constitutes a clear-cut mandate. In campaign discourse, the candidate stresses traditional attitudes and ideology and distinctions of his potential leadership. Electoral outcomes are therefore general rather than particular, barren of meaningful choice or voter influence on policy.

Behind the bland profile that the major parties normally present on policy

[8] E. E. Schattschneider, in Chambers and Burnham, 263.

stand several powerful realities of American society. With rare exception, American politics has been moderate politics, poor soil for nourishing ideological or major policy differences. Moderate politics is promoted by the wide diffusion of property, a large middle class, and a generous suffrage. The latter helps make government more balanced in its response to the different components of society. Social differences and conflicts have not been felt on a scale conducive to ideological parties.

The conflicts of American politics have rarely been vertical or class conflicts, but horizontal ones. In America, social and economic groups pursue differing goals and conflict with one another, but with a moderation that enables each to join in common cause with other groups at some expense to its own self-centered objectives. In Europe, on the other hand, the powerful class-oriented parties (for example, the Communist parties in France and Italy, and the Labour party in Britain) are usually unable to unite with parties oriented to a different class.

Franklin Roosevelt, exploiting the common interests of certain social and economic groups, could put together a Democratic coalition of the South, urban labor, racial and ethnic groups, which persisted through the 1940s, although it showed some weakening in the 1950s and 60s. Meanwhile, the Republicans maintained their own socioeconomic coalition of rural, Protestant, Anglo-Saxon, middle and upper class America. In the 1970s the appeal of Richard Nixon is essentially to these groups, whose visibility is heightened by their concentration in the suburbs. But in spite of these divisions the critics of parties argue that most of the time the parties are virtually indistinguishable in their ideological and policy positions.

A contrasting view, more approving of the party system, perceives significant differences between Republicans and Democrats. Thus the 1972 Democratic platform called for "immediate and complete withdrawal" of all U.S. forces in Indochina; amnesty for draft resisters; replacement of the welfare system with a guaranteed income plan of about $3,900 for a family of four; full employment with the government as employer of last resort; gradual tax reform; reduction in military spending; and enactment of a range of new social programs from day care to massive aid to the cities.

In contrast, the Republican platform supported President Nixon's terms for ending the Vietnam war, which allowed for its continuation, and it called for a strong defense establishment and rejected amnesty for war service resisters. Republicans opposed the principle of a guaranteed income. While the Democratic platform was silent on marijuana, the Republican opposed its legalization. The Democrats urged "federally funded and federally administered" health insurance, while the Republicans opposed "nationalized compulsory health insurance."

A perusal of other party platforms, actions of Presidents, and votes in Congress would reveal definable differences between the parties on civil rights, federal aid to education, medical care for the aged, regulation of labor-management relations, and other items on a lengthy list. A common element of the differences is the devotion of each party to certain idealized principles by which they evaluate programs or their parts. Thus Republicans tend toward decentralization of government activity, valuing state, local, and private action more than federal; a strict interpretation of the Constitution; a large role for private capital; a skeptical view of schemes for social equality. In contrast, modern Democrats are prone to centralization, promotion of social equality, a wider distribution of wealth, liberal interpretation of the Constitution. To the business executive or the ghetto resident, it does matter whether George McGovern or Richard Nixon is in the White House.

On controversial issues, the parties are apt to present a "center of gravity," clearly differentiating the policy preferences of Republican adherents from Democrats. One study found that among self-declared strong Democrats in the general adult population, those who thought government should "do more" for social welfare were almost four times as numerous as among strong Republicans. Those believing that government should do less were far more numerous among strong Republicans than strong Democrats. On the other hand, party differences were diminished by large numbers of both Republicans and Democrats who thought government was doing "about right." [9]

In the 1972 presidential campaign, Republican strategy (as well as Democratic) strongly focused on impressing voters that there were important and clear-cut differences between the parties and their candidates. The Republican platform charged that the rival party "has been seized by a radical clique which scorns our nation's past and would blight her future." On the Vietnam war, the platform said the United States should not perform an "act of betrayal" by overthrowing the Saigon government, and "we most emphatically say the President of the United States should not go begging to Hanoi." On the domestic side, the picture, according to the Republican platform, was one of sharp contrast. In the last Democratic administration (of Lyndon B. Johnson), "our horrified people watched our cities burn, crime burgeon, campuses dissolve into chaos." But after three and one-half years of Republican rule, the document stated, there was "a calmer sea, with a sure, steady hand at the helm." [10]

Parties as organizations

What the party is and what it can become, whether more responsible or not, depends critically on its nature as an organization. As a social unit the party consists of individuals who perform specific roles in a meaningful structure of interpersonal relations and communication channels. The party can also be visualized as a polity, a miniature political system, that distributes power, sets up authority structures, recruits leaders and workers, utilizes processes of representation, maintains electoral systems, defines goals, and resolves internal conflicts. How well or how badly these functions and processes are

[9] V. O. Key, Jr., *Politics, Parties & Pressure Groups,* 5th ed. (New York: Crowell, 1964), 217–18.
[10] *New York Times,* August 19, 1972.

performed goes far to determine how "responsible" parties are by democratic criteria.

Despite richness in organizational elements, the party differs significantly from that most highly structured of organizations, bureaucracy. While bureaucracy tends to depersonalization, strict observance of rules, discipline, and sanctions, the party is personalized, informal, and clientele-oriented.

Powerful environmental forces shape the parties—the nature of the political and constitutional system, political tradition and history, socio-economic conditions, the esteem accorded political work. Hence the federal governmental system provided for in the Constitution has fostered a federated party structure. High social mobility has avoided the monopolization of party offices and ranks by an aristocratic class, a tendency of European parties in less mobile societies. Party institutions, such as conventions and committee structures, are very much the product of history. In recruiting workers and candidates, parties have had to struggle against a strong vein of traditional social sentiment that disparages politics and views it as the refuge of second-raters and scoundrels.

The major parties exist in what is chiefly a competitive two-party system. The Presidency is a prize within the grasp of each party, the congressional electoral vote for each party tends to fall within the limits of 40 to 60 percent, and the states present mainly a two-party pattern. (The local party picture veers more sharply to one-party dominance.) Presumably, competition en-hances responsibility: the out-party acts as a watchdog over the performance of the in-party, and barks loudly at any lapses.

An unresolved question is whether party responsibility fares better in highly organized parties, or whether loose, even informal, organization affords better prospects. American parties are not easily classifiable under either alternative. Some political scientists feel that the party structure consists of numerous elites and sets of career classes that are highly differentiated in their self-consciousness. Others see the party as an open structure, marked by unstable tenure and uncertain personal relations among party associates. Power seems mercurial, quickly appearing and vanishing.

This disparity of views is also a sign of a dilemma that parties face. On the one hand, they must fulfill demands for "mobility" by providing op-portunities for the individual to rise quickly in influence and power. On the other hand, parties must provide "status" in order to attract leaders and workers, and this requires considerable stability in the allocations of power and functions. Adding to the strain is the voluntary character of the in-dividual's activity in the party. There are few real pressures the party can use to induce the individual to work under its banner. Likewise, the habit of parties to play down ideology tends to minimize the role of program and principles in drawing the individual into party activity.[11]

A comparison of the New York Democratic delegations to the national

[11] Samuel Eldersveld, *Political Parties: A Behavioral Analysis* (Chicago: Rand McNally, 1964), 10–12.

"Party membership is a matter of psychological attachment. . . ."

conventions in 1968 and 1972 illustrates the ebb and flow of power in parties. In 1968, the roster of New York delegates read like a "Who's Who" of the state party. But in 1972, more than 90 percent of the New York delegates were political unknowns even in the congressional districts they represented. Among those left out were the leaders of every county of metropolitan New York and the party leaders in the state legislature.[12]

If the criterion for a responsible party in mass democracy is that the party must adhere to a free and flexible membership policy, the American major parties measure up admirably. Membership is highly informal. There are no prescribed steps or tests by which one becomes a "Republican" or a "Democrat." An offer of work or money to the party of his choice will most likely be gladly accepted, unless he is an extremist, a Communist or a Bircher, whereupon he might not be welcomed. To vote in certain primaries, one must declare his affiliation with a given party, a simple act committed by the individual and subject to no serious review by the party. Chiefly, party membership is a matter of psychological attachment that ranges from the intense and enduring to the casual and transitory. Anyone imbued with the sense

[12] *New York Times,* July 4, 1972.

of belonging, or "party identification," tends to deem his party's cause his own. The forces prompting identification are not adequately known, although family influence is thought to be a large factor. Ordinarily, according to V. O. Key, Jr., 75 percent or more persons vote as their parents did. So absolute and blinding can partisan loyalty become that some voters may even act against their social or economic interests in order to be a true Republican or Democrat at all times.[13] An uncritical, blank-check tolerance may weaken the ability of the party to act responsibly, for blind devotion virtually empowers the party and its decision-makers to do anything they please.

Party organizations differ in cohesiveness, a quality that is a two-edged sword as far as responsibility is concerned. A tight-knit party, unified and disciplined, is more apt to get things done, to transform promises into policies. But these characteristics can be oppressive to another aspect of responsibility —the view that a party should be the channel through which various opinions are represented and expressed. Excessive unity can throttle that ideal.

Cohesiveness can be much affected by a variety of structural-functional factors. For example, greater cohesiveness is apt to be found when nominations are made by conventions rather than in a wide-open primary race. In a convention, conflicts may be worked out behind the scenes; compromises can be effected, bargains struck, and positions shifted, in quiet diplomacy. All these possibilities are barred in the typical primary, where conflict is open and public and therefore more difficult to manage by compromise.

To foster cohesion, to induce members and leaders to comply with party decisions, parties offer incentives and satisfactions—patronage and preferment, a political career, a boost to one's self-esteem, opportunities to influence policy-making, the thrill of a triumphant cause.

Finally, party organizations can be viewed as systems with layers of units —precinct, town or city, county, state, and nation, each more or less independently concerned with its own elections. Yet each higher level of organization normally values and seeks the cooperation of the next lower level or levels. This satisfaction cannot be evoked by command, but must be persuaded, whether by an attractive candidacy, a sense of common cause, or pragmatic inducements, such as the promised reward of office.[14] An important and uncertain question at the outset of McGovern's presidential candidacy was whether it could win the support of state and local leaders. The prospect at that point was unpromising. Mayor Richard Daley, whom the McGovern forces had denied a seat at the national convention, pledged support for all Democratic candidates but pointedly omitted mention of McGovern by name. Mayor Frank Rizzo of Philadelphia, a power in both city and state politics, pledged to do "everything in my power" to defeat McGovern. From New York Democratic leaders in the Bronx, Brooklyn, and Albany came signs that they would provide no real help. And in Texas, one of the most powerful of Democrats, John B. Connally, was soliciting support for Nixon among his

13 Key, 214.
14 Eldersveld, 9.

fellow party members. Concerning these defections a McGovern spokesman put on a brave face by declaring, in the fashion of Winston Churchill, "Mayor Rizzo's conversion to Republicanism, like Governor Connally's, has raised the intellectual level of both parties." [15]

The national party

It is difficult to see how a party can be responsible if it does not have a strong, effective national organization, yet on this standard the major parties are found wanting. An experienced politician has described the national organization of his party as "a loose affiliation of sovereign state parties, which meets as infrequently as possible, decides as little as possible, establishes no public policy whatsoever, but does manage to hold a convention every four years . . . [and] . . . raises fantastic sums of money." [16] In form, national party institutions have three parts: a national committee, a senatorial committee, and a congressional committee.

The contest for the Presidency is the most powerful force creating and maintaining a national party. That organization is made most visible by the national convention, which gathers every four years to nominate presidential and vice-presidential candidates and to adopt a national platform. Except for Congress, the convention is the one occasion when party members across the land are brought together.

Traditionally, each major party chooses delegates to its national convention by a complicated formula that acknowledges the state and local organizations as the foundations of the national party and that rewards the achievements of those organizations in recent elections. The 1972 Democratic National Convention introduced another ingredient in the sense that it sought to make the state delegations more representative of each state's population, an objective never entertained in the past. This shift in approach resulted from several Democratic reform studies, led by Senator George McGovern and Congressmen Donald Fraser of Minnesota and James O'Hara of Michigan. In effect the studies took the view that a responsible party should mirror the make-up of the population in its organization and deliberations. The reforms brought about important but by no means full achievement of these aspirations. These are some of the major changes evident in the 1,034 delegates to the 1972 Democratic convention:

• 358 delegates, or 34.6 percent, were women, three times the total for 1968, but well below the figure of 51 percent of the population that is female.

• 139 delegates were black, or 13.4 percent, which was double the 1968 figure. Since the total number of blacks was 9.2 percent of the national voting-age population, the McGovern guidelines were exceeded for blacks.

[15] *New York Times,* July 23, 1972.
[16] In Edward N. Costikyan, *Behind Closed Doors* (New York: Harcourt Brace Jovanovich, 1966), 153.

The Democratic National Convention included many women, blacks, and young people in 1972.

However, the Congressional Black Caucus had asked that 20 percent of the delegates be black, on the assumption that blacks provide that percentage of the Democratic vote.

• 239, or 23.1 percent, represented "youth," defined as thirty years of age or under. Of the voting age population nationally, about 31 percent are between the ages of eighteen and thirty.[17]

But the 1972 Democratic convention was unrepresentative in at least two major ways. The largest losers under the McGovern reforms, those who were underrepresented by the standards applied to other groups, were the white urban ethnics—Catholics mostly, but also Jews and Protestants. The pro-McGovern delegation of Illinois, for example, had only one Italian name and three Polish names among fifty-nine delegates. "Does that mean that only five percent of Chicago's voters are of Polish ancestry?" an observer asked. "If that were true a Republican would be mayor of Chicago."

In addition, the delegates who represented the young, blacks, and women were not typical of their groupings: they were more affluent and better educated. Thirty-nine percent of all the delegates held postgraduate degrees,

[17] *New York Times,* June 3, 1972.

Income distribution of convention delegates, 1972

Income level	Republican delegates	Democratic delegates	U.S. population
Under $5000	2%	5%	18%
5000-9999	5	10	32
10,000-14,999	13	20	27
15,000-25,000	28	31	18
Over $25,000	50	32	5

Source: *Washington Post,* August 19, 1972, p. A10.

compared with 4 percent of the population, and 31 percent had incomes over $25,000 a year, against 5 percent of the population. The black delegates had better incomes than the national norm for blacks: 19 percent had incomes over $25,000 and another 27 percent earned between $15,000 and $25,000.[18]

In addition to the delegates, the national convention includes an extended organizational structure. At the beginning of the convention, a slate of temporary officers is elected, the chief of whom is the temporary chairman who presides until the permanent organization is elected. By tradition, he makes the keynote address, an attempt to arouse the delegates with stirring themes. The convention also works through four major standing committees: Credentials, which hears challenges to the rights of delegations to sit and recommends a permanent roll of delegates to the convention; Permanent Organization, which recommends a set of permanent officers for the convention; Rules, which reports to the convention a body of rules to govern its proceedings; and Resolutions, which prepares a platform and presents it to the convention. Among the permanent officers is the permanent chairman, who, on election by the convention, replaces the temporary chairman as presiding officer.

A convention's real direction is apt to stem from an informal organization of bloc and factional leaders. A clearly dominant candidate may monopolize this organization. The 1972 Republican convention was dominated by Nixon forces in its major business of nominating candidates and adopting a platform. The McGovern forces had rather less sway at the Democratic convention, but they controlled the same outputs. The "control" of a convention is often qualified, however. The Nixon forces did not forestall a battle over the basis on which the delegates to the 1976 convention would be chosen, which found the larger, more liberal states arrayed against the smaller, more conservative states. And McGovern withheld pressing some further party reforms, in a desire not to deepen the disaffection of Democratic regulars, such as city and county leaders, who resisted them.

The oceans of oratory and behind-the-scenes buttonholing and maneuvering at the convention are directed to two great decisions: nominating the

[18] Michael Novak, "Three Myths of the McGovern Fantasy," *Newsday,* July 11, 1972.

candidates and adopting the platform. The latter is no tightly reasoned discourse on party principles, but a verbose declamation, more obfuscated than clear. Those in the political trade generally regard the platform cynically. Soon after his election, President Eisenhower was astonished when, on urging his congressional party brothers to rally behind the platform, he evoked only sardonic jest and counsel that such documents were not to be taken seriously. The denigration of platforms mirrors the frailty of parties as national organizations. Normally, the presidential nomination is a consensus emerging from previously contesting factions, and in which the party balances its need for appeal to the electorate with its own need for cohesion and vitality. Cohesion is sometimes beyond reach. At the Democratic convention of 1968, the anti-war group was dissatisfied, and in 1972, many party regulars were distressed.

In the four-year interval between national conventions, the agency acting for the national party is the national committee. The national committee members are chosen in each state by direct primary, by state party convention, by the state party committee, or by the state delegation to the national convention. The national committee provides direction for the presidential campaign, maintains the national headquarters, raises funds, conducts public relations, arranges for the next national convention, and fills vacancies on the national party ticket. The Democratic national committee performed this last function in 1972 when it named Sargent Shriver to replace Thomas Eagleton as the nominee for the Vice-Presidency. The committee's chief working executive is the national chairman, who often manages the presidential campaign, supervises the national headquarters, and pays off campaign debts. Although the national committee elects the chairman, he is virtually the hireling of the presidential candidate, from whom he takes his cues. In between campaigns, the chairman dispenses patronage, rallies support from the congressional party for the President's program, keeps the fires of party publicity high, and assists in the congressional elections. The chairman of the out-party, whose presidential candidate was defeated, typically faces a pile of unpaid bills, sagging party morale, and cantankerous factions displeased by defeat and ready to promote another candidate, whose nomination usually leads to his own replacement.

Each house of Congress has its own party organization, the senatorial and congressional campaign committees. Independent of the national committee, they are accountable to their respective legislative bodies.

At the national level, the party picture is one of dispersed power. State and local leaders go their own way, run their own shows, write their own rules, and, most of the time, treat the national committee with contempt. A similar indifference marks senators and representatives. Legislators deem their own organizations necessary as protection against the national committee's neglect.

The significance of the McGovern reforms is that they may soon shatter the American tradition of non-national parties. The 1972 convention reforms that were adopted move in that direction. As a first step, the national committee was trebled in size to include grassroots representatives, as well as certain party leaders, such as state chairmen, members of Congress, and governors. A second step calls for the new national committee to appoint a reform commission to prepare a new party charter and provide for restructuring of the party along even more national lines. In 1974, the committee is to call a national party conference for the adoption of the charter.[19] The continued progress of these moves may have been adversely affected by McGovern's defeat in 1972, despite the success of other parts of the Democratic ticket. And much will depend on whether the reforms become the basis of a genuine, broadly inclusive national party. They will not be if 1972 proves to have been an exclusive revolution, whereby the voices so long shut out in the past will now shut out those who had barred them from political power—the party regulars, for example, in the states and localities. However, the structural reforms themselves, the methods of delegate selection that stress principles of democratic representation, and the more popular emphasis of the party should endure in large degree. So seasoned an observer as Lawrence O'Brien, former national chairman, has said: "Never before has a political body so totally changed its way of doing business. There will be no turning back." [20]

State party politics

The tests of party responsibility must be applied to the state party organizations—they possess impressive power in their own right and they support the state governments, which in a federal system enact many policies with far-reaching effects.

The state parties cannot be envisioned as mere miniatures of the national structure, for they have sufficient resources and autonomy to work outside the national party and often in ways different from the two-party system. Nevertheless, there are ties and interactions between the two systems. Over decades, a correspondence appears in the fluctuations of state and national party fortunes (except in states with strong one-party structures).[21]

At the top of the formal structure in each state is the state committee, which ranges in size from a handful to a crowd, and whose authority varies widely. The state committee chairman is apt to enjoy the same close ties to the gubernatorial candidate as the national chairman does to the presidential candidate. The basic power-units of state politics are the county and city parties. In actuality, the state party is a loose union of these local parties, and the county chairmen and the local bosses act as the principal power-holders. Something of the potential strength of these local organizations is

[19] Clayton Fritchey, "Democrats to Start Becoming a National Party," *Newsday,* July 14, 1972.
[20] *New York Times,* July 13, 1972.
[21] V. O. Key, Jr., *American State Politics* (New York: Knopf, 1956), 34–47.

Organizational pattern of the major parties

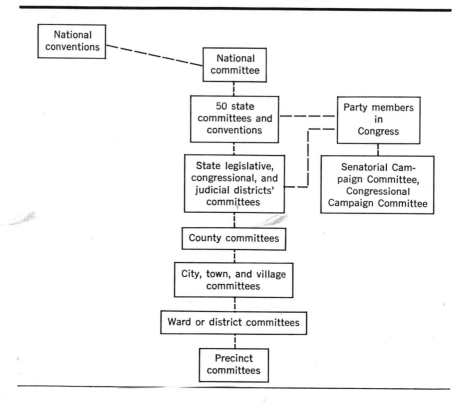

suggested by the comment of Joseph Cerrell, Hubert Humphrey's 1972 campaign manager in California: "The Democratic organization in this state is not worth a damn. There is more organization in one ward of Philadelphia than in all of California." [22]

Many state organizations violate any reasonable criterion of fair representation in party decisions and in the allocation of party resources. As the preserve of white middle and upper classes, they present a distorted picture, leaving out blacks, youth, the poor, and other categories of the less powerful. In the 1972 elections in Pennsylvania, for example, black Democratic workers in the industrial town of Homestead complained that their state and local parties provided little political activity in the slums, that the black community was being ignored. The black workers felt that candidates were trying to minimize the money they spent for black votes and were taking black voters for granted. "I tried to get more materials, like buttons and placards, to pass out and put up," a black worker said, "but headquarters hasn't sent them to me." [23]

The pattern of competitive two-party politics that prevails at the national

[22] *New York Times,* May 22, 1972.
[23] *New York Times,* April 16, 1972.

level is not generally duplicated in the states, where the structure of party systems is diverse. It will hardly comfort those friends of democracy who value competition as the key to responsible parties to learn that only half the states have competitive two-party systems. One standard for testing the presence of a competitive system is the popular vote for Democratic and Republican candidates for governor. If the vote usually hovers around a 50–50 dividing point, a competitive two-party system is deemed to exist. But if the vote divides extremely—say, 80 to 20—then the system is in effect one-party.[24]

In the competitive systems, the outcome of the state-wide election is often unpredictable, and the decisive electoral choices are made between parties rather than between rival leaders of factions of a single party. Both factors contribute to more responsible parties. If election outcomes are uncertain, candidates must be more attentive to voter needs and attitudes. And elevating the importance of parties relative to leaders, competition fosters the development of more enduring party principles and commitments to programs and policies. This kind of product of a broad consensus does not evolve as easily when politics is uncompetitive and the preserve of factional leaders. In that case politics is more personalized, more the mirror of the idiosyncracies of a string of passing leaders. But party competition is difficult to maintain since its presence depends on a web of factors. Among other things, it requires at least two complexes of divergent interests, which may embrace social, economic, geographic, ethnic, and religious factors. A common basis of division is the rural-urban rivalry, although this division is not always clear-cut; for example, urban-industrial wage earners may oppose propertied groups, both urban and rural. In the Northeast, the urban-rural cleavage may sometimes mask ethnic rivalries.[25] Not all differences serve democracy. What is important, however, is the opportunity to express differences and to make choices, basic elements of a democratic party system.

One-party states also have a kind of competition, the competition of factions. The factional systems of one-party states follow two distinct patterns —bifactional and multifactional. Some one-party states have a bifactional structure. For instance, in Democratic Mississippi, one faction, "the regulars," is white-dominated and the other faction, "the loyalists," is predominantly black. The regulars, headed by Governor William L. Waller, control state offices and state party machinery, but the loyalists are recognized by the national Democratic party. A decided push in 1972 for "unity" between the two factions was attributed to the need for a sixth-term candidacy of party regular Senator James O. Eastland. Facing a prospective challenge to his seniority rights and therefore to his chairmanship of the Judiciary Committee when the Senate convened in 1973, he could strengthen his position by having a unified party back home. The Democratic national committee, too, pressed for unity, so that Mississippi might be restored to the Democratic column in presidential elections. These Mississippi circumstances reveal the often tenuous nature

---

[24] Key, *American State Politics,* 286.
[25] Allan P. Sindler, *Political Parties in the United States* (New York: St. Martin's Press, 1966), 35–36.

of one-party factional competition—its vulnerability to the personal career needs of politicians, to guile and maneuver, and to the pressures of external forces.[26]

A one-party system may also have a multifactional structure, in which three or more groupings of politicians and their supporters back separate candidates. Florida, Arkansas, and Mississippi are among the states that illustrate this pattern. Typically, the factions are transitory groupings, whose guidelines for the voters remain blurred and whose implications for policy are unclear. There are occasional unpleasant side effects of multi-factionalism. It may induce demagoguery, or crude emotional appeals to the voters' prejudices and fears. And where the Constitution limits the governor to a single short term, it may result in a pattern of limited responsibility to party, obsession with manipulating influence and resources to sustain legislative and administrative backing, little incentive for policy planning, and temptation to use office for private gain.[27]

Some state parties have long been the focus of efforts to make them more democratic. The chief means relied on to bring about this transformation is the direct primary, a reform promoted by the Progressive movement and widely adopted in the early twentieth century. Presumably the people, instead of party bosses ensconced in smoke-filled rooms, determine the nominees. The direct primary was expected to make the parties more responsible in the sense that they would reflect voter preferences more directly and accurately. Unfortunately, the democratic dream has only been half-realized. Despite decades of primaries, boss-dominated parties remain, but they must be more solicitous of party members' views concerning nominations than they were in pre-primary days. Moreover, organization candidates must run the hazard of a primary fight, and frequently they fail.

Local party politics

"It is a serious matter," the French political scientist Maurice Duverger wrote of the United States, "that the greatest nation in the world, which is assuming responsibilities on a worldwide scale, should be based on a party system entirely directed towards very narrow local horizons." [28]

For the local party, the lowest and basic layer is the precinct, a party-defined subunit of a city. It is led by a captain or a committeeman, elected variously by caucus, convention, or direct primary, or appointed by higher authority. In larger cities, the next higher level is the ward or district, presided over by a leader and embracing several precincts. From these units, city councilmen or legislators are elected. The next higher level is the city or county committee, composed of precinct executives or their representatives,

[26] *New York Times,* June 12, 1972.
[27] Sindler, 31–35.
[28] In Demetrios Caraley, *Party Politics and National Elections* (Boston: Little, Brown, 1966), 227.

a major unit of the party machinery. In large cities such as New York or Chicago, the city organization far exceeds the county in superior resources and important offices, and is therefore the chief local unit. In most local areas, however, the county commands the resources to dominate local politics. The county organization not only participates in the selection of county officials, but may also contribute to the election of state legislators and congressmen. Often a political potentate, the county chairman links the county to the state organization and derives force from having under his command the great army of party workers who get out the vote. Party committees may also be established for state legislative, congressional, and judicial districts. Local parties are stronger and more cohesive than national and state parties. A mighty contributor to this strength is the frequency of one-party domination in county and city, even when the state is competitive.

In recent decades, powerful social forces have drastically changed local politics, particularly city politics. Between the Civil War and the New Deal, every big city had a party machine at one time. Typically, these party machines had a leader or "boss," who may have been the mayor or a nonofficeholder who wielded power behind the scenes. The machine controlled legislative, judicial, and administrative offices, and provided lower class voters with primitive welfare services—food and fuel to the poor, turkeys at Thanksgiving, personalized help for people tangled in the law, and political socialization. In return for these acts of "friendship," the machine solicited votes, particularly in the primaries, where machine leaders sought reelection. Despite their attentiveness to the people, the machines were a perversion of democracy, the antithesis of the responsible party. They thrived when voters placed a lower value on their votes than on the favors of the machines. Typically such a voter was little interested in issues and candidates.

After the New Deal, machines began to decline as government took over welfare activities, and per capita incomes and education levels rose during and after the war. The middle class, a constituency in which machines do not thrive, burgeoned. Many of the old-style machines dwindled away, while a few successfully adapted to their changing environment. One of the more conspicuous survivors is the Chicago machine of Mayor Richard J. Daley.

Some local organizations still busily perform services to recruit voters. A study of New Jersey precinct leaders found that they got work for the unemployed and poor, helped citizens victimized by rent gouging, got a neighborhood a traffic light, provided draft counselling to young men. Many contemporary organizations are still held together by rewards, influence, discipline, and ties to the community, despite the disclaimer of Meade H. Esposito, a New York City county leader, that "we're keeping this organization together with spit. There's no patronage." All but four of Esposito's twenty-three district leaders held state or municipal jobs like sanitation inspector, law assistant in Surrogate's Court, and deputy county clerk. A kind of career line, with movement from lesser to better jobs (judgeships, receiverships, guardianships), fosters discipline.[29]

[29] *New York Times,* June 1, 1970.

In those cities that have undergone changes, does city politics fill more adequately the criteria of responsible democratic party politics? One gain is represented by the decline of the machine boss. Typically he was a shadowy figure who ruled behind the scenes, luring voters with small favors while giving large rein and generous enrichment to selected businessmen, and keeping controversial local issues out of public discussion. In contemporary city politics, the old boss has generally been replaced by the public office-holder who is also the political leader: Robert Wagner and John Lindsay of New York, David Lawrence of Pittsburgh, and Kevin White of Boston. Today's big city mayor is often identified with the good government or reform tradition that flourished earlier in the century, and he aligns himself against political machines, fellow political leaders, and even the parties. To the good fortune of responsible party politics, he publicly discusses serious issues and develops programs addressed to significant local needs.

In the cities, as at the other levels of government, the nature of party organization is affected by governmental structure. Some cities, such as Chicago, Cleveland, and Los Angeles, choose the city council or legislature according to a district system, while other cities (Boston, Cincinnati, and San Francisco), elect councilmen-at-large—that is, by city-wide vote. The small district system tends to highlight the neighborhood and is responsive to the needs of ethnic groups composing it.[30] Neither system is clearly superior to the other when measured against the standards of responsible party politics. Both the neighborhood and the city as a whole are valid units of democratic representation, and it is arguable that a dual structure is more democratic than an absolute choice of one or the other.

Realization of the concept of the responsible party on the local level is hampered by the circumstance that metropolitan politics is the stronghold, if not the captive, of the Democratic party. Democratic organizations dominate the big cities, and in recent decades mayors and other city leaders have played important roles in national Democratic affairs. Likewise, the metropolitan centers have contributed significantly to Democratic presidential victories. The suburbs, in which most of the population is concentrated, are heavily Republican. But the suburban pattern has more variety, more division between Republicans and Democrats.

Party leaders
and workers

The standard party figures—the politician seeking office, the party leader waging the campaign, the party worker charged with getting out the vote— give life and substance to mass democracy. Their values, skills, and aspira-

[30] Edward C. Banfield and James Q. Wilson, *City Politics* (Cambridge: Harvard University Press, 1966), 123–24.

tions enable parties to function responsibly. Who are these vital figures? Do their own recruitment, purposes, and needs in undertaking political work harmonize with democratic ideals?

In a study of Republican and Democratic district and precinct chairmen in the Detroit metropolitan area, Samuel Eldersveld found that in neither party were these bodies of leaders "closed" social cliques. Rather, these leaders had assorted backgrounds, suggesting the parties had readiness of access. Although both groups had the same general social class orientation (middle class), they were familiar with lower class conditions through direct experience or the backgrounds of their fathers, who were factory workers, truck drivers, millhands, and machinists. Precinct leaders were even more diverse in social origins and status.

Presumably democracy is better served if the world of the party leader or worker is not excessively narrow in its associations, but reflects the diversity of society. Again, Eldersveld's findings are reassuring. Precinct captains were asked to identify the three people they "have worked with most closely in politics." More than one-third of the Republican respondents listed political associates from other occupational classes, and 60 percent of the Democratic blue collar leaders had white collar political associates, all indicative of "cross occupational" political relationships. Neither party had raised rigid occupational barriers.

Democracy is ill served if the party substructure is the pliable instrument of a self-serving elite. The study did not reveal the presence of a calculating elite of district leaders recruiting a corps of like-minded precinct leaders committed to maintaining the elite in power. The great majority of the precinct leaders interviewed had some self-generating reason for entering politics. For most party leaders and workers, the motivations were multiple, a synthesis of personal and impersonal interests.

The motivations that bring leaders and workers into party endeavor affect the possibilities of attaining responsible parties. If motivations are personal and self-interested, for example, the individual will be less prone to stress program and policy and less likely to commit himself to them. Generally, the Detroit study revealed that party leaders and workers have complex and multiple motivations. The motives of over two-thirds of the precinct workers studied were found to have changed after they began party work, and commonly personal goals and group goals, as perceived by party leaders, did not coincide. Social friendships and rewards and other personal satisfactions were the most important goals for precinct activists, including those who had arrived in top elite positions. Although they may have started out as idealists in the responsible party image, they soon came to expect personal satisfactions, which many cited in justifying their continuation in party work.[31]

Were the party people responsive to a predominant power orientation of the party? Or did they set idealistic goals? At the lower echelons, it was found, a large minority was not clearly conscious of the party as a power group. But

[31] Eldersveld, 50–55, 66–67, 242–43, 302.

party leaders revealed more consciousness of party power goals than did the general public. Republicans, a minority party in the Detroit area, rationalized their existence in other than power terms, and Republican precinct leaders tended to perceive their tasks as idealistic. In the more competitive precincts, the recognition of power goals increased.

Proposals

The 1970s have been and promise to continue to be an era in which party structuring and functioning are critically examined, leading to alterations in accord with the concept of a "responsible party." Both major parties have established study or reform committees. Although the important changes that have followed have occurred only in the Democratic party, much remains to be done to carry out proposals advanced in both parties. Here, gathered from some of the unfulfilled proposals, are guidelines for responsible parties for the 1970s.

1. The responsible party is conceived as one that is *representative* of the variety of society, the powerless as well as the powerful. As noted, neither party even approaches fulfillment of this concept. In both 1972 national conventions, women made sharp gains in representation, but they still fall well short of their percentage of the total population. Representation of blacks has markedly improved in the Democratic party but far less so among Republicans. Youth remains underrepresented in both parties.

A large agenda of unfinished business for improving representation in the Democratic party awaits action, owing to the postponement of reforms urged by the McGovern forces at the 1972 convention. Among them are:

• the expansion of party committees at all levels of party organization to include the so-called grassroots voters, particularly those traditionally left out of party deliberations (women, youth, blacks, Puerto Ricans, Chicanos, and the poor).

• a similar effort to improve the representation of such groups in party positions. Thus the McGovern reform plan calls for the selection of a woman as chairman of the 1976 national convention, with the position rotating between the sexes thereafter. The plan also proposes the creation of four co-chairman positions—both for the convention and its committees in 1976—representing blacks, youth, and other minorities.

• preferential presidential primaries to reflect the divisions of sentiment among party voters. More precisely, the plan calls for the abolition of winner-take-all primaries in 1976, the kind that enabled McGovern in 1972 to capture all 271 of California's delegate votes, even though he secured only 43 percent of the popular votes in the primary. The reforms also call for the abolition of crossover voting by Republicans in Democratic primaries, an arrangement that can distort primary outcomes.[32]

On the Republican side, the most sweeping reforms of representation have been proposed by an *ad hoc* congressional group, led by Congressman Thomas F. Railsback of Illinois, which looks to representation in the national convention of "all segments of the voting population," but rejects the concept of quotas.[33]

2. The contemporary reform proposals visualize the responsible party as one that permits broad, meaningful *participation* at all party levels and in every degree of party decision. Among the unfinished items on the McGovern reform agenda are these:

• stripping state chairmen and elected officials of much of their power and channeling decision-making generously to the reconstituted, more representative party committees and councils.

• creation of a special fund within the national party to subsidize the expenses of poor persons at national conventions or party councils.

• an exploration of the feasibility of holding the 1976 national convention on the campus of a large university so that needy delegates could use dormitory rooms and cafeterias.[34]

3. The responsible party, based on adequate standards of representation and participation, would be restructured to function better as a *policy-making* body. Here the most sweeping recommendations for change are made in a study by the Committee on Political Parties of the American Political Science Association. Impressed that "it is no longer safe for the nation to deal piecemeal with issues that can be disposed of only on the basis of coherent programs," the study calls for parties that will "provide the electorate with a proper range of choice between alternatives of action." Among other things, the study urged that national party platforms be adopted every two years and contain formulations of national principles to which all

[32] *New York Times,* June 25, 1972.
[33] *New York Times,* August 10, 1972.
[34] *New York Times,* June 25, 1972.

party candidates for public office at any level of government would be expected to adhere.[35]

But the framing of programs and the offering of choices must satisfy a competing, and sometimes contradictory, function of the responsible party, namely the task of keeping political differences within manageable bounds by reducing conflict and extracting consensus. "The accomplishment of party government," Pendleton Herring has written, "lies in its demonstrated ability for reducing warring interests and conflicting classes to cooperative terms." [36] Often platforms that appear evasive or inconsistent are in reality expressions of the compromise and consensus that enable clashing interests to live together in peace.

4. The concept of the "responsible party" might well be seen not merely in policy-making but also in a traditional function: as a link between administrative bureaucracy and the people. The genius of the bygone machine was that it humanized government in its dealings with the illiterate, the poor, the new Americans. In our presumably more sophisticated age, our parties, as Theodore Lowi has suggested, might forge a balance among the specialized bureaucracies, convey the people's feelings and needs to them, and communicate to the people the limitations bureaucracies struggle with. Parties could explain why the bureaucracy cannot do some things immediately, as well as when, possibly, they can be done—all for the sake of lessening public frustration and preventing the buildup of explosive public resentment. Lowi has called for a "new type of party machine composed of responsible partisans ... to help govern" the bureaucracies.[37] A vital task of the new party machine would be to inject again a humane element into bureaucratic dealings with the citizen.

Suggested Reading

Banfield, Edward C., and Wilson, James Q., *City Politics* * (Harvard University Press, 1966). Contains perceptive chapters on city party organizations and functioning.

Chambers, William Nisbet, and Burnham, Walter Dean, eds., *The American Party System: Stages of Political Development* (Oxford University Press, 1967). An analysis of the development of the American two-party system and its relationship with the social and political systems. Examines the functions and organizations of the parties and the tendencies to democratization.

Committee on Political Parties of the American Political Science Association, *Toward a More Responsible Two-Party System* (Holt, Rinehart and Winston, 1950). Advocates more disciplined, more centralized, and more program-oriented parties in the United States. This report is still the leading statement of this view.

---

[35] Committee on Political Parties, American Political Science Association, *Toward a More Responsible Two-Party System* (New York: Holt, Rinehart and Winston, 1950).

[36] Pendleton Herring, *The Politics of Democracy* (New York: Holt, Rinehart and Winston, 1940), 132.

[37] In Costikyan, 362.

Costikyan, Edward N., *Behind Closed Doors: Politics in the Public Interest* * (Harcourt Brace Jovanovich, 1966). An insider's account of the workings of New York City's politics, including primaries, campaigns, and functions of local political leaders. The author is a reform Democrat and former party leader.

David, Paul T., Goldman, Ralph M., and Bain, Richard C., *The Politics of National Party Conventions* * (The Brookings Institution, 1960). A thorough examination of national party conventions from a historical perspective, with emphasis on the role conventions play in the party system.

Duverger, Maurice, *Political Parties: Their Organization and Activity in the Modern State* * (Wiley, 1955). In this comparative analysis of parties in various countries Duverger, a French political scientist, explores the organization of different types of parties and their relationship to the electoral system.

Eldersveld, Samuel J., *Political Parties: A Behavioral Analysis* * (Rand McNally, 1964). An empirical study of local party organization in the Detroit area.

Hofstadter, Richard, *The Idea of a Party System* * (University of California Press, 1969). An analysis of the origins and development of key ideas concerning parties. Considers the functions of parties, including those of an opposition party. The treatment concentrates on the era of the Constitution's beginning and on the Jacksonian period.

Key, V. O., Jr., *American State Politics* (Knopf, 1956). Analysis of the American state party systems—types, organizations, and uses.

Key, V. O., Jr., *Politics, Parties, and Pressure Groups,* 5th edition (Crowell, 1964). The most thorough analysis available of American political parties. Analyzes party organization and processes, relations between parties and voters, and the role of parties in the governmental system.

Mandate for Reform, Report of the Commission on Party Structure and Delegate Selection to the Democratic National Convention * (Democratic National Committee, 1970). Presents specific proposals for reform for selecting delegates to the Democratic National Convention. Many of the proposals were used in the 1972 convention.

Saloma, John S., III, and Sontag, Frederick H., *Parties: The Real Opportunity for Effective Citizen Politics* (Knopf, 1972). A study of the major parties on the national, state, and local levels; examines strengths and weaknesses, successes and failures of the party system. Considers alternative ways of restoring control of political process to citizen voters and makes proposals to infuse new energy into the traditional party structure.

Sindler, Allan P., *Political Parties in the United States* * (St. Martin's Press, 1966). An overview of the American party system. Offers criteria for determining the presence of a competitive two-party system.

Sorauf, Frank, *Party Politics in America* (Little, Brown, 1968). A comprehensive analysis of American parties. Deals with their organization, electoral function, relationship to supporters in the electorate, and impact on government.

* Available in paperback edition

7

free
elections:
the American
voter

Not only is John Gardner, the philosopher-activist, distressed by the state of the major political parties, he is disenchanted with that hero of democratic theory, the average voter. Of that genre, Gardner, writing in 1970, observed,

> They are earning higher wages or salaries than ever before, buying more consumer goods, enjoying longer and more elaborate vacations—yet they defeat school bond issues, neglect elementary civic duties, allow their local government to fall into disrepair, nurse their prejudices—and complain. And grow fatter. They are angry at the way things are going but they will not help them get better.[1]

This picture of the voter as an indifferent prodigal son is at odds with more traditional and more optimistic assessments. According to the happier vision, every man is politically relevant and participates with reasonable willingness in the political system. He both contributes to and derives benefits from it. Major groups left out of the system wage arduous struggles to become genuine participants. The most recent effort has been made by blacks, who have assumed that their best potential asset, the means to a better life, is the vote. But this was no new action theory, for at one time or another all the great "underdog" groups in American experience—workers, farmers, immigrants—have used the vote in their struggle to overcome economic hardship, political deprivation, and low social status.

John Stuart Mill, the nineteenth-century English philosopher, idealized the vote in his essay *On Liberty*. To Mill, the vote was the climax of free public discussion, in which opinions on common affairs were expressed and criticized as steps toward the discovery of "truth." Unlike mathematics, "where there is nothing at all to be said on the wrong side of the question,"

---

[1] In Edward P. Morgan, "Are Americans Apathetic or Without Leadership?," *Newsday,* September 9, 1970.

on public issues "there is always some other explanation possible of the same facts." [2]

Discussion can simplify the voter's task by directing his attention only to those matters requiring choice or resolution. In Mill's view, the human faculties of perception, judgment, and moral preference can, by their nature, be exercised only in the making of choices. Choice-making has the important by-product of sharpening one's discernment of what is best, and, like muscles, that faculty improves with use. To Mill, choice-making, or its variant, voting, was nothing less than a key for man to other ways of life, each altogether different. "He who lets the world, or his own portion of it, choose his plan of life for him," wrote Mill, "has no need of any other faculty than the apelike one of imitation." [3]

Democracy's view of the voter

Since, in democratic lights, every man is politically relevant, resourceful democratic nations provide means for the citizen to act. The quickest and most convenient means of participation is the vote. The vote makes the ordinary citizen influential; it permits him to share in the most fundamental decisions of determining who shall govern and toward what ends. In contrast, the totalitarian dictatorship, while sometimes endowing the citizen with the vote, does not permit effective choice between opposing candidates and competing policy platforms. In the totalitarian state, the individual is a "participant subject" rather than an influential citizen. [4]

In democracy, the vote links government with the mass will. An election is the legitimate, orderly expression of popular preference—a systematic demonstration of the consent of the governed to public policies and the conduct of government. Electorates, looking back on the recent performance of governing elites, can choose to keep them in office or throw them out and install a new roster.

Elections may sometimes take a part in deciding policies, but more often they decide who the deciders shall be. In a nation as geographically extended as the United States and as socially diversified in ethnic, occupational, and regional characteristics, expressions of consent must be generalized rather than specific. There are definite boundaries between what voters can and cannot do. They cannot themselves initiate, prepare, and perform policy of some complexity. They cannot themselves govern. But this is to speak of elections only as a direct source of decision-making. Many a decision taken in the political

---

[2] John Stuart Mill, *On Liberty,* in Ernest Rhys, ed., *Utilitarianism, Liberty, and Representative Government: John Stuart Mill* (New York: Dutton, Everyman's Library, 1936), 96–97.

[3] *Ibid.,* 116–17.

[4] Gabriel A. Almond and Sidney Verba, *The Civic Culture* (Princeton: Princeton University Press, 1963), 4–5.

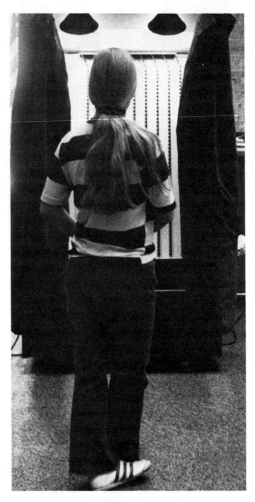

"The vote makes the ordinary citizen influential...."

system, in the legislature and by the executive, may be indirectly affected by elections. Once in office, elected officials are apt to weigh their decisions and policies for their likely impact on the voters in the next election.

In the American democratic system there is a pluralism of voting opportunities. No single election is a closed, self-contained enterprise. The voter, displeased by both major parties' candidates for President, can support candidates for other offices, such as senators or congressmen, whose policy outlooks are more agreeable to his own.

The voter presumably embodies several crucial virtues of democratic man. Since voting is an aggregate or mass process, the voter must be able to share values with others, and he must incorporate a multi-valued rather than a single-valued orientation. Without these capacities in the voter, the major parties could not function as agencies hospitable to the political brokers and compromisers who can weld diverse groups of people and values into a single cohesive force.

Theorists like John Locke and Jean Jacques Rousseau portray the citizen as essentially rational. To be sure, the Founding Fathers took a more reserved view of political man's rationality, but their contemporary, Tom Paine, perceived him to be under the influence "of reason and principle." With Paine, other theorists have visualized the citizen as voting in accord with sets of values or principles, whether conceived vaguely or humanely or in cold calculated self-interest. The voter was not seen as vacuous, indifferent, ignorant, or corrupt.

Voting and
the political culture

Voting is not an isolated, autonomous act. It is meshed with other elements of political life. Whether or not the voter will exercise his franchise, share in political discussion, or lapse into apathy, depends vitally on the political culture. That political culture embraces the voter's psychological orientation toward political objects—toward candidates, campaigns, issues, voting—which is crucial to his decision to vote or not. His "cognitive orientation" includes his knowledge and beliefs about the political system, about its roles, its incumbents, and its inputs and outputs. His "affective orientation" refers to his feelings about the political system and its elements. And his "evaluational orientation" embraces judgments and opinions about political objects, combining value standards and criteria with information and feelings. Data from a comparative study of "system affect" (attitudes toward the political system) among many nations afford reassurance for students of American politics. Queried whether they took national pride in some features of their government or political tradition, such as the Constitution, democracy, or political freedom, 85 percent of the Americans responded affirmatively, compared with 46 percent for the United Kingdom and 7 percent for West Germany.[5]

To flourish, the voter must live in a political atmosphere receptive to expressions of opposing viewpoints. Surroundings that are menacing rather than tolerant will suppress partisan feeling and genuine voter participation. To expend political energy and interest on the scale necessary for democracy, the voter needs the spur of a political culture of approving, widely held perceptions, beliefs, and norms.

Above all, the political culture can provide a sense of civic competence, indispensable for the maturing of the effective voter. As was mentioned in Chapter 1, the citizen who believes he has some influence over political decisions is more apt to use it. He is receptive to political communications and likely to initiate them. Studies reveal that compared with the citizen whose feeling of competence is low, the self-confident citizen is likely to be a more

[5] *Ibid.,* 102.

active partisan and voter, more satisfied with his political role, more committed to democratic values and ways.[6]

Who is the voter?

America's "middle voter" was identified at the outset of the seventies as "a forty-seven-year-old housewife from the outskirts of Dayton, Ohio, whose husband is a machinist." She is white, middle class, a high school graduate, with a family income of $8,622. Her brother-in-law is a policeman. She "is afraid to walk the streets alone at night," has "a mixed view about blacks and civil rights, because before moving to the suburbs she lived in a neighborhood that became all black"; she lacks the money to move if her new neighborhood deteriorates, and she "is deeply distressed that her son is going to a community college where LSD was found on the campus." [7]

This seemingly precise description should not deceive us into believing that the American voter is an uncomplicated political animal, easily explained. Any serious effort to fathom his mind and political habits must burrow through an extended labyrinth.

Group characteristics. From one perspective, the voter can be understood as a participant in a variety of group life: the family, his occupation or work group, the voluntary groups he belongs to, and his local community. Many citizens lean heavily on "opinion leaders" within these groups for guidance in voting. Voting studies disclose a high degree of family homogeneity in political attitudes and voting. Husbands and wives tend to be in blissful agreement in casting their ballots. According to a study, only one marital pair in twenty-two disagreed, and among parents and children, one pair in twelve disagreed.[8] Today that high consensus figure is weakened among the college-youth sector by disruptive issues such as the Vietnam war and shifts toward more self-determination in life styles. But youth also includes non-college youth who outnumber college youth and are less affected by these forces. On the eve of the 1968 elections, a Gallup poll disclosed that young people under thirty were more hawkish on the Vietnam war than people over fifty.[9]

The same sort of agreement prevails between the voter and his other close associates. He tends to vote the way his friends do and, to a lesser degree, his co-workers. Because the individual is apt to vote like others of his socioeconomic status, his social environment tends to be politically homogeneous. Most voters, therefore, lead lives of extraordinary political stability. Born into a Republican or Democratic family, the voter chooses as his spouse and friends

[6] *Ibid.*, 230–40, 257.
[7] In Richard M. Scammon and Ben J. Wattenberg, *The Real Majority* (New York: Coward-McCann, 1970), 71.
[8] Eugene Burdick and Arthur J. Brodbeck, *American Voting Behavior* (New York: Free Press, 1959), 57.
[9] Scammon and Wattenberg, 49.

persons whose views harmonize with his political heritage. By its very nature, a group assumes the sharing of common goals and characteristics. Conformity with the political opinions of the group rewards the individual with group acceptance and liking.

Are voting habits, then, so very stable? Indeed not. Individuals during a lifetime detach themselves from their primary groups and join new groups, in a move to another community, a change of jobs, association with another church or club. The voter's new social environment may significantly affect his political opinions. The voter often uses political preferences "instrumentally," to advance his acceptance in the new groups and move vertically in the social scale. In cases of horizontal mobility, such as a youth who rebels against his parents or a voter who moves from the city to the suburb or from the North to the South, the individual may adjust his political outlook to the new situation. Formidable leverage for change is exerted by groups into which the individual moves that espouse different norms for political opinions, values, and behavior. Theodore Newcomb's well-known study of a college community in the late 1930s, whose political atmosphere was liberal, demonstrated that its students from conservative homes rejected parental political opinions and switched to liberal norms.[10]

Demographic characteristics. Every voter is a walking catalogue of demographic characteristics. Biology; the societal frameworks in which one is born, reared, and passes his adult years; nationality, religion, and class, are all mighty forces that shape the individual's responses to politics—whether he votes and how he votes (see table).

Sex. How do men and women voters differ? The voting behavior of college-educated women appears to be little different from that of college-educated men, but the poorly educated woman is less likely to vote than her male counterpart. Male-female differences in voting habits, then, are widest among the least educated and diminish sharply at the opposite end of the spectrum. A 1959 study found that women, if unmarried, tend to share the political views of their fathers, but they will readily discard their father's views for their husband's.[11]

A 1972 poll by Louis Harris and Carolyn Setlow disclosed a growing interest among women in politics that is altering the picture of acquiescence and passivity portrayed in older research. In the Harris-Setlow poll, three out of five women questioned believed that women should be more active politically, although only one in six was actually active. The respondents were less likely to look to male leaders than their predecessors; instead, they sought "other women" to act in their behalf.

A poll of Princeton's class of 1962 and their wives, taken ten years after graduation, revealed that the wives were "more liberal" politically than their husbands, who were predominantly "liberal Republicans." The women favored a Democratic presidential candidate over Nixon by two to one. However,

[10] Burdick and Brodbeck, 165–70.
[11] *Ibid.*, 410.

Voting turnout of American social groups, 1968 and 1970

	Percent voting	
Social groups	1968	1970
Education		
8 years or less	54.5%	43.4%
9–11 years	61.3	47.1
12 years	72.5	58.4
More than 12 years	81.2	65.7
Family income		
Less than $3000	53.7	42.0
$3000–4999	58.2	45.0
$5000–7499	65.8	48.0
$7500–9999	73.1	55.3
$10,000 and more	80.4	66.2
Sex		
Men	69.8	56.8
Women	66.0	52.7
Age		
21–24	51.1	30.4
25–34	62.5	46.2
35–44	70.8	58.1
45–64	74.9	64.2
65 and over	65.8	57.0
Race		
White	69.1	56.0
Black	57.6	43.5
Residence		
Metropolitan	68.0	55.3
Nonmetropolitan	67.3	53.2
Occupation		
Employed	71.1	57.2
Unemployed	52.1	41.1

Source: U.S. Bureau of the Census, *Statistical Abstract of the United States, 1971* (Washington, D.C.: U.S. Government Printing Office, 1971), p. 365, Table 568.

when the husbands were asked whether their wives shared their political views, a full 88 percent answered "Yes." In the Harris-Setlow poll, 64 percent of the female respondents said that women did not vote the way their husbands told them to, and 60 percent of the males concurred. The Harris-Setlow study found women more sensitive than men to the poor, more peace-oriented, and more disposed to protect consumer interests. Other recent studies suggest that women have less party loyalty than men, react less to labels of "conservative"

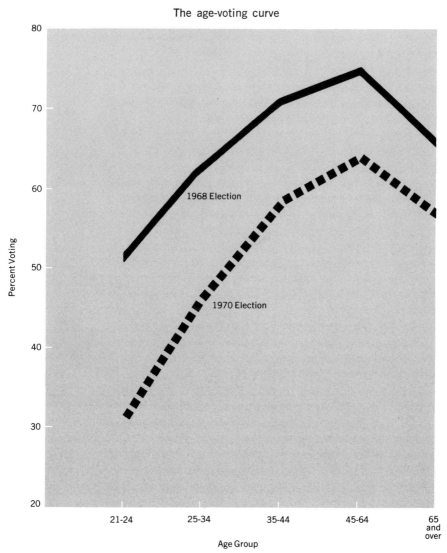

The age-voting curve

Source: U.S. Bureau of the Census, *Statistical Abstract of the United States, 1971* (Washington, D.C.: U.S. Government Printing Office, 1971), p. 365, Table 568.

and "liberal," and are more moved by issues and the character of the candidates.[12]

Age. When coupled with education or wealth, or both, age works a spectacular increase in voting until later years, in the sixties. The voting participation of the young is erratic.

In the 1968 elections, the news media fostered the impression that the nation's voting youth (those under thirty) were uniformly liberal, college-

[12] Gloria Steinem, "Women Voters Can't Be Trusted," *MS* (Summer 1972), 47–51.

educated, dovish on Vietnam, and ardent Kennedy and McCarthy intellectuals. But, in 1968, as at other times, youth was no monolith, but was riddled with political diversity. The young were slightly more likely to vote for George Wallace than were older voters, although they were also more pro-Humphrey. In political preferences the class gap between college youth and noncollege youth is greater than the generation gap between young people and their parents.[13]

The new young voter was a major strategic factor in the 1972 presidential campaign. In committing itself to a massive registration drive directed at the young voter, the McGovern camp assumed that it could win a critical eight million vote margin over Nixon among first-time voters. But the registration strategy almost backfired. Whereas college youth favored McGovern, noncollege youth gave most of their votes to Nixon. A CBS postelection survey found that Nixon attracted 46 percent of first-time voters, aged eighteen to twenty-four, while McGovern captured 52 percent, well below what his strategists had projected.

The CBS findings also indicated that only about 13 million, or 47 percent,

[13] Scammon and Wattenberg, 49.

of the 25.7 million new young voters turned out at the polls. One reason for the low turnout is that not all youths had a chance to register. According to Ridley Whittaker, director of the Student Vote, an organization directed at getting out the college vote, the chief obstacles to youth registration were not money, volunteers, or residency requirements, but limited time and the resistance of local election officials: "Everywhere . . . you're at the mercy of local officials' willingness to enlarge the times and places for registration." [14]

Religion. Voters in 1968 were mostly Protestant (68 percent), with Catholics comprising 25 percent and Jews 4 percent of the electorate. Catholics are concentrated in big cities, which traditionally vote Democratic. Waves of Catholic immigrants—Irish, Italian, Poles—have affiliated with the Democratic party. Many leaders of that party have been Catholic, and it has nominated the only two Catholic candidates for President, John Kennedy and Alfred E. Smith. Protestants are somewhat more likely than Catholics to vote Republican, while Jews constitute a solid liberal Democratic bloc. In 1968, 81 percent of them voted for Humphrey.[15]

In the 1972 campaign, the Nixon camp made a spirited bid for the religious vote. They courted Catholic voters and the ethnic groups on which they are based—Italians, Irish, and Poles. Among other things, representatives of the religious and ethnic press were brought to the Republican National Convention. The 1972 Republican strategy also centered on Jewish voters who, according to Herman Edelsberg, international affairs director for B'nai B'rith, liked what Nixon "is doing on Israel and Soviety Jewry. They are also concerned about law and order, particularly in the cities, and other social issues, and they find themselves more comfortable with Nixon's position than McGovern's. The Jews who reacted against Mayor Lindsay in New York will think twice before they vote for George McGovern." The Republican campaign strategy enabled Nixon to take a healthy minority of the Jewish vote and be the first Republican presidential candidate to win more than half the Roman Catholic votes.[16]

Occupation and Class. Persons of the same general socioeconomic status have about the same political attitudes, regardless of occupation. Occupation is chiefly important in defining the group of people with whom one works and thus the realm of primary group influence.

Socioeconomic status shapes both party and issue preferences. If one is a business executive, a doctor, or engineer, most likely he is also a Republican who looks askance at welfare programs and rising taxes. On the other hand, a black or a Puerto Rican living in a ghetto is prone to vote Democratic, in the belief that that party is more responsive to his concerns, and he favors public programs that are helpful to his needs—public health clinics, more schools, greater welfare benefits.

In the United States, class awareness is not a major factor in voting

[14] *New York Times,* July 23, 1972; November 9, 1972.
[15] Scammon and Wattenberg, 65.
[16] *New York Times,* May 7, 1972; November 12, 1972.

behavior. Contact with urban life increases class awareness so that its effect is greatest in large metropolitan areas, declines in smaller cities, and reaches a low in sparsely settled areas.

Nationality and Race. As groups, ethnic voters tend to vote for one party rather than the other, and to cross party lines to vote for a fellow ethnic. In New England, the Middle Atlantic, and eastern Great Lakes states, where ethnic groups are most concentrated, candidates have suffered many a gastronomic risk in order to eat their way into the hearts of ethnic voters.

For long decades blacks have been the victim of discrimination, intimidation, and violence; they have known the gap that lies between a legal right to vote proclaimed in the Fifteenth Amendment and meaningful exercise of that right. But thanks to the adamant black civil rights crusades of the 1960s, the passage of laws, and their enforcement, blacks now constitute a significant sector of the voting public. In the 1968 elections, nonwhites, comprising 11 percent of the population, cast about 9 percent of the vote. Their commitment to the Democratic party has been extraordinarily high, 85 percent in 1968 and 94 percent in 1964.[17]

Analyses preparatory to the 1972 presidential campaign suggested that the election could be swung by either major party through appeals directed at black, Spanish-speaking, Jewish, Italian, and Slavic voters. Together these groups make up 30 to 33 percent of the electorate, and they are concentrated in six major states, with 181 electoral votes, or two-thirds of the total needed to win the election—California, Illinois, New Jersey, New York, Ohio, and Pennsylvania.

The ethnic groups differ in percentages of voter turnout and in attitudes toward issues. Voter turnout in the elections of 1968 and 1970 was found to be decreasing among Northern blacks, Southwestern Mexican-Americans, and New York City Puerto Ricans, all strongly Democratic. In 1968, New York's Puerto Ricans cast fewer than half the ballots they did in 1960. Fewer than 35 percent of the eligible blacks in Brooklyn's Bedford-Stuyvesant section were registered as the 1972 elections approached. A 1972 study found that Italians and Slavs could no longer be taken for granted by Democrats, and that ethnicity had become less important for the Irish. The growing number of Italian-American voters in Republican ranks is suggested by Nixon's capture of 49 percent of their vote in New York in 1968, and Governor Rockefeller's reelection in 1970 with 65 percent of the vote. In New Jersey, Nixon's share of the Italian vote was 31 percent in 1960; in 1968 it rose to 40 percent.[18]

Any recital of demographic and group characteristics conjures up a vision of the voter as pliant, supine, a matchstick tossed about on a deterministic sea, rather than a rational human being weighing the dialectic of the campaign.

---

[17] Scammon and Wattenberg, 55–56.
[18] *New York Times,* May 7, 1972; Mark R. Levy and Michael S. Kramer, *The Ethnic Factor: How America's Minorities Decide Elections* (New York: Simon and Schuster, 1972), *passim.*

Sargent Shriver, the Democratic vice-presidential candidate in 1972, woos voters in the Spanish-American section of Denver.

Fortunately, not all voters are alike. Some are more independent and self-willed than others. And forces at work in politics can break them away from their accustomed moorings.

The candidate

Why in 1972 were photographs of President Nixon taken during his visits to Ireland, Italy, Yugoslavia, and Poland conscientiously distributed by the Republican National Committee to ethnic presses in cities around the country? Why was candidate Robert Kennedy photographed in 1964 wearing a ceremonial skullcap and on another occasion eating pizza with gusto? Because both Nixon and Kennedy were doing as countless other candidates have done, pursuing the vote, whether it be Jewish, Italian-American, or any other members of religious, ethnic, or racial groups. The candidate's standard function, on which his total campaign effort may succeed or fail, is to maximize support and minimize opposition. A classic example is New York state, with its 41 electoral votes. Nixon lost it in 1968 by 4 percent of the popular vote. That year he won only 15 percent of the state's Jewish vote, but in 1972 he apparently doubled that vote and carried New York with 59 percent of the vote.[19]

The candidate's approach to his campaign is shaped by his beliefs about how voters choose between candidates, how they evaluate his actions if he is an incumbent, and what strategy would win the needed votes. A study of the beliefs of candidates in Wisconsin's 1964 election revealed that candidates for the state legislature believe that voters are swayed more by the candidate's party identification than by the particulars of his contest, whereas candidates for state-wide offices or Congress attribute more impact on voters to their campaigns. An apparent by-product is the high level of party cohesion found in many state legislatures, since the elected representatives feel the key to electoral success is sturdy identification with one's party.[20]

The candidate is likely to have a campaign strategy that defines targets within the electorate, sets themes for speeches and literature, and provides a framework for the use of funds and the efforts of workers. Often the outlines of strategy are but dimly seen in the campaign's confusion. And candidates vary in capacity for strategic thinking; some prefer a flexible stance so that they can capitalize on breaks and counter the opposition's sudden ploys.

Strategy is sometimes conceived in terms of voters: getting faithful supporters out to vote, activating latent voter support, and attracting voters normally committed to the opposition. A key to Eisenhower's Republican success in 1952 was his annexation of 15 percent of the voters who styled themselves "strong" Democrats, while the comparable figure for Adlai Stevenson was 1 percent. In 1964, Johnson annexed 20 percent of the Republican vote, and postelection surveys in 1972 found that Nixon attracted 36 percent of the Democrats. Nevertheless, many a campaign strategist dismisses that type of achievement as rare and argues that the wiser course is to concentrate on the easier tasks—the first two voter categories—and to spend less time on winning over the opposition, particularly when the harvest, as Stevenson found, is apt to be light.[21]

Strategy that is conceived in terms of groups clashes with the candidate's need to appeal universally to all classes, races, and religions of his constituency. Appeal to one group risks offense to others. A candidate's demeanor toward a supporting group depends on his assessment of their motivations and expectations and on how important he thinks the group is for his election chances. The candidate may seek to build a coalition of groups, for which an important tool may be issue appeals. Thus Nixon's cultivation of his identification with law and order and with opposition to school busing was a vital part of his appeal to a variety of ethnic groups—Italians, Jews, Poles, and others who campaign strategists believed were deeply concerned with these

[19] *New York Times,* July 7, August 13, and November 8, 1972.

[20] John W. Kingdon, *Candidates for Office: Beliefs and Strategies* (New York: Random House, 1968), 38.

[21] M. Kent Jennings and L. Harmon Zeigler, *The Electoral Process* (Englewood Cliffs, N.J.: Prentice-Hall, 1966), 7–8; *New York Times,* November 9, 1972.

issues. The Wisconsin study disclosed that the candidate shies away from any precise *quid pro quo* for group support. But his response to groups generally indicates the boundaries within which he expects to act.

Campaign strategy also has a geographical dimension, which is striking in presidential elections. Because of the electoral vote system, candidates of both parties devote little effort to states strongly attached to one party.

The campaigning candidate makes tactical choices that have consequences for voter support and the quality of political discussion. Eisenhower excelled at assuming a lofty, above-the-battle, nonpartisan pose, dismissing criticisms of his farm policy as the "drivel" of "partisan orators" and "anguished politicians." Some candidates earnestly ignore their opponent's attacks, thereby limiting political discussion, while others reply, heeding the advice of Murray Chotiner, longtime counselor to Richard Nixon: ". . . when you answer it, do so with an attack of your own against the opposition for having launched it in the first place." [22] Apparently, this advice was heeded by John N. Mitchell when he was director of the 1972 Republican presidential campaign. The chairman of the Democratic National Committee, Lawrence O'Brien, had filed a lawsuit against the Republican Committee to Reelect the President for allegedly ordering a break-in at Democratic headquarters in Washington. In the spirit of Chotiner's counsel, Mitchell responded with the charge that the lawsuit "represents another example of sheer demagoguery on the part of Mr. O'Brien." [23]

The candidate presents an image to the voter. It may be a mirror of the inner man and his political soul, or it may be contrived, contoured at least partly by the candidate and his helpers. In 1932, Franklin Roosevelt, facing a despairing country bewildered by the economic depression, wisely chose to advertise himself as a daring, resolute champion of action. Occasionally, a candidate may be all genuineness. To the despair of his young workers, Eugene McCarthy had off-days when, consumed by boredom, he let it show, even to carefully selected audiences of influentials.

Democracy requires of an electoral campaign that the candidates meaningfully discuss the issues. The relation of the candidates to each other and to their audiences can vastly affect the worth of their discussion. Even a little mudslinging and name-calling may blast democracy beyond sight. Democracy also requires some kind of balance in the communicating abilities of the opposing candidates. Several conditions commonly threaten this balance. An incumbent who seeks reelection ordinarily enjoys solid advantages gained from his office—he is well known, what he says and does is widely reported in the media, and he may employ the manifold resources of his office to his candidacy's advantage. Candidates who have vied with John Kennedy, Nelson Rockefeller, and Averell Harriman also know the potency of a millionaire's

[22] V. O. Key, Jr., *Politics, Parties & Pressure Groups,* 5th ed. (New York: Crowell, 1964), 472.
[23] *New York Times,* June 21, 1972.

fortune. These less blessed rivals must scrounge for financial help and find comfort in the statistical evidence that rich men are no more assured of winning than poor men.

The campaign:
candidate and voter

According to democratic theory, the candidates, by waging their campaigns, help the voter make rational choices in casting his ballot. Rationality requires that the voter know what distinguishes the candidates and the likely consequences for public policy of their differences. Discussion too should reveal what manner of man the candidate really is, his character, style, and values, so that the voter may judge him accordingly.

But elements in the campaign militate against the rational ideal. Discourse with the voters is only one of the candidate's tasks; he must raise money and elicit support from interest group leaders and party personalities, efforts that cannot be crowned with success through rationality alone. The glittering prizes at stake in a campaign—jobs, huge contracts, direction of policy—are hardly conducive to an exclusively rational effort. The fact that the campaign is a contest between adversaries invites distortions and falsehoods, emotional appeals, and resort to debater's tricks. To the extent that it is rational, the campaign transpires within closely confined boundaries. Differences over issues are usually narrow, so that rival candidates vie to occupy the centrist position where most voters are concentrated.

Some campaigns stress "style" and avoid controversial particular issues. In 1948, Thomas E. Dewey waged a "style" campaign by claiming that his election would have a quieting, unifying effect. Meanwhile, he avoided discussion of specific new measures. His opponent, Harry S. Truman, stressed "position" on issues like housing, civil rights, health, labor-management relations. He advocated them with such fiery zeal that the crowds would cry "Give 'em hell, Harry!" A campaign may have a strong ideological focus, centering discussion on a single issue or philosophy—the pre-Civil War debates on slavery, Barry Goldwater's views on domestic policy in 1964, George McGovern's antiwar stand in 1972. Or, a campaign may have a weak ideological focus, in which discussion is diffused over many issues that rarely present opportunity for a position.

Issues vary in viability for different sectors of the electorate. There seems to be a direct relationship between increasing years of schooling and deeper grasp of issues. Education can provide the voter with a wide range of information on social, economic, and political problems that increases his awareness of issues, while those with little education lack the tools to comprehend them.

Gadgetry of mass appeal. "Voters are basically lazy," a television adviser to Nixon's 1968 campaign has written. ". . . Reason requires a high degree of discipline, of concentration; impression is easier." [24] Not surprisingly, television's political specialists value contrivance and image manipulation. In the light of Nixon's difficulties in adapting to television in 1960, nothing was left undone in 1968. A reserved man who prefers privacy, Nixon was made to give the impression on TV that running for President was a great joy; his ready tendency to perspire was countered with treated towels and extra cold air piped into his television chamber. The format and content of his spot commercials were shaped by the results of a test that had been given to selected viewers who registered their impressions of Nixon by choosing between pairs of adjectives: "wishy-washy/firm," "stuffed shirt/sense of humor." The packaged, integral image of the candidate, a "nationally advertised brand," displaced the discussion of issues and conflict. [25]

The year 1970 witnessed a speeding up of commercials. The older 5 minute spots virtually disappeared, and the 60-second spot yielded to the more popular 30-second spot, in which the layers of persuasion in sight and sound are more subtly compressed. The 4000 television spots used in Nelson Rockefeller's 1970 campaign for reelection as governor of New York (at a cost of $1.5 million) were supervised by Thomas P. Losee, of the advertising firm of McCann-Erickson, Inc., who had directed the "tiger in your tank" campaign of a major oil company. Linwood Holton used "confrontation" commercials in his successful race for the Virginia governorship in 1970; his Democratic opponent, William Battle, made use of moody, full-color films. A 1970 favorite was the testimonial, rendered in humble statement by anonymous individuals with whom viewers might readily identify. In a commercial for the Republican gubernatorial candidate in Texas, an earnest college girl declares, "Paul Eggers is one of us. He's a now sort of person"; after which a cowboy drawls, "I just like the way Paul Eggers talks." [26]

Radio and television have added vast reach to the candidate, but the limited time on the air requires him to put the issues more simply than before. Something of television's lethal power to circumscribe discussion is evident in this spot announcement used in the campaign of 1952: "Voice: 'Mr. Eisenhower, what about the high cost of living?' Eisenhower: 'My wife, Mamie, worries about the same thing. I tell her it's our job to change that on November 4.' " [27]

Candidates have had to cope with the idiosyncracies of the radio and television media. Television, as Gene Wyckoff has suggested, injects an artificial element into the campaign by transforming candidates into personal images. On television, Kennedy in 1960 appeared more in control, more firm, more likely to "stand up to Khrushchev" than Nixon, but on radio Nixon's

[24] Joe McGinniss, *The Selling of the President 1968* (New York: Trident Press, 1969), 36.

[25] *Ibid.*, 80.

[26] *New York Times,* October 24, 1970.

[27] In Stanley Kelley, Jr., *Political Campaigning: Problems in Creating an Informed Electorate* (Washington, D.C.: The Brookings Institution, 1960), 63.

resonant voice conveyed more command and determination than Kennedy's high-pitched voice and Boston-Harvard accent.[28]

One should not be driven to undue despair by the grosser manipulative possibilities of television. The medium has other uses, highly hospitable to democracy's needs. Televised debates and penetrating candidate-interview programs, in the style of "Meet the Press," afford invaluable close-ups of the real candidate. Interest groups and leaders, influential contributors and party leaders, and a goodly number of voters can prod the candidate to do something more than slick cavorting on the TV screen. In 1968, Nixon did not rest his campaign wholly on the artifices of his television craftsmen, but resorted to the radio for extended presentation of issues. The candidate's opponent too is a pressure. It was more difficult for Nixon to use a packaged campaign against Kennedy, whose TV prowess was great, than against Humphrey, whose prowess was modest.

But television's susceptibility to dramatic situations, capsulized statements, and emotional appeal bodes ill for democracy's rational ideals. It requires little argument to show that the spot commercial and much other televised political advertising are implicitly contemptuous of the ideal of the rational voter and serious discussion of important public issues. The proliferation of the TV commercial in a variety of forms is making it a serious pol-

[28] Gene Wyckoff, *The Image Candidates: American Politics in the Age of Television* (New York: Macmillan, 1968), 216.

luter of the political environment. In Great Britain, paid political announce-
ments on television are unlawful, and FCC member Nicholas Johnson has
noted, "The very idea of selling a politician in a spot ad, like merchandising
so much toothpaste, would be revolting to the Englishman." [29] Clearly, if the
abuse is to be regulated or overcome in America, much depends on the
cultural health and capacity for indignation of TV viewers.

New expertise, new technology. To exploit today's communications media as
well as traditional campaign techniques of rallies, literature, and newspaper
advertising, candidates are resorting to several types of expertise. Professional
campaign management firms may advise the candidate on how to allocate
his resources and what techniques to use; they generally supplement, if not
supplant, his political advisers. The professional firms may be used for some
specific purpose, such as devising a strategy, taking polls, organizing registration and telephone drives, preparing literature, developing broadcast commercials, or helping to raise funds. To carry forward their contrived assaults
to win the voter's favor, candidates also hire public relations firms, advertising
agencies, pollsters, media buyers, copy writers, computer analysts, and
producers of television commercials.

Public opinion polls have a number of uses. "In-depth" attitude polling
based on market research techniques helps the candidate decide early in the

[29] In *Newsday*, November 11, 1970, 13A.

campaign which issues to stress. Polling can gauge the impact of the candidate's efforts, the political usefulness of issues, the geographic areas where he is weak. Polls sometimes are employed for psychological impact; favorable results may convey a sense of winning to voters, workers, and contributors. On the other hand, a strong trend may induce complacency, causing voters to stay at home and campaign workers to ease up. McGovern attributed the decline of his lead in the 1972 California primary to these phenomena.

The computer revolution has invaded the realm of political campaigning. Computers perform clerical functions as well as provide sophisticated analyses of the campaign and the constituency. Computers can pinpoint swing areas and indicate where the campaigning candidate should go, what he should do, and how long he should stay. Using data from polls and the census, computers can simulate a campaign and test alternate strategies and the impact of issues on the electorate. The process, as a professional programmer claims, "enables the candidate to talk about the issues which interest the public . . . I believe this work can help restore the democratic process." [30] But it is also a process that favors a candidate who is pliant on issues. Carried to logical extreme, the process can reduce the candidate to an automaton and make the question of what he is really like—what his powers of judgment are, his values, his deep beliefs—more obscure to the voter. The voter needs such information to judge how successful the candidate will be as an office-holder, when in a sea of tasks, more formidable and various than those of the campaign, he will find the computer less useful as a crutch and shield.

Political technology at work. The campaign manager for Congressman Richard T. Hanna of California perused a folder with a thick pack of green-tinted computer print-outs stapled inside. "This is Alpha List C," he said, "Here are the names and addresses of 90,000 people in our district committed to vote for the congressman or strongly leaning that way. This is our majority, all laid out—the whole district targeted, voter by voter."

In behalf of Nelson Gross's 1970 Republican candidacy in New Jersey for a U.S. Senate seat, the political management firm of Bailey, Deardourff and Bowen of Washington, D.C., made a computerized analysis of the last four elections in 5,000 precincts. The analysis determined where incumbent Senator Clifford P. Case, a liberal Republican, ran best, and where Governor William T. Cahill, a moderate Republican, did better. A list resulted of 1,200 to 1,500 swing precincts that a Republican can carry, but does not always. A recorded telephone campaign, targeted for one million messages, concentrated first on these precincts; then as time permitted, calls were made to solid Republican areas, and finally to confirmed Democrats. The computerized precinct list also showed geographical areas into which Gross could usefully mail a "Case-oriented message" rather than one identifying his campaign with President Nixon.

Political technology can advise a candidate when moderate Democrats of

30 In *New York Times,* October 30, 1970.

limited political activity are most accessible (through newspaper advertisements in the sports section and late night television) and when active, conservative Republicans are best reached (through the radio between 7 and 9 A.M.). A similar precision applies to issues. A 1970 Republican congressional candidate in Minnesota's Sixth Congressional District was advised how to calm the differing anxieties of Lutheran and Catholic voters. To those who see something sinister in a candidate's scientific determination of the electorate's views of issues, a political technologist has replied that his work helps the democratic process because it "enables the candidate to talk about the issues which interest the public and not about those on which the public disagrees with him." If anything, this is an unduly restrictive view of the candidate's function, for it rules out any effort to change the electorate's opinion.[31]

The money problem

Political campaigning in a national election year has become fantastically expensive. In 1968, expenditures for all offices at stake, from city alderman to the Presidency, reached at least $300 million. About a third was spent on the presidential campaign, most of it in expensive drives by candidates seeking the nomination (Nelson Rockefeller, George Romney, Robert Kennedy, Eugene McCarthy).[32] The 1972 elections cost close to $400 million.

In a presidential campaign, enormous outlays are made for radio and television. Nixon's 1968 campaign alloted $12.6 million to broadcasting, Humphrey's $6.1 million, and Wallace's $.69 million. All political campaign spending on radio and television totaled $58.9 million in 1968, an increase of about 70 percent over 1964. A marked surge occurred in radio spending. In 1964 radio costs were $10.8 million; in 1968, they were $20.2 million.[33] Radio is attractive because its costs are lower than television's, it can reach trapped audiences like commuters on freeways, and, as Nixon discovered, speeches delivered on radio capture more press attention than do position papers simply released to the press.

Polls, computers, and their attendant experts add enormously to the costs of political campaigns. Even the traditional items of buttons, bumper stickers, posters, brochures, tabloids, and banners add up to solid expenditure. In an age of inflation, a sharp trend of rising costs afflicts all electoral units.

Money poses particular problems for democracy when the means of opposing candidates are unequal. This is especially so in national campaigns. The candidates cannot hope to canvass personally the length and breadth of the nation. Access to costly means of mass appeal—radio and television— becomes critical if each candidate is to exercise effectively his right to bring

[31] *New York Times,* October 30, 1970.
[32] Herbert E. Alexander and Harold B. Meyers, "A Financial Landslide for the G.O.P.," *Fortune,* 82 (March 1970), 164; *New York Times,* November 19, 1972.
[33] Herbert E. Alexander, "Communications and Politics: The Media and the Message," *Law and Contemporary Problems,* 34 (Spring 1969), 266.

his views to the electorate. Democracy is ill served when one candidate can overwhelm the communications media, leaving the other little heard and seen. Some attempt to control this potential hazard has been made in the 1971 Federal Election Campaign Act (see pp. 195–96).

Where the money comes from. All sorts of motivations prompt campaign gifts: concern for government policy; identification with a candidate or supporting group; an appetite for lucrative privilege such as government purchases, franchises, and protection from law enforcement; a craving for entrée by persons aspiring to party or community leadership, or who foresee the need for help with a political problem. The need for campaign money enables those who wield social power to convert it into political influence.

Most campaign gifts come from those otherwise involved in politics and better prepared for political life—with higher educational achievement and loftier economic status. Potent transitory influences affect giving—the candidate's appeal or his opponent's lack of appeal, the intensity of competition, which increases donations. Some contributors are faithful to their party from one election to the next; others are opportunistic, casting their lot with the likely winner.

A study of 50 of the nation's 250 wealthiest persons revealed that about two-thirds were campaign givers and that the very rich among these gave regularly. Members of wealthy families may contribute individually, yielding a substantial aggregate sum to a party. Or a wealthy family may divide its largess between the parties. In 1968, the IBM board chairman, Thomas J. Watson, gave to both major parties. The national Republican party's remarkable financial health in 1968 was owed chiefly to the return of large contributors, traditionally Republican, who had deserted Goldwater to support Johnson in 1964 and then reverted to their party more openhanded than before.[34]

Corporations with government contracts are faithful contributors. "Suppose," a critic has asked, "you represent one of the corporations that receives over $1 billion a year in Defense Department contracts. How much would it cost you to make a modest campaign contribution to *all* elected officials?" In 1968, officers or directors of 24 of the 25 top Pentagon contractors made political contributions.[35] Corporations are forbidden by law to contribute to federal election campaigns, but methods for indirect giving abound. Thus, officers of corporations can contribute as individuals and corporations can pay printing and other bills for candidates and post them on their books as "business expenses."

The same kind of prohibition and the same type of evasions pertain to labor unions. Union expenditure occurs through committees of individual unions and through the Committee on Political Education (COPE) of the AFL-CIO. These "educational expenditures" are made to inform members

[34] Alexander and Meyers, 105.
[35] *Ibid.*

about candidates and issues and encourage them to register and vote. Organized labor pursues a policy of "nonpartisan endorsement," but most of its expenditure by far favors Democratic candidates. Labor's impact is handicapped by the concentration of three-fourths of union membership in only one-third of the states.

Although in late decades the proportion of the population making campaign contributions has markedly expanded, 90 percent of the political money still comes from no more than 10 percent of the population. The day seems far distant when the yield from small donors will free the parties from acute dependence on big contributors. In state and local politics, freedom from big givers, especially among contractors, would be a major gain. One base that does not need broadening is the underworld; its contributions, while substantial, are not precisely known.

Campaign financing for presidential and congressional races was long regulated by the Corrupt Practices Act of 1925 and the Hatch Act of 1940. The Corrupt Practices Act bars corporations and the Taft-Hartley Act of 1947 bars labor unions from making direct contributions to federal candidates. All but three states regulate campaign financing for state and local offices. But, generally, the state laws have been easily evaded and their publicity and reporting provisions loosely enforced. Something of their sham was conveyed by the reaction of a Western attorney general after seeing a campaign's financial reports: "All of us are a bunch of liars." [36]

In 1971, the Federal Election Campaign Act was adopted, superseding the Corrupt Practices Act of 1925. Under the new act, any political committee that expects to raise or spend more than $1,000 in behalf of any candidate for the Presidency, Senate, or House must register with the Office of Federal Elections of the General Accounting Office. Hundreds of committees that evaded registration under the old law are covered by the new requirement. Campaign committees must report the sources of contributions received and campaign expenditures made. Two pre-election financial disclosures are necessary, one fifteen days and the other five days before the voting, and periodic cumulative reports are required later.

The act requires information about all contributors of more than $100, and it limits to $52,150, or 10 cents per resident of voting age—whichever is greater—a candidate's total spending for television, radio, newspaper, magazine, billboard, and telephone advertising. For the first time, the law limits the amount of money a candidate may personally invest in his own campaign —$50,000 for President, $35,000 for the Senate, and $25,000 for the House.

Corporations and labor unions continue to be barred from making direct contributions from corporate or regular membership funds. But the act sanctions a long-standing practice whereby corporations and unions maintain so-called voluntary political action funds. Thus corporate executives and employees and union members may pool their campaign contributions for

---

[36] Alexander Heard, *The Costs of Democracy* (Chapel Hill: University of North Carolina Press, 1960), 370.

transmission to parties or candidates selected by them, or for distribution as the managers of the funds see fit.

During the 1972 presidential campaign, Common Cause, the reformist citizens' lobby, sued to force the Nixon national campaign committee to disclose the sources of an estimated $10 million in contributions made before the 1971 law became effective. And the General Accounting Office, as monitor of the presidential campaign, charged that the Republican Finance Committee to Reelect the President had violated the new law for failing to keep detailed and exact account of some $350,000 in contributions.[37]

Are campaign money and its contributors a threat to democracy? Yes, if the contribution is a bribe and certainly it sometimes is. But if finance is viewed in the framework of the political process, the picture is more reassuring. Only some people have money, but most people, nearly all, have votes, and the two camps are often in conflict. Votes, not money, are the *sine qua non* of victory. And it must be remembered that men of wealth are not a monolithic legion. Their largess is tolerably well divided between the major parties. Finally, money being but one element in a campaign, there is no neat, reliable correlation between expenditure and results. The McGovern primary campaigns in 1972 were won by patient, careful grassroots work; monetary outlays were decidedly less than the big spending media campaigns of other candidates. In 1970, such big spending candidates as Richard Ottinger of New York and Howard Metzenbaum of Ohio won the primaries but lost the elections in their senate races. Even so, many an underdog candidate, for whom money is a scarce commodity, would gain small comfort from this mixed record. In 1970, Pat Driscoll, underdog Republican candidate in Michigan's Twelfth Congressional District, could not raise a thousand dollars to print and distribute leaflets with "seven issue ideas I worked out"—not a happy picture for democracy.[38]

Dirty politics

"Ten, nine, eight . . . three, two, one"—so began a political commercial to elect President Johnson in 1964. The countdown started with a small girl pulling the petals off a daisy and ended in a mushroom-shaped cloud on the television screen. The implication was that Goldwater's election would bring nuclear disaster ("The stakes are too high for you to stay at home"). This particular ad was pulled off the air for being "unethical," but it was in the tradition of campaign weapons of distortion and deceit that brutally assault the ideal of rational political discussion.

By the ancient art of mud-slinging, Grover Cleveland was depicted in his 1884 candidacy as a drunken saloon lounger and the epitome of immorality—father of an illegitimate child, which he denied. Cartoons featured an infant

[37] *New York Times,* April 7, August 27, and September 7, 1972.
[38] *New York Times,* November 1, 1970.

Mud-slinging in 1884: Cartoons portrayed Grover Cleveland as the father of an illegitimate child, constituting "one more vote for Cleveland."

labeled "one more vote for Cleveland." A photograph of Pat Brown, candidate for the California governorship, was placed in a pamphlet so that he appeared to be bowing deferentially toward a picture on the facing page of Nikita Khrushchev, truculent and demanding. Voter gullibility and hysteria are fertile fields for unscrupulous candidates.

Dirty politics seems also to have entered the contemporary age of political technology, as attested to by the so-called Watergate Caper of the 1972 presidential campaign. Five men, of whom two were former White House staff members in the Nixon administration, were apprehended during a break-in at the National Democratic Committee headquarters. They were charged with installing or removing eavesdropping devices in the office of the committee and with photographing committee papers. Other disclosures suggested widespread use of Republican undercover agents against McGovern and use of bogus letters to sabotage the primary campaigns of other Democratic candidates.

To counterweigh the malpractices, the press and other media can in cases of unfair personal attack give equal coverage to the responses to accusations. Probably the best check on malpractices is their frequent tendency to boomerang against their perpetrator. In a primary fight for the senatorial nomination, the polls showed that a merciless personal attack on Edward Kennedy by his rival Edward McCormack moved great numbers of voters to Kennedy's support. The federal government and some states bar the circulation of anonymous literature in campaigns, but enforcement is often difficult. A Fair

Campaign Practices Committee, composed of private, reform-minded citizens and hardheaded politicians, has developed a code of fair campaign practices and brings violations of its norms to the attention of the candidate and the public.[39]

How the voter
decides

As the hour approaches for the voter to go to the polling booth, how does he, in the turmoil of the campaign, decide how to cast his ballot? Like other human beings, the voter responds to what he sees and hears. His observations about political objects and events around him and the opinions of those he associates with sift through the machinery of mind and imagination to bring about his decision.

The main cogs of this machinery are the voter's beliefs and attitudes, cognition and evaluation, perception and emotion. They act on three in-gredients of the political world—candidates, issues, and parties. The voter's image of these political objects may seem ill-informed, but his behavior makes sense subjectively in terms of how they appear to him. The voter not only sees these elements of politics, but evaluates them. Within a short time, the voter's evaluative structure may change sharply. In 1948, voter evaluations were deeply rooted in the economic and social issues of the New Deal era, but in 1952 the evaluations shifted markedly to considerations of foreign affairs. Currently there seems to be something of a shift the other way—from foreign affairs to domestic needs.

Voters tend to have certain basic orientations toward the political world. Those with a strong candidate orientation respond to the personal attributes of the candidates in such reactions as "wheeler-dealer," "tricky," "sincere," "attractive." The voter who is issue-oriented deems questions of public policy paramount. Those candidates please him most who give promise of coping with these problems. Voters may be party-oriented, psychologically attached to their party and ready to respond to its appeals for support, regardless of candidates or issues.

The strongest attitudes are found in the partisan voter, who forms at-tachments to his party early in his adult years, influenced by family and reference groups; this identification typically gains strength throughout his life. Issues and the candidate's personality strongly influence the independent voter and the deviant voter (one who temporarily deserts his party to support the opposition). A voter of this genre is one who intended to vote for Adlai Stevenson in 1952 but changed her mind after he quipped, "Eggheads of the world unite. You have nothing to lose but your yokes." Repelled, the voter

[39] Bruce L. Felknor, *Dirty Politics* (New York: Norton, 1966), *passim.*

explained, "I can't visualize a President who is capable of making such flippant, witty remarks." [40]

But relatively few voters will change their attitude during a campaign. In 1956, only 20 percent of the voters decided how to vote during the campaign.[41] The force of events during an administration may affect far more voters than the blast of the campaign itself. Careful studies suggest that the Democrats had lost the 1952 election even before Eisenhower's nomination in July, thanks to massive desertions by their 1948 supporters displeased by the performance of the Truman administration. In his superb analyses of voting behavior, V. O. Key, Jr., concluded that probably the voter's primary role is one of appraising past events, past performance, and past actions. Voters are impressed more by performance than by promises, by the known more than the unknown. Voters, he concluded, fortunately for democracy, "are not fools." [42]

The voter's affiliations with various groups—social, economic, political— may cause his own voting to coincide with the dominant voting patterns of one or more of his groups. The groups vary in their voting solidarity, and group voting patterns may shift significantly from one election to the next. A vital factor in Kennedy's 1960 victory was the shift of nearly six Catholics in ten who had voted for Eisenhower in 1956.[43]

Most voters, needing to keep their attitudes intact, engage in selective perception: they watch on television the candidate they already approve and attend his rallies when he comes to town. Partisan voters will adjust their perceptions so that their image of current politics is consistent with their partisan image. But events like war, depression, urban rioting may penetrate the perceptual screen and change the voter's attitude. The voter's decision on election day springs from the interplay of his basic orientation and transient factors.

Voters can be classified according to their predispositions and habits in exercising their franchise. There are "core voters," who vote even when the campaign produces only a weak level of stimulation, and "peripheral voters," endowed with low political interest but who through strong stimulation by the election will go to the polls.

Within the electorate, Key discerned three major categories: standpatters, switchers, and new voters.[44] By far the largest of these are the standpatters, corresponding to the partisan voters, who vote for the candidate whose party they supported last time. Ranging from four-fifths to seven-eighths of those who vote, standpatters stand by the party even when they agree with the op-

[40] In Burdick and Brodbeck, 302.
[41] Angus Campbell, Warren E. Miller, and Donald Stokes, *The American Voter* (New York: Wiley, 1960), 78, 189.
[42] V. O. Key, Jr., *The Responsible Electorate* (Cambridge: Harvard University Press, 1966), 7.
[43] *Ibid.,* 119.
[44] *Ibid.,* 94–150.

position. Although a smaller category, switchers (corresponding to independent and deviant voters) number in the millions and move across party lines in both directions.

Switchers save the electoral system from undue rigidity. Not differing materially from standpatters in education and level of interest, they shift because of policy outlooks rather than psychological and sociological subtleties. Although they vote somewhat less regularly than standpatters, they most correspond to that hero of democratic theory, the rational voter. They are thinking voters, interested in issues, and refusing to take their cues from party leadership. To Key, the "new voters," who did not vote in the last election because they were too young or for other reasons, are a further force for flexibility in the political system.

But the standpatters too are democracy's anointed. Their steadfastness keeps the major parties within competitive bounds. The national voting pattern is consistently one of almost equal division between the parties. In the past one hundred years, neither party has won more than 65 percent of the presidential vote, and the average difference in successive presidential elections is 6 percent.[45]

Suffrage

A mark of democratic nations is the presence of universal suffrage (although not all nations with universal suffrage are democratic). To be effective by democratic standards, suffrage must be accompanied by the related freedoms of speech, assembly, and press and accomplished by the secret ballot, the voting machine, and other democratic means. In a federal nation such as the United States, universal suffrage must apply in all elections—national, state, and local. Universal suffrage did not burst suddenly from the political heavens, but materialized gradually as historic property qualifications were dropped and women, blacks, and youth were granted the vote.

Specific suffrage requirements are set by the states, subject to federal constitutional limitations, chiefly in the Fourteenth, Fifteenth, Nineteenth, Twenty-Fourth, and Twenty-Sixth amendments. Among the standard present-day requirements for suffrage are citizenship, necessary in all states; residence in the state, usually for one year; and a lesser term of residence in the county and voting district. Since Americans are a migrating people, residence requirements exclude about 5 percent of the potential electorate. In its 1970 extension of the Voting Rights Act, Congress included a provision permitting voters in every state to vote in presidential elections after living in the state for thirty days. The law also requires the states to permit absentee registration and voting. The extension prohibits the use of literacy and "good character" tests in all states. The required age of voters is provided for in the Twenty-Sixth

---

[45] Angus Campbell, Warren E. Miller, and Donald Stokes, *Elections and the Political Order* (New York: Wiley, 1966), 168, 182.

Black political potential in the South

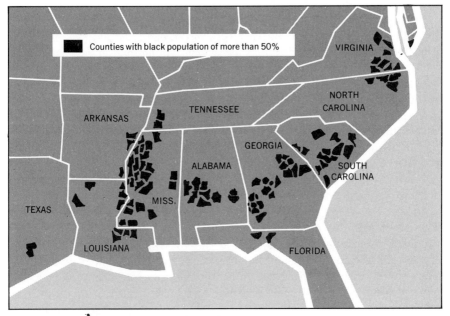

Source: *New York Times*, July 6, 1971, p. 1.
Data from U.S. Bureau of the Census.

Amendment, which stipulates that all citizens, eighteen years of age or over, have the right to vote in federal, state, and local elections.

Black voting rights. The extension of the suffrage in the United States to the black voter was the outcome of a long, harsh struggle. After the Civil War, the Thirteenth, Fourteenth, and Fifteenth amendments and the Reconstruction Act of 1867 seemed to enfranchise blacks. But whites soon reestablished control in the South, and deprived blacks of their vote by blatant subterfuges to which the Supreme Court gave its blessings. The most telling contrivance was the white Democratic primary, which the judiciary whittled away at, beginning in 1927, until in 1944 the Supreme Court finally overruled an earlier decision approving the white primary.[46]

The chief blows for the conversion of black citizens into effective voters were struck by a series of federal laws in the 1950s and 1960s, products of the civil rights movement. The most important, the Voting Rights Act of 1965, suspended literacy tests in many Southern counties, provided for federal examiners to register voters, and directed the Attorney General to institute court action against enforcement of poll taxes as a prerequisite to voting in state and local elections. In 1968, Southern blacks voted in far greater numbers than ever before—a 7 percent gain over 1964, while black voting outside the South declined 11 percent. The Southern achievement is credited to the Voting Rights Act of 1965, which was modified in 1970 and extended for

[46] *Smith v. Allwright,* 321 U.S. 649 (1944).

another five years, and to remarkably effective work in organizing and registering black voters.[47]

In spite of the gains, Julian Bond, a black civil rights pioneer, was distressed by the apathy of Southern blacks in the elections of 1970 and 1971. There was only spotty registration, occasional voting, and at best an embryonic political organization. Representative of the problem was Waterproof, Louisiana. In 1969 a Voter Education Project campaign there, in which Bond participated, caused black registrations to zoom from 100 to more than 600, a clear majority in the tiny town. But in the local 1970 elections, less than half of the eligible black voters cast a ballot. The fall-off was variously attributed to jealousies among competing black candidates, to the inability to perceive that politics can change the conditions of people's lives, and to the fact that "here in Waterproof," according to a local politician, "for the blacks and the whites, it's still yesterday." [48]

The act of voting. On the surface, the vote is an act involving simple, conventional choices—whether to vote at all, to vote straight Democratic or straight Republican, or to split the ticket, but beneath is a sea of motivations. The vote requires an expenditure of energy and time, an inconvenient scheduling of behavior. It imposes a relatedness to society and receptivity to communications concerning it. It may be used to vent an emotion—partisan loyalty, fear of nonconformity, support of policy, affirmation of democracy. Voting is instrumental behavior, a choice of means toward other ends, a step toward satisfying social wants. For most people, voting is their sole act of participation in political life.

For all the vast expenditure spilled on campaigns and the intense interest generated by presidential races, as a rule less than two-thirds of the eligibles vote. Legal barriers, particularly residence requirements, deprive great numbers, and personal obstacles eliminate many others. The several levels of government and the tradition of electing many subordinate officers requires the American voter to cast more votes per capita over a four-year period than any other voter in the world. This substantial demand and the general pattern of short terms of office serve to dissipate the voter's interest and activity. Although Western European voters vote in greater proportion, the American voter, with more demands made on him, turns out remarkably well.

Nonvoting ratios are highest among women, the young, blacks, nonunion labor, lower status groups (income, education, and occupation), white Southerners. The young voter's reduced turnout is attributed to lower income and therefore a less felt stake in society, to fluidity of occupational interest, geographic mobility, infrequency of home ownership, and less clearly defined relations with interest groups.[49]

In all, some 40 percent of the voting-age population typically do not vote in a presidential election. In an analysis of the nonvoter in the 1968 elections,

[47] Scammon and Wattenberg, 56.
[48] *New York Times,* August 8, 1971.
[49] Robert E. Lane, *Political Life* (New York: Free Press, 1959), 48–49.

Voting turnout in presidential elections, 1920–1972

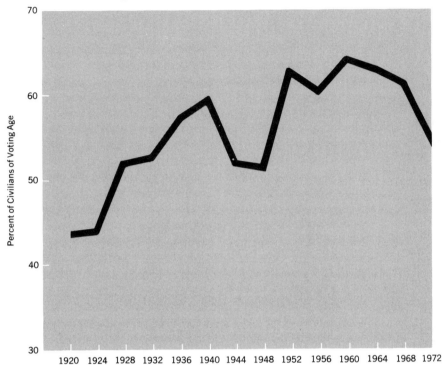

Source: U.S. Bureau of the Census, *Statistical Abstract of the United States, 1971* (Washington, D.C.: U.S. Government Printing Office, 1971), p. 364, Table 566; *New York Times,* November 12, 1972.

a Gallup poll discovered that about 5 percent were ineligible under existing voting laws, leaving the number of "eligible nonvoters" at 38 million. The reasons for their failure to vote were distributed as follows:

15 million were registered, but were uninterested or disliked the candidates
10 million could have registered but did not
7 million were sick or disabled
3 million were away from home
3 million could not leave their jobs
1 million did not obtain absentee ballots.[50]

Among these categories are at least 10 million persons with valid excuses for not voting, and the figure for voter turnout in 1968 can be adjusted from 60 to 73 percent. The 38 million eligible nonvoters are, however, an embarrassment to democratic ideals. In 1972, the voting-age population swelled by over 25 million, but the number of those who voted increased by only 2 million— 55 percent of the voting-age population cast their ballots; 45 percent did not. Why this large number? Political science research attributes much of it to the

[50] *New York Times,* December 10, 1968.

distracting demands of urban living, to personal preoccupations that exceed politics such as work, money, children. Nonvoting has its highest incidence among the less advantaged, which contributes to a tendency among candidates not to present programs directed toward their interests.

Election administration

Democratic ideals can become a mockery, the voter frustrated, campaign outlays of energy and money wasted, if elections are not administered efficiently and honestly. Elections, even for federal offices, are conducted by state and local governments, and state elections, though regulated by state legislation, are administered by local governments. The rather simple apparatus of electoral administration becomes crucial to fulfillment of democratic endeavor.

The initial, prevoting step of registration establishes a list of qualified voters in readiness for election day. Registration may be periodic or permanent. Permanent registration requires only a single appearance of the voter before registration officials and avoids the attrition of voters in the more demanding periodic registration. In the permanent system, registration lists are occasionally reviewed to eliminate disqualified voters.

Registration has led many Southern blacks into meaningful political participation, but in many non-Southern cities large proportions of blacks and Puerto Ricans fail to register. A careful study estimated that in Brooklyn, New York, blacks and Puerto Ricans comprise 30 percent of the population and 25 percent of the eligible voters, but not more than 15 percent of *registered* voters. The locally dominant Democratic party was not interested in registering them since its constituency viewed the unregistered voters "as a threat to most everything it valued." Lack of registration left these groupings unorganized, and in an era of decentralizing city services they forfeited influence "to groups unrepresentative of larger community interests"—to economically secure, safety-conscious blacks and Puerto Ricans and to "flamethrowing militants." [51]

That indispensable tool of modern electoral democracy, the secret ballot, emerged only after long struggle. Now used in all the states, the secret or Australian ballot (deriving its name from the continent in which it originated) is printed by public authority, bears the name of candidates of all parties, and is coupled with electoral administrative methods designed to assure the secrecy of one's vote.

But the ballot can also be used in a heavy-handed undemocratic manner. Particular candidates and minor parties often face formidable obstacles in getting places on the ballot. If petitions are required, the number of signatures can be set inordinately high and stipulated for all the state's counties, an uphill task in rural areas. Election administration officials, minions of the dominant party, may disqualify petitions and invoke court battles. The physical char-

[51] Arthur Kiebanoff, Senior Honors Thesis, Yale University, 1971.

acter of the ballot affects voting. Often the ballot is so long that the weary voter fails to vote on offices or measures toward the bottom or the confused voter makes a mistake in noting his preferences.

Although voting machines are authorized in three-fourths of the states for use in some or all localities, in recent presidential elections only about half the votes were cast by machine. Machines speed up the voting process, prevent fraudulent spoiling of ballots by election officials, minimize fraud and error in the count, and make the results quickly available. Procedures for tallying and reporting the vote are set forth in law. But hazards abound for honest error, especially where voting machines are not used. The long ballot, the often modest clerical competence of polling staffs, their weariness at the end of a long election day make slips in the count easy. In the United States electoral fraud is something of a hoary tradition, but V. O. Key concluded that it "occurs less frequently than is commonly supposed." [52]

One of the more hospitable havens of present-day seamy practice is Illinois, particularly Cook County, province of Chicago's Mayor Richard J. Daley. In 1960, Chicago delivered a long-delayed, improbable plurality of 319,000 votes for Kennedy, enough by 10,000 to offset Nixon's strength elsewhere in Illinois and deliver 27 electoral votes to Kennedy. In 1968, the once-burnt Nixon forces waged a poll-watching drive in Chicago (Operation Eagle Eye) to reduce the scale of the shenanigans. Nevertheless a reporter, disguised as a poll-watcher, witnessed Democratic election judges telling voters to pull the Democratic lever in the presence of silent "Republican" judges. The customary game was played out with the mayor and his downstate Republican foes each trying to finesse the other by holding back their count until they could ascertain the size of the total that had to be beaten.[53]

Election laws usually provide that the electoral results can be contested. Challenges are heard by election officials, the courts, and where legislators are involved, the legislative body. In some states, recounts are easily levied; in others, procedural barriers delay and hobble them. If readily available, a recount inspires election officials to more accurate workmanship. In his initial primary contest in 1972 with Congressman John Rooney of New York, Allard Lowenstein was narrowly defeated, according to the official result. Charging that there had been voting irregularities, Lowenstein successfully appealed to the courts, and another primary election was held.

Election outcomes

In a presidential election, not just one but hundreds of elections occur. In addition to the President, some senators, all representatives, and all manner of state and local officials are chosen. National and parochial influences vie with one another—a President's electoral strength may carry one senator into

[52] Key, *Politics, Parties & Pressure Groups,* 636.
[53] Lewis Chester, Godfrey Hodgson, and Bruce Page, *An American Melodrama, The Presidential Campaign of 1968* (New York: Viking Press, 1969), 760–61.

office on his coattails, while another senator may build his victory on local influences and personal strength. Separate voting for the executive and the legislature assures a mixed mandate. And the system of multiple elections (voting for executives and legislators at different levels of government) and the strong forces of electoral autonomy assure that elections can normally produce only a modest shift in the direction of public policy.

In general, the popular vote for lesser offices is more party-determined than the vote for President, and it fluctuates within a much narrower range. The party dominant in a congressional district often displays a remarkable capacity to withstand major fluctuations in the presidential vote. From 70 to 80 percent of the House districts will be represented by the same incumbent or party for five consecutive elections.[54]

The heavily fluctuating presidential elections present a variety of patterns. In the landslide victory, the most imposing display of electoral might in democracy, the electorate clearly expresses a lack of confidence in those who have been in charge of affairs. Franklin D. Roosevelt's defeat of Herbert Hoover in 1932 represented such an election. In an opposing kind of election, a reaffirmation of support or vote of confidence, the same coalition of voters prevails as constituted the majority in the previous election. Truman's 1948 victory utilized Roosevelt's New Deal coalition. In realigning elections, a party is returned to power by a new coalition of voters. The presidential victories of Eisenhower and Nixon were marked by success in Southern states, which represented the South's growing realignment from long-standing Democratic support to a new identification with the Republican party.

Some elections may be "critical." These bring enduring realignments of the electorate so that the disadvantaged party loses a succession of elections. The election of 1928 was of this type. Although Hoover, the Republican candidate, won, Republican strength suffered sharp declines in metropolitan and industrial areas, especially in the Northeast. The shift contributed to a series of Republican defeats, commencing in 1932 and continuing for two decades. This type of election too is impressive evidence of the electorate's impact, for it brings a broad redirection of public policy.[55]

This classification of elections valuably suggests the range of ways a democratic electorate can speak decisively. Elections determine more than who shall govern. They can redefine the direction of policy for years to come. They can express clear dissatisfaction with the performance of the incumbents, and the fact that such an expression can burst from the heavens disciplines those who govern. Retrospective judgments from electorates can be quite explicit—in 1968 they deemed the management of the Indochina war unacceptable. The election that is a vote of confidence confers invaluable prestige on an incumbent administration and renews momentum for its programs. Despite their imperfections, most American elections are a vindication of popular government.

[54] Jennings and Zeigler, 23.
[55] Key, *Politics, Parties & Pressure Groups*, 535–36.

Proposals

If good things can be made better, elections abound in opportunities for improvement.

1. Can democracy get a better return from the lavish investment in television campaigning? Conceivably, there might be more editorial endorsements of candidates by television stations, important for less affluent candidates, who cannot afford quantities of air time. The FCC encourages station editorializing so long as rebuttal editorials can be aired. Televised candidate debates and press confrontations might counter the impact of image manipulation. Prime-time programs might take the images apart, appraise them, and cultivate viewer comprehension of rational differences between the candidates.

Let radio and television provide reduced rates, or better still, free time for candidates on airwaves that belong to the people, and from which the communications entrepreneurs reap bounteous profits. Time might be allotted to candidates, the greater portion to major candidates and important offices. FCC member Nicholas Johnson favors barring the purchase of additional time and the use of any time in less than five-minute segments. When political propaganda or advertising techniques are used, Johnson suggests the station present the candidate as soon as possible in a setting over which he lacks control—a news conference, debate, or interview.[56]

2. Democracy would be better served if the candidates' outlays were equalized, if the built-in advantages of the incumbent were counterweighed by subsidies and communications facilities made available to the challenger. No less lights than Theodore Roosevelt and Harry Truman have proposed outright government subsidies for political campaigns. Among the resisters of the proposal are state and local organizations, which rightly fear a rush of power to national party organizations, and Republicans, in general, who usually are better financed than the Democrats in the present system of private political enterprise.

Conceivably, public disclosure laws, which now require the candidate to report publicly the sources and amounts of his financing for the campaign after his nomination, might be extended in coverage. Reporting requirements might be made to apply to primary nominations and include all important candidates and committees. If the past be a guide, such steps would be stoutly resisted by parties and legislatures.

3. To improve the quality of the campaign and reduce deceit and other malpractice, the reforms of several states might be used more widely. Oregon has a political criminal libel law, requiring the state's attorney general to act through the courts when a candidate is libeled. In effect, the candidate is freed of the image of a "bad sport" in initiating his own suit. The law has been applied only in extreme situations, and has therefore not succumbed to the danger of overuse. Most states and the federal government outlaw unsigned

[56] *Newsday,* November 11, 1970.

literature in campaigns. The laws assume that the voter must know the source of a political argument in order to evaluate it effectively.

Florida, Mississippi, and Nevada have "right of reply laws," which in the instance of a report of a damaging charge give the aggrieved candidate equivalent space and position in an early edition of the publication concerned. Under its "fairness doctrine," the FCC requires television and radio stations carrying personal attacks to offer the candidate at whom they are directed free time to reply.

4. Electoral administration in all the states should satisfy certain minimal standards, some notches above present practice. Permanent personal registration should prevail everywhere, and voting machines or electronic counters for paper ballots should be adopted in every state.

Let each state adopt a constitutional amendment permitting every bona fide resident to vote, with district residence requirements reduced to a minimum. Thirty days should be sufficient to prevent fraudulent voting and permit the preparation of voter lists.

And let every alert democratic citizen heed that timeless warning by Mr. Dooley: "A vote on th' tallysheet is worth two in the box." [57]

Suggested Reading

Alexander, Herbert E., *Financing the 1968 Election* (Heath, 1971). An extensive analysis of the costs of the 1968 election, with data on campaign contributors and comparisons of income and expenditure for the major parties. Alexander has made similar studies for the 1960 and 1964 elections.

[57] An astute commentator, inspired earlier this century by Finley Peter Dunne.

Berelson, Bernard R., Lazarsfeld, Paul F., and McPhee, William N., *Voting: A Study of Opinion Formation in a Presidential Campaign* * (University of Chicago Press, 1954). A study of voters' decision-making, based on interviews with voters of Elmira, New York, during the 1948 presidential campaign.

Campbell, Angus, Converse, Philip E., Miller, Warren E., and Stokes, Donald E., *The American Voter* * (Wiley, 1960). A study of voting behavior based on interviews and national voting samples, administered by the Survey Research Center of the University of Michigan.

Campbell, Angus, Converse, Philip E., Miller, Warren E., and Stokes, Donald E., *Elections and the Political Order* (Wiley, 1966). Further data and analysis of American voting behavior by scholars at the University of Michigan Survey Research Center.

Heard, Alexander, *The Costs of Democracy* * (University of North Carolina Press, 1960). Examines who contributes to campaigns and why, methods of fund raising, the regulation of campaign financing, and the implications of financing methods.

Kelley, Stanley, Jr., *Professional Public Relations and Political Power* * (Johns Hopkins Press, 1966). A landmark study of public relations techniques in campaigning both for candidates and for issues.

Key, V. O., Jr., *The Responsible Electorate* * (Harvard University Press, 1966). An analysis of voting behavior in presidential elections from 1936 to 1960. Contends that who voters vote for in presidential elections is closely related to their views on issues and policies.

McGinniss, Joe, *The Selling of the President, 1968* * (Trident Press, 1969). A readable and critical "inside" account of Nixon's television campaign in 1968.

Matthews, Donald R., and Prothro, James W., *Negroes and the New Southern Politics* * (Harcourt Brace Jovanovich, 1966). An incisive empirical study of the changing effectiveness of the Southern black voter and the factors that influence his participation in politics.

Phillips, Kevin P., *The Emerging Republican Majority* * (Arlington House, 1969). Contends that a new Republican coalition is emerging that will supplant the Democratic coalition as the majority party in national elections.

Polsby, Nelson W., and Wildavsky, Aaron B., *Presidential Elections* * 3rd edition (Scribner's, 1972). Analyzes the strategic factors that underpin the waging of a presidential campaign.

Scammon, Richard M., and Wattenberg, Ben J., *The Real Majority* (Coward-McCann, 1970). An analysis of contemporary voter attitudes that contends that candidates who occupy the "center" on issues are more likely to be elected than those who take more extreme positions on the right or left.

Voters' Time, Report of the Twentieth Century Fund Commission on Campaign Costs in the Electronic Era * (The Twentieth Century Fund, 1969). An examination of the rising costs of political campaign broadcasting and advertising, with recommendations for making television and radio more available to candidates.

White, Theodore H., *The Making of the President 1968* * (Atheneum, 1969). Similar volumes appeared for the elections of 1960 and 1964.* Vivid accounts of presidential campaigns, within a framework of contemporary social and cultural forces. Makes extensive use of interviews with political personalities involved.

* Available in paperback edition

8

leadership:

the

presidency

If a political system is to be made to work effectively, or if enormous power is to be used responsibly in foreign affairs, much depends on the calibre of presidential leadership. Leadership is a precious commodity in large-scale democracy; it can become hollow and faltering if it merely drifts in endless discussion. But a skillful leader can redefine issues in forms on which people more readily agree, give purpose to diffuse effort, raise society's aspirations and convert them into achievement.

The Presidency has enjoyed its most brilliant effectiveness in moments of leadership when the Chief Executive rallies public sentiment behind high purposes. Woodrow Wilson's New Freedom program of social justice and Franklin Roosevelt's New Deal were achievements of leadership that evoked the understanding and support of most of the people. According to Wilson, the Presidency occupies a unique place in the political system in its potentialities for leadership. "His is the only national voice in affairs," Wilson wrote. "Let him once win the admiration and confidence of the country, and no other single force can withstand him, no combination of forces will easily overpower him." [1] With the people behind him, the President can resist powerful interest groups, their lobbyists, and congressional spokesmen.

But leadership also means that the President sometimes may have to speak and act against public opinion that clings to views that he, according to his own best information and advice, knows to be inimical to the country's interests. This is an acid test of leadership that not all Presidents are willing to undertake. Wilson did in his doughty fight to bring the country into the League of Nations, the predecessor of the United Nations. But the country's predominant isolationist sentiment, faithfully represented in Congress, thwarted Wilson; subsequently his health buckled, and his fight failed.

Democratic leadership combines power with responsibility. In democracy, the leader is subject to criticism, thanks to the play of civil liberties, the presence of political opposition, and the freedom of the media to disseminate information. Responsible democratic leadership requires periodic elections, at

[1] In H. C. F. Bell, *Woodrow Wilson and the People* (New York: Doubleday, 1945), 113.

"Why I would like to be President: I would like to be President so I could live in the White House and ride around in big cars and helicopters and have big banquets and get on television whenever I wanted to and be in motorcades and parades and have my picture taken all the time."

which time the leader's performance is reviewed; if it is found wanting, the electorate can throw him out of office. Democratic leaders are subject to legal restraints on their powers, embodied in the Constitution and statutes and subject to judicial review. In democratic leadership, power and responsibility are locked in a continuous tension, and the political system struggles to keep the two elements in proper balance.

Presidential leadership has glamorous, almost monarchic dimensions—the acclaiming crowds, the waiting fleet of jets and helicopters, the retinue of counselors, the address to the nation. But Truman once described his presidential task in less enthralling terms: "I sit here all day trying to persuade people to do the things they ought to have sense enough to do without my persuading them. . . . That's all the powers of the President amount to." [2] Like other leaders, the President attempts to stimulate the behavior of others by communicating and by manipulating policy and program, money, manpower, and material. And like other leaders, he lives with the unpleasant reality that he can rarely command approval from everyone he serves.

Nor do the President's "followers" merely receive cues from their leader. "All leaders," observed Georg Simmel, "are also led as in countless cases the master is the slave of his slaves." [3] Leaders, including the President, act on the expectations of "followers" or "constituents." Society and its groups have needs that the President responds to. The most basic is maintaining the integrity and continuity of society itself. Social groups (constituencies) traditionally look to the President to guard them against external threat. But the type of response called for may change over time, and leadership behavior

---

[2] In Richard E. Neustadt, *Presidential Power: The Politics of Leadership* (New York: Wiley, 1960), 9.

[3] In Alvin W. Gouldner, ed., *Studies in Leadership* (New York: Russell and Russell, 1965), 20.

may alter accordingly. The vehemence of an Andrew Jackson and the intransigence of an Andrew Johnson were tolerable in the nineteenth century, but would be inappropriate in the dangers and sensitivities of the nuclear age.

The leader's attitudes, values, and skills may drive him to respond to group demands or deter him from responding. The economic depression of the 1930s called for highly innovative leadership that could restore shattered public and business confidence. But President Hoover held to the philosophy that it is not the place of the national government to initiate action. Instead he favored state and private action, altogether a frail back for the herculean task of lifting the country up from the depths of the depression. Neither was Hoover the kind of person who could inspire the nation and restore its damaged self-esteem. The Presidency "is not a showman's job," he said, "I will not step out of character." [4] He read his infrequent radio addresses in a dull monotone that quickly lost his audience. Hoover's successor, Franklin Roosevelt, brought an activist philosophy and exhortative gifts that inspirited the nation and restored confidence.

People have made studies to try to figure out what distinguishes leaders from nonleaders, effective leaders from ineffective ones. So far no one has been able to identify a set of attributes (IQ, height, particular skills, and so on) that consistently characterize leaders or effective Presidents. Warren Harding and Franklin Pierce excelled as orators and would have delighted a Hollywood casting director looking for someone to play the ideal stereotype of the President—yet their Presidencies appear near the bottom of most ratings of leadership-effectiveness.

Constitutional provisions
for the Presidency

Much of the crucial language of the Constitution setting forth the President's powers in Article II is sparse and general. It provides that "the executive power shall be vested in the President" but gives no clear definition of executive power.

But the Constitution also vests in the President certain specific powers. He is commander in chief of the army and navy of the United States. He is empowered to grant reprieves and pardons for offenses against the United States. The Constitution provides that the President shall make various appointments with the advice and consent of the Senate—ambassadors and ministers, justices of the Supreme Court, and other officers.

The Constitution gives the President important legislative powers and establishes him as a key participant in lawmaking. He is directed to deliver what has become known as the State of the Union message and to communicate special messages on further subjects to Congress. Legislation that Con-

[4] Theodore G. Joslin, *Hoover Off The Record* (New York: Doubleday, 1934), 18.

gress passes requires his approval to become law. And if he vetoes it Congress can override his action only by obtaining a two-thirds vote in each house. In addition, the President "on extraordinary occasions" can convene one or both houses.

In foreign affairs, he is empowered to make treaties, with the consent of two-thirds of the Senate. And he is empowered to receive the ambassadors and ministers of other nations. In both foreign and domestic affairs, he is charged to see that the laws are faithfully executed. As for other provisions, the Constitution specifies his qualifications, selection, and impeachment.

These formal provisions of the Constitution give only a limited view of the President's powers. Indeed, they do not give a hint of the enormous power that has accrued to the office as history has proceeded. The Constitution itself reflects a struggle between the concept of executive power as subordinate to the legislative power and the concept of executive power as autonomous and self-directing within broad latitudes. The tension between the two concepts has never ceased. As the debate over the President's power in the Vietnam war testifies, it persists today.

Over the decades and centuries, presidential power has expanded by the assertion and skill of the incumbents—Jackson, Wilson, the Roosevelts, and the entire line of Presidents since the Second World War. Presidential power has increased in response to society's demands for protection against economic depression, for social justice, for national security and survival, especially in the nuclear age.

Presidential tenure. The Constitution better enables the President to provide leadership by endowing him with substantial tenure. The elected term of four years contrasts with the meagre one-year term given to most state governors at the time the Constitution was framed, robbing their office of power and influence. The President used to be eligible to run indefinitely, but following Franklin Roosevelt's marathon four terms the Twenty-Second Amendment limited the incumbent to only two terms.

The Constitution anticipates interruptions of tenure by the incumbent's resignation, death, disability, or impeachment. No President has resigned, and only Andrew Johnson has been subjected to impeachment procedure, only to be saved by a single senatorial vote. Lawmakers were galvanized into clearing up some troubling, unanswered constitutional questions about disability by President Kennedy's assassination, which aroused speculation over the chaos of uncertainties had he remained alive but helpless.

The Twenty-Fifth Amendment, passed in 1967, authorizes the President, on deeming himself disabled, to notify the Speaker of the House and the President pro tempore of the Senate in writing. If the President cannot or will not give notice, the Vice-President supported by a majority of the Cabinet or such other body as Congress might provide, could advise the congressional officers of the President's inability. The Vice-President then becomes Acting

President for the duration of the President's inability. The amendment also prescribes steps for the President, recovered from his disability, to resume the powers and duties of his office.

Leadership in democracy requires the continuous availability of its highest civilian officers—otherwise government might be taken over by illegitimate power, including the military. To make certain that the Presidency is always filled is a concern of both the Constitution and statute. Attention focuses on the Vice-Presidency. The Twenty-Fifth Amendment specifies that whenever it becomes vacant, the President can nominate a new Vice-President who will take office when confirmed "by a majority vote" of both congressional houses. The Succession Act of 1947 provides for a line of officers to succeed to the Presidency when something happens to both President and Vice-President. In sequence come the Speaker of the House; then the president pro tempore of the Senate, followed by the heads of the Cabinet departments. With all the successors concentrated in Washington, the law does not respond to what seems to be common sense in the nuclear age: some presidential successors ought to be located outside the national capital.

Selecting a President

To attain his office, the President must survive a rigorous selection process that tests his political acumen and skill, factors highly relevant to leadership. In past times, the process was sweetened by the idea that "any boy can become President." Ideally suited for the democratic principle that leaders should emerge from a broad base, the idea embodies a middle class emphasis on success and the myth of a mobile open-class society, generally discredited in recent years as people have become more sensitive to the unacknowledged class boundaries that present real obstacles and prevent the mobility of blacks and other deprived groups.

The thirty-six men who have been President also reveal that the reality is different. Presidents emerge from solid white middle-class or upper-middle-class backgrounds. Their fathers have been professionals, proprietors, officials, and farm owners, rather than low-salaried workers, servants, and farm laborers. And in achievement before gaining office, Presidents have attained a status far beyond the log cabin. Twenty-four of the thirty-six incumbents have been lawyers, a profession that nurtures skills highly useful in politics, and one that can be left temporarily and returned to more readily than other callings.[5]

Winning the presidential nomination transpires in a kind of free enterprise political system. A lengthy apprenticeship in the party is not a prerequisite, for the presidential nomination has fallen to persons outside the party altogether. Generals, after a successful war, are a favorite resort for parties eager for a winner. The generals may have no party affiliation—they may never even have

[5] Donald R. Matthews, *The Social Background of Political Decision-Makers* (New York: Doubleday, 1954), 23–24.

voted. Some Presidents—Hoover and Eisenhower, for example—were approached at one time or another by representatives of both major parties. Usually, however, the nomination is won by a politician who has served his party well and has held a leading position, say, as Vice-President, governor, or senator. But the aspirant should not be so dogmatic that he offends major factions of his party, nor so partisan that he alienates voters of the opposition party—his own party's success may depend on their crossing party lines at election time. Typically, he tends to be more pragmatic than ideological, more prone to shift and adjust on issues than to hold tenaciously to fixed positions.

Choosing the delegates. In recent presidential elections, the nomination has been all but won before the national convention of the party meets to make the official decision. The crucial struggle takes place months before the convention when delegates committed to various candidates are selected in each state. (The national party determines the total number of delegates and their allotment among the states.) Delegates function largely as a ratifying body at the convention when the majority of them are committed on the first ballot to one candidate. If the issue is in doubt, however, many ballots may be required at the convention to determine the party nominee. In 1924, when a two-thirds vote of the delegates was necessary to nominate, the nomination of John W. Davis required 103 ballots.

Methods of delegate selection vary from state to state, and are constantly changing. In some states, the state party leaders or committeemen designate some of the delegates. Some states have voters elect representatives to a state convention, which chooses the delegates to the national convention. In other states, primary elections allow the voters of each district to elect a slate of delegates committed to a particular candidate. More and more states are instituting preferential primaries in which the candidates divide the delegates according to the proportion of the vote they won. A few states allow the candidate with the most votes in the primary to take all the delegates. There is an almost infinite variety of state practices.

The delegate selection system is criticized for its excessive variation from state to state and for violating the principle that all registered voters wherever they live should have identical roles in nominating the candidate. The present system tends to allot the major influence to the party organization and sharply limits the impact of the young, the poor, and the urban minorities. The winner-take-all primary is attacked as inherently undemocratic, but states have been reluctant to substitute the preferential primary because they feel it might weaken the state's influence at the national convention by dividing its delegates.

The Democratic party has initiated many reforms in its delegate selection system, as specified by the party's McGovern Commission. The states, for example, were given guidelines as to the number of minorities that should be represented among the delegates. Party members in states with unrepresentative delegations were given an opportunity to challenge them and seat representative delegates. As a result the 1972 Democratic National Convention was attended by greater numbers of blacks, young people, women, Chicanos, Indians than had ever attended a convention before. Eighty percent of the delegates were attending for the first time. This new coalition of delegates provided the impetus to nominate George McGovern. In the 1972 Republican convention, women achieved strikingly better representation than in 1968, although they fared somewhat less well in representation than did Democratic women in 1972. Blacks and youth also made gains at the Republican convention in 1972 but again on a scale more modest than their gains in the Democratic convention.

In the struggle to win delegate support prior to the convention, candidates tend to pursue certain strategies. For instance, the "dominant leader," such as an incumbent first-term President, normally has a clear unrivaled claim to renomination and seeks only to prevent a contest from developing. Nixon succeeded in doing so in 1972 although Lyndon Johnson was unable to prevent it in 1968. The "organization man" strategy, suitable for the candidate who stands well with party leaders, has its prototypes in the 1968 campaigns of Nixon and Humphrey, who both enjoyed formidable strength in the regular party organization then. This strategy treats primaries somewhat incidentally, although regarding them as useful, and values the delegates' "second choice" support. Often, the delegate discharges his obligation to the voters of his state by voting on the first roll call for the candidate of their choice; after that, he may switch his vote to another candidate favored by his state party or party faction. A "popular hero," such as McGovern was among certain constituencies in 1972, seeks to create a groundswell in resorting to the primaries. He may bypass some state leaders who look askance at his type of candidacy. McGovern's nomination was achieved in 1972 because of a snowballing success in the primaries and in spite of the bitter opposition of an army of state and local leaders.

The convention. Behind the noisy jumbled exterior of the national convention an intense, rational enterprise is conducted by the rival candidates and their managers. When the result is in doubt, the candidate himself may be on hand, pleading his case before state delegations and superintending his forces. From a cottage outside the Los Angeles Sports Arena, in 1960, John Kennedy and his floor managers had direct communications lines to "state shepherds" who roved the convention floor with walkie-talkie sets. McGovern and Humphrey both had a network of aides courting the delegates at the 1972 convention.

Promotion of candidacy is apt to employ any one or more common tactics. The "test of strength," prompting a roll-call vote in early sessions of the convention, provides an accurate indication of the strength of the respective camps well before the vote on the nomination. More by necessity than by choice, the McGovern forces obtained such a roll-call vote when they challenged the removal of 121 McGovern delegates from the California delegation.

*President Nixon and Vice-President Agnew, following their renomination
at the Republican National Convention in 1972.*

The outcome both increased McGovern's delegate strength and revealed its
magnitude. The "bandwagon" is a psychological contraption, intended to
maximize the impression of a candidate's strength, to prompt others to rush
aboard for the potential political advantage of helping to build the winning
side. The "steamroller" prompts a faction that captures control of the convention to employ its power mercilessly in convention decisions against the
opposition. The Goldwater steamroller at the 1964 Republican convention
made it difficult for a dissenter like Nelson Rockefeller to gain the floor and
be heard. Amid boos and catcalls, Rockefeller reminded the delegates that
"this is a free country." A smoother steamroller assured Nixon's renomination
in 1972. The sole dissenting vote was cast for Congressman Paul McCloskey
(Calif.), and this was done with careful apologies and only because it was
required by state law. The "deal," by which the candidate makes an agreement
concerning the disposal of the Vice-Presidency, Cabinet, or other posts, increases his delegate support and helps unite the party.

    The convention is responsible for adopting a platform. This may be a bland
exercise, or it may spark a bitter fight as the Vietnam plank did in the 1968
Democratic convention. After the platform is adopted the presidential

The 1972 presidential candidates "press the flesh" in their campaigns.

nomination takes place. Following nominating speeches for the various candidates, balloting begins with a roll call of states. The chairman of each state delegation announces its vote, which can be united or divided. If the announced vote is challenged, the delegation is polled. Ordinarily the nomination occurs on the first ballot; if not, further ballotings are taken until a majority is attained. Johnson in 1964 and Roosevelt in 1936 were nominated simply by acclamation.

Next on the agenda is the nomination of the Vice-President, who is generally singled out beforehand by the presidential nominee. Usually the Vice-President is expected to "balance the ticket," by hailing from a section of the country different from the President's or representing different constituencies. Nixon's choice of Spiro Agnew of Maryland in 1968, a strong advocate of law and order, was viewed as a bow to Southern supporters who clinched Nixon's own nomination on the first ballot.

The campaign. In the course of the campaign, the nominee must make strategic decisions about the coalition of groups he wants support from. He is guided by the combination of states and electoral votes he hopes to rally for victory. Kennedy's 1960 strategy focused on nine large states (New York, Pennsylvania, California, Michigan, Texas, Illinois, New Jersey, Ohio, and Massachusetts) comprising 237 of the 269 electoral votes then required to elect a President. In his stand on issues and the program he championed, Kennedy concentrated on the needs of city-centered groups in these heavily industrial-urban states. In his 1968 and 1972 campaigns, Nixon pursued a Southern strategy by taking a reserved stance on civil rights issues, opposing school busing, and giving a commitment to law and order.

The nominee may support issues to which he feels personally committed. Thus McGovern gave a top priority to his opposition to the Vietnam war despite a Louis Harris poll during the campaign showing that 55 percent of the voters supported the Nixon administration's heavy bombing of North Vietnam, while only 32 percent opposed it.

Presidential candidates have become increasingly dependent on television campaigning to project their views—and their image. Nixon's 1968 campaign staff was full of men from advertising and television who meant to project a new image of Nixon, correcting what they saw as his natural deficiencies. Instead of the "grumpy, cold, aloof Nixon" lacking in humor, a man who seemed to be "forty-two years old the day he was born," the managers, by controlling the style and atmosphere of the candidate's television appearances, transformed him into someone who delighted in communicating with the people and derived "great joy" from seeking the Presidency.[6] In such a television campaign, issues and conflict politics are muted, a tactic that does not perceive electoral democracy as resting on serious discussion of significant problems.

But even in the age of television, the candidates still "get out to the people" in personal appearances. The local speech, the slow drive down Main Street, the walk through the streets, and "pressing the flesh," as Lyndon Johnson called it, were major activities of both sides in the 1972 presidential race. Not only the candidates but their families and clans toured the byways. Air travel enables the candidate to appear in several or most regions of the country in a single day. The same major cities may be visited and revisited. After a few weeks of the 1972 campaign, Pittsburgh had been visited so many times by the national Democratic ticket that local leaders were grumbling

[6] See Joe McGinniss, *The Selling of the President 1968* (New York: Trident Press, 1969).

that most of their effort was spent organizing rallies and receptions for their visitors, leaving little time for local contests.

Posters, buttons, and literature are as important as they were a century ago, and the registration drive, the exhorting telephone call, and the offer of a ride to the polls on election day signify that getting out the vote remains a prime job of the campaign and its workers.

The election. In the voting booth in November, the citizen appears to be choosing a President; actually he is choosing electors. The Constitution has provided that the President be elected by an electoral college, or, more precisely, by fifty electoral colleges, that is, one in each state. In each state and the District of Columbia one elector is chosen for each senator and representative that state has in Congress. Each elector has one vote, and a majority of the total number of electors is necessary to choose a President. Electors are chosen by the general ticket system, which applies the principle of "winner take all." The party carrying a state in the presidential contest, even if it won by only a few votes, wins all the state's electors, and the minority party or parties get none. If no candidate receives a majority, the Constitution directs the House of Representatives, with each state having one vote, to choose the President from among the three candidates receiving the largest number of electoral votes.

Why do we adhere to this system? Why not institute direct popular election of the President, which would best harmonize with the Supreme Court's ideal of "one man, one vote" voiced in its apportionment decisions? Such an alternative would imperil the two-party system by giving additional parties weight and influence; the winner-take-all procedure in the electoral college– general ticket system denies any proportional representation for third and fourth parties and thus discourages their remaining long in the field. A multiparty system would diminish the vigor of the Presidency by causing the office to rest on a narrower foundation of popular support.

The present electoral system encourages party factions to modify their differences so that they might present a united front adequate to capture the Presidency. The present system also draws more attention to the problems of cities than is likely under alternatives. Parties now make a point of concentrating on large states, with their wealth of electoral votes, and on their great cities, which may control the outcome of the election. Finally, a direct popular election of the President would sometimes require a run-off election, which is costly in money, delay, and public uncertainty about leadership.

The nature of presidential roles

The elected, tenured President exercises leadership through a complex of roles comprising his office. He is party leader, legislative leader, administrative leader, chief diplomat, commander in chief, and chief decision-maker, among other roles. His performance in a role is shaped by situations, critical and minor, and by his personality—his attitudes, values, and skills.

A role embraces rights and obligations—what is due and what is owed. For example, interpreting his relation to the Indochina war, Nixon claimed "the constitutional right," derived from the commander-in-chief clause, to continue to wage war in that area. And he saw also his task as one of obligation. He justified his dispatch of American troops into Cambodia to seek out enemy sanctuaries as part of his "responsibility—to use his powers to protect American forces when they are engaged in military actions." [7] Obligations, as Nixon made clear, may not just impose burdens; they can remarkably expand the presidential role by providing cause for action.

The President's roles are enlarged or curtailed by the expectations of different constituencies at home and abroad, all of whom have stakes in what he does. Their expectations have great range, from which the President may select in any given situation. Some expectations may be historical in their roots. America's past glories and military successes shape the expectations of many citizens looking at how any incumbent President conducts the Indochina war. For many of these people, who have learned of America's invincibility from schoolbook histories, Nixon struck a happy chord when, in a report on the war, he said "America has never been defeated in the proud 190-year history of this country. And we shall not be defeated in Vietnam." [8] But expectations are not impervious to change. They may alter over time from the erosion of events or by the President's own design. The plodding, dispiriting Vietnam war makes it unlikely that any President in the future could affirm the pledge of Kennedy's inaugural, to fight "any foe," wherever he may be, "to assure the survival and success of liberty." A public thoroughly tired of the Vietnam war could not bear such words.

The President's leadership roles have boundaries. In one view, he is surrounded by watchful, assertive boundary-setters, empowered to draw lines within which he is expected to perform. The Supreme Court and other federal courts monitor the President's conduct in light of the Constitution and other laws and push him back when he exceeds them. Hence the Court forced Truman to release the steel mills that were seized in face of a pending labor strike that threatened to cut off production needed in the Korean war. [9] Congress is another boundary-setter and, like the courts, may be both restrictive and expansive. Time and again Congress has given Nixon far larger appropriations for social programs than he requested, and in effect prodded him to take a larger role than he wanted. The vast executive bureaucracy, with its appointed, tenured personnel, may encourage the President or deter him. And the electorate is a boundary-setter so powerful that it can throw the President

---

[7] "Interview with the President on U.S. Foreign Policy," New York Times, July 2, 1970.
[8] "Transcript of President's Address to the Nation on Vietnam," New York Times, April 21, 1970.
[9] Youngstown Sheet and Tube Company v. Sawyer, 343 U.S. 579 (1952).

and his party out of office if his performance is unacceptable. The Washington community, the world's capitals, and historians are apt to judge Presidents and what they do as leaders by their ability to maintain, or even to enlarge, the boundaries of their office.

The goals and preferences of a President's leadership roles may be the same as or different from those of his various publics. Presumably his influence expands as he articulates and achieves the things his countrymen want most. Other parts of the political system are then more apt to respond to his demands and needs; the electorate will more readily and enthusiastically keep him in office. For this shared political bliss to transpire, that President does best who instructs himself in what the people want and how they are faring. The modern public opinion poll may both simplify their task and occasionally mislead them. Presidents resort to all sorts of contrivances to determine how popular their conduct is. Franklin Roosevelt relied on his observant, far-travelling wife and on his administrator of public works, Harry Hopkins, whose tasks took him about the country. Harry Truman, in need of impressions of Midwestern agricultural opinion, dispatched his friend Leslie Biffle, secretary of the Senate, to that region, where, disguised as a farmer, he ferreted out true local sentiment.

But the President who excels as a leader excels at pursuing significant goals at the risk of dissonance with group will. He must, if necessary, be willing to sacrifice popularity to policy. In 1793, many Americans favored the French over the British in their European conflict; American sympathies were fanned by the fiery rhetoric of France's minister to the United States, Citizen Edmond Charles Genêt. Demand for war with Britain mushroomed, but Washington, convinced that the young nation must not squander its precious strength in war, chose a policy of neutrality. In the press and in public meetings, he was mercilessly maligned, and even his safety was imperiled. "Ten thousand people in the streets of Philadelphia," wrote Vice-President John Adams, "day after day threatened to drag Washington out of his house, and effect a revolution in the Government, or compel it to declare war in favor of the French revolution and against England." [10] But neutrality remained Washington's policy and it prevailed.

Party leader

The President is leader of his party. But in this role he is handicapped by a lack of effective national party institutions. Much of the power and money of the major parties is concentrated in state parties. The loyalties of national legislators run to state and local parties, which nominate them. Sometimes a legislator seeking reelection may lessen his chances if he identifies too much with the President's policies. In a 1966 Louisiana Democratic primary in the

[10] In James E. Pollard, *The Presidents and the Press* (New York: Macmillan, 1947), 37.

Sixth Congressional District, the little-known John R. Rarick toppled the incumbent of twenty-four years, Congressman James Morrison, who had voted for the 1965 Voting Rights Act. "He's got the LBJ brand on him," Rarick said time and again of Morrison. Rarick's victory statement revealed the basis of his campaign: "I guess by now LBJ knows he don't own the 6th District of Louisiana. I guess by now the federal spies and CORE know they couldn't scare all the people away from the polls." "Federal spies" alluded to a ruling by a federal panel at New Orleans that under the 1965 Voting Rights Act federal observers could help illiterates vote in the polling booths.[11]

A few Presidents, a Jefferson and a Jackson, excelled as party leaders and dominated the governmental machinery. But because success in party matters depends so much on personal skill, the role has never stabilized. In the free personal enterprise and minimum discipline of the national party structure, the chief rivals and detractors of the President's leadership may abound within his own party. Lyndon Johnson's principal opponents were all Democrats: Senator J. W. Fulbright led congressional critics of his Vietnam policy, followed close behind by the Democratic Senate Leader, Mike Mansfield. Johnson's chief challengers to his reelection were Democratic senators Eugene McCarthy and Robert Kennedy, whose strength influenced him not to seek renomination.

To make his way as party leader, to induce his fellow party members to move in his direction, the President is able to manipulate certain resources. The most historic is patronage, or the dispensing of offices and jobs. Once a busy concern of nineteenth-century Presidents, patronage has been reduced to a shadow of its former self by the merit system in civil service. Even when a federal appointment is within the power of patronage, the President may be subject to "senatorial courtesy," or the obligation to confer with the senator or senators from the state where the office is to be filled. The Senate will almost invariably reject a presidential nominee when the senator who is owed courtesy objects. In effect, senatorial courtesy transfers the distribution of patronage within a state from the President to senators of his party.

The President can also manipulate a vast pork barrel of executive branch expenditures for military contracts, highways, and other public works construction. The President may distribute the largess of federal expenditure more bountifully to the constituencies of legislators who vote faithfully for his programs than those of legislators whose support is spotty.

The President may use program and policy to recast the make-up of his party, to attract into its ranks groups that are indifferent or attached to the rival party. Franklin Roosevelt wrought a major transformation of the Democratic party by constructing a new coalition of votes. Major laws of his administration—the Social Security Act, the National Labor Relations Act, and work relief laws—appealed to city-centered groups, labor, blacks, the new immigrants, women, and intellectuals. Blacks were weaned from their

[11] Atlanta *Constitution,* September 26, 1966.

traditional attachment to the Republican party, and labor came to regard the President as an unfailing champion. With all this, Roosevelt also was careful in his innovations not to offend the South, his party's traditional bastion.

President Nixon appears engrossed in a quest to convert the Republican party from its long-standing minority status into a voting majority. One vision of this transformation sees the party dominant in the nation's heartland, in the South, in California, and in the suburbs everywhere, with the Democratic party retaining its black support in the North and South as well as command-ing votes from the Northeast and Pacific Northwest.[12] Pursuing what some regard as a "Southern strategy," the Nixon administration slowed the pace of school integration in 1969–70 and nourished other policies that aroused protests from black civil rights leaders.

Legislative leader

Modern Presidents are spoken of as "chief legislators" and "the third legisla-tive house," so involved are they in lawmaking. Yet for all his prestige, the President may toil in vain, particularly in social legislation.

Historically, Congress tends to follow the President's lead in three types of situations. One is the crisis of war or economic depression, when survival of the social system is at stake. Franklin Roosevelt in the Great Depression and Presidents of both world wars enjoyed full congressional support. A second situation is national security and foreign affairs, particularly from the end of the Second World War until recently, when widespread disillusionment with the prolonged Indochina war set in. The Marshall Plan, NATO, the Korean war—these are monuments to interbranch cooperation induced more by Communist pressure than by magic of presidential leadership.

The third situation blooms in an abnormal political climate highly favor-able to the President. In 1964–65, Johnson was the beneficiary of lopsided majorities in both congressional houses following his massive victory over Goldwater. The election produced an unusually large crop of seventy-one freshmen Democratic congressmen, who proceeded to support the President more than 80 percent of the time on roll-call votes. (Since freshmen legislators tend to come from "unsafe" districts, they depend to some extent on the President's support for reelection and are prone to follow his lead.) With such imposing political resources, Johnson in 1965 presided over more innova-tive social legislation than any other President in any other single session of Congress in the twentieth century. The list included medical care for the aged under Social Security, the first comprehensive aid-to-education legislation, a voting rights law, a broad housing program with rent subsidies for low income families, and programs for combating serious diseases and air and water pollution. Most of these measures had been on the presidential agenda for twenty years. Well could Johnson hail the Congress of 1965, "my Congress," as the greatest Congress ever.

[12] *New York Times,* July 13, 1969.

A more frequent scenario of interbranch relations is deadlock. Kennedy's urban-oriented program met rejection and delay in Congress, particularly in the House. In the Nixon era, similar results appeared, only the ideological roles were reversed. By comparison, Congress was liberal and urban-oriented and the President conservative. Much of the interbranch conflict centered on the budget and appropriations: Congress made huge additions to the President's requests for funds—in fiscal year 1969, the President's budget was augmented by $3 billion.

In part, the Nixon-Congress conflict was an election-year struggle for the reins of power and a means for Congress to assert itself after a rush of power to the executive in foreign affairs. It was also a fight over priorities between a Republican President and a Democratic Congress. Nixon stressed military priorities, support for the Indochina war, and "fiscal responsibility" through restrained expenditure, especially in social areas, to check inflation. Democratic leaders, on the other hand, urged increased domestic expenditures for education, pollution control, and health—"The needs of the people will be given top priority," as Majority Leader Mike Mansfield put it. Nevertheless, Democratic congressional liberals simultaneously presented the uncharacteristic spectacle of advocating tax reductions to enable private citizens to spend more money. The paradox of favoring more federal expenditure but providing less money for it moved Charles Schultze, former budget director of the Johnson administration, to write, "When the chips are down on tax cuts, those who talked about priorities for pollution control and education and an end to hunger voted for a different set of priorities—for beer and cosmetics and white-wall tires." [13]

Legislative-executive relations may be transformed from disagreement and inaction into consensus and action, with the President leading the effort. For years prior to the Education Act of 1965, bills providing general aid to education were wrecked on the issue of public aid to church-related schools. Through discussions with the principal interest groups in conflict—the National Education Association and the National Catholic Welfare Council—the Johnson administration developed a formula acceptable to both: to aid not schools as such but children, whether in public or private schools. The consensus was incorporated into an administration bill, and with the two education lobbies supporting it, a new law was passed without major amendment. A deadlock of decades was finally broken.

Nevertheless, it was not consensus, but checks and balances and potential conflict that the Founding Fathers built into the Constitution in congressional-presidential relations. Each branch is responsible to different constituencies: the President is elected by a national majority or plurality; Congress by local constituencies. National and local viewpoints are thus injected into national politics, with each deemed necessary and valid in a nation as diverse and extensive as the United States. Different terms of office for the President and the congressional houses fortify the differences of constituency.

The principle of checks and balances is observed in functions shared by

13 *New York Times,* December 20, 1969.

the President and Congress. Both branches participate in lawmaking, appointments, treaties, and the like, and positive action can seldom occur without a consensus of the two branches. Furthermore, Congress makes specific demands on the President, prompting President Eisenhower once to observe rightly, "I am part of the legislative process." The contemporary President is expected to put an agenda before Congress and promote it. The Constitution requires him to deliver to Congress a State of the Union message, which usually delineates the scope of his legislative programs for the coming year. In 1921 Congress passed the Budget and Accounting Act requiring the President to give an annual budget message that explains the massive executive budget (which the act also empowered him to prepare) and spells out work programs and costs to achieve goals outlined in the State of the Union message and to continue ongoing programs. In 1946 Congress passed the Employment Act requiring the President to deliver an annual economic report that specifies policies to maintain employment and production at high levels, combat inflation, and satisfy economic needs. Many special messages on the President's own initiative may focus on single policy areas like education, civil rights, and foreign aid.

Theodore Roosevelt began the practice that contemporary Presidents follow of supplementing their messages with actual drafts of bills. The President and his aides promote his programs by a kind of private, unofficial, almost invisible politics that exploits the influence of personal contact, patronage, and pork barrel. The tête-à-tête in the White House or legislative office, the presidential phone call to the undecided legislator, the accommodations and compromises necessary to patch together a legislative majority— all these may be used by the President trying to move a major bill through Congress. A legislative liaison team of the White House staff handles many of these duties. The President may also take his legislative program to the people. Theodore Roosevelt was the first of the modern Presidents to make use of popular appeals in order to swing public opinion to his side. In civil rights crises of the 1960s, when, for example, black students applied to Southern universities or blacks sought access to public facilities, Kennedy and Johnson, in television addresses, expounded to the nation the rights and moral obligations involved. These efforts helped develop a public climate that was more receptive to new civil rights legislation, which Congress soon enacted.

The President also participates in a later stage of lawmaking when a bill, passed by both houses of Congress, comes to him for approval or veto. Several choices are open to him. He can sign the bill and make it become law. He can abstain from signing, in which case it becomes law after ten congressional working days. If Congress adjourns within the ten days, the bill dies (pocket veto). Finally, the President can veto the bill by sending it back to Congress with a message stating his objections. A roll-call vote in each house can override the veto, but this seldom happens because a two-thirds majority is required. Often a President's threat to veto can shape legislation while Congress is considering it.

President Nixon confers at a breakfast meeting with House leaders Hale Boggs and Gerald Ford. Also attending are Richard Cooke of the congressional liaison office, and General Alexander Haig, staff assistant to Henry Kissinger.

Modern Presidents use the veto to express all kinds of disapproval, and Franklin Roosevelt was its chief brandisher with 631 vetoes. Since the President has only a general veto and not an item veto as some governors do, he must accept or reject a bill as a whole; he cannot veto particular items and approve the rest. The arrangement inspires legislators to add riders or provisions that may be little related to the bill, which the President may reluctantly accept if he wants the other parts of the bill enough.

Administrative leader

To exercise leadership, to take policy initiatives and carry them out, to deliver on his promises, the President depends on support from the nearly three million civilian employees of the executive branch. Their expertise, possession of government's material resources, and virtual monopoly of the capacity to act make them vital cogs in the President's leadership performance.

Help for the President. In exerting leadership, the President is aided by a host of helpers, advisers, and councils. The most traditional of his helpers are the Cabinet, consisting of the department heads such as the Secretaries of State, Defense, Treasury, and others who meet with the President presiding.

The Executive Office of the President is an umbrella-like structure, under which are clustered the President's staff agencies. Most of the units of the Executive Office deal with continuous large-scale processes in the Presidency and involve substantial expert staffs, procedures, records, and jurisdictions. Budgeting is one of these processes; it is handled for the President by the Office of Management and Budget.

The White House Office consists of about two dozen assistants to the President and a large clerical force. Among the assistants to President Nixon is the assistant for national security affairs, Henry Kissinger, whose influence equals, if it does not exceed, that of the Secretaries of State and Defense. Likewise, the influence of assistant John Ehrlichman in domestic policy surpasses that of most department heads. Other White House aides, like the press secretary and the appointments secretary, discharge functions that are important to the everyday functioning of the Presidency. Still other assistants help with tasks of personal and political importance to the President— drafting his speeches, planning election campaigns, and providing policy and political advice on key decisions.

Every recent President has made some reorganization of his staff, an act that in itself suggests enterprising leadership. In a major overhaul in 1970, Nixon created the Domestic Council which advises on domestic policy and oversees its implementation. It consists of department and agency heads and is guided by Ehrlichman. In addition, Nixon transformed the old Budget Bureau into the Office of Management and Budget. The new structuring was expected to give the President a kind of information he has sorely needed: evaluations of the performance of agencies and programs, a means to compare what is promised with what has been or can be accomplished.

Limits on the President. Although he presumably presides over the executive branch, the President is far from being its master. Congress, for one, is a potent presence. Acts of Congress determine what the departments do and give them the authority to do it. Congress also prescribes structure and operating procedures, and it can require Senate approval of new bureau chiefs and investigate agency performance or review an agency's policy when it comes to Capitol Hill annually for appropriations. Congressional standing committees and subcommittees also may watch protectively over the agency, aided and abetted by interest groups whose needs it serves.

Often congressional surveillance is directed to keeping the agency within bounds desired by interest groups, however different they are from the President's view of the agency's mission. These differences may be seen to operate on the unfortunate statistic of 14,000 workers who are killed each year because of occupational hazards, and the two million more who suffer disabling injuries. Federal laws regulating occupational hazards are limited in coverage, and the Labor Department, which administers them, seldom invokes their mild penalties. Business lobbyists have convinced Congress that safety

White House aides John Ehrlichman and Henry Kissinger meet with the President.

standards can be best administered by the states. The lobbyists also induce Congress to hold appropriations down for enforcement activities, so that the Labor Department's inspection staffs are able to visit only between 2 and 3 percent of all the plants covered by law. The Labor Department has reported that "the vast majority" of plants have no meaningful safety and health programs. Both Presidents Johnson and Nixon criticized the spotty character of state laws and called for expanded federal effort. President Nixon has urged that "the quality of the work place" is "a critical factor for Government attention," but Congress continues to handcuff the Labor Department with limited authority and meagre appropriations.[14]

On occasion, the courts may thwart the President when he asserts administrative leadership. Although the Constitution says nothing about the President's power to fire people, the Supreme Court in *Myers v. United States* [15] seemed to find an unlimited authority when President Wilson removed a postmaster. The case emboldened Franklin Roosevelt to remove a Federal Trade Commissioner, William E. Humphrey, because of their policy

[14] *New York Times,* January 2, 1970.
[15] 272 U.S. 52 (1926).

differences, but the Court in *Humphrey's Executor v. United States* [16] ruled that officials who wield legislative and judicial power as Humphrey did are immune to presidential removal except as Congress stipulates. Congress did not consider the policy difference between Humphrey and Roosevelt as a ground for Humphrey's removal.

The bureaucracy itself can resist the President. It can delay and dilute what he wants done. President Kennedy, for example, eagerly awaited new policy proposals for Latin America to develop in the State Department, but little was forthcoming. Eventually he turned to other quarters, to the White House staff and to old hands from previous administrations who were brought back.

A contemporary Republican President, an Eisenhower or Nixon, faces a largely Democratic bureaucracy, one mostly recruited during that party's long dominance of the White House and therefore sympathetic to views sometimes at odds with those of the Chief Executive. In the Nixon administration, HEW employees have openly protested the priority given the Vietnam war over their department's work. Democratic Presidents have generally been spared such pressure.

Even the President's staff can hobble his leadership. Eisenhower, meaning to provide leadership of high ethical resolve, pledged himself to create an administration "as clean as a hound's tooth," only to have his chief assistant, Sherman Adams, driven from its ranks for unethical conduct. Encouraged by his staff's gross miscalculations, Kennedy floundered in a nightmarish fiasco, the abortive invasion of Cuba's Bay of Pigs in 1961. Critics see Nixon surrounded by iron rings of White House assistants that not even Cabinet Secretaries can penetrate. George Romney, Secretary of Housing and Urban Development, complained that for long stretches he was unable to reach the President by telephone.[17] Interior Secretary Walter Hickel, in a letter to the President that somehow was "leaked" to the press, urged better communication between the President and the young, as well as between the President and the Cabinet. Hickel recommended presidential meetings with Cabinet Secretaries "on an individual and conversational basis" as a step toward "greater insight into the problems confronting us all, and . . . into the solutions of these problems." [18]

Chief diplomat and
commander in chief

In sweeping language the Constitution establishes the President as commander in chief of the armed forces and vests in him "the executive power" that includes powers usually belonging to heads of governments. The President

[16] 295 U.S. 602 (1935).
[17] *New York Times,* May 10, 1970.
[18] *New York Times,* May 7, 1970.

makes treaties, "by and with the advice and consent of the Senate . . . provided two-thirds of the senators present concur." The President can also make "executive agreements" with foreign powers, which do not have to be reviewed by the Senate and are authorized by the executive power clause, the commander-in-chief power, and any statutes or treaties that accord the President the right to make such agreements. The President appoints ambassadors and other public ministers and consuls, with the Senate's advice and consent. But he alone receives the diplomatic representatives of other nations, which is in effect a power to recognize new governments without consulting Congress. On the other hand, Congress has the power to enact laws for the tariff and international monetary affairs, to appropriate funds for foreign aid, and to declare war.

Foreign affairs and national security have provided some of the most severe tests of presidential leadership. Presidents have led the country successfully through horrendous wars. Washington and Van Buren triumphed in their ordeal of leadership by keeping the nation at peace when their countrymen preferred war. The nation has been spared, thanks greatly to presidential leadership, the scourge of devastation and dismemberment. Reflecting the built-in ideal of balanced government, both Congress and the Chief Executive have enjoyed periods of being on top. The legislative hand was uppermost in the entry into the War of 1812 and the Spanish-American War in 1898, in the rejection of American membership in the League of Nations, and in the isolationist policies prevailing between the two world wars.

Since the Second World War, power has moved dramatically to the President. The era of nuclear weapons and the Communist threat on most continents have increased the President's power to the point that he has been able to get almost anything he wants from Congress. Not until the war in Vietnam had been waged for a long time did the President encounter significant resistance on Capitol Hill. Since the Second World War all decisions of magnitude in foreign affairs have been presidential, which he could make in secrecy and freedom, informing Congress and the people only close to or after the event. In effect, the larger the issue, the more freedom the President has had to act on it. Thus Truman used the atomic bomb against Japan and sent troops to Korea; Kennedy launched an indirect invasion in Cuba and engaged in confrontation with the Soviet Union over emplacement of missiles in Cuba; and all recent Presidents have fought in Indochina. In none of these decisions was Congress a significant participant.

The dragging, frustrating war in Vietnam brought sharply into question the President's power to conduct war if Congress has not declared it. (The Constitution, however, does not require Congress to declare war if it wants war.) Historically, the President as commander in chief has deployed the armed forces and has directed their use to protect American lives and interests. Of America's eleven serious, extended violent engagements with another country, only five have entailed a declaration of war: the War of 1812, the Mexican War, the Spanish-American War, and the two world wars. No declaration of war was made or requested for the naval war with France (1798–1800), the first and second Barbary wars (1801–05 and 1815), the Mexican-American clashes (1914–1917), and the Korean and Indochina wars. Controversy over the respective powers of Congress and the President has been free of judicial intervention. Holding that the respective powers of Congress and the President in this area are "political questions" on which it does not rule, the Court has left the question to combat and accommodation between the other branches.

In the 1950s, conservatives in Congress launched the Bricker Amendment to pare back the President's power to make treaties and executive agreements, fearful that they would commit the nation to upholding in other countries civil rights and other social policies not yet adopted domestically. A forceful effort by President Eisenhower staved off the amendment. Following the entry of American forces into Cambodia in 1970, Congress approved the Cooper-Church Amendment to a bill authorizing the sale of military supplies and equipment to foreign governments. The amendment, the first "wartime" restriction on a President, bars presidential expenditure without congressional consent and in effect makes it impossible for the President to keep troops and advisers in Cambodia. As the amendment gained momentum in the Senate, the President, presumably to head it off, announced that by June 30, 1970, American forces "of all kinds" would be out of Cambodia.[19] The longer the Indochina war persists, the more vulnerable the President is likely to be to limitations of the Cooper-Church type, attached to appropriations he can ill afford to reject.

Far more than Congress, the electorate has been a check on the President. Dissatisfied with his management of a war, it may cast him or his party out of office. In 1952, the public, restive under the extended Korean war, voted the Democrats out of the White House and elevated Eisenhower, who had promised to "go to Korea" to help end the war. Likewise, a disgruntled public dismissed the Democrats in 1968 for, among other reasons, their failure to manage the Vietnam war effectively.[20] War is a high-risk enterprise for presidential leadership. Unless he wins it quickly, the President is in deep political trouble, particularly in an age when television brings war's horrors into everyone's living room.

Conflict manager and
decision-maker

"There are no easy matters that will come to you as President," Eisenhower counseled the incoming President Kennedy. "If they are easy, they will be

[19] *New York Times,* May 17, 1970.
[20] Philip D. Converse, et al., "Continuity and Change in American Politics: Parties and Issues in the 1968 Election," *American Political Science Review,* LXIII (December 1969), 1083.

settled at a lower level." [21] Some of the most intense and tortuous conflicts a President faces may stem from conflicts between his roles. He adjudicates between their competing demands by giving priorities to one role over another. Thus Nixon, faced with his economic role to combat inflation and his social role to maintain and ·improve social programs, made a series of choices giving priority to the former over the latter. But the President's priority-setting seldom follows a consistent pattern. It may vary by occasion, over time, and by role elements. Though generally unhappy with huge appropriations for social programs, Nixon advocated new approaches to welfare, including a guaranteed minimum income, that involved increased outlays. In an office like the Presidency, which concentrates responsibilities in a single individual, roles blur; the President in performing a single act may impinge on several roles, and he may not consciously change hats in moving from role to role.

In addition, the President has several constituencies—including the national electorate, domestic interest groups and leaders, the bureaucracy, Congress and its substructures and personalities, and foreign leaders—and each constituency makes demands on him. The electorate wants peace and prosperity. West Germany wants the continued presence of a large American force. Israel wants more fighter aircraft to counter Soviet aid to Egypt. Blacks want more and better jobs. Often these demands conflict. Antiwar leaders demanded immediate and total withdrawal from Vietnam, which to military commanders was treason. Nixon's most articulate Southern supporters cannot abide school integration; prestigious black leaders, whose wrath he cannot ignore, demand it.

In coping with his constituents' expectations, the President may pursue an erratic course, with actions acceptable to different constituencies at different times. Nixon's Supreme Court nominations of Clement Haynsworth and Harrold Carswell pleased Southerners and their leading spokesman in the administration, Republican Senator Strom Thurmond of South Carolina. These and other moves infuriated the NAACP chairman, Bishop Stephen G. Spottswood, to the point of accusing the administration of being antiblack. But weeks later it was Thurmond who agonized after it seemed the administration in several moves was taking a hard line toward forced integration in the South. Thurmond lamented that the administration had become wedded to a "Northeast philosophy." [22]

To maintain links with his various publics, the President must depend on his ability to communicate persuasively concerning progress toward goals, the problems that will be encountered, and the changes that will be necessary. Each President has his own method and style of persuasion, a reflection of personal chemistry and talent. Eisenhower derived mileage from his fame as a general and from a winsome manner that gave credence to the assertion of the day, "I like Ike." Kennedy charmed his audiences with wit and eloquence, and Johnson sought to overwhelm them with Southern-style persuasion. Nixon

[21] Television interview, December 17, 1962.
[22] *New York Times,* July 18, 1970.

compensated for lesser capacities of public inspiration by adroit timing and
use of facilities that modern communication technology provides. He skillfully
used the news conference to advocate his policies and resorted to such innovations as a televised veto of an Education Appropriations bill to dramatize his
objections. To deemphasize the Presidency's Eastern connections, he has
established a "Western White House" in California, and he occasionally
moves important staff conferences from Washington to other cities—to Chicago
to discuss pollution and to Indianapolis to review urban problems in 1970.

A scourge of presidential communication with the public is the "credibility
gap," which is prone to appear in wartime. Wilson's 1916 candidacy for reelection was eased by his campaign slogan "He kept us out of war," and
Franklin Roosevelt, seeking reelection in 1940, assured the mothers of
America that their sons would not fight again in a foreign war. Each statement immediately preceded the nation's entry into a world war. In the

endless, slippery Vietnam war Presidents have had difficulty keeping their promises. Johnson promised in his 1964 campaign that he would not send American boys halfway around the world to do what Asian boys should do, and Nixon campaigned in 1968 on the basis of a "secret plan" to end the war.

Some constituencies are more disposed than others to criticize a President's performance, or the state of the nation under his leadership. Their mission is to expose inadequacy, to innovate, to replace a blemished present with a better future. The clergy, the press, and the academic community are recruiting grounds of presidential critics. When Lincoln faltered in issuing the Emancipation Proclamation, the clergy pushed him to take the step. In the modern black civil rights movement the clergy have pressed the Chief Executive to move faster and faster. Clergy, most notably the Berrigan brothers, and many of the academic community, both faculty and students, have coalesced in the antiwar movement.

Constituencies may hinder a President in his attempts to resolve conflicts. A President seeking to improve the nation's balance of payments may find he is at the mercy of business investments abroad. Attempting to slow the pace of inflation, he can be thwarted by business price policies and labor's wage demands. A constituency that is displeased with a President may impose sanctions against him. Sanctions have variety and range—some are slight and others severe—but they all are intended to restrict the President or compel him to work within constituency expectations. For example, in 1904 business magnates, displeased by Theodore Roosevelt's energetic social reforms, began to look about for a more conservative presidential nominee, a step they were careful to let the President know about.

The expectations of the constituencies are not entirely self-willed. They may be shaped by anticipations of likely presidential behavior on the basis of his past performance. The more unanticipated his conduct and the more it fails to conform to prevailing ideas, the more severe the resistance to it and the shriller the outcry. Franklin Roosevelt, moving to overcome a hostile Supreme Court by "packing it," or adding new members to assure a court favorable to his New Deal program, employed a method so unexpected and so unconventional that it sparked one of the fiercest struggles of American politics.

Faced with conflict and the need for decision, the President may indulge in avoidance behavior. Eisenhower abstained from entering into civil rights conflicts on the basis that they were matters of the private citizen's conscience and choice. Most national politicians today refuse to take a stand on the controversial abortion issue, referring to it as a "state" question. Or the President may engage in partial avoidance—compromise. He may compromise in a single event or in a series of episodes. President Nixon, to keep his welfare reform measure alive in Congress, agreed to various modifications proposed by Democratic legislators. He accepted a proposal by Senator Ribicoff (D., Conn.) to allow a year of "field tests" of the family assistance program before it would go into operation. Then Nixon urged the Senate Finance Committee, where his measure had long been stalled, to report it out and give the Senate "a chance to work its will." [23]

Where patterns of conflict persist or repeat, the President may seek to control them by institutionalizing them. Budget-making, supervised by the President's Office of Management and Budget, disposes annually of literally thousands of conflicts emerging from constituency demands.

There are several other ways a President may handle conflict and reach a decision. The conflict may be a simple choice of values: Presidents who aspired to land a man on the moon had to choose, in allocating the mammoth outlays, between the exultation, prestige, and scientific value of a moon landing and the prodigious needs of the inner cities. When constituency expectations are involved in a conflict, the President may decide primarily on the basis of legitimacy, or whether what a constituency wants is "right" or "wrong." Presidents Kennedy and Johnson, addressing the nation in civil rights crises, stressed standards of conduct for whites toward blacks in terms of doing "what is right." But a President's orientation to constituency expectations may also be one of expediency. He may give priority to sanctions over legitimacy or right. Presumably he keeps a kind of tally sheet, recording the sanctions likely to be thrust on him if he chooses this course or that, and his ultimate choice may be for a course involving the lightest sanctions. Both Kennedy and Johnson edged toward a recognition of the People's Republic of China, but the likely costs of such a step—the certain outcry of critics within their own party and the opposition party—deterred them. Another pattern is a hybrid of the last two—a moral-expedient orientation. Soon after Pearl Harbor, Roosevelt announced that henceforth "Dr. New Deal" would vacate the Washington scene for his successor "Dr. Win the War." Roosevelt was articulating the supreme need to win the war as quickly as possible, but it was also a decision that had the general approval of his constituencies. The President's sense of their needs happily coincided with their expectations.

How and whether the President leads, his willingness to bear the risks of leadership and the wrath of constituents if he violates their expectations, depends centrally on the President as a person—his values, character, and style. The President's own values can prompt him to ignore certain problems and controversies or they may cause him to act eagerly. The quality and bent of his leadership may depend on his character, or his general stance toward himself and his environment. The President's style politically links his character with the office. Applying a scheme of general character tendencies, James David Barber classified Presidents Lyndon Johnson and Richard Nixon as "Active-Negative." The "active" label is derived from a spectrum of possible behavior ranging from activity to passivity. The "negative" label denotes the attitude the Presidents have toward their activity. Accordingly, Barber interpreted the behavior of Johnson and Nixon as denoted by an aggressive stance, intense effort with low personal reward, compulsive activity, and the use of politics to compensate for power deprivations. An understanding of the

[23] *New York Times,* August 29, 1970.

President's personality tendencies may indicate to those who structure his staff the kind of arrangements necessary to counterbalance them. Thus if a President makes major decisions with excessive privacy and too little consultation, it would be desirable to structure his so that it would be drawn, with its information and advice, more into the decision-making process.[24]

Proposals

1. No one would oppose an entreaty to make presidential selection more democratic. The more elusive question is: how? Some would abolish the national convention and the electoral vote and substitute a national presidential primary and popular election. Others would retain the national convention, but reform it. They urge that proportional representation be given to rival candidates in each state and that greater representation be allotted to the blacks, the young, women, and others presently badly underrepresented. There has been a general impression that the national conventions are excessively dominated by county chairmen, district leaders, and governors who have limited interest in national issues and the positions of candidates. The 1972 Democratic convention gave hope this view need no longer prevail.

2. What should be the respective roles of the President and Congress in war-making? Senator Jacob K. Javits (R., N.Y.) has proposed a bill that would bar the President from committing American troops to hostilities for longer than thirty days without obtaining congressional consent. The President could take action to repel a sudden attack against the United States or its forces, protect the lives and property of American nationals, and comply with national commitments such as mutual defense treaties. After thirty days, the hostilities could not be continued except by "affirmative legislative action."

The proposal seeks to protect the President's discretionary authority as commander in chief to take emergency actions in the absence of a congressional declaration of war. Simultaneously it seeks to place congressional checks on the use of his authority by requiring the President to obtain approval for sustained hostilities.[25]

But could American troops ever be disengaged from violence simply by congressional action? And what would be the effect of this proposal on the United States in the estimation of its allies and the calculations of its opponents? As the debates on the Cooper-Church resolution made clear, questions concerning the desirable roles of Congress and the President are not readily answered.

3. Legislative-executive deadlock can halt progress in meeting mountainous social problems. A frequent obstacle is Congress' internal organization —committee chairmen chosen by seniority, their broad arbitrary powers, the

[24] James David Barber, *The Presidential Character* (Englewood Cliffs, N.J.: Prentice-Hall, 1972).
[25] *New York Times,* June 16, 1970.

influential House Rules Committee. Proposals to alter these and other congressional processes might speed the progress of social legislation. But a President too little committed to general social improvement may also be an obstacle. Some attribute the presence of such a Chief Executive to the dominance of political machines and managers in his selection and look to more popular participation in the nominating processes as the key to obtaining more socially aware Presidents. Still others wearily dismiss legislative-executive deadlock as simply a reflection of society's own indifference to its problems. The political branches cannot be expected to act when society is not ready to. But an assertive President—a Theodore Roosevelt who saw the Presidency as "a bully pulpit"—would not permit society to slumber. "The President," Truman once said, "has got to set the sights."

Suggested Reading

Barber, James David, *The Presidential Character: Predicting Performance in the White House* (Prentice-Hall, 1972). A creative, insightful analysis of presidential character and style and their influence on decision-making. Barber skillfully interprets the behavior of Presidents, using twentieth-century incumbents as examples.

Bell, Wendell, Hill, Richard J., and Wright, Charles R., *Public Leadership* (Chandler, 1961). A useful introduction to a study of leadership; explores various approaches to the subject and techniques of empirical study and includes discussion of presidential leadership.

Burns, James MacGregor, *Presidential Government* * (Houghton Mifflin, 1965). A challenging interpretive study of the Presidency—its contemporary problems as an office and its potentialities. Offers recommendations for improving the office.

Corwin, Edward S., *The President: Office and Powers* * 4th edition (New York University Press, 1957). A classic study of the historical development and the legal powers and problems of the Presidency. Deals with major presidential roles.

Fenno, Richard F., Jr., *The President's Cabinet: An Analysis in the Period from Wilson to Eisenhower* * (Harvard University Press, 1959). A cogent treatment of the development and functioning of the Cabinet and its place in the political system.

Gouldner, Alvin W., ed., *Studies in Leadership* (Russell and Russell, 1965). A useful collection of essays on various aspects of leadership. Discusses types of leadership, leadership techniques, leadership-group relations, and leadership traits.

Hargrove, Erwin C., *Presidential Leadership: Personality and Political Style* * (Macmillan, 1966). Interesting analysis of leadership types among twentieth-century Presidents. Gives particular attention to presidential needs and values.

Koenig, Louis W., *The Chief Executive* * revised edition (Harcourt Brace Jovanovich, 1968). Analysis of the various roles of the President and leadership processes.

Neustadt, Richard E., *Presidential Power* * (Wiley, 1960). An informed analysis of problems faced by modern Presidents in the exercise of power.

Petrullo, Louis, and Bass, Bernard M., eds., *Leadership and Interpersonal Behavior* (Holt, Rinehart and Winston, 1961). A valuable compilation of readings on leadership that analyzes the nature of roles, varieties of leadership situations, and linkages between leaders and groups.

Reedy, George E., *The Twilight of the Presidency* * (NAL-World, 1970). A critical examination of the Presidency. Reedy, a former press secretary to President Johnson, contends that the President's excessive removal from political reality has detrimental consequences for the quality of leadership.

Rossiter, Clinton, *The American Presidency* * revised edition (Harcourt Brace Jovano-vich, 1960). A concise treatment of the Presidency, with emphasis on presidential roles.

Sorensen, Theodore C., *Decision-Making in the White House* * (Columbia University Press, 1963). A valuable analysis of the nature of presidential decision-making, by a former aide to President Kennedy. The author makes effective use of his background in the Kennedy administration.

* Available in paperback edition

9

responsive
bureaucracy

To many who criticize contemporary American society, its most repelling feature is its impersonalization. In much of day-to-day living, it is all too easy to feel that one is a mere number on a computer card—a phone number, an Army service number, a credit card number, employee number, account number, student number. A list of numbers is a list of anonymous entities; as numbers we enjoy no significant differentiation as human beings. Democracy, which developed with the specific purpose of valuing each individual for his uniqueness, seems to be mockingly denied in the jungle of big organizations that process, use, regulate, and discard him.

Not a few contemporary youth contrive to withdraw from the world of big organizations, and try to develop new life styles that represent humanistic values. Some of them succeed in finding ways of living that provide them with authentic, personal experience; some, however, blink away the fact that contemporary society with its soaring populations, its mountainous demands for food, shelter, education, and other essentials, requires a complex industrial economy to sustain it. Without big organizations of some kind, modern society would dissolve into a chaos of unspeakable suffering, and democracy would be unattainable with countless citizens deprived of life's essentials.

The really crucial question for democracy is: if we must have big organizations, can their impersonality be reduced, their hard-shelled insensitivities softened to the point that they acknowledge the dignity and worth of man? No better terrain for probing this question is available than the national executive branch. Largest of America's administrative organizations, it suggests that complex, large-scale civilization cannot be conducted without having great aggregates of individuals joined together by authority, discipline, and common purpose. Giant business organizations are also run as massive regulated enterprises, but their goals are different from those of the government bureaucracy. Business is oriented to profit-making and efficiency; when objective goals like these are sought, impersonality is often an inevitable result. Public organizations, on the other hand, help sustain man as an effective citizen and human being by applying humane values through services that profit-oriented organizations are disinclined to undertake.

Because public bureaucracy has many intertwinings with politics, we can strive to make it responsive to the needs of individual man and the interests

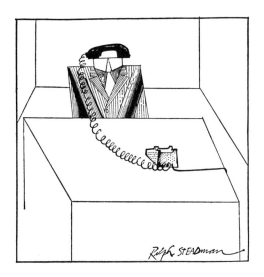

of all the people. Democratic theory permits the popularly elected representatives to choose administrative officers for delegated tasks and powers and to provide for the recruitment of personnel with the kind of specialized knowledge and skill that neither the elected nor appointed representatives possess. The specialized personnel are endowed with tenure. This ensures they will not be removed for political reasons and their competence and skill will continue to be available. Although seemingly removed from popular control, they still function within an environment of constraints and pressures conducive to democratic responsiveness. A large question for democracy emerges. How is the public bureaucracy to be kept responsive and accountable to popular political authority without impairing the inherent advantages of expertise and experience, protected by a tenure necessary for attracting qualified personnel? Pursuit of this inquiry requires a look at several intrinsic qualities of the national executive branch.

Nature of the
national executive branch

The national executive branch consists of departments and agencies—like the Treasury Department, the Tennessee Valley Authority, and the Veterans Administration—and its nearly 3 million civilian employees include Secretary of State William Rogers, White House assistant Henry Kissinger, FBI agents, and the local mailman. The numbers are almost doubled if the armed forces are counted. All are responsible for carrying out laws and directives from Congress and the President.

In social background, the national bureaucracy is more broadly represen-

The executive branch

THE PRESIDENT

Executive Office of the President

The White House Office
Office of Management and Budget
Council of Economic Advisers
Council on Environmental Quality
Domestic Council
National Aeronautics and Space Council
National Council on Marine Resources
  and Engineering Development

National Security Council
Office of Economic Opportunity
Office of Emergency Preparedness
Office of Intergovernmental Relations
Office of Science and Technology
Office of Telecommunications Policy
Special Representative for Trade Negotiations

Departments

Department of State
Department of the Treasury
Department of Defense
Department of Justice
Department of the Interior
Department of Agriculture
Department of Commerce

Department of Labor
Department of Health, Education, and
  Welfare
Department of Housing and Urban
  Development
Department of Transportation

Agencies, boards, and commissions

Administrative Conference of the
  United States
Advisory Commission on Intergovernmental
  Relations
American Battle Monuments Commission
Appalachian Regional Commission
Atomic Energy Commission
Canal Zone Government
Central Intelligence Agency
Civil Aeronautics Board
Commission of Fine Arts
Commission on Civil Rights
District of Columbia
Environmental Protection Agency
Equal Employment Opportunity Commission
Export-Import Bank of the United States
Farm Credit Administration
Federal Coal Mine Safety Board of Review
Federal Communications Commission
Federal Deposit Insurance Corporation
Federal Home Loan Bank Board
Federal Maritime Commission
Federal Mediation and Conciliation Service
Federal Power Commission
Board of Governors of the Federal Reserve
  System
Federal Trade Commission
Foreign Claims Settlement Commission
General Services Administration

Indian Claims Commission
Interstate Commerce Commission
National Aeronautics and Space
  Administration
National Capital Housing Authority
National Capital Planning Commission
National Foundation on the Arts and
  Humanities
National Labor Relations Board
National Mediation Board
National Science Foundation
Panama Canal Company
Railroad Retirement Board
Renegotiation Board
Securities and Exchange Commission
Selective Service System
Small Business Administration
United States Postal Service
Smithsonian Institution
Subversive Activities Control Board
Tax Court of the United States
Tennessee Valley Authority
U.S. Arms Control and Disarmament Agency
U.S. Civil Service Commission
United States Information Agency
United States Tariff Commission
Veterans Administration
Water Resources Council

tative of society than are Congress and the President, whose social bases are concentrated in the middle and upper middle class. Studies of the backgrounds of federal bureaucrats reveal remarkable heterogeneity, in sharp contrast to European bureaucracy, which draws its employees from the same class. The American public service is accessible to most people regardless of status. Religions, races, skills, economic interests are better represented in the national executive branch than elsewhere in society.

In ethos, the executive branch is democratic, working within the framework of law, interacting with the organs of constitutional government, and taking more pains than most enterprises to subscribe to the principle of "equal pay for equal work." Career advancement is remarkably faithful to the ideals of merit and equal opportunity. Well could Theodore Roosevelt contend concerning federal personnel practices, "The merit system . . . is in its essence as democratic and American as the common school system itself." [1]

In breadth, the executive branch compares with a university faculty; scarcely a matter of human concern is unrepresented in its ranks. Simple mention of the Post Office, the Selective Service System, and the Internal Revenue Service suggests how far-reaching and decisive is the effect of organizations of the executive branch on the lives of almost everyone.

The largest component of the national bureaucracy is the Defense Department, which absorbs nearly half the federal budget in conducting the Indochina war and maintaining a huge military establishment. The executive branch includes a vast apparatus for foreign affairs: the State Department and the embassies and missions overseas; the Agency for International Development, which administers the foreign aid program; the United States Information Agency; and the Central Intelligence Agency. Many executive agencies are devoted to rendering benefits and services: the Department of Housing and Urban Development clears slums and plans urban renewal projects; the Office of Economic Opportunity administers and coordinates poverty programs; the Agriculture Department provides an array of services for the farmer and the rural community; the Interstate Commerce Commission regulates the conduct of private enterprises—their rates, safety, and quality of service.

National executive organizations vary in form. The largest units are departments and agencies, with a single head, a secretary or administrator. Each has deputies and aides. The secretary's aides consist of one or more undersecretaries and at least several assistant secretaries responsible for one function or for several related programs. These deputies are usually a mix of political appointees and career civil servants. Below the top executive level are the major constituent units of a department, sometimes called "administrations" (the Manpower Administration of the Labor Department) or "bureaus" (the Federal Bureau of Investigation of the Justice Department), in which operating responsibilities are concentrated. Although bureaus and

---

[1] In Frederick C. Mosher, *Democracy and the Public Service* (New York: Oxford University Press, 1968), 202.

Executive personnel

Organization	Employees in United States	Employees outside United States	Total paid employees, January 1970
Executive Office of the President	4,044	—	4,044
Executive Depart- ments	2,354,031	216,078	2,570,109
Agriculture	105,241	1,243	106,484
Commerce	30,449	374	30,823
Defense	1,083,865	178,935	1,262,800
HEW	106,280	—	106,280
HUD	14,777	—	14,777
Interior	67,284	596	67,880
Justice	36,084	421	36,505
Labor	10,407	72	10,479
Post Office	739,060	2,401	741,461
State	11,323	30,224	41,547
Transportation	61,049	1,140	62,189
Treasury	88,212	672	88,884

Source: Chart number 1907-0-42-355 (Washington, D.C.: U.S. Government Printing Office, 1970).

administrations may be headed by political appointees, the great mass of their employees are members of the career civil service.

The executive branch also embraces the independent regulatory commissions (like the Civil Aeronautics Board, the Securities and Exchange Commission), which are headed by a bipartisan plural executive or commission appointed for fixed terms that exceed the President's. They are located outside the departments and the President's formal line of command. Another distinctive unit is the government corporation. Agencies such as the Tennessee Valley Authority and the Federal Deposit Insurance Corporation provide services of a quasi-business character; they resemble in function and structure the business corporation and operate more flexibly than the departments.

The national executive branch enjoys several monopolies of function and specialization (exploration of space, the armed forces, the Foreign Service) but most of its activities resemble those of nongovernmental agencies—deciding, doing, administrating, performing such "executive" functions as budgeting, disbursing, planning, choosing personnel, and the like.

The bureaucracy also "legislates," or makes rules binding on the public and authorized by congressional statutes. The national bureaucracy conducts hearings and trials to enforce its rules. Although Congress may provide how the adjudication is to be performed, agencies enjoy large discretion concerning their hearings' procedures and records. Some agencies in handing down decisions will set forth their reasons like a higher court does, while other agencies simply announce the results. Some agencies accept findings of fact by their civil service hearing examiners; others in dealing with appeals may largely ignore the examiners' work and make their own findings of fact.

In their other related activities, agencies receive complaints from private sources. The Federal Trade Commission gets complaints concerning deceptive business practice; the Interstate Commerce Commission reviews complaints concerning services, charges, and other conduct by railroads and truckers. Agencies also have "application cases"; individuals and groups applying to engage in some activity require administrative approval—a license, for example, to operate a television station. Agencies like the Veterans Administration and the Bureau of Old-Age Survivors Insurance of the Department of Health, Education, and Welfare (HEW) determine the individual's eligibility for benefits. Agencies can apply sanctions. The Federal Communications Commission, for example, can revoke the licenses of radio and television stations, but it rarely takes that step, preferring instead to warn informally against offensive behavior.[2]

Problems of bureaucracy

As key participants in a dynamic democratic order, the bureaucratic organizations of the national executive branch must be responsive to the needs of the nation and the individual citizen, but certain limitations hamper them. Bureaus are often victims of the *rigidity cycle:* as the bureau grows, its internal division of labor tends toward ever more intensive specialization. Overall perspective diminishes as each task is fragmented into smaller parts. Coordination becomes more difficult because more people are involved in each decision. Decisions are delayed, superfluous procedures and reports luxuriate, and proposed action must survive a labyrinth of multiple approvals. The organization displays a low capacity for swift or innovative action.

Another bureaucratic malady inhibiting democratic responsiveness is *dysfunction,* when the stability achieved from tenure and individual rights is gained at the expense of qualitative performance. Although the personnel system protects the employee against arbitrary treatment, it fails to provide incentives that would encourage imaginative planning and dynamic administration. Instead it fosters a mediocrity that thrives on security. Bureaucracies are also subject to *technical myopia,* when the expert derives from his specialization the unshakable conviction that his judgments are "objectively" superior to those of anyone else.

Nor is democracy aided when the bureaucrat, moving up the career ladder, becomes highly *conforming,* mirroring the values and behavior of the

[2] For fuller treatment, see Peter Woll, *American Bureaucracy* (New York: Norton, 1963), 61–72.

personnel system, shunning disagreement with colleagues and disturbances of his organization's design and mission.[3] This attitude fosters a conservative inclination for existing policy and an unfriendly climate for innovation. Excessive administrative *discontinuity,* rather than excessive stability, hampers some organizations. A prime example is the foreign aid program; since the Second World War it has been assigned to six different agencies directed by eleven different administrators—circumstances that make operating effectiveness agonizingly difficult.

Various writers, including sociologist C. Wright Mills, see the national bureaucracy not as the servant of popular democracy, but as its transgressor. Members of the bureaucratic elite participate in a kind of interlocking directorate with a general governing elite of public and private leaders who direct the nation.[4] Mills's thesis seems highly dubious for the United States where power is fragmented by occupation, section, and jurisdiction. Nevertheless, one is aware of elites for particular bureaucratic programs; a relatively small group of persons, some official and some private, exert a dominant influence on policy. Their power seems derived less from wealth or general prestige than from status as acknowledged specialists or professionals in their program field. A growing problem for democracy is the need to obtain knowledge about the membership, coordination, and control of these numerous elites.

It is estimated that nearly one-third of all government employees are engaged in professional and technical work.[5] This increased professional emphasis is a mixed blessing for bureaucracy. Daniel Bell and Don K. Price see a new society emerging in which older values and distributions of power favoring property, wealth, production, and industry will yield increasingly to knowledge, education, and intellect—all strengths of public bureaucracy.[6] Apart from the political appointees at the top, public leadership is embracing an ever wider array of professions affiliated with the missions of the organizations in which they function. But the older professions may be staunch defenders of existing and perhaps obsolete approaches. The intra-agency and interagency terrains may be battlegrounds for struggles between the old and the new, among the professions and within them. Mindful of these conflicts, Chief Executives such as Theodore Roosevelt and John F. Kennedy have sought to speed development of new programs by promoting civil servants who represent points of view at variance with those of the old professionals.

A final and significant problem for democracy is that Congress and the

[3] A contrary view, which sees some bureaucrats as innovative, is provided in Morris Janowitz, *The Professional Soldier, A Social and Political Portrait* (New York: Free Press, 1964), and John E. Harr, *The Anatomy of the Foreign Service: A Statistical Profile* (New York: Carnegie Endowment for International Peace, Foreign Affairs Study No. 4, 1965).

[4] C. Wright Mills, *The Power Elite* (New York: Oxford University Press, 1956).

[5] Mosher, 103.

[6] Daniel Bell, "Notes on the Post-Industrial Society," *The Public Interest,* I (Winter 1967), 24–35; Don K. Price, *The Scientific Estate* (Cambridge: Harvard University Press, 1965), 15–16.

President must depend on the bureaucracy in several important ways. Political organs legislate and direct, but only the bureaucracy can implement. Entrapments and obstacles stud the path of implementation. Faulty administrative judgments, miscalculations, and omissions can drain policy of effectiveness. Bureaucracy controls the manner in which it chooses to implement decisions: it can refine, redefine, and reject. Bureaucratic subordinates can effectively kill top-level decisions by overcomplying with them or interpreting them literally.

Policy-makers also depend on the bureaucracy for a constant supply of relevant, accurate, and meaningful information. Each administrative subordinate is a data filter for his superior, and this filtering is often a difficult, critical task for human judgment. One of the more devastating failures occurred when a lieutenant chose not to report to superiors information from his subordinate that vast, unaccounted-for numbers of aircraft, according to the radar screen, were approaching Hawaii. Their mission, as it was later discovered, was to bomb Pearl Harbor.

Bureaucracy and the political system

How well bureaucracy serves democracy depends crucially on how effectively it is linked with the political system. Bureaucracy is more apt to respond to human needs and desires if its conduct is monitored by outside sources rather than closed off and left to its own will. For democracy to advance, bureaucracy must be kept in balance with other institutions of political society—the courts, the legislature, the Chief Executive. Otherwise, society will be afflicted by inherently undemocratic features of bureaucracy—its stress on hierarchy and elites and its tendency to haughty, all-knowing expertise.

The Constitution. We depend most fundamentally on the Constitution to keep bureaucracy on the democratic path. The Constitution does not deal explicitly with bureaucracy; the framers could hardly have anticipated its enormous present-day importance. Yet in indirect ways the Constitution contributes importantly to control over the functioning of bureaucracy and its place in the governmental system. In creating the three branches of government, the Constitution did not give one branch exclusive control over the bureaucracy. It vested substantial controlling powers in Congress, which can create, reorganize, and terminate administrative agencies and regulate their conduct through its power of appropriation. The Senate must give its consent to major administrative appointments. But the Constitution also vested the executive power, the commander-in-chief power, and other authority and duties in the President. Thus in effect the Constitution made the two political branches competitors for exerting dominion over the executive branch. But the judiciary was not left out. Constitutional amendments, particularly the Bill of Rights, require that the national bureaucracy observe civil liberties, subject to the monitoring eye of the courts.

In addition, the federal system of government established by the Constitution requires the national bureaucracy to carry out many programs and policies through federal-state cooperation. Historic sectionalism and a dispersed economy have nurtured a decentralized federal bureaucracy that utilizes field organizations heavily. Finally, thanks largely to the Constitution, the national executive branch is shaped by the principle of pluralism to which other major political institutions are also subject.[7]

Political responsiveness

From the constitutional arrangements spring several concepts of how the executive bureaucracy should conduct itself in a democracy. Bureaucracy should be politically responsive; that is, it should seek honestly and efficiently to interpret and carry out the public will expressed through political processes and institutions. Bureaucracy should respond promptly and faithfully to changes in that will. According to a corollary principle, bureaucracy should live a life of political neutrality. If the people are sovereign in a democracy, and the public employee is merely the people's servant, he must be separated from any special ability, derived from his position, to influence the people's political judgment. Thus the Hatch Act of 1939 bars political activity for civil servants.

The concepts of political neutrality and responsiveness work most readily when the executive branch merely carries out policies adopted by Congress and the President. More difficult is the commonplace practice of bureaucracy to develop and recommend policy and to interpret and implement it after approval by political authorities. Can bureaucracy act neutrally in these more involving relations? The dilemma has fostered efforts to distinguish between policy development and policy execution—between holders of policy or political positions, where presumably political responsiveness is most important, and administrative personnel. The latter are permanent civil servants, recruited and governed by merit standards and politically neutral, this time in the sense that they command only a minor voice in determining public policy. Policy or political personnel are grouped on "Schedule C," a listing of political appointees whose selection, tenure, and other conditions of employment are exempted from merit standards. In a change of administration, many of these employees also depart. But difficulties beset the attempted separation of political and administrative positions. Agencies such as the State Department rely heavily on career personnel in policy-making. And what is "political" or what is "administrative" may be abruptly changed by the rise and fall of public concerns and issues.

[7] Woll, 49–57.

Political support. No bureau can survive without external political support. Departmental political leaders may lend such support. Even more conducive to assured survival is the good will of the congressional appropriations committees and subcommittees and the favor of the interest groups with which the bureau deals. A standard concern of bureaus is maintaining and increasing their political support. In fact, this bread-and-butter task even predates a bureau's existence; bureaus are created only after political pressure or some social need, which is politically recognized, achieves sufficient force to bring the bureau into being. For example, the Interstate Commerce Commission was created because of agrarian discontent over heavy-handed railroad freight charges, and the Securities and Exchange Commission came into being after the stock market crash of 1929 revealed gross malpractices.

In pursuing its quest for support the bureau takes on aspects of the pluralist political system in which it exists. No bureau or department can attach itself to a cohesive enduring majority, because there is none. Just as no single interest group can represent the popular will, neither can any department or bureau. They therefore serve not one but several masters—interest groups, Congress, and the President—a reality that bars the autonomous, omniscient bureau, the neat harmonious organization pattern, the logical unity so alluring in theoretical conceptions of bureaucracy. American pluralist politics do not permit it.

Bureaucracy
and interest groups

To make their way politically, bureaus of the executive branch have several locus points of responsiveness, and not the least of them are interest groups. Bureaus provide the groups with enduring or institutionalized representation in the governmental system. They promote the groups' interests and respond to their needs by providing such services as research and subsidies or by adopting policies that will promote the well-being of the group. Normally, bureaus welcome the groups' good will and, even more, their active support. Above all, the bureaus seek to avoid displeasing the groups, for fear they might protest to Congress, the parties, or the Chief Executive. These are the seeds of the political responsiveness of the bureaus to the interest groups.

The bureaus generally represent specific interest groups. The Agriculture, Labor, and Commerce departments, for example, signify specialized concern for the triad of great economic entities: the farmer, the laborer, and the businessman. Organizations like the American Farm Bureau Federation and the National Rural Electric Cooperative Association watch closely the programs and operating decisions of the Department of Agriculture and its subunits. The AFL-CIO maintains a similar vigilance over the Labor Department, as do various business organizations over the Department of Commerce.

Departments are organized to respond to subdivisions of interests in the groups. Thus the Labor Department is concerned not only with the working man, but its Women's Division is devoted to working women. The Department of Commerce is attentive not only to large-scale enterprises but includes a Small Business Administration. Scientists can turn to HEW's National Institutes of Health, sportsmen to the Interior Department's Bureau of Fish and Wildlife Service, and educators to HEW's Office of Education.

Interest groups prefer to deal with a single major purpose department such as the Labor Department, as opposed to a multipurposed one like the Department of Health, Education, and Welfare. They want to know where responsibility for decisions lies and not have to compete for attention with rival programs and therefore rival combinations of interest groups. Accordingly, the American Legion strenuously and successfully insists that health services for veterans be lodged not in HEW, but in the Veterans' Administration.[8]

Interest groups watch closely the programs and decisions of the departments and subunits. Occasionally they try to influence the selection of appointees outside the merit service. If they cannot actually determine the selection decision, they often can get it vetoed. In 1970 HEW Secretary Robert Finch proposed to appoint Dr. John Knowles as head of the U.S. Public Health Service. Knowles was reform-minded and articulate about what he deemed inadequate American health care, but the American Medical Association, which challenges the contention that the health care system needs reform, opposed the appointment. Rallying support from Minority Leader Senator Everett Dirksen and from key members of the White House staff, the AMA forced Finch to withdraw Knowles's name.[9]

Pressure groups may also bring about the appointment of advisory committees composed of representatives of various interests affected by a bureau's or a department's programs. Sometimes interest groups influence policy at public hearings that are required on proposed regulations. Or in some bureaus citizens and groups file written comments on proposed legislation. The enforcement of policy also triggers keen interest group concern and pressures, which have much to do with whether policy is enforced vigorously, half-heartedly, or not at all. In 1969, Herbert E. Ley, Jr., freshly ousted as Food and Drug Commissioner, said that he was under "constant, tremendous, sometimes unmerciful pressure from the drug industry," as he advanced policies for consumer protection and that some days he "spent as many as six hours fending off representatives of the drug industry." [10] Interest groups failing to secure the cooperation of bureaus may move against them through Congress and the courts. But in many an instance bureaus cherish group support, as the National Park Service does when it looks to conservation groups to back its efforts to set aside more land for public use.

[8] James W. Davis, Jr., *The National Executive Branch* (New York: Free Press, 1970), 141.
[9] *New York Times,* May 26, 1970.
[10] *New York Times,* December 30, 1969.

Finally, bureaus and interest groups may ally in order to manipulate congressional committees and subcommittees. For decades the FBI received the red carpet treatment in Congress; its every wish was granted, a privileged status that drew strength from the bureau's ties with state and local law enforcement associations, which no congressman up for reelection wished to offend.

Democracy is ill-served when bureaucratic responsiveness to groups is distributed unevenly. A 1970 study of the U.S. Forest Service found the agency excessively responsive to the timber industry and other commercial interests and far less so to recreation interests. Over an eight-year period, budgetary requests for timber sale management were trimmed only 5 percent while those for recreation were cut 55 percent.[11] There is plenty of evidence that groups with superior resources and sophistication fare better in their bureau dealings than those less favorably constituted. A representative of a community action program of the "war against poverty" concluded that "the poor in this society can only survive if they learn how to maneuver successfully within the bureaucracies." For the poor, one of the more baffling features of bureaucracy is the elaborate division of work and responsibility permitting "delaying, stalling, dodging, and buckpassing." [12]

Despite group assertiveness, it would be grossly erroneous to portray public employees simply as minions of organized interests. Many bureau leaders excel at achieving goals connected with public interest and are motivated at least partly by altruistic loyalty. Although no single conception of public interest can be unequivocally identified as the one best policy or decision, officials commonly have their own conception of public interest in pursuing their tasks. It functions as a guideline or standard that the official applies to his conduct. Sometimes officials deem the public interest to be the pursuit of a specific policy goal, such as the promotion of a nuclear non-proliferation treaty. Other times officials may be absorbed in promoting goals closely connected with self-interest—goals promising survival or growth of their offices or organization. Still other officials may see their task as manipulating competing interest groups to a kind of stand-off, while allowing the needs of unrepresented interests or of the nation itself to advance.

Bureaucracy and Congress

Bureaucracy participates in an elaborately intertwined partnership with Congress. In pursuing their "errand boy" duties for constituents, congressmen depend on the cooperation of the bureaus. Nearly half the legislation that

---

[11] *New York Times,* June 6, 1970.
[12] In Robinson O. Everett, ed., *Anti-Poverty Programs* (Dobbs Ferry, N.Y.: Oceana Publications, 1966), 198.

Congress considers originates in the executive branch, and on the average two-thirds of all public bills enacted stem from that branch.[13] Eager to promote a pet public bill, a legislator knows that among the allies he must find, few, if any, exceed in importance the administrative agency with jurisdiction over implementing his proposal. Legislation altering benefits for veterans will suffer a poor future without support from the Veterans Administration.

Congress tends to legislate in general terms and delegate the power of more detailed law making to the administrative agencies. Thus Congress in creating the National Labor Relations Board and the Federal Communications Commission said simply that these bodies shall regulate relevant private conduct in a "just" and "reasonable" manner and in the "public interest."

Congress is apt to be watchful of how the bureaus use their delegated power. An individual legislator, acting on his own, can publicize flaws in agency performance, an embarrassment bureaus normally seek to avoid. As Christmas, 1970, approached, for instance, Congressman James G. O'Hara (D., Mich.), sponsor of the Child Protection and Toy Safety Act of 1969, urged in a public letter to the HEW Secretary that the agency use the act's powers to bar dangerous toys still on the market, which included a blowgun dart that a child could suck into his lungs and a large steel-tipped dart used in a lawn game.[14]

In environmental matters, individual congressmen and committees have been gadflies to spur the administration into more serious effort. Early in the Nixon administration, Congressman Henry S. Reuss (D., Wis.) criticized the Federal Water Quality Administration (FDQA) of the Interior Department for failing to recommend to the Justice Department the filing of suits against forty companies discharging mercury into the nation's waterways. FDQA responded that it was giving the plants time to reduce their discharges, but added, doubtless spurred by the push from Reuss, that suits would be filed "if any companies ignore warnings." [15]

The most consistently powerful means of inducing bureaucratic responsiveness is the key congressional function of overseeing the executive branch through the appropriations committees and subcommittees, special investigating committees, and program and policy hearings in standing committees like Agriculture and Banking Currency. Each agency is subject to at least an annual review session on Capitol Hill, culminating in a "contractual agreement" between congressional committees and top administrators. In return for statutory authority and funds supplied by the appropriations committees, the bureaucracy in effect promises to achieve certain goals or results. Subsequently the committee reviews bureaucratic performance of its promises.

Congressional investigations can be a powerful impetus for the administrator's accountability, and they also can grind political axes of the congress-

[13] Davis, 14.
[14] *New York Times,* November 3, 1970.
[15] *New York Times,* October 21, 1970.

Congressman George Mahon, chairman of the House Appropriations Committee, reviews departmental appropriations requests piled up on his desk.

men involved. After nearly a year of the war on poverty program, a House investigating subcommittee, following hearings in eleven cities, charged that local political machines had been enabled to organize "giant fiestas of patronage . . . to feed their political hacks at the trough of mediocrity." The development was lamented as blocking the involvement of the poor in program development contemplated in the poverty legislation.[16]

Critics of Congress' large capacity to intrude in executive affairs complain that it tends to bring disarray to orderly administration, to undermine the supervisory function of the Chief Executive, and to inject narrow, particularistic considerations into broad-gauged programs. When the war on poverty program was originally considered in Congress, its provisions were addressed especially to the needs of blacks. But members of the North Carolina delegation, meeting in the Speaker's office, demanded absolute assurances that Assistant Secretary of Defense Adam Yarmolinsky, who had helped prepare the poverty program and who had vigorously supported the rights of black servicemen in Southern states, would have nothing to do with the new program's administration. Executive representatives made a quick telephone call to the White House and Yarmolinsky "was sacrificed without ceremony or ado." [17]

[16] Everett, 200.
[17] Daniel P. Moynihan, *Maximum Feasible Misunderstanding: Community Action in the War on Poverty* (New York: Free Press, 1969), 91.

Because of its steady partiality to property interests, Congress may some-times check bureaucracy's readier tendency to represent interests more akin to public welfare. A favorite congressional tactic is to legislate principles and ideals pleasing to the general body of constituents and then hobble their effectiveness by making inadequate provision for their enforcement. For example, in 1970 Congress made the Defense Department agencies responsible for recovering excessive profits from military contractors but allowed them only "minuscule staff and funds" to scrutinize the billions of dollars spent on defense procurement. Consequently, the staff was forced to rely on the con-tractors' reports of costs and profits rather than examining them in-dependently.[18]

Congress can also thwart efforts to pass laws creating administrative agencies promoting popular interests. This frustration has long attended the thus far futile effort to pass legislation creating an independent consumer pro-tection agency.[19]

All too often there is a "triple alliance" of bureau, congressional com-mittee or subcommittee, and relevant interest groups, who develop an endur-ing consensus on policy that dominates decisions in the executive and legis-lative branches. Unrepresented groups may be forgotten, the larger public interest neglected, and the President and Congress as a whole defied. A not uncommon spectacle is the bureau chief who, having lost a budgetary decision in the review by the Office of Management and Budget at the presidential level, will have the cut restored, often with interest group support, by ap-pealing (indirectly) to "his" congressional subgroup.

Bureaucracy
and the courts

Congress entrusts judicial power to the bureaus, in effect constituting a net-work of administrative judicial systems. Independent regulatory commissions like the Federal Trade Commission and the National Labor Relations Board and departments like Agriculture, Defense, and HEW exercise important judicial responsibilities. The Veterans Administration, for example, decides several million cases of benefit questions a year. Quality of service, prices, rates, and licenses are at stake in administrative litigation involving telephone, electric, and gas utilities, transportation and communications facilities, and the conduct of enterprises such as banking. Some systems of administrative justice provide for appeals within the agency. Administrative justice is often more efficient than the regular courts since each commission deals only with a particular kind of case and the entire procedure is handled by those who are experts in solving the kinds of problems involved. Administrative justice is thus swifter and far less costly.

[18] New York Times, March 3, 1970.
[19] New York Times, December 3 and 4, 1970.

Although the executive branch has its own judicial powers, it is still, in some respects, subject to review by the national judicial system. The courts can review administrative performance to determine whether the executive officers are acting consistently with authorizing statutes and the Constitution. The courts may intervene when the agency itself asks that its rules be enforced: Selective Service, for instance, may take the young man to court who fails to report for induction, whereupon the court may review Selective Service procedures and conclude that the man was improperly classified. The victim of bureaucratic arbitrariness can resort to the courts when administrators fail to perform official duties.

Court review as a means of promoting agency responsiveness has marked limitations, however. In the overwhelming body of cases, the courts refuse to substitute their own decisions for those of the agency, and in only a handful of the thousands of agency decisions each year does an aggrieved party resort to the courts. Naturally, agencies tend to go to the courts only when they have strong cases. As for the appeals of private individuals, the courts are far more accessible to elites than to the poor, who are most often aggrieved but cannot afford the legal fees required.

Bureaucracy and the President

Potentially, the Presidency is the most imposing instrument available for maintaining the responsiveness of the executive branch. The Constitution makes the President the chief administrator. The general investiture of the executive power in the President, his designation as commander in chief, his initiative in making appointments and treaties, his power to require the opinions of his department heads, his messages to Congress, and his duty to see that the laws are faithfully executed—these all contribute to establishing the President as the superior officer of the executive branch. Congress has reinforced this position by empowering the President to prepare the annual budget for the executive branch and to reorganize its agencies and functions.

To assist the transformation of the President into a true chief administrator, Franklin D. Roosevelt's Brownlow Committee (Committee on Administrative Management) proposed in 1937 that a clear, uninterrupted line of command and responsibility run between top and bottom and that the President's span of control be reduced to a manageable scale by consolidating agencies, including the regulatory commissions, into a limited number of departments. Furthermore, it was found that the President needed help from an ample White House staff wielding controls in his behalf for planning, personnel, and fiscal management.

Although giant strides toward fulfilling the Brownlow proposals have been taken in expanding the White House staff in the President's behalf, the departments are still as dispersed as ever. In his 1971 State of the Union speech

Proposed Reorganization of the Departments and Major Functions,
Transmitted to Congress, March 25, 1971

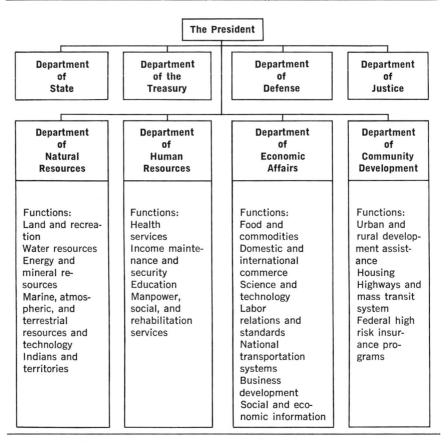

Source: Office of Management and Budget, *Papers Relating to the President's Departmental Reorganization Program* (Washington, D.C.: U.S. Government Printing Office, March 1971), p. 25.

Nixon pressed for a consolidation of the eleven executive departments into eight, but nothing has been done since to implement this suggestion (see chart). The reality is that the President cannot command and expect automatic obedience, given the power of the bureaus, buttressed by interest groups and congressional committees. Like other wielders of authority, he often finds that his orders are heeded when the official or bureau concerned feels it is in its interest to obey.

If a program has importance and magnitude, it is apt to exceed the boundaries of a single bureau or department and so rely on the Presidency for coordination. The poverty program, for instance, in its initial years was chiefly under the aegis of the Office of Economic Opportunity (OEO) and included some 9 or 10 programs, but there were an additional 250 related Great Society ventures administered by 15 other agencies, embracing projects for education, manpower, health, welfare, housing, urban renewal, and economic development. Only the President possessed authority to direct and coordinate the branch-wide effort. He alone could give meaning to the ambitious goals, launch initiatives for bold legislative programs, set priorities for allocating funds, shape the alignment of numerous, competing agencies, and decree broad policies.

Probably the worst disaster befalling the poverty program was President Johnson's subsequent change of attitude toward it. In 1964 he proclaimed "unconditional" war on poverty, but in 1967 he declared to a key legislator that it was hardly his favorite program, and his legislative message that year spoke only of a "strategy against poverty." Sargent Shriver, a prestigious figure in the early days of the poverty program, was relieved of his command of OEO, dispatched to France as ambassador, and replaced by a little-known career civil servant. The public importance of the program declined so much that when the Poor People's March reached Washington the following year, it seemed unaware of OEO and its director.[20]

But while agencies directing an innovative and controversial program like the war on poverty depend heavily on the President, other agencies may not. If they are graced with high public prestige like that accorded the FBI (especially under its late director, J. Edgar Hoover), if they enjoy close cooperation with effective interest groups as the Army Corps of Engineers does, they can conduct their affairs with little expectation of presidential intervention, or else successfully defy it. After a tempestuous political existence in the Roosevelt era, the Tennessee Valley Authority developed such favor among those it served that it successfully repulsed a large effort by the Eisenhower administration to diminish its activity.

President Kennedy once exclaimed: "I can get more done at the White House in a day than the State Department can in a week." With this outburst, he expressed his exasperation with the slow pace of bureaucracy. And nowhere is this more apparent than in innovation. What bureaucratic innovation there is tends to be elaborately researched and negotiated. Mostly, however, the bureaucracy wants to perpetuate existing policy, the foundation on which routines are built that enable the bureaucracy to cope with daily demands on its resources. Presidents, on the other hand, are driven toward innovation by many factors—the occasional crises that reveal the inadequacy of prevailing policy, the pressures of lesser problems that converge on his office and cannot be quieted except by innovative steps, his desire to distinguish his administration from his predecessors' and command a good page in history (most likely, according to the evidence, when the President innovates).

To speed innovation in the bureaucracy, Presidents may search the bureau-

---

[20] Moynihan, 4–5.

cratic line for members with new ideas. From Dr. Harvey Wiley, an Agriculture Department bureau chief, Theodore Roosevelt secured the formulations that developed the eventual food and drug program. And Presidents may venture outside the executive branch for innovative thinking. Kennedy, Johnson, and Nixon have utilized task forces of distinguished private citizens to design new programs. Through the toil of seventeen of these task forces, Nixon could consult a shelfful of potential programs on aging, air pollution, marijuana, welfare, women's rights, and other subjects for the seventies and beyond.

Presidential staff agencies. In overseeing the executive branch, the President is aided by an array of staff agencies such as the White House Office, the National Security Council, and the Office of Management and Budget. All function directly in the President's behalf and are closely geared to the operations of his office. In contrast, the departments and bureaus are more removed from the President and their operating responsibilities are geared to major governmental functions like collecting taxes, administering old age pensions, and equipping the nation for defense.

Of the presidential staff agencies, the one closest to the Chief Executive is the White House Office. As mentioned in Chapter 8, the White House Office includes several dozen assistants to the President, of whom the most important to Nixon have been Henry Kissinger for national security affairs and John Ehrlichman for domestic affairs. These assistants, personal appointees of the President, provide links with Cabinet and sub-Cabinet officials, with bureau chiefs, and with legislators, party leaders, and interest group representatives concerned with bureaucratic functioning. The precise assignments given White House assistants differ with each President.

The Office of Management and Budget, into which President Nixon reorganized the former Bureau of the Budget, is a powerful arm of the President for reaching the bureaucracy. In addition to overseeing the budget for the entire executive branch, the Office evaluates bureau programs in terms of costs and benefits, fosters program planning and management improvement, oversees bureau involvement in the development of legislation, and coordinates their statistical programs. Other presidential agencies, such as the Council of Economic Advisers, the National Security Council, the Domestic Council, the Office of Science and Technology, combine advisory, supervisory, and coordinating functions, linking the President and the bureaus. Typically, they coordinate related work being done by many agencies.

The President often makes major policy decisions aided by *ad hoc* teams drawn from his own staff and the departments. Thus President Nixon's initial decisions on the anti-ballistic missile program (ABM) included as participants the Secretary and Deputy Secretary of Defense, the Presidential Assistant for National Security Affairs, the Secretary and Undersecretary of State, and the Director of the Arms Control and Disarmament Agency. Departmental participants were aided by bureau staffs: for four weeks the Deputy Secretary

President Nixon meets with the National Security Council, including the head of the CIA, the chairman of the Joint Chiefs of Staff, the Secretary of State, and Henry Kissinger.

of Defense conferred daily with the Defense Department's director of research and planning and the acting Assistant Secretary for Systems Analysis, who, in turn, were aided by staff specialists.[21]

A focus of the President's staff agencies is the bureau chief, the main link between the career corps of his organization and the presidential administration. The bureau chief may be a civil service career man. If he is an outsider, he is apt by training and experience to be highly suited for the bureau's program and to have professional stature. He is the chief intermediary for the program interests of his bureau and its personnel and the world of politics represented by top departmental leadership and the President and his staff. That the conjunction of program and politics can be a volcanic pressure point is amply illustrated by experiences of HEW bureau chiefs in the Nixon administration.

[21] *New York Times,* March 19, 1969.

When Leon E. Panetta was ousted as head of HEW's Office for Civil Rights in 1970, he attributed it to the administration's slowing of school desegregation and the hostile pressures of White House aides. Coincidentally with these pressures, the ABM debate raged in Congress. The opposing sides were closely matched and Senator John Stennis of Mississippi (Armed Services Committee chairman) played a leading part, supporting the administration in its wish to go ahead with the ABM project. Panetta, whose task was to enforce civil rights policy, said that Stennis, through White House staff connections, was exerting heavy pressure on him to slow down school desegregation. When Stennis let it be known that he would be willing to leave his senatorial service (and thus his leadership in pushing the ABM through Congress) in order to "help Mississippi in its educational problems," Panetta was soon forced to depart for private life.[22] Dr. James E. Allen, Jr., likewise was compelled to leave his post as Commissioner of the Office of Education when the administration made it impossible for him to fulfill his personal commitment to school desegregation.

In another HEW quarter, the head of the Public Health Service, Dr. Roger O. Egeberg, complained that both his departmental top command and the presidential staff were not taking his advice on health matters, and that symptomatic of his low estate was his exclusion from membership on an informal White House committee dealing with health.[23]

Personnel systems

The responsiveness of bureaucracy can be enhanced by policies and practices of personnel administration. Deeply pervading the federal personnel system is the principle of merit, itself the foundation of democratic responsiveness. As embodied in the Pendleton Act of 1883, the basic federal personnel law, and succeeding legislation, the merit principle allows anyone to compete for positions and win appointment by demonstrating merit in examinations well regulated for objectivity. Aptitude and achievement rather than social class are the criteria for selection. Likewise advancement in the service is based on observed performance, or merit. Precise job classifications are merit-centered, designed to assure "equal pay for equal work."

Despite the pervasiveness of the merit principle, personnel administration in the executive branch is not a monolith. It is true that most employees— some two million—come under the jurisdiction of the Civil Service Commission, which administers examinations, classification, pay, and other personnel legislation and functions. But the pay of blue collar workers—about a quarter of all federal employees—is set by local wage boards. The Foreign Service in the State Department, the Tennessee Valley Authority, and the Atomic Energy Commission have their own merit systems, permitting significant innovations and adaptations to their special needs.

[22] *New York Times,* March 1, 1970.
[23] *New York Times,* May 26, 1970.

Democracy cannot thrive without adequate performance of bureaucratic functions. The federal government has to recruit a competent civil service, and to do so, it must compete in the general talent market with private employment. This is no easy task. A study has found that the appeal of federal employment is lowest among persons with better education, higher occupational attainments, and more technical skills—persons whom government needs most and for whom competition is keenest. According to the study, the major attractions of the federal service are job security, steady income, good retirement benefits—all incentives more likely to appeal to people with relatively low levels of aspiration since people who hope to achieve things are more responsive to incentives like challenge and possibilities of advancement.[24] Fortunately many agency employees are persons of excellent competence who find greater scope and excitement in dealing with public policy and the advance of human values than in the narrow concerns of profit-centered private enterprise.

For democracy's sake, bureaucracy must not only recruit but retain competent personnel. Administration—the bureaucracy—must be responsive to the human beings who compose it, to their feelings, career aspirations, and self-protective ways. Management must be alert to the impersonalizing effects of computers and other work-saving machines, to the possibility that the fetish of efficiency and objectivity may obscure the organization's humane purposes. Such concerns stir interest in supervisory training, employee development programs, fringe benefits, and arrangements for democratic or participative management, which seek to give employees a voice in decisions that concern them. Thus far, however, participative management is largely a slogan, lacking form and substance.

There have been recent instances of employee assertion. In 1970 fifty Foreign Service officers signed a letter to the Secretary of State protesting the United States operation in Cambodia. Top management chided these mostly younger officers below the middle grades for taking a step that was "unprofessional" and "embarrassing to the Administration," but they were assured that no punitive measures would be applied.[25] This of course remains to be seen; perhaps these officers will not advance as quickly as if they had not signed the letter.

The State Department personnel have not been alone in resorting to protest. Justice Department employees responsible for civil rights administration publicly protested the Nixon administration's policies in that field. Activist employees of HEW, unhappy with the war and school segregation policies of the Nixon administration, launched the HEW Action Project and hired a full-time director to press for reforms within the department. The group has concentrated on increasing its membership, on making itself a catalyst for isolated government workers, and on improving communications between workers and those in authority. It is also pressing for vigorous

---

[24] Franklin P. Kilpatrick, Milton C. Cummings, Jr., and M. Kent Jennings, *The Image of the Federal Service* (Washington, D.C.: The Brookings Institution, 1964), 117–40.
[25] *New York Times,* May 21, 1970.

Employees of the Department of Health, Education, and Welfare march past the White House in protest of the Indochina war. The employees expressed a wish to "take our concerns directly to the Administration."

enforcement of employment rights of women and minorities and for establishment of day-care centers for HEW employees. In general, the group wants to function, according to its director, as "a completely democratic organization, serving as a good outlet for employees to go in any direction they want." [26]

Unionization and collective bargaining are increasing in the federal government. Federal unions are stressing grievance procedures and working conditions not covered by law. In the future, unions may seek a role in examinations, classification, and other personnel processes. Some observers anticipate confrontations between unionization and the merit tradition. Another likelihood is that a growing union presence will throw more features of personnel administration open to congressional consideration and public discussion.

Administrative processes

Key administrative processes contribute significantly to keeping the executive branch responsive to popular needs. *Programming* and program development focus on particular needs and open the door to grand-scale if not grandiose

[26] *New York Times,* October 5, 1970.

objectives. The original antipoverty program of 1964, for example, chose to do nothing less than eradicate poverty for thirty-five million poor. Programs incorporate strategies, tactics, and basic concepts. The poverty program was to focus on helping youth in a long-term investment approach to breaking the intergenerational cycle of poverty. Major strategies were put into operation by a series of programs—the Neighborhood Youth Corps, the Job Corps, VISTA, and the College Work Study Program. The poverty program was to funnel direct federal aid to local communities instead of using the states as conduits, for the states are not always sympathetic to the cities, where poverty is concentrated. The community action program concept was developed to spark the creation of new institutions and innovating and coordinating mechanisms in local communities involving local citizens.

The method of *organization* in a bureaucracy can heighten responsiveness to popular need and will. Organization allocates power, rights, resources, and responsibilities. Those who create or revise organizations can structure them on the basis primarily of purpose, process, area, or clientele—that is, group together bureaus contributing to a common purpose (State Department), bureaus utilizing employees with similar or related skills (Public Health Service), bureaus serving the same area (Tennessee Valley Authority), or the same clientele (Veterans Administration). By its method of organization, the TVA is presumably more responsive to the Tennessee River region than if, say, it were a subordinate unit in the Interior Department. And the Veterans Administration is more responsive to veterans' needs, more integrative in treatment, than if veterans' services were scattered among many agencies. On the other hand, grouping several functions under a broad purpose permits grand-scale strategies for major problems, such as the war on poverty.

Budgeting utilizes analytical and informational processes to allocate resources to programs and agencies. Budget-making evokes negotiation and bargaining, intensive application of the politics of who gets what. Interest groups concerned with the programs maintain alert watch over the budget's development and its transformation into appropriations by Congress. Year by year, agencies tend to increase their budgets, but they must also keep the confidence of those who review the budgets, including the congressional appropriations committees. Thus their requests must appear reasonable in the light of past increases.

Budget-makers in the bureaus receive guidelines from the Office of Management and Budget (OMB) and cues from speeches by the President and other administration leaders indicating interest in this or that program. After the bureaus prepare their requests, they are reviewed at the top departmental level and at the presidential level by the OMB. In scrutinizing agency budgets, the OMB considers a bureau's present and potential workloads, expressed in quantified terms. Cost-benefit data must also be developed for departmental and OMB reviews. At those levels decisions are shaped by the availability of funds and the need to allocate them among competing demands that invariably exceed the amount available.

The national executive branch also utilizes budgeting methods known as PPBS or PPB (Planning, Programming Budgeting System). PPB groups programs according to broad objectives. It seeks to integrate the processes of planning, programming, and budgeting, to develop multiyear programs and financial plans for making annual budget decisions, and to devise alternative courses of action, each accompanied by quantitative analyses of program costs and effectiveness. Where possible, PPB employs computer technology. Originally developed in the Defense Department, PPB is being introduced in other departments and agencies. Wrongly handled, PPB could impede the public responsiveness of bureaucracy. Critics fear that an obsession with quantitative measurement may undervalue the quality of administration and ignore political costs and gains.[27]

Administrative procedures prescribe the steps of bureaucratic action. The procedures adopted have much to do with how responsive the executive branch is. In the case of the poverty program, for example, administrative decisions led to heavy reliance on community action programs, whose procedures were set forth in the "Community Action Program Guide." Proclaiming that the heart of the program was the "mobilization" of the poor themselves, the guide specified "traditional democratic techniques" such as group forums and discussions, nominations, and balloting, block elections, petitions and referendums, newsletters to neighborhood leaders and potential leaders.[28]

Coordination among several or more agencies responsible for segments of a shared program is needed to secure maximum benefit from the use of resources when they are scarce, as they nearly always are. Commonly, programs with multibureau or agency participants become objects of personal and organizational struggle. Higher executives may encourage and manipulate the wrangling to foster more bureaucratic responsiveness to themselves. Such competition is not always undesirable: it tests opinion, evokes information that might otherwise never reach the top, and creates opportunities for high level decisions instead of mere ratification of formulations made at lesser bureaucratic levels.

Nevertheless, competition and conflict must be regulated to avoid complete chaos. Coordinating mechanisms channelize conflicts and provide for their resolution. Interdepartmental and intradepartmental committees representing the organizational participants are one kind of coordinating mechanism. Or a "lead" agency may seek to provide coordination, as the OEO did for the many participating agencies of the poverty program. Or presidential assistants and organizations like the Office of Management and Budget and the National Security Council may provide coordinating facilities.

Each method has its flaw. In time, interdepartmental committees often falter in effectiveness as department secretaries begin to withdraw their interest and support. Lead agencies are often hobbled when other participating

---

[27] Davis, 193; see generally, Aaron Wildavsky, *The Politics of the Budgetary Process* (Boston: Little, Brown, 1964).
[28] Moynihan, 97–98.

agencies make end-runs to the White House and Congress. Forceful presidential assistants tend to shield the Chief Executive from issues and influences he should be aware of; weak or ineffective assistants are easily circumvented.

Proposals

The problem posed at the beginning of this chapter still stands: as far as the future can be envisaged, bureaucratic arrangements will be necessary for sustaining and regulating human society; and the more sophisticated they become, the greater is the danger of a lack of contact between government organizations and the individual human beings they are set up to serve.

1. There is growing interest in the device of the ombudsman, used in Sweden and several other countries to make bureaucracy more responsive to the individual citizen's rights and grievances. The Swedish ombudsman is elected by a parliamentary committee for a four-year term, is eligible for reelection, and has no responsibility to the executive. Anyone can appeal to him; he has unlimited access to bureaus and he can admonish and prosecute any official for improper performance of duties. Foreign experience shows that the ombudsman is enormously effective in keeping officials aware of their public accountability.[29] Conceivably, if applied to the United States, there might be one or more ombudsmen for each department or agency.

England utilizes Citizens' Advice Bureaus (CAB) to increase responsiveness and accountability by informing citizens about bureaucracy. CAB offices, manned by hired and volunteer help, are located in libraries, churches, settlement houses, and casework agencies. They explain the functions and operations of government agencies, and they advise the citizen of his rights so that he can challenge wrongful bureaucratic action. In recent years, CABs have answered more than a million queries annually, and their sturdy effectiveness makes the idea worth considering for the United States.[30]

2. The administration of civil rights, poverty, urban renewal, and other social programs has suffered in late years from a serious credibility gap. Generally, what administration accomplishes falls far short of what political leaders promise, and this is the worst imaginable case of irresponsiveness. In public speeches, Presidents have committed themselves to goals of almost utopian scale, raising expectations that can never be satisfied by administrative and political realities. Serious damage is done when people's expectations crumble into disillusionment.

To diminish the credibility gap, the Office of Management and Budget and the Domestic Council created by President Nixon may play important parts. When new programs are designed, these administrative agencies are to provide the President with information hitherto in short supply—measured forecasts of what the program can accomplish within given intervals, a year, two years,

---

[29] Walter Gellhorn, "The Swedish Ombudsman," *Yale Law Journal*, 75 (January 1965), 10.

or more. Projections are revised as the programs proceed. Although the President is literally swamped with all sorts of information, he has been most severely handicapped by serious information gaps on agency performance. The new machinery is expected to equip him with this information.

Until he has this type of information in hand, the President himself must refrain from injecting into campaign speeches and State of the Union messages high-flown schemes and fantastic promises that no administrative system, even at optimum performance, could possibly fulfill.

3. Innovations of administrative technique are badly needed. Particularly in domestic programs the concept of centralization has prevailed since the New Deal era nearly four decades ago. We are only beginning to realize the possibilities of decentralization and citizen participation. Many urban programs could be advanced by joint public and private action, in which European experience is far richer than ours. Little use has been made of potential volunteer manpower that could be so fruitfully addressed to urban problems— the retired businessman and professional, women of middle years whose family responsibilities have diminished, high school and college youth whose talents might be applied part time, or in lieu of military service. It seems certain that budgets and paid manpower for the massive administrative tasks of helping urban people will long be woefully inadequate.

In the future, both centralization and decentralization will have their uses. Centralization can be the source of equality in the standards of administrative policy and performance in various regions of the country, thereby contributing to social justice. Historically, centralization has been the route to major innovative social policy and its general availability to the people. But it has been handicapped by impersonalization and obliviousness to individual differences. At its best, decentralization enables administration to see the individual in his own world, amidst his full complement of positive and negative elements, so it can respond more accurately to his needs and desires. At its worst, decentralization is a favorite refuge of those opposed to policies that enhance social justice, knowing that it is often easier to defeat them locally than nationally. It is hoped that future administration will utilize the best features of both centralization and decentralization.

Suggested Reading

Altshuler, Alan A., ed., *The Politics of the Federal Bureaucracy* * (Dodd, Mead, 1968). A valuable treatment of the federal bureaucracy in the context of the political forces that interplay with bureaucratic operations.
Davis, James W., Jr., *The National Executive Branch* * (Free Press, 1970). A useful description and analysis of the federal executive branch and its workings. It relates

---

[30] Mildred Zucker, "Citizens' Advice Bureaus: The British Way," *Social Work* (October 1965), 85.

the executive agencies to the general political system and illuminates budget and personnel processes.

Downs, Anthony, *Inside Bureaucracy* * (Little, Brown, 1967). A well-rounded, insightful analysis of bureaucracy and its functioning. Examines types of bureaucratic personalities, ideology, conflict, and innovation, among other topics.

Gawthrop, Louis C., *Bureaucratic Behavior in the Executive Branch* * (Free Press, 1969). A cogent examination of the nature of bureaucracy and its processes. Bureaucracy is also seen in its relations with the political and social systems.

Mosher, Frederick C., *Democracy and the Public Service* * (Oxford University Press, 1968). An excellent analysis of bureaucracy's relationship to democracy. Provides extensive background on the nature of federal civil service, explores the trend toward professionalism and its implications, and other developments significant for democracy.

Rourke, Francis E., *Bureaucracy, Politics, and Public Policy* * (Little, Brown, 1969). An excellent analysis of the role of bureaucracy in the making of public policy. Considers different approaches to policy-making in bureaucratic agencies.

Sayre, Wallace S., ed., *The Federal Government Service* * (Prentice-Hall, 1965). Several political scientists analyze historic influences on the federal service, its relation to presidential and congressional politics, and its personnel processes. Explores the image of federal employment and the trend to a career system.

Simon, Herbert A., *Administrative Behavior* * 2nd edition (Macmillan, 1957). A classic analysis of behavior and decision-making in administrative organizations. The book has influenced the studies of others on bureaucracy and has been the chief base for Simon's own work on administrative organizations.

Wildavsky, Aaron, *The Politics of the Budgetary Process* * (Little, Brown, 1964). An invaluable examination of the federal budgetary process—its politics, both inside and outside the executive branch, and the behavior of its participants.

Woll, Peter, *American Bureaucracy* * (Norton, 1963). Examines the federal bureaucracy within the constitutional and political systems. Explores a variety of federal agencies, which are viewed as possessing their own political and legal systems.

* Available in paperback edition

10

popular

representation:

congress

"Politics produces few saints," former U.S. Senator Paul Douglas has written.[1] Most U.S. congressmen bear this statement out. Nevertheless, an occasional member of Congress pursues what conscience and judgment suggest are required in the country's interest, and he acts despite formidable obstacles, costs to his career, the displeasure of colleagues, and the likelihood of failure.

Consider, for example, Donald Riegle, a young Republican congressman from Flint, Michigan. Chief among those who had induced Riegle to abandon a budding business career for politics had been Richard Nixon. But as the Nixon administration proceeded, Riegle became increasingly distressed by his perceptions of its profile. The war continued in Vietnam, with incursions into Laos and Cambodia; the administration was addicted to a "Southern strategy" that blocked any serious treatment of urgent domestic problems; and "citizen faith in the whole self-government process was continuing to deteriorate." In speeches, in votes on bills and resolutions having to do with the war, in parliamentary maneuver, and in supporting the Republican presidential candidacy of fellow congressman Paul McCloskey of California, Riegle transposed his convictions into action.

Over the months that he expressed his conscientious insurgency, Riegle faced an array of pressures, obstacles, and penalties that would have deterred most individuals. Not surprisingly, he became persona non grata at the White House, and his name was removed from the White House invitation list even for such routine events as bill-signing ceremonies and prayer services. Many a House Republican colleague became distant and others warned Riegle to change his ways. Key figures in the state party, whose approval congressmen value, became suspicious, spoke disparagingly of his political judgment, and muttered that he was "too stupid to realize that [his] activities are probably destroying [his] future within the Republican party." The House Republican leader, Gerald Ford, an old friend, warned, vaguely but ominously, "Don't be too surprised if the rug is pulled out from under you." There were

[1] Paul H. Douglas, *In the Fullness of Time* (New York: Harcourt Brace Jovanovich, 1971; 1972), 236.

other tribulations. Riegle figured that the odds were "fifty-fifty" that his phone was bugged. Influential citizens of his constituency attacked him publicly, and a spokesman for the most powerful force in his district, General Motors, warned that he was fast becoming to Republican politics what Ralph Nader was to the economy, or more specifically to General Motors, and that he might be "opposed" in the next primary.

Good friends admonished Riegle to do as business executives do and become "a team player," but the young congressman rejected this counsel:

> In Congress, being a team player means acquiescing without a fight. It means staying silent while the wrong things are done. Being a team player in the House means throwing the game. . . . Either the compromises you have to make to achieve your goal wind up destroying you or you find when you finally reach that goal that it's far too late to do anything about the issues that used to motivate you.[2]

Theories of representation

Riegle's behavior is a tolerable approximation of a theory of the legislator and his function of representation formulated by Edmund Burke, an eighteenth-century English essayist and member of the House of Commons: the representative, applying "his mature judgment, his enlightened conscience," should serve his constituency's interest but not necessarily its will. Periodically, in elections, the constituency can review its representative's performance and dismiss him if it is displeased. As a senator, John F. Kennedy articulated the Burkean view when he said:

> The voters selected us . . . because they had confidence in our judgment . . . [to] determine what were their own best interests, as part of the nation's interests. This may mean that we must on occasion lead, inform, correct, and sometimes even ignore constituent opinion, if we are to exercise fully that judgment for which we were elected.[3]

A rival theory holds that the representative should follow the "mandate" of his constituents, or their will as expressed in elections, instructions, and by other means. The representative finds out as best he can what his constitu-

---

[2] Donald Riegle, *O Congress* (New York: Doubleday, 1972). Quotations are on pp. 13, 38, 69, and 91.

[3] In Malcolm E. Jewell and Samuel C. Patterson, *The Legislative Process in the United States* (New York: Random House, 1966), 397.

ents want and faithfully mirrors it in his legislative conduct, particularly voting. Thus as a congressman, John Kennedy, despite his Burkean aspirations, voted for a tariff on codfish, a historic major industry of his constituency; it was the single important exception of a political career committed to reduction of trade barriers between nations.

Both theories fit into the conceptualization of representative government fashioned by John Stuart Mill, the nineteenth-century English political economist. For Mill, democracy is most practically consummated by representative government, through which "the whole people . . . exercise through deputies periodically elected by themselves the ultimate controlling power." [4] When people cannot assemble to make common decisions because of their numbers or because they are scattered over a large area, they choose deputies or representatives to make laws.

Mill holds that representative government, centered in a lawmaking body elected by the people, is the most desirable of all governments. The popular legislature permits "the supreme controlling power" to remain with the community. The citizen not only has a voice in deciding who will govern, but he and his fellows actually serve as lawmakers, which brings them directly into the governing process. The popular legislature best serves the maxim "that the rights and interests of every or any person are only secure from being disregarded when the person interested is himself able, and habitually disposed, to stand up for them," either by being present or by choosing others to represent him in whom he has trust. Representative government most assures that "general prosperity . . . is more widely diffused." [5]

How effectively does Congress reflect Mill's ideals of representative government? To answer this question we must look at the entire congressional operation, for as will be seen, virtually every facet of Congress affects "representation." Congressional procedures, the distribution of power among the members, their social organization—all these variables help determine how accurately or imperfectly Congress measures up to Mill's standards.

A full evaluation of Congress's representational qualities also requires scrutiny of its many roles, especially its most important one, lawmaking. Most of the debate in political science writing over the effectiveness of Congress centers on its lawmaking function. Congress also has certain other specific functions assigned by the Constitution. It proposes amendments to the Constitution; it is empowered to declare war; it can impeach and try the President and other civil officers. Congress regulates the conduct of its members and can decide whether a prospective member has been properly elected or should be seated. The President must submit treaties and certain appointments to the Senate for "advice and consent." And in another key role, Congress oversees and supervises the conduct of the executive agencies.

[4] John Stuart Mill, *Representative Government,* in Ernest Rhys, ed., *Utilitarianism, Liberty, and Representative Government: John Stuart Mill* (New York: Everyman's Library, Dutton, 1936), 228.
[5] *Ibid.,* 207–08.

Representation in
public policy-making

A major, if not the most important, end product of congressional representation is public policy, embodied in laws that Congress enacts, appropriations it provides, and appointments to executive office that the Senate approves, among other means.

Domestic policy. Article I of the Constitution enumerates sweeping powers for Congress in domestic matters—the power to regulate interstate and foreign commerce, to tax, to regulate agriculture, to provide a currency, and the like. Congress can affect centrally almost every present-day issue of importance. Gains have been made in combating pollution primarily because of a series of congressional air and water pollution laws. The success of consumerism depends heavily on the scope of congressional legislation and the vigor of enforcement that congressional financing permits—prospects that appear unlikely until a far more effective congressional consensus develops. Civil rights, school desegregation, open housing, and voting rights have all been the subject of legislation. In the 1970s, the school busing issue is taking on crucial congressional dimensions.

In deciding about public policies, Congress makes choices between conflicting values and between the interests and sentiments attached to those values. Congress becomes the battleground of competing claimants. Take the "truth-in-lending" law, passed in the Johnson administration after more than a quarter century of struggle. Prior to the law, many borrowers did not realize that personal finance companies charged interest by the month and that 3½ percent a month was the equivalent of 42 percent a year, since interest was also charged for unpaid interest. Banks and department stores were also less than candid in their credit policies.

The effort to pass legislation requiring full disclosure of such policies aroused against it such powerful organizations as the American Retail Association, the U.S. Chamber of Commerce, the American Bankers Association, and the American Bar Association, whose aid was invoked by department stores, mail order houses, used car dealers, and all manner of manufactured goods interests. On the Senate Banking and Currency Committee, which considered the legislation, all Republican members except Clifford Case of New Jersey opposed the bill and heavy inroads were made among the Democrats. One such Democrat was himself in the small-loan business. In addition, the power groups were represented by Washington law firms composed of influential Democrats, who had labored in the liberal vineyards of the New and Fair Deals but were now being richly rewarded from their transfer of commitment.

Arrayed on the other side, in favor of the bill, were priests and professors and officers of mutual savings banks, who advanced the simple intellectual argument that it was only fair and just that the consumer know how much he was paying for credit. They pointed out that although lack of information hurt nearly everyone, the poor suffered most. Well-publicized committee hearings held in many cities, timely books, and ingenious compromises that shocked perfectionists finally produced a law. As Senator Paul Douglas, a leader of this long fight, watched the President sign the bill, a few tears came to his eyes, for "a small group of the common people without money or much political influence had finally and at least temporarily prevailed over the massed power of the financial, industrial, legal, and political Establishment." [6]

The hard struggle for consumer protection continues, without let-up. In 1972, as Congress neared the close of its session, important consumer groups struggled, unsuccessfully for the most part, to bring consumer bills to a vote. The lobbying victories in 1972 flowed to industry pressure groups instead. A no-fault automobile insurance plan, designed to provide fairer settlements for auto accident victims and less expensive auto insurance rates, was killed in the Senate after heavy lobbying against it by trial lawyers and segments of the automobile insurance industry. In the House, action was blocked on a bill that would give the Federal Trade Commission specific authority to issue trade regulation rules against unfair or deceptive selling and advertising practices. [7]

In legislating on public policy, Congress makes a diversity of detailed decisions. This operating principle is consistent with the theory of representation. If a legislature is representative, it gives greater effect to the will of its constituents by legislating in detail. Congress's strong penchant for diversity of decision is evident in the military draft legislation adopted in 1971. Among other things, Congress established a nationalized lottery call (eliminating the local board quota system), restored authority to draft college students, expanded the procedural rights of draft registrants, authorized a program to treat and rehabilitate drug addicts and alcoholics in the armed forces, set a 2.5 million personnel ceiling on the forces at active strength, and a 130,000 limit on the number of men who could be drafted in fiscal year 1972.

Underlying these details were even broader decisions, on which the legislative battle concentrated—Congress rejected the President's proposal to establish an all-volunteer army, and it turned down a proposal of some of its members to cut by one-half American troops stationed in Europe and to set a firm deadline on the withdrawal of American troops from Indochina. Instead, on the latter point, a "sense of Congress" resolution was adopted urging the President to negotiate a cease-fire for the Vietnam war and to withdraw American troops at the earliest possible date, pending the release of all U.S. prisoners of war. [8]

Foreign policy. Although Congress is ordinarily the dominant force of domestic policy-making, its impact in foreign policy and national security policy has

---

[6] Douglas, 523–35.

[7] *Christian Science Monitor*, August 26, September 7 and 14, 1972.

[8] *Congressional Quarterly Almanac, 1971* (Washington, D.C.: Congressional Quarterly, 1972), 259.

declined over the years, and power has flowed to the President. Nevertheless, the Constitution confers substantial powers on Congress: the power to declare war, to raise and support armies, to appropriate funds on which the entire national security apparatus and activity depend, to pass laws, to create and revise administrative structures, and the Senate to pass on appointments of many foreign policy makers.

Yet, despite considerable congressional opposition to the Indochina war reflecting growing opposition in the country, and despite solid effort and some success by legislative doves, Congress proved incapable of halting the war. Congress did succeed in barring the use of funds for military operations in Cambodia, and the Senate approved (but the House rejected) the cutting off of funds for the Vietnam war by a specified date. The more conservative House has regularly been a graveyard of the doves' proposals, although in an unusual turn of events the House Foreign Affairs Committee in July 1972 approved legislation that would order a termination of American involvement in the war, subject only to a limited cease-fire with North Vietnam and release of American prisoners.[9] Undeniably, congressional pressures helped speed President Nixon's moves to reduce American forces in Vietnam, but Congress took no decisive step to halt the war, as it could have done by manipulating its appropriations power.

The member of Congress and his constituency

A cardinal principle of Mill's theory of representation is that the legislator faithfully represents the will and needs of his constituent. Elections permit at least two possible ways for the constituency to shape or control the policy actions of its representative. By one, the constituents can choose a representative who shares their views to such an extent that in following his own convictions in Congress he does what they want. The representative's own policy attitudes are the bridge between constituency opinion and his actions. A second means of constituency control is for the representative to follow his perceptions of constituency opinions in order to win reelection: although his views may not be the same as theirs, he promises to do what he thinks they want. The perceptions connect constituency opinion and his actions.[10] Thus, a Michigan congressman who had been an unswerving hawk on the Vietnam war was suddenly confronted by the enlargement of his constituency by 40,000 Michigan State University students, thanks to the Twenty-Sixth Amendment and court rulings. In anticipation of the coming elections and the probable dovelike preferences of his new constituents, the representative began to reconsider his position on the war.[11]

John Stuart Mill's idealized theory of legislator-constituency relations is

[9] *New York Times,* July 25, 1972.
[10] Warren E. Miller and Donald E. Stokes, "Constituency Influence in Congress," *American Political Science Review,* LVII (March 1963), 50.
[11] Riegle, 109.

somewhat disabled by findings which reveal that most Americans are almost totally uninformed about issues discussed in Congress. Thus the legislator does not always have a clear signal to follow. At most, the average citizen holds general opinions about how the country should be run—how far, for example, a government should go to achieve welfare objectives, improve civil rights, and cope with the war in Vietnam. People base their responses to particular questions on these general expectations, and issues on which Congress might vote are judged according to these broad evaluative standards. Like their constituents, most congressmen have only general conceptions of how far government should go in welfare and other policies.

Studies also reveal that people are largely unaffected by knowledge they might gain of what the congressman says and does on policy questions. The dominant influence in voting in congressional elections is identification with party. But, according to these studies, there is a kind of vindication for Mill since members of Congress nevertheless are influenced by the belief that people do evaluate their voting records. Of a sample of congressmen opposed for re-election, more than four-fifths said the outcome had been largely determined by the electorate's response to their performance. Evidence discloses that in roll-call voting the congressman's behavior is strongly influenced both by his own policy preferences and by his perceptions of his constituency's preferences. Paradoxically, this sturdy regard for the constituency prevails despite the imperfect information the representative has about these preferences and the slight awareness the constituency normally has concerning his policy stands.[12]

Constituents impose other demands on the member of Congress. He is their "errand-boy," handling citizen needs and grievances with the executive branch. A license rejected or a benefit denied is a matter that looms large in the life of the individual citizen, and it may prompt him to write to his congressman for help. Senator Paul Douglas considered himself a kind of "ombudsman" or public defender for his constituents, one who could "reduce excessive delays and rescue living, breathing people from the file of unanswered papers. The farther away an official is from the people the greater are these delays."[13] One congressman periodically mailed about 15,000 postcards to constituents announcing that he would be in a certain area at a certain time and inviting them to drop by and discuss anything that was on their mind. Setting up a card table, usually in front of a grocery or drug store on a town's main street, he collected an extraordinary array of items on which people needed help.

Constituencies consist not only of people, but also of territory, and the Constitution provides different geographic bases of representation for the two congressional houses. The Senate, representing the states, grants to the 300,-000 inhabitants of Alaska the same representation as to the 20 million inhabitants of California. For the House, the Constitution requires that

[12] Miller and Stokes, 50–56.
[13] Douglas, 152.

representation be apportioned among the states "according to their respective numbers," and that House seats be reapportioned every ten years based on the national census. By law, Congress has limited House membership to 435, and the state legislatures determine the boundaries of each congressional district within each state.

Court rulings require that all congressional districts in a state must be absolutely equal in population ("as nearly as is practicable one man's vote in a congressional election is to be worth as much as another's" [14]), and that any variance, "no matter how small," must be justified. The effect of the new standards has been a shift of about 10 percent of House members to the suburbs; rural areas sustained the chief losses, followed by the central cities. After the elections of 1972, for the first time more congressmen will come from suburban areas than from either cities or rural districts.[15] But representation embraces more than mere numbers of human beings; it affects territories with distinctive life styles and interests, denoted by the "suburb" and the "inner city." In insisting on the "one man, one vote" principle, the courts are diminishing the impact of the rural and central city sectors and their ability to extract benefits. The realigned system of representation, while superficially equal, affirms the superior influence of the suburbs and of the industries that are increasingly concentrated there.

The ability of a congressman to represent his constituency is affected by the time and energy he devotes to other roles, and much may depend on how he sees these roles relative to representation. Some members, for example, perceive little connection between the legislation they promote and constituency attitudes toward them expressed in the quest for reelection. "The legislative and reelection functions are not really closely related," a congressman has said. "You can be a superb legislator and yet by neglecting the 'how do I get known to the voter?' question you will be a superb ex-legislator. Conversely, you can be a great fellow with the voters and a mediocre legislator." [16]

The quality of representation of constituents may be modified by the personal career interests of a member of Congress. He may approach his congressional work in terms of its capacity to speed his upward political mobility. Career lines are far from standardized among legislators. Some members are happy to remain congressmen or senators; others see their offices as stepping stones to other offices. Johnson and Nixon followed career paths that led from the House of Representatives to the Senate, the Vice-Presidency, and the Presidency. Kennedy followed an identical route except for the Vice-Presidency. For many legislators, the career path leads to leadership within his particular house, and his progress may depend importantly on his observance of behavioral norms likely to enhance his prestige and influence

---

[14] *Wesberry v. Sanders* (1964), 376 U.S. 1.
[15] *New York Times,* April 12, 1971.
[16] Charles Clapp, *The Congressman, His World as He Sees It* (Washington, D.C.: The Brookings Institution, 1963), 53.

there. Skills in parliamentary tactics are not considered essential to success. In bygone days when oratory was admired, Clay, Webster, and Calhoun could build congressional reputations on their prowess in debate, but they have no counterparts on the contemporary scene. A full-length speech by a Fulbright or a Mansfield derives importance from its substance rather than its style, and its impact is less on the members than on the public.

How representative is the representative of society?

According to John Stuart Mill's prescriptions, representative government should as far as possible mirror the different strands of opinion in society. Opinions presumably are best represented by those who hold them or have sustained the experience that produced them. A test of opinion representation is the social backgrounds of legislators. Ideally, they should reflect the diversity of society. Logic suggests that similarities of social background of the representative and the represented will produce public policies more responsive to the needs of the constituent. Implicit in this contention is the assumption that the poor man best represents the poor, the farmer the farmer, and so on. How well does Congress satisfy this ideal of representation? Is Congress a microcosm of American society with all its social variety?

Not really. In Congress, there is a much higher proportion of people from middle and upper class background than in the general population. Fathers of senators and representatives are more often professional or businessmen than fathers of persons in the general population. Likewise, the representatives themselves, when first elected, usually are from the higher ranges of the class structure. They are more likely to be lawyers and bank presidents than plumbers or policemen. More so than the ordinary job-holder, the member of Congress has high occupational mobility. He is a careerist "on the make." In education, he well surpasses his constituents, typically having not only a college education but postgraduate education as well, in law or other fields.

Although the United States in its population distribution is now an urban and suburban nation, legislators, like other principal office-holders of the federal government, were reared predominantly in small towns. In other words, after growing up under one pattern of population distribution, they are passing their mature years in another pattern, a discrepancy with consequences for the representative system. Sixty-four percent of the senators of the 1960s grew up in rural and small-town environments, 17 percent in medium-sized cities, and 19 percent in metropolitan areas. Some think, however, that the small-town background of most senators helps qualify them for the tasks of representation. The small-town child is often exposed to a cross-section of the community, to those "above" and "below" his social position, giving models of behavior that the secluded farm and the socially segmented big city are less apt to provide.

In its members' sex, religion, and race, Congress is also unrepresentative of the nation. In the Ninety-Third Congress (1973–75), blacks and women were underrepresented in both houses. Although blacks comprised about 11 percent of the population, there were only sixteen black representatives and one black senator. No senator and only fourteen representatives were women. In the Ninety-Second Congress, Roman Catholics for the first time became the largest religious denomination in Congress, with 101 representatives and 12 senators. Only two senators and twelve representatives in that Congress were Jews. Foreign-born citizens are barely represented at all. The decided preferance is for citizens of Anglo-Saxon backgrounds.[17]

The nature of congressional social backgrounds contributes to and reinforces the major cleavages in Congress, which are economic and racial. The sympathies and interests of one group of legislators, ordinarily the dominant group, are largely identified with the possessors of wealth and power, or the economically successful. Those legislators of another group, usually a minority, are more sympathetic to the less successful, to the poor, to the lower middle class, and even to those with minor power—the small farmers, small businessmen, and wage earners. Members of Congress are also divided between those who support white supremacy and those who assist racial justice. Generally, the two divisions are mutually reinforcing. Those strongly committed to white supremacy tend to line up in defense of wealth and privilege, while those who defend the racial underdogs support the less powerful.

Why are the less powerful so noticeably absent from congressional ranks? For one thing, one senator has noted, "Elections cost too much and political life is too precarious for those who live on the ragged edge." [18] However, a social and economic interpretation of legislative behavior must be used cautiously. Some of the wealthiest legislators, as the three Kennedys suggest, may be defenders of deprived people.

Safeguards
for representation

Mill would surely agree that popular representation is no self-sustaining political plant; it requires nourishment and protection. Above all, it needs to be protected by constitutional arrangements. The Founding Fathers fortunately and carefully did this by providing for representation in Congress

---

[17] Jewell and Patterson, 102–11; Donald R. Matthews, *U.S. Senators and Their World* (Chapel Hill: University of North Carolina Press, 1960), 16–23; *Congressional Quarterly Weekly Reports* (January 15, 1971), 126; *New York Times,* November 9, 1972.

[18] Douglas, 197.

in the first article of the Constitution. Representation is made complex by the fact that Congress is a bicameral (two-house) system of representation, with both houses strong, self-willed participants. Each enjoys separate elections, different constituencies, and both shared and separate powers.

To discharge his function of representation, the congressman or senator requires effective freedoms to meet, speak, and vote. The Founding Fathers were sensitive to these needs and made careful provision for them. The rules and customs of each house reinforce the constitutional safeguards. These rules assume that no representative, deliberative body can function successfully unless courtesy is observed and unless congressmen expressing a minority opinion have the same rights as majorities. Accordingly, the senator or congressman functions within a social system that can modify his representational behavior. The effectiveness of any structure of personal relations such as Congress depends on the ability of the participants to pursue reasonably predictable behavior, permitting common, stable expectations about another's conduct. The congressional social system, like other such systems, consists of norms—what group members are expected to do under given circumstances. A leading norm, a representative observed, is "that you shouldn't do harm to a colleague if you can avoid it. You have to live with these people. You need their votes just as they need yours." [19]

Congressional norms may be highly formalized, like the published rules; others, like the seniority system in committees, may be strongly traditional although unwritten. Any new member soon becomes conscious of a number of informal, unwritten rules. Prominent among these are concentration on legislative work, specialization and expertise as a means of influence, and courtesy and reciprocity. Courtesy makes cooperation possible between legislators who represent rival constituency viewpoints or otherwise compete. Reciprocity, which involves a personal exchange of assistance or a willingness to compromise over provisions of legislation and procedural issues, markedly facilities the discharge of congressional business. A related norm is that reciprocity can be cast aside when major concerns of constituencies are involved.[20] The typology of norms is presented in the table on the next page.

Norms are buttressed by cues, such as friendly tips from colleagues concerning a legislator's performance, and by penalties. "Woe to a member who has failed to clear matters properly," wrote Congressman Clem Miller, referring to the introduction of legislation. "Both parties have elaborate machinery that will halt the consent action." Much minor legislation, important to constituents, and therefore to the member, advances by "unanimous consent," a procedure by which legislative colleagues withhold objections. But for an errant congressman, Miller noted, "From out of nowhere can come an objection." [21]

[19] Clapp, 13.
[20] Jewell and Patterson, 371.
[21] Clem Miller, *Member of the House: Letters of a Congressman* (New York: Scribner's, 1962), 84.

Typology of legislative norms

Degree of formality or visibility	Description	Manifestation in Senate
High	Highly formalized written rules	Rules, standing orders, committee rules, precedents, rulings of chair
Intermediate	Well-established, traditional, unwritten rules	Senatorial courtesy, the seniority rule
Low	Informal, unwritten rules	Apprenticeship, specialization, courtesy, reciprocity, institutional patriotism, etc.

Source: Malcolm E. Jewell and Samuel C. Patterson, *The Legislative Process in the United States* (New York: Random House, 1966), p. 362.

Although the congressional houses possess a formidable apparatus for conformity, it also is a mark of Congress that considerably more than any other country's national legislature it permits wide individuality in the performance of certain roles. Congressman Don Riegle was impressed with how much his own style differed from that of Congressman Bill Steiger, both of whom were the same age and had come to Congress at the same time. To Riegle, Steiger (R., Wis.) was an "inside man," highly conversant with the complicated internal legislative process: the day-to-day piecemeal adjustments, the perfecting amendments, above-average participation in floor debate, "the base touching and necessary courtesies to senior members, the laughing at their unfunny jokes." Steiger was a dependable team player who learned "how to dissent occasionally without burning his bridges." In contrast, H. R. Gross, ranking Republican member of the Post Office Committee, is a maverick of twenty-three years' standing, often opposed to the leadership and often punished. "You know," he said, ". . . the one thing that makes this job worthwhile is being able to say and do what I think is right." [22]

A key to Gross's freedom (and that of other legislators) is his relation to his constituency. It is his employer, with the right to hire and fire him. Neither the congressional power centers—party leaders, committee chairmen, and others—nor Congress itself can supersede this dominating power of the constituency. The relationship makes it easier for the legislator to vote independently of house and party influences.

Some legislators use their freedom to promote innovative public policies: Congressman Aimie Forand advanced legislation for what became the

[22] Riegle, 67.

Medicare program, Congressman Henry Reuss initiated the idea of the Peace Corps, Senator George McGovern has drawn attention to world and domestic food problems, Senator Walter Mondale to auto safety, Senator Philip Hart to consumer labeling.

The committees

Congress utilizes several types of committees. Most important are the standing or permanent committees, seventeen in the Senate and twenty-one in the House (see table). There are also select or special committees to investigate specific problems. They can report their findings, but they cannot bring up legislation for consideration on the floor, as the standing committees can do. Joint committees, composed of members of both houses, are used for routine, ceremonial, and investigative purposes and can ease coordination between the houses.

Members are assigned to committees by a committee on committees within each party in each house. Their choices are submitted to the party caucus, consisting of all members of the party in the particular house, but the caucus never rejects the choices. Personal, partisan, and seniority factors are important in making the assignments. Weighty consideration is usually given to helping the legislator in his relations with his constituency and his quest for reelection. There is also a tendency to appoint senior congressmen to preferred committees and to leave less desirable committees to freshmen.[23]

Definite liberal-conservative patterns appear in committee make-up. In 1971, two key House committees that traditionally have been bastions of conservatism received a jolt when a few liberals were assigned to them. Two critics of the Indochina war were added to the Armed Services Committee and four liberals to Appropriations, including Louis Stokes of Ohio, the first black ever to sit on the committee. This small step toward a better ideological balance inspired one congressional veteran to speak of "a real revolution." To head off the injection of this unwanted new blood, Appropriations Committee Chairman George H. Mahon of Texas tried, unsuccessfully, to reduce the size of his committee and thus eliminate the need for new members. Major credit for the "revolution" has been given to the new House leadership, Speaker Carl Albert (Okla.) and Majority Leader Hale Boggs (La.), who reportedly were determined "to prove that theirs was not going to be a conservative administration, partial to the South." [24]

A critical part of the representative's or senator's legislative life is passed in committees. Typically, all legislators serve on them. House members serve on one or two standing committees, and senators usually on two or three. To build up influence, necessary if he is to represent his constituents effectively and influentially, the legislator must succeed in committee work. "Congres-

---

[23] William L. Morrow, *Congressional Committees* (New York: Scribner's, 1969), 44.
[24] *New York Times,* February 1, 1971.

Congressional standing committees

Senate standing committees	House standing committees
Aeronautical and Space Sciences	Agriculture
Agriculture and Forestry	Appropriations
Appropriations	Armed Services
Armed Services	Banking and Currency
Banking, Housing, and Urban Affairs	District of Columbia
Commerce	Education and Labor
District of Columbia	Foreign Affairs
Finance	Government Operations
Foreign Relations	House Administration
Government Operations	Interior and Insular Affairs
Interior and Insular Affairs	Internal Security
Judiciary	Interstate and Foreign Commerce
Labor and Public Welfare	Judiciary
Post Office and Civil Service	Merchant Marine and Fisheries
Public Works	Post Office and Civil Service
Rules and Administration	Public Works
Veterans' Affairs	Rules
	Science and Aeronautics
	Standards of Official Conduct
	Veterans' Affairs
	Ways and Means

sional government is committee government," Woodrow Wilson rightly said.

Just as Congress and its members do, committees provide representation for value conflicts. The assignment of legislators to committees, the presence of majority and minority parties on the committees, the conduct of hearings with outside witnesses appearing in behalf of rival interests, all contribute to the representation of competing values. Some see the committee as a broker, effecting compromises and consensus among various interest groups that champion differing values in its forum.[25]

But some committees represent certain values better than others. For instance, a sacred political tradition gives at least one Texas Democrat a seat on the House Ways and Means Committee, which handles tax and revenue legislation. What prompts this solicitude is the need to "protect" the oil depletion allowance, a great boon both to Texas oil millionaires and, in the past, to the Democratic party into whose coffers huge sums of campaign

[25] Morrow, 235.

money from grateful oil interests have flowed. Some committees are stronger than others, and not surprisingly, values associated with strength benefit proportionately. Thus the more conservative House Democrats cheerfully support the assignment of their liberal party colleagues to such a "liberal" committee as Education and Labor. They know that so long as the Appropriations Committee remains a conservative stronghold, they can put the brakes on "spendthrift liberals." [26]

Some committees reveal a decided regional imbalance, and most committees display another marked bias or unrepresentativeness: they are a happy hunting ground for organized interest groups. Legislation to benefit the grower, the refiner, the distributor, the importer, and the exporter emerges easily. Less organized groupings—the young, the old, the consumer—gain scant recognition. The presence of members friendly to powerful interests is taken for granted in some committees. Organized agricultural interests regard the Agriculture Committee as their preserve; mineral and grazing interests claim the Interior Committee for themselves. Democrats regularly placate organized labor by assigning pro-labor representatives to the Education and Labor Committee, and Republicans please the National Association of Manufacturers by appointing pro-business members to that same committee. Committees are typically structured to afford representation to a diversity of well-organized interest groups; the resulting balance precludes any group or coalition of groups from continuously dominating committee affairs. The effect is to promote conflict between the groups and their spokesmen.

In more solid contributions to representation, committees champion states' rights in legislation, help preserve balance between the national and federal principles of the Constitution, maintain Congress as a counterpoise to a powerful bureaucracy, and respond to the individual legislator's needs to enhance his influence, develop specialized knowledge and skills, and acquire prestigious group identity.

The rules committee. The House Rules Committee, a standing committee, has been characterized as "the most powerful and the most irresponsible organ of the House" and "a dignified oligarchy." The fifteen members of the committee in effect determine which legislation will be considered on the floor of the House. The committee reports to the House special orders or rules setting the time and terms of debate on a bill. In exchange for a rule, the committee may require that the bill be modified, and the rule it grants may help or hinder a bill's chances.

The Rules Committee, a stronghold of conservatives of both parties, applies a heavy hand to social legislation. On a single day in 1970, the committee refused to give a rule on two key social bills, a consumer bill and a bill giving the Equal Employment Opportunity Commission authority to stop discrimination in hiring by industry and labor unions. Both bills had passed the Senate by big majorities. The committee chairman, William F. Colmer

[26] Riegle, 144.

The House Rules Committee often turns a deaf ear to consumer complaints.
Chairman William Colmer appears to be doing so as he meets with
a group seeking action on consumer legislation in 1970.

(D., Miss.), blocked action simply by not scheduling hearings. The Rules Committee's sidetracking action stirred Congressman Ben Rosenthal (D., N.Y.), the consumer bill's manager, to denounce the committee's inaction as a "desecration of the legislative process," as "anticonsumer and pro-business." "It is outrageous that these men can prevent the House from working its will." [27]

The chief assault on the Rules Committee's arbitrary might was levied in 1961 by President Kennedy, with indispensable help from Speaker of the House Sam Rayburn. The committee was enlarged by the addition of two liberal Democrats to offset its conservative tilt. Since that day, the committee has not been so consistently a bottleneck to social legislation.

On several grounds, the Rules Committee would horrify John Stuart Mill's ideals of democratic representation. The ratio of majority members to minority is always kept at 2 to 1, regardless of the ratio in the House. The committee is also unrepresentative geographically: Southern Democrats and

[27] Clayton Fritchey, "One-Man Roadblock in Congress," *Newsday,* December 7, 1970.

Midwest Republicans currently predominate. A similar imbalance prevails in the overrepresentation of rural areas as compared with urban, a mighty factor in the committee's provincial conservatism.

Party committees. Senators and representatives function as party men, and the party committees in each house reinforce this loyalty. As mentioned, each party in each house has a committee on committees whose members represent the country's principal regions. For their respective parties, they assign members to standing committees. Given the importance of standing committees in legislation, these decisions are most consequential.

Campaign committees of each major party in the House and Senate assist in the electoral campaigns of members. Sometimes this assistance is not evenhanded. It is reported that in the 1970 elections Senator John G. Tower, chairman of the Republican Senate Campaign Committee, allotted nearly twice as much in party funds to the unsuccessful campaign of his fellow Texan and conservative, George Bush, as to any other Senate candidate. Some other Republicans who faced difficult campaigns received not a cent.[28] In both houses each party has a Policy Committee, a title that exaggerates its functions. Rather than make policy, it either becomes a supporting arm of the majority and minority leaders or lapses into disuse.

Congressional
leadership

One disturbing reality that Mill's rational model of representation could not take into account is that not all the representatives in the two houses of Congress are equal in influence and power. In the network of organizations and suborganizations that make up Congress, some indeed are leaders of imposing power—the Speaker of the House, for instance, is often spoken of as the most powerful officer, after the President, in the federal government. Congressional leaders are of two main types: seniority leaders, or the chairman and ranking minority members of the standing committees, and elective leaders, chosen by party caucus or conference in each house.

The power an individual congressman accumulates through leadership is highly valued by his constituents. For example, an appeal to citizens of the Tennessee Fourth District to reelect Joe Evins (D.) described him as "a very coveted congressman because of the powerful positions he holds"—a member of the Appropriations Committee, ranking high in the list of seniority (seventh among thirty Democrats on the committee), and chairman of such important appropriations subcommittees as those on Independent Offices (such as the Federal Trade Commission) and the Department of Housing and Urban Development, Public Works, and the Atomic Energy Commission. The AEC has major installations in Evins' district, and regarding its budget he "is in

[28] *New York Times,* October 2, 1970.

the driver's seat." Perhaps the most eloquent testimony of Evins' power was the establishment of a field office of the Federal Trade Commission in Oak Ridge, a unique privilege for a community of its size.[29]

Committee chairmen: the seniority rule. "I know not how better to describe our form of government in a single phrase," wrote Woodrow Wilson, "than by calling it a government by the chairmen of the Standing Committees of Congress." [30] A cardinal feature of "this disintegrate ministry," as Wilson called the chairmen, is their selection by the principle of seniority, an unwritten custom by which committee chairmanship automatically goes to the member of the majority party who has the longest uninterrupted service on that committee.

The seniority rule is one of the most controversial and contested aspects of Congress. It outrageously distorts the ideals of balanced representation entertained by John Stuart Mill. When Democrats control Congress, most committee chairmen are Southern Democrats, and in Republican Congresses, Midwesterners dominate; in both situations rural areas are far more represented than urban. In age, committee chairmen are older than the average ages of their congressional houses. In 1971, the average age of the combined membership of Congress was 53.7 years. The average of senators was 56.4 years and of representatives 51.9 years. In strong contrast were the ages of standing committee chairmen, which for the Senate ranged from forty-two to seventy-nine, with an average of sixty-five, and for the House ranged from forty-four to eighty-four, with an average of sixty-eight. The most elderly of the House patriarchs in 1971 included William Colmer (Rules), who was seventy-nine, and Emanuel Celler (Judiciary), eighty-one, and in the Senate, Allen Ellender (Agriculture), seventy-nine, and Clinton Anderson (Aeronautical and Space Sciences), eighty-one. The elderly, rural characteristics of the chairmen tend to make them conservative and inhospitable to social legislation.

The chairmen have enormous powers. They set meeting times, appoint subcommittees and their chairmen, assign bills to subcommittees, hire committee staffs, lead the floor debate on bills approved by their committees, and serve on conference committees of the House and Senate to iron out interhouse differences over a bill's provisions.

Indicative of the potentially wide range of the committee chairman's power is the career of Senator James O. Eastland (D., Miss.), chairman of the Senate Judiciary Committee. In 1956, liberals opposed his initial appointment to the committee because of his denunciation of the Supreme Court's 1954 decision outlawing segregation in public schools. As chairman, Eastland has consistently opposed civil rights legislation, weakened its provisions, delayed its passage, and forced civil rights advocates to resort to extreme parliamentary tactics to circumvent his committee.

[29] *The Oak Ridger* (Oak Ridge, Tennessee), October 22, 1970.
[30] In Morrow, 31.

"Maybe We'd Be More Convincing If We Could Bust Out Of Here"

From Herblock's State of the Union (Simon & Schuster, 1972).

Eastland's committee also deals with all aspects of the judiciary, including court appointments. In order to secure the appointment of Thurgood Marshall, a black, to the Second Circuit Court, the Kennedy administration sweetened what for Eastland was a bitter pill to swallow by recommending the appointments of Harold Cox and J. Robert Elliott to district court judgeships in Mississippi and Alabama. Both appointees turned out to be bitter-end segregationists.[31] According to President Johnson, Eastland opposed the nomination of Abe Fortas to become Chief Justice because of a speech by Fortas stressing the similarity of the Jewish and black struggles for equality, which Eastland interpreted as a conspiratorial call for Jews and blacks to take over America.[32] Eastland has taken more kindly to the entire series of Nixon's nominations to the Supreme Court. Eastland is also a member of the Agriculture Committee and coincidentally an enthusiastic participant in the federal farm subsidy program. In 1969, his cotton farm was credited with receiving $146,000 in subsidy payments.[33]

There is another side of the coin to the seniority principle. It is attractive because it is automatic. It avoids the factional and personal struggles that

---

[31] Arthur M. Schlesinger, Jr., *A Thousand Days: John F. Kennedy in the White House* (Boston: Houghton Mifflin, 1965), 698.

[32] Lyndon Baines Johnson, *The Vantage Point: Perspectives on the Presidency 1963–1969* (New York: Holt, Rinehart and Winston, 1971), 546–47.

[33] *Congressional Quarterly Almanac, 1970* (Washington, D.C.: Congressional Quarterly, 1971), 649.

might flame if other methods were used. And seniority helps assure that the chairman is well steeped in congressional ways. According to former Speaker Champ Clark, "a priest or a preacher who has just taken orders is not immediately made a bishop, archbishop, or cardinal. In every walk of life 'men must tarry at Jericho till their beards are grown.' " [34]

Elected party leaders. Most members of Congress vote with the majority of their party most of the time, a phenomenon indicative of another dimension of representation. The member is in a real sense a representative of his party; typically he bears a sense of party loyalty, vague feelings of party tradition, and an awareness of belonging fortified by the experience of his electoral contests. Without his party's label, he would have almost no chance to win. In Congress, he depends on it for cues for voting on a wide range of issues. One of the senator's and congressman's first acts at each new congressional session is to participate in his party's caucus or conference to choose party officers. [35]

The most exalted of these officers is the Speaker of the House of Representatives, in many ways the representative of the representatives. Both parties nominate candidates in a party caucus, and sometimes there is contention between rivals in the caucus. But the election, conducted by the whole House, is mostly form, for the vote proceeds customarily along party lines. Thus the majority party's candidate is nearly always elected Speaker. The Speaker's representativeness is enhanced by the fact that he is usually someone who stands near the center of the range of his party's opinions. The present Speaker, Carl Albert (D., Okla.), has labored to bridge the gaps between Democratic factions, ranging from what some call the Northern "bomb-throwing liberals" to the Southern "boll weevils."

Once an office of virtually absolute power, the Speakership was trimmed back by a congressional revolt in 1910. Nevertheless, its powers remain substantial. The Speaker presides over House sessions and is expected to interpret and enforce the rules with fairness to everyone. Yet he is also expected, as a party leader, to advance his party's fortunes. The Speaker has a major voice in naming members of the powerful Rules Committee and, when he wants to, strongly influences other committee appointments. He designates members of special investigating committees, and he can participate in debate and vote. But the most important elements of his power are the force of his personality and the esteem in which he is held. Much of former Speaker Sam Rayburn's large influence was said to have come from "innumerable kindnesses, favors, compliments, and courtesies afforded Members, their families, and their constituents." [36] The longest-tenured Speaker, Rayburn served intermittently for seventeen years from 1940 to 1961. His meetings with House leaders and

[34] George Goodwin, Jr., "The Seniority System in Congress," *American Political Science Review,* LIII (June 1959), 412–36.
[35] See David B. Truman, *The Congressional Party* (New York: Wiley, 1959), 145–47.
[36] In Richard Bolling, *House Out of Order* (New York: Dutton, 1965), 65.

intimates, known as the "Board of Education," were held in a House hideaway where, over bourbon and branch water, they planned strategy and swapped stories.

The Senate has no leadership figure comparable to the Speaker. The Constitution designates the Vice-President to preside over its sessions, and the Senate elects a President pro tempore to preside in his absence, but neither of these officers possesses significant power; whatever impact each has depends on his personal influence.

In both houses, each party chooses a floor leader, so that both the Senate and the House have a Majority and Minority Leader. The House Majority Leader is usually the chief strategist and tactician on the floor for the majority party. He arranges the schedule of debate, in consultation with the Speaker, the Rules Committee, and, to a degree, the Minority Leader. One reason the House has been the burial ground for antiwar measures is that these leaders cast up obstructions against scheduling the measures for debate. According to one dovish congressman, when antiwar bills remain bottled up in the Rules Committee, the Speaker and other leaders will publicly complain about the committee's arbitrariness, while at the same time they privately urge the committee chairman to keep the bills immobile.[37] Since the Senate is more informal than the House and depends less on rules, the scheduling function of the Majority Leader is chiefly limited to arranging the order in which bills are considered.

A Majority Leader facilitates representation by seeking to build a consensus among legislators who only partially agree, and whose differences may be encouraged by differences between their constituencies. Lyndon Johnson, one of the most successful of Senate Majority Leaders, respected the differences of the senators he endeavored to persuade: "The thing you must understand is that no man comes to the Senate on a platform of doing what is wrong. They will come determined to do what is right. The difficulty is finding an area of agreement." Johnson's formidable persuasive gifts were supplemented by favors he performed for the individual senator—helping move his pet legislation and arranging for assignments to special committees, appropriations for subcommittees, and appointments to represent the Senate at international meetings. Johnson was the center of the communications network of his senatorial party, which often enabled him to provide invaluable intelligence for a cooperating senator. Adept at parliamentary technique, he could coach a senator caught in a procedural snarl on how to get what he wanted.[38]

The whips (a name and function borrowed from Britain's Parliament) are also chosen by party caucus in each house. Like the leaders, whips enable members of common or reconcilable points of view to join in a voting force. The Majority Whip and Minority Whip keep informed of the attitudes and voting intentions of their party members and are responsible for getting them to the floor when votes are taken.

[37] Riegle, 171.
[38] Ralph K. Huitt, "Democratic Party Leadership in the Senate," *American Political Science Review,* LV (June 1961), 337–38.

Help for the
congressman

To represent his constituency effectively, whether in doing its "errands," introducing legislation, or deciding how to vote, the senator or representative receives several kinds of aid from his House and from congressional institutions. Each member has an allowance for a personal staff, the size of which reflects the size of the constituency. Its most important members are one or two administrative assistants, in many ways "assistant senators" or congressmen. Well educated, politically experienced, often with prior employment in the executive branch, they deal with the departments, prepare speeches, manage public relations endeavors, and advise their chief on issues.

In addition, there are committee staffs, both clerical and professional. Although the latter lack legal tenure, they accumulate long service with the increasing practice of committees to regard them as nonpartisan and to continue their employment from one Congress to the next. Often highly competent, with invaluable contacts in the executive branch and Congress, the professional staffs oversee research, arrange hearings, prepare bills, make inquiries to the departments, and help prepare legislation for the floor and for conference committee stages. A committee staff often develops a proprietary interest in a bill—it may have originally drafted it—and is alert to clues of concessions necessary to pass the bill. Both committee staffs and members of Congress can use the research resources of the Legislative Reference Service of the Library of Congress and the bill-drafting skills of the lawyers employed by the House and Senate Legislative Counsel.

Rapidly developing in recent decades, congressional staffs have been viewed as a principal counterweight to the enlarging influence of the executive branch. The executive has enjoyed swiftly ascending influence in legislation because of the advantages of unrivaled resources of facts and technical competence, central elements of legislative decisions. The expert congressional staffs are now able to supply these elements and often provide a kind of doublecheck on the executive departments. But Congress's increasing dependence on staff research is criticized by those who raise the question of whether decisions may not be shaped more by the staffs than by the congressmen themselves.

Congress at work:
lawmaking

A major preoccupation of the member of Congress is lawmaking, the supreme act of representation. He introduces and promotes legislation desired by his constituents or required according to his own best judgment of situations arising in society. But other legislators may reach an opposite judgment or represent constituents with different wills. Compromises usually must be made by the legislative participants in order to build a majority for a law to pass.

The end product, legislation or laws, comprises rules that are binding on the entire community and derive force from the representativeness of the law-makers.

Congress expresses its will through bills, which become laws when approved by both houses and by the President, or passed over his veto (see table). Often the houses express themselves in a joint resolution, which is not readily distinguishable from a bill except that it deals with situations that presumably are temporary. An example is the Gulf of Tonkin Resolution, which expressed congressional support for the President to "take all necessary measures to repel any armed attack against the forces of the United States and to prevent further aggression" in Southeast Asia. Both bills and joint resolutions require presidential approval. Other kinds of resolutions require the approval only of both chambers, or by merely one house. For example, a "sense of Congress" resolution to end the Vietnam war at the earliest possible date is considered by the two houses only and does not go to the President.

The vigor of the representative principle is upheld by the freedom of each senator and congressman to introduce bills. But all bills, once introduced, are not equal, unfortunately for the representative principle. A bill's chances for success depend on the influence of its sponsors and on whether it is important and controversial. Only a small part of the several thousand bills and resolutions introduced each session ever emerge from committee; still fewer are voted on by the houses. In the second session of the Ninety-First Congress (1970), for example, 7,487 bills and resolutions were introduced and referred to committee. But only 505 bills became law.[39] Interest groups and executive departments are alert to combat any bills that displease them. A legislator's chances are enormously enhanced if he can get the subject matter of his bill incorporated into the President's program for legislation.

Committee consideration. In both houses, bills are normally referred to the standing committees that have jurisdiction over their subject matter. For important bills public hearings may be held, where testimony is given by interest group and executive agency spokesmen and other concerned persons. Hearings may attract public attention to a bill, provide time for the political climate to change, and ease the acceptance of the bill's policies. Sometimes minority positions are not even aired at hearings; they remain unarticulated unless argued by the committee's minority members.

Bills may also be considered in a committee's executive, or closed, session, which bars the public but at which testimony may be taken. The committee also usually amends or votes on a bill in closed executive sessions. If a majority of a committee will not support the bill, that is, "report" it to the "floor" for action by a particular house, its life is ended. Congressional committees and subcommittees have been criticized for holding excessive numbers of executive sessions. One study revealed a range for many committees of from 30 to 47 percent. Senator William Proxmire has protested: "In most cases

[39] *Congressional Quarterly Almanac,* January 15, 1971, 136.

A typical way a bill becomes law

Introduction	Introduced in House		Introduced in Senate
Committee action	Referred to House committee	(Committee holds hearings, recommends passage)	Referred to Senate committee
Floor action	House debates and passes		Senate debates and passes
		House and Senate members confer, reach compromise	
	House approves compromise		Senate approves compromise
Enactment into law		President signs into law	

Source: Adapted from *Congressional Quarterly Almanac 1970* (Washington, D.C.: Congressional Quarterly, 1971), p. 3.

there is no reason for the exclusion of the press and the public from committee sessions where proposals are put to a vote. And yet . . . about 90 percent of the definitive decisions made by Congress are made in committee . . . in secret executive sessions. . . . There is no justification for excluding the public . . . it is their government." Others contend that the executive session permits committee members to escape the observation of the more highly organized interest groups and to speak and vote more freely for general concerns.[40] The Legislative Reorganization Act of 1970 requires that all committee sessions be open, unless closed by majority vote—but this is an option exercised all too frequently.

Getting to the floor. A bill can reach the floor of either house by being favorably reported out of committee. If that were the only way, the handful of men comprising a committee could thwart the will of constituencies and their representatives, and therefore Mill's ideal of representation, but congressional procedures set up alternative routes to the floor. For example, in the House, a bill bottled up in a standing committee, including the Rules Committee, can be brought to the floor via a discharge petition signed by a majority, or 218 members. The procedure is seldom invoked, however, because of the large number of signatures required and the legislators' disinclination to offend the chairman and the committee holding the bill. In the Senate, where there is no Rules Committee comparable to the House's, bills move more readily from the standing committees to the floor.

In both houses, bills reported favorably from committee go on the

40 Morrow, 98, 101–02.

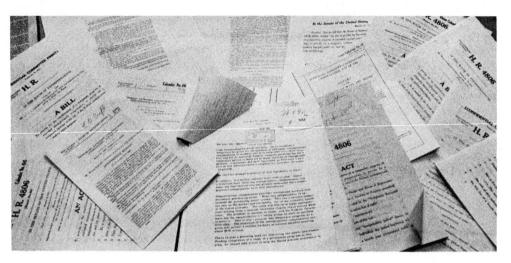

calendar. In the Senate the less controversial bills are taken up in the order in which they are reported. For important or controversial measures, the majority leader, after consultations, makes a motion for their consideration. In the House, the Rules Committee, the Speaker, and the Majority Leader reach a consensus for the sequence in which bills are considered, the limitations on debate, and the bill's substance, and if no consensus develops, the Rules Committee may act on its own.

Floor consideration. Floor debate seldom changes votes, but it helps focus public attention on a bill and permits more time for the undecided to learn how the political winds are blowing and for further consensus to develop.

House debate is highly regulated and less susceptible to dilatory tactics than in the Senate. The most important House debates occur in the Committee of the Whole House on the State of the Union, a device that allows less than a quorum of the full House to conduct business. Proceedings there are guided by the bill's managers, and time is divided between those speaking for and against.

The Senate has a proud tradition of unlimited debate; it imposes few controls and tolerates the filibuster, a procedure by which a minority of senators seeks to frustrate the majority by literally "talking a bill to death." The filibuster may be stopped by cloture, a vote by two-thirds of the Senate membership to close off debate, but it is rarely invoked. Used by both liberals and conservatives, Northerners and Southerners, filibusters have greater impact near the end of a session, when, eager to promote other pressing measures whose advance is blocked, the leaders agree to drop the bill against which the filibuster is directed.

Congress votes. Most constituents are ignorant of how their representatives vote on a given measure, even if a roll-call vote is taken. Lobbyists, interest groups, and party leaders do keep track of voting records. Legislators take roll-call votes seriously because they make a public record. Other types of voting, such as the standing vote and the voice vote, leave no record for the constituent to inspect. Until recently members were also able to escape recording by using the teller vote, a procedure by which the legislators simply file down the aisle and are counted. But in 1970 the Legislative Reorganization Act began requiring that names be recorded at teller votes. Even being recorded for a vote sometimes doesn't tell the full story, however. By an unrecorded voice vote, a legislator may support amendments curtailing a bill, but he may ultimately go on record in the roll call as voting for the bill, creating the impression that he supported it.

In 1973, the House of Representatives replaced the traditional roll-call method with a computer-operated electronic voting system, which can cut voting time in half. It also permits immediate retrieval of current and past voting information at the push of a button. Scoreboards, looming high over the House chamber, flash information much in the fashion of those used in a football stadium. (The system was, in fact, designed by a former professional football player.)

The conference committee. Often the versions of a bill may differ in the House and Senate. For most bills, differences between the two chambers' versions are settled when one house simply accepts the language of the other. Only on controversial bills or where differences are strong—true for less than a tenth of all bills—is a conference committee of the two houses appointed by the presiding officers. Generally, it comprises the chairman of the relevant standing committee of each house plus members of his committee that he recommends. His recommendation normally includes the senior members of both parties of his committee, and, if a subcommittee was involved, its senior members.

A conference committee is anything but a showcase of representation. Because only congressmen with considerable seniority tend to be appointed, three-fourths of the House members in 1970 had never attended a conference meeting. Under the rules, conferees are supposed to represent the position taken by their house, but they often do not. In 1970, the House voted $200 million for work on the SST, and the Senate voted no money at all for the program. Among the conferees, however, four of the seven senators had voted for full funding for the plane. One of them was Democratic senator Warren G. Magnuson of Washington, home state of Boeing aircraft, which had a huge stake in the outcome. A staunch backer of the SST, Magnuson made perfectly clear beforehand his intention to support the plane in the conference. After a remarkably brief consultation (three hours), the conferees approved a $210 million appropriation for the plane.[41]

Decisions of the conference committee cannot be amended when reported back to the houses for final vote. The houses can only accept or reject. Rejection sends the bill back to conference, with or without instructions.

[41] *New York Times,* December 21, 1970.

A bill-signing ceremony. President Nixon signs into law the Postal Reorganization Bill.

Pressures, however, are usually so great to get some kind of bill passed that the conference report is often accepted. If so, the bill goes to the President.

The President chooses. Representative of the national popular constituency, as he likes to regard himself, the President approves or vetoes the bill prepared by the representatives of the other constituencies, the states and the congressional districts. He can sign the bill or simply allow it to become law without his signature by neither signing nor vetoing the bill within ten days after he receives it. In approving, he can state his objections to parts of the bill and urge Congress to revise them at a later date.

If he vetoes, he may append a message, often directed as much to his national constituency as to Congress, underscoring differences between himself and his opposition. Messages accompanying President Nixon's vetoes of an HEW appropriation and of a hospital construction bill depicted him as a foe of inflation and watchful of government parsimony, while the Democratic Congress was pictured as callously free-spending.[42] By two-thirds vote of each house, Congress can override the President's veto. He avoids that danger by using the "pocket veto": if Congress adjourns within ten days of the President's receiving a bill, he can kill it by simply taking no action—by pocketing it. Historically this type of veto has been used near the end of a session, but President Nixon has given it new scope. During a short Christmas week adjournment in 1970, Nixon brandished the pocket veto to kill a $225 million medical education bill. What Congress might have done had it had the opportunity to override the veto is suggested by the overwhelming legislative vote

[42] *New York Times,* January 27 and July 1, 1970.

for passage—64 to 1 in the Senate and 346 to 2 in the House. Irate liberal Democrats cried that the President was outrageously violating constitutional intent and historic practice; others threatened to go to court and predicted with alarm that the day was coming when "we'd be risking vetoes any time we adjourned from Friday night until Monday morning." [43]

Overseeing
the executive

A vital function of the representative legislature, wrote John Stuart Mill, is "to check by criticism, and eventually by withdrawing their support, those high public officers who really conduct the public business, or who appoint those by whom it is conducted." [44] Congress is well suited to satisfy Mill's prescription, for it is undoubtedly the most powerful legislative body in the world in dealing with the executive. Today contrasting ideological tendencies enlarge interbranch differences. In Democratic Presidencies, the Chief Executive is apt to be more liberal than Congress, while in Republican Presidencies, Congress appears more liberal. Differences between the branches are also enlivened by what Congressman Richard Bolling (D., Mo.) sees as a sturdy streak of parochial pride. "A close reading of speeches by congressional seniors," he has written, "makes it quite apparent that . . . each congressional seat is in the nature of a bit of their transplanted home territory from which they conduct legislative and verbal forays against two alien bodies, the executive and judicial, that threaten the domestic peace and tranquility." [45]

A watchful Congress seeks to check administrative distortions of legislative intent. It works to prod administration into efficient performance and to expose corruption. Congress excels in keeping administration more sensitive to popular opinion than it might be otherwise. Congressional investigations of the executive branch provide a way to counter bureaucracy's burgeoning dominance of expertise and information.

The Appropriations Committee of each house exercises considerable power in overseeing the executive. Committee members mean to protect Congress's power of the purse, an attitude that disposes them to scrutinize departmental activity, to ferret out unnecessary expenditure, and to reduce budgetary estimates, although with the gaping proviso that constituency interests be served. The temper of the committee is suggested by a member's comment, "These [executive] agencies spend all their time . . . trying to think up ways to hoodwink us." [46]

As a former member of the House Appropriations Committee, Secretary of Defense Melvin Laird can fully attest to the possibilities. A favorite tactic

---

[43] *New York Times,* December 31, 1970.
[44] Mill, 241.
[45] Bolling, 117.
[46] Richard F. Fenno, *The Power of the Purse* (Boston: Little, Brown, 1966), 316.

HEW Secretary Elliot Richardson
testifies at a hearing of the Senate
Labor and Public Welfare
Subcommittee in 1971. Congress has
responsibility for overseeing the
executive branch.

of the Secretary is to load the Appropriation committees aboard the Navy yacht *Sequoia* and make a run up the Potomac while serving drinks, roast beef, and split lobster tails, and inducing a bipartisan congressional quartet to sing, gravel-throated George Andrews (D., Ala.), Congress's best raconteur, to tell a few stories, and Congresswoman Charlotte Reed (R., Ill.), former vocalist of Don McNeill's Breakfast Club, to render "September Song." But ordinarily the Appropriations committees shun luxury. The House committee's meeting room is spartan and drab, with old tables, worn brown swivel chairs, and a half dozen faded scenic prints set on pale green walls. The room gives little clue that its users divide up $200 billion each year.[47]

Congressional surveillance of an agency is most intense when its mission concerns controversial domestic problems like civil rights and poverty and government's role in employment policy. A director of the U.S. Employment Service, attempting to set up a single employment office in the District of Columbia, wrote that he "leased building space and fixed the date for opening the office. I was then called before the House committee to review and explain our plans. The chairman wanted to know how the desks were going to be laid out to see whether there was going to be adequate segregation. We

[47] Riegle, 76.

did very little without thinking about consulting a congressional committee." [48]

But the function of overseeing has another side of the coin. Congressmen are all too willing to grant money or approval when it will benefit their constituents, a concern known as the "pork barrel" factor. A Public Works Committee member may seek a new federal park for his district, or a member of the House or Senate Space Committee may try to attract the National Aeronautics and Space Administration to build in his district; they train at least some attention on whether the agency programs will please their constituents and thus gain votes for the next election. Doubtless, legislative discontent over administration policy on the Vietnam war has sometimes been modified by the prosperity the war has brought to many states and congressional districts.

Other congressional functions

In several other functions Congress represents the entire people or performs a national duty. The Constitution empowers it to originate amendments. If the electoral college fails to choose a President, the House of Representatives does so, and the Senate decides in a similar lapse for the Vice-President.[49] Both houses represent and exercise a national trust in the impeachment of public officers; the House initiates charges, and the Senate sits as a court of judgment. As well, the Senate serves as an executive council in providing the President with its advice and consent for appointments and treaties.

By constitutional direction, Congress makes laws governing the line of succession to the Presidency after the Vice-Presidency, as in the Presidential Succession Act of 1947. And Congress originated the Twenty-Fifth Amendment, which provides that a vacancy in the Vice-Presidency can be filled by an appointment made by the President and approved by Congress, and vests in Congress duties concerning the existence and termination of disability of the President.[50]

Bargaining

The member of Congress representing his constituents hopes to produce laws reflecting their will, but laws are made only by joining with other members, who represent constituents of possibly different sentiments. Voting majorities of members must somehow be constructed to reconcile or attentuate differences of interest and view. The process is complex because there are so many

[48] Morrow, 176–77.
[49] For further discussion of the amending process, see Chapter 3, and of Congress and presidential elections, see Chapter 8.
[50] For further discussion, see Chapter 8.

points of decision—committee, subcommittee, floor action, and conference—
and power is dispersed. The lack of a ready majority enhances the power of
alert minorities to halt a bill's progress. Much will depend on who its supporters are (committee chairmen, party leaders, respected members, the
President), where they are located (on the committee or subcommittee
reviewing the bill, on the Rules Committee), and how intensely they feel
about the bill. All these criteria apply equally to those opposed to the bill.

The process that aids the building of coalitions among members to process
and eventually pass bills is the mechanism of bargaining. Bargaining appears
in many forms. It may be non-negotiated, as when the decision-maker takes
a step that anticipates the reactions of others. Bargaining at early stages is
often of this type. Bargaining that is negotiated is evident in simple reciprocity, or logrolling: a congressman, by word or act, says to another, "You
give me what I want and I'll give you what you want."

The ideal of balanced representation is not served when one legislator is
overpoweringly skillful and successful in bargaining. The late Senator Robert
S. Kerr (D., Okla.) was one of these; a colleague described him as "a keen
and remorseless bargainer, who usually won the lion's share of any spoils that
were divided." Pious, populistic, and a persuasive orator of liberal themes,
Kerr proclaimed that his working philosophy was that he was opposed only
"to any deal that I am not in on." In bargaining Kerr was adept at logical
argument, and when it suited his purpose he could let fly volleys of cutting
and witty ridicule or fiery denunciation. His altogether effective manner was
heightened by a gigantic body, thundering voice, and the prestige of enormous
wealth. "He was more feared than liked," a Senate colleague wrote, "and the
vast majority, not caring to tangle with him, preferred to go along, lest they
excite his anger." Encouraged by such passivity, Kerr did wondrous things.
As a member of the Senate Finance Committee he sponsored and protected
from all peril the oil depletion allowance, the most generous of tax giveaways.
While chairman of the Joint Congressional Committee on Space, he installed
the chief of his petroleum company as administrative head of the new space
agency. He dreamed of transforming the shrunken Arkansas River in Oklahoma into a crowded artery of commerce with steel mills and industries on
its banks, and to speed the coming of that day he dotted his state with
federally built dams and lakes.[51]

Bargaining may transpire in compromise, the application of the "half a
loaf is better than none" philosophy. To gain support for a bill or its parts,
a policy or figure somewhere between two extreme positions is agreed on.
Where such flexibility is not possible, another kind of bargaining may occur—
"side-payments," or nonpolicy rewards and punishments, may be dangled,
say, by a Majority Leader, a committee chairman, or a presidential aide to
induce a legislator to contribute his vote. The currency of side-payments
includes appointive positions (judgeships, postmasterships, and other patron-

[51] Douglas, 235.

age), institutional positions (committee and subcommittee assignments, party positions), and resources (campaign contributions and aid, more staff, travel opportunities and expenses).

Bargaining suffuses executive-legislative relations, as the passage of the Emergency Employment Act of 1971 demonstrates. President Nixon had earlier vetoed similar legislation, but this time, contrary to expectations, he approved it. Why this change of presidential sentiment? Nixon's sudden receptivity was assisted by events—something had to be done to pare down existing high levels of unemployment, which were threatening Nixon's victory in the approaching 1972 election. In addition, the White House was under intense pressure from mayors, governors, and Republicans in Congress facing the coming election test "to do more" about the unemployment problem. Once the President agreed to the public jobs concept, which he had scorned in his veto message, Senator Jacob K. Javits (R., N.Y.) and others in Congress worked out compromise language that the White House would accept. Thus, whereas Nixon had objected to the earlier legislation as a "dead-end entrapment in permanent public subsidy," the new law was designed to assist career advancement and to develop new nonsubsidized careers for the worker. Liberal legislators were pleased that job funds could be used in a broad variety of fields, such as the environment, health care, education, public safety, recreation, and housing, and the President was placated by the two-year limit on the law (the earlier legislation would have had no time limit). In approving the new law, Nixon hailed it for providing "speedy relief." [52]

Among many legislative politicians and in much political writing, bargaining and compromise and the pragmatic skills necessary to effect them in a pluralistic society are regarded as highly valuable arts, even as supreme virtues. Paradoxically, idealism is suspect as the real enemy of attainable good. But while the pragmatic approach is often fruitful, it easily becomes negative, devalues issues, confines leadership to adjustment. It has yet to be proven adequate for dealing with deep social cleavages, such as race and urgent urban problems, or for breaking cleanly with past policy and embarking on new or strongly ideological programs. For those power-interests that oppose these programs, Congress, with its bargaining, provides an ideal strategic terrain for blocking and killing them. [53]

Congress evaluated

Compared with other national legislatures, Congress excels at giving representation to local, state, and regional diversity and interest. The Constitution contemplates that these smaller constituencies are as deserving of representa-

[52] *New York Times,* July 13, 1971.
[53] Lewis A. Froman, Jr., *The Congressional Process: Strategies, Rules and Procedures* (Boston: Little, Brown, 1967), 16–33.

tion as the national constituency, identified with the Presidency and the totality of Congress. But to those who seek rule by national majorities, Congress seems an anathema. Presidents, particularly those elected on platforms calling for innovative social legislation, generally meet rebuff in Congress, particularly in the House with its small constituencies. (The larger Senate constituencies tend to resemble the urban-rural balance of the President's electorate, the nation, and in that chamber he encounters less difficulty.) In recent Republican Presidencies, Congress has assumed a more liberal stance toward social legislation than the Chief Executive, and so deadlock persists.

Congress's most ardent critics see it as distressingly slow, fiddling while social institutions burn. Major health and education legislation, for example, idled on the congressional agenda for two decades before they were passed, and the Equal Rights Amendment was only recently passed, after decades of delay. On some questions, Congress has dawdled so long that it has forfeited policy-making to the other branches. Both school desegregation and legislative reapportionment were initiated by the Supreme Court, for segregationists controlled the relevant congressional committees and other key legislators owed their careers to malapportionment. In an era of drastic change, some critics see Congress as suffering from an "institutional adaptation crisis," having acquired excessive immunity to demands for innovation. Congressman Richard Bolling has asked, "Will the nation learn to improve itself by means of other institutions and thereby push the Congress to the outskirts of American society?" [54]

The dispersal of power in Congress and the multiple barriers created by the rules and procedures favor conservative interests and the status quo. Important social legislation can be passed only with arduous effort and bargaining that yields readily to compromise and concession. Less organized interests—the young, the consumer, urban dwellers—fare notably less well in Congress than organized moneyed interests. Congress will readily pass an oil depletion allowance and oil import quotas in genuflection to the American petroleum industry, but a proposed rat control program for the cities draws only merriment and jest. Instead of adding to the bureaucracy, one legislator suggested that the federal government hire and subsidize a million cats.

Proposals

Congress is a top priority item in any quest for improving American democracy. It is the strongest representative legislature in the world. No other national legislature has as much effect on public policy, on the conduct of the executive, and on the temper and concerns of society. Not without

[54] In Robert Bendiner, "Congress in the Age of Aquarius," *New York Times,* January 19, 1970.

cause, a careful student of Congress has written, "The Congress of the United States is the world's best hope of representative government." [55] But this does not mean that Congress cannot be improved.

1. The feature of Congress on which reformers have concentrated is the seniority system, which produces committee chairmen, often of conservative persuasion, who indulge freely in personal power, a gross affront to the ideal of representation. The alternatives to the seniority system include selection of chairmen by party caucus, rotation among senior committee members, election of the chairman by committee majority. Some propose an age limit of seventy years for chairmen and the setting of meeting dates, agenda, and other procedures by majority committee vote instead of the chairman's decision. To begin, Democrats might well follow the example of House Republicans, who now elect by secret ballot the ranking Republicans on each committee.

2. To deter legislators from considering personal economic gain in representing certain constituent interests, reformers have called for elimination of conflicts of interest, full disclosure of a member's financial holdings and income, and his influence on executive departments and regulatory agencies. While alert to apply such standards to the executive and the judiciary, Congress has been loath to clean its own stables.

3. The tendency of congressional power centers to underrepresent liberal members might be curtailed if legislative party institutions were strengthened. The key party organ is the House or Senate party caucus. Conceivably, the caucus might distribute committee seats with a better balance among liberal and conservative viewpoints. Possibly this would result in committee members more disposed to seek needed policy changes, to cooperate with relevant individuals and groups, and to attract public support. Instead of obdurately resisting change, Congress might lead in its management.

Suggested Reading

Burns, James M., *The Deadlock of Democracy* * (Prentice-Hall, 1963). A cogent analysis of Congress's inadequacies in responding to national needs. Argues that there is actually a four-party system consisting of distinctive congressional and presidential wings of both major parties.

Clapp, Charles L., *The Congressman: His Work As He Sees It* * (The Brookings Institution, 1963). Informative disclosures about the work of congressmen, made by a representative sample of congressmen in a series of discussions.

Clark, Joseph S., *Congress: The Sapless Branch* * (Harper & Row, 1964). An illuminating examination of Congress by a former senator and an advocate of congressional reform. Critical of the seniority system, Clark explores alternatives to it.

Fenno, Richard F., Jr., *The Power of the Purse: Appropriations Politics in Congress*

[55] Ernest S. Griffith, *Congress: Its Contemporary Role,* 4th ed. (New York: New York University Press, 1967).

(Little, Brown, 1966). A careful, full-scale examination of the appropriation process in both houses, with particular focus on the appropriations committees and subcommittees.

Froman, Lewis A., Jr., *The Congressional Process: Strategies, Rules, and Procedures* * (Little, Brown, 1967). A convenient, clear explanation of congressional procedures. Particularly valuable for its analysis of bargaining and coalition-building.

Green, Mark J., Fallows, James M., and Zwick, David R., *Who Runs Congress?* * Ralph Nader Congress Project (Bantam Books, 1972). A candid report on how Congress and congressmen function. Views the people, politics, power structures, and pressure groups that influence America's lawmakers.

Matthews, Donald R., *U.S. Senators and Their World* * (University of North Carolina Press, 1960). Empirical analysis of the U.S. Senate in 1960. Focuses on occupational and geographical backgrounds of the senators, their functions in the Senate, and their general political environment.

Morrow, William L., *Congressional Committees* * (Scribner's, 1969). A useful analysis of congressional committee processes, within the general context of congressional and executive branch politics.

Peabody, Robert L., and Polsby, Nelson W., eds., *New Perspectives on the House of Representatives* * 2nd edition (Rand McNally, 1969). A valuable collection of articles on many aspects of the House—committees, leadership selection, and legislative-executive relations.

Polsby, Nelson W., *Congress and the Presidency* * (Prentice-Hall, 1965). A readable portrayal of the legislative and executive branches, with emphasis on the distinctive features of the House and Senate.

Riegle, Donald, *O Congress* (Doubleday, 1972). A revealing account of the political world of a congressman by a House member from Michigan.

Saloma, John S., III, *Congress and the New Politics* * (Little, Brown, 1969). An overview of the legislator's work. Discusses congressional decision-making and information processing. Evaluates congressional performance and considers proposals to strengthen Congress.

Truman, David B., ed., *The Congress and America's Future* * (Prentice-Hall, 1965). A useful collection of essays on various aspects of Congress. Includes recommendations for improving Congress.

Truman, David B., *The Congressional Party* (Wiley, 1959). A landmark study of congressional leadership and the relationship between the make-up of the congressman's constituency and his behavior in the House.

* Available in paperback edition

11

equal

justice:

the

courts

Every sightseer in Washington, D.C., sees emblazoned on the marble palace that houses the Supreme Court the ideal, "Equal Justice Under Law." Many another American courthouse bears similar sentiments: "Equal and Exact Justice to All Men of Whatever State or Persuasion," "Justice Is Denied to No One," "Impartiality Is the Life of Justice as Justice Is of Good Government," "Where Law Ends, There Tyranny Begins."

But the inscriptions on the courthouses' exteriors are not always matched by what transpires inside. In the Wyoming State Penitentiary at Rawlings, a young prisoner from northern Wyoming is serving from ten to twelve years for a $7.50 armed robbery. Another young prisoner from the southern part of the state who committed the same crime and collected $124 was sentenced to two to three years. "A crime like robbery shocks the people in northern Wyoming," the warden explained. "Those who live along U.S. 30 in southern Wyoming are a lot more blasé about it." [1]

Daily in the misdemeanor arraignment court of Los Angeles, crowds of 100 to 300 defendants are gathered and pressed into a small space between the counsel table and the courtroom railing. Somehow bailiffs shepherd the defendants into lines. "By the time the defendant appears before the judge," a former magistrate of this crammed dispensary of justice has written, "frequently his only objective is to get out of the courtroom as fast as possible. . . . Under such conditions, it is possible that defendants plead guilty without adequate knowledge of the charges against them." [2]

It is in trial courts such as these that most citizens experience their only encounters with organized justice. But these are scenes that are hardly compatible with even the most modest aspirations of democracy. What, then, is an ideal system of justice in a country of the size and character of the United States? Where has that system gone wrong?

[1] In Howard James, *Crisis in the Courts* (New York: David McKay, 1968), 144.
[2] Harry W. Jones, ed., *The Courts, the Public, and the Law Explosion* (Englewood Cliffs, N.J.: Prentice-Hall, 1965), 113.

Democracy
and justice

"Man's capacity for justice," Reinhold Niebuhr, the theologian, has written, "makes democracy possible, but man's inclination to injustice makes democracy necessary." [3] Theorists and practitioners of democratic government have long been preoccupied with establishing even-handed justice that prefers no class or race over another, that protects essential rights of free men, that deliberates their fate rationally and fairly.

The legal system responds seriously to these ideals. In criminal cases it enables the powerless individual and the resourceful, strong government to clash on relatively equal terms before an independent judge. The defendant can choose his own counsel or accept an appointed counsel if he is indigent. The prosecutor labors under a substantial burden of proof: he must establish beyond reasonable doubt that the accused committed the alleged crime. The introduction of evidence is carefully regulated, and many forms of testimony that might conclusively demonstrate the defendant's guilt are barred. The defendant need not take the stand unless he wishes; if he chooses, he can have the protection of a jury trial. Twelve fellow citizens who represent not the government but the conscience of the community determine his guilt or innocence, after which he has rights of appeal.

Democracy anticipates that quarrels will erupt between its citizens. But democratic society, indeed any society, cannot function in the rampant strife that would result from settling quarrels by brute strength. Courts are devised to settle civil disputes by procedures of litigation that are a kind of war conducted with verbal weapons. Things that society values highly—liberty, property, religion—are protected, and legal norms are enforced in an even-handed way. By imposing rules on the disputants, the courts again to some degree are equalizers, enabling the individual to defend his rights and property against stronger private adversaries.

According to the ideals of democracy and justice, the courts must shun any appearance of arbitrariness. Their behavior is expected to produce an atmosphere of responsibility, rationality, and predictability. They cherish the principle of *stare decisis,* by which an earlier decision applies later in a similar case, although federal judge Charles E. Wyzanski, Jr., usefully warns us that these "judgments are not predictable by lawyers as eclipses are by astronomers." [4] Nonetheless, the democratic public expects markedly different behavior from their judges than from their legislators and executives. The latter are politicians who promote partisan advantage, bargain and compromise, and engage in controversy. But the judge is expected to be controlled, decorous, impartial. Judges wear a uniform, a robe, which, Jerome Frank

---

[3] Reinhold Niebuhr, *The Children of Light and the Children of Darkness* (New York: Scribner's, 1960).

[4] Charles E. Wyzanski, Jr., *Whereas—A Judge's Premises* (Boston: Little, Brown, 1965), 28–29.

noted, "gives the impression of uniformity of the decisions of the priestly tribe." [5]

Dimensions of crime

Concerned democracy affords not only the judicial protection of a fair trial to the accused criminal. If he is convicted, it will work to rehabilitate and restore him as a fully functioning member of society. If he cannot be restored, he deserves at least to be treated with humanity and decency. Ideal democracy can withhold its dispensations from no one.

For contemporary American democracy, the ideals pose mountainous tasks. Even before it became a burning topic of political rhetoric in the elections of 1968 and 1970, crime was a massive problem, and it continues to swell. In 1970, there were forty-three arrests for every thousand persons (not including traffic offenses). Between 1960 and 1970, according to FBI data, violent crimes and property crimes together increased 176 percent. The sharpest rises have occurred in narcotic drug law violations, which in 1970 rose 44 percent in a single year. In the election year of 1972, the FBI's combined crime index suddenly assumed a rosy hue when a mere 7 percent rise was reported for 1971. Because of a slowed rise in crimes against property, that overall figure obscured a marked rise in violent crimes (11 percent).[6]

As a concept, "crime" is a net that encompasses widely varying behavior —gambling, possession of marijuana, robbery, murder—and a leading cause of recent upsurges in the incidence of crime is the continuing expansion of its definition.

Common law crimes. Crimes that break the common law include burglary, murder, assault, robbery, rape. Such crimes are heaviest in areas with low income, physical deterioration, welfare dependency, racial and ethnic concentration, broken homes, working mothers, high disease rates, overcrowded and substandard housing and educational facilities, and other adverse social circumstances. Crimes of violence are the preserve of young males, with eighteen to twenty as the peak years.[7] Although, statistics show the number of crimes to be distressingly high, the absolute number of those who commit the crimes is reduced by recidivism, repeating offenders. Estimates of recidivists among prisoners range from 40 to 60 percent.

Irwin R. Brownstein, a justice of the New York State Supreme Court in Brooklyn, recommended to a state legislative committee in 1972 that the

[5] Jerome Frank, *Courts on Trial* (Princeton: Princeton University Press, 1950), 256.
[6] Federal Bureau of Investigation, *Uniform Crime Reports for the United States* (Washington, D.C.: U.S. Government Printing Office, 1970), 5, 35; *Christian Science Monitor,* August 29, 1972.
[7] James, 150; President's Commission on Law Enforcement, *The Challenge of Crime in a Free Society* (Washington, D.C.: U.S. Government Printing Office, 1967), 34, 44.

Crime rates in the United States, 1940–1970

| Year | Crimes against property[1] | | Crimes against persons[2] | | |
	Number per 100,000 population	Rate of increase	Number per 100,000 population	Rate of increase	Rate of increase of population
1940	460	—	98	—	—
1950	580	26.1%	116	18.4%	14.9%
1960	920	58.6	148	27.6	18.5
1970	2381	147.0	360	126.0	13.3

[1] Includes burglary, larceny of $50 or more, and auto theft.
[2] Includes murder, forcible rape, robbery, and aggravated assault.
Source: FBI Annual Reports and U.S. Bureau of the Census, *Statistical Abstract of the United States, 1971* (Washington, D.C.: U.S. Government Printing Office, 1971), p. 5, Table 2; p. 140, Table 216.

legislature enact mandatory minimum sentences for multiple offenders (recidivists), who, he said, were spreading the "plague" of crime. Granting that the jailed offender would probably gain little in the way of rehabilitation, the justice contended that "while this defendant is incarcerated, he is not going to murder, rob, mug, rape, burglarize, assault or steal from anyone."

Brownstein was himself a product of a poor area of Brooklyn and in his earlier judicial career felt "compassion for the guy who is in trouble." He often invited defendants to his home and helped them to get jobs or enter drug rehabilitation programs. He stressed that he has not lost his compassion for defendants, particularly first offenders, who are the most responsive to rehabilitation. But he noted that of 328 cases on his calendar, all but 12 involve multiple offenders, and that after considerable experience with this pattern, "It became clear to me that many of these people had made crime a vocation. . . . I learned that the criminal is often a devious, manipulative, bad person." If multiple offenders are imprisoned for lengthy terms, "the crime rate would drop so sharply as to stagger the imagination." Brownstein, who described downtown Brooklyn at night as a "war zone," carries a revolver when he walks his dog; he once fired at two young thugs who were beating a seventy-two-year-old man and managed to rescue the victim.

Brownstein's testimony was attacked by many lawyers, including the chief of the Legal Aid Society's criminal division, who called the proposal a "vote of no confidence in the judiciary." [8]

Like offenders, the victims of common law crimes are concentrated among the lower classes. Risks of victimization from forcible rape, robbery, and burglary are highest in the lowest income groups and decrease steadily at higher income levels. (Larceny, on the other hand, falls most heavily on the highest income groups.) The costs of crime to democracy are perceivable

[8] *New York Times,* September 29, 1972.

both in the losses of crime victims and in the erosion of the quality of life. In a study of high crime areas in two large cities, 43 percent of the respondents said they stayed off the streets at night because of their fears of crime; 31 percent traveled only by car and cab at night; 35 percent no longer spoke to strangers; 20 percent said they would like to move to another neighborhood because of the fear of crime.[9]

White collar crime. "The financial cost of white collar crime," wrote Edwin H. Sutherland, "is probably several times as great as the financial cost of all crimes customarily regarded as 'the crime problem.' " [10] In pursuit of sales and profit, businessmen compile a high rate of lawbreaking by embezzlement, restraint of trade, misrepresentation in advertising, financial fraud, antitrust violations, infringement of patents, price fixing, violating pollution regulations.

If anything, Sutherland's estimate is too low and too limited. It does not take into account the social harm to the community, the injury to life and health of individual citizens. And the financial loss to consumers and to government amounts to many times over the losses incurred by common law offenses of burglary, robbery, and larceny. The latter crimes are recorded in the national crime index, but white collar crimes are not; the absence of data is a shield behind which such crimes can all the better be pursued. Loose, fragmentary definitions of corporate crime and grossly inadequate enforcement reinforce a social system in which that crime can function and even flourish.

Justice treats white collar crimes unequally with common law crimes. He who robs the corner grocery store lands in jail. He who steals a railroad becomes wealthy, respected, and sufficiently powerful politically to preserve his immunity. Daniel Drew, a pious fraudulent robber baron of the nineteenth century, observed that "law is like a cobweb; it's made for flies and the smaller kinds of insects, so to speak, but lets the big bumble bees break through."

Unlike common law offenses, white collar crime is impersonal and diffuse in its victimization; those affected are often unaware of the harm done to them. The social class incidence of white collar crime is exactly opposite that for common law crime. For the latter, high incidence occurs in the lower socioeconomic class. White collar crime is the preserve of the upper socio-economic class.

The chief difference between the two crime categories lies in the use of judicial and administrative processes for dealing with offenders. For white collar crimes these processes are highly irregular and incomplete. Also, they are easily thwarted because white collar crime is continuously evolving in subtle new methods and sophistication. Something of the quiet, ingenious proliferation of method is evident in the practice of medicine, one of the least criminal of professions. Today's criminal and antisocial medical practices include illegal sales of narcotics, illegal services to underworld criminals,

---

[9] President's Commission on Law Enforcement, v.
[10] Edwin H. Sutherland, *White Collar Crime* (New York: Holt, Rinehart and Winston, 1949; 1961), 12.

fraudulent reports and testimony in accident cases, falsified income tax returns, unnecessary treatment and surgical operations, restriction of competition, fee-splitting, overcharging for services to Medicare, welfare, and other public programs.

Some white collar crime is inadvertent, but most is deliberate. As in lower class crime, many offenders in business criminality are consistent offenders. Of seventy corporations that Sutherland studied, 97.1 percent had two or more adverse decisions.[11] Often white collar crimes are highly organized. Lucrative antitrust violations have been based on gentleman's agreements, pools, patent agreements, cartels, and other intricately structured arrangements. Business groups lobby the legislatures to hold down appropriations for enforcement, and they try to influence the selection of administrators and the drafting and passage of legislation. For them, the construction of a loophole in a law is a creative and rewarding act.

A key element of criminology is the conception of oneself as a criminal. The conception virtually does not exist in white collar crime. The businessman who violates the law does not lose status among his business associates. He suffers that loss only if he violates the business code, and indeed he is admired if he expresses contempt for government, the quality of its personnel, and the "impracticality" of law. Often, however, government personnel are among his staunchest admirers, a sign of the cultural homogeneity of civil servants and businessmen and the aspiration of many government employees to move one day into lucrative and prestigious business positions.

Organized crime. Crime in America has another major dimension—organized crime—which is a cross between common law and white collar crime. Variously called the Mafia, Cosa Nostra, the mob, and the syndicate, organized crime was estimated by the President's Commission on Law Enforcement in 1966 to operate in 80 percent of the cities of more than a million people.[12] Typically, this kind of crime thrives on a variety of illegal activities—gambling, narcotics, loansharking, labor racketeering, among others. Organized crime also infiltrates a number of legitimate industries, such as food products, restaurants, garbage disposal, securities, and realty. As standard activity, organized crime cultivates politicians and police and often corrupts them. FBI documentation once credited organized crime with virtually running the city of Newark, New Jersey, during the mayoralty of Hugh Addonizio, who subsequently was jailed. As one knowledgeable state official informed a state legislative committee at the time, "Official corruption in New Jersey is so bad that organized crime can get anything it desires."[13]

The world of organized crime, vividly depicted in "The Godfather," is for the most part the domain of racketeering "families" organized in a strict

---

[11] *Ibid.,* 217.

[12] President's Commission on Law Enforcement, 191.

[13] Fred J. Cook, "The People v. the Mob; Or, Who Rules New Jersey?" *New York Times Magazine* (February 1, 1970).

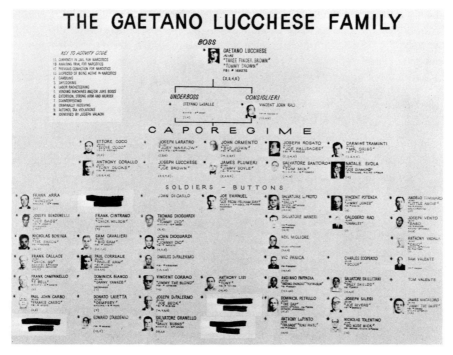

A Mafia "family tree."

hierarchical structure running from boss and underboss down through the lieutenants to the soldiers. A key figure is the counselor, a tactician skilled in avoiding the entrapments of the law.

An ordinary criminal and a member of a crime family are not accorded equal justice. A New York State Joint Legislative Committee on Crime found that the rate of dismissals and acquittals for racketeers was five times that of other defendants. On the same day, for example, New York Supreme Court justice Domenic S. Rinaldi sentenced two defendants. One, Paul Vario, a captain in the Mafia family of Thomas Lucchese, pleaded guilty of bribing a police officer. Vario, whose criminal record began in 1925 and included a conviction for rape, could have been given a year in jail; instead, he was fined $250. The second defendant Justice Rinaldi sentenced that day was Luis Guzman, nineteen years old, who was given up to five years in a reformatory for robbing a drugstore.[14]

Why this preferential treatment for the mob? "Obviously the skill of counsel is one reason racketeers do better," an assistant district attorney has said. "They can afford better lawyers." Most judges treat organized crime figures leniently for certain offenses like gambling, which they look on as victimless crime and even as a welcome relief after a heavy load of violent

[14] *New York Times,* September 27, 1972.

crimes. This form of unequal justice is also fostered by the tendency of judges to come up through political organizations and to build up obligations along the way. "At the same time racketeers cultivate political figures," a prosecutor has said, "and when their people get in trouble they try to use whatever influence they have." [15]

Servants of justice

The most demanding test of equal justice occurs in the citizen's encounters with the criminal law. Whether fairness will prevail depends on the behavior of several standard participants.

The police. The police issue citations, summonses, warrants, and make arrests that bring defendants into court on criminal charges. Police enjoy large discretion whether or not to arrest. Often they develop policies discriminating between various kinds of violations, ignoring some and making arrests for others, with or without intention to prosecute. Thus in Detroit, police have long arrested drunks to get them off the streets. Treated as "Golden Rule Drunks," they are released without charge or offense when sober.

Police discretion can be abused. Individual police may discriminate between young and old, long hair and short, white and black. Many a police manual suggests ruses and ploys for handling the accused—feigning sympathy and solicitude, falsely identifying him with other crimes to induce his confession to the current offense, playing two suspects off against one another and declaring that one has confessed, stressing that the accused's nervousness betrays his guilt. In *Miranda v. Arizona* (1966) and *Escobedo v. Illinois* (1964),[16] the U.S. Supreme Court intervened to bar interrogation of suspected persons without their consent unless defense counsel is present. Confessions, unless spontaneous and unsolicited and secured through the accused's deliberate waiver of his right to remain silent, are barred. However, a 1971 decision held that a statement inadmissible as evidence under the earlier rulings might still be used in court to contradict the suspect's testimony.[17]

The prosecutor. The prosecutor is an attorney empowered by the national, state, or county government to seek indictments and contend for conviction of accused criminals. In most states, the prosecutor is the county's district attorney. Usually elected, he is often the most visible of local officials, a skilled cultivator of the press, and politically ambitious. In lesser jurisdictions, prosecutors are part time and often young lawyers with little trial experience.

Like the police, the prosecutor enjoys broad discretion to ignore offenses or to prosecute. The prosecutor often becomes a *de facto* judge, deciding guilt or innocence and the concessions to be made to a cooperative defendant who

[15] *New York Times,* September 25, 1972.
[16] 384 U.S. 436 (1966) and 378 U.S. 478 (1964).
[17] *New York Times,* February 25, 1971.

will plead guilty and forfeit a trial. One of the prosecutor's more powerful weapons is the multiple indictment. A single event producing an offense can lead to an indictment of several counts. The severe punishment possible from conviction on all counts helps speed the accused into accepting a lesser plea. Among the other cards in the prosecutor's hand are recommendation of the amount of bail, if any; deciding when the case will appear on the calendar; and selecting the term—in effect the judge—to try the case.

The prosecutor is of necessity committed more to selective justice than to equal justice. He has only limited resources of budget and staff and an overwhelming number of cases. As well, there are not enough police to arrest all law violators, judges to try them, and jails to hold them; and even if there were, society would not tolerate total law enforcement.

The criminal lawyer. Despite his critical importance in the dispensing of justice, the criminal lawyer, defender of the accused, holds a low place on his profession's totem pole. His more respected and influential colleagues shun what they consider to be the profession's "dirty work." Criminal law practice is frequently a venture in personal influence. Vital to the criminal lawyer's successful functioning is his network of personal relations with other members of the criminal justice system—the police, court clerks, probation personnel, and the bail bondsmen. They may steer business his way, inform him of significant developments in a case, bend some regulation in his favor. On the other hand, the best-known lawyers tend to be criminal lawyers. Edward Bennett Williams and F. Lee Bailey enjoy this present fame, because of their demonstrated skill in protecting the rights of unpopular defendants, whose guilt is virtually assumed, and often in winning their cases.

Many factors suggest that the defense attorney–client relationship is not wholly consecrated to the goddess of Justice. Often the defense attorney has to restrain his commitment to a particular client's interest for the sake of preserving his network of contacts in the judicial system. And clients are made to understand that the full commitment of professional expertise, inside knowledge, and personal connections depends on payment of fees—in advance. Paradoxically, in most criminal cases, the defense attorney profits best by limiting their duration and scope. Seeking to avoid a trial, which overwhelming data show that he most likely will lose, he performs less as gladiator than as agent-mediator who brings the accused around to pleading guilty. The defense attorney thereby "helps" both his client, by saving him from the severer penalty of a trial, and the court, by lightening its burden. Everyone concerned—the police, the prosecutor, and the judge—wants to terminate the litigation with minimum expenditure of time and money, and the defense lawyer influences, coaxes, and wheedles his client into accepting that situation.

The trial judge. The judge, Aristotle said, is "living justice." The slogan that ours is a "government of laws and not of men" conceals the fact that the law is not so exact that one reasonable judge will interpret it in precisely the same way as another. A further misconception is that a trial judge is watched over by appellate judges. Relatively few cases are appealed; even when they are, the trial judge's determinations of fact are definitive, and in most cases only the facts, not the law, are in controversy. The trial judge is truly the key man in the system of justice.

Harry W. Jones has written that "only a man of first-rate capacity can make sound, split-second decisions on questions of criminal law and procedure, exercise sentencing responsibilities thoughtfully and wisely under exhausting pressure of time, and improve procedures." [18] While many judges approximate the ideals suggested by Jones, all too frequently others fall well below them. Many are hacks, placed on the bench for long service to their party. Some resort to the bench as semiretirement from arduous law practice. Others are simply incompetent lawyers seeking a better living. In the intensity of a trial, a judge's shortcomings are magnified. Some are inattentive and lazy; others abrasive, short-tempered, prejudiced. Some are weak, permitting others to push them around. Weakness is all the more indulged since a judge is ruler of his own kingdom and largely hidden from public view. No superintendent, no critical public opinion makes him work or restrains him from abuse. Everywhere there is deference, from the retinue of court attendants, many of whom owe their jobs to him, and from lawyers who practice before his bench and find life easier if they have his favor.

The jury. There are two kinds of juries. The grand jury, usually consisting of from sixteen to twenty-three persons, sits in criminal cases to decide whether to grant a prosecutor an indictment, in effect an accusation against someone considered guilty of a serious crime. The prosecutor must prove there is enough evidence against the defendant to warrant his being brought to trial.

The jury that hears his trial and determines his innocence or guilt is a petit jury, consisting of six or twelve members. To many, juries are the shining knights of equal justice, twelve persons from all walks of life bringing to the trial court more experience and insight, more understanding of man's motives, than can any single judge. Justice is safeguarded by secret deliberations, which protect the jury's freedom from fear of retaliation. A leading New York justice, Bernard Botein, values juries for bringing the compassion of the community into the courtroom to soften for some defendants the harshness of the law. Although occasional critics are disparaging of juries—H. L. Mencken said that, next to throwing dice, trial by jury was the best method for ascertaining guilt thus far devised—recent research casts them in a favorable light. A University of Chicago Law School study found that although individual jurors might be forgetful or confused, the "net intelligence" of the group was "miraculous," their decision moving by and large with the weight and direction of the evidence. Juries, the study found, deliberate longer in difficult cases than in easy cases, and they are prone to even-handed justice—willing to tolerate the defendant's violation of the law if everybody else is

[18] Jones, 128–29.

violating, hostile to preferential treatment in which the dominant partner in a crime gets more lenient treatment.[19]

The trial court

Trial courts, in which most cases both begin and end, are "inferior" or "petty" —limited to minor civil and criminal cases—and "superior"—of general jurisdiction, covering the more serious civil and criminal cases. Most courts are manned by professional judges. Some are presided over by justices of the peace, apt to be untrained laymen, but they are a declining breed. Specialized tribunals such as family and juvenile courts draw on the expertise of probation officers, social workers, psychiatrists, and others, and permit more flexible proceedings.

In physical appearance alone, trial courts afford wide variety, from cold, cavernous structures of dirty marble in big cities to a justice of the peace court in Oklahoma City housed in a converted storefront building, with metal-framed, chicken-wire glass windows, an American flag thumbtacked to the wall, four bare bulbs dangling on electric cords, pictures of Indians scattered on the walls, a collection of unmatched chairs and old pews, and a desk— the judge's bench—on a wooden platform.[20]

In metropolitan areas, mass production justice reigns. In 1970, for example, Philadelphia's Court of Common Pleas, a superior trial court, was faced with 91,980 cases and managed to dispose of 67,402 of them by year's end.[21] To keep their heads above the incessant litigious floodtide, trial courts rely heavily on pretrial procedures. More than two-thirds of the civil cases do not get beyond the preliminary stages and are settled out of court, sometimes with the judge's help. Most criminal cases never come to trial and about 90 percent of these are settled by negotiation, or plea bargaining, between the prosecutor and the defendant, with or without an attorney.

Plea bargaining. The common pretrial practice of plea bargaining is a procedure many miles removed from the fair-minded exactitude of equal justice. As noted earlier, metropolitan prosecutors and judges, under heavy caseloads, prefer to settle cases out of court to save time, staff energies, and expense. The prosecutor is in a bargaining position because he can decide what charge(s) to make against the defendant. Initially, he may charge the defendant with a serious offense he knows he cannot prove, expecting to reduce the charge in exchange for a guilty plea. The defendant too may prefer to bargain rather than face trial, fearful that the prosecutor and judge will be displeased

---

[19] Harry Kalven, Jr., and Hans Zeisel, *The American Jury* (Boston: Little, Brown, 1966), 287–313.
[20] James, 38–39.
[21] *New York Times,* March 8, 1971.

if he insists on his day in court and that a jury will convict him on the greater charge.[22]

In Chicago, for example, the prosecutor proposed a one-to-three-year prison sentence for a defendant caught in a laundry company swindle. Defense counsel deemed it too severe, and after much haggling, the defendant was given five years' probation and ninety days in the county jail. Defense counsel noted that if his client demands a trial "and is found guilty, he can expect a two-to-five-year sentence. If a jury finds him guilty, the prison term will probably be four to eight years. That's the penalty imposed for taking up the court's time." [23]

Advocates of plea bargaining point out that overburdened metropolitan courts cannot try all cases coming to them and that the quality of justice would suffer without the heavy pruning of cases by plea bargaining. It permits flexibility and certainty in a rigid, often erratic system, mitigates the harshness of mandatory sentences, and helps law enforcement needs when leniency is exchanged for information from the accused. But critics point out that dangerous offenders can manipulate the bargaining to win unjustifiably lenient treatment, or that prosecutors threaten harsh sentences disproportionate to the alleged offense. Worst of all, many who are innocent plead guilty rather than run the risks and higher penalties of a trial. Lamentably, both prosecutors and judges contribute to such fabricated injustices.

Bail. Bail procedures often show flaws under the glaring light of equal justice. When the court is not certain a defendant will appear for trial, it may require bail, a sum of money the defendant must put up to gain his freedom until his day of trial. If he does not show up, he forfeits the bail. The amount of the bail depends on the seriousness of the crime and the defendant's reputation, although busy courts have little time to investigate. Lacking money, as he usually does, the defendant may secure a bail bond, which obligates the signer (the bail bondsman) to pay the face value or bail if the defendant fails to appear for trial. The bail bondsman receives a fee, perhaps 10 percent of the bail.

Bail discriminates against the poor. A New York study disclosed that 25 percent of those arrested could not furnish bail of $500 (in effect, $25 for a bail bond fee), 45 percent failed at $1,500, and 63 percent at $2,500.[24] Those unable to post bond, including the innocent, are shunted off to jail to await trial; in larger cities this may be a matter of months. In New York state, of 3,500 jailed and untried defendants studied, 556 had their charges eventually dismissed. Consequently, 16 percent of those in jail, although innocent, were treated like other prisoners. Chances are that the jailed innocent defendant will lose his job, and, as with other imprisoned defendants, the preparation of his case becomes more difficult. Among other things, he cannot help his

[22] Herbert Jacob, *Justice in America* (Boston: Little, Brown, 1965), 155–56.
[23] James, 153.
[24] President's Commission on Law Enforcement, 131–32.

attorney round up witnesses and share in interviewing them. Studies of New York and Philadelphia courts show that those who are unable to post bond and remain in jail are far more likely to be found guilty and to receive more severe punishment than those who are free to help prepare their defense.[25] Some improvement was provided by the federal Bail Reform Act of 1966, which required federal (although not state or local) judges to release defendants before trial except in cases for which death was the possible punishment or where there was cause to believe the defendant would flee. Bail could still be set, but a defendant could not be held if he could not pay it.

Delay. One of the most destructive foes of justice is delay. Anyone arrested in Cleveland in midsummer on a serious charge will be fortunate to have his day in court by Christmas. A New Yorker whose auto is hit by another car will be unable to collect a penny in five years, even though his medical expenses pile up, if the other driver's insurance company haggles over a settlement. Delay corrodes justice. It deprives the citizen of a basic public service, the courts, when he most needs it. With the lapse of time, evidence deteriorates and the likelihood of justice being done diminishes. Delay places an unhealthy emphasis on a bargained settlement and lessens public confidence in the courts.

Why is delay so prevalent? Although metropolitan populations have soared, many courts have the same number of judges as they did several decades ago. In many cities, more judges are precluded because courtrooms are unavailable to accommodate them. There is a surfeit of lazy judges. Many judges work hard in their chambers and on the bench, but others keep a twenty-five- or thirty-hour workweek, despite case backlogs. Many courts close down for two months in the summer. Criminal and auto-accident cases are usually handled by only a small part of the local bar. In Cleveland, a study disclosed that 55 lawyers, from a bar of about 3,000, try 82.3 percent of these cases. Busy lawyers require many continuances, or postponements. Expert witnesses, such as doctors or psychiatrists, are also busy professionally, and cause delay. Many judges criticize the police for overwhelming the courts with "cheap cases." "There are wolves out there, and you keep sending me chipmunks and squirrels," a Philadelphia judge shouted at police who concentrated on petty offenders while violations more costly to the community remained untouched.[26]

Sentencing. An exceedingly arbitrary feature of criminal cases is sentencing. Some judges give great weight to the recommendations of the prosecutor, probation officer, or social worker, and the climate of public opinion. Other judges are customarily severe with those charged with serious crimes against the person, such as robbery and rape, while others may be affected by the defendant's dress, age, length of hair, race, and nationality. In a federal

[25] Jacob, 155.
[26] *New York Times,* March 8, 1971.

district court in the same month, a defendant who took $15 from the Post Office drew six months in jail, while a "more respectable" defendant, who misapplied $150,000 from a bank, drew probation.[27]

Superficially, the ideal of equal justice is fulfilled if the judge metes out the same punishment for given categories of offenses, with little attention to the particular offender and his personal circumstances. But in a sophisticated democracy, equality of vengeance as the manifestation of equal justice yields to reformation and deterrence, in which emphasis is shifted from fitting punishment to the crime to fitting it to the offender.

State appellate courts

State courts include appellate courts and the trial courts previously discussed; they are the backbone of the judicial system. The great bulk of court cases materialize under state law and from the fact that cases of less than $10,000 cannot ordinarily be brought in federal courts, but must be pursued in state courts. The state of New York alone has eight times as many justices as the federal courts. If justices of the peace are excluded, New York still has twice

[27] *New York Times,* September 27, 1972.

as many justices. A vastly greater volume of cases are disposed of in New York each year than in the entire federal court system, and the state's judicial budget well exceeds that of the federal government.[28]

In less populated states, there is a single appellate court usually known as the Supreme Court, to which cases come from trial courts. Some larger states have an additional tier of intermediate appellate courts, from which cases go to the Supreme Court.

Most state Supreme Courts have no choice but to hear all cases that are appealed. Some require complete, printed transcripts of the trial, others only partial, typed transcripts. Appellate courts that hear oral arguments (not all do) do so without a jury, and decisions are settled by a majority of the justices. Although comprehensive statistics are unavailable, New York and California appellate courts, for reasons that are not clear, have experienced no significant change in case volumes in recent years, in contrast to the strong upsurge in the trial courts.

Most likely, what Judge Jerome Frank called "the upper court myth" is at work. Despite the fact that appeals are freely available, relatively few cases are appealed. According to one estimate, trial courts determine fully 90 percent of case outcomes.[29] But certainly the mere availability of appellate courts helps gain fair trials for many litigants who might not otherwise obtain them. Some trial judges, knowing their work can be reviewed, are proud of having few of their decisions reversed and are sensitive to the professional denigration implicit in appellate reversals.

How are state justices selected? Surely equal justice cannot be well served by judges of indifferent professional competence. Responding to democratic credo, justices in most states are subject to popular election. But there are problems. The voter is generally apathetic and ignorant about judicial candidates. According to one study, 81 percent of those who voted in New York City could not name the judicial candidates for whom they had voted. The real decision-makers are the few political leaders who nominate the judges, and very often their favor, as former U.S. Attorney General Herbert Brownell has noted, "shines on mediocre candidates."[30] Politicians use judgeships to repay political debts and to provide geographic and ethnic balance to party tickets.

Seeking to escape the politicians' influence, some states employ the non-partisan election. But it is a mirage, since it frees the parties of whatever responsibility they feel to provide tolerably competent candidates, and factors of race, religion, and other judicial irrelevancies persist. In a few states, the governor can appoint judges with the approval of one legislative house. But the governor depends heavily on recommendations from his political advisers and is subject to political pressures.

To elevate judicial professionalism and subordinate politics, some states

[28] Delmar Karlen, *The Citizen in Court* (New York: Holt, Rinehart and Winston, 1964), 23.
[29] Jones, 131–32.
[30] *Ibid.*, 156.

follow the Missouri Plan. A merit selection procedure, it utilizes a nominating commission consisting of the chief justice of the state as chairman, three lawyers elected by members of the state-wide bar, and three nonlawyer citizens appointed by the governor. Except for the chief justice, who provides insight into the political function, commission members are barred from holding public or party office. For any judicial vacancy, the commission provides a slate of three nominees, from which the governor must choose one. The plan injects into the selection process professionally qualified nominees and goes far in insulating the act of judicial selection from the contamination of political waters.

Judicial tenure, too, is a factor in equal justice. Among the states, judicial terms vary widely; it may be for life, for ten years, six, and four, among others. Few competent lawyers will give up their practices for a short term on the bench. Longer terms afford the time and experience valuable for becoming a good judge, and they foster independence and detachment, both vital ingredients of justice. But tenure that is too ironclad can promote lassitude and arbitrariness, corrosive of vital justice. Many states provide periodic reelection of judges, but this opens up the same political Pandora's box that afflicted their original selection. The Missouri Plan employs a procedure of periodic noncompetitive reelection. The justice's name appears on the ballot without partisan designation. If a majority of votes are negative, or if the judge does not file for retention, a vacancy exists that is filled by the Plan's procedure of appointment. The reelection feature of the Plan has won the approval that has also favored its other parts. To take care of gross judicial misconduct, states have impeachment and other removal processes.[31]

Bureaucratic justice

One Los Angeles judge handles 60,000 intoxication cases a year, 250 a day. A "makesheet" from the Police Record and Identification Bureau provides data concerning each defendant's previous arrests, and then, as the judge has explained, "we have the defendant himself, and at a glance you can have some information as to whether he is in good shape or a physical wreck or on the verge of d.t.'s, whether he is well dressed or in rags, etc. . . . Then, if he wishes, the defendant may make a statement." [32] Mirroring the impersonality of urbanization, metropolitan justice has become bureaucratized justice, heavily committed to routines and perfunctory treatment of the individual.

This system is altogether contrary to the idealized version of due process embodied in the Constitution and in U.S. Supreme Court decisions. According to the ideal, criminal justice will be served through a formal adversary procedure, with strict rules of evidence, and a full, fair, open trial by jury, exploring thoroughly the question: Is the accused innocent or guilty? From

[31] Henry J. Abraham, *The Judicial Process,* 2nd ed. (New York: Oxford University Press, 1968), 41.
[32] Jones, 113–14.

arrest to sentence, the proceedings must be free of coercion and threat.

The historic constitutional ideal has been supplanted by an administrative-bureaucratic version of due process, superficially responsive to the older forms but far removed from their substance. To cope with high-volume mass justice, bureaucratic due process employs strategies and evasions calculated to evoke pleas of guilty and substitutes manipulative judicial administration for the jury trial and the combat of adversaries. In his study of a metropolitan court, for example, Abraham Blumberg found that in a given year, of 5,073 cases of indictments found by a grand jury, only 145, or 2.85 percent, were disposed of by trial.[33]

In the system of "justice without trial," the presumption of innocence is negated. In fact, it is turned around. The principal participants—police, prosecutors, defense attorneys, and judges—all assume that persons accused of crime are guilty and that their task is to work out the punishment. As the endless lines of accused are processed, the participants of the judicial community tend to develop a routinized callousness. Administrative justice concedes that those accused are entitled to counsel, but his presence does not produce a court-centered adversary contest. The most respected prosecutors and defense attorneys are those who respond "reasonably" in a system where most defendants are "guilty" of some crime.

Likewise, the psychological approach to criminology that would view the criminal as a "sick person" serves to elaborate bureaucratic justice. According to this approach, the court becomes something more than a legal agency; it is one of several clinics in the individualized treatment of offenders. The participating psychiatrist, psychologist, or social worker purports to replace punishment with the scientific treatment of crime, but he actually only validates legal judgments in terms of medical and social sciences and thereby reinforces the roles of the accusers and the accused. Psychiatry has become an inherent part of judicial bureaucracy, available at virtually every stage of a criminal proceeding, and often without the consent or cooperation of the accused. In effect, psychiatry can be used to deprive the defendant of due process, including the privilege against self-incrimination and the right to a trial. Once a psychiatrist has determined that the accused is "mentally ill" and unable to stand trial, he is more than likely to be confined in a mental hospital for a longer interval than if he had been simply convicted of a crime. The probation officer, psychiatrist, and social worker, instead of fortifying the image of individual worth and dignity projected in the Bill of Rights, may subject the defendant to a jargon of disparagement. Their professional reports may speak of him as "depraved," "psychopathic," "immature," "inadequate," "shiftless," and other terms of vague diagnostic significance.

The ideal of individualization, of rehabilitating the offender by attacking scientifically his specific ills, however intrinsically laudable, is subordinated to bureaucratic discipline; the psychiatrist and the social worker, eager for promotion or professional recognition, harmonize with the organization, while the offender they "serve" is manipulated to satisfy the organization's needs and

[33] Abraham S. Blumberg, *Criminal Justice* (Chicago: Quadrangle Books, 1967).

goals. The traditional official goals of the criminal court based on the old values of due process and equal justice have been displaced in modern mass society by goals of maximum production, efficiency, and organization-centered career advancement.

Poverty, race, and justice

In the fifties and sixties, a favorite and rewarding resort for poor and deprived groups was the United States Supreme Court where, for example, the principle of school desegregation was given legal status. But, then as now, other elements of the judicial system were far less friendly. Local courts are often a part of the social apparatus that exploits the poor. Store owners on the fringe of the slums rationalize that they do the poor a favor by extending them credit at interest of 100 or 200 percent. When poor people falter in repaying, the store owners can go to court and take their wages.

Community Action for Legal Services, Inc. (CALS) of New York City, funded by the federal antipoverty program, made a three-month study of civil, family, and Supreme Court judges in 1970. It cited thirty instances of judicial intemperance and prejudice against the poor. The cases involved landlord-tenant disputes, marital and family relations, consumer fraud, and welfare actions. The study disclosed that some judges told poor clients from the bench that their CALS lawyers were "not helping them," delivered court-room speeches displaying antipathy to all welfare recipients and partiality to landlords, and threatened CALS lawyers with contempt citations for raising substantive opposing points. But the study notes that these judges were the exception rather than the rule, since "the majority of judges conduct them-selves according to the highest judicial standards." [34]

Criminal justice arrests and punishes blacks in numbers disproportionate to whites. *Uniform Crime Reports* discloses that blacks are arrested three or four more times than whites, although comprising only 11 percent of the population. Likewise, convicted blacks comprise three or four more times their proportion of the population; according to data from *National Prison Statistics,* they number about one-third of the nation's prison population. Racial data are hampered by difficulties of defining race. One study found that 40 percent of the offenders contributing to "Negro" crime totals are either half or more than half white. [35]

Although data are unavailable, the widespread belief exists that blacks, Chicanos, and Puerto Ricans, far more than whites, are subject to illegal arrest, arrest on weak suspicion, illegal detention, and physical abuse by police. Data from local studies (no national judicial statistics are available)

[34] *New York Times,* December 21, 1970.
[35] Marvin F. Wolfgang, *Crime and Race, Conceptions and Misconceptions* (New York: The American Jewish Committee, 1964), 36.

show that blacks are jailed more than bailed, and that well beyond the proportions for whites, blacks are convicted with little evidence and sentenced to severe punishments of long duration. Not all studies support these findings, however. A Philadelphia study of twenty-one judges disclosed no racial differences in sentencing practices.[36]

Law enforcement officials who are poorly paid or are from poor backgrounds may be particularly unfavorably disposed toward blacks. Stanley Schrotel, former police chief of Cincinnati, has observed that "we are calling on policemen to make judgments in situations highly charged with racial overtones. Yet that white policeman is originally from a socioeconomic level a cut below the mean. From a group that has strong negative feelings about Negroes." [37]

Can blacks get a fair trial? When Bobby Seale, national chairman of the Black Panther party, was indicted in 1970 on charges of conspiracy and of murder of a Panther member whom Panthers claimed was a police informer, Kingman Brewster, president of Yale University and a lawyer, expressed skepticism that black revolutionaries could receive a fair trial in the United States today. Brewster was proved wrong in this case. Seale was acquitted, and he soon resumed his place in the Black Panther party.

Justice for blacks was again tested in 1972 when Angela Davis, a former philosophy instructor at the University of California at Los Angeles, stood trial for murder. She was accused of buying the guns that were used in an escape attempt by a convict standing trial. In a gun battle outside the courthouse, the judge, the convict, and his rescuer were killed. Under California law, if Miss Davis had supplied the guns, she would be equally guilty with those who attempted the escape. Her trial was also preceded by dire forecasts about the capacities of American justice. Again the prophesies did not materialize, and a jury acquitted Miss Davis.

But some say that the question of a fair trial is a moot point if the defendant can never come to trial. They point out that many Panthers have been systematically killed in a campaign of genocide against the group by police. Relations between Panthers and police have always been at high tension. In Oakland, California, where the Panthers were founded, the black militants, armed with guns and a knowledge of statutes, kept a watch on police activities to see that black rights were observed. Although Panthers saw themselves as a self-defense organization, they were given to incendiary utterances about the police (coining the term "pig" as a synonym), and they prompted FBI Chief J. Edgar Hoover to call them the "most dangerous and violence-prone of all extremist groups." [38]

Conflict and violence erupted between Panthers and police, and a Panther lawyer asserted that by 1970 twenty-eight Panthers had been "murdered" by

[36] *Ibid.,* 48.
[37] James, 101.
[38] *New York Times,* July 14, 1970.

police, a figure that was accepted as established fact by the *New York Times,* the *Washington Post,* and civil rights leaders like Roy Innis and the Reverend Ralph D. Abernathy. Subsequently the figure was challenged by Edward Jay Epstein, a writer on legal subjects. After examination of nineteen cases cited by the Panthers, Epstein found that police had no involvement in nine of the cases and in six others Panthers were killed by policemen who had first been seriously wounded. Epstein found only one instance—the killing of Fred Hampton and Mark Clark by the Chicago police on December 4, 1969— showing questionable police conduct that might lend support to the claim of a police conspiracy against the Black Panthers.[39]

Criminal justice for the poor. The judicial system treats the poor of any ethnic group differently from the nonpoor. By nature of their condition, they are less able to hire counsel, pay bail, utilize psychiatric services, employ expert witnesses and investigatory assistance. In effect, the elements of due process are more available to some—those favored with economic well-being—than to others. For all their deprivation of legal resources, the poor overwhelmingly dominate the criminal court. A study of the cases handled by the probation division of a metropolitan court found that of the 3,643 persons investigated only 8 percent were—because of education, occupation, and income—"non-poor." [40]

Crime data, however fragmentary, suggest that a major attack on crime and the creation of the longed-for state of law and order must be directed at the social and physical conditions of the poor American. The fertile soil of crime consists of low income, unskilled occupations, unemployment, family disruption, drug addiction, and poor education. Together they reap a heavy psychological harvest of frustration and damaged self-esteem.

Crimes relating to narcotics exact a devastating toll from the poor. Although narcotics crimes have a growing incidence in the suburbs, their numbers in the cities and especially in the ghettos are soaring beyond belief. Estimates vary greatly, but some calculations attribute as much as three-quarters of all serious crime in Washington, D.C., and New York City to drug addiction. To keep himself supplied each day, a heroine addict must make large cash outlays, which an ordinary job, if he is fortunate enough to have one, cannot provide. He is driven to steal money or merchandise that can be converted into money. Muggings, hold-ups, burglaries, and even murder befall the addict's victims, and in the ghetto, these are usually his fellow poor. For the addict, crime becomes a way of life. Among all age groups, close to 90 percent of those arrested for violating laws while on addictive drugs had criminal records.[41]

[39] Edward Jay Epstein, "The Panthers and the Police: A Pattern of Genocide," *The New Yorker,* 46 (February 13, 1971), 45.
[40] Blumberg, 40–41.
[41] Richard Harris, *The Crisis of Law, Order, and Freedom in America* (New York: Dutton, 1970), 28.

Legal aid

"You can't call a lawyer if you haven't got a dime." So runs the slogan of the Legal Aid Society, an organization devoted to providing free legal service to indigents. In New York City alone, Legal Aid handles each year a quarter of a million requests for assistance. But there are still great numbers of people who need legal aid and lack information about access to it. Poor people tend not to seek counsel as they would medical service; they are restrained by the belief that lawyers' fees are exorbitant.

More and more organizations are providing legal aid services—settlement houses, local bar associations, law school clinics, and tax-supported legal aid bureaus. Each source of assistance has its own eligibility tests. Usually the individual must be poor enough to be unable to afford his own counsel and must have the kind of case that his source of aid will take. Some sources, for example, refuse divorce cases, deeming divorce a luxury inappropriate for indigents.

The quality and benefits of legal aid vary widely. The assigned counsel may be a junior member of the bar with little trial experience or the chance name drawn from a list of all the lawyers of the county. Assigned lawyers work without adequate pay, may have to take time from their regular practice, and may not be especially qualified for the kind of case involved. Legal aid societies have one or several capable and experienced men at the top, but they place the brunt of their work on young attorneys, barely starting out and only briefly associated with the organization. A fledgling lawyer is ill-matched with the career men of the prosecutor's office, experienced in criminal trial work. And most aid societies have not enough funds to handle the magnitude of cases. A Chicago study estimated that 60 to 80 percent of accused criminals lacked adequate access to legal representation.[42]

Many cities have a Public Defender, some at substantial salaries, which attract experienced and talented men fully capable of competing with the prosecutor. The Public Defender may also have a corps of assistants and investigators; under some plans, he may contract business to private law firms. In New Jersey he is appointed by the governor with the advice of the state senate, has cabinet level status, and works through regional representatives in major urban areas. But Defender's offices may also be training grounds for inexperienced lawyers. And they require substantial appropriations that are not as readily provided as they are for the prosecutor's needs. Many cities limit the Defender to misdemeanor cases in municipal courts and utilize court-appointed attorneys in more serious cases.

The national
judicial system

The national judicial system includes several levels of courts created by Congress under Article III of the Constitution: the Supreme Court, 11 circuit courts of appeals, and 88 district courts, employing more than 400 judges. There are also legislative or more specialized courts, such as the Tax Court and the Court of Military Appeals. By far, the chief business of national courts is the interpretation of national statutes and administrative and judicial regulations and decisions.

The Supreme Court and lower national courts may occasionally declare acts of Congress invalid—on the average there has been less than one per court term in the last quarter century. Although that power is not explicitly stated in the Constitution, Chief Justice John Marshall reasoned that the Supreme Court possessed it in *Marbury v. Madison* (1803).[43] National courts also review state statutes and actions for their compatibility with the federal Constitution, a busy procedure in recent years in civil liberties cases.

In effect, the United States has a dual court system. The federal Constitution, statutes, and administrative laws may be adjudicated in either state or federal courts. The dual system often causes varying interpretation of legal doctrine from state to state—in essence, unequal justice. But in the momentum

---

[42] Samuel Krislov, *The Supreme Court in the Political Process* (New York: Macmillan, 1965), 217.
[43] 1 Cranch 137.

of the civil rights movement of the sixties, a black citizen, well aware of the biases of Southern state judges, valued the option of taking his case to federal courts, in which the new civil rights doctrines evolved.

The jurisdiction of federal courts, according to Article III, applies to cases involving a question of federal law (derived from the Constitution, statutes, and treaties); admiralty and maritime cases; controversies involving certain types of parties such as ambassadors, the United States, a state, citizens of different states, and foreign states or citizens. In practice, federal court civil cases are about evenly distributed among those involving a federal question, those in which the United States is a party, and those between citizens of different states. In some civil litigations—admiralty, bankruptcy, patents, and copyrights—federal courts have exclusive jurisdiction. In other federal civil cases, both the national and state governments have jurisdiction. Federal trial courts enforce the federal criminal law in trying offenses against narcotic, postal, customs, and immigration laws, and cases involving interstate kidnapping and interstate prostitution. Most ordinary crimes are dealt with by the states.

Federal district courts. The eighty-eight United States district courts are trial courts of general jurisdiction. There is at least one in each state and large states have more. Only criminal trials make extensive use of juries, for the right to a jury is waived in more than half the civil cases. Federal district judgeships are prized political plums. Appointees are more apt to emerge from a routine political career than be a distinguished lawyer or legal scholar. The latter type flourishes in the appellate courts.

The Courts of Appeals. The principal appellate courts are the Courts of Appeals (circuit courts), one in each of the eleven judicial circuits into which the nation is divided. The circuits are geographically defined to equalize the caseload. Circuit courts hear cases on appeal from lower federal courts and from federal administrative agencies, but they lack power to review actions of state courts. Under federal law litigants have the right to one appeal, and circuit courts must hear all appeals brought from federal district courts. Nonetheless, these seemingly admirable provisions for equal justice are limited by the high costs of appeals—attorney's fees, reproduction of briefs, extra psychological strain, and an average prolongation of eighteen months for the case.

Circuit court decisions are ordinarily final; few appeals rise to the Supreme Court. Chiefly, circuit courts perform as watchdogs of the district courts to avert gross injustices. Each federal trial court acts in the knowledge that its decisions can be reviewed, although in fact few are.

The specialized courts. The specialized courts—Court of Claims, the Customs Court, Court of Customs and Patent Appeals, the Tax Court, and the Court of Military Appeals—dispose of cases in which private parties press some grievance against the government. These may include an inventor who contends that the Patent Office wrongfully refused to issue him a patent or an importer who protests Customs officials' assessments of the economic value of goods or a taxpayer displeased by rulings of the Internal Revenue Service.

Administrative support. Federal courts are assisted by an administrative structure that includes the Judicial Conference of the United States, chaired by the Chief Justice of the Supreme Court and participated in by justices from the various federal courts. The conference formulates rules of procedure for the national courts and deals with other judicial policy. The Administrative Office of the United States Courts, whose chief officers are selected by the Supreme Court, performs many tasks for federal courts below the Supreme Court: the hiring and pay of subordinate personnel of federal courts, analyses of dockets and workloads, provision of facilities and supplies, arrangement of seminars for judges. The Department of Justice performs such support functions as the operation of a federal police system, the bringing of prosecutions and the argument of cases on appeal, management of federal prisons, and the screening of nominations for the federal judiciary.

The Supreme Court. The highest court in the national system is the Supreme Court. It hears cases on appeal from both state courts and lesser federal courts and is the final adjudicative body for all cases. Unlike most other appellate courts, the Supreme Court can choose the cases it wishes to hear. In a typical three-year period, 5,967 cases were filed with the Court, but only 322 were disposed of with full opinions. Of these, 69 percent were appeals from lower federal courts and 31 percent appeals from state courts.[44] By maintaining strict selectivity, the Court has avoided entrapment in the mass production justice of the lower courts.

If equal justice presupposes that a body of well-qualified justices will scrutinize the merits of the individual case, the Supreme Court fulfills this criterion so strikingly that Anthony Lewis contends it is "the last stronghold of personal responsibility for decisions." [45] No other court matches the Supreme Court in power and prominence. It can respond to the ideal of equal justice by spotlighting inequities in public policy and in the political system, such as school segregation and distortions in legislative apportionment. Further, it can commence lengthy sequences of remedial actions by all branches of government, at all levels.

The Supreme Court exercises original jurisdiction—sits as a trial court— in a few types of cases, such as those involving ambassadors and suits between states, as stipulated in Article III of the Constitution. According to the article, Congress can enlarge or restrict the Court's appellate jurisdiction. In creating administrative agencies such as the Interstate Commerce Commission, Congress provided for the appeal of certain cases decided by the commission to

[44] Jones, 11.
[45] *New York Times Magazine* (January 17, 1965), 56.

federal courts. The arrangement permitted ultimate appeal to the Supreme Court.

The Court has little to do with disputes between individuals. Equal justice in this category, a mass production task, is left to other courts. In criminal justice, the Court has been more involved, insisting at times on the accused's right to counsel, fair trial, and fair procedures, but taking a more relaxed view of searches and seizures. In reviews of state criminal justice, the Court has been erratic. As John P. Frank has noted, the Court makes "distinctions so fine that the general run of state trial courts can be expected to pay little attention to them." The Court's conceptions of justice may support the status quo or act as a force of change in economic questions. In an antitrust case, it may allow the gigantic United States Steel Corporation to swallow up a smaller company, concluding that "it is not for courts to determine the Nation's economic development." But on another day, under the same antitrust laws, the Court required the breaking up of the elephantine Standard Oil trust.[46]

Normally, the Supreme Court sits from October through June in a sedate, formal atmosphere. The lawyer, usually outfitted in morning clothes, is allowed one half hour to argue his case before the black-robed justices. The justices can interrupt—and use up time—with questions.

On Fridays, the justices meet in conference to discuss and vote on pending cases and applications seeking review for other cases. The Chief Justice presides over this secret meeting. He enjoys superior opportunities for influence derived from the prestige of his position, his role as chairman of the conference, and his power to assign the writing of opinions by the justices when he is with the majority. Once asked how the conference proceeds, Justice Hugo Black replied, "The Chief Justice, if he is with the majority, states that case to the majority and gives his views of what the law should be. . . . He speaks first, and then the next man in rank speaks . . . and so on down to the bottom . . . then . . . we cast a formal vote." [47]

The ranking justice among the majority decides who will write the Court's opinion. In addition, each justice is free to write his own dissenting opinion or concurring opinion. The Court customarily hands down its opinions on Mondays. As the words are read in the courtroom, they are analyzed for their consequences for society, their meaning for constitutional processes, and their clues to the future direction of the Court, which is usually known by the name of its Chief Justice, now "the Burger Court."

This is also to say that the Supreme Court works within a political context and the justices have a political texture. The Court's decisions bear political implications for society. In civil rights, for example, the Warren Court (under Chief Justice Earl Warren) acted at a time when Congress and the executive did little or nothing. Likewise, when the other branches did nothing

---

[46] John P. Frank, *Marble Palace: The Supreme Court in American Life* (New York: Knopf, 1968), 221.

[47] In *Congressional Quarterly Weekly Reports* (January 3, 1969), 9.

The "Burger Court," June 1972. Front row: Justices Potter Stewart, William O. Douglas, Chief Justice Warren E. Burger, Justices William J. Brennan, Jr., and Byron R. White. Back row: Justices Lewis Powell, Thurgood Marshall, Harry A. Blackmun, and William Rehnquist.

to remedy the inequalities of representation, the Supreme Court intervened with its reapportionment decisions. Typically, the Court cannot get too far ahead of public opinion, but as the Warren Court shows, it can respond to need for change.

The Court can also retreat from these positions, as the current Burger Court illustrates. Thanks to President Nixon's appointments, the Supreme Court has reconsidered some of the positions taken by the Warren Court on civil liberties. Reflecting President Nixon's identification with the law and order issue in political campaigns, the Burger Court has pared down Warren Court holdings protecting the rights of those who are arrested and those who become criminal defendants. Previous civil rights decisions have also been trimmed back.

The Supreme Court seems by its nature the very antithesis of popular rule. Its unelected justices have life-tenure and can influence, if not decide, public policy. Despite these seeming limitations, the Court contributes importantly to democracy. The Court's function of judicial review helps keep the democratic machine in balance, forestalls one part from dominating the others, and the machine itself from running off wildly in one direction. The Court is not a sustained barrier to the popular will, but checks it momentarily, if at all, and adjusts to it in the long run. It is the Court that personifies the basic democratic charter, the Constitution, by infusing spirit and life into its general language through interpretation and by sparing it from rigidity and disuse in a changing world. The justices help democracy function by sorting out the enduring values of society and asserting them and by applying what the legislature and the executive see largely as abstractions to an actual case. Only then does equal justice attain its fullest meaning.

Corrections

The final element of the judicial system is "corrections." This extreme euphemism embraces all institutions and officers devoted to the punishment or rehabilitation of offenders—jails, prisons, reform schools, wardens, probation and parole officers, psychiatric and social workers.

Of the offenders who provide the business of corrections, some are committed irrevocably to criminal careers, some are continuously capable of violent crimes against their fellow citizens, others are responsive to conventional values, and probably most are aimless and uncommitted to goals of any kind. Adding to the complexity of corrections is the wide diversity of offenders—perpetrators of common law crimes, alcoholics, narcotics addicts, sex deviants, victims of senility. Typically, these many special types of offenders are dealt with in large, general purpose programs.

Correctional activities are handicapped by the jungle of political subdivisions, each level of government being largely independent of the other. The federal government lacks control over the states, which are responsible for most prison and parole programs, while probation is frequently tied to county and local governments. The county lacks jurisdiction over the jails of cities and towns. In the maze of jurisdictions, corrections readily contribute to the inequality of justice.

Correctional institutions do not correct; they constitute the poorest conceivable preparation for successful reentry into society, for they generally reinforce the patterns of deviance and destructiveness that society rejects. An estimated 80 percent of correctional manpower is devoted to custody and maintenance, with only a small percent assigned to treatment and rehabilitation as a primary function.[48] The disproportion reveals excessive preoccupation with retribution, or extraction of the offender's debt to society. Adding to the problem is that many offenders are the most troublesome citizens—the violence-prone, the misfits and failures, the unrespectable and the irresponsible —types that society prefers to keep out of sight.

For the prisoner, justice and democracy stop at the jailhouse door. With little exception, life in jails and prisons is barren, brutal, and degrading. The prisons are grim and fortresslike, with tiers upon tiers of cells arranged essentially for security. Impersonality reigns in dress, in marches from cells to dining halls and shop, in assignment of identifying numbers. Conversation is often restricted. Typically, the prisoner is little rewarded for his work—a few cents a day. Women inmates are treated even worse: they get no pay for household tasks, which are presumed to be "women's work." A wide chasm

[48] President's Commission on Law Enforcement, 162.

An example of constructive correctional action: graduation exercises at the Manhattan House of Detention, October 1972.

divides the inmates and staff. Overcrowding, sadistic guards, sexual exploitation, deaths unknown to the outside world—these are standard fare of prison life.

The bloodiest explosion of prison inadequacies occurred at New York State's Correctional Facility at Attica in 1971. The troops and police who were called in to quell the riot ended up killing thirty inmates and nine guards who were hostages. Congressman Charles Rangel (D., N.Y.), a member of an investigating committee, exclaimed angrily, "The shooting was all over the place. It was unbelievable." After the shooting ended, convicts complained that they had been forced to run a gauntlet naked between lines of club-wielding state troopers.

Attica drew attention to the deep crisis of many prisons in the country. But hardened, budget-pinched prison administrators can do little to improve conditions. Sheer desperation fuels the convicts' hopeless revolt: "If we can't live like human beings, at least we can die like men," chanted the inmates in the teeming Attica prison yard. The list of twenty-eight demands that was ultimately accepted by state officials at Attica sounds like a bill of rights that a democratic society is prone to take for granted, even for prisoners who live at the edge of existence: a healthy diet, religious freedom, adequate medical care, noncensorship of outside publications except when prison security was imperiled. Ironically, many of the demanded reforms were similar to those aspired to for some time by the State Commissioner of Correction, Russell Oswald. But the bloody abortive revolt served only to delay them and to divert attention and resources to maintaining security.[49]

There are occasional cases of constructive action. To prepare inmates for their return to competitive society, a federal corrections project in Washington, D.C., seeks to duplicate capitalistic, competitive living, in which the inmate works, has income, pays for his wants, and manages his funds. New Jersey's Highlands program places the inmate in a "synthetic culture," where he learns to work for what he wants, to fight with words instead of his fists, to take criticism. The Huber Law of Wisconsin permits prisoners in county jails, including those guilty of felonies, to work in adjacent communities during the day and to serve their sentences at night. A 1971 federal court of appeals decision, declaring that the time was long past when prisoners could be treated "as temporarily a slave of the state," recognized that safeguards exist against arbitrary treatment of prisoners; it barred punishment for merely expressing their views, restricted censorship of their mail, and upheld their right to sue prison officials for violation of their constitutional rights.[50]

Proposals

1. It is better to prevent crime than to cure it. This is probably the most rewarding principle for the future viability of the judicial system. The surest means of prevention is to provide a stake in American life for all Americans. Social justice lays a firm foundation for law and order.

A program of prevention would seek to strengthen the family as an institution, concentrate more resources in slum schools, and enhance employment opportunities. The President's Commission on Law Enforcement proposed that a Youth Services Bureau be established in each community to which juveniles could be referred by police, courts, parents, and social agencies for counseling, education, recreation programs, and job placement. Prevention of crime should also concentrate on the prevention of drug addiction, which fuels the fastest growing type of crime.

2. Criminal justice needs a broader range of techniques to deal with offenders, which suggests the importance of related sociological and psychiatric research and heightened attention to the study of criminal law and criminal trial work in the law schools.

3. Structural changes are needed in the court system. The presence of numerous, autonomous courts with fragmented and overlapping jurisdictions often poses the problem of choosing the right courts; errors, easily made, are

---

[49] "The Attica Tragedy," *Newsweek* (September 27, 1971), 22–38.
[50] *New York Times,* February 25, 1971.

costly in legal fees and delay. A troubled family might have to traverse several courts. Proposals would call for family courts equipped to deal with the whole range of family problems.

States increasingly are abolishing justice of the peace systems and replacing other minor courts with district or county courts. District courts, established throughout a state with broad jurisdiction, are commonly staffed with legally trained, full-time personnel, thus avoiding the tendency to "unequal justice" in part-time, mediocre local courts. District courts also provide better records, important for appeals, and more uniform practice.

To further promote equal justice through uniform judicial standards and administration, we might make the daily operation and efficiency of all courts in a state the responsibility of an Administrative Board of the State Judicial Conference (analogous to the national judiciary's Conference), consisting of the state's chief justice and four justices from major judicial subdivisions.

Certain offenses—gambling, drunkenness, vice, narcotics addiction, traffic violations—might be taken out of regular court procedures, where they contribute enormously to workloads, and be handled by administrative tribunals assisted, where necessary, by social, psychological, and psychiatric professionals. Such a procedure would free the courts to handle more serious offenses in the fashion of traditional due process. But to avoid the worst aspects of bureaucratic justice the services rendered by professionals must be humanized and individualized, directed to the specific person, to his situation and needs.

4. The courts, with their high case volume, badly need professional management. Judges should be relieved of nonjudicial duties. A professional administrator, preferably a nonlawyer, might direct staff functions, organize court budgets, oversee quarters management, collect statistical information, improve coordination with other participants in criminal justice—the police, defense attorneys, and the district attorney. Judges, as public servants, should be more subject to public scrutiny, their jobs made more demanding, their performance raised to higher levels of productivity.

There are acute shortages of other professional personnel—too few probation officers to advise judges whether defendants should be paroled or held on high bail, too few qualified correctional officers to deal adequately with prisoners.

5. To combat one of the worst perpetrators of injustice—delay—states might adopt California's requirement that trials be held within a certain time limit; otherwise the accused is released. Lawyers might be required to make all their pretrial motions—a frequent source of delay—in a single omnibus proceeding. Some courts successfully employ a "certificate of readiness," a statement signed by lawyers that they are ready for court, after which a firm trial date is set.

In auto-accident cases, where delay is notorious, "no-fault" insurance settlements would avoid or reduce litigation, or jury trials might be abolished and recourse made to a tribunal system similar to that used to determine

LePelley in The Christian Science Monitor © 1972 TCSPS

Getting somewhere?

workmen's compensation. In addition, many states have adopted or are considering no-fault divorce laws.

Administrative responses to the growing crisis of court backlogs would include a lengthening of the widely prevalent short judicial day, full court schedules in summer months, more use of night courts, and temporary assignment of justices with lighter workloads to courts that fall behind.

6. Bail, often so automatic and undifferentiated among defendants and so burdensome to the poor, might be subordinated to a general requirement that a judge release a defendant on his own recognizance before trial unless he finds that the release would not reasonably assure the defendant's reappearance or would be an undue risk to community safety.

7. In the course of an investigation of the Attica riot, a special commission in New York came to some conclusions as to how prisons and jails should function. Prisoners should have the rights of other citizens, except that of liberty of person. They should be given maximum amount of freedom to conduct their own affairs and should accept social responsibility from the outset. The prisons ought to be staffed with persons motivated to help, including ex-inmates. The prisons should be opened up to the community and inmates allowed to participate in work-release programs. Community and professional groups should be encouraged to participate in the life of the prison.[51]

A project group of the San Francisco architectural firm of Kaplan and

---

[51] *Attica: The Official Report of the New York State Special Commission on Attica* (New York: Bantam Books, 1972), xvi–xviii.

McLaughlin has recommended we build fewer jails. Jails are self-fulfilling prophecies in that they create their own populations. More use should be made of parole, probation, work release, and fines. Those jails that are built should be smaller, community based, nonrepressive, and allow a full range of opportunity and choice in environments and activities. The group even suggests competitive jail and parole systems, recognizing that competitive systems work elsewhere in society. As a means of forcing public awareness of what needs to be done in the correctional institutions, one of the members of the project suggested that a period of time in jail be a part of every school curriculum. This would serve to educate students in the functions of institutions and also bring community reform to the jails.

Judicial reform, it must be conceded, is one of democracy's more uphill struggles. Popular interest is difficult to generate and therefore politicians give it low priority. Lawyers, politicians, judges, bail bondsmen, and others have strong vested interests in the creaky, antiquated status quo, and they take unkindly to changed procedures. All along the judicial front political parties fear loss of patronage. Laymen, many battered reformers testify, must do the reform tasks themselves. But let no one forget the warning of Arthur T. Vanderbilt, late Chief Justice of New Jersey: "Judicial reform is not a sport for the short-winded."

Suggested Reading

Abraham, Henry J., *The Judicial Process,* 2nd edition (Oxford University Press, 1968). An excellent introduction to the judicial process that analyzes the workings of the courts on the federal, state, and local levels.

Blumberg, Abraham S., *Criminal Justice* * (Quadrangle Books, 1967). A useful analysis of the bureaucratization of judicial processes, including those concerning corrections and rehabilitation. Assesses the consequences of this development.

Botein, Bernard, *Trial Judge* (Simon and Schuster, 1952). An informed and revealing examination of the work of a trial judge by a distinguished former trial judge.

Jacob, Herbert, *Justice in America: Courts, Lawyers and the Judicial Process* (Little, Brown, 1965). An excellent treatment of the entire judicial process; considers its limitations as well as its possibilities. Includes a particularly useful analysis of judicial policy-making.

James, Howard, *Crisis in the Courts* * (David McKay, 1968). Contains data and analysis of the contemporary crisis of overburdened courts, the causes of delays, and the possibilities of judicial specialization. Explores all the principal parts of the judicial process.

Jones, Harry W., ed., *The Courts, The Public and the Law Explosion* (Prentice-Hall, 1965). Explores the nature and consequences of the ever increasing demands on judicial processes. Offers useful proposals for dealing with the court crisis.

Kalven, Harry, and Zeisel, Hans, *The American Jury* * (Little, Brown, 1966). A comprehensive study of the jury system, exploring its usefulness to both democratic and judicial processes. Contains highly informative data.

Shapiro, Martin, *Law and Politics in the Supreme Court* (Free Press. 1964). A study of the Court's role in major fields of public policy. Explores the methods, rationales, and limitations of the Court's handling of public policy issues in each field.

Sutherland, Edwin H., *White Collar Crime* * (Holt, Rinehart and Winston, 1949; 1961). A pathbreaking study of one of the fastest growing areas of crime. Delineates differences between white collar crime and other kinds of crime.

The Challenge of Crime in a Free Society: A Report by the President's Commission on Law Enforcement and the Administration of Justice * (U.S. Government Printing Office, 1967). A valuable study by a presidential commission appointed to examine crime and its implications for a democratic society. Provides data and analysis for different types of crime and makes important recommendations concerning the court system, the police, and correctional administration.

Wolfgang, Marvin E., *Crime and Race, Conceptions and Misconceptions* (American Jewish Committee, 1964). A sociologist's analysis of different types of racial discrimination in criminal justice. Describes the difficulties of securing adequate racial data in this area.

Zeisel, Hans, Kalven, Harry, Jr., and Buchholz, Bernard, *Delay in Court* (Little, Brown, 1959). Informed analysis of the causes and extent of various kinds of judicial delay. Explores the consequences of the problem and ways of dealing with it.

* Available in paperback edition

12

free
men:
civil
liberties

"Those who deny freedom to others," wrote Lincoln, "deserve it not for themselves, and, under a just God, cannot long retain it." A century later, in the 1960s and 70s, both the denial of freedom and its assertion were evolving into subtle new forms, raising questions that friends of democracy cannot easily answer and that even Lincoln might find difficult to judge. William Kunstler, the attorney who specializes in defending radical clients, contends that freedoms are widely violated and gutted, and that even the few that are exercised are meaningless because the political system is unresponsive. "Nothing will change anything in this country," Kunstler has said, "until the people go into the streets."

Certain of freedom's dilemmas surfaced in the massive 1971 May Day arrests in Washington where thousands had gathered to protest the endlessly protracted Indochina war. Although Senator John V. Tunney (D., Calif.) and others warned against "foolish and useless acts" that might ruin several months of hard work by real peace advocates, guerilla forays tied up traffic, slashed tires, and overturned trucks, in a proclaimed, but futile, objective to "stop the government." Police countered with the largest mass arrest in the nation's history. Among the 13,400 arrested were innocent bystanders, including six mental patients who were walking with their attendants. "Just bring them in and lock them up," police were ordered, in blatant disregard of civil liberties and normal arrest procedures. "I took these steps," the capital police chief explained, "because I felt they were necessary to protect the safety of law-abiding citizens and to maintain order in the city." [1]

Violations of civil liberties and their victims are limited to no one creed or class. Several weeks before the Washington demonstrations, a representative of the Polaroid Corporation was prevented from speaking on color theory at Harvard by screaming, chanting disrupters. They were resentful that Polaroid had not withdrawn all its activity from South Africa in protest of racism, but

[1] *Newsweek* (May 17, 1971), 24–29.

The jails in Washington, D.C., could not accommodate all those arrested at the May Day demonstrations in 1971.

had chosen instead to pay equal wages to people of all races (a radical policy in South Africa). In vain did Professor Archibald Cox plead to the disrupters, "Freedom of speech is indivisible. You cannot deny it to one man and save it for others. . . . The price of liberty to speak the truth as each of us sees it is permitting others the same freedom." [2]

Freedom's place in democracy

Without certain kinds of freedom democracy cannot exist. The freedom to speak, to write, to hear others, to petition, to vote, supports political life. Together these freedoms affirm Carl L. Becker's contention that of all the forms of government democracy alone has "the cardinal principle that free criticism and analysis by all and sundry is the highest virtue." [3] If democracy is in its quintessence government by the people, then, as James Madison said, "the censorial power is in the people over the government, and not in the government over the people." [4]

[2] Anthony Lewis, "The Freedom to Speak," *New York Times,* March 29, 1971.
[3] Carl L. Becker, *Freedom and Responsibility in the American Way of Life* (New York: Vintage Books, 1955), 37.
[4] In Irving Brant, *The Bill of Rights: Its Origins and Meaning* (Indianapolis: Bobbs-Merrill, 1965), 236.

Nondemocratic governments must control, direct, restrain public opinion to assure their continuance. But popular democracy cannot be truly paramount, or self-governing, where government can punish its critics, or silence them by threat. Such a government can be studded with democratic forms— a representative legislature, popular elections, and the secret ballot—but these forms are reduced to empty symbols if enforced conformity and passive acquiescence supplant freedom to choose and to criticize. Modern democratic man values both the political freedom to share in determining group purposes, and the individual freedom to carry on his own private purposes and to realize his potential—in effect, freedom from the state. Through freedom, democratic man proclaims the supreme value of his personality.[5]

Freedom can be defined in terms of freedom *from,* freedom *to,* and freedom *for.* Most commonly, it is described as freedom from, as the absence of external constraints. But we are subject to all sorts of physical constraints, and to live satisfactorily with our fellow human beings we submit to social constraints. Freedom may also be abridged by another form of external constraint—political constraints imposed by the legitimately exercised power of the state. Moreover, the absence of external constraints (freedom from) signifies little if we lack ability and means to achieve purposes that we value (freedom to). Our freedom to do things must exist within the context of opportunities that will give our aspirations significant prospects of being realized. A child dropped in the middle of a desert is free from eating spinach, but in actuality is free only to starve. Genuine freedom requires opportunities as well as rights.

The American political system does not value all freedoms equally. Certain freedoms are deemed to be of the utmost importance, and these we speak of as "civil liberties." The central and most authoritative rendering of them is the Bill of Rights, the first ten amendments of the Constitution. These include the right to life, liberty, and property, to free speech, a free press, freedom of assembly and of worship, and other comparable freedoms. By its incorporation in the Constitution, the Bill of Rights is placed beyond the reach of simple majorities, beyond the chance outcomes of political controversies and elections, and beyond official whims. Conceptions of basic freedoms are not static; today many contend that civil liberties must include the assurance of minimal levels of economic subsistence and protection against arbitrary private power, such as the paper mill that pollutes a lake.

In a democracy the state is part of a larger order, society. The state is a means to certain ends of society, but not to all ends, nor does it embrace all interests and activities. Civil liberties draw a line between society and the state and shut the state out of a realm that is deemed inviolably private—the home, the church, the tastes of the individual. In contrast, the totalitarian systems acknowledge no distinction between the state and society. They

[5] Herbert J. Muller, *Issues of Freedom: Paradoxes and Promises* (New York: Harper & Row, 1960), 33.

claim the right and power to dominate all society, whether in business, religion, literature, education, and recreation or, on the scale of George Orwell's *1984,* in all of life, with privacy abolished.

Freedom is a fragile commodity. The majority risks the loss of its status should a minority, by exercising free speech, convert sufficient numbers to its view. Champions of civil liberties face the logical trauma that some may use their protected freedom of speech to induce the suppression of civil liberties. Above all, "civil liberties" is a highly sophisticated concept; it requires us, for instance, to understand why we allow an individual to remain silent because, citing the Fifth Amendment, he says he may incriminate himself. "If he is innocent," we may reason, "he ought to tell us, and if he is guilty, this right should not concern us." Unrestrained by responsibility, freedom becomes license, and democratic societies wrestle with the tantalizing, elusive problem of how freedom and responsibility can be reconciled to best effect.

"Freedom is not free," wrote Edmond Cahn.[6] Political freedom can be costly; it can agitate society, divert energies, ignite strife. Easily violated, freedom is never secure. Its preservation requires arduous, unflagging effort, and constant vigilance remains its price.

Is freedom adequately protected?

Freedom's chief protection is the Bill of Rights. Elsewhere in the Constitution further safeguards are provided—the prohibition of a bill of attainder (legislation aimed at a particular individual) and the Thirteenth, Fourteenth, and Fifteenth amendments, which emerged from the Civil War and provide for the transfer from slavery to freedom and citizenship. The Bill of Rights specifies what government may not do and the procedures it must observe if it acts against the individual. Originally the Bill of Rights restricted only the federal government, but in 1868 the Fourteenth Amendment extended many parts to the states.

In the light of present-day realities, the Bill of Rights has serious omissions. It embodies the older view of freedom as the absence of restraint and gives scant acknowledgment to freedom's affirmative dimensions—the right to work, the right to education, the right to medical care. And for all the deserved reverence accorded the Bill of Rights, we should not be blind to the fact that many people's freedoms may time and again be violated without redress. Administrative agencies can make short shrift of the citizen's liberties in actions that never come into public view or attract only scant attention. The Federal Bureau of Land Management can fence people out of public lands, with public money paying for the fences, all for the convenience and enrichment of a few ranchers. Private persons and organizations too can,

[6] Edmond Cahn, ed., *The Great Rights* (New York: Macmillan, 1963), 11.

with impunity, limit the freedom of others. Labor unions severely restrict access of blacks to work as skilled laborers, condemning them to unskilled jobs.

The apparatus of civil liberties includes the courts, which, as James Madison predicted, "will consider themselves in a peculiar manner the guardians of those rights." [7] The constitutional language of freedom, "intended to endure for ages to come," is expressed in general phrases—"due process," "unreasonable searches and seizures"—whose meaning in specific times and situations must be interpreted, the task of judges. For the democratic judge, the Constitution and its Bill of Rights are authoritative texts to equip him with legitimate standards of decision and embolden him to overrule legislative or administrative action that violates civil liberties.

Yet there is respected opinion that attaches small significance to the judicial function. The eminent judge Learned Hand once said that "Liberty lies in the hearts of men and women; when it dies there, no constitution, no law, no court can save it; no constitution, no law, no court can even do much to help it. While it lies there it needs no constitution, no law, no court to save it." [8] Thanks to the "hearts of men," black children were segregated from whites in public schools for a century after the Civil War, until a court decision helped change the minds, if not the hearts, of some men to the point that by 1971 a majority of Southern schools were integrated. Yet it must also be acknowledged that the Court's positive contributions sometimes seem more enduring than the condition of men's hearts. Former Justice Arthur Goldberg, assessing the Supreme Court's performance over almost two centuries, hailed the Court for never overruling precedent "to any significant degree" to lessen human liberties.[9] Generally the court has done honor to the position taken by its distinguished member Oliver Wendell Holmes, who wrote, "I . . . probably take the extremist view in favor of free speech, in which, in the abstract, I have no very enthusiastic belief, though I hope I would die for it."

Nevertheless, court opinions interpreting civil liberties often grant them less scope than their literal constitutional language. The Constitution bars Congress from "abridging the freedom of the press"—a provision the courts extend through the Fourteenth Amendment to the states—but the language, as judicially interpreted, does not grant an absolute right. Libelous statements, for example, are not protected. In *Beauharnais v. Illinois*,[10] the Court approved state antihate legislation that made it a crime to publish statements exposing persons of any race, color, creed, or religion to contempt, derision, or obloquy. There and in other cases, the Court applied a balance of interests test, holding that restriction of press freedom is constitutional if the public interest furthered by the legislation outweighs exercise of that freedom in importance.

[7] In Norman Dorsen, *Frontiers of Civil Liberties* (New York: Pantheon Books, 1968), 62.
[8] *Ibid.*, 19.
[9] *New York Times,* April 13, 1971.
[10] 343 U.S. 250 (1952).

The courts distinguish between prior and post restraints, which government may venture to impose on publications to head off criticism of officials. Prior restraint, that is, censorship, is barred. In 1971, the Supreme Court affirmed this position when it blocked the government's attempt to suppress publication in the *New York Times* and the *Washington Post* of the secret Pentagon history of the Vietnam war.[11] Post restraint, which is subject to the balance of interests test, involves sanctions or remedies arising after publication. Thus courts often take the view that a person may be held responsible for the effect of his words or writings. The line between prior and post restraints is sometimes fuzzy. The case of *Near v. Minnesota*[12] involved a state law that branded as a public nuisance any periodical that regularly published obscene, lewd, or scandalous material. Using this law the district attorney had obtained an injunction against future publication of a weekly newspaper that mixed antisemitism with charges of corruption in Minneapolis politics. Was this prior restraint and censorship? Five Supreme Court justices said it was and four said it was not.

In grappling with freedom of religion, the Court has had to cope with a tangle of objectives set by the Constitution and Congress. The First Amendment forbids laws "prohibiting the free exercise of religion" and laws "respecting an establishment of religion," such as the creation of an official church. For the sake of free religious practice, the Court has invalidated laws requiring door-to-door religious solicitors to secure a police permit, children of Jehovah's Witnesses to salute the flag in school despite their religious scruples, and an alien seeking naturalization to swear that he will defend the country by bearing arms that his religious convictions oppose. The establishment provision, however, has come into conflict with the attempts by all levels of government to respond to burgeoning demands for education in both public and parochial schools. Court decisions, which have been numerous, follow a somewhat erratic course.[13]

In a key case, *Everson v. Board of Education*,[14] the Court upheld a town ordinance reimbursing parents for bus fares spent to send their children to either public high schools or Catholic parochial high schools. And state subsidies of bus transportation of children to parochial schools were upheld as aiding the child rather than the church. The Court also approved programs permitting children to leave school early for religious instruction.[15] But the Court swung the other way in holding that the establishment clause forbids sectarian instruction on public school property during school hours, an officially composed nondenominational prayer for public school children, and obligatory Bible-reading and recitation of the Lord's Prayer in public schools.

That the Court is continually faced with the task of adapting general civil

---

[11] *New York Times v. United States,* 703 U.S. 713 (1971).

[12] *Near v. Minnesota,* 283 U.S. 697 (1931).

[13] See Paul G. Kauper, *Civil Liberties and the Constitution* (Ann Arbor: University of Michigan Press, 1962), 3–52.

[14] 330 U.S. 1 (1947).

[15] See Milton R. Konvitz, *Expanding Civil Liberties* (New York: Viking, 1966), 14–41.

liberties provisions to new circumstances is evident in rulings on free speech and expression in the 1960s and 70s, an era of demonstrations for black civil rights and against the Vietnam war. In the quieter 1930s, the Court in *Hague v. CIO* [16] declared that the use of the streets to assemble, discuss public questions, and communicate thoughts was part of the privileges and immunities and rights of citizenship. In more recent cases, the right to this public forum has not been absolute, but has been constrained by general convenience and the needs of public peace and order. In balancing the competing claims of order and free expression, the courts allow regulation of the time, place, and manner of assembly and expression. Maintaining the public interest in regard to the flow of pedestrian and vehicular traffic implies the power to restrict the size of a group of picketers and to regulate the route of a march. In interpreting the Voting Rights Act of 1965, and in passing on incidents stemming from the related march of that year from Selma to Montgomery, Alabama, the Court made it a duty of the government to protect unpopular marchers and demonstrators from hostile onlookers.

The concept of the "public forum" is steadily enlarging to include areas technically private but that acquire a public character. Thus labor picketing of the parking lot of a privately owned shopping center, the distribution of anti-Vietnam war leaflets in privately owned railroad stations, and access to the privately owned radio and television stations to discuss unpopular causes, have all received judicial sanction.

One of the harsher realities of the world of civil liberties is that their assertion through court action is costly and must necessarily be selective. The school segregation cases of 1954 cost about $200,000, and the average civil liberties case that has gone through a federal appeals court adds up to a bill of about $5,000.[17] Costly litigation heightens the importance of such nonprofit organizations as the American Civil Liberties Union, the NAACP Legal Defense and Educational Fund, the American Jewish Congress, and such federal agencies as the Civil Rights Commission, the Civil Rights Division of the Department of Justice, and the Equal Employment Opportunity Commission, which carry the brunt of civil liberties litigation.

A major weapon of attack is the "test case" conducted by a new breed of advocate, the civil liberties lawyer, who is steeped in both labyrinthian governmental functioning and legal technicalities. A crucial question yet to be answered satisfactorily is whether the civil liberties test case really results in lasting gains, or whether, all too often, wins only an immediate victory, whose principles are eroded by wily opponents and must be continually relitigated. Certainly this has been the pattern in the school segregation cases and school prayer cases, where the courts ruled in favor of civil liberties but many local officials have slithered about in obvious reluctance to comply with court holdings.

[16] 307 U.S. 496 (1939).
[17] Konvitz, 70.

There is a danger in relying too much on litigation to improve civil liberties. Crucially important is the cultivation of understanding among local officials, whose domain is where most people's rights are observed or abused. Healthy local attitudes will gain far more for civil liberties than occasional selective visitations by the United States Supreme Court.

The tension of authority and freedom

"When legislation touches freedom of thought and freedom of speech," wrote Justice Felix Frankfurter, "such a tendency is a formidable enemy of the free spirit." [18] In a democracy, the tension between authority and freedom pervades political life. In fact, psychological research has provided us with corresponding labels for certain personality types commonly encountered in a democratic society. These labels, "authoritarian" and "democratic," bear important consequences for civil liberties. As a type, the authoritarian, whether an official or a private citizen, is devoted to fixed ideology and procedure and is single-minded about the correctness of his goals and the means of fulfilling them. He justifies his conduct as sanctioned by an authority —God, an elite, or scientific method—and takes a disparaging view of the mass of men, deeming them manipulable, misinformed, incapable of thought, their political perceptions beclouded by sentimental values.

A contrasting type is the "democrat," who stresses freedom, equality, the dignity of man. Even more significant, he is committed to processes of free and open inquiry in selecting and fulfilling goals. Above all else, the democrat values the process of choice itself; he is open to alternatives and flexible in his plans. He views his fellow men optimistically, as capable of reason and compromise, cooperative, and, like himself, committed to an open society. Both the "authoritarian" and "democratic" types may be radical or conservative.[19]

Seldom in American life do we encounter anyone who fulfills either type. Rather, most public figures are a mixture of the two. Thus Franklin Roosevelt at one time aided countless men through New Deal programs of social security, relief for the unemployed, cheap electric power from the Tennessee Valley Authority, all adding to man's self-esteem and bringing relief from freedom-crippling pressures. But the Franklin Roosevelt of another day, of the Second World War, sanctioned the uprooting of thousands of Japanese and Japanese-Americans from their West Coast homes and employment and their removal to government camps, a pale variant of the concentration camps against which the war was presumably being fought. Like many persons, Roosevelt's behavior mixed elements of the opposing authoritarian and demo-

---

[18] 341 U.S. 494, 556 (1950).
[19] June L. Tapp and Fred Krinsky, *Ambivalent America: A Psycho-political Dialogue* (Beverly Hills, Calif.: Glencoe Press, 1971), 3.

cratic types. The conflict and tension that he and other men at various levels of official life experience are mirrored in shifting behavior, as the official responds to the demands of specific situations and seeks to maintain a balance imposed by himself and the political culture.

Society itself wrestles with a similar ambivalence in its institutions and experience. Elements such as nationalism, militarism, police, hierarchy and subordination in the work situation represent authoritarian emphases. On the other hand, religious ideals, the arts, and humanitarian endeavor bear democratic colorations.

Given the breadth of human variation, democracy must be hospitable to all personality types; it cannot expect to one day be filled exclusively with democratic personalities. In any case, it does not follow that the democracy is best whose people conform most to the democratic personality type. Authoritarian personalities are useful, if not essential, for certain roles involving the exercise of authority. In other roles they are at least harmless, while in still others they are clearly harmful, and democracy provides defenses against them. Hence a function of the electoral process is to expose and sift out authoritarian types who seek certain offices. Authoritarian types function acceptably only when they are subject to "authority," that is, when they are regulated by defined roles and are accountable to still higher authority. Thus the authoritarian can be tamed and confined to acceptable boundaries by "authority."

No society, including democracy, can dispense with authority. Through authority people seek order and safety, realizing that they cannot enjoy freedom without a social order capable of protecting their life and pursuits and without a military system capable of protecting them from external threat. Political scientist Carl J. Friedrich sees authority not as blind order-giving or naked assertion of dominion over others, but as "the ability to issue communications which are capable of reasoned elaboration." Another political scientist, George Catlin, concludes that "for the purposes of political science, authority is neither in itself good or bad. It carries no poison." [20]

The extreme of authority is authoritarianism, but democracy too has its extremes of disobedience and insurgency. The Bill of Rights permits dissenters to use many forms of expressions in order to bring others to accept their beliefs; they may speak, write, hold mass meetings, parade, and demonstrate. But dissent sometimes takes the form of civil disobedience, to borrow Thoreau's term, in which the dissenter deliberately violates a law. In a common tableau of his conduct, the civil disobedient eventually defers to the law by accepting arrest and punishment. The disobedient views his behavior as expressive of a conscience offended by unjust laws and policies. Martin Luther King, Jr., represented this attitude when he said, "I submit that the individual who disobeys the law, whose conscience tells him it is unjust and who is willing to accept the penalty of staying in jail until the law is altered,

[20] *Ibid.,* 49.

For Martin Luther King, Jr., enduring principles stood above the law. Here he is leading a voting rights march from Selma to Montgomery, Alabama.

is expressing at the moment the very highest respect for the law." [21] In this view, enduring principles stand above the law, and the function of law is to facilitate their expression and preservation.

"Disobedience," argues federal judge Charles E. Wyzanski, "is a long step from dissent." To Wyzanski and other critics, civil disobedience attacks democracy itself, rejects representative government and the courts, and the rule of law. However nobly defined are its motive, objective, and method, disobedience often induces others to take up lawbreaking for self-determined reasons that may be far less justifiable. When civil disobedience flaunts one law, it subverts all laws. By implication the civil disobedient claims that the children of light are morally privileged to break the law, but, one may retort, so, in fairness, ought the children of darkness to be privileged. Finally, these critics maintain, civil disobedience, however peaceful and well-intentioned, may spawn disorder that can quickly break into violence.[22]

In the behavior of many civil disobedients, political scientist Paul F. Power discerns a pattern of "responsible" civil disobedience that is open and unsecretive, deliberate rather than accidental, a clearly unlawful act stemming from "conscientious" dissent rooted in moral or religious beliefs, a concrete objective of public reform, and exhaustion of all legal remedies before disobedience begins. According to Howard Zinn, if the particular civil disobe-

[21] Martin Luther King, Jr., "Love, Law and Civil Disobedience," *New South,* 16 (January 1961), 8.

[22] Tapp and Krinsky, 195–99; Lewis H. Van Dusen, Jr., "Civil Disobedience: Destroyer of Democracy," *American Bar Association Journal,* 55 (February 1969), 123–25.

dience is morally justifiable, the jailing of the perpetrator is immoral, "and should be opposed, contested to the very end." Christian Bay and others hold that the means employed need not be "nonviolent." [23]

Bay contends that civil disobedience can advance human values no longer served by majoritarian institutions because of distortions of the rule of law and representative government. Disobedience then becomes a means to a future that banishes poverty and violence and expands human rights. But will the disobedients who reject today's imperfect democracy restore a democracy in the better world of tomorrow? Far too many revolutions have substituted for a flawed order a new one that is equally, if not more, repressive. Bay's better society appears to involve the dropping of an old elite for a new elite of radicals who would produce bold policies, which is hardly a scenario of popular democracy.[24]

Who respects freedom?

Research of recent decades enables us to look at this question from several perspectives—from the standpoint of class as a shaper of individual attitudes, from the standpoint of other social indexes (education, religion, sex, and geography), and from the standpoint of personality types.

Citing both foreign and national studies, Seymour Martin Lipset, in *Political Man,* concludes that extremist and intolerant movements are more likely to be based on the lower classes than on the middle and upper classes. Nazism and Fascism attracted lower class support first and gained the support of other classes later. Ethnic prejudice and proclivity for totalitarian principles are consistently disclosed in studies of public opinion, religion, family patterns, and personality structure of members of the lower class. Such people are prone to reject equal rights for minority groups, to hold intense nationalistic sentiments, and to be the most unfavorably disposed toward civil liberties.

Many elements of lower class life produce this profile. Poor education, meagre participation in political and other voluntary organizations, minimal reading, and authoritarian family ways are the rule. The life of the poor spins a psychological web that restrains them from effective democratic participation. The poor develop habits of submission and are confined to a narrow world by little access to sources of information and by inadequate verbal facility. These circumstances weaken their self-confidence and inhibit their participation in the political process. Receptivity of the lower classes to authoritarianism is enlarged by economic insecurity, which increases the farther down one is in the economic scale. Insecurity fosters hostility toward

[23] Paul F. Power, "On Civil Disobedience in Recent American Democratic Thought," *American Political Science Review,* LXIV (March 1970), 44–46.
[24] Christian Bay, "Civil Disobedience," *International Encyclopedia of the Social Sciences,* Vol. II, 484–85.

scapegoats and acceptance of the drastic, short-term solutions of extremist groups.

The higher educational attainment of the middle class reduces its authoritarian responses, and according to studies, the well-educated upper middle class is the least "authoritarian." But particularly gratifying for advocates of democracy is the *independent* effect of education. A study of auto workers with low educational attainment found them more authoritarian than auto workers with more education. This study establishes that even where other social factors are unfavorable, education has an independent effect and benign long-term significance.[25] Based on this finding, today's rising education levels for the general population augur well for democratic gains.

Samuel Stouffer studied the influence of a variety of social factors on tolerance of nonconformity in the era of the 1950s, when Senator Joseph R. McCarthy was deep in his hunt for Communists.[26] Stouffer had been impressed by the fact that historically a pattern of ebb and flow has persisted in American civil liberties: repressive interludes such as the post-Revolutionary Alien and Sedition Acts, the Know Nothing party preceding the Civil War, and the Ku Klux Klan of the Reconstruction period, have always been followed by periods when the "sober second thought of the people" prevailed and reasserted civil liberties. A vital democratic resource, accordingly, is an enduring residual regard for freedom, which although perhaps temporarily eclipsed is eventually reasserted.

Interviewing 6,000 men and women in all walks of life and in all parts of the country, Stouffer sought to tap not transient opinion, but latent attitudes or predispositions. Among his findings were that community leaders, tending to be responsible and thoughtful citizens, are more likely than the rank and file to give a "sober second thought" to the dangers involved in denying civil liberties to those whose views they dislike. Different types of leaders, however, harbor different attitudes: leaders of women's clubs, the American Legion, and the DAR are less tolerant of a Socialist speech than the chairman of the school board or the president of the bar association. Older people tend to hold stauncher conformist attitudes than younger people at the same educational level. But in *all* age groups the better educated are more tolerant than the less educated.

In other findings, women, including those with high levels of political interest, are less tolerant of nonconformists than men, nonchurch-attenders are more tolerant than church attenders, and city people more than rural folk. The citizen of the metropolis has contact with a greater variety of people whose values are different from, or even repugnant to, his own. The West, according to Stouffer, contains the largest proportion of relatively tolerant people, followed by the East and Middle West, and then the South. To what

[25] Seymour Martin Lipset, *Political Man* (New York: Doubleday, Anchor Books, 1963), 87–102.
[26] Samuel A. Stouffer, *Communism, Conformity, and Civil Liberties,* Revised Ed. (New York: Wiley, 1967).

extent intersectional migrations since Stouffer's survey have altered these conclusions remains to be researched and likewise the effect of the fast-growing suburbs, which seem to blend the higher tolerance of the city with the lower tolerance of the countryside.

Both the need for civil liberties and the disposition to honor them for others are functions of personality. Giuseppe Di Palma and Herbert McClosky sampled a cross section of Minnesota adults and national adults to determine what influences govern the acceptance or rejection of the dominant political and social values of society. They tested the adults for attitude conformity on such items as "The idea that everyone has a right to his own opinion is being carried too far these days" and "Poor people should look out for themselves." [27] For this purpose, conformity and deviation were defined as the degree to which an individual American subscribed to the beliefs held by more than 70 percent of the American people, as measured by survey data derived from questionnaires administered in the middle and late 1950s.

Conformity, as conceptualized in the study, was by no means the equivalent of instant yea-saying, suggestibility, or gullibility, but was indeed the inverse. Here the conformer was not one who affirms belief after belief regardless of content and the contradiction of one belief by another. Instead the conformer discriminately recognizes which of the countless beliefs he encounters society has accepted or rejected.

Those who conform for the most part to majority attitudes, the researchers found, are "by substantial margins" better adapted socially and psychologically than the deviants, those who reject most of them. The conformers are more intellectually oriented, more politically aware, more proficient in cognitive skills. They manifest greater self-esteem and less anxiety than the deviants and are less directed by aggression and inflexibility. To some degree, social maladaptation of the deviant reflects personality traits that independently influence his ability to recognize and understand the norms.

Deviants, the studies found, of both college and noncollege backgrounds, fail to absorb the value of the "American Creed" respecting tolerance, faith in freedom and democracy, political and social equality, procedural rights, and the like, as effectively as conformers of comparable education. Deviants are more prejudiced, more politically cynical, and more responsive to extreme right wing and left wing values, which the majority, and especially the majority of the educated, reject.

The deviant was found to be a suggestible individual, vulnerable to aberrant opinions that a more selective mind would reject. The suggestibles are low in self-esteem, psychologically vulnerable, anxious, guilt-ridden, cautious, fearful of failure. Laurence J. Gould has found that such deviants show less curiosity about the reasons for their own judgments and those of the majority, are less sensitive to the feelings of others, and less aware of the more subtle

---

[27] Giuseppe Di Palma and Herbert McClosky, "Personality and Conformity: The Learning of Political Attitudes," *American Political Science Review*, LXIV (December 1970), 1054–73.

and informal norms in social situations.[28] A study of the Berkeley nonstudent as a deviant subculture confirms these findings, but also reveals him as autonomous, free in impulse expression, and displaying an experimental, intellectual, and complex orientation toward social experience.[29]

Big brothers:
technology and bureaucracy

A cardinal distinction of democracy, in contrast to totalitarian states, is its respect for the privacy of the individual and the group, the legitimacy of the individual's pursuit of nonpolitical purposes—the arts, literature, sports, and personal retreat for reflection and critical thought. "The free man is the private man," wrote Clinton Rossiter, "the man who still keeps some of his thoughts and judgments entirely to himself." [30]

American democracy is committed to such ideas as the family as an autonomous unit and religion as a matter of personal choice and observance. But privacy is not an absolute right. Some private behavior can be oppressive to democracy—anonymous influences over public life that penalize the general citizenry, conspiracies that threaten democracy's survival, crime luxuriating beyond reach of reasonable law enforcement methods. The public's "need to know" is occasionally the countervalue of privacy.

A delicate problem is posed: how can the precious right of privacy be maintained in a proper balance with government's need to inform itself of the private behavior of individuals and groups and even, in exceptional circumstances, to regulate their conduct?

The increasing surveillance of private individuals and groups by law enforcement agencies and a growing array of government bureaus may prompt one to question whether the proper balance is being preserved. In his thorough study, *Privacy and Freedom,* Alan Westin makes three general classifications of surveillance: (1) physical surveillance of a person's location and acts through optical and acoustical devices, without his knowledge or against his will; (2) psychological surveillance through oral and written tests and other devices to extract from an individual information that he may not give willingly or wittingly; (3) data surveillance through the collection, exchange, and manipulation of documentary information about individuals and groups by data-processing machines, particularly computers, on a scale that seriously threatens privacy.[31]

---

[28] Laurence J. Gould, "Conformity and Marginality: Two Faces of Alienation," *Journal of Social Issues,* 25 (April 1969), 39–63.
[29] David Whittaker and William A. Watts, "Personality Characteristics of a Nonconformist Youth Subculture: A Study of the Berkeley Non-Student," *Journal of Social Issues,* 25 (April 1969), 65–89.
[30] In Milton R. Konvitz and Clinton Rossiter, eds., *Aspects of Liberty* (Ithaca, N.Y.: Cornell University Press, 1958), 16–17.
[31] Alan F. Westin, *Privacy and Freedom* (New York: Atheneum, 1967), 68.

In 1971, Christopher Pyle, a former Army intelligence captain, testified in a Senate hearing that the Army acquired and stored information on the political activities of thousands of Americans. He is holding a copy of a photo taken on a college campus.

Public protests against both the Indochina war and the resultant low priority of urgent domestic problems have spurred the compiling of detailed dossiers on the lives of millions of those dissenting citizens. Documents brought to light in 1971 revealed that high civilian and Defense Department aides of the Johnson administration mapped out a far-flung domestic intelligence effort amid the widespread civil disturbances of 1967–68. Thousands of civilians were placed under military surveillance—civil rights activists, black militants, antiwar protesters, establishment politicians, and, with becoming respect for the polarities of American politics, the Black Panthers and the Ku Klux Klan, the NAACP and the John Birch Society, the Students for a Democratic Society and the Daughters of the American Revolution. The military intelligence operation extracted information from local police and the FBI and deployed its own agents posing as members of the groups, as newsmen, or as interested bystanders. A black agent registered in a university course in black studies to report on fellow students. Another joined the Youth International party (Yippies) and slept alongside its candidate, a pig named "Pigasus," during a counterinauguration, paralleling President Nixon's inauguration in Washington in 1969.[32]

[32] *New York Times,* January 18 and April 17, 1971.

An Army intelligence report on "The Crazies," who allegedly were to have seized a Staten Island ferry in March 1969.

Senator Sam J. Erwin, Jr., chairman of a subcommittee on constitutional rights, concluded in 1971 that the Department of Health, Education, and Welfare "probably maintains more personal data on individuals than any other Federal department." [33] The department's and society's mightiest tool for raking in data is the Social Security number, which is required for growing numbers of purposes—voter registration affidavits, telephone company records, military records, driver's licenses, death certificates, insurance policies, and other forms. In an age of computerized data exchange, the Social Security number bids fair to become a universal identifier for an individual from birth to death, and simultaneously his worst enemy, opening doors on his privacy. When critics pressed to regulate governmental data collection and dissemination activity, including use of the Social Security number as an identifier, Assistant Attorney General William H. Rehnquist declared that the Justice Department would oppose any such legislation. "Self-discipline," he added, "on the part of the executive branch will provide an answer to virtually all of the legitimate complaints against excesses of information gathering." [34]

Fortunately, more restraints are available than the weak reed of bureaucratic self-discipline. Constitutional safeguards against unreasonable searches and seizures and self-incrimination are applicable, and the law of trespass, locally enforced, bars entry onto someone's property without his permission. Wiretapping is regulated by the Omnibus Crime Control Act of 1968, which

[33] *New York Times,* March 16, 1971.
[34] *Ibid.*

reflects a body of earlier court decisions. According to this act, it is illegal under most circumstances for government officials or private citizens to wire-tap messages. In national security situations, the President may permit bug-ging, but otherwise, federal and state officials must petition the courts for permission and show the same probable cause that is required for a search warrant. In the rising black civil rights movement of the 1950s and 1960s, the Court upheld "associational privacy" in banning an Alabama law requir-ing the NAACP as an out-of-state corporation to submit its membership and officer lists prior to admission in the state. In other rulings, the Court has identified, although more tentatively, "political privacy" (which, it noted, is subject to "the right of the State to self-protection"), the right to anonymity in public expression, and the privacy of the body or inviolability of the person. Expanding judicial recognition of privacy gives hope that the courts will soon subject governmental intrusions on privacy to the requirements of due process. A due process test might require that surveillants use the methods that least violate privacy. Those employing the wiretaps, bugging, or whatever might have the burden of proof that techniques less deleterious to privacy are not available.

An array of counterdevices also protect the fortresses of privacy. Corpora-tions use "floating room" systems to ensure privacy at conferences, and jamming and detection devices continue to become available at tolerable cost for "bug protection." Better professional and ethical standards of enforcement officials are basic needs; doctors, lawyers, accountants, psychologists, and other professionals are awakening to their responsibilities to democratic man in collecting and using personal data.[35]

The economics of freedom

Freedom rests on an economic base. The individual can more readily enjoy freedom if he has economic means, and private associations can more effec-tively join in the competition of ideas in a pluralistic society if they can afford to disseminate their communications. These truths are clearly evident in the fundamental communications systems, the free exercise of which freedom depends on—the press, radio, and television. Unfortunately, strong economic trends are afoot in each that are inimical to the interests of freedom.

The media. Freedom of the press is being jeopardized by the steady movement toward monopoly of the local press by profit-hungry entrepreneurs who build chains by buying up competing media—the local radio and television stations, daily and weekly newspapers, and even "shopper" publications. Thanks to this long-forming trend, in the late 1960s there were no competing daily news-papers in seventeen states, and in each of twenty states there was only one city

35 Westin, 382, 398.

with competing papers. A 1971 study reveals the decided push toward one-newspaper communities: [36]

Total number of dailies	1,748	
Total number of cities with dailies	1,511	
Total number of one-daily cities	1,304	(86.3%)
Total number of cities with single morning and single evening paper under the same ownership	141	
Total number of cities with "joint operation" but separate ownership of morning and evening newspapers	21	
Total number of cities with two or more competing dailies	37	(2.5%)

Several economic forces have accelerated the trend to newspaper monopoly. Not the least of these are spiraling costs of newsprint, labor, equipment, and ink, and costly strikes. Another is the spreading technique of the joint operating contract between two or more papers of a city to eliminate competition in key areas of production; advertising and circulation, for

[36] Hillier Krieghbaum, *Pressures on the Press* (New York: Crowell, 1972), 158.

instance, offer joint rates, which are only slightly higher than the rates for one publication. These price fixing deals practically assure that no new newspaper will be established since its advertising and circulation rates must be sold at below cost to meet the unfair competition of jointly operated papers. High newspaper profits and even lusher radio-TV yields enable chains to expand further in all the media.

No regulatory policy has yet successfully intervened to turn back the monopolistic tide. Whenever the Justice Department or the Federal Trade Commission tries to act, the monopolists cry out that "freedom of the press" is in peril, conveniently forgetting that the intended beneficiaries of a free press are not the news purveyors, but the news consumers. Instead of protecting press competition from economic strangulation, the courts apply doctrines that further monopoly. Under the Supreme Court's "failing business" doctrine, for example, no antitrust case exists when one newspaper buys another that is failing and acquisition by the buyer is the best means of salvaging the paper.

The area of free speech most damaged by press monopoly is local news and issues, for which national news magazines like *Time* and *Newsweek* can provide no remedy. For millions of Americans, the First Amendment is dead on local affairs; without competing media, the published fare of political discussion is limited to what the single owner chooses to provide. The local radio and television stations might offer competition, but increasingly they are owned by the same entrepreneur who owns the newspaper.

The economics of television are also inhospitable to freedom. The industry's orientation is to profits, huge, ballooning profits. Having a television franchise, one favored entrepreneur has said, is like receiving "a license to print money." Soaring profits accrue both to the local stations and to the chains or national networks like NBC and CBS. The great bulk of local programming is provided by the chains.

Program fare is bland and unvaried, prompting former Federal Communications Commission chairman Newton Minow to behold television as "a vast wasteland." Television's heavy dependence on a few big-spending advertisers invites censorship of news and entertainment content. Procter and Gamble, easily television's largest advertiser, bars from its programs material unfavorable to business, and especially to grocers and druggists. Chrysler, a major munitions manufacturer, killed a proposed war story program, "Barbed Wire," in 1966 because the plot was too antimilitary, and a gas company eliminated from a series on the Nuremberg trials all references to gas as a cause of death in Nazi concentration camps.

An elaborate economic-technological structure undergirds the networks, TV's oligopoly. Decades ago, RCA (NBC) induced the FCC to establish television channels by assigning them on the extremely limited UHF spectrum, in lieu of other choices leading to a more crowded, competitive field, with less profits and more program variety. Although individual stations are licensed, the networks, the giants of the industry, are licensed by no one, but are subject only to minor regulation by the FCC. This leniency facilitates concentration on profits rather than on public interest.

To protect their monopolistic position, the networks have unmercifully opposed potential competitors like "pay" or subscription TV (STV) and community antenna (cable) television (CATV). With unstinting cooperation from station owners, movie producers, and movie theater owners, the networks have blocked pay TV. Among other things, they have paid huge sums to acquire first-run movies and professional sports rights, while NBC's David Sarnoff has cried, "Keep American radio and television broadcasting free to the public!" To counter the emerging CATV, the networks have bought heavily into that enterprise.

Much of CATV's future awaits pending decisions by Congress, the FCC, the Justice Department, and the courts, but if the past be a guide the networks will prevail through their practiced manipulation of the political system to their own use. Should the FCC thwart them, which is unlikely, they can apply to friendly congressional subcommittees to launch investigations. In that benign atmosphere, they can employ their favorite weapons, the filibuster and documentary inundation. In investigation or pending decision, the networks can be counted on to submit lengthy pleadings and impressively authored and expensively produced reports and studies. When the FCC expressed concern over the networks' control of programming, they forthwith hired Arthur D. Little, Inc., the prestigious management consulting firm, to prepare a massive rebuttal, "Television, Program Production, Procurement, and Syndication," chapter and verse of which were quoted endlessly by industry witnesses to the FCC, on Capitol Hill, and in news releases.[37]

Hope for a way to meet democratic needs lies in the more competitive and growing suburban press and in the resurging weekly press. The latter, a historic hotbed of grassroots democracy, is published by a local owner and treats local politics and events. Although chains are making some inroads, their impact thus far is attributable largely to the economy of central printing, which relieves the publisher of maintaining expensive, cumbersome equipment and storage space and reduces his payroll.

Less liberty for the poor and dependent? In today's welfare state, government distributes benefits not only to the poor but to most citizens at some time in their lives. Two out of three college students attend publicly supported institutions, more than two million persons live in public housing units, nine out of ten wage earners are eligible for Social Security. Veterans' benefits, aid to families with dependent children, farm subsidies, vocational rehabilitation training—these are typical of programs with masses of beneficiaries.

Benefits of a given program are not available to all persons, but only to those satisfying prescribed qualifications—public housing applicants must have low incomes, a welfare mother must have dependent children and no other means of support, and for old age assistance one must attain a certain

[37] *Ibid.,* 156.

age. Administrative officials can arbitrarily deny or halt public benefits, with an impunity protected by legal doctrines unfavorable to the beneficiaries and by the general circumstance that those most dependent on government's largess are worst situated to contest its decisions in the courts. Only a shadow of the civil liberties available to the person accused of a crime are accorded the government beneficiary. The criminally accused has rights to notice of charges made against him, a jury trial, representation by counsel, restrictions on evidence introduced against him, and appeal. Few of these safeguards apply in the denial or withdrawal of a government benefit.

In according greater civil liberties to the criminally accused than to those dependent on government benefits, the legal system overlooks the harsh reality that loss of a benefit can become "punishment" far more severe than a court-imposed fine. A state university student, facing punishment for a demonstration or a sit-in, can better bear a modest fine than expulsion from his university and a stigmatized inability to continue his education at public expense. One easily imagines the superior importance of benefits to defined legal rights in occurrences such as these: A baby froze to death in Arlington, Virginia, because its parents, recently arrived in the state, were ineligible for welfare under a one-year residence requirement. Public school teachers in Seward, Alaska, and Susanville, California, were discharged for making public statements critical of local school board policy. A welfare caseworker in Oakland, California, was fired for refusing to participate in predawn raids to check on clients' homes.[38]

Of all the categories of government beneficiaries, whether foundations, students, or gentlemen farmers, those whose liberties are most flimsily protected are the poor. The most exploited of that genre is the welfare recipient, whose dependence is also the greatest. A favorite object of welfare restrictions is the unmarried mother. Most states reduce or deny benefits to otherwise eligible mothers if a man is living with the family, even though he has no legal obligation to support the children and indeed may be incapable of doing so. Welfare mothers are often required to accept any employment that happens to be available, which tends to press them into menial and farm field work; their service is often a kind of subsidy to their underpaying employer. In some states the mother may be removed from welfare rolls on accepting employment, even though her wages may be lower than her welfare pittance.

The welfare recipient is subject to varieties of surveillance corrosive of privacy and dignity. The privacy of many a welfare recipient has been trampled by "midnight raids" and searches, unannounced inspections made without warrants, to check eligibility, with the explicit or implied threat that refusal to cooperate will terminate assistance. But a New York court decision provides a glimmer of hope for civil liberties in upholding a client who refused a caseworker entry and whose benefits were consequently terminated.[39]

[38] Robert M. O'Neil, *The Price of Dependency: Civil Liberties in the Welfare State* (New York: Dutton, 1970), 18–19.
[39] Charles Reich, "Midnight Welfare Searches and the Social Security Act," *Yale Law Journal,* 72 (June 1963), 1347; *Steward v. Washington,* Welfare Law Bulletin No. 9 (July 1967), 4.

The great majority of states impose residence tests, many with a three-year waiting period, which can work hardships. In 1966, Mrs. Vivian Marie Thompson moved with her baby from Boston, where her husband had abandoned her, to Hartford, to be near her mother. Connecticut, which requires one year of residence, denied her welfare application. Fortunately, she was sustained month to month by contributions from Hartford's Catholic Family Service.[40]

Welfare agencies decree what needs shall be budgeted and what new resources should be tracked down, decisions to which the recipient must respond or face reductions of his allotments. Federal law lets the states decide whether mothers are "appropriate persons" for jobs or training whose small children would be placed in publicly supported day-care centers. During congressional debate over the legislation establishing the work/day-care tandem, Senator Joseph Tydings (D., Md.) exclaimed, "We cannot take children from their mothers and place them with thirty or fifty other children into bare prison-like rooms where they are warehoused like so many cardboard boxes all day while their mothers work in order to remain on the welfare rolls."

The poor fare little better in other sectors of governmental life. In many cities women with illegitimate children are systematically excluded from public housing projects. These projects are hated, James Baldwin has written, "because they reveal the real attitude of the white world." Often a single serious criminal violation will bar an otherwise qualified applicant from public housing projects. The applicant who is told why his application is rejected or the tenant who is given reasons for his eviction is the exception rather than the rule. But encouragement comes from a federal court of appeals case criticizing the New York Housing Authority's failure to promulgate selection standards,[41] and from New York state courts which require that constitutionally valid reasons be given a tenant for his eviction. Administrative agencies can tighten procedures in behalf of the poor at any time, and sometimes they have.

Decisions of most regulatory agencies are easily appealed to the courts by the aggrieved party, but for the welfare recipient or housing applicant it is another story. Review procedures are labyrinthian and textually obscure to the beneficiary who is required to "exhaust" administrative remedies before resorting to the courts. Because of litigious delays, the recipient may have to scrounge for other support to tide him over, after which he may be told his case is "moot" because he no longer needs the benefit. In contrast to the casual, obscure appellate procedures for welfare recipients, Robert O'Neil is impressed with the impeccable due process observed after the disputed 1968 Kentucky Derby, when a ruling disqualified the winning horse, Dancer's Image, for having been drugged. When the owner demanded a hearing, it transpired within a week. Meanwhile the purse money was held and the official record suspended. When the original ruling was affirmed, it was appealed to the Kentucky Racing Commission for even more elaborate hearings with

[40] O'Neil, 265.
[41] Promulgating standards: *Holmes v. New York City Housing Authority,* 288 N.Y.S. 2d 159 (App. Div. 1968).

attorneys, witnesses, cross-examination, expert testimony, and a 3000-page transcript of the record. And when the appeal was decided against Dancer's Image, the owner moved to appeal again. As between race horses and welfare clients, the preferences of civil liberties are clear.[42]

The black
civil rights movement

The most painful failure of American democracy has been the persistent exclusion of blacks from its privileges. But failure, as Swedish sociologist Gunnar Myrdal has pointed out, is also "America's incomparably great opportunity for the future." [43] The contemporary black civil rights movement is one of the main thrusts for opportunity.

Despite emancipation and the constitutional amendments that followed (Thirteenth, Fourteenth, and Fifteenth) outlawing slavery and granting the black man "the privileges and immunities" of citizens, including the vote, his world, well into the twentieth century, has consisted of the "Jim Crow" room in restaurants, the poll tax, "Negro quarters" in the cities, inferior segregated schools, terror from the Ku Klux Klan, racial discrimination in employment.

After flickers of change in the Second World War and the postwar years, the Supreme Court in 1954 made a great breakthrough in *Brown v. Board of Education*,[44] which held that segregation in public school education was inherently discriminatory and therefore unconstitutional. Legislation in the form of the Civil Rights Act of 1957 took care of some of the other deprivations. The act enabled the federal government, by serving civil injunction, to assist anyone deprived of his right to vote, and enlarged the administrative apparatus of civil rights. A second law (1960) plugged loopholes of the first by providing for federal voting referees to register blacks when local officials would not, but neither act bore much fruit. President Eisenhower, in whose administration the laws were passed, gave slender support.

Meanwhile, from the mid-fifties onward, a civil rights movement was flowering. It began in 1955 when Mrs. Rosa Parks, a black seamstress, sat down in the white section of a Montgomery, Alabama, bus because her feet hurt. Arrested for violating the segregation laws, she was aided by Reverend Dr. Martin Luther King, Jr., and other clergy of the city who instigated mass boycotts and Gandhi-type passive resistance in a dynamic religious crusade. Led by clergy and young people, white and black, the civil rights movement undertook sit-ins at lunch counters and demonstrations at hotels, movie theatres, and amusement parks. Freedom riders, white and black, protested segregation in buses and at terminals, a hazardous pursuit that met with sniper fire and savage beatings.[45]

[42] O'Neil, 314.
[43] In Anthony Lewis, *Portrait of a Decade* (New York: Random House, 1964), 14.
[44] 347 U.S. 483 (1954).
[45] Lewis, *Portrait of a Decade*, 71–90.

Rosa Parks touched off the Montgomery bus boycott, and the civil rights movement of the 1950s.

With the advent of a new decade and John F. Kennedy's administration a new era in civil rights began—a "beautiful start," Roy Wilkins, NAACP leader, has termed it. Accelerating change occurred in every aspect of race relations, and always with federal involvement. The administration brought suits in behalf of the black voter (even in Sunflower County, home of Mississippi's powerful Senator James Eastland), induced the ICC to ban bus and rail segregation, attacked employment discrimination through clauses in government contracts and requirements that federal agencies hire substantial numbers of blacks, prohibited discrimination in much federally aided housing, and quickened the pace of school desegregation. At his death, Kennedy had before Congress proposals for the most sweeping civil rights legislation in history.

His successor, Lyndon Johnson, whom Wilkins has hailed for giving "the greatest impetus to civil rights in the history of our country," saw the proposals through to enactment in the Civil Rights Act of 1964. The act barred racial discrimination in all public accommodations affecting interstate commerce and in all publicly operated facilities, promoted fair employment standards in business and in labor unions, authorized suspension of federal funding of state or private programs that permitted racial discrimination, barred different standards for white and black voting applicants and made a sixth-grade education a "rebuttable presumption" of literacy, provided for

*Voter registration in Selma, Alabama,
following passage of the Voting Rights
Act of 1965.*

mediation of racial disputes, and authorized the Attorney General to bring
enforcement suits in public accommodation and school segregation violations.

To increase voting rights, seen as a primary means to a better life, civil
rights leaders resorted to peaceful marches, sit-ins at local courthouses, and
demonstrations, which were often beset by violent attacks, mass arrests, and
murders. President Johnson urged passage of what became known as the
Voting Rights Act of 1965, which suspended literacy and other voting tests
that fostered discrimination, empowered federal examiners to order registration, required federal approval before new state or local voting laws could
take effect, and enabled the Attorney General to challenge state and local
poll taxes. The force of the 1965 Act was soon felt. In the 1968 presidential
election, the proportion of qualified Southern blacks who voted was higher
than anywhere else in the country.

Thanks to the civil rights movement, the number of black state representatives and senators has strikingly increased, and blacks have been elected
to local offices in the North and South, including the mayoralties of major
cities—Cleveland, Newark, and Gary, Indiana. Many Southern restaurants,
hotels, motels, hospitals, and theatres have opened their doors, although this
is a firmer pattern in large cities than in smaller towns. Substantial rises have

occurred in black white collar employment and in technical jobs for skilled black workers; highly qualified blacks have won access to major positions in business, education, and government. The generally depressed economic situation of blacks was attacked by poverty program projects such as Head Start, VISTA, and the Job Corps. But these gains seemed, at best, only slight to the National Advisory Commission on Civil Disorders (Kerner Commission), which warned in 1968 that "our nation is moving toward two societies, one black, one white—separate and unequal." [46]

Richard Nixon was elected without black support, and his stance toward the civil rights movement has displeased its leaders. In 1970, Bishop Stephen G. Spottswood, NAACP chairman, complained "that the national administration has made it a matter of calculated policy to work against the needs and aspirations of the largest minority of its citizens." [47] The administration's exaltation of law and order, its selection of Supreme Court nominees with blemished records on civil rights, and its retreat from the national commitment to abolish the dual school system, have dismayed civil rights leaders. Even when the Supreme Court upset the administration's dallying policies in 1969 and ordered an end to school segregation, root and branch, at once, Nixon declared he would do no more than the existing law required and underscored his preference for the neighborhood school over school busing. Toward housing policy, Nixon has also been reserved, pledging enforcement of existing prohibitions against discrimination but rejecting federal leverage to force local communities to accept low- and moderate-income housing. Access to such housing in the suburbs is viewed by civil rights groups as vital if growing concentrations of blacks in inner cities are to be reduced. In these several postures, Nixon appears unwilling to pursue civil rights goals at the sacrifice of his standing with the largely white, largely suburban, and partly Southern constituency that elected him. [48]

Fortunately, that constituency tolerates greater exertion in the economic sector. Nixon has avowed commitment to "black capitalism," although critics disparage the effort actually extended. He has moved to reform the welfare system in order to add to poor families' income and halt the break-up of black families. To foster "equal job opportunities," the Nixon administration has offered the "Philadelphia Plan," which submits guidelines for hiring minority construction workers on federally assisted projects. In these cases black leaders lament the modesty rather than the direction of the administration's efforts.

As the seventies begin, the black rights movement faces a crisis of strategy. The crisis is fired by growing disillusionment and frustration over the slowness of change, despite the laws, the programs, and the promises. For all their gains, blacks have been losing ground to whites in their high unemployment and school drop-out rates and their consequent vulnerability to drugs and

[46] *Report of the National Advisory Commission on Civil Disorders* (New York: Bantam Books, 1968), 1.
[47] *New York Times,* June 30, 1970.
[48] *New York Times,* May 21 and June 12, 1971.

crime. And as the price of integration, white society persists in demanding the subordination of black culture.

Of the available choices for blacks, there remains the now traditional strategy of racial integration incorporated in the *Brown* case and the Kerner Commission's *Report on Civil Disorders* and symbolized by the mayoralty of Kenneth A. Gibson of Newark. Gibson, elected with black and white support, maintains that his city, in desperate straits now, can survive only if racial harmony replaces the racial divisions that have exploded into rioting.

A second strategy is represented by Gibson's local rival, the author Le Roi Jones (Imanu Amiri Baraka), who is publicly committed to driving whites from positions of authority and has taken giant steps in his purpose by gaining power in Newark governmental agencies. Also of this strategic school is Roy C. Innis, national director of CORE (Congress of Racial Equality). Innis feels that the black thrust should be not toward racial integration, but toward black control of the "instruments of power—the schools, the police and the hospitals" in their communities. Like Innis, many black leaders now of this view had earlier advocated integration.[49]

The strategy most insistently set forth at 1970 conferences of black leaders was "black nationalism" and "Pan Africanism," which beholds America as two nations, one black, one white. Only a nation controlled by black people, the leaders contended, can end discrimination in housing, bring fair employment, more black teachers and schools, greater medical aid, more blacks on television. Black nationalism rejects a present order "structured with blacks at the bottom," with 35 to 50 percent of young blacks unemployed and roaming the streets, potential victims of the drug traffic. They reject a system in which blacks generally are highly vulnerable to the economic recession of the seventies. Blacks, therefore, must "revolutionize America so that politics will be put in command of economics." The path to black nationalism is community control and the substitution of socialism for capitalism; capitalism is viewed as exploitative of blacks and socialism as best suitable for blacks "who are concerned about the total humanity of this world." Black spokesmen differ in their concepts of violence and its appropriateness, and whether and how empathic whites should be involved in the black struggle.[50]

Other rights movements

The 1960s and 70s have been rich with other movements to gain rights for groups that have long suffered deprivation. The women's liberation movement is a massive effort of a broad variety of feminist groups and thought to overturn the structure of male-dominated society. After passing through a con-

[49] *New York Times,* September 9, 1970 and June 19, 1971.
[50] *New York Times,* September 9, 1970; Floyd B. Barbour, ed., *The Black Seventies* (Boston: Peter Sargent Publisher, 1970), 22–43, 300.

*Jean Westwood and Anne Armstrong,
top women in the major parties.*

sciousness-raising phase, the movement has turned to politics to promote such high priority issues as equal pay for equal work, day-care centers, and repeal of abortion laws. A vast feminist lobbying effort pushed an Equal Rights Amendment through Congress and on to adoption by many states. In the 1972 election year, women made impressive gains in the major parties. Forty percent of the Democratic delegates were women and 35 percent of the Republican. For the first time, the Democrats chose a chairwoman, Jean Westwood of Utah (who resigned in December after McGovern's decisive defeat). The Republicans elected a co-chairwoman, Anne Armstrong of Texas (who resigned to take a position in the Nixon administration). The issue that most unites the women's liberation movement is the repeal of all abortion laws, based on the tenet that a woman has the right to control her own body. Many feminists content that there should be an end to governmental interference in all reproductive and sexual matters.[51]

Puerto Ricans and Mexican-Americans (Chicanos) have also been moving to improve their rights, whose easy violation has been attributed by

[51] Dierdre Carmody, "Feminists Are Shifting Emphasis from Persons to Politics," *New York Times,* August 22, 1972.

Congressman Herman Badillo (D., N.Y.) to "the continuous deterioration of conditions in which the Spanish-speaking live and the apathy shown to their problems by governmental institutions." The La Raza Unida party of Mexican-Americans and Puerto Ricans is pledged to work for a Chicano political movement independent of the major parties. The Chicano party endorsed neither McGovern nor Nixon in 1972, and in other elections, such as the governorship of Colorado, it advanced its own candidates. "We don't need the red necks," said Chicano leader Albert Gurule. "We must cut the umbilical cord from the gringo." The La Raza party has had to struggle with differences of perspective and interest that divide the small, largely rural Chicano communities from the urban Chicano slums. As a bond, and to build identity, the Chicanos are stressing their ties with the culture of ancient Mexico.[52]

"Red power" is the slogan of growing numbers of American Indians intent on securing greater self-determination, a policy President Nixon has advocated. Much of the Indians' attention has centered on the Bureau of Indian Affairs of the Interior Department; the bureaucracy there has been accused of subverting the self-determination effort. Gradually, key Bureau posts have been filled with officials who are sympathetic to the President's view. The reformist Indians are seeking more autonomy on the reservations so that they can develop their own business enterprises and skills and other resources that might procure at least the beginnings of democracy for them.[53]

Proposals

What ought to be done to make freedom more vigorous and secure in the 1970s in a society favored with an admirable charter, the Bill of Rights, but which of necessity maintains a network of authority sometimes harmful to freedom?

1. The Bill of Rights should be extended to include basic positive freedoms. Surely among these are the right to a minimum income, the right to work, to education, to health care. To reject these freedoms is to confess that society is narrow, callous, and still the captive of social Darwinism. "Let the unemployed man lie starving," Edward Sparer reminds us, "let the sick woman die because an affluent society won't provide her with minimal medical treatment, and you have killed off the speaker, the writer and the worshipper. You have preserved those rights only for the comfortable and the affluent. The reason we need a constitution is to protect the rights of the weak, the powerless and the dispossessed." [54]

2. As for the television networks and their voracious profit-making at the expense of quality and public affairs programming in which democracy has a stake, we might heed the counsel of former FCC chairman Newton Minow

[52] *New York Times,* November 29, 1971.
[53] *New York Times,* September 22, 1971.
[54] In O'Neil, 287.

that federal licensing be extended to the networks. Experience amply suggests that federal regulation through licensing can counterweigh advertisers' pressures for mass appeal, low-level fare. But a danger lurks in the arrangement, particularly in an era when government has been warring with the media; federal licensing may be used to inhibit the expression of views that run counter to those that government cherishes.

3. Senator Sam J. Ervin's subcommittee on constitutional rights has been studying government's rapidly increasing collections of information, their injustices to the citizen, and the chilling effect the consciousness of being watched can have on political participation, especially dissent. Legislative proposals are pending that would give the citizen the right to know what the government knows about him and that would subject collection of information to controls. Another proposal would require each government agency having a file on a citizen to apprise him of it, permit him to see it, make factual corrections, and rebut derogatory information. Other proposals would restrict the kinds of information collected, establish standards for accuracy, and apply a "forgiveness principle"—expunging information after it has served its immediate purpose or becomes irrelevant or outdated. Pending legislation, however, makes exemptions for pretrial investigations and for national security, which critics lament is already too big a shelter for unjustifiable invasions of privacy.[55]

4. For the poor, the chief victims of administrative indifference to rights, full-time lawyers who specialize in problems of poverty are needed in the courts and legislatures and before administrative agencies. An attractive model is the neighborhood law office that is part of, or well integrated with, a general community service program, enabling its attorneys to work closely with social workers and other administrators. The office should reach out for clients who are often ignorant of the law and regard it as an enemy. The poor might be helped by the creation of a new class of legal technicians—subprofessionals or "para-lawyers"—conversant with proverty's routine and standardized problems and working under lawyers' supervision.[56]

5. If we subscribe to the proposition that an integrated society is more appropriate for democracy than a dual society, one white and one black, the political and social systems will need to magnify their commitment to that society enormously. Martin Luther King's observation that $300,000 is spent to kill one Viet Cong compared with $50 to help each American poor person still rings true. Many call for a "freedom budget" of perhaps $20 billion a year for the next decade to transform the ghettos and to enhance the quality of the lives of their people, leading to their full-fledged participation in society.

Money and programs are futile without large-scale cross-institutional efforts to conquer prejudice, the most formidable barrier to integration. Involved is the arduous, obstacle-laden task of inducing schools to educate for racial equality, business practices to be nondiscriminatory, churches to re-

[55] *New York Times,* March 22, 1971.
[56] Dorsen, 303–07.

formulate doctrines in order to teach more emphatically that prejudice is a sin. Sometime ago the psychologist Gordon W. Allport posed the essential criteria for eliminating prejudice and crossing the threshold to genuine integration: (1) the groups in contact possess equal status; (2) they seek common goals; (3) they are cooperatively dependent on each other; and (4) they interact with the positive support of authority.[57] But even if these difficult steps are taken, prejudice may persist within us. As Anatole France described one of the characters of his novels: "He flattered himself on being a man without any prejudices; and this pretension itself is a very great prejudice." [58]

Suggested Reading

Aron, Raymond, *An Essay on Freedom* (World, 1970). An introductory essay on freedom and its underpinnings in a pluralist society. Aron, a French political philosopher, also discusses forces that are inimical to freedom.

Brant, Irving, *The Bill of Rights: Its Origins and Meaning* (Bobbs-Merrill, 1965). A useful account of the background of the Bill of Rights and its subsequent interpretation in key Supreme Court decisions. Also analyzes questions concerning civil liberties and the behavior of extremists.

Dorsen, Norman, *Frontiers of Civil Liberties* (Pantheon, 1968). A discussion of the test case technique and the civil liberties lawyer, and their contributions to civil liberties. Deals with issues concerning draft resisters, demonstrations, and the poor.

Glock, Charles Y., and Siegleman, Ellen, eds., *Prejudice U.S.A.* * (Praeger, 1969). A valuable compilation of readings that focus on prejudice against blacks and efforts to cope with the problem. Includes discussions of the black civil rights movement, the impact of the communications media, and ways of reducing prejudice.

Konvitz, Milton, *Expanding Liberties* (Viking, 1966). A useful examination of court decisions on major contemporary civil rights issues. Explores critically the implications of the court holdings.

Krieghbaum, Hillier, *Pressures on the Press* (Crowell, 1972). The best general compendium on the state of the media, with data and analysis on monopolistic trends, newspaper chains, government press agents, broadcasting economics, and corporate power. Offers proposals for dealing with the problems involved and their threat to civil liberties.

Lewis, Anthony, *Portrait of a Decade: The Second American Revolution* * (Random House, 1964). A readable examination of the black civil rights movement of the 1950s and 60s—its leaders, strategies, and major episodes, and the role of the courts, Congress, and the Presidency.

O'Neil, Robert M., *The Price of Dependency: Civil Liberties in the Welfare State* (Dutton, 1970). An analysis of how the civil liberties of some of those seeking government benefits are impaired, including students, welfare recipients, tenants of public housing, and civil servants.

Pfeffer, Leo, *Church, State and Freedom* (Beacon Press, 1967). An excellent analysis of the relationship of religion to the constitutional system. The question of public aid

[57] Charles Y. Glock and Ellen Siegelman, eds., *Prejudice U.S.A.* (New York: Praeger, 1969), 188–89; Gordon W. Allport, *The Nature of Prejudice* (New York: Doubleday, 1958), passim.

[58] *The Crime of Sylvestre Bonnard,* Part II, Chapter 4.

to parochial schools is explored in terms of public policies and court doctrines, as are questions involving conscientious objectors, faith healers, and others with civil liberties issues deriving from religion.

Rucker, Bryce W., *The First Freedom* * (Southern Illinois University Press, 1968). A definitive, very readable survey of the mass media—their economics, concentrated power, operating practices, and the dangers for civil liberties. Offers remedial proposals.

Stouffer, Samuel A., *Communism, Conformity, and Civil Liberties* * (Wiley, 1967). An examination of which groups in the community react to anticommunist excesses. Compares the responses of leaders and rank and file, young and old, various social classes, and other categories.

Tapp, June L., and Krinsky, Fred, *Ambivalent America: A Psychological Dialogue* * (Glencoe Press, 1971). An imaginative presentation, drawing on various writers, of the continuing conflict between the "authoritarian" and the "democrat" in American culture and the political system.

Westin, Alan F., *Privacy and Freedom* (Atheneum, 1967). Discusses the effect on privacy and freedom of improved electronic eavesdropping devices. Examines practical difficulties facing the courts and offers useful proposals.

* Available in paperback edition

13

diversity
in unity:
the states
and federalism

When Paul Powell, Secretary of State of Illinois and for thirty-six years a public servant, died in 1970, his body lay on the same catafalque that once held Lincoln. Hundreds of officeholders crowded in the capitol's crepe-draped rotunda to pay him honor, and high officials declared in tribute that there had passed "a man of deep compassion who truly loved people," "a natural leader who never lost the common touch." Subsequently, the eulogies faltered when huge amounts of cash stuffed into shoe boxes, envelopes, and a bowling bag were discovered in Powell's hotel suite and office safe. His estate was estimated to be worth nearly $3 million, even though his highest annual salary had been $30,000 as Secretary of State.

Conjectures as to the source of this remarkable hoard focused on lobbyists, especially racetrack, trucking, banking, and insurance lobbyists, on businessmen eager for lucrative state contracts, and even on soda dispenser concessions in the capitol. As a legislator, Powell tirelessly helped the horse racing tracks by keeping their state taxes low; he was rewarded with thousands of shares of stock, purchased at ten cents a share and valued at four dollars in his estate. During his career, Powell was accused of receiving huge amounts of money from trucking companies anxious to avoid weight regulations. Steady sources of income were the kickbacks or contributions from patronage employees and the "testimonial dinners" that the Secretary of State threw for himself with lobbyists and contractors as faithful and generous participants. "I can smell the meat a-cookin'," he would shout to party workers near election time, stirring visions of juicy spoils, and adding "My friends eat at the first table" and "If you can't get a meal, take a sandwich." Most of Powell's fortune was left to the Johnson County Historical Society in his native Vienna, Illinois, to preserve his home as a museum and shrine.[1]

[1] *New York Times,* January 15, 1971.

The shame
of the states

Paul Powell's career was not a bizarre aberration, but a product of the skilled practice of a brand of politics prevailing in many states. Generally, political science research agrees that state lobbying, characterized by relaxed ethics, highhanded methods, and plush entertainment, is "dirtier" than national lobbying. Robert Engler's studies disclose that in the state capitals the oil industry uses crude lobbying practices that would be unthinkable in Congress, and Lester Milbrath found more bribery in the states.[2] Some industries burrow deep into those sectors of state government that have the most to do with their affairs. In New York State, an assemblyman beholding the banks' encroachment in the state Banking Department cried, "As far as the public is concerned, we could get along without the Banking Department and just let Chase Manhattan take over its functions."[3] But the worst feature of lobby-ridden state politics is its unrepresentativeness. The less organized and the less well-off—the slum dweller, the consumer, the aged, the young—have a decidedly minor role in lobbying

The distortions of representation are invited by the low visibility of state politics. The average citizen is not as concerned about the affairs of his state as of his city or nation (see table). Less immediate than the city and less glamorous than the country, the states are consigned to a limbo of indifference. M. Kent Jennings and Harmon Zeigler developed cognitive maps indicating those aspects of politics more salient to the individual than others. Their study found that interest in state politics among those with less education is slight to begin with. But the higher a person's formal education, the less interest he evinces in state politics for the greater is his concern with broader environments. Nor does it seem to matter if a state is politically strong and active—the people of states with larger electoral turnouts and powerful governors are no more likely to follow state affairs than people living in states of opposite tendencies.[4]

Of all the levels of government, the states today appear least relevant to our time, given excessively to drift and narrowness of view and presenting a jungle of obstructions to urgent social needs. The failure of state governments to modernize—70 percent of the detail-laden state constitutions were written in the nineteenth century—paralyzes their executives, produces legislatures little interested in critical social problems, and sustains political parties barely capable of advancing beyond patronage and plunder.

[2] Robert Engler, *The Politics of Oil* (New York: Macmillan, 1961); Lester Milbrath, *The Washington Lobbyists* (Chicago: Rand McNally, 1963). See also Herbert Jacob and Kenneth Vines, eds., *Politics in the American States* (Boston: Little, Brown, 1965), 103–04.

[3] *New York Times,* March 12, 1971.

[4] M. Kent Jennings and Harmon Zeigler, "The Salience of American State Politics," *American Political Science Review,* LXIV (June 1970), 523–35.

Salience of governmental affairs at four levels[1]

Level of governmental affairs	Rank of how closely followed			
	First	Second	Third	Fourth
International	20%	16%	22%	42%
National	32	31	26	10
State	17	33	27	22
Local	30	20	25	25
	99%[2]	100%	100%	99%[2]
	N=983	983	983	983

[1] Data drawn from the University of Michigan Survey Research Center's 1966 election study, utilizing a national sample of the adult population.
[2] Total percentages do not equal 100% due to rounding.
Source: M. Kent Jennings and Harmon Zeigler, "The Salience of American State Politics," *The American Political Science Review,* LXIV (June 1970), p. 525, Table 1.

The sorriest victims of the states' antediluvian ways are the big cities. The people in need who are concentrated there are turning increasingly to Congress, the Supreme Court, and the federal administration, where they hope to win greater attention and sympathy. Data on the states' performance bear them out. Although state taxes and expenditures have increased more rapidly than federal, the states have shown a far more marked disposition to expand their normal services than to respond to new dimensions of urban and metropolitan problems. Indicative of the imbalance is the pattern of state participation in federal grant-in-aid programs. In 1970, thirty-seven states were participating financially in the federal airport construction program, and twenty in building local sewage treatment facilities. In contrast, only eleven states were assisting financially in urban renewal, ten in urban mass transportation, and four in local hospital and medical facilities construction.[5]

The states haven't always been laggers. Traditionally, the states have been laboratories of democracy, pioneering in many areas of public policy—the direct primary, the initiative and referendum, female suffrage, banking, railroad and public utility regulation, unemployment compensation, old age pensions, and factory inspection. For decades, the states have carried out well such traditional functions as education, highways, general health, prisons and training centers for juvenile offenders, and a host of regulatory functions that affect us when we hunt, fish, drive a car, marry, practice law or medicine, or enter callings for which we must have a license.

Above all, the states are distinctive political and cultural entities. In a country of insistent centralizing forces, the rights of the states impose a healthy

[5] The American Assembly (Alan K. Campbell, ed.), *The States and the Urban Crisis* (Englewood Cliffs, N.J.: Prentice-Hall, 1970).

decentralizing influence. While generally supportive of the needs of national unity, the states respond to the citizen's interest in maintaining his individuality expressed in the things that count most in his daily life—his vocation, family, recreation, his regional and local culture, for which the states provide protection and services. For all their blemishes, states perform other indispensable democratic functions: they recruit political participants and train political leaders, and they provide for domestic programs to such an extent that their combined expenditure exceeds that of any other level of government.

The state legislature

In structure and process, the state legislatures bear resemblances to Congress. Except for Nebraska's unicameral legislature, the states have two-house legislatures, one based principally on area, such as counties, and the other on population. Like Congress, state legislative membership is subject to requirements of age and citizenship, plus other qualifications not expected of national legislators, such as residing in the state a certain length of time. State bodies are smaller than Congress, but they vary in size, from 17 in Delaware's and Nevada's upper house to 67 in Minnesota; from Delaware's 35 in the lower house to New Hampshire's 400. Terms of office are also uneven, with a general pattern of two years in the lower house and four in the senate. Legislative leaders—the Speaker and the senate Majority Leader—are often more powerful than their counterparts in Congress. Most state legislatures have strong committee systems similar to, and often exceeding in power, that of Congress.

Pay and allowances, once low, are improving, and sessions limited by agrarian tradition to an interval from after Christmas to spring planting time, every other year, are tending to annual and longer sessions. Generally, the pattern of lawmaking resembles that of Congress respecting initiation of bills, committee hearings, floor debate, and voting, although the states must cope far more with trivial, usually noncontroversial, bills. As in Congress, a bill's fate depends most on the committee to which it is assigned. If state legislatures have so many resemblances to Congress, why do they evoke the most sweeping lamentations heard about any American political institution?

Rivalry and factionalism. One of their worst offenses is that the legislatures often fail to provide a balanced representation of sectional divisions and rivalries within their borders, leaving the losers in the battles for public policies feeling deprived and isolated and sometimes engendering separatist tendencies. After the battering that New York City's fiscal proposals suffered in 1971 from the legislature dominated by "upstaters," Mayor John V. Lindsay called for the conversion of the city into the fifty-first state. The endless struggle between great metropolitan centers and upstate and downstate is a common pattern of state politics. Like New York City, Los Angeles, Omaha,

Detroit, Cleveland, Philadelphia, and Boston are all aggrieved by being constantly shortchanged by the state legislature; they claim to yield far more to the state in tax revenues than the value of policies they receive in return.

Opposing geographic regions assume other forms. Water-rich northern California is at constant loggerheads with water-poor southern California because of consequent differences over public policies. East Texas, Southside Virginia, and the anthracite region of Pennsylvania are intrastate regions that have each developed superior cohesion and assert political influence well beyond economic or popular strength. In recent decades, the older urban-rural and intrasectional rivalries have been complicated by the rapid emergence of a new dimension, the suburb. How the cities lose out in the urban-suburban contest is discussed later in the chapter.

State legislatures may be deterred from making broad attacks on major social problems by their tendency toward factionalism. Even states with strong political parties may succumb to intraparty factional turmoil and paralysis. A divided government, where each major party controls a legislative house or the legislative branch is dominated by one party and the governorship by the other, may also prevent legislatures from enacting bold assertive policy.

The life of the state legislator. The state legislatures are pushed into a posture of underachievement and indifference to social problems by attitudes of the members that are rooted in the nature of the legislature itself. Its pay, appointments, and life style are hardly inspiring or ennobling. The typical legislator must either leave his family at home or rent a place for them at the capital for the session, and he must make continual junkets back home to attend political party and community functions. Much of his time in the capital must be passed in hotel bars where most business is done, even though these may not be his preferred habitat. The low average pay of the legislator will barely meet his living expenses in the capital. Since few people can afford to remain away from their regular employment for three months every year, or even every other year, the quality of state legislators suffers.

The distasteful legislative life leads to a high turnover. In most states between one-third and two-thirds of the legislators are serving their first term. Those who serve only one or two terms are generally not defeated but retire voluntarily, complaining typically: "Being in the legislature has hurt my law practice and cost me money," "It is a nervous life," "too uncertain and hazardous." [6] The result is an incongruous situation for democracy. The voter is deprived of opportunity to pass judgment at the polls on the incumbent legislator's performance, and must rely on platforms and campaign promises to choose between candidates. Democracy cannot thrive if its offices are not prizes eagerly sought, but are instead burdens to be cast off at the first opportunity.

The tattered dimensions of legislative life are woven into the legislators' perceptions of their role. From interviews with Connecticut legislators, James

[6] In Jacob and Vines, 170–71.

David Barber developed a set of role types. Many legislators were classified as Spectators, who attended sessions regularly, but seldom introduced bills or participated in debate, found legislative service "diverting," had a low opinion of themselves as legislators and little interest in leadership positions. Less likely than other types to have more than a high school education and thus with fewer prospects, they were more willing to run for reelection. The Advertisers, another role type, valued legislative life for making contacts and publicizing their business. Most were lawyers, and the wide variety of other occupations represented tended toward advisory or sales relationships with clients and customers. After one or two terms, the Advertiser hoped to amass enough publicity to advance his occupational career significantly.

Another type, the Reluctant, had been dragged from retirement and a prestigious position in a rural community. Generally indifferent to political advancement, he was disinclined to leadership positions and important committee posts and deemed himself less effective than the average legislator. The only type conceivably sparked by interest in social or urban problems was the Lawmaker, who concentrated on the serious work of the legislature, was eager for innovative laws, and delighted in getting programs established. Young, well-educated, and a hard campaigner, he aspired to important roles in the legislature and meant to build for himself a strong political future.[7]

State parties:
uncertain instruments
for policy

State parties show attractive potential as responsible constructive organs of public policy. Intertwined with national parties and serving as sources of nominations and campaigns for national office, state parties might be expected to derive broader perspectives from their enlarged environment, including appreciation of urban problems. State parties can also choose among widely different styles of organization, leadership, and campaigning, ranging from the sedate hustings of Vermont to the roaring embroilments of Texas. Unfortunately, the reputations of state parties fall far short of their hopeful auguries. Instead, they rival the urban organizations in perpetrating two great blemishes of American democracy—corruption and mediocrity.

Party machines. A recurrent form of the state party is the political machine, whose leaders are innocent of both ideas and ideals. The Byrd organization of Virginia developed by the late Senator Harry F. Byrd, which is now in eclipse but not without capacity to revive, was the most powerful of machines. Identifying itself with Virginia's history and stirring Virginians' pride in their state, it supplied genteel leaders and candidates, employed ramrod discipline

---

[7] James David Barber, *The Lawmakers: Recruitment and Adaptation to Legislative Life* (New Haven: Yale University Press, 1965).

and ultimately race prejudice to maintain its power, and administered a philosophy of conservative individualism, which kept social expenditure in such tight rein that Virginia enjoyed treasury surpluses while other states, responding to citizen needs, ran up deficits.

Old-style machines persist in Massachusetts, New York, New Jersey, Pennsylvania, Ohio, and Arizona. Patronage is their principal currency, and kickbacks from government workers and contractors and finagled elections are their stock in trade. The machine unifies politicians bent on securing control of the public treasury; in exchange they render such public services as education and highways and protection of economic groups. They are inspired not by social problems and policy, but by personal profit extracted from politics through means foul and fair. When an upstate Pennsylvania machine politician learned that the opposition was crying, "Give the Court House Back to the People," he retorted, "Let the people build their own court house. This one is ours, and we mean to hold onto it!" [8]

Party patterns. States vary in how the parties fit into the state. At one extreme are the Southern states, which in state politics tend to be dominated by a single party, traditionally the Democratic. At the other extreme are highly competitive two-party states where one party enjoys control over at least one house of the legislature and alternating control over the other house and the executive.

The one-party system is by no means a way to unbroken unanimity. Frequently there are turbulent primary contests for its nominations. On the face of things, the voter is then given a choice, but, unfortunately, this choice may be limited to personalities and the voter may have little knowledge of what the candidates stand for. In two-party contests, the voter is more aware of the general philosophy, viewpoint, and performance of a party reflected in the individual candidate. One-party systems are characterized by factionalism, so that factional alliances supersede party politics in the legislature. Factions cluster around issues, regions, and personalities, including flamboyant types like Huey Long in Louisiana and Herman Talmadge in Georgia. Factions may be long enduring, such as the Long and anti-Long alignments and the Byrd machine and its opponents in Virginia, but a frequent pattern is multifactionalism: candidates for major office form their own transient coalitions, which regroup as new candidates appear in later contests.

In two-party systems, the parties are certain to play some role in the legislature, although their significance varies among the states. Two-party politics often presents a problem of appearance versus reality. Even where two parties exist in a state, the real competition may still be between factions rather than parties. At the close of the 1960s, only about one-fourth of the states had genuine two-party competition, and in less than two-thirds of them

---

[8] In James Reichley, *States in Crisis: Politics in Ten American States* (Chapel Hill: University of North Carolina Press, 1964), 243.

did the second party have any real chance of soon winning the governorship or the legislature.[9] The seventies, however, are bringing trends toward additional competitive two-party systems. Republicans are making inroads into the solid Democratic states of the South and Southwest: Virginia, Louisiana, Texas, North Carolina, and Florida have witnessed a growth of Republican strength. And California, long a Republican state, has become competitive. Mobility, urbanization, and rising educational levels should provide sophisticated voters in coming decades who are more generous to social need, less tolerant of political exploiters, and capable of penetrating the sham of state politics.

Malcolm Jewell suggests that responsible parties are the best available, although imperfect, means to a more responsible legislature, and one therefore more responsive to urban problems. The ideal he proposes would be two parties reasonably competitive in the state generally, as well as in many legislative districts; each would be capable of winning full control of the government and each would be identified with defined programs and policies, affording the voter real choice. Choosing between gubernatorial and legislative candidates, the voter can advance at least a broadly outlined program.[10]

The complexities lurking beneath the surface of this ideal are suggested by Thomas Flinn's study of party responsibility in the states. He found that officeholders will vary in how they respond to their party. Those beset by the insecurity of a narrow victory are less likely to be loyal to party positions than those who win by wide margins. Party influence on legislators increases with district size and complexity and length of term, but party support is less forthcoming from legislators of socially homogeneous districts. In addition, is was found that a state does not have to have an intensive party organization and leadership pressures on legislators in order to have party cohesion, as in Connecticut and New York. In states with weak, divided party organization—Minnesota and Ohio, for example—cohesion is also impressive.[11]

Interest groups
in state politics

From the standpoint of democratic ideals, the state legislatures are all too easily dominated by interest groups, powerful and propertied and heedless of the needs of the underrepresented and the unorganized. Testimony comes from every side. Scarcely had Luther Hodges been elected governor of North Carolina in 1954 when a lobbyist of twenty years' experience approached him and said, "Let's you and I take a bottle of Scotch and go up to my room

[9] Charles R. Adrian, *State and Local Governments,* 2nd ed. (New York: McGraw-Hill, 1967), 158.
[10] Malcolm E. Jewell, *The State Legislature: Politics and Practice* (New York: Random House, 1962), 129.
[11] Thomas Flinn, "Party Responsibility in the States," *American Political Science Review,* LVIII (March 1961), 60–71.

and set up your senate committees." [12] Following the close of the New York legislature's 1971 session, Betty Furness, the state's first consumer affairs adviser, resigned; she charged that the legislature was more interested in protecting industry than the consumer ("Industry doesn't advise the legislature, it pretty well controls it"). Referring to her unit-pricing bill, Miss Furness added, "I really felt skunked on that. I don't want the food industry writing my bills. I also had three prescription drug [pricing] bills. . . . I didn't expect to lose them all." [13]

The specific interest groups with power vary from state to state. Gas and oil companies are powerful in Texas, iron and sugar interests in Colorado, truckers and loan sharks in Missouri. In New York, the education lobby rivals the juggernaut strength of the huge insurance companies. But the relative strengths of general categories of interest groups are similar in the states. In a study of legislators' perceptions of salient interest groups in California, Ohio, New Jersey, and Tennessee, John Wahlke found that business interests ranked first in all four states. Ranking second in general salience in three states was education, which tied for third in the fourth state. Labor interests ranked third or tied for it in all four states.[14] Surprising was the relatively low rank of agriculture in salience.

Wahlke found that the state's political culture is a significant factor in distinguishing its mode and style of pressure politics. Norms and expectations peculiar to each state system are widely transmitted and circulated among the population; consequently, legislators have acquired potential responses appropriate for their legislature and state political system even before they take office.

Presumably democracy is better served if interests are diversified, competitive, and representative. Is this an obtainable ideal? New interests do appear frequently. And as some states have become industrialized, interest group competition has been enhanced by the rise of organized labor. Labor is especially influential in legislative delegations from the more sizable cities. The relationship between labor and the Democratic party is apt to be close in states passing from a rural or business-dominated society to a more complex political system. In such advanced industrial societies as Massachusetts and New York, labor also reaches *de facto* understandings with Republicans in bargaining and negotiating in the legislative arena. Unfortunately, labor's usefulness for the resolution of urban problems seems definitely limited. Although interested in public services and equitable tax structures, labor has demonstrated little desire for broad innovative community programs. Ideologically, labor prefers to cooperate with other groups in preserving and improving existing community organizations.

---

[12] Luther H. Hodges, *Businessman in the State House* (Chapel Hill: University of North Carolina Press, 1962), 20.

[13] *New York Times,* July 13, 1971.

[14] John C. Wahlke, et al., *The Legislative System: Explorations in Legislative Behavior* (New York: Wiley, 1962), 314.

Other interest groups have a broader vision of public problems. Among those the legislator commonly encounters are the League of Women Voters, the Parent-Teacher Association, and state, city, and county governmental agencies and personnel. School teachers are usually well organized and persistent in presenting their demands. Other groups putting pressure on legislators are the press, those on welfare, and the unemployed. Sometimes reorientations on the part of certain groups will serve the interests of the traditionally unrepresented. Some business lobbies, for instance, have come to appreciate that the states can play a constructive role in cooling urban racial tensions, and interests like the housing industry have an immediate financial stake in state aid to the cities.

The governor

"The governor is not the executive; he is but a single piece of the executive," Woodrow Wilson, who later became governor of New Jersey, once complained.[15] What troubled Wilson was the practice for many state officers— the Attorney General, the Controller, the Secretary of State—to be popularly elected, and for boards and commissions not to be subject to the governor's direction, as logic would suggest, but to report to the legislature. The governor is further handicapped in some states by a short term of two years and by ineligibility for reelection. Even today, Wilson's complaint applies to a majority of states. Weakened or dispersed executive power favors the highly organized groups and neglects groups that struggle in the bog of urban problems.

Fortunately, in our own and Wilson's time, the governor is more than an executive. He symbolizes the state as a social and political entity; he speaks for all the people, whether of slum or suburb; and his concerns embrace both business prosperity and rural poverty. More than any other of the state's political personalities, he is identified with the "general public good." Responsibility for initiating major state-wide programs falls on him, and few important undertakings can advance without his leadership.

Many of the roles the governor performs resemble the President's, done on the smaller scale of state politics. Like the President, the governor is a popular leader, aided by a press secretary or public relations counselor who nurtures a favorable image and seeks to influence the timing and substance of relevant news stories. On major issues, the governor can "go to the people" via the media, and many governors have regular, often weekly, press conferences. In 1971, Governor John J. Gilligan of Ohio went to the people on a tax issue. Ohio's taxes, expressed as a percentage of personal income, were lower than any other state's except those of New Hampshire, and Ohio spent less on public services on a per capita basis than the five poorest states. Gilligan proposed to expand both taxes and services. To win public support

[15] In Adrian, 216.

for his bold program, Gilligan distributed to television stations a series of short documentaries on the state's problems. He was forced to this recourse when the vice chairman of the legislative Finance Committee growled that his group would "cut that program up so badly that even the Gilligan funeral homes [the governor's family business] won't be able to handle it." [16]

In many states the governor is the most powerful single force in legislation. Governor Huey Long of Louisiana personally lobbied on the floor of the legislature for his bills, and one Kentucky governor sat beside the presiding officer during critical roll calls. Governors or their aides have been known to watch the vote from the balcony. More commonly, the legislator is simply called into the governor's office and asked to support a bill. The governor speaks with the force behind him of patronage, contracts, and public works construction. Many a legislator would consider a new highway in his district as a more than fair exchange for his vote on a particular issue.

In his more formal efforts, the governor presents his program in an annual or biennial message comparable to the President's on the state of the union, followed by special messages. His budget also conveys his program. The governors in half the states can call the legislature into special session. In this way he can specify the matters to be considered, which increases his influence on the legislative agenda. Most governors gain leverage by being able to veto items in a bill, although legislators may blunt the item veto by combining objectionable and unobjectionable items in the same clause. In several states, the governor has an "amendatory" veto by which he specifies the changes that would make the bill acceptable.

For all their influence, most governors are inadequately endowed to face the formidable legislative power structure. In most state legislatures, the speaker of the house, the presiding officer of the senate, and the chairmen of the principal standing committees enjoy enormous power, which flourishes with the neglect of rules, formal and informal, affecting legislative life; leaders arbitrarily select committee slates and chairmen and make other dispensations that enhance their influence on the individual member. The leaders' actions are given little coverage in published official records and the press, and this obscurity enlarges their power to manipulate against the governor. Many a governor fights back as party leader. Party competitiveness in states with genuine two-party systems fosters a discipline that the governor can exploit. In one-party states, the governor's strength depends on the factions he manages to attract and on his native political skills.

A sizable list of governors have performed on the heroic scale. New York's strong, achieving governors include the Roosevelts (T. R. and F. D. R.), Charles Evans Hughes, Alfred E. Smith, Herbert Lehman, Thomas E. Dewey, and Nelson Rockefeller. In California, Hiram Johnson, after gaining the governorship in 1911 with the slogan, "Kick the corporations out of politics," pushed through legislation to tame what then numbered among the mightiest corporations, the railroads. During his term, 1959–66, Edmund G.

[16] *New York Times,* March 17, 1971.

"Pat" Brown won from the California legislature increases in personal income, business, and luxury taxes that enabled him to expand the state's services. He also established a Fair Employment Practices Commission and an Office of Consumer Counsel.

Many governors, although still a minority, have had their powers strengthened. A switch to the short ballot has eliminated the election of numerous executive officers and concentrated authority over state agencies in the governor. Excessively large numbers of agencies, often overlapping in function, have been consolidated into a manageable number—a dozen or so—and independent boards or commissions reduced or eliminated. The governor has been provided with a personal staff and Cabinet, executive budgetary power, and control of expenditure. In the executive department, the personnel system has been based on the merit principle, which usually gives the governor a more competent staff.

The rise of a strong governor pattern is one of the brighter hopes for more constructive responses from the states to social need. When Terry Sanford, former governor of North Carolina, consulted the governors in the mid-1960s on the powers they lacked "which could aid you significantly in effecting your programs," they replied overwhelmingly with a catalogue of wanted powers of the strong governor type. "To be able to lead," Sanford concluded, "the governor needs to be freed from the barbed wire of antiquated constitutional barriers." [17]

Another hopeful sign for gubernatorial response to social need is the rising interest of Republican governors in gaining urban voting support. Democrats have traditionally depended on urban votes whereas Republicans have tended to write it off. But in Pennsylvania, Massachusetts, and Illinois, Republican gubernatorial candidates have sought to ally with municipal reform movements against Democratic city machines. In other populous states, Republicans have courted urban voters with promises of more state aid to the cities. But promises are many—on the part of both Republicans and Democrats—while accomplishments are few.

The cities:
stepchildren
of the states

So far the states have largely refrained from launching the major initiatives desperately needed in the cities. Only one governor, former New Jersey governor Richard Hughes, has presented what deserves to be called a full-scale state urban program; other governors and legislators have been full of excuses for doing little. One serious inhibition on legislative effort is the high political risk of providing for the expanded fiscal program needed to aid the cities: rising taxes are a political graveyard for governors and legislators.

[17] Terry Sanford, *Storm Over the States* (New York: McGraw-Hill, 1967), 187.

Where outlays have been increased, they have—in this inflationary era—gone chiefly to buttress normal services, with little thought for *adding* to these services.

The malaise of state-urban relations is contributed to by marked differences in their political cultures. By one count, in thirty-one states city populations live in political cultures different from those of surrounding areas.[18] Urban politics has increasingly become a channel for assertion by deprived people, mobilized by aggressive leaders and confrontations. The politics of outlying areas has tended to be the domain of the "establishment" in state government. State politics is the terrain where the two cultures clash. Thus far the states are more prone to resist and reject than to alleviate urban problems, which are their constitutional responsibility.

Unlike the federal Constitution, a document of delegated powers, the state constitutions endow the states with plenary, or absolute and complete, powers. Among them is the power to create local governments and to grant them such powers as the states see fit. Generally, the states have been niggardly in yielding powers, many of which are highly crucial to present-day urban problems—powers to tax, zone surrounding areas, regulate housing, provide or improve mass transportation, and acquire open space. The states can control the dividing lines between local governments, a power used largely to maintain the crazy quilt of local government patterns that handcuffs the cities in coping with problems that cross local boundaries.

Some states provide for municipal "home rule," which purportedly grants increased powers to the cities, but is often a misnomer of unjustifiable optimism. Some states' constitutions do not grant the powers to local governments directly; instead they authorize or instruct the legislature to dispense home rule powers, a mandate the legislature may ignore completely. Home rule may be limited to one or two of the largest cities or extended to all cities and even to lesser units. The definitions of local power range from very general to very specific.

In many ways, home rule has boomeranged against the larger cities. The fact that it facilitates the incorporation of municipalities has enabled the expensive residential suburban area, by incorporating itself, to avoid annexation by a neighboring municipality with formidable school, health, and racial problems. Industrial enclaves can incorporate and thereby spare themselves school taxes of adjoining municipalities, whose inhabitants they employ but for whose children's education they don't want to pay. They can also use incorporation to sidestep local regulations of pollution. And despite the home rule movement, the cities still remain badly handicapped by state-imposed limitations on expenditure, the level of indebtedness, and the kinds of taxes they can levy. Such limitations make the cities more dependent on state largess.

Coupled with the crippling limitations on urban powers is the states' reluctance to use their own ample powers to deal with city problems. If they

[18] Daniel J. Elazar, *American Federalism: A View From the States* (New York: Crowell, 1966), 184.

wanted to, states could induce a more rational organization of local government, make their aid systems more responsive to local needs, and assume financial responsibility for many functions performed locally. To the cities, the states are a tantalizing spectacle of governments enabled by law and resources to take bold initiatives, but disinclined to do so, even as the avalanche of urban problems grows increasingly formidable.

The neglect of the cities is partly a product of political demography. The Census Bureau's "Standard Metropolitan Statistical Areas" distinguishes between central cities (50,000 population or more), inhabitants of their surrounding suburbs, and persons residing outside these areas (outstaters). According to the 1970 census, city dwellers comprised 31.4 percent of the population, suburbanites 37.2 percent, and those in nonmetropolitan areas, 31.4 percent. Only in New York and Arizona did more than 50 percent of the population live in cities. In every other state, even in the most industrialized, city people are a minority of the population. City political strength is further reduced by being divided among parties and candidates in state-wide elections and by rivalries among the cities themselves, which, of course, vary in size, need, and political culture. New York City, for example, which in 1970 had 39 percent of the state's population, has suffered reduced political influence in the state because of the ineptness of its dominant party, the Democrats, and because of the long-standing antagonism of the state's other cities. Another factor of demographic politics is the increasing concentrations of blacks in the cities, which is accelerating the trend toward black city halls and white state capitols. Finally, the larger city delegations to the state legislatures are all too often the offspring of machines, creatures of undistinguished competence and cramped horizons and, in short, unworthy ambassadors of complex city problems.

While the city has been in disarray, the rural squirearchy has functioned smoothly in state legislative politics. The quarrel with their conduct in the seats of power as leaders and committee chairmen is not that they have been totally unresponsive to the city, but that they have just not been responsive enough. In general, they excel in what their rural constituencies appreciate— providing superior highways, land grant universities, decentralized public school systems. To urban problems they accord a secondary status, regulating them with the rural virtue of frugality.

Legislative reapportionment has somewhat reduced the rural sway by elevating the fast-growing suburbs, particularly in the legislatures of New York, California, Illinois, Pennsylvania, Michigan, and New Jersey. Both geographically and politically, the suburbs lie between the cities and the countryside, resulting in something of a net gain for the cities since suburbs are accustomed, as Daniel Moynihan has noted, "to spending a lot of money." [19]

The suburbs share certain problems with the city—mass transit needs, water pollution, vanishing open space, slum pockets. Since many suburban-

[19] The American Assembly, 180.

ites work in the cities, they are at least exposed to city problems, if not affected by them. But as yet the suburbs show little tendency to ally with the cities; they look askance at high city taxes, plundering city political machines, expanding welfare roles. Alarmed at the growing exodus of lower class groups from the inner cities toward the suburbs, they manipulate their state and local political power to block state housing construction programs from coming into their territory. The outcome of such state politics is to concentrate racial groups in the cities and to provide services for the cities whose quality is well below suburban levels for education, transportation, health care, water supply, garbage disposal, air pollution control, and public safety. The suburbs' sturdy success in the state legislatures has inspired the aphorism that many states are governments "of the cities, by the county, and for the suburbs."

The city-state horizon is not altogether cheerless. Drawing inspiration from the federal government's Model Cities program, the Pennsylvania Partnership City program and Connecticut's Community Development Action Plan are attacking the housing, health, and education problems of urban neighborhoods. There is rising agitation for state takeover of certain local functions. Small and heavily populated states such as Massachusetts and Connecticut are virtually local governments themselves, and Massachusetts is much involved in the operation of metropolitan service districts for the Boston area. Similar administrative patterns are developing in other states. State administration of education and welfare is increasingly advocated in the light of the states' broader and less restricted tax resources and the sharp variation in local resources for such services.

More than twenty states have established some kind of agency for local affairs, known by such titles as State Department of Community Affairs and State Department of Urban Development, a clue to rising state concern for local problems. Thus far, however, these offices seem strongly oriented to preserving the status quo rather than introducing basic governmental changes. With prodding from the federal government, the states have generously encouraged the formation of councils of governments (COGs)—voluntary associations of local governments and elected officials—to facilitate discussion and study of local problems. COGs have made strides in regional planning in the San Francisco bay area and elsewhere, but critics see them also as mere watchdogs of an inadequate status quo. A few states have passed laws liberalizing annexation procedures and tightening controls over separate municipal incorporation.[20]

State politics
as tax politics

"The question is, how can we afford to pay for things we would like to afford, and in many instances the things we need to afford?" Governor Howard Pyle,

[20] This discussion of urban-state relations draws on The American Assembly, *The States and the Urban Crisis, passim.*

once asked the Arizona legislature.[21] These words well suggest that one of the essentials of state politics is tax politics.

Although state taxes are rising faster than federal and local taxes, many states have not tapped their most lucrative tax sources and in levying new taxes have not adopted productive rate schedules. Most states levy a property tax, a general sales tax, and a broad-based income tax, and many impose taxes on tobacco products, gasoline, and the transfer of real estate and stocks and bonds. In the fifty states together, according to one study, sales taxes represented 58 percent of state revenues, personal and corporate income taxes more than 23 percent, property taxes 2.7 percent, with the remainder from miscellaneous taxes and license fees.[22]

By their nature, state taxes oppress the poor. The sales tax is a regressive tax—that is, its burden is lessened as the ability to pay increases. Since the sales tax on food, fuel, and other necessities applies equally to all, rich and poor, the poor must inevitably spend a larger percentage of their income on the tax than do those of higher income. But state legislators favor it because it is easy to collect, the public accepts it as a relatively painless imposition, and it holds up in times of economic decline. State income taxes also tend to be regressive, falling most heavily on those of lower income. Unlike the more progressive federal income tax, state income taxes increase only slightly as income increases.

Corporation income or profits taxes produce about two-thirds as much revenue for the states as the personal income tax, but the great bulk of the yield is concentrated in only four states—California, New York, Pennsylvania, and Wisconsin. In other states, the corporate income tax is usually a mere token.

States have been prone to hold in check their taxes on business so that they might attract new industry (and more jobs, more revenue). Many states advertise favored tax arrangements for new plants, and all states employ industry hunters who attempt to entice prospective industry (see illustration on p. 384). States issue free revenue bonds to finance new industrial buildings. And in a glass case in the middle of the Salt Lake City airport terminal is a display with the caption, "Utah is a free port state. No property tax on inventory held for out-of-state shipment. If stored in California, the tax would add more than 20 percent to your storage cost each year."

But the barrier of corporate tax protection gives hope of being stormed. As more and more states have found it necessary to institute some form of corporate income tax, a less defensive way of thinking has come to light. In 1971, for example, when Connecticut was engaged in painful deliberations over adoption of an income tax, fears were expressed that industries would go elsewhere. "Where . . . are they going to move?" a union leader snapped. "Are they going to move back to New York with Rockefeller's tax package?" [23]

Business lobbies originally led resistance to the state income tax, but the

[21] In Reichley, 45.
[22] The American Assembly, 37.
[23] *New York Times,* March 20, 1971.

rising federal income tax has ignited general voter hostility to all state tax increases. In confrontations with tax politics, voters are at their blindest, irrational worst. In the late 1960s, Nebraska's voters defeated a proposal to add a state income tax and simultaneously abolished the state property tax, leaving their state for a time with no major tax sources. In 1972, the New Jersey legislature rejected a proposal for an income tax. The tinderbox of voter feelings forces state legislators to conjure up special, preferably hidden, taxes that will be least likely to arouse political resentment. As yet, the most constructive suggestion for enabling the states to find their way out of the impasse of tax politics has been supplied by a New England legislator: "The only way we could get a realistic and workable tax program in this state is if the legislature from Oregon sat in our capitol and made our tax laws, and our legislature sat in Oregon and did the same for them." [24]

[24] In Sanford, 26–27.

The states
and the federal system

What the states are and what they can become is shaped by their place in the federal system. The destinies of urban areas, too, are touched by federalism, which determines the respective powers of the national government and the states to deal with their problems. Political scientist William Riker has defined federalism as consisting of at least two levels of government that rule the same lands and people. Each level has at least one area of action in which it is theoretically autonomous and a guarantee, usually constitutional, of that autonomy.[25]

American federalism is sustained by several political institutions. The U.S. Senate represents the states, the President is a product of votes rendered state by state, and the national judiciary interprets the Constitution in ways that preserve the federal arrangement, as by separating states' rights from national rights. The major parties reflect the federal system in organization and devote themselves to determining the respective roles of the federal government and the states. The decentralized parties work to perpetuate a parallel governmental decentralization. Through Congress, they make certain that provisions are incorporated into laws retaining for the state and local governments important roles in the exercise of functions entrusted to the national government, such as unemployment compensation.[26]

Federalism protects and capitalizes on the states' quality of diversity; it permits flexibility and innovation in the complicated American political system. Under federalism, there are many gateways for ideas and action, so that their fate is seldom settled by a single arbiter. Federalism allows for a variety of responses on matters for which there is no vast enduring majority, but on which opinions justifiably differ and fluctuate. On numerous questions of public policy, many answers are better than one answer. The formidability of writing a single law on a complex social subject such as abortion is suggested by the fact that in a single year of the late 1960s, twenty-three states were weighing changes in their laws.

Despite the carefully honed structure of federalism, jurisdictional separations are not meticulously maintained. Rather, an opposite tendency applies: when a problem reaches the point of public concern, it becomes the concern of all publics at all levels of government, regardless of the niceties of structure. People unable to obtain satisfaction from their state governments will seek outside assistance—sometimes from local government, more often from federal. Likewise, citizens disconcerted by national action may turn to the states for succor. Thus Martin Luther King, Jr., seeking civil rights for blacks in the South, looked to the national government; white Southerners, disaffected by the resulting national policy, looked to their states for recourse. The national-state interplay gives the states an important part in virtually all

[25] William H. Riker, *Federalism* (Boston: Little, Brown, 1964), 11–13.
[26] Elazar, 49–51.

federal domestic programs, a part that is neither minor nor hollow. In welfare programs, for example, Washington sets standards, but the states, within limits, determine the size of welfare payments and eligibility for different types of assistance.

The late Morton Grodzins argued that American federalism was a system of "multiple cracks," each denoting a part of the legislative and administrative process where the national and state levels of government join, and which individuals and groups might more easily penetrate to influence policy. The result is a "chaos" of overlapping jurisdictions and decision-making, which helps preserve the openness of the system. In an era of large-scale government, democracy gains in this system because there are many points at which citizens and groups can influence decision-makers. A kind of built-in balance of power perpetuates the system. If one level of government seems to dominate an activity, the other can make its influence felt politically, or through money, or through an interchange of professional administrators.[27]

Intergovernmental sharing ranges over virtually the entire front of domestic policy. Any listing of metropolitan problems is also a listing of national problems—or, more precisely, of national urban problems. Of the several forms of intergovernmental cooperation, the most important are the grants-in-aid—federal transfers of funds to the states and federal or state transfers to local governments for defined purposes, usually subject to a degree of supervision and review by the granting government. The states are not mere conduits of federal funds; rather, as William Anderson put it, the relationship reflects the principle that "political power, like electricity, does not run all in one direction." [28] The grant-in-aid system enables the states to administer functions bearing a national interest and thereby, in effect, acquire a measure of control over national policy. The states can utilize this administration as a check on the national government.

The long history of grants-in-aid reaches back to the land grants of the eighteenth century. Current grants center on inner city and metropolitan problems—welfare, education, health, open space, model cities, air pollution, ghetto schools, poverty, water and sewer facilities, health services. Some newer programs bypass the states: the aid moves from Washington directly to local governments, attesting to the states' proven inadequacy in dealing with central city problems.

Typically, grants-in-aid have a cost-sharing or fund matching requirement that the participating states and localities must satisfy. The grants may be of a project nature, such as building a highway, or on a formula basis, the apportioning of money according to need or fiscal capacity. Population and per capita income are frequent variables. In the formula grant, the federal government is a kind of equalizer of the disparities among the states in what they need and what they can afford. Grant programs are hailed for providing

[27] Morton Grodzins, *The American System* (Chicago: Rand McNally, 1966), *passim*.
[28] William Anderson, *The Nation and the States, Rivals or Partners?* (Minneapolis: University of Minnesota Press, 1955), 2–3, 204.

A session of the National Governors' Conference in 1968 at which New York's Nelson Rockefeller, Florida's Claude Kirk, and California's Ronald Reagan show a willingness to cooperate.

services in areas where the tax base is small, for increasing the capacity of state governments to meet its demands, for enabling state legislatures to initiate programs they would otherwise have found impossible. Critics of aid programs decry their fragmentation of federal programming, their overlapping and uncoordinated character, the sometimes excessive national control that ignores area differences and special needs, and the tendency toward "functional autocracy," by which specialists at all governmental levels ally themselves against external controls.

The several levels of government promote cooperation and sharing through conferences, exchange of services, lending of equipment and personnel, and the performance of functions by one government for another. Formal cooperation may be expressed in contract (for example, the exchange of personnel for joint enforcement of the law) or by compact. Compacts, provided for in the federal Constitution, are made between states, with congressional approval. The federal government may or may not participate in them. The Port of New York Authority is based on a 1922 compact by which New York and New Jersey through the Port Authority cooperatively administer a host of transportation enterprises. The Southern Regional Educational Compact permits states with poor professional training schools to send students to other states with the tuition being billed to the sending state.

States cooperate with one another through mutually supported organizations like the Council of State Governments, which does research and functions as a clearing house for common state concerns. It also serves as a secretariat for various organizations of state officials, such as the National Governors' Conference, the National Legislative Conference, and the Conference of Chief Justices. By their own decision many states have adopted uniform state laws, designed by the National Conference of Commissioners on Uniform State Laws, to keep pace with American mobility and change. Most states have enacted a uniform commercial code and a uniform narcotics drug act, among other laws. Both among the states and with the federal government, cooperation is eased by professional associations in health, education, welfare, law enforcement, and other areas in which shared professional interests and aspirations evoke a high degree of cooperation. Professionals tend to identify more with the function performed than with the government served.

Those who despair over the decline of the central cities and the fate of its people shrug off these cooperative undertakings as too little and too late. Beneath the cooperative façade, the states jealously preserve their sovereignty and act as selectors of federal programs that, however directed to the central city, they then adapt to their rural and suburban biases. City problems are limited to piecemeal treatment, and the pace set by the cumbersome structure and haphazard machinery seems incorrigibly slow.

Toward innovative
state policies

Is there any hope for the central city, where need and pressure are greatest, in a political system in which the states retain a large role and are the least likely of all governmental levels to view city problems with sufficient sympathy?

In early theoretical formulations, V. O. Key contended that party competition enables lower status groups to assert their own interests more effectively by creating some semblance of organized politics and lessening the difficulty of sorting out political actors and issues. In his analysis of New England state politics, Duane Lockard contended that states with complex economies would more likely have competitive parties since the two-party principle flourishes in a diversity of economic interests. And this diversity makes it difficult for a few powerful interests to dominate policy.[29] Subsequent studies in the 1960s have contradicted the Key-Lockard observations and concluded that any tie between party competition and social welfare expenditures is spurious.[30]

Charles F. Cnudde and Donald J. McCrone tested Key's contention that party competition provides political organization useful to the have-nots in their 1969 study of four state expenditure policies—per pupil expenditure, old age assistance, unemployment compensation, and aid to dependent children. Cnudde and McCrone concluded that party competition was important only for per pupil expenditure and old age assistance. Concerning aid to dependent children and unemployment compensation, they found that party competition was of minor importance. Hence, competition was only sometimes helpful to have-nots in seeking useful policies.[31]

Ira Sharkansky and Richard Hofferbert found that different social and economic characteristics have varying relevance for policies. Their relevance also varies between areas of policy. A strong association was found between party competition and voter turnout, on the one hand, with affluence on the other. Thus citizens are more likely to participate in politics and parties are more likely to compete where residents are well educated and relatively wealthy. Welfare and education policy is, in turn, significantly dependent on the association of party competition, voter turnout, and affluence. Thus, when a state is wealthy and shows high voter turnout and strong party competition, it is likely to score high on the level of welfare and educational services.

In contrast, highway and natural resources policy appears most dependent on the level of industrialization in the state, in an inverse relationship: well-developed highways and fish-game programs accompany low levels of industrialization and population concentration. Clearly, the level and scope of public services cannot be improved by manipulating merely one political or structural characteristic of state government, such as party competition. In addition, careful studies are needed of the contributions of dynamic leaders and strong traditions, particularly the prevailing values of a state's cultural environment.[32]

Because serious attacks on urban and metropolitan problems require novel and experimental approaches, the states' capacity to innovate is at a

[29] V. O. Key, *Southern Politics in State and Nation* (New York: Vintage Books, 1949), 307; Duane Lockard, *New England State Politics* (Princeton: Princeton University Press, 1959), 336–37.

[30] Richard E. Dawson and James A. Robinson, "Inter-Party Competition, Economic Variables and Welfare Policies in the American States," *Journal of Politics,* 25 (May 1963), 265–89; Thomas R. Dye, *Politics, Economics and the Public* (Chicago: Rand McNally, 1966).

[31] Charles F. Cnudde and Donald J. McCrone, "Party Competition and Welfare Policies in the American States," *American Political Science Review,* LXIII (September 1969), 858–66.

[32] Ira Sharkansky and Richard I. Hofferbert, "Dimensions of State Politics, Economics, and Public Policy," *American Political Science Review,* LXIII (September 1969), 867–79.

premium. Understanding of forces that bring states to innovate becomes important. Jack L. Walker has concluded on the basis of preliminary evidence that state decision-makers are likely to adopt new programs when they become convinced that their state is relatively deprived, or that some need exists to which other states in their "class" have already responded. These tendencies illuminate the importance of specialized systems of communication among the states, especially through the professional associations of state administrators.[33]

One innovative policy that has come to pass is President Nixon's plan for "general revenue sharing," which Congress enacted in somewhat modified form in 1972. Doubtless a landmark in federal-state fiscal relations, the plan in effect transfers a portion of federal revenue collections to the states with few limitations on their use. It remains to be seen whether the fears of those who objected to the plan will be realized—namely, that a lower quality of state and local performance will supplant national action, that states less sensitive to urban problems will siphon off federal funds for other purposes, that national priorities expressed in urban terms will be modified, and that the civil rights guarantees of federal programs will be watered down.

Proposals

Despite the striking interdependence of factors shaping state politics, improvements are worth making piecemeal—if for political reasons they cannot be done simultaneously—because they can accumulate. Improvements are called for in state institutions, in policies, and in state relations with the cities and metropolitan areas, the national government, and the federal system. In weighing changes, one must consider differences among the states in size, geography, economic development, urbanization, and political culture.

1. It would be useful to explore the desirability of general state constitutional revision. The precise prescriptions of state constitutions now in force are often drags on state progress and strongholds for interest group protection. Instructive for state reform is the relative brevity and general language of the federal Constitution, which is less sheltering of interest groups and more adjustable to change.

2. To rescue the legislature from captivity to a rural tradition of parsimonious self-denial, part-time status, and free-style interest group orientation, changes in workaday aspects of legislative life are necessary: annual sessions in all states rather than biennial in some, a decent annual salary, fewer constitutional restrictions on tax and spending powers, mandatory periodic reapportionment, smaller legislatures to make the members more important and visible, competent professional staffs and bill drafting, comprehensive law revision, a legislative library and reference services, adequate offices, a few

[33] Jack L. Walker, "The Diffusion of Innovations among the American States," *American Political Science Review*, LXIII (September 1969), 880–99.

strong standing committees of broad jurisdiction, codes of ethics, and ethics committees empowered to review lobbyists' activities. Chances for legislative improvement are dim unless political leaders, the mass media, and educational and civil institutions undertake to make the public more aware of the problems.[34]

3. The governor too is often the victim of historic and limiting constitutional provisions. In a day of grave urban problems executive action should be encouraged rather than suppressed, and we would do well to eliminate certain serious restrictions on gubernatorial power. The two-year term in states should be replaced by a four-year term, with reeligibility for at least one term. The governor should have full budget-making authority to enhance his capacity as planner and coordinator of the executive branch. He needs tools of policy analysis to weigh present decisions for their long-term implications and to measure the costs of solving a problem against the costs of doing nothing. The governor and the lieutenant governor should be the only elected executives on the ballot. Like the President, the governor needs the power to reorganize executive agencies and eliminate boards and commissions that are beyond his jurisdiction, and he needs an expanded office alert to new ideas, especially those that are paying off in other states.[35]

4. By every indication, state politics in the foreseeable future will not tolerate the many measures necessary to reduce the fragmentation and impotence of local governments and to transform them into larger units more capable of dealing with serious local and metropolitan problems. Nevertheless, suggested here is an ideal model, constructed without concern for immediate difficulties.

The states should create a single, expandable area-wide unit of government for each metropolitan community. Smaller subgovernments would be retained to protect local diversity and a sense of small community representation in the larger metropolitan context. All other local governments would be abolished. To forward such arrangements, the states must develop clear statements of the goals to be accomplished by local reorganization. The states too would need to provide incentives—financial and program inducements— to spur local governments to reorganize. The successful consolidation of little red school houses into larger school districts is instructive for this model.[36]

5. To extricate the cities from the quagmire of constitutional and statutory restraints on home rule, the Model State Constitution of the National Municipal League provides that a city may exercise any legislative power or perform any function that is not denied in its charter nor to cities generally or of its class and that is within any limitations set by the state legislature.

---

[34] See *State Legislatures in American Politics, Report of the Twenty-ninth American Assembly* (New York: The American Assembly, Columbia University, 1966), 5–9, *passim.*

[35] Sanford, 190–203.

[36] The American Assembly, *The States and the Urban Crisis,* 80–82.

In effect, the provision would diminish home rule as a constitutional issue and make it more a political question to be worked out between the cities and the state legislature. It would enable the cities to take the initiative, with the prospect that the state legislature would be less likely to act negatively merely to defeat the city's decision.[37]

Clearly the states must overcome the image that prompted disparagement from two big-city mayors. Former mayor Joseph Clark of Philadelphia views the states as "the weak link" in today's government and finds local governments, especially the larger cities, "more sophisticated, more mature." To which Mayor Ivan Allen of Atlanta adds, "What is decried by many as 'federal encroachment' has been the salvation of Atlanta." [38]

Suggested Reading

Barber, James David, *The Lawmakers* * (Yale University Press, 1965). An empirical study of Connecticut legislators and their work. Analyzes several types of legislators and their goals.

Campbell, Alan K., ed., *The States and the Urban Crisis* * (American Assembly, Prentice-Hall, 1970). Analyzes the states' role in the contemporary urban crisis. Discusses state tax and expenditure policies, home rule, the federal government's role; offers proposals for improvement.

Elazar, Daniel J., *American Federalism: A View From the States* * (Crowell, 1966). A leading survey of the problems of federalism in the United States, with stress on the directions of change.

Grodzins, Morton, *The American System* (Rand McNally, 1966). A cogent analysis of the nature of American federalism and the governing principles of its operation, with an approving appraisal of the results.

Hodges, Luther H., *Businessman in the Statehouse* (University of North Carolina Press, 1962). An informative account of the trials and satisfactions of the governor, by a former governor of North Carolina.

Jacob, Herbert, and Vines, Kenneth, eds., *Politics in the American States: A Comparative Analysis* (Little, Brown, 1965). A useful introduction to state politics, with focus on such factors as the physical and social environment, the varieties of political participants, and the rules of the political process and their attitudinal base.

Jewell, Malcolm E., *The State Legislature: Politics and Practice* * (Random House, 1962). An excellent analysis of the internal structure and operations of the state legislature and its relation to the external political world.

Ransome, Coleman B., Jr., *The Office of Governor* (University of Alabama Press, 1956). The leading study of the work of governors and trends of their offices.

Reichley, James, *States in Crisis: Politics in Ten American States* (University of North Carolina Press, 1964). A readable study of the politics and economic and social problems of selected states. The discussion includes relevant federal and local politics.

Riker, William H., *Federalism* (Little, Brown, 1964). An analysis of federalism, its structure, the major concepts that underlie it, and its consequences. Considers the relation of federalism to freedom.

[37] *State Legislatures in American Politics,* 5–9.
[38] The American Assembly, *The States and the Urban Crisis,* 153–54.

Sanford, Terry, *Storm Over the States* (McGraw-Hill, 1967). A former governor of North Carolina examines the contemporary weaknesses of the states, and their causes. Stresses the effect of interest groups, news coverage, tax policies, national programs, and outmoded constitutions.

Wahlke, John C., et al., *The Legislative System: Explorations in Legislative Behavior* (Wiley, 1962). A comparative study of state legislators and their roles. Emphasizes the importance of interest groups, parties, and the political culture.

* Available in paperback edition

14

---

the

---

grassroots:

---

local

---

politics

One of the more surprising results of 1971's municipal elections was the victory in Berkeley, California, of a coalition of young liberals and radicals, who won the mayoralty and three of four council seats. This is a pattern that conceivably might be repeated in other college towns. "Students are finally showing some political sophistication," observed the president of student government at the University of California. "Maybe we can't change things overnight at the national level, but we've certainly shown we can affect local politics." And a youth named Tim, who was selling flowers to passersby, added, "For the first time, we've stopped talking about the abuse of the system and worked through it, and we succeeded." [1]

These are testimonials to one of the oldest and most venerated visions of government in America—"grassroots democracy," the conviction that small political units permit the purest fulfillment of popular rule, that the government closest to man, his work, and his home is best responsive to his need and will, and under his watchful eye can most safely be entrusted with power. In local life, the citizen escapes his faceless, numbered fate in the national mass. He is most completely an individual in his own community; he knows those who govern and is known by them. Daily he can watch their performance and hold them to account.

The praises of local politics have long been sung by leading public thinkers. Perceiving that size was no equivalent of greatness, the Greeks searched for a political unit that, by permitting "an organic sense of structural difference," afforded perfection of human development. They exulted in their discovery of the small community as the locale where the good life could be best pursued. After the day of the Greeks, a long succession of continental thinkers hailed the virtues of the small community, and in the United States, Jefferson and Jackson extolled the individual citizen in his locality, a happy

---

[1] *New York Times,* April 8, 1971.

Warren Widener and his wife at campaign headquarters celebrating his victory in the mayoralty race in Berkeley, 1971.

combination for liberty, independence, and integrity. Both leaders and the political movements that clustered about them ascribed to the community an inherent right to govern itself free from excessive intervention by remote authority, especially the state legislature. From such thinking, the idea of "home rule" was born.

To its admirers, the small community provides means and opportunity for people to participate in public affairs, to share in decision-making, and to derive a sense of competence from doing so. If they make mistakes, the consequences do not blaze on the catastrophic scale of national affairs. The small community is a bulwark against concentrated power. Of all the levels of government it is the most conserving of the delicate balance between necessary collective action and preserving the individual's identity. Even while asserting his freedom and individuality, the member of the small community discovers a harmonious relation of man to man and of man to government. The intertwining of his life with his neighbors', their shared beliefs and experiences, their common interests in the everyday life of the community, the intimacy of personal relations, develop the sense of integration so valued by Plato and Aristotle.

But what of cities? Are the virtues of the small community lost in the big city, offspring of technology and modern social and economic organization? Not necessarily, argues Jane Jacobs, a present-day student of the cities. The city is a sequence of neighborhoods, and the neighborhoods embody the sterling qualities of community. Cities offer varieties of neighborhoods—from great ethnic enclaves to high income areas, which derive identity from their inhabitants, their shops and merchants, and their community spirit, which makes good Samaritans of neighbors.[2] Life in the city offers both privacy and contact, and leaves the individual largely free to define for himself the balance between the two. The city surpasses the small community in affording a broader spectrum of human experience in the arts, in the variety of social life and economic opportunity, in the diversity of human expression. Too often the tight integration of the smaller community becomes oppressive conformity, while the great city invites cosmopolitan living in ways consistent with human freedom.

The city: can the grassroots be preserved?

Nowadays, however, the cities are hobbled by massive inequalities that negate democracy. Ghettos abound, and as the middle class flees to the suburbs, the many very poor live in desperate contrast to the few very rich. Poverty is ugly and pervasive; fear supplants neighborliness, and congestion and crime overwhelm even the hardiest good Samaritan.

The cities vary in the severity of their problems. There are crisis cities— New York, Cleveland, Detroit, Newark, St. Louis—where decay and loss of jobs and wealth to the suburbs have caused difficulties that seem beyond the power of city officials to overcome. Newark is a microcosm of almost every kind of urban trouble—decayed schools, dilapidated housing, the highest local property taxes in the nation, badly depleted economic resources, a severe racial riot in 1967, deepening racial divisions, the highest crime rate in the country, and soaring rates of unemployment among slum youth. Like growing numbers of cities, Newark recently voted for a black mayor, Kenneth A. Gibson, whose election was widely hailed as a victory for black political power, and in the perspective of this chapter, as a triumph of grassroots politics. "But what kind of power is it," Mayor Thomas J. D'Alesandro of Baltimore asked, "to preside over disease, poverty, and pestilence? . . . What is there to rejoice in?"[3] Another kind of city, typified by Indianapolis, Memphis, Kansas City, and Houston, faces problems smaller in scale and that seem locally manageable.

As befits grassroots politics, the city contains many power centers. Some are less compatible with grassroots principles than others in promoting the enlargement and consolidation of political power rather than the grassroots ideal of small political units. The city's citizens must continuously remind the political actors that their function is representative and temporary, subject to review and redefinition. The several categories of principal participants in

[2] Jane Jacobs, *The Death and Life of Great American Cities* (New York: Random House, 1961), 59–120.
[3] *New York Times,* April 26, 1971.

Washington, D.C. In the cities, "the many very poor live in desperate contrast to the few very rich."

city politics include the public officials, the party leaders, the bureaucracies, a variety of nongovernmental groups, the communications media, and the officials and bureaus of state and national governments.

The public officials—executives, legislators, and judges—man separate branches of government, each of which serves different constituencies with distinct expectations and demands. Unfortunately for the grassroots ideal, officials vary in public visibility: most legislators, judges, and lesser executives function in secluded anonymity, while the chief executive constantly occupies the spotlight. Party leaders keep politics competitive—they select candidates for office, operate machinery that candidates need to win votes, and help acquaint the voters with candidates and issues.

Although structured according to some kind of merit system, the city bureaucracies—the teachers, policemen, firemen, sanitation workers, and transit workers—are not a monolith but self-conscious, cohesive groups, with their own bargaining organizations. They make self-interested demands on the city in return for performing the services on which the community depends. Another category of participants in city politics is that of the private citizens at the grassroots who are deeply interested in what government does and form associations of varying durability and cohesiveness—a permanent citizens' budget commission or an *ad hoc* group of mothers lining up their baby carriages across a busy intersection to force the installation of a traffic signal. The news media have a special place as channels through which all kinds of participants, the powerful and the powerless, reach the general public. Despite engrossment in their own worlds, the federal and state bureaucracies are imposing forces in city politics—they provide services to the city, grant funds, offer local officials opportunities for higher office, and oversee the local bureaucracies.

Each participant views city politics not simply as a grassroots enterprise, where the voice of the people is to be detected and heeded, but as a grab bag of stakes and prizes. Some look to further their careers, win employment, obtain a share in the city's vast market for goods and services. Other participants seek "intangible" rewards—particular policies and programs, or alterations in operating procedures.

City politics is also the politics of cleavage. The poor favor high levels of expenditure for welfare, housing, and sometimes schools, and rarely oppose any kinds of outlay. Upper-income groups want good public services when they are directly benefited, but are decidedly less approving when benefits accrue to the poor; middle-income groups, harried by mortgage and credit payments, prefer low spending levels.[4]

The city's governmental institutions can be organized in ways that advance or hamper the grassroots principle. The city council or legislature may be elected from the city at large, that is, by the entire city, or from wards or districts. In recent years, the trend has been toward at-large election; in cities of over 10,000 population, 60 percent elect their councilmen-at-large and 23 percent solely from districts, while the remaining 17 percent combine the at-large and district principles. The experience of many cities discloses that a district or ward system is more compatible than an at-large system with grassroots interests, for power is more widely dispersed, the citizen enjoys more points of access to influence politics, neighborhoods and ethnically defined areas are better represented, and minorities are better able to win recognition.[5] But diffused power can also work against minorities by insulating middle- and upper-class neighborhoods, and by diluting the central city government's ability to respond to minority needs.

Cities have adopted different types of executive structures, some more and some less compatible with particular grassroots principles. At first glance, the most compatible form might appear to be the weak mayor system, still widely used in the smaller cities, which permits dominance by the popularly elected council and council-oriented administrative boards. But many cities seeking vigorous leadership more capable of responding to grassroots needs have adopted the strong mayor system, which reduces the number of elected officials (a sacrifice of grassroots participation), decreases or abolishes administrative boards, and establishes a chief executive with sizable resources of legislative and community leadership, supported by a professional civil

---

[4] This discussion has drawn on Wallace S. Sayre and Herbert Kaufman, *Governing New York City* (New York: Russell Sage Foundation, 1960), Chapter II.

[5] Edward C. Banfield and James Q. Wilson, *City Politics* (Cambridge: Harvard University Press, 1966), 89–95.

service. Another variant of the strong executive is the council-manager plan. A city manager, appointed by the council, supervises the administrative departments, appoints and removes their heads, prepares and administers a budget, and initiates matters for the council's consideration. An elected mayor and council presumably take care of "policy-making," while the manager, a professional administrator, handles "policy execution." The council-manager plan prevails in middle-sized and smaller cities.

Interestingly, the trend toward the strong chief executive has paralleled the trend of increasingly deteriorating problems in the cities. In the face of dire problems, the cities are opting for positive progressive leadership. If anything, as the 1971 elections show, the cities' desperation has linked a strong executive more with grassroots politics. In San Jose, California, Oklahoma City, and Dallas, the winning mayoralty candidates ran a kind of "people's campaign," stressing participatory democracy and a spirit of renewal. San Jose's new mayor, Norman Y. Mineta, a Japanese-American, defeated a field of fifteen candidates while advocating a tax increase and open housing, and in Oklahoma City, Patience Latting thoroughly shook up politics in her city while winning on a reform ticket.[6]

Racial politics. At the grassroots, city politics is racial politics. The most striking fact of the city is racial division, and its politics is confrontation between black and white. The black mayor has come into his own—in 1971 there were fifty-five—but many mayors, white and black, function as coordinators between the races. Thus D'Alesandro, white mayor of Baltimore, saw himself as "a bridge between black and white." He considered this function temporary, however, because "black political power is coming," with the steadily rising proportions of blacks in city populations. True to this prophecy, D'Alesandro subsequently did not seek reelection, while Richard G. Hatcher, a black power mayor, was reelected in Gary, Indiana.

Virtually any major social problem of the cities is simultaneously a racial question. Crime, delinquency, education, housing, unemployment, all bear racial dimensions. For instance, it is estimated that more than 70 percent of the families displaced from their homes by urban renewal and highway projects are nonwhites; their unemployment rate is at least double the national average, and they account for 20 percent of the incidence of juvenile delinquency, although they comprise only 12 percent of the total population. The struggle to overhaul outmoded city and metropolitan government structures is held back by racial factors: the white suburbs fear that closer governmental alignment with the cities will open the gates to black intrusion on their residential preserves. In turn, the black is wary of restructuring that might reduce his burgeoning power in city politics.

In the great cities, blacks, living in huge enclaves and disaffected by the harsh treatment dealt them by society, are a grassroots constituency of vast need and potential turmoil, on the scale that Kenneth B. Clark alluded to

[6] *New York Times,* June 14, 1971.

when he wrote, "The dark ghettos now represent a nuclear stockpile which can annihilate the very foundations of America." While conceding that the solidarity of ghetto peoples is essential to bettering their condition, Edward Banfield sees them in the short run as *"the* serious problem of the cities," a threat to peace and order, and in the long run as capable of pressures that compel the pursuit of politics in ways less democratic, less heedful of individual rights, and less able to act in the common interest than the present political order.[7]

What pushes the black into his unhappy state in the ghetto? He is the most recent unskilled, relatively low-income newcomer to reach the city from a backward rural area. He was lured not by glittering, misleading promises but by the prospect that life on the declining farm would be markedly improved on by the cities' opportunities for jobs, housing, and schools. The black man's tragedy is that he reached the city so late, long after the waves of other immigrants, and in such great numbers in so short a time. Historically, other groups of urban immigrants have emerged from the purgatory of the slums to a happier place in society, and ethnic politics was a transitional phenomenon. As ethnics assimilate, new unities and issues replace the old, and the politician who once thrived on ethnic politics fades away. The tantalizing question is: Will black ghetto life and politics bend to this sequence?

Class politics. Relevant to this question is the circumstance that city politics at the grassroots is also class politics. Much of the prejudice dealt out to blacks, Banfield suggests, is not racial, but class prejudice. What whites often perceive as "Negro" behavior is actually lower-class behavior.[8] In the larger cities black class structure, compared to white, embraces a large, economically backward lower class. Banfield believes that if the large cities retain their present vast lower classes—and there is every indication that they will— little gain can be made on their problems, and this sector of the grassroots will remain oppressed. Though good jobs may be offered to all, some will remain regularly unemployed. If slums are razed, the new housing that replaces them will be turned into new slums. Despite a guaranteed income—should that proposal transpire—and despite enhanced welfare payments, squalor, despair, and disease will persist. In Banfield's bleak assessment, many of the slum dweller's problems and, by middle-class standards, his unpromising future can be laid to his lower-class orientation.

Another interpretation of the city ghetto is provided by Stokely Carmichael and Charles V. Hamilton in *Black Power*. They consider the oppressor of the ghetto to be the contemporary middle class. The college-educated, salaried administrators, whose chief interest is to gain more objects for service, management, and control, need a permanently expanding dependent clientele and organizational power to protect their function. Simultaneously, the lower

[7] Quotations are in Edward C. Banfield, *The Unheavenly City* (Boston: Little, Brown, 1968; 1970), 13.
[8] *Ibid.*, 76.

Drawing by Handelsman; © 1972 The New Yorker Magazine, Inc.

"I can remember this neighborhood before it became uninhabitable."

class has been transformed from a productive segment to a permanently unemployed one, for its value, Carmichael and Hamilton contend, "is no longer labor, but dependency." Both classes are perceived in daily battle, manifested by demonstrations and controversies sparked by issues concerning education, housing, and welfare administration.

It is in the cities, with their great concentrations of blacks, Carmichael and Hamilton suggest, that the crucial issue of public control of technology will be determined. Because the people of the ghetto are the expendables of corporate power, they may be motivated enough to use popular power to question, resist, and possibly even to guide, democratically, automation to better, more humane purposes. Black people in increasing numbers hold the balance of electoral power in the largest cities. By addressing that power to the problem of corporate technology, they would apply grassroots politics to a consequential national issue.[9]

Herbert Gans suggests in *The Urban Villagers,* a study of the West End

[9] Stokely Carmichael and Charles V. Hamilton, *Black Power* (New York: Random House, 1967), 148–49.

of Boston, that city politics is class politics with implications for grassroots ideals.[10] The West End is a slum with a heavy concentration of lower-class, second-generation Italian-Americans. There, as in countless similar urban situations across the country, the public bureaucracies that administer such "caretaker" functions as education, social work, public recreation, and public health are manned by middle-class personnel, who apply middle-class values to their work. A danger lurking in this process is that they may impose middle-class values on those whose presumed disposition is to reject them. The grassroots principle would insist that at a minimum the behavior patterns and values of the working class subculture should be understood and taken into account by the professional and bureaucratic caretakers. The best assurance for achieving this objective is the political involvement of the affected lower and working classes.

To conduct this study as a participant-observer, Gans resided in the West End. He found that cultural and emotional barriers prevented satisfactory interaction between the "urban villagers" and the caretakers. Most West Enders were convinced that the police, the bureaucracy, elected officials, and the courts conspire endlessly to deprive citizens of what is rightfully theirs. Government agencies were the instruments of the individuals who ran them, most of whom were corrupt. The working class scorned middle-class reform movements in Boston as simply devices for shifting graft from the pockets of politicians to the coffers of bankers and businessmen. West Enders had difficulty in perceiving the presence of an "objective" bureaucracy. Few of them worked in offices, public or private, and many repeated the sardonic tale of how a man with a long Sicilian name finally got a job in the Irish-dominated city government by changing his name to Foley. Another experience fostering a distasteful impression of local government was the eventual extensive redevelopment of the West End, which obliterated homes of lower-class people to permit the construction of luxury apartments.

In a defensive reaction, West Enders had as little to do with government as possible; when necessary they looked to the politicians of their area to act as intermediaries. Political apathy among West Enders was so high that they did not systematically protest to the City Hall the redevelopment project, which crushed their existence as a subcommunity. Other serious consequences flowed from this lack of grassroots participation. Politicians who represented them did not have the benefit of pressure from citizen groups in seeking concessions in the legislature or at City Hall. In any case, once a candidate was elected, he became relatively independent of his constituents, except for doing favors and voting right on the few issues that concerned them. Eventually, he too fell within the West Enders' perceptions of being "corrupt" and of having been "bought."

Gans's study revealed that among the worst political lackings of the working and lower classes were (1) their inability to organize to secure political representation; (2) a general inability to understand bureaucratic behavior, which encouraged an overreliance on conspiratorial explanations of the out-

[10] Herbert J. Gans, *The Urban Villagers* (New York: Free Press, 1962).

side world that were often inaccurate; and (3) a widening gap between themselves and the larger society. Meanwhile the middle-class bureaucracy was misperceiving the lower class as simply a frustrated version of the middle class, unable to gain access to middle-class opportunities and services. But the inadequacy of this approach is reflected in the general failure of the bureaucratic caretakers to win lower-class people over to middle-class culture. Simply providing more schools, playgrounds, and health facilities contributes little or nothing to improvement of lower-class life. As a start toward improvement, the bureaucratic caretakers need to realize that the lower-class subculture, like others, has its own distinctive prerequisites of opportunities, education, income, and occupation. Here grassroots politics is the only effective kind of politics whether through the direct political and even administrative involvement of the lower class, or through the conversion of middle-class bureaucracy to attitudes and processes more attuned to the needs and culture of the lower class.

The suburbs:
grassroots
of the middle class

The suburbs are definable by geography and habitation. They occupy the country immediately outside the city and are the preserve of the middle class, molded by its values, institutions, and way of life.

Suburbs differ. Some number among the nation's oldest towns; others like Reston, Virginia, are freshly created, planned communities. Many so-called suburbs are better spoken of as outer cities. Pasadena, Texas, near Houston, has exploded from a small suburban town to a "city" with a population of nearly 100,000; it combines today's problems of pollution with yesterday's small-town concepts. Suburban variety complicates the politician's life. "Campaigning in the new suburbia drives you crazy," complained a politician from De Kalb County, Georgia, which includes a corner of Atlanta and soared from more than 150,000 to 416,000 in the 1960s. "It's different from one neighborhood to the next." [11]

Suburban politics. Those who idealize the suburbs behold them as the return of the small town, even of the ancient Greek's ideal community. The suburbs are an escape from big organizations, including the big city ("so big that no one counts"), and provide a way of life based on spontaneous cooperation, voluntary neighborliness, and genuine participation.

But between this ideal and reality, as Herbert J. Gans found in his study *The Levittowners,* there exists a yawning gap.[12] Admittedly, suburban government transpires within a general democratic framework in the sense that the voters have life-and-death power over government and its officials, which

[11] *New York Times,* May 31 and June 2, 1971.
[12] Herbert J. Gans, *The Levittowners* (New York: Pantheon Books, 1967), *passim.*

can be wielded in periodic elections. But in between elections local citizens play only a minor role in governmental affairs. And the elected official's relations with citizens tend to become distant and controlled. As part of the governmental structure, the official typically concludes that he can make it work only by keeping citizens at a distance, by minimizing response to and feedback from citizens, and by not raising or taking stands on issues.

In Levittown, citizens reinforced this controlled process by communicating very little with their local government, school board, or other agencies. Meetings of elected bodies were poorly attended, and even public hearings evoked low citizen turnout, except when there was a fight. The reason seems to have been that most government activities did not touch their everyday lives and interests. Many Levittown decisions encompassed matters of interest only to the officials and their staffs, or centered on satisfying requirements of county and state governments or requests for licenses and approval from builders and businessmen. Citizens hesitant about communicating with officials were aware, from past observation and experience, that politicians are often unresponsive; they rebuff the petitioner with vague generalities and infrequently are of genuine help with individual requests. Notions of "altruistic democracy" also made their relations unproductive: the prevailing view was that because officials serve the community and the public interest, their behavior is impartial and dedicated and their decisions are morally proper.

In Levittown and other communities, a distinction must be made between the apparent or performing government, on the one hand, and the actual one, on the other. In the first, officials listen to citizen views and in public meetings appear to vote on the basis of what they have heard. The second embraces the "backstage," secret, and far more meaningful deliberations of the actual government. Ordinarily, the interested citizen has little impact on the actual government, but he can sometimes penetrate the official façade by resorting to a conflict strategy, by creating enough disagreement to force the actual government to reveal itself.

The opposition party, sniffing for lapses by the existing government as the route to power, may take up the citizen's cause. The most common intervention strategy is to make a public statement demanding a specified decision. Often the public statement is couched in terms of moral appeal. A favorite appeal is the call for "leadership," and a more extreme moral appeal is the charge that officials are unfair, politically motivated, or paid off. Such attacks are usually defeated by stronger counterattacks mounted by officials, which enable them to discredit the interveners as agitators. For interveners who have neither numbers nor power, the introduction of new "facts" and "ideas" is often the most effective strategy. But interveners fare best if they can display visible political support. Levittown's decision-makers were most impressed by sizable, repeated turnouts of personally concerned citizens such as parents whose schoolchildren would be affected by a decision, citizens living in an area that would be rezoned.

The Levittown interveners were of several types. Most individuals or groups were *ad hoc*. Continuing or permanent interveners tended to become interest groups of the type that are consulted before decisions relevant to their concerns are made. An exception was the "cosmopolitans," continuous interveners who were largely unorganized and not consulted regularly. For the most part, college-educated professionals with upper-middle-class life styles, they visualized the community according to national and even world standards. Their high value of education led to demands for a superior school system, with facilities for adult education, and enlargement of cultural resources. Espousing liberal reform politics, they valued expertise in the governmental structure, nonpartisan politics, master planning, and a maximum of selfless citizen participation. Skilled in political controversy and fact-gathering, they excelled, despite their small numbers, at extracting concessions and compromises; and they functioned most successfully as technicians and experts in behalf of majority demands. A weakness of Levittown's cosmopolitans was a style that antagonized others, for they tended to represent themselves as idealists defending what they considered to be the public interest against selfish, unenlightened forces. In Levittown, the most effective individual intervener was the expert; he was especially valued by middle-class citizens confident that specialized knowledge can overcome "politics," toward which they took a disparaging view.

In this suburban dimension, grassroots participation constitutes a kind of dialectic, in which officials seek to maintain the actual government in an equilibrium and the citizen-interveners to penetrate or even upset it. The continuing struggle involves decision-makers, interveners, political parties, and other organized components of the suburban political community.

Suburbs and the central city. In large degree, the suburbs are a product of the continuing migrations of recent decades in which the advantaged are fleeing the disadvantaged. Vast numbers of blacks are left to the core city, as the middle class flees to avoid their welfare and service costs. Census data for 1970 corroborate the warning of the National Advisory Commission on Civil Disorders that America is moving "toward two societies, one black, one white —separate and unequal." Where blacks do penetrate the suburbs in substantial numbers, it is the municipalities just over the border from the central city. "They feel that at least they are not living in the inner city," the black city manager of one such municipality has said. In upper-income suburbs, there is salt-and-pepper integration, scatterings of well-to-do blacks here and there, but it is insignificant.

The accelerated flight of the whites in the 1960s has produced sharp declines in the populations of major cities and striking gains in the suburbs. Of nine major cities, according to the 1970 census, all but two—Los Angeles and Houston—showed declines. The sharpest drops were recorded by St. Louis (19 percent) and Cleveland (15.6 percent), while their surrounding metropolitan area swelled in total population. As a frequent pattern, cities and towns closest to the central city show population losses while com-

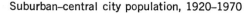

Suburban–central city population, 1920–1970

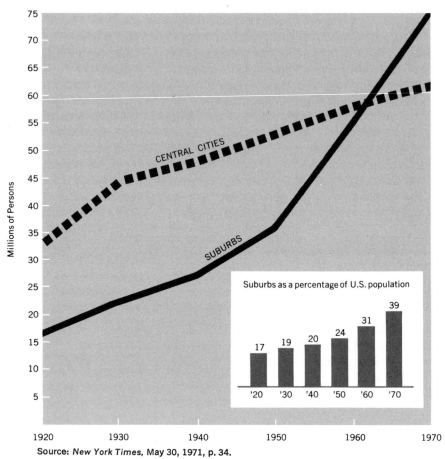

Source: *New York Times*, May 30, 1971, p. 34.

munities farther removed show rises of spectacular proportions. The trend augurs declining political influence for city people, despite their desperate needs.

Most suburbanites look askance at the central city and its volcanic problems; the upper-income resident views with horror the prospect of annexation or the creation of metropolitan-area government, and the lower-income suburbanite fears that the city will provide and tax him for services he does not want. Black middle-class suburbanites show similar disdain for poorer blacks in the central city. According to the black city manager of East Cleveland, the cry of both blacks and whites is, "We don't want that mess from Cleveland coming out here." [13]

Many central cities are writhing in the strangleholds of their suburbs.

[13] *New York Times*, June 2, 1971.

The fifty wealthiest counties [1]

County	Median income	County	Median income
1. Montgomery, Md.	$16,710	26. Prince Georges, Md.	12,450
2. Fairfax, Va.	15,707	27. Monroe, N.Y.	12,423
3. Nassau, N.Y.	14,632	28. Conta Costa, Calif.	12,423
4. Du Page, Ill.	14,458	29. Geauga, Ohio	12,411
5. Marin, Calif.	13,935	30. St. Louis, Mo.	12,392
6. Oakland, Mich.	13,826	31. Washtenaw, Mich.	12,294
7. Westchester, N.Y.	13,784	32. Orange, Calif.	12,245
8. Rockland, N.Y.	13,753	33. De Kalb, Ga.	12,137
9. Arlington, Va.	13,743	34. Dakota, Minn.	12,120
10. Bergen, N.J.	13,597	35. Suffolk, N.Y.	12,084
11. Anchorage, Alaska	13,593	36. Baltimore, Md.	12,081
12. Howard, Md.	13,472	37. Arapahoe, Colo.	12,063
13. Somerset, N.J.	13,433	38. Hartford, Conn.	12,057
14. Morris, N.J.	13,421	39. Jefferson, Colo.	12,045
15. Johnson, Kan.	13,384	40. Honolulu, Hawaii	12,035
16. San Mateo, Calif.	13,222	41. Putnam, N.Y.	11,996
17. Macomb, Mich.	13,110	42. Middlesex, N.J.	11,982
18. Fairfield, Conn.	13,086	43. McHenry, Ill.	11,965
19. Lake, Ill.	13,009	44. Lake, Ohio	11,964
20. Waukesha, Wis.	12,795	45. Kane, Ill.	11,947
21. Norfolk, Mass.	12,749	46. Richmond, N.Y.	11,894
22. Montgomery, Pa.	12,747	47. King, Wash.	11,886
23. Ozaukee, Wis.	12,620	48. Tolland, Conn.	11,874
24. Union, N.J.	12,593	49. Middlesex, Mass.	11,860
25. Santa Clara, Calif.	12,456	50. Delaware, Pa.	11,822

[1] Among all counties of 50,000 or more population, as measured by median family income in the 1970 census.

St. Louis, for example, contains only about 27 percent of the population of its metropolitan area, and many of its poor neighborhoods extend right to the city limits. The suburban area around it has become dominant in almost every important particular—industry, wealth, and political power—while the central city has been left with most of the poor, a declining tax base, and little means of spreading the burden. According to the 1970 census, all fifty of the nation's wealthiest counties, as measured by median family income, are in the suburbs (see table).

In effect, the suburbs are a device of segregation at the grassroots, separating tax resources from governmental services, the ability to pay from the locus of need, and thereby committing vast city populations to a life of misery. Ironically, much of the wealth of the suburbs is generated by the employment of its citizens in the city, but in tax and expenditure policies, the city's contribution is coldly discounted. "The suburbs are a kind of Robin Hood in reverse," Mayor Joseph Alioto of San Francisco has put it, "taking from the poor and giving to the rich. . . . The suburbs reap the benefits." [14]

[14] *New York Times,* July 21, 1971.

Metropolitanism: consolidation of the grassroots?

Can the cities and the suburbs—these two altogether different worlds existing side by side at the grassroots—ever meet and permit a synchronizing of means and need? Some suggest they can through common participation in metropolitan government. Fewer local governments through consolidation into metropolitan governments would mean more tax nourishment and improved local effectiveness. Without metropolitan government how could Cuyahoga County, Ohio, obtain the county-wide cooperation of Cleveland and fifty-nine other towns and cities on planning issues? Without metropolitan government the suburbs, despite numbers and power, will remain largely masses of little islands, unable to join efforts and control the forces that shape their future. And without metropolitan government the citizen will exercise a minimum of influence on such matters as major highways, bridges, parks, and economic policies that transcend his own local government units, but are vitally important in his everyday affairs.

At this time, however, most metropolitan areas abound in various and sundry local governments. Twenty-four metropolises—or about one of every nine—have 200 or more local units. Most prolific is the Chicago Standard Metropolitan Statistical Area (SMSA) with 1,060; Philadelphia is not far behind with 963. Many local units are small. About one-half of the municipalities of SMSAs have fewer than 2,500 inhabitants, and the territories of many cover less than three square miles—these grassroots are minuscule.

Types of local government. Among the more numerous components of local government are *municipalities,* established to provide such local services as law enforcement and fire protection to the inhabitants of urban and suburban settlements. By nature, municipalities were intended to include only a small portion of the land area of a state. *Towns,* especially in New England, the Middle Atlantic states, and Michigan and Wisconsin, have taken on many municipal-type functions. In other states—Indiana, Illinois, the Dakotas, Nebraska, and elsewhere—town governments perform limited functions of maintaining minor roads and certain aspects of social welfare. Chiefly they persist as valued sinecures for the political faithful.

Counties were founded to help the state government fulfill its tasks— assisting judges of the state court system, conducting elections, recording legal documents, providing services to rural areas, and law enforcement. Because of their responsibilities to the state, the entire state is divided into counties. In the modern era of the burgeoning metropolis, county activities have markedly expanded, embracing functions usually identified with municipalities (fighting communicable diseases, administering airports, hospitals, welfare assistance, and recreation areas).

Special districts, which comprise 62 percent of local governments, administer only one function. Most commonly this function is schools, but they are also used for airports, housing, sewage disposal, rapid transit, recreation, and highway construction. Independent of the voters, of other governments, and largely of the state legislature that creates them, special districts can do very much as they please. As a species of decentralization, they are at the grassroots but not of it.

Fortunately, the hordes of local government units do not conduct themselves altogether as isolated, self-willed entities, oblivious to fellow governments and common problems. There is a vast network of cooperative agreements for libraries, personnel services, public welfare, public health, purchasing, tax assessment and collection. These agreements are often temporary, based mostly on specific state authorizations, and they apply to services more than to facilities. Cooperation has been spurred by the intensity of some functional problems and the desire to avoid the creation of a more powerful and inclusive metropolitan government. Cooperative understandings, arranged by local administrators or sanctioned by local legislatures, are easier to establish than more formal arrangements requiring voter approval. Such cooperation sometimes even transcends central city-suburban cleavages.

A handful of metropolitan regions have metropolitan councils, including Detroit, Washington, D.C., San Francisco, and Salem, Oregon. These councils are voluntary associations of governments and key officials, whose powers are advisory, recommendatory, and coordinative. The Detroit Council, a pioneer, has made regional aviation and water studies, compiled the area's plans of public works programs, and endorsed bills for presentation to the state legislature. Critics, however, scorn the councils as toothless tigers capable of little bite on the status quo.

Patterns of consolidation. In the welter of adjustment to the metropolitan age, several major patterns are discernible among local governments. The one-government approach features large-scale municipal annexation (pursued most notably by Oklahoma City, which has amassed the largest city area in the United States) and city-county consolidation. An example of city-county consolidation is Davidson County, Tennessee, which includes Nashville. Davidson has an elected metropolitan county mayor and council. Functions that the county performs on an area-wide basis include schools, public health, police, courts, welfare, housing, streets and roads, while urban governments handle more intensely local functions—additional police protection, fire, sewage disposal, street lighting and cleaning. Nowadays, the one-government approach has little momentum. Grassrooters dismayed by the sizable enlargement of the local government unit object to this approach. Small government units are disinclined to subordinate themselves in consolidation and grapple with unwelcome problems, and there exists a strong belief, often valid, that many functions can be better performed by smaller units than by the metropolitan county.[15]

More satisfying to grassroots sentiment is the two-level or federal concept,

---

[15] John C. Bollens and Henry J. Schmandt, *The Metropolis* (New York: Harper & Row, 1965), 437–38.

in which one or more area-wide functions are allotted to an area-wide government, while local functions (more numerous and substantial than those in the metropolitan county plan) remain with local units. The result is a metropolitan-local system. The two-level arrangement sometimes uses the metropolitan district, approximating or coinciding with the metropolitan area, which is limited to a single service—water, transit, sewage disposal—or a few activities. Another variation is the comprehensive urban county plan by which the county performs some functions of area-wide significance, while the municipalities perform essentially local services. An illustration is Florida's Dade County, which includes Miami. Despite titanic struggles with local and state forces, Dade County has accomplished managerial reforms, is administering a uniform traffic code and an expressway system, and has constructed a seaport. The county has been handicapped by a lack of effective political leaders and civic organizations, by legal restrictions, and by meagre controls over the municipalities. Worst of all, according to one county manager, has been "the political opposition that municipal officers have placed in the path of almost every area-wide endeavor attempted." [16]

Metropolitanism is growing, supported by such interest groups as the Chamber of Commerce, the League of Women Voters, and builders and contractors eager to escape conflicting local building codes and zoning practices. But powerful forces at the grassroots limit metropolitanism to piecemeal advance rather than sweeping victories. Local officials fear the loss of power and prestige, labor unions are skeptical, and political parties, more interested in controlling offices than in making metropolitan policy, remain indifferent. State politicians behold metropolitan leaders as potential competitors.

Those interested in the urban poor have not been encouraged by their encounters with metropolitanism. In Baltimore County, consisting of 600 square miles without a single incorporated city, critics assert that the absence of community governments makes it difficult for the individual's view to be heard. Houston, in effect a metropolitan government because of Texas' generous annexation laws, has not applied its powers to poverty, housing, and schools, but instead has chosen to tax itself at the lowest rate of the twenty-five largest cities.[17] In the consolidated metropolis, the grassroots can also be fiscally malnourished.

Citizen participation

Grassroots theory presupposes that the citizen is eager to participate in many aspects of local affairs. There are many inducements to do so. In the local community the individual meets with the larger society and culture. There he directly confronts society's institutions and regulations and functions in organized relationships with other human beings. In addition, the citizen is

[16] *Ibid.,* 470.
[17] *New York Times,* June 3, 1971.

BLOCK ASSOCIATIONS CAN MAKE A DIFFERENCE !

SEE WHAT THEY HAVE DONE FOR THE COMMUNITY.

COME ON A BUS TOUR WITH US

TO SEE THE DIFFERENCE BETWEEN ORGANIZED AND UNORGANIZED BLOCKS.

SEE WHAT YOU CAN DO:

FOR SAFER STREETS

FOR CLEANER STREETS

FOR A GREENER BLOCK

DATE: OCTOBER 2ND   TIME: 6: 30 P. M.

MEETING PLACE: ASSEMBLYMAN TONY OLIVIERI'S DISTRICT OFFICE/ 209 E. 76th ST.

---

sometimes self-interested—he participates to protect his property or business. Other times, he is driven to participate in order to satisfy his family's needs for local public facilities or services, particularly in education and recreation. The motivational proddings are many, and not everyone possesses them in equal degree.

Participation appears to be affected by one's sense of community identification. For some, the local community is little more than a residence or a place of livelihood, and their contributions are the indispensable ones of producers, consumers, and taxpayers, while sharing little, if at all, in civic life. Others shoulder the burdens of voting, serving on school committees, and aiding in charity drives. Alas, according to one study, citizen participation does not rank high in citizen pride. A sampling of metropolitan Dayton, Ohio, residents was asked, "If someone who didn't know the Dayton and Montgomery area asked you what you were proudest of about it, what would you tell him?" More than half of the respondents stressed the area's cleanliness and beauty; others noted its prosperity and friendliness; but only one in fifty testified to a pride in citizen interest and participation.[18]

The modern city harbors mighty forces that deter participation. The city's bigness and elaborate specializations make the citizen's direct participation difficult, if not ineffective, and engenders numbing feelings of helplessness. The citizen is compelled to focus his attention and energies on his livelihood and to minimize his civic life. Although size, typically, may not afflict the suburbanite, specialization does. How does his participation compare with the city dweller's? The results of studies are mixed. A survey of electoral participation in forty-five communities of various sizes in Los Angeles County over a seventeen-year period disclosed little relation between community size and voting turnout.[19] However, the Dayton area survey found

---

[18] *Metropolitan Challenge* (Dayton, Ohio: Metropolitan Community Studies, 1959), 29–30.
[19] Lawrence W. O'Rourke, *Voting Behavior in Forty-Five Cities of Los Angeles County* (Los Angeles: University of California, Bureau of Governmental Research, 1953), 104.

that suburban residents are more likely than central city residents to belong to child-centered organizations and social and hobby clubs, but less inclined to participate in civic-oriented groups. The low participation of the suburbanite in the latter might be explained in terms of his being content with his community as it is; none of the competing political choices significantly threaten community norms or the established order.[20]

In a study of four middle-sized Wisconsin cities, Robert Alford and Harry Scoble examined six categories of factors thought to be major influences on local political involvement: social status, activity in organizations, community attachment, religion and ethnicity, political motivations, and sociopolitical environment. Social status and organizational activity, they found, were the most important characteristics linked with local political involvement. Political motivations or predispositions—measured by the indices of civic duty, political efficacy, and political alienation—were relatively less important. Even less important as an influence on local involvement was the individual's sociopolitical environment, as measured by social status and voting turnouts of the ward of residence.[21]

The most common and accessible form of grassroots participation is voting. Does the grassroots quality of an election affect voting? Apparently not, according to data revealing that voting behavior at the local level is generally similar to that of state and national elections.[22]

Studies of voting turnout show that turnout is generally higher in cities with "unreformed" political structures and sharper class or ethnic cleavages. Voting turnout is higher—not lower—in cities with less well educated populations, most likely because political issues in these cities are founded on bread-and-butter economic interests and are posed more explicitly and visibly than in the middle-class suburbs. Lineberry and Fowler have found that "reformed" cities (those with a manager-council, nonpartisan elections) were less likely to be responsive to divisions among their people than unreformed cities. Reformed cities, they inferred, have "removed" party as an influence for aggregating interests; consequently their political structures would be less integrated with their social structures than those of unreformed cities.[23]

The clear message of these studies is that the grassroots principle is essentially political—its utility and validity rest on politics. To diminish or remove politics from local affairs is to drain the grassroots ideal of its importance and of its potentially sizable contribution to democracy. Thus reforms such as at-large and nonpartisan elections reduce grassroots effectiveness and other so-called democratic reforms have had little offsetting impact.

[20] *Metropolitan Challenge,* 228; Bollens and Schmandt, 240–41.
[21] Robert R. Alford and Harry M. Scoble, "Sources of Local Political Involvement," *American Political Science Review,* LXII (December 1968), 1192–1205.
[22] Bollens and Schmandt, 223.
[23] Robert L. Lineberry and Edmund P. Fowler, "Reformism and Public Policies in American Cities," *American Political Science Review,* LXI (September 1967), 706. See also Robert R. Alford and Eugene C. Lee, "Voting Turnout in American Cities," *American Political Science Review,* LXII (September 1968), 796.

Elites
and the grassroots

The presence of elites in local politics is an intolerable violation of the grassroots ideal. At the grassroots, every man's opinion is relevant, and one or a few men's voices must not steadily dominate others. In recent years, many studies have grappled with the question: Who really runs the local community? Few, if any, of the studies support the sweeping grassroots response that it is "all of the people all of the time." Is grassroots thinking merely an exercise in fantasy?

Chief of the early studies is sociologist Floyd Hunter's *Community Power Structure*,[24] which aimed to discover the influentials in "Regional City," a pseudonym for Atlanta, Georgia. Hunter submitted lists of known governmental, business, and civic leaders to a panel of six persons, each informed and active in local affairs, who rated the reputed leaders according to their relative power. Hunter discovered that a "power structure" ruled Regional City consisting of about forty "power leaders," most of them businessmen. This finding was not unrelated to the nature of Regional City, a focal point for transportation, finance, and commerce ("the business of Regional City is business"). The machinery of government, Hunter maintained, was used "for the attainment of certain goals coordinate with the interests of the policymaking group." [25] With the blessing of the power leaders, projects move ahead; without it, all is becalmed. Community-wide issues pass through a committee structure dominated by power leaders, and policy is carried out by a responsive bureaucracy. In Regional City, the politician has little place except as an agent of the power leaders, and grassroots democracy finds no fertile soil.

A sharply contrasting view of local politics appears in Robert A. Dahl's *Who Governs?*,[26] a study of a city far less oriented to business and industry—New Haven, Connecticut. Instead of a highly centralized power structure, Dahl found a pluralistic or dispersed arrangement of community decision-making. Many individuals possess influence, and each asserts himself within a rather limited scope and only on certain questions—one set of actors controls issues of urban renewal, but if building a new hospital is at stake, another combination of leaders sets the course. In Dahl's New Haven, the business leaders who rule Hunter's Atlanta are but one of many influential groups or power clusters.

Dahl distinguishes between "direct" influence, possessed by relatively few, and "indirect" influence possessed by a great many. In the open, pluralistic system of New Haven, political leaders embody many of the most widely held values and goals of society. Whenever major popular values alter, the

---

[24] Floyd Hunter, *Community Power Structure* (Chapel Hill: University of North Carolina Press, 1953; 1968).
[25] *Ibid.,* 102.
[26] Robert A. Dahl, *Who Governs? Democracy and Power in an American City* (New Haven: Yale University Press, 1961).

politicians follow each swing of the pendulum. By sharing common values with political leaders and candidates, the great mass of those less involved in politics "can be said to 'govern.' " [27] But the impressive popular—grassroots— influence depends supremely on two institutions: elections and competitive parties.

In a 1961 study of six major community decisions in Chicago, Edward Banfield concluded that the supposition that a power elite pulls the community's wires is groundless.[28] Banfield also found multiple subunits of influence concentrating on particular sectors or issues of policy. In the convolutions of this dispersed power structure, many persons and groups, each independent and self-willed, must be brought into a consensus for every significant issue or proposal. No single unit of influence could decide or act for Chicago as a whole or formulate or carry out any general policy. Only from the clash and accommodation of multiple views and pressures could decision or policy ultimately emerge.

The presence of Chicago's tightly disciplined political machine did not alter one jot the general functioning of multiple influence centers. Notwithstanding their power, the mighty machine's leaders, rather than initiate proposals themselves, preferred to "ratify" proposals laid before them by local groups, especially after they had arranged their own consensus. When groups continued to disagree, the machine's elected officials delayed decision as long as possible while still receiving and even encouraging their pressures. Estimating the "representativeness" of the pressures, the officials picked up cues that sparked their judgments of how the issue was viewed by the public at large, for the elected machine official followed the course of doing what "a broad cross section of the community wants." The grassroots have their place in the gyrations of the country's most formidable local machine.

Peter Bachrach and Morton Baratz attack the pluralist approach and suggest that community power has "two faces"—one evident in the outcomes of the overt decision-making process, and the other manifest in the capacity of individuals and groups to prevent issues or contests from arising that would threaten their interests. Thus, nonissues and nondecisions are revealing indicators of community power, and instead of asking "who rules," one would investigate what procedures and rules of the game operate to *prevent* issues from arising. The focus of inquiry would be on which persons or groups, if any, gain from those rules, and which, if any, are handicapped by them.[29]

The weight of these many studies is that the folks at the grassroots are not mere ciphers in the hands of an omnipotent elite who manipulate community decisions. Grassroots people assert themselves through groups, political leaders, parties, and elections, and their force is substantial enough to make it difficult, if not impossible, to identify the elite that runs the city.

---

[27] *Ibid.,* 91.
[28] Edward C. Banfield, *Political Influence* (New York: Free Press, 1961).
[29] Peter Bachrach and Morton Baratz, "The Two Faces of Power," *American Political Science Review,* LVII (December 1962), 947–52.

Often it is clear that no one runs it—decisions and policies accumulate, snow-balling into results that no one intended or even contemplated.

The national government
and the grassroots

By all the force of logic, the national government is anathema to grassroots politics. Its preference for centralization, its remoteness from local affairs, the fact that most of its decision-makers hail from places other than a given local community and in no wise depend on its approval, would lead the grassroots to expect little nourishment from Washington. But logic is not always a sure guide to politics, and, paradoxically, the federal government since the 1960s has launched some of the most striking innovations in grassroots democracy yet known in American experience.

One is urban renewal, or the effort of governmental agencies and private groups to eradicate slums and halt blight in the cities. Local renewal agencies are granted federal funds and the power to condemn run-down neighborhoods, tear down the buildings, and resell the cleared land to private developers at a reduced price. The dispossessed slum dwellers, according to federal law, are to be relocated in "decent, safe, and sanitary" housing. Urban renewal also aims to create new tax revenues for the cities and halt the rush of middle-class whites to the suburbs.

Federal and state laws require that citizens of the community participate in renewal planning. Funds are to be spent and powers exercised "in the public interest," which is to be ascertained by open communication between officials and citizens. Apart from indulgence in the democratic ideal, participation has a pragmatic side: an apathetic or hostile community might obstruct fulfillment of a renewal project and bitter, protracted conflict might sap public confidence in a costly enterprise.

In a study of the interractial Hyde Park–Kenwood renewal project, near the University of Chicago, Peter Rossi and Robert Dentler examined the contribution of citizen participation.[30] Neighborhood and block groups shared in a "Community Conference," which proved highly effective in defining the public interest, formulating concepts of general interest that often overrode more self-interested quests for specific benefits, and organizing a mass base of support.

In contrast, the Seaside-Hammels project in New York City was virtually barren of citizen participation. People most affected by the project, those who lived on its site, had no significant voice in deciding whether or not there was to be a project, and what kind it would be. The attitude underlying these barren results is revealed by a project administrator who proclaimed, "Neigh-borhood groups are crap." In his study of New York City renewal projects,

[30] Peter H. Rossi and Robert A. Dentler, *The Politics of Urban Renewal* (New York: Free Press, 1961).

J. Clarence Davies found that even with participatory procedures, widespread feelings of alienation reigned among neighborhood groups and individuals, who were convinced that the city officials involved were corrupt and that the project was a plot to enrich real estate interests. Not surprisingly, a citizen's stakes in the project do much to shape his judgment of it. Small businessmen stand to lose most, particularly those engaging in a marginal enterprise that is highly dependent on the nature of the neighborhood population, and home-owners, with an economic and emotional investment in their houses, are often the most embittered.[31]

Far too often citizen participation is a sham. Renewal can destroy a grass-roots environment, chase away slum dwellers, and import selected newcomers for many luxury and a few middle-income housing projects, or provide in-expensive land for expanding colleges, hospitals, and shopping centers.[32]

In its antipoverty program, the federal government has also tried to in-volve the grassroots, this time the poor, in administration and policy-making. The antipoverty act of 1965, which launched the "war on poverty," requires "the maximum feasible participation of the residents of the areas and the members of the groups served," that is, the poor themselves, in the community action programs (CAPs). These programs include social services (remedial education classes, transporting the poor to the doctor), new opportunities (food cooperatives, subsidized business ventures), and changes in middle-class-oriented institutions (schools, hospitals, community chests).

The poor's participation was first seen in grandiose terms. "In effect," said Sargent Shriver, the program's original director, "we are asking those who hold power in the community to 'move over' and share that power with those who are to be helped." [33] Grassroots democracy was challenged as never be-fore: Could inarticulate, uneducated poor people, with low self-esteem and no administrative experience or parliamentary skill, share in decision-making with powerful and sophisticated community representatives?

Ralph M. Kramer made comparative studies of five California commu-nities and the participation of their poor in the poverty program.[34] In San Francisco, conflict between the mayor and minority leaders preempted any meaningful involvement of the poor themselves. Eventually, a coalition of ethnic minority groups, led by civil rights activists, triumphed over the mayor. Ostensibly, the poor were running their own program, since each target area organization (TAO) or neighborhood in which a community action program was established called for the war on poverty to be fought through direct involvement of the poor. Poor residents chose their own governing board for

---

[31] J. Clarence Davies III, *Neighborhood Groups and Urban Renewal* (New York: Colum-bia University Press, 1966).

[32] James Q. Wilson, ed., *Urban Renewal: The Record and the Controversy* (Cambridge: MIT Press, 1966), 538–39.

[33] In Robinson O. Everett, ed., *Anti-Poverty Programs* (Dobbs Ferry: Oceana Publications, 1966), 28.

[34] Ralph M. Kramer, *Participation of the Poor: Comparative Community Studies in the War on Poverty* (Englewood Cliffs, N.J.: Prentice-Hall, 1969).

Four modes of the resident poor's participation in the poverty program

Goal	Content of activity	Role of the poor
1. Participation in policy-making by representatives of the poor	CAP policy-making	Governing board members

Issues

Participation by the poor in a tripartite coalition	or	**Control** of the CAP Board by the representatives of the poor who constitute a majority of the members

Goal	Content of activity	Role of the poor
2. Target area feedback and utilization of service	Program development	Social service consumers

Issues

Centralization of power in the CAP with advisory functions delegated to the target area organization	or	**Decentralization** of power, with planning, policy-making, and administrative authority vested in the target area organization

Goal	Content of activity	Role of the poor
3. Redistribution of power to affect changes in community policies	Social action	Political constituency

Issues

Social service programs: community organization used mainly for information and referral purposes	or	**Political power:** community organization used to foster social action and community development

Goal	Content of activity	Role of the poor
4. Job experience	Employment in CAP	Staff members

Issues

Merit system qualifications for employment of indigenous people	or	**Patronage** as reward for loyalty or both merit and loyalty as criteria for employment

Source: Ralph M. Kramer, *Participation of the Poor* (Englewood Cliffs, N.J.: Prentice-Hall, 1969), p. 4.

the TAO, and the results ranged from an overall indigenous board in one area to virtually no representation of the poor in another. Most of the "poor" who were involved were not impoverished, but were working- or middle-class persons.

All five communities that Kramer studied were pressured to increase the representation of the poor in governing boards and to grant greater autonomy and policy-making power to the neighborhood organizations. Leadership and the ability to build coalitions were major factors in enlarging the impact of the poor. In San Francisco and Santa Clara County, relatively young, politically astute spokesmen of minority organizations with backgrounds in the civil rights movement saw an opportunity in the poverty program to organize the poor with federal sanction. In Santa Clara County, a Mexican-American coalition gained allies among labor, religion, and the NAACP.

Different communities developed different patterns in disposing of issues. In some, the community "climate" was more receptive to consensual modes of decision-making, and officials were responsive even to mild pressures asserted in behalf of low-income people.

In other communities, the consensual pattern was aided by the lengthy experience of previous social service projects, which supplied indigenous participants capable of promoting the interests of the poor, plus a nucleus of white liberal supporters in the community. In still other communities the CAP became the focus of a struggle for control between, on the one hand, civil rights activists and minority politicians and, on the other hand, the local officials, worried that the poverty program would be captured by those who did not owe allegiance to the mayor.

A common question concerning participation is: Who speaks for the poor? Typically, CAPs took place in target areas with high concentrations of impoverished minority families and individuals, the pressures of program deadlines, limited staff, and many imponderables. Several patterns of representation emerged. In one, a single organization or combination of several existing neighborhood organizations was sought out to be the major source of the new official body for target area participation. In another, a completely new organization was created either through a series of decentralized, area-wide elections, or by selecting the TAO's membership at several public meetings. The common result was a "creaming" process: those persons most accustomed to participating in voluntary associations were skimmed off the top and became the nucleus of the representatives, thereby excluding most of the hard-core poor.

Elections did not alter this result. Their impact was limited by the laxity with which they were conducted, the flexible criteria for candidates, small voter turnout, and the failure to maintain constituency organizations after the election. Representation was also hampered by relatively little concern for accountability, disruptive factionalism, and the representative's lack of a sense of accomplishment, plus the structural and sociopsychological barriers to the poor's participation rooted in the realities of poverty itself. Although the CAPs created new centers of minority influence, none affected the prevailing structure and balance of power in any significant way.

On the positive side, participation forced the professional staffs to meet target area representatives on a regular, formalized basis, which meant that program plans had to be discussed and poor people's reactions taken into account. Governmental and community influentials, representing the established centers of power, confronted minority persons as peers for the first time. The gains have clearly outpaced the losses and CAPs have become regular, established institutions in nearly any city of size.

Like the antipoverty program, the 1965 federal Model Cities program called for "widespread participation." Selected cities were to demonstrate how blighted neighborhoods could be renewed, both physically and in the quality of life, by a concentration of federal and local programs, with a high degree of local and citizen control. But Model Cities is even more susceptible to City Hall control than the poverty program. Federal legislation specifically requires that funds be controlled by City Hall, which George Romney, Nixon's Secretary of Housing and Urban Development, said must have "final control and responsibility." [35]

Proposals

For all the bold new projects of the 1960s the races have become increasingly divided between the central cities and the suburbs, prompting one black political leader to remark that the day will soon come when black people residing in the central city will charge white suburban people admission to partake of the city's economic and cultural attractions. Clearly, the nation's sorest domestic vulnerability is at the grassroots. At this late hour, can anything be done?

1. John V. Lindsay, speaking from experience as a Republican, a Democrat, and a fusion mayor, has called for the recognition or chartering of "national cities." Noting that cities like Houston, Detroit, and Philadelphia are each larger than fifteen of the fifty states, and that the budget of New York City is larger than the budget of New York state, Lindsay proposes that the federal government grant a number of national cities special powers. He anticipates that twenty-five cities with populations over 500,000 would qualify, and perhaps others as well.

No longer would national cities be supplicants to their states, resolutely indifferent to city problems. The chartered national cities would deal directly with Washington on matters of trade, finance, and social welfare, and they could receive broader federal financial support than under the present system, by which the juiciest financial resources slide to the suburbs beyond the city's reach. National cities, under the Lindsay plan, would have "independent authority on issues of local concern and urban development." Local grassroots politics would persist and possibly flourish even more than it does now, despite the paradox of a stronger federal presence.[36]

2. If tradition, apathy, and powerful political forces prevent adoption of the plan of national cities, then let us have metropolitan area governments,

[35] *New York Times,* December 15, 1969.
[36] *New York Times,* June 9, 1971.

possibly patterned after the successful Metropolitan Council of the Minne-apolis–St. Paul area. Unlike other metropolitan councils whose powers are feeble, the "Metro Council," as Minnesotans call it, has power with teeth. It has the power to tax and to coordinate the overall physical, social, and eco-nomic development of the 3,000 square mile area. The Council wields authority over functions that affect the entire area—highways and sewage disposal, for example—while leaving to local government those functions that can better be fragmented, such as schools and police.

How did this political miracle alight in Minnesota? Like other cities, Minneapolis–St. Paul experienced massive migrations to the suburbs and deterioration of the inner cities, and in the 1960s these rising problems became acute. The crisis-ridden municipalities joined business and civic interests in pressing for a governmental instrument that could deal effectively with major area-wide problems. The state legislature created the council of fifteen members, a cross section of the area's civic and business leadership appointed by the governor. Ostensibly a part-time responsibility, the Council has been so effective, and therefore busy, that some of its members spend their full time canvassing their districts for citizen opinion and applying the council's broad authority.[37]

3. To enable the suburbanite, or for that matter, any citizen, to penetrate the apparent or performing government and reach the real government—in other words, genuine grassroots politics—Herbert Gans has proposed the revival and extension of the traditional American civic association. This would be a forum for meetings and publications, which would enable people to air their opinions on important issues and would report the results of community public opinion polls on these issues. Using high school students to publish a newspaper and reports, the association could both reduce costs and contribute to the education of the students in the social sciences. Deficits could be fi-nanced by municipal subsidy. The association could add diversity to local political discussion, increase grassroots involvement, and facilitate citizen feedback by publication of letters containing ideas and grievances.

To succeed, the civic association would have to be deliberately political rather than pursue the traditional and usually futile course of being "above politics." Sometimes it need not take sides, but always it would seek to draw out opposing opinions, and thereby force officials to discuss local issues meaningfully. The association's members and officers would be drawn from all political groups, party factions, and local interests. Its effectiveness would depend on its ability to attract widespread citizen support in order to make decision-makers pay attention to its activities and findings.[38]

4. There is an array of possible structural changes in local government, which, if effected, might brighten the future of grassroots politics. Both political communication and the decision-makers' responsiveness might be improved

---

[37] *New York Times,* February 7, 1971.
[38] Gans, *The Levittowners,* 359–60.

by enlarging local elective bodies. Boards and councils of three, five, or even nine men (rarely are there women members) cannot adequately represent the diversity of most communities, especially their less powerful minority citizens. A board of fifteen to twenty officials would enable voters to express opinions on a broader basis and give more exposure to minority views.[39]

5. The local participation aspects of the war on poverty are, despite their flaws, a valuable contribution to grassroots democracy and ought to be built on. Democratic pluralism is patently ungenuine if minority members of the community, most usually the powerless and the deprived, are left out. In many communities, the CAP demonstrated that participation by low-income people can increase their stake in society and, by diminishing their feelings of powerlessness, can raise their morale and social effectiveness.

What might be done to improve the local participation of the poor? First, since the poor are not a homogeneous group with shared class consciousness and a common set of demands and needs, there is no single structure for participation nor one set of goals that is desirable for all. Flexibility and variety seem to be the most useful qualities of any structuring for the poor's participation. The possibilities of flexibility are greater than the CAP experience has revealed. Emphasis might be given to the development and support of functional organizations like mutual benefit associations and cooperatives, in which low-income persons would constitute the policy-making board and staff as well as the users and beneficiaries. Stemming from individual and neighborhood needs, these organizations would vary in scope and size—from child-care cooperatives and food buying clubs to credit unions and neighborhood organizations.

The neighborhood corporation is a feasible means for enabling low-income residents to acquire a power base. Democratically structured, the neighborhood corporation would conduct a wide range of enterprises for the benefit of the neighborhood as consumers and employees. Self-governing, single or multipurposed, accountable to residents and stockholders, the neighborhood corporation could avoid some of the electoral dilemmas that afflicted the TAOs and might establish or revitalize democratic processes in low-income areas. Admittedly, there would be many hazards, not the least of which is that the neighborhood corporation may acquire the worst habits of bureaucracy.

Other steps toward improving the impact of the poor at the grassroots might include strengthening their social, religious, and civic organizations by providing them with staff, technical assistance, funds, and other resources enabling them to operate their own programs. Efforts to organize poor people around shared needs should focus not so much on poor persons as such, but rather on members of social groupings, such as agency clients, ethnic minorities, or participants in a functional or mutual-benefit organization.[40]

---

[39] *Ibid.,* 361–62.
[40] Kramer, 269–73.

Suggested Reading

Banfield, Edward C., *The Unheavenly City: The Nature and Future of Our Urban Crisis* *
  (Little, Brown, 1970). In this analysis of urban society and politics, Banfield contends
  that the "urban crisis" is sometimes exaggerated.
Donaldson, Scott, *The Suburban Myth* * (Columbia University Press, 1969). Challenges
  many generalizations about the suburbs and stresses their variety. Usefully explores the
  implications of suburban living and politics for democracy.
Gans, Herbert J., *The Levittowners* * (Pantheon, 1967). Analyzes the politics of a suburban community and illuminates its discrepancies with democratic ideals. Offers
  remedial proposals.
Gilbert, Charles E., *Governing the Suburbs* (Indiana University Press, 1967). An insightful analysis of the suburbs and their governmental problems. Deals with different
  kinds of suburbs.
Gottmann, Jean, *Megalopolis* * (Twentieth Century Fund, 1961). A study of the largest
  urbanized sector of the United States, the coastal northeast.
Hawley, Willis D., and Wirt, Frederick M., *The Search for Community Power* *
  (Prentice-Hall, 1968). An excellent analysis of the considerable debate that has developed over the question of who exercises community power. Draws on the work of
  both sociologists and political scientists.
Kramer, Ralph M., *Participation of the Poor: Comparative Community Studies in the
  War on Poverty* * (Prentice-Hall, 1969). Illuminating comparative study of the war
  on poverty in a number of California communities. Stresses the limitations of poor
  people in politics as well as their strengths.
Rossi, Peter H., and Dentler, Robert, *The Politics of Urban Renewal* (Free Press, 1961).
  A leading study of the politics of urban renewal and of neighborhood participation.
  Deals with the role of city hall politics.
Sayre, Wallace S., and Kaufman, Herbert, *Governing New York City* * (Russell Sage
  Foundation, 1960). A comprehensive study of New York's government and politics.
Wilson, James Q., *Urban Renewal: The Record and the Controversy* * (MIT Press, 1966).
  An invaluable study of urban renewal politics in different communities. Evaluates urban
  renewal as a response to urban problems and analyzes the political effectiveness of
  neighborhood organizations as participants.
Wood, Robert C., *Suburbia: Its People and Their Politics* * (Houghton Mifflin, 1959).
  A study of suburban politics, social values, and governmental problems.

*Available in paperback edition

15

war

and

peace

"Foreign politics," wrote Alexis de Tocqueville, "demands scarcely any of those qualities which are peculiar to a democracy; they require, on the contrary, the perfect use of almost all those in which it is deficient." [1] Democracy thrives on consensus-building processes and equitable rule-making, but in the international system, states are discrete, rules few, enforcement weak, power relatively unregulated, and conflict easily provoked. World affairs are dominated by the selfish phenomenon of nationalism, which is less than a wholly satisfactory mold for democracy.

Nationalism embodies an egotism that beholds other states and their people as potential enemies, and such democratic values as love of neighbor and fairness toward others are superseded by absolute assertion of self-interest. Only "individual men" and not the nations of which they are a part, according to theologian Reinhold Niebuhr, "are able to consider interests other than their own in determining the problems of conduct, and are capable *on occasion,* of preferring the advantages of others to their own." [2] Representing the worse rather than the better side of man, nationalism facilitates the dominance of collective passions and emotions over the democratic ideals of rationality and objectivity. "My country right or wrong," a spirit engendered by nationalism, readily places a premium on such undemocratic behavior as aggression, secrecy, and deceit.

Nationalism tends to inflate the executive branch, which can indulge more efficiently in these undemocratic behavior patterns than can the other governmental branches. The executive can make key foreign policy decisions with absolute secrecy, in gross violation of democratic norms. There was no public debate about whether the United States should become a nuclear power; the entire initial program was enveloped in wartime secrecy. Such public debate as took place on the desirability of advancing from atomic to hydrogen bombs was retrospective rather than prospective, since it was oc-

---

[1] Alexis de Tocqueville, *Democracy in America* (New York: Vintage Press, 1937), Vol. 1, 243.
[2] In Harry H. Davis and Robert C. Good, *Reinhold Neibuhr on Politics* (New York: Scribners, 1960), 84.

casioned not by regularly applicable procedures, but as a by-product of hearings concerning the continued eligibility for security clearance of J. Robert Oppenheimer, a leading atomic scientist. The executive's control over foreign policy subjects democracy to a malady describable as "the pride of leaders." [3] The chief executive may develop such a personal stake in the success of a policy, such as one for the Vietnam war, that he will not abandon his course of action, no matter how high or ill-advised are its costs.

If they do not already pertain to war, foreign policies may lead to war, which history has made too frequent an aspect of the human condition. In war, democracy is always a loser. Democracy has a special stake in peace, in whose hospitable climate it fares far better than in the oppressive rigors of war. War endangers civil liberties, imbalances the powers of government by enlarging the executive, shifts public funds from programs needed to promote a just and good life at home to the machines of war, which can only destroy. Yet, like any nation-state, a democratic one has the fundamental obligation to survive, to protect its citizens from external danger, to perpetuate itself as a form of government rather than yield to the threatening tyrant who means to destroy its processes.

The Communist system

Contemporary American democracy's dilemmas in foreign affairs are compounded by the nature of its principal competitors, the Communist nations. By western democratic standards, the Communist powers possess several characteristics inimical to peaceful foreign policy. In Communist lands there are special inducements for the pride of leaders to manifest itself. The leaders function as priests of the revealed religion of Marxism-Leninism; they are its absolute interpreters, guardians, and aggrandizers. Claiming infallibility in thought and action, they can extract from the citizen an absolute duty to obey. It is but a short step to the "cult of personality," the worship of an individual leader, a Mao or a Stalin, as the charismatic incarnation of Communist truth and virtue. According to the leaders' interpretations of their dogma, a non-Communist state such as the United States is perceived not as democratic, but as capitalistic, exploitative, and deteriorating, soon ripe for overthrow by proletarian revolution. These are not the most propitious findings for the cause of peace.

In their respective stances toward foreign policy, the western democracies and the major Communist powers differ radically. The democracies are status quo oriented; they are prone to uphold existing political boundaries, to profess "respect for international obligations and treaties," to treat issues of technology and human rights as domestic rather than international. The Soviet Union tends toward an opposite position on these criteria. Since the Second World

[3] See Hans J. Morgenthau, *A New Policy for the United States* (New York: Praeger, 1969), 155–56.

President Nixon being welcomed to Peking in 1972.

War, Soviet policy has been expansionist, leading to the conquest of Eastern Europe and a part of the Balkans, pressure on Turkey, increased presence in the Mediterranean and the Indian Ocean, recovery of interests in China following the Yalta Conference of 1945, supply of armaments to North Korea and North Vietnam. To seize power in less developed countries the Communists have perfected guerrilla warfare techniques, supplemented by social and economic theories and promises pitched to strong popular desires, such as the redistribution of land to tenant cultivators.

Despite these and other inauspicious factors, the Communist landscape affords views of trends hospitable to peaceful, constructive relations with the western democracies. Contemporary communism is far less monolithic, less overshadowed by the Soviet Union, than in the past, to the point that the Communist system has become polycentric. Thus Communist Yugoslavia, China, Albania, and Rumania pursue policies determined not by the Soviet Union, but by their own peculiar national qualities and needs. These Communist nations cooperate or compete with one another and with western democracies to advance their individual interests. For all its thorny formidability, Communist dogma is largely silent on how relations between Communist sovereign nations should be conducted, and the stirrings of a give-and-take procedure among equals point toward more a democratic than a totalitarian framework. (Distressing exceptions—Czechoslovakia and Hungary among them—suggest that equality is reserved for countries more removed from the Soviet orbit.) Communism too can resort to constructive pragmatism: witness the reception of President Nixon and his entourage in Peking in 1972 after decades of mutual Sino-American denunciation. Nixon followed that visit with one to Moscow.

Finally, in some Communist lands there are faint signs of democratic freedoms. When a Russian youth, Pavel Litvinov, dared to walk in Moscow's Red Square in 1968 with a placard demanding that the Soviet Union "Get Out of Czechoslovakia," he was arrested, tried, and imprisoned for five years. This was progress. "In Stalin's day," Averell Harriman, former ambassador to Moscow, noted, "he would not have gotten to Red Square. He would have been grabbed before, and his body would never have been seen again." [4]

Varieties of American foreign policy

In facing a world of dangers and opportunities, American democracy has pursued foreign policies that have become traditional or at least recurring. One is *isolationism,* which draws inspiration from Washington's Farewell Address, warning the nation against the dangers of "entangling alliances." It was manifested in public insistence that American troops "come back home" promptly after the two world wars, in effect abandoning situations that the United States had helped to create to other influences, including after the First World War, Hitler. A hazard of the disillusionment over the Vietnam war is that it may revive the false supposition that the external world can safely be abandoned to its own turbulent self. As indiscriminate abstention, isolationism scorns foreign aid programs and blinks away any responsibility for the outside world, four-fifths of which barely subsists on one-fifth of the world's resources. A withdrawn American democracy would push on the other, less powerful democracies the task of competing with totalitarian states for influence in the international system.

Opposite in extreme, and even more vigorous, is the policy of *globalism,* denoted by indiscriminate involvement and absolute confidence in the competence of American power to protect our interests anywhere, anytime. Its most sweeping expression appeared in John F. Kennedy's inaugural address in 1961: "Let every nation know, whether it wishes us well or ill, that we shall pay any price, bear any burden, meet any hardship, support any friend, oppose any foe to assure the survival and success of liberty." [5] An operating example of globalism was the Truman Doctrine, formulated in 1947 to provide aid to Greece and Turkey against threatened Communist encroachment.

[4] W. Averell Harriman, *America and Russia in a Changing World* (New York: Doubleday, 1971), 100–01.
[5] In *New York Times,* January 21, 1961.

United States mutual defense and collective security agreements [1]

Far East

Security treaty with Australia and New Zealand

Mutual defense treaty with Philippines

Mutual defense treaty with Nationalist China

Security treaty with Japan

Mutual defense treaty with South Korea

Southeast Asia Treaty Organization (SEATO): Australia, Britain, France, New Zealand, Pakistan,[2] Philippines, Thailand, United States

---

Europe

North Atlantic Treaty Organization (NATO):
Belgium, Britain, Canada, Denmark, France, Greece, Iceland, Italy, Luxembourg, Netherlands, Norway, Portugal, Turkey, United States, West Germany

---

Latin America

Inter-American Treaty—Organization of American States (OAS):
Argentina, Barbados, Boliva, Brazil, Chile, Colombia, Costa Rica, Dominican Republic, Ecuador, El Salvador, Guatemala, Haiti, Honduras, Mexico, Nicaragua, Panama, Paraguay, Peru, Trinidad-Tobago, United States, Uruguay, Venezuela

---

[1] In the Middle East, the United States is not a signatory member of the Central Treaty Organization (CENTO; Britain, Iran, Pakistan, and Turkey), but it does provide arms, funds, and participants in economic, antisubversion, and military committees.
[2] On November 8, 1972, Pakistan announced that it was withdrawing from SEATO.

The Truman Doctrine visualized the world as divided into two main camps, democratic and totalitarian. It pledged the defense of free democratic nations everywhere against "direct or indirect aggression" and against "subjugation by armed minorities or by outside pressure." [6] Its principal tool, *containment,* applies counterforce, whether political, economic, or military, to check the maneuvers, direct and indirect, of the Soviet Union and other Communist powers.

In the spirit of globalism, the United States since the Second World War has followed an assertive foreign policy on all the continents and has structured a series of worldwide alliances in mutual defense pacts like NATO and SEATO. Balance of power has been a chief object of this foreign policy. As an Atlantic power, the United States has kept a wary eye on developments in the European continent. America intervened in two world wars to maintain a balance of power when Europe was threatened by German hegemony, and since the Second World War the United States has maintained troops in Europe and joined NATO to guard against possible Soviet dominance on the continent. NATO (North Atlantic Treaty Organization) consists of the United

[6] In Morgenthau, 179.

States and Canada and thirteen nations of western and southern Europe, who are pledged to defend each other against attack. NATO has its own command systems and forces contributed by the member countries. Through NATO, the United States long hoped to have an integrated European military system, but this has not materialized, and the United States has felt compelled to maintain a sizable force in Europe on its own.

As a Pacific power, the United States has sought to check Communist expansion in Asia. In its commitment to wars in Korea and Vietnam the United States has tended to equate local Communist movements with the more major and more outreaching ones. It has also tended to assume that the balance of power considerations are the same in Asia as in Europe—that the rice surplus countries of Southeast Asia are as strategic as the industrial nations of western Europe. The principal Asian alliance of American sponsorship is SEATO (Southeast Asia Treaty Organization), which has amounted to little more than a mutual defense pact among the participating nations. In a separate action, induced by France's determination to withdraw forces from South Vietnam in 1956, the United States took over responsibility for maintaining a non-Communist regime there south of the 17th parallel.

Events have served to distinguish the realities of globalism from its rhetoric. For example, containment could not prevent the Communist takeover of mainland China in 1949, and the difficulty and costliness of containing communism in Southeast Asia has long been apparent. Richard Nixon gave signs of moving away from the well-worn containment policy. He announced that "after a period of confrontation, we are entering an era of negotiation." [7] He followed this announcement with visits to mainland China, the Soviet Union, Rumania, and other Communist powers. In addition, he promulgated the Nixon Doctrine, which looks toward sharp reductions in American forces overseas, furthered by heavy withdrawals from South Vietnam and Taiwan and enlarged responsibility of local peoples for their own defense.

American foreign policy is most often *moralistic,* a by-product of democracy's latent smugness, its tendency to oversimplify its environment, to see itself as good, indeed exemplary, and opposing forms of government as evil. Woodrow Wilson beheld the First World War as a glorious crusade for universal democracy: the dragon to be slain was autocratic government. The international dimensions of Lyndon Johnson's Great Society program combined moralistic Wilsonian globalism with faith in the rightness of the "American dream": "We mean to show that this nation's dream of a Great Society does not stop at the water's edge. It is not just an American dream. All are welcome to share in it. All are invited to contribute to it." [8] But holding up America to other nations as a model that they ought morally to follow has drawbacks. It unduly minimizes the tenacity of ruling classes, particularly in developing countries, to perpetuate the status quo, and it overlooks the fact that most other nations do not enjoy to the same degree the rich environmental

[7] Richard Nixon, *U.S. Foreign Policy for the 1970s, A New Strategy for Peace* (Washington, D.C.: U.S. Government Printing Office, February 18, 1970), 2.
[8] In Morgenthau, 86.

blessings of the United States—bountiful natural resources, geographic separation from scenes of international strife, and a rational hard-working people who can readily take advantage of high social mobility.

The United Nations

American utilization of the United Nations as an instrument for advancing its foreign policies has been erratic. One reason for this is that the UN is paradoxically structured so that peace and democracy, which we have been assuming are altogether harmonious, are competing concepts. As to peace, the UN is predicated on the assumption that it can endure only if the big powers want it to; consequently, the UN's Security Council is the domain of five great powers (the United States, Britain, China, France, and the Soviet Union). Their unanimous votes are necessary on all substantive measures, enabling any one of the five to veto a resolution supported by the other four and the ten additional members elected for a term of two years by the General Assembly. The democratic ideal of equality is upheld by the Assembly in which each member nation, regardless of its power, has one vote. But the UN's principle of peace supersedes the principle of democracy because the Assembly can only debate and recommend while the Council alone can make binding decisions.

United Nations agencies

Economic Commission for Latin America ECLA	International Telecommunications Union ITU
Economic and Social Council ECOSOC	UN Conference on the Application of Science and Technology to Developing Areas UNCAST
Food and Agriculture Organization FAO	
International Atomic Energy Administration IAEA	UN Conference on Trade and Development UNCTAD
International Bank for Reconstruction and Development IBRD	UN Development Program UNDP
	UN Educational, Scientific, and Cultural Organization UNESCO
International Civil Aviation Organization ICAO	
International Development Association IDA	UN Industrial Development Organization UNIDO
	UN Institute for Training and Research UNITAR
International Finance Corporation IFC	
International Labor Organization ILO	World Health Organization WHO
International Monetary Fund IMF	World Meteorological Organization WMO

How serviceable has the UN been for the maintenance of peace, a precondition of democracy in all countries? The UN Charter bans the use or threat of force in international relations and guarantees each member nation its territorial integrity and security. But the UN has stark moments of ineffectuality, such as when the great powers act unilaterally—the Soviet Union putting down the Hungarian uprisings of 1956 and occupying Czechoslovakia in 1968, or the United States landing Marines in Santo Domingo in 1965. Impotence is also exposed when the great powers confront one another or take opposite sides on an issue: the UN could do little to halt the war between India and Pakistan in 1971 because the Soviet Union backed India and the United States favored Pakistan. Fortunately, UN peace-keeping has enjoyed conspicuous successes, particularly its interventions in Lebanon, the Congo, and Cyprus, where civil war threatened and the UN in effect performed the duties of domestic government. Since its expansion in the late fifties and sixties to include many nonaligned nations, the UN has been much less dependable for American purposes, a circumstance that has led the United States increasingly to bypass the UN's peace-keeping possibilities. The pride of nations works its spell.

American commitment to the UN was particularly buffeted by the admission of Communist China to the world organization in 1971 and the ejecting of an old ally, Nationalist China. Vigorous lobbying by the United States Ambassador to the UN, George Bush, failed to stave off the defeat. For years many nations had restively followed the American lead in voting to keep Communist China out, but the well-publicized preparations for

Nixon's journey to mainland China broke the ranks of American supporters.

Since the China defeat, Congress has been reluctant to assume as much responsibility for the UN's bill. In 1972 it applied the axe to its appropriation for the UN and, with the Nixon administration's approval, lowered its share of the UN budget from 31.52 percent to 25 percent. The State Department explained that it was "unhealthy" for the world organization to depend excessively on payments by one member. Meanwhile UN Secretary General Kurt Waldheim was asking for a 5 percent increase to cover costs in 1973.[9]

The decision-making network for foreign policy

The Executive Office. Particularly in decision-making, as we saw in Chapter 8, foreign affairs and national security are the more private and removed realms of the Presidency. Formidable structural and traditional elements are at work. The President's powers are vested in him personally; he does not share them with any other body, except in the case of treaties and certain appointments, which need the approval of the Senate. As head of the executive branch, the President commands the sinews of action: the armed forces, foreign aid, appropriated funds, a vast bureaucracy. The swift development in the last three administrations of a powerful assistant to the President for national security affairs (successively McGeorge Bundy, Walt W. Rostow, and Henry Kissinger) further magnifies the President's personal power.

Nixon's 1970 reorganization of the National Security Council (NSC) enhanced Kissinger's role and influence. The reorganization provides for a number of interdepartmental committees or groups as part of the NSC structure, all of which closely involve Kissinger. An Interdepartmental Review Group, chaired by Kissinger and composed of top officials from State, Defense, and other agencies, reviews foreign policy issues and options before they are presented to the President. Kissinger is also chairman of an interdepartmental group that reviews the national security budget, and he is at the center of still other groups that make contingency plans for possible crises and review the implementation and performance of established policies.

Kissinger's growth of power has been accompanied by a growth of staff, approaching as high as 100 assistants, a resource that emboldens the White House to reject departmental judgments and substitute its own. Both the White House and the departments, of course, can favor peace-serving positions. Thus Nixon overruled the Joint Chiefs of Staff when they opposed unilateral elimination of stocks of biological weapons, but the chiefs successfully counseled restraint when in 1969 an unarmed U.S. spy plane was shot down off the coast of North Korea and the outraged President's initial inclination was to bomb airfields in retaliation.[10]

The National Security Council was originally meant to concentrate on

[9] *New York Times,* August 22, 1972.
[10] *New York Times,* January 21, 1971.

such national security matters as the defense budget and military strategic and tactical doctrine but successive Presidents have transformed it into a foreign-policy-making body. In the latter role, the function of three of its seven statutory members—the Secretary of Defense, Chairman of the Joint Chiefs of Staff, and the Director of the CIA—tilt the NSC toward military and intelligence viewpoints that are disposed to perceive world affairs apprehensively, in terms of threats and capabilities. Only one NSC member, the Secretary of State, is suited to speak for the peaceful processes of diplomacy.[11]

The Department of State. Because it is responsible for conducting diplomatic relations, the State Department is functionally predisposed to maintain peace. An eruption of war is a revelation of professional failure. Unfortunately, democracy's interest in peace has been impaired by the generally reduced effectiveness that has befallen the State Department since the Second World War. Presidents are prone to speak of it disparagingly; Kennedy called it "a bowl of jelly," and Nixon, soon after taking office, was described as "now more determined than ever to turn the place upside down." [12]

What ails the State Department? Partly its troubles stem from the complexity of foreign policy itself, its incorporation of a diversity of ingredients including political, economic, cultural, psychological, and informational elements, all of which must somehow be woven together into policy. As bureaucracies are wont to do, the State Department provides elaborate specialization for these elements, to the point that responsibility is excessively divided and easily evaded. The splintering of work into many pieces compels heavy reliance on "coordinating" or "clearing" horizontally among bureaus and offices before ascending the chain of command. An instruction to an ambassador, for example, can require up to twenty-seven signatures for clearance before it is dispatched.[13] "Clearing" is a voracious consumer of man-hours committed to telephone calls, committee and staff meetings, and constant redrafting of policy development papers to reflect the elaborately qualified, almost Byzantine assent of those who do the clearing.

Policy initiatives develop so slowly that the State Department and its Foreign Service personnel largely forfeit innovative foreign-policy making to others. According to the important departmental self-study, "Diplomacy for the 70's," the department concentrates "on the end of daily routine, while other departments, Defense, CIA, the White House staff have made more important, innovative contributions to foreign policy." [14]

The State Department and the Foreign Service are excessively separated from the domestic political world. Both parties of interest suffer. As John

[11] John Franklin Campbell, *The Foreign Affairs Fudge Factory* (New York: Basic Books, 1971), 267–69.
[12] In Campbell, 6.
[13] *New York Times,* January 18, 1971.
[14] U.S. Department of State, *Diplomacy for the 70's: A Program of Management Reform for the Department of State* (Washington, D.C.: U.S. Government Printing Office, 1970); *New York Times,* January 18, 1971.

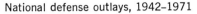

National defense outlays, 1942–1971

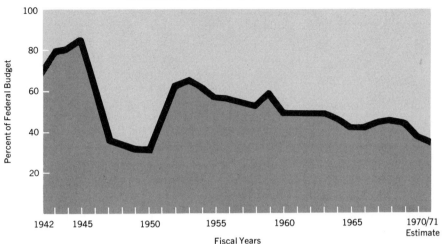

Source: *U.S. Budget for Fiscal Year 1971* (Washington, D.C.: U.S. Government Printing Office, 1970), p. 83.

Franklin Campbell suggested, the diplomat can bring a sense of reality about the outside world to domestic rhetoric.[15] Likewise, in his presumed dedication to perpetuating peace, the diplomatic careerist could enjoy greater impact if he appreciated the nature of domestic forces and interests working for peace.

The military. Since the Second World War, many have become gravely concerned lest the huge American military establishment overwhelm the democratic society it is supposed to protect. Even a President such as Lyndon Johnson, who very much depended on the military, became suspicious: "The generals," he said, "know only two words—spend and bomb."[16]

Can democratic society confine the military within salutary limits? The Founding Fathers deliberately established civilian supremacy over the military, most immediately by subordinating the armed forces to a civilian commander in chief, the President. Fortunately, the contemporary era of an expanded military presence has been accompanied by extension of the principle of "civilianization." For example, the defense establishment's heavy dependence on advanced industrial technology and modern management techniques has fostered interpenetration of these disparate worlds and the emergence of a new breed of "military managers" who more resemble the civilian organization man than the traditional "heroic leader" of the military establishment. However, this development has an underside: it provides the foundation for the military-industrial complex and its spreading influence in domestic society.

[15] Campbell, 66–67.
[16] In Adam Yarmolinsky, *The Military Establishment* (New York: Harper & Row, 1971), 31.

Military strategy is no longer the exclusive domain of military profes-sionals. The rise of civilian experts became strikingly evident in the Kennedy-Johnson administrations, particularly during Robert McNamara's tenure as Secretary of Defense. His innovative budget techniques and cost-benefit analyses accelerated the centralization of civilian authority in the Pentagon. In the Nixon administration that authority has become somewhat less cen-tralized.

Since many elements enter into national security decisions, the military are thrown into constant association with the State Department and other civilian agencies in hammering out policy. Unfortunately, a frequent effect of this interplay is the ascendance of military influence in foreign policy. Military policy-makers impress the civilians with the dire need to halt Communist expansion, with the importance of reducing opportunities that embolden the Soviet Union to initiate war, with the absolute imperative of avoiding any serious American disadvantage should war come. Like the military, civilian policy-makers then become prone to judge events and contingencies in terms of enemy capabilities rather than intentions.

Important to democracy's future and the prospects for peace is the state of the professional military mind. A comparative study of West Point cadets and Dartmouth college students found that the cadets are decidedly less libertarian on such matters as dealing with protesters and screening campus speakers, and were more hard-nosed on foreign affairs. To the solace of libertarian democracy, it was also found that graduates of colleges such as Dartmouth often hold senior posts in the national security establishments, where presumably they can keep some check on their less democratically attuned associates.[17] The present wave of military unpopularity seems likely to foster a narrower range of applicants for the service academies from more conservative social backgrounds.

Intelligence. "One of the greatest dangers of the cold war mentality," writes Harry Howe Ransom, "is that it tends to ape the adversary." [18] In resorting to major intelligence activity, American democracy is adapting to a hostile environment by taking up undemocratic ways, or a process that is an art of many parts, both covert and overt. Intelligence includes information about another country's economic life, internal political issues, military strength, its present and future leaders, its purposes. The information can be garnered from the press, library research, interviews with visitors and refugees, or by spying. Increasingly information is gathered by electronic and other technical means. Information must be interpreted for meanings relevant to decisions, for trends, for clues of possible intent. Interpretations lead to "estimates," or projections into the future by means of studied responses to such questions as "What will be the effects of American economic policy on Soviet-Japanese

[17] *Ibid.,* 81–82.
[18] In Harry Howe Ransom, *The Intelligence Establishment* (Cambridge: Harvard Uni-versity Press, 1970), 244.

relations?" and "What are the probable developments in Chinese Communist nuclear capabilities?"

Close to a score of agencies engage in foreign intelligence work, including the State and Defense departments, the Atomic Energy Commission, and the Federal Bureau of Investigation. The most controversial is the Central Intelligence Agency (CIA), which conducts its own intelligence operations, coordinates those of other agencies, and reports to the President and the National Security Council. The CIA is unique among organizations in the freedom it enjoys from budgetary and other administrative controls and from customary congressional surveillance. The CIA thus commits a double affront against democracy: it pursues undemocratic functions free even of normal democratic checks.

This privileged secrecy fuels criticism of the CIA when it bungles, which is not infrequent. There have been a string of miscalculations in Southeast Asia, like the political assassinations attributed to the CIA's orders to Green Beret detachments of the Army in Vietnam. The disastrous Bay of Pigs invasion in Cuba was predicated on faulty estimates from the CIA. The CIA's more egregious lapses have evoked limited reorganizations, not all of them restrictive or corrective. In a 1971 overhaul, President Nixon enhanced the coordinating powers of the CIA Director over the intelligence community and established an intelligence committee, headed by Kissinger, within the National Security Council, thus strengthening White House control.[19]

Rounding out the foreign affairs administrative structure is the United States Information Agency (USIA), which includes the Voice of America and carries on diverse information and propaganda activities abroad. Various cultural exchange programs are handled chiefly by the State Department.

Domestic influences
on foreign policy

In foreign affairs, the United States, like other nations, pursues goals and interests that derive definition from the domestic political system. The paramount national interest is to secure a world environment that will not unduly threaten or disrupt the internal cultivation of democratic social values.

The chief interpreter of what the interest requires is the President. He dominates foreign policy to an extent he does not approach in domestic policy. Most of the time he gets his way in dealings with Congress; since the Second World War he has not been defeated on a single major issue relating to foreign policy. Even in the rising unpopularity of the Vietnam war, he has remained in command, with only minor concessions and adjustments.

Nevertheless, there are outer limits to congressional acquiescence to foreign policy, beyond which the usual forces of political conflict and checks and balances regulate the President. The amount of funds appropriated for foreign

[19] *New York Times,* November 6, 1971.

Should Congress End The War?

We who are in the U.S. Senate and the House of Representatives know that Congress must vote within the next few weeks on whether to cut off funds for the War in Vietnam.

We are convinced that the best way to get the funds cut off is to get the ballot which is reproduced at the left into every communications medium in the country.

This ballot asks citizens to vote yes or no on the question of whether the Congress should cut off funds for the War in Vietnam.

Every American must be given a chance to register his or her
ion ᴏ ᴛʰⁱ ⁱˢˢ

An advertisement placed in papers across the country in 1972 by Peace Alert USA, whose national co-chairmen were Senators Harold Hughes and Alan Cranston and Congressmen Donald Riegle and Paul McCloskey.

aid is an annual struggle, with Congress typically scaling down presidential requests drastically. Congress is especially sensitive to contributions to international organizations; it questions their value and utility for American purposes. Congress is also touchy on world trade rules that trespass on the historic legislative role in determining tariff policy. Toward centers of prickly, well-publicized criticism, such as the Senate Foreign Relations Committee, the administration is apt to strike a reserved and wary stance.

Can Congress stop the war in Vietnam? Yes, if it wants to. Congress can withhold appropriations for waging the war, or in providing appropriations can specify a date beyond which funds are not to be available for the war. Why has Congress not done these things? In 1970 Senators George McGovern (D., S.D.) and Mark Hatfield (R., Ore.) promoted an amendment to an appropriations bill that would cut off funds for the Vietnam war after December 31, 1970, but the amendment was defeated. Later, an amendment sponsored by Senators John Sherman Cooper (R., Ky.) and Frank Church (D., Idaho) barring funds for military operations in Cambodia was successful.

In 1972 Senators Church and Clifford Case (R., N.J.) promoted an amendment prescribing a cutoff of funds for American hostilities in Indo-china by the end of 1972. When adequate Senate support failed to materialize, another formula was tried to attract more votes. The Case-Church plan was revised to tie the cutoff of funds to the release by North Vietnam of all American prisoners of war. Ultimately, the amendment passed the Senate by a narrow margin when a still further condition was added for an internationally supervised cease-fire.[20]

A second major attack by Senate critics of the Vietnam war has been a war powers bill, sponsored in 1971 by Senators John C. Stennis (D., Miss.), chairman of the Armed Services Committee, and Jacob K. Javits (R., N.Y.), who seek to avoid American involvement in future wars like Vietnam simply by presidential decision. Under the war powers bill, the President could use the armed forces "to the extent reasonably necessary" to (1) repel any armed attack on the United States or its armed forces; (2) prevent or defend against an imminent nuclear attack on the United States, "but only if the President has clear and convincing evidence" that such an attack is imminent; (3) evacuate American citizens from any foreign country where they face "an imminent threat." In such emergency situations, the President could use the armed forces for only thirty days without obtaining congressional authorization.

The Stennis bill would bar the President from using United States forces to cope with an attack on a nation with which the United States has a defense treaty, without congressional authorization. That authorization would also be required for American military personnel to serve as advisers to foreign armies engaged in combat, which was an early step in the American involvement in the Vietnam war.[21] A version of the Stennis bill was passed overwhelmingly by the Senate in 1972.

When antiwar efforts succeed in the Senate, they face failure in the House, which has regularly supported the President and the war. With rare exception, the House Foreign Affairs Committee kills antiwar measures. If they should miraculously survive, they get stuck in the Rules Committee, which has been unflagging in supporting the war. Leaders of the House Foreign Affairs Committee made clear that they regarded the Stennis bill as an undesirable, if not unconstitutional, encroachment on the President's powers as Commander in Chief.[22] In the struggle to end the war, the Senate has been consistently vanquished by what amounts to an alliance between the House and the President.

The President uses his considerable power and political skill to defeat antiwar measures. In 1972, President Nixon was able to slow legislative opposition by his summit conferences at Peking and Moscow. Many legislators felt that while those ventures were in progress, they must stand behind the President. The engrossment of senators and representatives in their own election campaigns in 1972 and the Paris peace negotiations with North Vietnam

[20] *New York Times,* May 17, 1972.
[21] *New York Times,* May 12, 1972.
[22] *New York Times,* April 14, 1972.

conducted by Henry Kissinger also deterred members of Congress from taking action to curb the President. Finally, the Nixon administration has been vigorous and resourceful in battling on Capitol Hill against any significant restriction on presidential power. When, for example, the war powers bill gained momentum, the administration countered with a plan that would require the President merely to submit a report to Congress when he commits the armed forces to hostilities. This was acceptable to the House but not to the Senate, and the upshot was no enactment of war powers at all, which was exactly what the administration wanted.[23]

Appropriately for democracy, public opinion can be a formidable force that the President, for all his dominance, must reckon with. Growing public disfavor with the Vietnam war was a mighty factor in inducing President Johnson to stop the bombing in North Vietnam. But a purposeful President can, with the rich, flexible resources of his office, often outmaneuver dispersed public opinion. Nixon removed American troops from South Vietnam but extended the range and intensity of certain aspects of the war through heavy bombing of North Vietnam, despite a strong antiwar sentiment on the part of many Americans. According to studies, members of the general public are more isolationist in their beliefs than their political leaders.

Gabriel Almond sees public opinion on foreign policy as generally expressive of popular moods that fluctuate between extremes of indifference to world developments and oversimplification of foreign problems, between optimism and pessimism, between the desire to withdraw and the determination to intervene and set the world aright. Continuously involved and effective is what Almond calls the "attentive public," well-educated, informed, and concerned individuals and groups, including influentials and opinion-makers like editors, educators, clergy, and TV commentators. The general public, wallowing in their shallow moods, are supposedly pliant to the touch of these prestigious sources.[24]

In foreign affairs, interest groups are rather less varied and numerous than they are in domestic affairs. Virtually unique is the peace movement of the late 1960s. At that time various groups espousing civil rights, black nationalism, pacifism, and general left-wing opposition to prevailing American politics united in opposing the Vietnam war. Intensely committed, they employed mass demonstrations, civil disobedience, and violence.

The most forceful antiwar demonstrations occurred in 1970 when President Nixon unexpectedly announced that American troops had crossed into Cambodia to attack Communist forces. Although the President stated that this was not an invasion of Cambodia, outraged public opinion disagreed. Shortly after the announcement four youths were shot and killed at Kent State University by Ohio National Guardsmen, who had been sent there to monitor campus unrest. Tragedy was repeated later that spring when two black stu-

---

[23] *Ibid.*
[24] Gabriel A. Almond, *The American People and Foreign Policy* (New York: Harcourt Brace Jovanovich, 1956).

dents at Jackson State College in Jackson, Mississippi, were killed by state highway patrolmen who opened fire on their dormitory. The shock of these events unified moderate and radical campus opposition to the President. Protests took place on more than 400 campuses, and many colleges suspended classes. A year later, May Day 1971, massive protests were staged in major cities across the country. The aggressive campaign of civil disruption in Washington resulted in the largest mass arrest in American history.

How useful are the protests, which for all too many participants mean the risk of life and limb and arrest? Protests did not stop the war, but they provided the public with forceful reminders that a little-seen war existed. They induced public opinion to question the war and to oppose particular war policies. The resulting climate induced President Johnson to step down after his first full term, and it was a powerful force in bringing President Nixon to make huge withdrawals of American troops from Vietnam. The task of arranging and conducting the protests provided practical experience in organization and developed political skills. In getting out the vote for George McGovern in the primaries in 1972, the young veterans of the antiwar movement outdid the party professionals, and secured the nomination of a candidate opposed to the war.

A final influence on foreign policy is the party, although the play of party politics normally is far less vigorous in foreign than it is in domestic affairs. The major parties tend to avoid disagreement on the general body of foreign policy. Nevertheless, the long drawn-out Vietnam war has become an issue for the party out of power, as was the Korean war in 1952, when Eisenhower reaped a rich harvest of votes for promising to "go to Korea" to end the war. Particular issues of national security, especially when they touch the sensitive nerve of survival, may come to the forefront of an election campaign. In 1960, Kennedy gained much mileage from an alleged missile gap.

Economic foreign policy

"With God's help," a senator once orated in a campaign address, "we will lift Shanghai up and up, ever up, until it is just like Kansas City." [25] Into this grandiose promise and into the attitudes of Americans generally toward foreign aid is poured a mixture of aspirations and concerns. A humanitarianism, which well befits democracy, is one ingredient. It is expressed in Harry Truman's "Point Four" program of aid to the newer, developing countries, making the benefits "of our scientific advances and industrial progress available" to the "more than half of the people of the world . . . living in conditions approaching misery." [26] But foreign aid has other, usually more intense and self-serving purposes—checking the advance of communism, disposing of un-

[25] In Campbell, 178.
[26] In Louis W. Koenig, *The Truman Administration* (New York: New York University Press, 1956), 277.

wanted surplus agricultural commodities, providing new markets for American industrial exports. The confusion of motives complicates and unstabilizes the planning and administration of foreign aid.

Foreign aid is administered through an array of instruments including loans repayable at low interest, nonrepayable grants, and human resource development in the recipient country through technical assistance or instruction and training. Social resource development (civil service and hospitals) stresses institution-building and modernization and involves the donor perhaps too deeply in the affairs of the recipient country. But the knowledge and skill imparted by foreign aid can be better prolonged through institutions than through individuals.[27]

Foreign aid's chief organizational habitat is the Agency for International Development (AID), which takes foreign policy guidance from the State Department. AID maintains missions abroad that are often criticized as oversized (to the point of outnumbering the regular diplomatic mission), prone to occupy the best of scarce office space, and disposed to "run" the local programs unilaterally. AID is responsible for carrying out programs of financial and technical assistance to less economically developed nations, mostly in Asia, Africa, and Latin America. It sends abroad specialists in health, education, agriculture, and other fields. Through direct loans, AID offers other countries long-term, low interest funding for projects like highways, schools, hospitals, and dams. AID also makes loans to international financial institutions, such as the International Bank for Reconstruction and Development (World Bank), the Inter-American Development Bank, and the Asian Development Bank. Increasingly, American aid is being channeled through these institutions rather than through direct aid to particular countries.

Foreign aid is beset by problems. It has never been popular in Congress, and each year Capitol Hill deals heavy blows to the President's financial requests. "We cut the gizzards and some of the liver out of the bill," cried Congressman Otto E. Passman (D., La.), whose subcommittee reviewed the appropriation bill for fiscal 1973. But Passman's rejoicing obscured the fact that his committee recommended, and the House approved, a massive appropriation of $4.2 billion in economic and military assistance.[28] Since much AID money stays in the country to purchase commodities and to hire technical experts, Congress eventually provides that agency with sizable funds.

In the task of "building democracy" in less developed countries, the United States may do little more than undergird the local authoritarian regime, now educated and modernized by means of foreign aid. The aid program may be unappealing to local people resentful of any kinds of outside pressures that disturb their established ways of life. This is true even of the Peace Corps, one of the most successful of aid agencies and redolent with good will.

Foreign aid has other problems. Military aid and supporting economic aid tower over aid that is not militarily connected. Moreover, a crisis psychology

---

[27] John D. Montgomery, *Foreign Aid in International Politics* (Englewood Cliffs, N.J.: Prentice-Hall, 1967), 26–68.
[28] *New York Times,* September 22, 1972.

dominates the patterns of allocation: aid is funneled most generously to nations at or near the Communist periphery. Finally, for decades, foreign aid has been an object of resentment of the groaning American taxpayer, who, according to poll studies, opposes its size and cost. The fact that foreign aid commands slender domestic interest group support makes it prey to frequent reorganization and turnover in leadership.

Except for foreign aid, economic foreign policy is the domain of business and governmental elites. Befogged in convoluted technicalities, trade and monetary policy have been found to be realms of ignorance and indifference for the general public, evoking heavy responses of "don't know" to information-testing questions.[29] Consequences for democracy ensue from the separation of the interested few from the uninterested many. The nexus between business interests and related executive agencies, such as the Treasury and Commerce departments, is close and comfortable. The banking community and the Treasury Department promote their shared interests through the International Monetary Funds (IMF) and the World Bank.

Ordinarily, the President has considerably less to do with economic foreign policy than with military policy. A powerful exception to the general pattern of presidential remoteness developed in a series of moves by President Nixon in 1971. He was then faced with a sluggish economy and approaching national elections, a politically ominous combination. To jog the domestic economy, Nixon decided to reduce the inflow of foreign goods. He imposed an import surcharge, proposed the most lavish U.S. export subsidy in history, and prodded East Asia into a "voluntary" restraint agreement on steel. He moved aggressively to improve the U.S. balance of payments and terminated the convertibility of the dollar, thereby removing the linchpin of the international monetary system, whose smooth functioning is vital to the world economy. Because of domestic political processes, American democracy was speaking in protectionist and nationalistic accents, reversing the practice of contemporary Presidents to resist protectionism and lead the world toward freer trade.[30]

Nuclear weapons and arms control

This generation is the first to hold a veto power over the continuation of mankind, an arrogant posture utterly alien to democracy. The Pandora's box from which this lamentable power has sprung is filled to overflowing with nuclear weapons. The United States and the Soviet Union possess them in such degree that French sociologist Raymond Aron has written: "It is on the fear of atomic apocalypse that we must base our hope that the directors of

[29] Ernst B. Haas, *The Web of Interdependence: The United States and International Organizations* (Englewood Cliffs, N.J.: Prentice-Hall, 1970), 58.
[30] C. Fred Bergsten, "The New Economics and U.S. Foreign Policy," *Foreign Affairs,* 50 (January 1972), 199–200.

the great powers will be wise." [31] That wisdom is regulated by the balance of terror maintained between the two foremost nuclear powers, the U.S. and the U.S.S.R. The key ingredient of the present balance is the second-strike or retaliatory capacity to inflict a devastating counterblow after the aggressor's initial attack has pulverized much of the victim nation. A hopeful presumption for democracy and for future mankind is that the anticipated damage of the second strike will deter any would-be aggressor from launching a first strike.

The general workability of the balance of terror principle is dependent on several other conditions. One is the possibility that the balance can be disturbed, if not disrupted, by the development of new, ever more powerful and sophisticated weapons systems. The possibilities include both offensive and defensive systems.

Another fragile condition is that each side must maintain the impression of an absolute determination to retaliate after the rampant radioactive devastation of a first attack. The psychological underpinnings of deterrence would crumble if the potential aggressor came to believe that his opponent, although possessing the weapons, would be disinclined to use them. Each side is therefore under pressure to publicize an impregnable resolve to deliver a second strike.

Maintaining this impression may even require decision-makers to traverse a morass of nuclear doomsday brinkmanship. In the Cuban missile crisis of 1962 President Kennedy was called on to determine how far the Soviet Union would go in its purpose of establishing missile sites in Cuba—whether it was bluffing or in earnest, to the point of going to war. At best, decision-makers writhe in a nightmare of paradoxical uncertainty. "Yet a nation," Hans Morgenthau wrote, "cannot determine with certainty when the other side is bluffing without the test of actual performance—a test which it is the very purpose of mutual deterrence to avoid." [32]

While maintaining the nuclear power balance the United States and the Soviet Union are negotiating to regulate the weapons race through techniques of arms control. These techniques include all the forms of military cooperation between potential enemies to reduce the likelihood of war, its scope and intensity if it does occur, and the political and economic costs involved in preparation for war. Through arms control potential enemies cooperate in mutual regulation of their military establishments. They reduce or limit national capabilities for wartime destruction, as well as reduce the incentives that may lead to war or heighten its destructiveness. All these purposes may be advanced through formal negotiated agreements and through self-control, abstinence by one or both sides from a provocative action. Unfortunately, arms control may sometimes not be altogether conducive to general peace.

---

[31] Raymond Aron, "Political Action in the Shadow of Atomic Apocalypse," in Harold D. Lasswell and Harlan Cleveland, eds., *The Ethic of Power* (New York: Harper & Row, 1962), 445.

[32] Hans Morgenthau, "The Four Paradoxes of Nuclear Strategy," *American Political Science Review,* LVIII (March 1964), 24.

Thus if arms control reassures the major powers against the outbreak of general war, it may remove a major inhibition on lesser or local wars.[33]

In the nuclear age, arms control has been an element of national policy at least since the Eisenhower administration, when the President came to apprehend the catastrophic consequences of a spiraling arms race. Negotiations begun by Eisenhower and continued by Kennedy led to the partial test ban treaty of 1963, a triumph shadowed by the unwillingness of two nuclear powers, China and France, to adhere to the treaty. Under UN auspices, a 1966 treaty outlaws nuclear weapons in space. A similar treaty exists for Antarctica. A nuclear nonproliferation treaty (1968) bars the nuclear powers from aiding other nations in the development of nuclear weapons and other nuclear explosive devices. Arms control also includes the "hot line" emergency communication link between the White House and the Kremlin.

In the seventies, U.S.-U.S.S.R. efforts have centered on strategic arms limitation talks (SALT). At his mid-1972 Moscow summit meeting, President Nixon agreed to a treaty limiting antiballistic missile (ABM) defensive systems. ABM missile deployment under the treaty is to be restricted to 200 missiles at two sites in the United States and the Soviet Union. In addition, the President entered into an executive agreement limiting the number of intercontinental ballistic missiles (ICBMs) and submarine missiles. In these landmark Moscow agreements, each side in effect made a tacit admission of its defenselessness in the face of nuclear attack and rejected the horrendously expensive and probably unattainable goal of first-strike capability. But the Moscow agreements have gaping loopholes that suggest the need for a future agenda of arms limitation. The agreements place no limitation on the number or power of the warheads that may be affixed to the permitted number of missiles. Nor does the freeze affect efforts on both sides to make existing systems even deadlier. Hardly had the ink dried on the Moscow agreements when the United States was moving ahead with the development of a B-1 superbomber and the Trident submarine, an advanced vessel designed to carry twenty-four nuclear-tipped missiles with a range of more than 5,000 miles.[34]

Arms control has stirred up rough waters for the superpowers and their alliances. Some non-nuclear nations fear that the nonproliferation pact will deprive them of access to nuclear technology and consequently hamper their industrial development. To allay these fears, the nonproliferation treaty commits the nuclear powers to a special aid program to preclude this penalizing effect and guarantees that peaceful nuclear experiments will be shared in by all. Sentiment expressed in some nations, such as Japan and Germany, contends that nonproliferation condemns them to lasting inferiority and to possible blackmail from nuclear states that have not subscribed to the treaty, such as France and Communist China.

[33] Thomas C. Schelling and Morton H. Halperin, *Strategy and Arms Control* (New York: The Twentieth Century Fund, 1961), 2–5.
[34] *New York Times,* June 2, 1972.

Some critics, looking anxiously in this eleventh hour for a tolerable future for mankind and democracy, dismiss arms control as a mere palliative and preach the absolute necessity of the stronger medicine of disarmament. The mere existence of weapons, they argue, may provoke their use. Moreover, modern weaponry unleashes an unremitting avalanche of waste and grossly distorts American budgets to the detriment of urgent social needs. These critics believe that weapons unduly enhance the influence of the military strategist and suffuse society with military values. To work for the elimination of military weapons would eventually eradicate the most disruptive suspicions among nations since they need no longer fear violence and threats to their survival. Disarmament could become a giant step toward other forms of international cooperation; it might lead eventually to a world state.

Among the roadblocks to serious disarmament is the problem of inspection. A nation that faithfully lives up to its part of the agreement wants safeguards against the possibility that the other nation has cheated and is therefore superiorly armed. Inspection techniques are especially difficult in the cases of production of bomb parts, laboratory projects, and the manufacture of conventional weapons dispersed among several or more plants. The production and testing of multiple, independently targeted nuclear warheads (MIRV) are not detectable by existing spy satellites. Both the SALT talks and the Moscow summit conference in 1972 failed to produce any agreement for on-site inspection, and the United States had to settle for a Soviet pledge that there will be no interference with inspection by spy satellites of compliance with existing agreements. Both nations agreed to set up a committee to examine charges of violations. But even these seeming gains for inspection are offset by the large body of nuclear weaponry not embraced in agreements— for example, the United States "tactical" fighter bombers in Europe and the estimated 700 middle-range Soviet missiles aimed at western Europe.[35]

[35] "Disarmament: A Big Step," *Newsweek* (May 29, 1972), 42–43.

For decades, mutual suspicion has bedeviled U.S.-U.S.S.R. efforts at disarmament, resulting in a thorny dilemma: when nations distrust each other, an effective inspection system is indispensable, but because they do not trust each other, an effective inspection system becomes unacceptable for fear that it will be abused for intelligence purposes. The inspection problem is exacerbated by the contrasting natures of the superpowers as open and closed societies. In the free and open society of the United States, where important decisions are visible and publicly scrutinized, few violations of a disarmament agreement would go undetected and escape political debate. In the Soviet's closed society, the absence of a free press and opposition parties would shroud most violations in secrecy.

In addition to the impasse on inspection, disarmament efforts are frequently hobbled by disagreement on parity, a mathematical formulation expressing top or lower limits of each nation's armament efforts.

Even more serious, an arms race may manifest deep underlying political differences and rivalries between nations, a circumstance in which disarmament itself can work no great magic. As George Kennan has suggested, "to attempt to remove the armaments before removing these substantive conflicts of interests is to put the cart before the horse." [36] Finally, serious, or eventually complete, disarmament implies world government, a drastic reconstituting of political power for which no national governing elite anywhere has manifested its approval or tolerance.

Overcoming war

How war occurs. If people and nations are adamant against relinquishing their arms, can war be avoided or its incidence reduced by other means? Those who have sought to explain why wars occur discern many causes in addition to armaments. In some analyses, the cause of particular wars is an event—an act or a personality. In others, it is a complex of human motives, ideals, and values; in still others it is the operation of impersonal forces, conditions, processes, and relations. The outbreak of the First World War, for example, has been variously attributed to national mobilizations, ultimatums, the ambitions of rulers, explosive events, alliances, a revanchist drive to recover lost territories, the machinations of munition-makers and international bankers, and the perfidy of diplomats.

In a passage of brave "thinking about the unthinkable," Herman Kahn perceived several ways in which nuclear war might erupt. *Inadvertent war* might occur through mechanical or human failure, including pathological behavior. To Kahn, this is the most likely of causes. Less probable is war by *miscalculation,* resulting from policy-makers' misperceptions, misunderstandings, and failure to think through the consequences of actions. Nuclear war

[36] George Kennan, *Russia, the Atom and the West* (New York: Oxford University Press, 1958), 29.

The Vietnam war.

may also occur by *calculation,* or a decision-maker's judgment that nuclear war with all its costs appears less undesirable that the abysmal "peace" of living under an invading tyrant dedicated to mass extermination or other hideous aberrations. Finally, Kahn suggests the danger of *catalytic war,* ignited by a third party or nation consciously contriving to start war between the superpowers, with the hope of emerging as the dominant nation after their mutual destruction.[37]

How to avoid war. Fortunately, although history is replete with wars, it is also rich in the abundance of wars avoided and conflicts settled through negotiation. For the sake of the future of democracy and mankind, the avoidance of thermonuclear war, with their prospect of horrendous destruction, is a matter of all too obvious urgency. After identifying fear and suspicion as major causes of violent conflict, Charles Osgood posed a scheme that he called

[37] Herman Kahn, *Thinking About the Unthinkable* (New York: Avon Books, 1962), 41–61.

"Graduated Reciprocation in Tension-Reduction," or "Graduated Unilateral Disengagement," in effect a reversal of the arms race and a calculated "peace offensive" designed "to induce reciprocation by the enemy." According to Osgood, the United States must take the initiative in creating an atmosphere of confidence and trust through a sequence of unilateral acts that its opponents will perceive as reducing external threat. These acts should be accompanied by explicit invitations to reciprocate, but they should be executed regardless of whether the opponent agrees. The unilateral initiatives would be continued over extended periods of time; they would be diverse in form and widely publicized. They would be graduated in risk potential, but not to the point of endangering our "heartland." [38] A major obstacle would be the fashioning of sufficient domestic political consensus to initiate the effort and to maintain it in the face of a possible string of the opponent's rebuffs.

Wars always deal with issues that can be settled by other means. Between the nations of today's world, there exists no actual or conceivable conflict of interest that cannot be resolved peacefully. But the most formidable difficulty in putting this simple truth into operation is that it has not been accepted by the family of nations as a high priority social value. War persists because as an institution it is not yet subordinate to the social system it is supposed to serve. If ever the priority of peaceful negotiation should be attained, it would be through a world order far superior to whatever semblance of that order we have now.

The solution is touched by optimism. Many historians and sociologists believe that man has been evolving, gradually but steadily, toward conceptions of universal peace, justice, and freedom. Sociologists stress that as persons in different groups communicate with one another regularly, they tend to form common opinions, and these in the long run synthesize the values and technologies of the communicating groups into a common culture and value system, leading to common interests, goals, and standards, and to cooperation to realize them. Cooperation is the path to common policies and the construction of an organization to enforce the law and achieve the policies.[39]

Must the hoped-for world order be a world democracy? Yes, Pope John XXIII argued in an extraordinary encyclical letter, "Pacem in Terris" (1963). Since all members of the human family are involved, Pope John contended, the universal common good must be promoted. A worldwide public authority imposed by the force of the more powerful nations would not by definition be democratic, and it would become the instrument of one-sided interests. Just as in the individual political community, so in the world community, pursuit of the common good requires due regard to each human being. Among other things, adequate observance of the common good must

[38] Charles E. Osgood, *Alternative to War or Surrender* (Urbana: University of Illinois Press, 1962).

[39] Quincy Wright, "Toward a Universal Law for Mankind," in Richard A. Falk and Saul H. Mendlovitz, eds., *The Strategy of World Order*, Vol. 1, *Toward a Theory of War Prevention* (New York: World Law Fund, 1966).

acknowledge as fundamental "the right of free movement in the search for truth . . . and also the right to a dignified life." [40]

The human factor. Is it true, as some pessimists argue, that war can never be shaken off because of some baseness in human beings that savors violence and destruction? An overwhelming body of psychological research emphatically agrees that "war is not born in man." While aggressive behavior is an essential antecedent to war, it is clearly not its sole or effective cause. For all its violent nature, war affords only a small portion of those who engage in it the direct opportunity to vent aggressive drives. Dependence on draft laws to secure an adequate military force attests to the absence of any general human zeal for violence. Man also has counterbalancing tendencies, which his detractors overlook, such as his sturdy disposition toward affiliation and cooperation.

Although war cannot be convincingly ascribed to a single human motive, such as aggressiveness, various human factors may contribute to its onset. We, including our leaders and decision-makers, are prisoners of our perceptions to the point of overlooking the paths to peace and seeing only those that lead to war. We perceive according to our training and experience, according to our mental set and expectations, and according to our wishes. Often the opinions and attitudes two contending nations entertain of each other are mirror images. Ample evidence suggests that the Russian view of Americans reflects our view of them; that is, they consider us dangerous, warmongering, untrustworthy, while they are peace-loving and honorable.

Wars are facilitated by man's seemingly infinite capacity to rationalize, to interpret his behavior in ways that make it seem just and reasonable. Hence many a war has "liberated" the oppressed and given expression to "the will of God." In the nuclear age, one of the more hazardous psychological mechanisms for the sake of future peace is *denial,* the assumption that an unpleasant experience has never occurred, or that a present dangerous situation does not exist. Consequently, many people display a relative lack of concern over the possibilities of nuclear war, behavior that responds to overwhelming threat by simply denying its existence. [41]

Proposals

In providing for its own defenses in an age of totalitarian states and nuclear weapons, American democracy, as we have seen, resorts to intrinsically nondemocratic processes—the military, intelligence, propaganda—and faces the task of managing them in ways that are most compatible with democratic

[40] Pope John XXIII, *Pacem in Terris: Peace on Earth* (New York: Paulist Press, 1963); in Falk and Mendlovitz, 111–16.

[41] See Otto Klineberg, *The Human Dimension in International Relations* (New York: Holt, Rinehart and Winston, 1964), and Joseph H. de Rivera, *The Psychological Dimension of Foreign Policy* (Columbus, Ohio: Charles E. Merrill, 1968).

values. Since peace is the most propitious environment for democracy's nurture, American democracy has a special stake in avoiding war and building a world order. Within the framework of limiting necessities, that is, the duty of any nation to see to its survival by maintaining an adequate military force and intelligence activity, what improvements might be aspired to?

1. As the agency whose function is to conduct international relations through diplomacy and negotiation, the State Department needs badly to be restored to preeminence in the governmental system. Clearly, it can do so only with the President's approval and support. What changes might make the department more attractive to him?

The department suffers grievously from overstaffing, and proposals for personnel slashes run as high as 50 percent. Overstaffing multiplies useless work, slows and smothers innovation (important to the President), and creates excessive chains of commands. About half of State's employees administer rather than plan policy, an imbalance that overwhelms the policy bureaus with administrative paperwork and liaison activity. A languishing Policy Planning Council might be restored to earlier vigor and its once proud function of intellectual inspiration in a highly bureaucratized department.

Most likely, the economic and international organization bureaus of the department will play a growing role in the new world of the 1970s and 1980s. To their ranks as well as to other policy sectors of the department talented and ambitious young people must first be attracted and then retained as they mature in their working careers. With very few exceptions, ambassadorships should be limited to career personnel.[42]

2. Although intelligence is an indispensable function in today's diplomacy, its blunders and misfortunes, the blows of uncontrollable events, and its remoteness from normal democratic controls have tarnished its prestige and alienated much of the intellectual community, on whose support it critically depends. Harry Howe Ransom has proposed that the CIA be divided so that the branch for covert operations, which has stirred the worst outcries, is separated from that for research and analysis. The former, embracing espionage, counterespionage, and political warfare, among other things, badly needs control by responsible political authority. The President himself, or the State Department acting in his behalf, should oversee it, carefully weighing risks against possible gains, and the likely consequences of failure and debacle.

In recent years, debate has periodically risen and subsided over the desirability of tighter congressional surveillance of the CIA through a joint committee patterned after the Joint Committee on Atomic Energy. The committee's staff would watch over CIA operations, and the committee itself would provide a forum for expression of congressional doubts and criticisms and proposed improvements. Hampering the proposal's progress is general congressional satisfaction with existing surveillance by the Appropriations and Armed Services Committees, with repeated effective CIA investigations

[42] Campbell, 230; Charles W. Yost, "The Instruments of American Foreign Policy," *Foreign Affairs,* 50 (October 1971), 66–68.

in recent years, and with a functioning Board of Consultants on Foreign Intelligence Activities, comprised of qualified private citizens who advise the President regularly and report findings at least twice a year. Equally inhibiting is the view that unlike atomic energy, which is a subject for general legislative consideration, intelligence activities are "peculiarly the prerogative of the Executive." [43]

3. A joint congressional committee has been proposed for another vital sphere—examining the relationship of military spending to other spending and establishing priorities between them. For all the elaborateness of present budgeting and appropriation practices, nothing even approaching this kind of rational, deliberate priority-setting is now provided.

We might build on the Secretary of Defense's practice of delivering to the Congressional Armed Services Committees—and in declassified or "sanitized" form to the public—an annual statement on the military posture of the United States. President Nixon's annual message on world affairs is an important step in this direction for foreign policy, but to assure fair competition in the priority sweepstakes the Secretary of State should prepare an annual formulation of American foreign policy. Similar policy statements would be helpful from the director of the Arms Control and Disarmament Agency and from the major domestic departments. National priority setting is a central task of Congress. It needs an organized body of policy choices—which it now lacks—to determine the variations of emphasis on military spending, agricultural subsidies, and school lunches. [44]

4. Of the UN's many ailments, few are more disconcerting than its faltering efforts at peace-keeping. Wars rage despite the towering ideals of its Charter. The effectiveness of the Security Council is paralyzed by the veto, and the General Assembly by the proliferation of small nations among its members—eighty-five small states, representing 10 percent of the world's population and 5 percent of the world's economy, can make decisions by the required two-thirds vote. Increasingly the Assembly affords only an illusion of action by voting resolutions for propaganda purposes on colonialism, racism, economic development, and similar issues without any expectation that they will be implemented.

To make the Assembly effective in the important function of peace-keeping, a system of weighted voting might be used that would better equate power and responsibility in UN decision-making. Toward this end, a policy panel of the United Nations Association has proposed the building of "coalitions for peaceful settlement." Assembly members joining a coalition would agree in advance to accept as binding a resolution adopted by a specified majority. Different coalitions, cutting across geographical and ideological blocs, would form on different issues, such as international narcotics traffic or aircraft hijacking. Implementation of agreed-on action programs might replace some

43 Ransom, 166–67.
44 Yarmolinsky, 49–53.

of the present flood of propaganda resolutions voted by irresponsible majorities.

Conceivably, the coalition procedure might be used to develop a standby peace-keeping force. Specified units in the armed forces of participating nations would receive training for emergency service in the international peace-keeping force. The participating nations would also have logistical support and financing in readiness so that any operation by the international force could start up quickly. Thus far the Soviet Union has blocked the creation of a standby peace-keeping force by insisting that the Security Council, where the Soviet can apply its veto to the force and its use, make the key decisions, rather than the Secretary General as other nations have proposed. According to some estimates, if the United States took the lead in the coalition approach to a peace-keeping force, some twenty to twenty-five nations would join and eventually the Soviet Union might also. America, which shows weariness of its taxing unilateral role of global policing, might welcome an enhanced UN capability for collective security.[45]

Suggested Reading

Buchan, Alastair, ed., *A World of Nuclear Powers?* * (American Assembly, Prentice-Hall, 1966). Thoughtful discussion of nuclear power and the spread of its use among the nations. Explores methods and problems of control.

Campbell, John Franklin, *The Foreign Affairs Fudge Factory* (Basic Books, 1971). A witty, informed examination of the entire foreign affairs establishment. Acutely analyzes problems pertinent to democracy and weighs the possibilities of their improvement.

de Rivera, Joseph H., *The Psychological Dimension of Foreign Policy* (Merrill, 1968). Contains an excellent analysis of perception, communication, and bargaining in international relations. Examines the nature of hostility and means of controlling conflict.

Falk, Richard A., and Mendlovitz, Saul H., eds., *Toward a Theory of War Prevention* * (World Law Fund, 1969). A useful collection of materials from a wide range of authors on many aspects of the problem of preventing war. Examines various explanations of the causes of war.

Fulbright, J. W., *The Arrogance of Power* * (Random House, 1966). Fulbright, the chairman of the Senate Foreign Relations Committee, takes a critical look at the United States foreign policy pretensions.

Haas, Ernst B., *The Web of Interdependence: The U.S. and International Organizations* * (Prentice-Hall, 1970). Examines the changing American stances toward the United Nations and reviews American relations with other international organizations.

Halberstram, David, *The Best and the Brightest* (Random House, 1972). A series of vivid, in-depth portraits of the men in the Kennedy and Johnson administrations who made the decisions that drew us into Vietnam. Halberstram, a journalist, has done extensive research and interviewing for this book.

Klineberg, Otto, *The Human Dimension in International Relations* * (Holt, Rinehart and

---

[45] Robert Kleiman, "How to Make the U.N. Work," *New York Times,* September 19, 1971.

Winston, 1964). A skillful psychological analysis of the nature and causes of aggression and of the possibilities of overcoming war.

Lewin, Leonard, *Report From Iron Mountain* * (Dial Press, 1967). A fanciful exploration of society's problems following the elimination of war.

Morgenthau, Hans J., *A New Foreign Policy for the United States* * (Praeger, 1969). An excellent analysis of the major elements of American foreign policy, with particular attention to relations with the Soviet Union and Communist China.

Ransom, Harry Howe, *The Intelligence Establishment* (Harvard University Press, 1970). An analysis of intelligence processes and of participating agencies. Contains an especially useful critique of the CIA.

Rostow, W. W., *The Diffusion of Power, 1957–1972* (Macmillan, 1972). Examines America's world role from 1957 to 1972, from Sputnik to Peking. Rostow was foreign policy adviser to three American Presidents.

Schelling, Thomas C., and Halperin, Morton H., *Strategy and Arms Control* * (Twentieth Century Fund, 1961). A cogent examination of the nature and problems of arms control. Deals with problems of inspection, evasion, and maintaining strategic balance.

Yarmolinsky, Adam, *The Military Establishment* * (Harper & Row, 1971). An informed analysis of the professional military, the Defense Department, and their relations with the Presidency, the State Department, and the CIA. Yarmolinsky served in the Defense Department in the Kennedy and Johnson administrations.

*Available in paperback edition

16

the
quality
of
life

Many phenomena are woven into the quality of a nation's life: Bach and the Beatles, the state of the medical arts, the incidence of crime, levels of employment, distribution of income, nutritional standards, the inventive genius of a Bell, an Edison, and the faceless scientists who developed the computer. Although there are many contributors to the quality of life, no person or organization ranges so widely as the national government over the sprawling gamut of human affairs—whether it is putting a man on the moon, aiding the arts, massively concentrating on a cure for cancer, or reducing racial oppression. The national government can innovate policy and apply a wealth of bureaucratic skills and quantities of money that no other organization of society can even approach in scale. Much of the quality of life depends on the political will that motivates the government—what troubles it resolves to attack, what injustices it chooses to ignore.

Yet, for all its power, government has been unable to forestall the rise of what in effect are two quite different Americas. One is the preserve of the business corporation, which dominates the economy by utilizing advanced technology. More bureaucratic than entrepreneurial, it is relatively independent of the market place. Corporate America is denoted by affluence, conforming employees, and devotion to essentially private rather than social objectives. There is a second America, which Michael Harrington calls "the other America." It is typified by the old-fashioned market economy, where "one finds transients, such as migrant farm laborers and casual restaurant employees, and the steady workers in the shops of cockroach capitalism." [1] While the first America is affluent, the second staggers under chronic depression and unemployment. Its showcase is the urban ghetto.

---

[1] Michael Harrington, *The Other America* (New York: Macmillan, 1962). The quotation is from Michael Harrington, *Toward a Democratic Left* (New York: Macmillan, 1968), 57.

Corporate America

On many grounds, leading economists have lauded the contemporary business corporation. Adolf Berle views the corporation, monitored by government regulation, as "the most successful in the modern world. It has done more for all of its population than any other, without ignoring or glossing over its deficiencies." [2] It has achieved a level of production never attained by any other large population and has perfected techniques of distribution to a point where only a fraction of the American people have fear of catastrophic want, in the sense that it haunts millions of people in India and Pakistan. The corporation's achievements have been gained without any general impairment of civil liberties, without imprisonment, exile, torment, or concentration camps.

If the corporation digresses from acceptable social purposes—if, for example, it worships unduly at the shrine of growth and maximum profits—its behavior is subject to internal modification. One of the leading apologists of the contemporary corporation, John Kenneth Galbraith, is confident that corporate personnel recruited from the intellectual and scientific community, whose learning and talents are indispensable for operating the "technostructure" to which the corporation is wedded, constitute a regulatory force that will prompt decisions "responsive to the larger purposes of society." [3] Galbraith's confidence is rooted in the liberalizing influence of the universities, in which the corporate experts were trained and whose society-serving values they absorbed. Corporate excesses are therefore regulated and controlled by enlightened personnel from within and by a watchful government from without.

But today from many sides comes criticism, even condemnation of the corporation. The more sweeping indictments portray it as the master of society, as the exploiter, and ultimately the destroyer, of nature and man. It impoverishes and dehumanizes, pollutes and corrupts, and deprives Americans of control of the machinery of their society. [4] Organization predominates, and the individual passes his years making his way through a world directed by others. For the men (seldom women) at the corporate top, their organizations represent hard-core structures of affluence, safely beyond the reach of the competitive struggle of the old-fashioned marketplace. High corporate position brings privileges beyond income, tax advantages, and chargeable business costs—it brings the favors of debtors and wooers.

In the eyes of Ralph Nader and his "Raiders," the great corporations are addicted to antisocial behavior to the point that the consequent damage is worse "than all the depredations of street crime." [5] Profits and policies are

---

[2] Adolf A. Berle, *The American Economic Republic* (New York: Harcourt Brace Jovanovich, 1963).

[3] John Kenneth Galbraith, *The New Industrial State* (Boston: Houghton Mifflin, 1967), 399.

[4] See, for example, Charles A. Reich, *The Greening of America* (New York: Random House, 1970).

[5] Edward F. Cox, Robert C. Fellmeth, and John E. Schultz, *"The Nader Report" on the Federal Trade Commission* (New York: Richard W. Baron, 1969), 90.

pursued at the expense of the quality of life: the automobile industry, for example, has lagged in introducing a collapsible steering column that would measurably reduce traffic accident fatalities, and in equipping vehicles with pollution-reducing devices.[6] Cars, buses, and trucks are estimated to contribute nearly half the air pollution in the United States—its serious toxic ingredients are associated with a significantly high incidence of morbidity and mortality from emphysema, chronic bronchitis, lung cancer, and heart disease. Corporations also engage in deceptions of the type that finds a leading soup company using marbles in its ads to make its product appear richer than it was. Corporate enterprise easily bends government to its influence and gains lucrative privileges. The government withdrew an antitrust proceeding against ITT, which proffered a contribution to the expenses of the 1972 Republican National Convention. The ages-old preferential tax laws for the corporate wealthy—a "welfare program for the rich"—enabled the billionaire petroleum magnate, Jean Paul Getty, to pay an income tax in the 1960s of only a few thousand dollars, equivalent to that for a middle-income engineer.[7]

The other America

The other America was discovered in the sixties—in John Kennedy's 1960 presidential campaign in Appalachia, in Harrington's book, in the marshaling of data for Lyndon Johnson's war on poverty. During the relatively prosperous Eisenhower years of the 1950s, millions of people, it was found, did not share in the economic feast. Rather they constituted a more or less permanent underclass for whom prosperity was beyond reach. They resided in "depressed areas," communities and entire regions whose economic tempo lagged far behind that of the rest of the country. Above all, they were concentrated in the urban ghetto, where rates of unemployment, particularly for youths, were staggering. So impressed was the Johnson administration with the prevalence, misery, and potential danger of the underclass that "war" was declared on "poverty" in 1964 as the top-priority item of the national agenda.

Increasingly, as the poverty program has proceeded, the underclass has been more systematically defined. In the later 1960s, the Labor Department developed a concept of "subemployment" to take in two groups: the long-term unemployed, who sustain fifteen weeks or more of unemployment during the year, and those earning less than $3,000 for year-round, full-time work. (The minimum earnings figure is revised upward from time to time.) The subemployed were found to comprise 10 percent of the working population, and the rate in ten urban slums was 34 percent.[8] Since the poverty program's launching, the geography of poverty has somewhat shifted. A 1970 Census

---

[6] Ralph Nader, *Unsafe at Any Speed* (New York: Grossman, 1965), 48, 99.
[7] Philip M. Stern, "Uncle Sam's Welfare Program—for the Rich," *New York Times Magazine* (April 16, 1972).
[8] Kermit Gordon, ed., *Agenda for the Nation* (New York: Doubleday, 1968), 50.

Bureau study showed that poverty was growing faster in the suburbs than in the cities, a change attributed to the growing urbanization of the suburbs and the tendency of rural migrants to move directly to suburban sections rather than to central city areas.[9]

The underclass has certain ethnic contours. Of the 25.5 million people living in poverty in 1970 (that is, living below a certain income level for a family of four), 30 percent were blacks and about 9 percent were persons of Spanish-speaking background. Even more dramatic are the proportions of various ethnic groups who live in poverty. Among all blacks, 34 percent are poor, and among all persons of Spanish-speaking origin, 24 percent are poor.[10]

Northern black members of the underclass mostly live in the ghetto, a definite geographic area of the community in which masses of blacks are involuntarily restricted. The ghetto results in *de facto* school segregation and an invariably inferior education, which in turn reinforces the central condition

[9] *New York Times,* November 14, 1971.
[10] *Ibid.*

of excessive black unemployment and underemployment. Membership in the underclass exacts other tolls. Life expectancy of nonwhites is lower than for whites in all age groups in the prime working years. Nonwhite maternal mortality rates are four times that of whites, and approximately 50 percent more nonwhite infants die within one month of birth than white infants.[11]

Both private enterprise and government may add significantly to the misery of the poor. Urban ghettos are a fertile field for credit frauds, rackets, and deceptive business practices. Not surprisingly, the prime targets of the Watts riots were the establishments of merchants whose price gouging and credit practices were costly to the poor. To spokesmen for the poor, Phases 1 and 2 of the Nixon administration's wage-price stabilization program hurt poor people since they stabilized the advantages of the affluent, white, and well-organized citizens.[12]

Poverty can soil and tatter the entire fabric of life. Psychiatrist Robert Coles and three other doctors depicted this life in "Children of Mississippi," a report growing out of a tour of seven Delta counties in 1967:

> We saw children being fed communally—that is by neighbors who gave scraps of food to children whose own parents had nothing to give them . . . they are also getting no medical attention whatsoever. They are living under such primitive conditions that we found it hard to believe we were examining American children of the twentieth century![13]

Government as promoter

Toward the two Americas of affluence and poverty, government may assume stances that are simultaneously beneficial to both. When the economy is in an interlude of strong growth, the ranks and plight of many of the underclass are reduced. Governmental policies may promote and maintain that growth. Indeed, the Employment Act of 1946, a landmark piece of legislation, specifies a clear responsibility of the federal government "to use all practicable means . . . to promote maximum employment, production and purchasing power." To further these lofty ends, the federal government manipulates fiscal policy to promote or check the tempo of the economy. Fiscal policy embraces public expenditures, the quantity of money in circulation, taxes, and interest rates, all of which have consequences for levels of employment and the availability of work for the underclass.

The government also benefits a variety of clients—businessmen, farmers, veterans, and students, among others—by providing subsidies and services.

---

[11] Gordon, 122.

[12] *New York Times,* January 9, 1972.

[13] In Nick Kotz, *Let Them Eat Promises: The Politics of Hunger in America* (Englewood Cliffs, N.J.: Prentice-Hall, 1969), 9.

The Commerce, Labor, and Agriculture departments, and the Small Business Administration, for example, perform research and render advisory services for their respective clienteles. The huge annual appropriations for highways are, in effect, a lavish public underwriting of the automobile industry and bus and trucking enterprises. Tariffs protect American industries from underselling by foreign competitors; in this way the high prices and profits of domestic oil and steel corporations are safeguarded, and the domestic textile industry is protected from overwhelming competition from the more cheaply produced textiles of Japan.

Government as regulator and protector

Government at all levels also regulates private economic enterprise and affords a measure of protection to those who may be harmed by its abuses. Much of federal regulation is conducted by the independent regulatory commissions. The Federal Communications Commission (FCC) watches over radio and television and interstate telephone and telegraph enterprises; the Securities and Exchange Commission (SEC) over the stock market and securities sales; the Interstate Commerce Commission (ICC) over ground and water transportation; the Civil Aeronautics Board (CAB) over the airlines; and the Federal Trade Commission (FTC) regulates industry in general for fair trade practices. Typically, the commissions are created in an era of reform such as the progressive era of Woodrow Wilson and the New Deal of Franklin Roosevelt. During an initial interlude, the commissions typically pursue their task with a measure of reformist zeal, but as time passes they become increasingly friendly and protective to the industry they presumably regulate. Eventually the commissions become diligent protectors of industry, but feeble regulators.[14] Their obligations to consumers and the public interest are accorded a low priority. Industry pressures and legislators who are friendly to particular industries induce this trend, as do the ambitions of commissioners and their staffs, who after serving with a commission may move into more lucrative careers in the industry they are charged to regulate. William H. Tucker, for example, chaired the Interstate Commerce Commission when it handed down some rulings favoring Penn Central. Tucker later left the ICC to take a position as a vice-president of Penn Central.[15]

If they so desire, the regulatory commissions are quite capable of regulating themselves, as the FTC proved a few years ago. In their 1969 study, Nader's Raiders deplored the FTC's droning regulatory pace and seeming obliviousness "to the billions of dollars siphoned from poor and middle-class

[14] See Marver H. Bernstein, *Regulating Business by Independent Commission* (Princeton, N.J.: Princeton University Press, 1955), *passim*.
[15] Robert Sherrill, *Why They Call It Politics* (New York: Harcourt Brace Jovanovich, 1972), 174–75.

consumer alike by deceptive practices hiding shoddy and harmful products and fraudulent services." [16] Spurred by the Nader report and a sharply critical American Bar Association study, President Nixon appointed a new chairman, Caspar Weinberger, who served a brief but vigorous service before moving to the Office of Management and Budget. During Weinberger's tenure the FTC was restructured to permit more stress on the agency's chief concerns, deceptive practices and consumer protection. The commission suddenly manifested a new "toughness." It announced, for example, that henceforth all major industries must supply substantive data in support of their advertising claims, such as the advertised contention of a major manufacturer that its tire "stops twenty percent quicker." At last the FTC was overcoming a long-standing timidity and attacking a leading industrial corporation. Previously, with rare exception, it had limited its assertiveness to smaller enterprises.

Despite such gains, one FTC commissioner concluded that under the leadership of Weinberger's successor the FTC, as well as other independent regulatory agencies, were still not sufficiently responsive to the public interest and required "radical structural reform." [17]

Commissions are not the only regulatory organizations. Government departments also regulate—the Agriculture Department oversees the cotton and grain exchanges, the Department of Labor regulates the minimum wage and maximum hour laws, and the Food and Drug Administration (FDA) of the Department of Health, Education, and Welfare covers two vital consumer subjects. Does it matter if regulation is done by a department or by an independent commission?

Although the FDA is less able than the FTC to ignore the violations of large powerful industries and challenge only minor enterprises, the FDA through most of its history has based its policies on trust of business practice and reliance on voluntary methods of regulation. Congress encouraged this tendency by leaving the agency largely without funds to do anything else. In such a framework, industry-government relations are sometimes cozy. In 1962, disclosures revealed that the chief of the FDA's antibiotic division had received over one-quarter million dollars from the drug industry in the preceding eight years. An FDA Citizens Advisory Committee, whose members were chosen by this same amply rewarded division chief, issued a report in 1962 urging that mandated self-inspection and self-regulation should eventually supersede FDA regulations and enforcement. The chairman of the drug subcommittee of the Advisory Committee was a former HEW assistant secretary, then engaged in private Washington food and drug law practice, whose clients included Richardson-Merrell, Inc., the American manufacturer of thalidomide. This drug, promoted for the relief of nausea in pregnant women, was eventually removed from the market after fetal deformities were attributed to it.

[16] Cox, et al., 29.
[17] Mark V. Nadel, *The Politics of Consumer Protection* (Indianapolis: Bobbs-Merrill, 1971), 65.

"Artificial coloring, artificial flavoring, artificial glop, artificial slop, artificial this, artificial that . . ."

In the late 1960s, thanks partly to several sensational episodes, such as the thalidomide disaster, that attracted congressional and public attention, the FDA underwent reorganization. For a time the agency stressed enforcement and closer surveillance of the drug industry. The new leadership at one juncture even denounced the drug industry as irresponsible and unworthy of trust. But, as in the case of the FTC, there was no enduring transformation of the FDA into a vigorous, effective champion of consumer interests. Despite the research of two decades from multiple sources, both within and outside of FDA, of chromosome damage induced by cyclamate, a sugar substitute used in food products, the agency did virtually nothing. Finally, in 1969 HEW imposed a ban on the use of cyclamates. HEW Secretary Robert Finch announced the action with an air of reluctance and cited only the least impressive evidence of their harm. One month later, HEW rescinded the ban. Congressional investigations disclosed that FDA's scientists bitterly protested the step, and in late 1970 a total ban on cyclamates was restored.

The heroes, if any, in this shabby history are the members of the news media who exposed the dangers of cyclamates, congressional investigators, and FDA bureaucrats willing to risk their careers.[18] The absence of a coherent,

[18] *Ibid.,* 69–76.

effective consumer interest group structure places a great burden on these sources.

New regulatory consumer movements. Efforts to improve the quality of American life have much at stake in the burgeoning consumer movement of the late 1960s and the 1970s. The consumer interest has the moral force of more or less coinciding with the public interest, and it can be pragmatically defined to include every individual, group, or organization. To a high degree, consumerism is a consensus issue, with tenets on which there is ready agreement. It is therefore attractive to candidates as a cause whose espousal is good politics. It is also an inexpensive issue, involving no large public outlays.

On the other hand, consumerism is a low intensity issue, one that people care about, but not deeply. This makes the consumer movement dependent on crisis (preferably scandal) and the chance presence of egregious, newsworthy personalities. Consumerism got a large boost in 1966 when auto safety legislation was pending and General Motor's crude harassment of consumer advocate Ralph Nader came to light. Senator Abraham Ribicoff (D., Conn.) exploited the opportunity this event presented by holding hearings on the auto safety issue and the attempted intimidation of a legislative witness. The resulting, thoroughly publicized furor prompted the Johnson administration, eager to preserve its image of progressiveness on social questions, to draft an auto safety bill. But Nader promptly denounced it as a "no-law law" and Ribicoff called for tougher legislation. Senator Warren Manuson (D., Wash.), chairman of the Commerce Committee, which considered the bill, did not mind striking a blow for consumerism as a step toward broadening his base of political support. Together, these forces overwhelmed the mighty automobile industry, so long feared by politicians. The industry, as one journalist observed, proved in this instance to be "a paper hippopotamus." [19]

The movement for consumer regulation is a crowded political stage whose many players include the President and his White House Office. The two Roosevelts prominently supported food and drug legislation and Lyndon Johnson made consumer protection a major item of his legislative program. In his first year in office, President Nixon proposed legislation that his supporters hailed as a "consumer's bill of rights" (but which Ralph Nader termed as inadequate). The White House Office includes a consumer affairs aide, Mrs. Virginia H. Knauer in the Nixon administration, who presses within presidential councils for stronger consumer legislation.

The Nixon administration started strongly on the consumer question but subsequently checked its interest. Mrs. Knauer, with White House backing, initially gave her support to legislation that would create an independent consumer protection agency with authority to represent consumer interests in proceedings before federal regulatory agencies and courts. But when a vote came at the end of the 1972 session to bar further debate on the bill and

[19] *Ibid.,* 141–42.

Disposition of senators toward consumer protection, by party

	Scale score					
	1–4 (Most favorable)		5–8		9–12 (Least favorable)	
	Percent [1]	Number	Percent [1]	Number	Percent [1]	Number
Northern Democrats	79.2	38	26.0	7	6.1	2
Southern Democrats	12.5	6	53.9	14	9.1	3
Total Democrats	91.7	44	80.8	21	15.5	5
Republicans	8.3	4	19.2	5	84.9	28
Totals	100	48	100	26	100	33

[1] Percentage of scale category occupied by party category.
Source: Mark V. Nadel, The Politics of Consumer Protection (Indianapolis: The Bobbs-Merrill Company, 1971), p. 107.

allow the Senate to vote on the measure, the bill's sponsors failed by three votes to obtain the two-thirds majority needed to invoke cloture. It was generally conceded that the White House could have supplied the necessary votes. Senator Ribicoff proclaimed that "the bill is dead for the year and there should be no doubt where responsibility for killing it rests—squarely on the Nixon administration." [20]

Despite this setback, Congress has generally taken the consumers' interests to heart. The exceptional numbers of subcommittees dealing with consumer affairs testify to the growing political importance of the question. Congress has passed a substantial body of consumer legislation: auto safety (1966), truth-in-packaging (1966), meat and poultry inspection (1968), and truth-in-lending (1968). What causes the legislation to be passed? Sometimes publicized crisis or scandal may be a precipitating event. The balance of sentiment within a congressional committee may be important as well as the inability of resisting industry to maintain a united front. Even more important is the crusading skill of a person like Ralph Nader. Nader believes that the worst abuses against consumers are perpetrated by the largest corporations rather than by fly-by-night operators, and that no one deserves to be harmed

[20] New York Times, October 6, 1972.

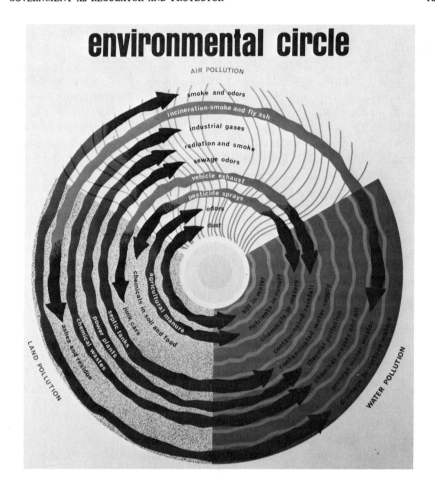

environmental circle

AIR POLLUTION

or cheated, whether he cares about it or not.[21] Nader is a magnet for information, a skilled exploiter of publicity, and an efficient mobilizer of his Raiders, a corps of students who have studied government agencies and whose work is institutionalized in a Center for the Study of Responsive Law.

But the millennium for the consumer is still far off. Government agencies responsible for administering laws dealing with auto safety, inflammable fabrics, and hazardous substances are weak and understaffed, business deceit still luxuriates, and not the least danger of the consumer movement is that the public may be lulled into believing that serious problems have been solved.

New regulatory environmental movements. The attention now being accorded to ecology has belatedly sparked the individual's awareness that he and his fellow human beings are not alone in the world, that his behavior meshes with nature in patterns extending beyond historical time. The individual and nature

[21] Nadel, 144–45, 178–79.

react to each other; their transactions are always circular, producing a mutual feedback.[22] Classical democracy, which views the individual as autonomous and self-sufficient, is no longer adequate in an age sensitive to ecology.

Human beings are becoming more aware of their abuse of the ecosystem. In Lake Erie, for example, with its huge mounds of decaying fish and algae piling up on the shore, the biological balance is so upset that the lake seems near "death." Vast abuse has been committed by household detergents whose phosphate content overburdens the waters with organic matter, by synthetic insecticides such as DDT that kill off natural insect predators of the target pest, by such nonbiodegradable products as synthetic fabrics, aluminum furniture, pop-top beer cans, and nonreturnable bottles. Industry in general has long enjoyed a virtually unrestricted license to batter nature; a worshipped economic growth and rising affluence have been attained at exorbitant ecological cost.

Environmental politics has its own ecology of multiple interacting parts. As an issue of rising popularity, it has been taken up by many executive and legislative committees and subcommittees and has touched off intense squabbles over jurisdiction. Generally, Congress has taken more initiative in pollution problems than has the President. It has anticipated problems sooner, been more responsive to public opinion, and has regularly improved the quality of legislation emanating from the executive branch. For instance, Congress set up the Environmental Protection Agency with substantial powers instead of providing a weaker arrangement that Nixon proposed. The two branches differ far less regarding appropriations. Although the committees steadily approve executive requests for funds, they seldom increase them and then only marginally.[23]

All three of the last Presidents have been activists in environmental lawmaking. But the heroic posture has sometimes been a mask for political gamemanship. Lyndon Johnson, for example, to promote his claim that even while fighting the Vietnam war he was diligently pumping more money than ever into social programs to improve the quality of life, and simultaneously balancing the budget, was driven to lease sales of the outer continental shelf to private oil companies, including the channel off Santa Barbara, California. Although it helped "balance the budget," the sale was but a prelude to the disastrous oil spill that caused enormous damage to Santa Barbara's beaches and wildlife.[24] Despite his support of major new legislation for water and air pollution, President Nixon has favored leaving pollution enforcement in the hands of the states, which ensures that industry, which is powerful in state politics, will have a strong say in what happens.

The Nixon administration has instigated criminal action against the owners and executives of companies that discharge industrial waste into rivers

[22] Robert Disch, ed., *The Ecological Conscience* (Englewood Cliffs, N.J.: Prentice-Hall, 1970), 56–57.

[23] J. Clarence Davies III, *The Politics of Pollution* (New York: Pegasus, 1970), 73.

[24] James Ridgeway, *The Politics of Ecology* (New York: Dutton, 1970), 146–47.

Outlays for major
environmental quality programs
(in millions of dollars)

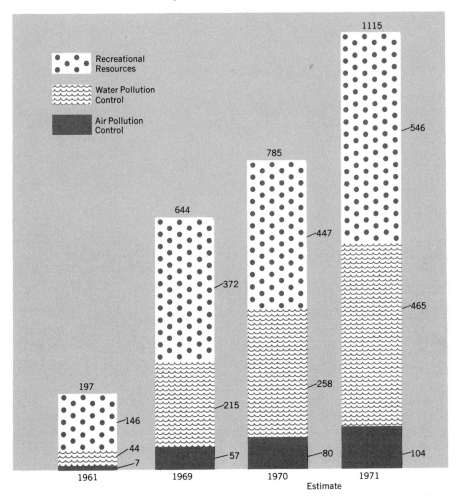

Source: *U.S. Budget for Fiscal Year 1971* (Washington, D.C.: U.S. Government Printing Office, 1970), p. 28.

and harbors.[25] But these steps were taken under long-standing federal laws respecting rivers and harbors. The executive was only doing what, legally, it was supposed to do.

In 1970 Nixon submitted a reorganization plan to Congress to create the Environmental Protection Agency. EPA was to concentrate responsibility for federal antipollution programs that had previously been scattered among a

[25] *New York Times,* November 5, 1971.

dozen agencies. The EPA's duties cover the environmental gamut—water and air pollution, solid waste disposal, registration of pesticides, the setting and enforcement of environmental radiation levels. In one forceful action in 1972, William D. Ruckelshaus, administrator of EPA, denied the automobile industry's request for a year's postponement of the sharp reduction in exhaust pollutants required for 1975 models under the Clean Air Act of 1970.[26]

Environmental politics is a jungle of interest group pressures and counter-pressures. Mighty industries that pollute and mean to escape or minimize regulation have allies in key sectors of the governmental apparatus. The Interior Department has long been a dedicated lobby for the oil and gas industries. According to a 1970 survey, most of the state boards primarily responsible for cleaning up the nation's air and water are heavily weighted with industry representatives of the principal sources of pollution.[27] Bureaucratic ties are also characteristic of the older conservation pressure groups, such as the North American Wildlife Federation and the National Audubon Society, which stress such traditional conservation values as beauty and wise use. The newer conservation groups cover a wide spectrum but are primarily the domain of the middle class. They include Ralph Nader's corps of investigators, the Sierra Club, and New Left organizations such as Ecology Action of Berkeley, California, which participated in the People's Park campaign there, performs symbolic destruction of automobiles, and is a splinter wing of the Peace and Freedom party.

Inevitably, given the almost boundless breadth of ecology, the pressures of groups suffer from diffusion. They represent conflicting values: the older groups echo the political mainstream, and the new conservationists, bearing overtones of the New Left, are concerned with the total environment and see unfettered technology as guaranteeing the world's destruction. Meanwhile the rest of society struggles under an unresolved conflict of values—their desire to improve the polluted environment and their appetite for gadgets and prosperity, which, so far anyway, they seem to prefer.

Government services

For the welfare of its citizens and the quality of their lives, government engages in a multitude of services, whether by providing subsidies to corporate farmers or striving to improve the life chances of a ghetto youngster oppressed by poverty and inferior education.

What prompts government to provide a new service or expand an old one? New discoveries of problems or of societal imbalances may trigger pressures. Ralph Nader and fellow crusaders did so for job health and safety legislation when they discovered that "elk and deer are better protected than working

[26] *New York Times,* May 13, 1972.
[27] *New York Times,* December 7, 1970.

Lining up for unemployment checks in Detroit, Michigan.

men and women." [28] Disaster may spur the innovation of social policy. A 1970 fire in an Ohio nursing home whose smoke caused most of the thirty-two deaths was attributed to carpeting that met suggested federal guidelines governing flammability. The tragedy launched an effort to establish stiffer guidelines. [29] The values of political leaders, their perception of their constituencies' value preferences, the capabilities of social science learning and technique to identify, analyze, and prescribe for society's problems are all determinants of the welfare function. Other forces that are operative are suggested in the following discussion of some major governmental services.

Employment and unemployment. A devastating blow to the quality of life is unemployment. It strikes most heavily among the lower income classes, but it is a growing threat to middle class professionals. During periodic economic recessions it generally reaches high and unacceptable levels to the point that voters want to throw out those in office and bring in the other party. Apart from the material suffering imposed by unemployment on adults, and on their children as its most innocent victims, unemployment is a seed of alienation, a mood that is reinforced by segregation or concentration of the unemployed, particularly blacks in the compound of the urban ghetto.

The principal weapons for combating unemployment or alleviating its effects derive from the New Deal of the 1930s. The federal Social Security Act of 1935 established unemployment insurance programs to pay benefits to unemployed people. Federal and state taxes on employers, and in three states on employees, finance the program. Each state has an unemployment

[28] *New York Times,* November 15, 1970.
[29] *New York Times,* April 5, 1970.

insurance program, but the amount of the benefits and the period for which they are provided vary substantially among the states. Although most benefits run for twenty-six weeks, a typical maximum weekly payment of $45 is far from adequate for an unemployed worker and his family.

A feature of the New Deal that has continued on a more diminished scale is work relief for the able-bodied jobless on public works projects. Originally, schools, roads, bridges, and sidewalks were built under the concept, and today it can be argued that American society has a huge backlog of neglected public works needs. But expenditure for such purpose is severely limited and is proportionately far less relative to the gross national product and the labor force involved than it was in the New Deal. Implicit in work relief for the jobless is the concept that government recognizes and fulfills an obligation as "the employer of last resort," which guarantees employment opportunities to everyone in intervals of diminished private employment.[30] No able-bodied person need be unemployed if political society wills that he should not be.

Health. There is a cliché that American medical care is "the best in the world," but the record betrays glaring deficiencies when compared with data for other nations. The United States ranks first in the world in the percentage of gross national product devoted to health care but eighteenth in male and eleventh in female life expectancy. The American infant mortality rate is worse than that of a dozen nations; it is almost twice as high as that in Sweden. Health care is a realm of class and racial discrimination—its high cost and the absence of any general public insurance program tend to make care most available to those who are well-off.[31]

Why must the world's richest nation suffer these lamentable deficiencies? Studies blame the antiquated style of medical practice—a cottage industry in a scientific-technological age—the shortage and maldistribution of doctors and hospitals, the extraordinary success of the American Medical Association as a pressure group in opposing remedial action, the circumstance that the United States is the only major nation in the world without national health insurance.[32]

The federal government's principal insurance program is Medicare, which is part of Social Security and derives financial support from Social Security taxes. Available to persons sixty-five years old and over, Medicare helps to pay hospital bills, and for those subscribers who pay a modest extra monthly charge, it also pays part of doctor bills. The great preponderance of those enrolled carry the additional coverage. For the poor there is Medicaid, based on health care programs conceived by the states, with inevitable variation from state to state. In most programs the federal government pays half the costs and the states and sometimes counties the remainder. Medicaid is vulnerable

[30] Robert Theobald, ed., *Social Policies for America in the Seventies* (New York: Doubleday, 1968), 31.

[31] Ed Cray, *In Failing Health* (Indianapolis: Bobbs-Merrill, 1971), *passim.*

[32] Barbara and John Ehrenreich, *The American Health Empire* (New York: Random House, 1971), *passim.*

to drastic cutbacks, of the type ordered by Governor Ronald Reagan of California in 1970: in the face of rising costs, he made cutbacks to the point that for a period only emergency medical care was available.[33]

For general reform, the Nixon administration looks to improved private health insurance plans while Senator Edward M. Kennedy, source of the chief rival plan, looks to national health insurance. But critics of both plans point out that health insurance is by no means synonymous with health care.

Education. Contemporary national education programs are highly vulnerable to unfriendly thrusts from both congressional and presidential politics. Education becomes easily snarled in the self-serving politics of individual legislators in strategic positions, and proposed outlays are almost invariably subject to drastic slashing in the House Appropriations Committee.

Why do education interests falter at the national level? By long tradition, education is a concern of state and local politics, where it derives the great bulk of its financing. Education pressure groups—teacher organizations and PTAs—are most effective at state and local levels, and lack aggressive, venturesome representatives at the national level. The National Education Association, which lobbies in Washington, is a pale image of these qualities. In national politics, education is disunited by controversy over aid to parochial schools and by the contrasting interests and perspectives of state colleges and universities and private institutions. Also at work is an historic current of anti-intellectualism, which manifests itself in politics.

The confusion of legislative politics puts the President in a strategic position to influence the final result. In 1965 Lyndon Johnson, who aspired to be known as the "Education President," guided the passage of the first general federal aid to education, the Elementary and Secondary Education Act and the Higher Education Act. This legislation provides aid not to schools but to children on the basis of economic need and concentrates expenditure on the urban and rural poor. The federal government also provides general purpose grants, funds for textbooks, libraries, and teacher training, and aid for handicapped children. For higher education, there are federal scholarships, federally insured loans for college students, and federal support for student employment, library book acquisitions, and graduate student fellowships.

In the Nixon years, the presidential posture toward education changed. In messages to Congress, Nixon contended that education needs reform more than money and counseled against increasing federal outlays until educational inefficiencies are eradicated. (It is intriguing to imagine the application of this principle to the military budget, the moon shots, or to public outlays generally.) President Nixon's other major involvement in educational policy has been his opposition to busing to achieve racial integration in the schools.

Although federal outlays for education in both the Johnson and Nixon years have been relatively high, a national educational crisis is underway. City schools are deteriorating in quality as the middle class flees to the suburbs,

[33] *New York Times,* December 25, 1970.

and higher education struggles with a financial crisis. Many universities and colleges, including New York University and such well-endowed institutions as Yale and Columbia, struggle with growing deficits. A modest congressional appropriation for higher education in 1972, together with suggestions from the Nixon administration that the funds be released sparingly, add up to but a token response to a serious problem. As yet the political system has demonstrated no real capability for dealing adequately with the contemporary needs of education, a key element of functioning democracy.

Housing. The government's effort to improve the quality of life through better housing, particularly for the poor, has been little more than a treadmill of futility, although there has been no lack of programs. The principal responsibility for housing is vested in the Department of Housing and Urban Development (HUD), a progeny of Johnson's Great Society program. The comprehensive housing law that created HUD in 1965 also included the innovation of rent supplements for low-income families. The Model Cities program, established by legislation in 1966, was entrusted to HUD. At the outset of the 1970s, Congress had provided $1.3 billion for Model Cities in 150 communities.

The federal government's multi-billion dollar housing war is fought on other fronts. Low- and middle-income homeowners are assisted by the Federal Housing Administration (FHA), which insures the mortgages. A partiality to low-risk loans has prompted the FHA to concentrate its support of housing in the white suburbs rather than in the urban slum, thus contributing substantially to the problem of residential segregation. Federal housing laws and appropriations have supported urban renewal projects in nearly a thousand cities. But this effort too is criticized for its partiality to building luxury apartments for upper income groups, while lower income families are shifted from one deteriorating area to another. Early in the 1970s, about one-fourth of the two million housing units built or rehabilitated benefited from federal subsidies.[34]

Despite the billions of dollars spent, the housing picture keeps getting worse rather than better. "Fairmont Manor," a federally subsidized, 110-unit garden apartment complex in Philadelphia for low- and moderate-income families, is bedeviled with the standard problems and frustrations—shoddy construction, poor management, crime, and drug traffic. Broken windows, peeling paint, litter-strewn lawns, thin walls, and windows that do not work plague its residents. The project gained national prominence when federal courts ruled that federal projects could no longer be administered in a fashion that fosters the concentration of minorities in the central cities.[35] Reacting to the federal court decision, HUD adopted a new policy banning the construction of subsidized housing in neighborhoods of high minority concentration; its effect was substantial. A black mortgage banker in Chicago observed,

[34] *New York Times,* February 20, 1972.
[35] *New York Times,* November 2, 1971.

A plan to inject low-income housing in a middle class neighborhood in Forest Hills met with heavy community resistance.

"There is a moratorium on housing in the central city. No applications are being approved." [36] Yet when housing for the poor was to be intermixed with middle class neighborhoods, as in a proposed plan for Forest Hills, Long Island, the resulting outcry halted the project and prompted a drawn-out search for a workable compromise. Housing remains a bog of costly dilemmas.

Welfare and poverty. The nature of public welfare programs and their problems have been discussed in Chapter 5. In effect, the welfare system commits huge aggregations of people (one in six in New York City) to a quality of life vastly inferior to the life of other people. Most people on welfare are condemned to live in poor housing; their children receive no more than an inadequate education; the entire family suffers from malnutrition; and their problems and needs are treated with bureaucratic indifference. Yet welfare is also salvation from a far worse fate—from even more depressed levels of life. Welfare programs at least feed, clothe, and house people who otherwise would be destitute.

Welfare rolls, which continue to soar in the cities, are now also a phe-

[36] *New York Times,* April 18, 1972.

nomenon of the suburbs. A 1971 study found that in suburban Westchester County, adjacent to New York City, the welfare population had doubled in the preceding five years. The study disclosed that these suburban welfare recipients were different from the stereotype of their urban counterparts, which portrays them as newly arrived migrants with the limited vision and purpose of the lower class. Most of Westchester's welfare recipients had lived in the county for years or had come to take jobs there that they later lost. Many recipients had close ties to their neighborhoods, even though their housing conditions may have been poor, and they held high aspirations for their children.[37]

The most ambitious formulation to obliterate poverty was President Johnson's "war on poverty," launched in 1965. The effort embraced a variety of programs: *manpower programs,* designed to provide jobs or job training for the poor; *individual improvement* programs, including education and health, directed to changing at an early and more fundamental level the factors that prevent people from utilizing job and other opportunities; and *community-betterment programs,* to alter the oppressive environment that holds the poor down. The Nixon administration proposed an *income maintenance program,* based on a guaranteed annual income, but Congress did not approve it. The administration, in turn, has rejected counterproposals from members of Congress.

Administration of the poverty program is housed in the Office of Economic Opportunity, with support from other departments and agencies. OEO's units include Volunteers in Service to America (VISTA), a "domestic Peace Corps" that trains young persons to work in poverty areas and other situations of social need; and Community Action Programs, involving federal grants for programs administered by local groups.

The poverty program reflects several strategies that have enjoyed fluctuating degrees of ascendance. Initially, the program pursued a dual strategy of jobs plus services. It was not enough to create jobs; the poor had to be prepared for them through services provided by government—education, vocational training, health services, counseling, and placement. Many of these services were remedial, and others were meant to help young people long before they entered the labor market, commencing in the preschool years (Head Start). Job creation measures therefore had to be accompanied by job preparation measures, and sometimes the two were combined, as in the Neighborhood Youth Corps, which combined "work training" with "work experience."

After some years of experience with the poverty program, a group of administrators and scholars concluded that services and opportunities were not enough. An "income redistribution" strategy was also necessary, for the poor's overriding flaw is that they do not have enough money. These critics favored a mix of job and income maintenance strategies. Still other social scientists look on poverty as a condition of insufficiency of housing, basic

[37] *New York Times,* November 7, 1971.

services, education, and political and social participation, to which marginal improvements in income could never adequately respond.[38] To grapple with the complexities of poverty is to discover the current limitations of social science learning and technique.

Social action analysis

The severity of social problems, their enormous consequences for the individual and the community, and the costly annual federal outlays, which have soared from $30 billion to $110 billion in ten years, put a premium on the use of systematic analysis for social policy. To begin with, we need answers to seemingly simple questions: How many people are poor? Where are they? Who are they? Why are they poor? Who is in bad health?

At least two developments in recent years have markedly enhanced the ability to answer these questions. One is the improvement and wider utilization of sample survey techniques, and the other an extraordinary increase in the data processing capacity of computers. When the war on poverty began in 1963, governmental administrators had only the vaguest impressions of how many people were poor and who they were. An arbitrary income of $3,000 was set as the "poverty line" for a family. Lack of technical capability in utilizing census and other data barred a more sophisticated definition of the poor that would have allowed for differences in family size and between living on the farm and in the city. In the seventies, a more sensitive and useful definition of poverty makes allowance for family size, location, and other characteristics. A special census survey, the Survey of Economic Opportunity (SEO) has been developed to provide more refined and accurate information about low-income groups. Problems persist—for example, many poor people, and especially men in their twenties, fail to respond to the survey, and incomes are frequently underreported. Nevertheless, better data influence the way officials think about problems, and not a few old myths have been dispelled. One myth was that most of the poor are black mothers with lots of children living in large cities. Although many poor can be thus described, most are white and over half of all poor families have male heads.[39]

More sophisticated data contribute invaluably to the analytical work on which new social policy proposals are based. President Nixon's welfare reform measure is an example. Armed with varieties of analyzed data, the policymakers gained new insights into what was wrong with the existing welfare system. The data collected enabled analysts to estimate the distribution of benefits under alternative plans for welfare reform and envisage which welfare recipients would win and which would lose under each plan. Likewise, the several possible plans could be compared in terms of cost, their effective-

---

[38] James L. Sundquist, ed., *On Fighting Poverty* (New York: Basic Books, 1969), 243–47.
[39] Data on social service spending from the *New York Times,* May 25, 1972. Concerning social action analysis, see Alice M. Rivlin, *Systematic Thinking for Social Action* (Washington, D.C.: The Brookings Institution, 1971), 11–12.

ness in reducing poverty, their impact on work incentives, and other factors. Decision-makers are employing several widely established techniques that contribute to systematic analysis. Preeminent among these is budgeting, or more precisely PPBS (Planning, Programming, Budgeting System), described in Chapter 9 (see p. 264).

PPBS and other similar decision-making approaches utilize cost-benefit analysis. Thus, if insufficient resources are available to spend on both neighborhood schools and neighborhood health clinics, which should be favored? Analysts would total the costs and benefits of each and favor the program with a higher excess of benefits over costs. Doubtless, funds would be provided for both programs, but the crucial question is whether additional funds would bring more benefits in one program than in the other.

For some programs, costs are less easily estimated than for others—the costs of finding a cure for cancer are more uncertain than estimates for building a neighborhood school. And cost-benefit analysis cannot set values on less measurable elements such as self-reliance and the satisfactions of clean air and outdoor recreation. On the other hand, cost-benefit analysis induces greater precision about what is being bought in budgets and appropriations and for whom. Measurements of the outputs of social action programs facilitate analysis of the relative effectiveness of various ways of bringing them about, and they help to hold administrators accountable to their clienteles and provide incentives for more effective management.[40]

Another analytical technique is the "tax model," which has been adapted to use for social programs. As this model is applied, a sample of federal tax returns is entered on a computer tape together with programs estimating the increase or decrease in tax yields and the effect on various categories of taxpayers of defined changes in the tax base or rates.

Analysis also focuses on "outputs" that are deemed desirable and measurable—for example, reading skills and subject-matter knowledge in education. Analysis may shed light on how these are best produced and leads to an interest in "inputs" to education—types of teachers, curriculum, and teaching methods. This analytical approach assumes that a functional relationship exists between the kinds and quantities of resources used and the results produced.[41]

These techniques too have limitations. Inputs and outputs are often confused and inadequately described. Because there is little collected information about a given individual over extended periods of time, the effect on him of specific social services is difficult to ascertain. Social service systems are not particularly organized to facilitate study of their effectiveness. Little is known of the impact of decisions in one program on other programs, a question that is sometimes of intense political and administrative importance. Application of analytical techniques takes place against a disspiriting background of rising dissatisfaction with social services. Nor have analytical techniques and the

40 Rivlin, 60.
41 *Ibid.,* 70.

political system of which they are a part been able to prevent the occurrence of calamities that impose hardship on millions of people, such as the high level of unemployment stemming from the economy's slowed pace in the early 1970s. Finally, it is imperative that research and analysis not become substitutes for action. Action is more essential than touching all the bases of analytical research.

Rejection of liberal pluralism

Both political scientists and political activists have expressed doubt concerning the capacity of the political system to improve the quality of life. Indeed, some activists are so agitated by the system's inadequacies that they are committed to its overthrow and to the substitution of a new and presumably more competent system.

"The End of Liberalism." In *The End of Liberalism,* Theodore Lowi cites the inadequacies of pluralism as a central feature of the American political system. He defines the American variant of pluralism as "interest group liberalism." It is liberal in the sense that it seeks to use government in a positive, expansive role, and interest groups are the key component because, as Lowi states, interest group liberalism "sees as both necessary and good that the policy agenda and the public interest be defined in terms of the organized interests in society." [42] Organized interests are viewed as representative of most aspects of the individual's life. Groups check one another as each presses its claims on society, and government's role is to ensure access and to ratify agreements and accommodations deriving from competing leaders and their claims.

But, Lowi points out, the interest group principle incorporates serious liabilities. It erodes political responsibility by surrendering programs to the groups and shutting out the general public. Interest group liberalism creates privilege, which is removed from any corrective touch because it is clothed with the authority and prestige of the state, whether the actor involved is the National Association of Manufacturers or the National Association for the Advancement of Colored People. Even when a program clearly purports to uplift the quality of life of the poor, the chief effect of the resulting administrative arrangements is to create privilege and push the quality of life to a lesser place. An urban redevelopment program thus becomes the means by which the building industry legitimizes some of its more questionable policies, such as relaxed standards for the quality of materials used. Community organization for the poverty program provides leverage for ambitious individual spokesmen for the poor and for particular churches and organizations pressing for recognition as the channel of legitimate demand. The more aggressive

42 Theodore J. Lowi, *The End of Liberalism* (New York: Norton, 1969), 71.

can use their power for self-aggrandizement rather than for the good of the larger group.

The impact of the government-interest group alliance is essentially conservative. Apart from creation of privilege and evasion of popular rule, both hallmarks of conservatism, the alliance is the source of solid resistance to change. Because change imperils privilege and threatens entrenched leadership, interest group oligarchies work mightily to fend it off. Whatever beneficial change occurs generally comes at the beginning of a program; over the rest of its long course the program defies change, raising doubts about the capacity of government agencies for justice. Government's inability to respond effectively to worsening social problems has created what Lowi terms a crisis of public authority, of which the symptoms are the protests and riots by a burgeoning variety of distressed citizens and groups.

In the light of this analysis, political leadership capable of commanding mass appeal to offset group power becomes a prized instrument of change. General social movements like Populism of the late nineteenth century and Progressivism of the early twentieth century are also valuable, although rare. The protest and disorder they stir up may, if all goes well, lead to innovative social policy.[43]

The New Left. The most emphatic critic of the quality of life in present society is the New Left. New Left manifestations range from fringes of the otherwise "mainstream" movements that supported the presidential candidacies of Eugene McCarthy and Robert Kennedy in 1968 and George McGovern in 1972, to an extreme represented by the Students for a Democratic Society (SDS), its Weatherman faction, and other alienated components of the civil rights movement. One difficulty in securely identifying the new radicalism is its disinclination to spell out its ideological goals with any precision.[44]

Far clearer is what the New Left is against. It rejects present American democracy, for all its evolution over nearly two centuries, as hopelessly corrupt and oppressive. Rhetoricians of the New Left spurn as bourgeois the values that are at the core of conventional democracy: freedom of speech, tolerance of differences, change through discussion and consent rather than through violence, and the general legitimacy of democratic practice. At any one time, the New Left concentrates on a few, readily defined, highly visible issues such as the war in Southeast Asia, racism, and poverty. The inability of the political and economic systems to respond sufficiently to these problems incites the New Left's sweeping indictments. Radical wrath falls not merely on American political institutions, but extends to quasi-public institutions— the universities, banks, and to a lesser degree, trade unions.

The chief ideologist of the New Left is Herbert Marcuse, who deems

[43] See Theodore J. Lowi, *The Politics of Disorder* (New York: Basic Books, 1971).
[44] William P. Gerberding and Duane E. Smith, eds., *The Radical Left* (Boston: Houghton Mifflin, 1970), 3.

American society so resistant to change that only revolutionary pressures from without can alter the present system. An advanced industrial society, Marcuse contends, excels at barring change, and democracy and tolerance are themselves barriers to necessary revolutionary overthrow.[45]

On the positive side, the New Left has helped to underscore the towering problems of contemporary American politics that a torpid political system has responded to with what are at best half-gestures. But the New Left zealot's disposition to "take the law into his own hands" frees him from a cardinal democratic principle—accountability. While he judges and condemns society for its offenses, he acknowledges no source that is to judge his behavior, and therefore lives and acts free of responsibility and culpability.

The New Left is also denoted by a vague millenarianism, or belief in an ultimate utopian system, which contributes to its alienation from, and driving impatience with, existing institutions. What will replace the present shambles of inadequacy? The New Left's answers are more implicit than explicit. But if recent experience with social programs is a dependable guide, there is no sure road to a society with a dramatically improved quality of life; there is only complexity and uncertainty. Political resolve, expenditure of billions of dollars, and even revolutionary overthrow are not enough, given the technical intricacies of today's social problems as compared with government's tasks in the past.

Historically, government has excelled in mailing out pension checks, letting contracts, and selling electrical power. Results were easily observed, and it could be safely assumed that if federal money were spent on a particular objective, it would be achieved. But in the sixties and seventies, federal responsibilities have gone far beyond the traditional one of spending money. In the poverty program, government provides a whole range of direct services—preschool programs, job training, and medical care. Despite vast expenditure, problems get worse rather than better, and often an effort directed at one problem multiplies other problems.

How objectives or programs are to be achieved has become a most crucial question. Social science skills are badly needed to help improve the levels of program success. Simplistic explanations and resolves, whether they emanate from radicals, liberals, or conservatives, fall into the category of nonsolutions.[46]

Proposals

Fortunately, proposals for improving the quality of American life abound. The following relate to several of the more prominent issues of this chapter.

[45] Herbert Marcuse, *One Dimensional Man* (London: Routledge and Keegan Paul, 1964), xii. See also Christopher Lasch, *The Agony of the American Left* (New York: Knopf, 1969), 172–73.
[46] Jack Rosenthal, "Epitaph for the Great Society," *New York Times,* May 25, 1972.

1. In the latter days of the Johnson administration, an HEW study proposed that the President issue a "Social Report," just as he does an "Economic Report." [47] The proposed report would permit a periodic stock-taking of the social health of the nation. Social indicators would show how well the nation is doing with its problems, would give them more visibility, and facilitate more informed judgments on national priorities. The report would contribute toward a better evaluation of programs in public and political discussion. In reviewing accomplishments and problems, it would provide insight into how different measures of national well-being are changing or ought to change. In his Social Report, the President might give prominence to some social problems in democratic politics that would not otherwise be articulated because they are not newsworthy or are not represented by interest groups.

2. For the current movement against environmental pollution to function on a scale appropriate to the severity of the problem, Anne Morrow Lindbergh has called for either a return to or the creation of "earth values." The earth and its preservation stand as a primal value in which the human race can root itself. From earth values spring human values. "But to have earth values," Mrs. Lindbergh has observed, "we must extend our vision and see the earth as a whole, as the astronauts saw it and as the ecologists have begun to see it." [48]

Various kinds of organizational structuring have been proposed to cope with environmental problems. George F. Kennan, former ambassador to the Soviet Union and Yugoslavia, is among those who advocate the creation of an International Environmental Agency, staffed primarily by scientists and engineers, who, Kennan hopes, would be "true international servants," not restricted by the national interest of individual governments. Concentration on environmental abuse as a national problem seems futile since polluted air and contaminated coastal waters move about without respect to national boundaries. "Indeed," Kennan argued, "the entire ecology of the planet is not arranged in national compartments; and whoever interferes seriously with it anywhere is doing something that is almost invariably of serious concern to the international community at large."

The international organization, as he envisages it, would collect and disseminate information on all aspects of the environmental problem. It would help coordinate research, establish international standards on environmental matters, and, eventually enforce rules covering all activities affecting the environment on the high seas, in the stratosphere, outer space, and possibly the Arctic and the Antarctic. Above all, the organization must have at heart the interests of no one nation or commercial concern, but simply those of mankind and his "animal and vegetable companions, who have no other advocate." [49]

[47] U.S. Department of Health, Education, and Welfare, *Toward a Social Report* (Washington, D.C.: U.S. Government Printing Office, 1969), xi–xiii.
[48] *New York Times,* February 2, 1970.
[49] *New York Times,* March 20, 1970.

A stride toward handling conventional problems internationally was taken at the UN conference on the environment held in Stockholm in 1972. The conference adopted a lengthy declaration of principles, including one calling for nations to give each other information on contemplated actions with environmental impact and for "the elimination and complete destruction" of nuclear weapons and all other means of mass destruction. The declaration, which requires ratification by the UN General Assembly, looks toward the establishment of a new UN coordinating unit for environmental matters.[50]

3. To those who are disenchanted by the New Left but desire bolder, more serious responses than are now offered to society's problems, Michael Harrington's formulations for a "Democratic Left" may be intriguing.[51] He rejects the older liberalism, symbolized by the New Deal, as inadequate for contemporary necessities; in effect, the New Deal has become the status quo. The private business community, which the New Deal was designed to save, has learned to use the welfare state to serve its interests, and Harrington confidently predicts that the private board rooms that created environmental problems will propose to solve them for a handsome price and in the wrong way. The maneuver is not out of conspiracy or malevolence, but out of a desire to protect investments and maximize profits.

Instead of the hazy apocalypse envisioned by the radical left, Harrington seeks a specific program for infusing a complex technological order with a democratic and humane spirit, a program that would appeal to both radicals and more traditional reformers. In essence, he seeks to convert the theory that the public "owns and controls" the welfare state into actuality. He wishes, simply, to make it possible for the people to insist that public monies be spent on public purposes. When tax funds are used to support major transformations of society, the decisions should be democratically debated and determined. Instead of public policy dominated by interest groups, Harrington looks for the selection of priorities "through the democratic process." This would require the creation of agencies for "democratic planning" and better assure the allocation of more of the country's resources "according to the criteria of social need."

The chief vehicle for transforming American politics would be a new "majority party of the democratic left," in whose ranks Harrington visualizes blacks, the poor, the rebellious young, "working people" of the modern technology who have a nonmaterial interest in basic change, and others untainted by prosperity or power.

But questions remain. Could a voting majority be mobilized around the program banner of a "democratic left"? Does not Harrington visualize an American politics that would be far more ideological than it normally is, with its preference for pragmatic accommodation? And might not components of the new majority as they gain strength also become self-centered and self-aggrandizing, just as others who attained power have?

---

[50] *New York Times,* June 17, 1972.
[51] Michael Harrington, *Toward a Democratic Left* (New York: Macmillan, 1968).

However, these are not sufficient grounds for cynicism and resignation. Democracy, in one perspective, is an ideal, so lofty and rigorous that it eludes full achievement by fallible human beings and their institutions. But democracy is also a reality, or a complex of realities, which constitute a partial achievement of the ideal—substantial civil liberties, civil rights, and a host of social equalities. Enough is achieved in the democratic reality and the probability of further gains is sufficiently strong to make the struggle to improve on the reality always worthwhile. As Winston Churchill suggested, if democratic government, with all its faults, sometimes seems to be bad government, the thought is comforting that all other forms of government are worse.

Suggested Reading

Commoner, Barry, *The Closing Circle* (Knopf, 1971). An informed analysis of the environmental crisis in all its major dimensions. Explores the causes of the crisis and the possibilities of remedial action.

Cox, Edward F., Fellmeth, Robert C., and Schultz, John E., *"The Nader Report" on the Federal Trade Commission* * (Baron, 1969). An important report by "Nader's Raiders" on the ailments of the Federal Trade Commission. Provides useful insights into the workings of the regulatory process.

Davies, J. Clarence, III, *The Politics of Pollution* * (Pegasus, 1970). Explores the many political facets of water and air pollution and their regulation. Deals chiefly with the national government, but also discusses state and local government roles.

Dubos, René, *Reason Awake: Science for Man* * (Columbia University Press, 1970). A well-written discussion of how and why science and technology are used in ways inimical to the quality of life. Urges that politics challenge technological expertise.

Gordon, Kermit, ed., *Agenda for the Nation* * (Doubleday, 1968). Discusses a broad range of problems, including poverty, race relations, welfare reform, and tax policies, that need to be improved in the seventies.

Harrington, Michael, *Toward a Democratic Left* * (Macmillan, 1968). A leading American Socialist philosopher and activist analyzes the kind of political coalition that is necessary, and how to form it, to deal constructively with serious social problems.

Lowi, Theodore J., *The End of Liberalism* * (Norton, 1969). Explores the antagonisms that interest group liberalism has toward public interest and the general improvement of the quality of life. Lowi views interest groups as a self-serving, conservative force.

Nadel, Mark V., *The Politics of Consumer Protection* * (Bobbs-Merrill, 1971). An overview of consumer politics, with particularly useful discussion of the Food and Drug Administration, the Federal Trade Commission, and Ralph Nader.

Nader, Ralph, *Unsafe at Any Speed* * (Grossman, 1965). Nader's exposé of the automobile industry's affronts to the consumer; the first of a series of reports that brought Nader to the forefront of the consumer movement.

Ridgeway, James, *The Politics of Ecology* * (Dutton, 1970). A readable, far-ranging discussion of the ecological crisis in its political dimensions. Examines the Nixon administration's policies and the value of various remedial proposals.

Rivlin, Alice M., *Systematic Thinking About Social Action* * (The Brookings Institution, 1971). Examines the usefulness of social science techniques for planning, executing, and evaluating governmental social programs. A former Assistant Secretary of HEW, the author discusses the limitations of social science knowledge and the consequences for program strategies.

Schultze, Charles L., *The Politics and Economics of Public Spending* * (The Brookings Institution, 1968). Analyzes the federal budget as a political enterprise to realize social goals. Stresses budgetary techniques of systematic analysis.

Sundquist, James L., ed., *On Fighting Poverty* (Basic Books, 1969). Valuable discussion of different approaches to the problem of poverty, types of poverty programs, and their political contexts.

Theobald, Robert, ed., *Social Policies for America in the Seventies* * (Doubleday, 1968). Explores a wide range of contemporary social and economic problems and a variety of possible responses to them.

*Available in paperback edition

the

declaration

of

independence *

The unanimous Declaration of the thirteen United States of America.

When, in the Course of human events, it becomes necessary for one people to dissolve the political bands which have connected them with another, and to assume, among the Powers of the earth, the separate and equal station to which the Laws of Nature and of Nature's God entitle them, a decent respect to the opinions of mankind requires that they should declare the causes which impel them to the separation.

We hold these truths to be self-evident, that all men are created equal, that they are endowed by their Creator with certain unalienable Rights, that among these, are Life, Liberty, and the pursuit of Happiness. That, to secure these rights, Governments are instituted among Men, deriving their just Powers from the consent of the governed. That, whenever any form of Government becomes destructive of these ends, it is the Right of the People to alter or to abolish it, and to institute new Government, laying its foundation on such Principles, and organizing its Powers in such form, as to them shall seem most likely to effect their Safety and Happiness. Prudence, indeed, will dictate that Governments long established should not be changed for light and transient causes; and, accordingly, all experience hath shewn, that mankind are more disposed to suffer, while evils are sufferable, than to right themselves by abolishing the forms to which they are accustomed. But, when a long train of abuses and usurpations, pursuing invariably the same Object, evinces a design to reduce them under absolute Despotism, it is their right, it is their duty, to throw off such Government, and to provide new Guards for their future Security. Such has been the patient sufferance of these Colonies; and such is now the necessity which constrains them to alter their former Systems of Government. The history of the present King of Great Britain is a history of repeated injuries and usurpations, all having in direct object the establishment of an absolute Tyranny over these States. To prove this, let Facts be submitted to a candid world.

He has refused his Assent to Laws the most wholesome and necessary for the public good.

He has forbidden his Governors to pass Laws of immediate and pressing importance, unless suspended in their operation till his Assent should be obtained; and when so suspended, he has utterly neglected to attend to them.

He has refused to pass other Laws for the accommodation of large districts of People, unless those People would relinquish the right of Representation in the legislature; a right inestimable to them and formidable to tyrants only.

He has called together legislative bodies at places unusual, uncomfortable, and distant from the depository of their Public Records, for the sole Purpose of fatiguing them into compliance with his measures.

* The original spelling, capitalization, and punctuation have been retained.

He has dissolved Representative Houses repeatedly, for opposing, with manly firmness, his invasions on the rights of the People.

He has refused for a long time, after such dissolutions, to cause others to be elected; whereby the Legislative Powers, incapable of Annihilation, have returned to the People at large for their exercise; the State remaining in the mean time exposed to all the dangers of invasion from without, and convulsions within.

He has endeavoured to prevent the Population of these States; for that purpose obstructing the Laws for Naturalization of Foreigners; refusing to pass others to encourage their migrations hither, and raising the conditions of new Appropriations of Lands.

He has obstructed the Administration of Justice, by refusing his Assent to Laws for establishing Judiciary Powers.

He has made Judges, dependent on his Will alone, for the tenure of their offices, and the amount and payment of their salaries.

He has erected a multitude of New Offices and sent hither swarms of Officers to harrass our People, and eat out their substance.

He has kept among us, in times of Peace, Standing Armies, without the Consent of our legislatures.

He has affected to render the Military independent of and superior to the Civil Power.

He has combined with others to subject us to a jurisdiction foreign to our constitution, and unacknowledged by our laws; giving his Assent to their Acts of pretended Legislation:

For quartering large bodies of armed troops among us:

For protecting them, by a mock Trial, from Punishment for any Murders which they should commit on the Inhabitants of these States:

For cutting off our Trade with all parts of the world:

For imposing Taxes on us without our Consent:

For depriving us, in many cases, of the benefits of Trial by Jury:

For transporting us beyond Seas to be tried for pretended offences:

For abolishing the free System of English Laws in a neighbouring province, establishing therein an Arbitrary government, and enlarging its Boundaries, so as to render it at once an example and fit instrument for introducing the same absolute rule into these Colonies:

For taking away our Charters, abolishing our most valuable Laws, and altering fundamentally the Forms of our Governments:

For suspending our own Legislatures, and declaring themselves invested with Power to legislate for us in all cases whatsoever.

He has abdicated Government here, by declaring us out of his protection, and waging War against us.

He has plundered our seas, ravaged our Coasts, burnt our towns, and destroyed the Lives of our People.

He is at this time transporting large Armies of foreign Mercenaries to compleat the works of death, desolation and tyranny, already begun with circumstances of Cruelty and perfidy scarcely paralleled in the most barbarous ages, and totally unworthy the Head of a civilized nation.

He has constrained our fellow Citizens, taken Captive on the high Seas, to bear Arms against their Country, to become the executioners of their friends and Brethren, or to fall themselves by their Hands.

He has excited domestic insurrections amongst us, and has endeavoured to bring on the inhabitants of our frontiers, the merciless Indian Savages, whose known rule of warfare, is an undistinguished destruction of all ages, sexes and conditions.

In every stage of these Oppressions, We have Petitioned for Redress, in the most humble terms: Our repeated Petitions, have been answered only by repeated injury. A

Prince, whose character is thus marked by every act which may define a Tyrant, is unfit to be the ruler of a free People.

Nor have We been wanting in attentions to our British brethren. We have warned them from time to time of attempts by their legislature to extend an unwarrantable jurisdiction over us. We have reminded them of the circumstances of our emigration and settlement here. We have appealed to their native justice and magnanimity, and we have conjured them by the ties of our common kindred, to disavow these usurpations, which, would inevitably interrupt our connexions and correspondence. They too have been deaf to the voice of justice and consanguinity. We must, therefore, acquiesce in the necessity, which denounces our Separation, and hold them, as we hold the rest of mankind, Enemies in war, in Peace Friends.

WE, THEREFORE, the Representatives of the UNITED STATES OF AMERICA, in GENERAL CONGRESS assembled, appealing to the Supreme Judge of the World for the rectitude of our intentions, DO, in the Name, and by Authority of the good People of these Colonies, solemnly PUBLISH and DECLARE, That these United Colonies are, and of Right, ought to be FREE AND INDEPENDENT STATES; that they are Absolved from all Allegiance to the British Crown, and that all political connexion between them and the State of Great Britain, is and ought to be totally dissolved; and that, as FREE and INDEPENDENT STATES, they have full Power to levy War, conclude Peace, contract Alliances, establish Commerce, and to do all other Acts and Things which INDEPENDENT STATES may of right do. AND for the support of this Declaration, with a firm reliance on the protection of divine Providence, we mutually pledge to each other our Lives, our Fortunes, and our sacred Honour.

the

constitution

of the

united states

of america*

We the people of the United States, in Order to form a more perfect Union, establish Justice, insure domestic Tranquility, provide for the common defence, promote the general Welfare, and secure the Blessings of Liberty to ourselves and our Posterity, do ordain and establish this Constitution for the United States of America.

Article I

Section 1. All legislative Powers herein granted shall be vested in a Congress of the United States, which shall consist of a Senate and House of Representatives.

Section 2. The House of Representatives shall be composed of Members chosen every second Year by the People of the several States, and the Electors in each State shall have the Qualifications requisite for Electors of the most numerous Branch of the State Legislature.

No Person shall be a Representative who shall not have attained to the Age of twenty-five Years, and been seven Years a Citizen of the United States, and who shall not, when elected, be an Inhabitant of that state in which he shall be chosen.

[Representatives and direct Taxes shall be apportioned among the several States which may be included within this Union, according to their respective Numbers, which shall be determined by adding to the whole Number of free Persons, including those bound to Service for a Term of Years, and excluding Indians not taxed, three fifths of all other Persons.] [1] The actual Enumeration shall be made within three Years after the first Meeting of the Congress of the United States, and within every subsequent Term of ten Years, in such Manner as they shall by Law direct. The Number of Representatives shall not exceed one for every thirty Thousand, but each State shall have at Least one Representative; and until such enumeration shall be made, the State of New Hampshire shall be entitled to chuse three, Massachusetts eight, Rhode-Island and Providence Plantations one, Connecticut five, New-York six, New Jersey four, Pennsylvania eight, Delaware one, Maryland six, Virginia ten, North Carolina five, South Carolina five, and Georgia three.

When vacancies happen in the Representation from any State, the Executive Authority thereof shall issue Writs of Election to fill such Vacancies.

The House of Representatives shall chuse their Speaker and other Officers; and shall have the sole Power of Impeachment.

Section 3. The Senate of the United States shall be composed of two Senators from each State, [chosen by the Legislature

* The Constitution and all amendments are shown in their original form. Parts that have been amended or superseded are bracketed and explained in the footnotes.

[1] Modified by the Fourteenth and Sixteenth amendments.

thereof,] [2] for six Years; and each Senator shall have one Vote.

Immediately after they shall be assembled in Consequence of the first Election, they shall be divided as equally as may be into three Classes. The Seats of the Senators of the first Class shall be vacated at the Expiration of the Second Year, of the Second Class at the Expiration of the fourth Year, and of the third Class at the Expiration of the sixth Year, so that one-third may be chosen every second Year; [and if Vacancies happen by Resignation, or otherwise, during the Recess of the Legislature of any State, the Executive thereof may make temporary Appointments unil the next Meeting of the Legislature, which shall then fill such Vacancies].[3]

No Person shall be a Senator who shall not have attained to the Age of thirty Years, and been nine Years a Citizen of the United States, and who shall not, when elected, be an Inhabitant of that State in which he shall be chosen.

The Vice-President of the United States shall be President of the Senate, but shall have no vote, unless they be equally divided.

The Senate shall chuse their other Officers, and also a President pro tempore, in the absence of the Vice-President, or when he shall exercise the Office of the President of the United States.

The Senate shall have the sole Power to try all Impeachments. When sitting for that purpose, they shall be on Oath or Affirmation. When the President of the United States is tried, the Chief Justice shall preside. And no person shall be convicted without the Concurrence of two thirds of the Members present.

Judgment in Cases of Impeachment shall not extend further than to removal from Office, and disqualification to hold and enjoy any Office of honor, Trust, or Profit under the United States: but the Party convicted shall nevertheless be liable and subject to Indictment, Trial, Judgment, and Punishment, according to Law.

Section 4. The Times, Places and Manner of holding Elections for Senators and Representatives, shall be prescribed in each state by the Legislature thereof; but the Congress may at any time by Law make or alter such Regulations, except as to the Places of Chusing Senators.

The Congress shall assemble at least once in every Year, and such Meeting shall [be on the first Monday in December,] [4] unless they shall by Law appoint a different Day.

Section 5. Each House shall be the Judge of the Elections, Returns and Qualifications of its own Members, and a Majority of each shall constitute a Quorum to do Business; but a smaller number may adjourn from day to day, and may be authorized to compel the Attendance of absent Members, in such Manner, and under such Penalties, as each House may provide.

Each House may determine the Rules of its Proceedings, punish its Members for disorderly Behavior, and, with the Concurrence of two thirds, expel a Member.

Each House shall keep a Journal of its Proceedings, and from time to time publish the same, excepting such Parts as may in their Judgment require Secrecy; and the Yeas and Nays of the Members of either House on any question shall, at the Desire of one fifth of those Present, be entered on the Journal.

Neither House, during the Session of Congress, shall, without the Consent of the other, adjourn for more than three days, nor to any other Place than that in which the two Houses shall be sitting.

Section 6. The Senators and Representatives shall receive a Compensation for their Services, to be ascertained by Law, and paid out of the Treasury of the United States. They shall in all Cases, except

[2] *Superseded by the Seventeenth Amendment.*
[3] *Modified by the Seventeenth Amendment.*

[4] *Superseded by the Twentieth Amendment.*

Treason, Felony, and Breach of the Peace, be privileged from Arrest during their Attendance at the Session of their respective Houses, and in going to and returning from the same; and for any Speech or Debate in either House, they shall not be questioned in any other Place.

No Senator or Representative shall, during the Time for which he was elected, be appointed to any civil Office under the Authority of the United States, which shall have been created, or the Emoluments whereof shall have been increased, during such time; and no Person holding any Office under the United States shall be a Member of either House during his continuance in Office.

Section 7. All Bills for raising Revenue shall originate in the House of Representatives; but the Senate may propose or concur with Amendments as on other bills.

Every Bill which shall have passed the House of Representatives and the Senate, shall, before it become a Law, be presented to the President of the United States; If he approve he shall sign it, but if not he shall return it, with his Objections, to that House in which it shall have originated, who shall enter the Objections at large on their Journal, and proceed to reconsider it. If after such Reconsideration two thirds of that House shall agree to pass the bill, it shall be sent, together with the objections, to the other House, by which it shall likewise be reconsidered, and if approved by two thirds of that House, it shall become a Law. But in all such Cases the Votes of both Houses shall be determined by Yeas and Nays, and the Names of the Persons voting for and against the Bill shall be entered on the Journal of each House respectively. If any Bill shall not be returned by the President within ten Days (Sundays excepted) after it shall have been presented to him, the Same shall be a Law, in like Manner as if he had signed it, unless the Congress by their Adjournment prevent its Return, in which Case it shall not be a Law.

Every Order, Resolution, or Vote to which the Concurrence of the Senate and House of Representatives may be necessary (except on a question of Adjournment) shall be presented to the President of the United States; and before the Same shall take Effect, shall be approved by him, or being disapproved by him, shall be repassed by two thirds of the Senate and House of Representatives, according to the Rules and Limitations prescribed in the Case of a Bill.

Section 8. The Congress shall have Power To lay and collect Taxes, Duties, Imposts and Excises, to pay the Debts and provide for the common Defence and general Welfare of the United States; but all Duties, Imposts and Excises shall be uniform throughout the United States;

To borrow money on the credit of the United States;

To regulate Commerce with foreign Nations, and among the several States, and with the Indian Tribes;

To establish an uniform Rule of Naturalization, and uniform Laws on the subject of Bankruptcies throughout the United States;

To coin Money, regulate the Value thereof, and of foreign Coin, and fix the Standard of Weights and Measures;

To provide for the Punishment of counterfeiting the Securities and current Coin of the United States;

To establish Post Offices and post Roads;

To promote the Progress of Science and useful Arts, by securing for limited Times to Authors and Inventors the exclusive Right to their respective Writings and Discoveries;

To constitute Tribunals inferior to the Supreme Court;

To define and punish Piracies and Felonies committed on the high Seas, and Offenses against the Law of Nations;

To declare War, grant Letters of Marque and Reprisal, and make Rules concerning Captures on Land and Water;

To raise and support Armies, but no Appropriation of Money to that Use shall be for a longer Term than two Years;

To provide and maintain a Navy;

To make Rules for the Government and Regulation of the land and naval forces;

To provide for calling forth the Militia to execute the Laws of the Union, suppress Insurrections and repel Invasions;

To provide for organizing, arming, and disciplining the Militia, and for governing such Part of them as may be employed in the Service of the United States, reserving to the States respectively, the Appointment of the Officers, and the Authority of training the Militia according to the discipline prescribed by Congress;

To exercise exclusive Legislation in all Cases whatsoever, over such District (not exceeding ten Miles square) as may, by Cession of particular States, and the acceptance of Congress, become the Seat of the Government of the United States, and to exercise like Authority over all Places purchased by the Consent of the Legislature of the State in which the Same shall be, for the Erection of Forts, Magazines, Arsenals, dock-Yards, and other needful Buildings;—And

To make all Laws which shall be necessary and proper for carrying into Execution the foregoing Powers, and all other Powers vested by this Constitution in the Government of the United States, or in any Department or Officer thereof.

Section 9. The Migration or Importation of such Persons as any of the States now existing shall think proper to admit shall not be prohibited by the Congress prior to the Year óne thousand eight hundred and eight, but a tax or duty may be imposed on such Importation, not exceeding ten dollars for each Person.

The privilege of the Writ of Habeas Corpus shall not be suspended, unless when in Cases of Rebellion or Invasion the public Safety may require it.

No Bill of Attainder or ex post facto Law shall be passed.

[No capitation, or other direct, Tax shall be laid unless in Proportion to the Census or Enumeration herein before directed to be taken.] [5]

No Tax or Duty shall be laid on Articles exported from any State.

No Preference shall be given by any Regulation of Revenue to the Ports of one State over those of another: nor shall Vessels bound to, or from, one State, be obliged to enter, clear, or pay Duties in another.

No Money shall be drawn from the Treasury, but in Consequence of Appropriations made by Law; and a regular Statement and Account of the Receipts and Expenditures of all public Money shall be published from time to time.

No Title of Nobility shall be granted by the United States: And no Person holding any Office of Profit or Trust under them, shall, without the Consent of the Congress, accept of any present, Emolument, Office, or Title, of any kind whatever, from any King, Prince, or foreign State.

Section 10. No State shall enter into any Treaty, Alliance, or Confederation; grant Letters of Marque and Reprisal; coin Money; emit Bills of Credit; make any Thing but gold and silver Coin a Tender in Payment of Debts; pass any Bill of Attainder, ex post facto Law, or Law impairing the Obligation of Contracts, or grant any Title of Nobility.

No State shall, without the Consent of the Congress, lay any Imposts or Duties on Imports or Exports, except what may be absolutely necessary for executing its inspection Laws: and the net Produce of all Duties and Imposts, laid by any State on Imports or Exports, shall be for the Use of the Treasury of the United States; and all such Laws shall be subject to the Revision and Control of the Congress.

No State shall, without the Consent of Congress, lay any duty of Tonnage, keep Troops, or Ships of War in time of Peace,

---

[5] *Modified by the Sixteenth Amendment.*

enter into any Agreement or Compact with another State, or with a foreign Power, or engage in War, unless actually invaded, or in such imminent Danger as will not admit of delay.

Article II

Section 1. The executive Power shall be vested in a President of the United States of America. He shall hold his Office during the Term of four years, and, together with the Vice-President, chosen for the same Term, be elected, as follows:

Each State shall appoint, in such Manner as the Legislature thereof may direct, a Number of Electors, equal to the whole Number of Senators and Representatives to which the State may be entitled in the Congress: but no Senator or Representative, or Person holding an Office of Trust or Profit under the United States, shall be appointed an Elector.

[The Electors shall meet in their respective States, and vote by Ballot for two persons, of whom one at least shall not be an Inhabitant of the same State with themselves. And they shall make a List of all the Persons voted for, and of the Number of Votes for each; which List they shall sign and certify, and transmit sealed to the Seat of the Government of the United States, directed to the President of the Senate. The President of the Senate shall, in the Presence of the Senate and House of Representatives, open all the Certificates, and the Votes shall then be counted. The Person having the greatest Number of Votes shall be the President, if such Number be a Majority of the whole Number of Electors appointed; and if there be more than one who have such Majority, and have an Equal Number of Votes, then the House of Representatives shall immediately chuse by Ballot one of them for President; and if no Person have a Majority, then from the five highest on the List the said House shall in like Manner chuse the President. But in chusing the President, the Votes shall be taken by States, the Representation from each State having one Vote; a quorum for this Purpose shall consist of a Member or Members from two-thirds of the States, and a Majority of all the States shall be necessary to a Choice. In every Case, after the Choice of the President, the Person having the greatest Number of Votes of the Electors shall be the Vice-President. But if there should remain two or more who have equal votes, the Senate shall chuse from them by Ballot the Vice-President.] [6]

The Congress may determine the Time of chusing the Electors, and the Day on which they shall give their Votes; which Day shall be the same throughout the United States.

No person except a natural-born Citizen, or a Citizen of the United States, at the time of the Adoption of this Constitution, shall be eligible to the Office of President; neither shall any Person be eligible to that Office who shall not have attained to the Age of thirty-five years, and been fourteen Years a Resident within the United States.

[In Case of the Removal of the President from Office, or of his Death, Resignation, or Inability to discharge the Powers and Duties of the said Office, the same shall devolve on the Vice-President, and the Congress may by Law provide for the Case of Removal, Death, Resignation, or Inability, both of the President and Vice-President, declaring what Officer shall then act as President, and such Officer shall act accordingly, until the disability be removed, or a President shall be elected.] [7]

The President shall, at stated Times, receive for his Services a Compensation, which shall neither be increased nor diminished during the Period for which he shall have been elected, and he shall not receive within that Period any other Emolument from the United States, or any of them.

Before he enter on the execution of his Office, he shall take the following Oath

---

[6] *Superseded by the Twelfth Amendment.*
[7] *Modified by the Twenty-fifth Amendment.*

or Affirmation:—"I do solemly swear (or affirm) that I will faithfully execute the Office of President of the United States, and will, to the best of my Ability, preserve, protect, and defend the Constitution of the United States."

Section 2. The President shall be Commander in Chief of the Army and Navy of the United States, and of the Militia of the several States, when called into the actual Service of the United States; he may require the Opinion, in writing, of the principal Officer in each of the executive Departments, upon any subject relating to the Duties of their respective Offices, and he shall have Power to Grant Reprieves and Pardons for Offenses against the United States, except in Cases of Impeachment.

He shall have Power, by and with the Advice and Consent of the Senate, to make Treaties, provided two thirds of the Senators present concur; and he shall nominate, and by and with the Advice and Consent of the Senate, shall appoint Ambassadors, other public Ministers and Consuls, Judges of the supreme Court, and all other Officers of the United States, whose Appointments are not herein otherwise provided for, and which shall be established by Law: but the Congress may by Law vest the Appointment of such inferior Officers, as they think proper, in the President alone, in the Courts of Law, or in the Heads of Departments.

The President shall have Power to fill up all Vacancies that may happen during the Recess of the Senate, by granting Commissions which shall expire at the End of their next Session.

Section 3. He shall from time to time give to the Congress Information of the State of the Union, and recommend to their Consideration such Measures as he shall judge necessary and expedient; he may, on extraordinary occasions, convene both Houses, or either of them, and in Case of Disagreement between them, with respect to the Time of Adjournment, he may adjourn them to such Time as he shall think proper; he shall receive Ambassadors and other public Ministers; he shall take Care that the Laws be faithfully executed, and shall Commission all the Officers of the United States.

Section 4. The President, Vice-President and all civil Officers of the United States, shall be removed from Office on Impeachment for, and Conviction of, Treason, Bribery, or other high Crimes and Misdemeanors.

Article III

Section 1. The judicial Power of the United States, shall be vested in one supreme Court, and in such inferior Courts as the Congress may from time to time ordain and establish. The Judges, both of the supreme and inferior Courts, shall hold their Offices during good Behaviour, and shall, at stated Times, receive for their Services, a Compensation, which shall not be diminished during their Continuance in Office.

Section 2. The judicial Power shall extend to all Cases, in Law and Equity, arising under this Constitution, the Laws of the United States, and treaties made, or which shall be made, under their Authority;—to all Cases affecting ambassadors, other public ministers and consuls;—to all cases of admiralty and maritime Judisdiction;—to Controversies to which the United States shall be a Party;—to Controversies between two or more States;—[between a State and Citizens of another State;] [8]—between Citizens of different States,—between Citizens of the same State claiming Lands under Grants of different States, and between a State, or the Citizens thereof, and foreign States, Citizens or Subjects.

In all Cases affecting Ambassadors, other public Ministers and Consuls, and those in which a State shall be Party, the supreme Court shall have original Jurisdiction. In all the other Cases before mentioned, the

[8] *Modified by the Eleventh Amendment.*

supreme Court shall have appellate Jurisdiction, both as to Law and Fact, with such Exceptions, and under such Regulations as the Congress shall make.

The trial of all Crimes, except in Cases of Impeachment, shall be by Jury; and such Trial shall be held in the State where the said Crimes shall have been committed; but when not committed within any State, the Trial shall be at such Place or Places as the Congress may by Law have directed.

Section 3. Treason against the United States, shall consist only in levying War against them, or in adhering to their Enemies, giving them Aid and Comfort. No Person shall be convicted of Treason unless on the Testimony of two Witnesses to the same overt Act, or on Confession in open Court.

The Congress shall have power to declare the Punishment of Treason, but no Attainder of Treason shall work Corruption of Blood, or Forfeiture except during the Life of the Person attainted.

Article IV

Section 1. Full Faith and Credit shall be given in each State to the public Acts, Records, and judicial Proceedings of every other State. And the Congress may by general Laws prescribe the Manner in which such Acts, Records and Proceedings shall be proved, and the Effect thereof.

Section 2. The Citizens of each State shall be entitled to all Privileges and Immunities of Citizens in the several States.

A Person charged in any State with Treason, Felony, or other Crime, who shall flee from Justice, and be found in another State, shall on demand of the executive Authority of the State from which he fled, be delivered up, to be removed to the State having Jurisdiction of the crime.

[No Person held to Service or Labour in one State, under the Laws thereof, escaping into another, shall, in Consequence of any Law or Regulation therein, be discharged from such Service or Labour, but shall be delivered up on Claim of the Party to whom such Service or Labour may be due.] [9]

Section 3. New States may be admitted by the Congress into this Union; but no new State shall be formed or erected within the Jurisdiction of any other State; nor any State be formed by the Junction of two or more States, or parts of States, without the Consent of the Legislatures of the States concerned as well as of the Congress.

The Congress shall have Power to dispose of and make all needful Rules and Regulations respecting the Territory or other Property belonging to the United States; and nothing in this Constitution shall be so construed as to Prejudice any Claims of the United States, or of any particular State.

Section 4. The United States shall guarantee to every State in this Union a Republican Form of Government, and shall protect each of them against Invasion; and on Application of the Legislature, or of the Executive (when the Legislature cannot be convened) against domestic Violence.

Article V

The Congress, whenever two thirds of both Houses shall deem it necessary, shall propose Amendments to this Constitution, or, on the Applicaion of the Legislatures of two-thirds of the several States, shall call a Convention for proposing Amendments, which, in either Case, shall be valid to all Intents and Purposes, as part of this Constitution, when ratified by the Legislatures of three-fourths of the several States, or by Conventions in three-fourths thereof, as the one or the other Mode of Ratification may be proposed by the Congress; Provided that no Amendment which may be made prior to the Year One thousand eight hundred and eight shall in any Manner affect the first and fourth Clauses in the Ninth Section of the first Article; and that no State, without its Consent, shall be deprived of its equal Suffrage in the Senate.

[9] *Superseded by the Thirteenth Amendment.*

Article VI

All Debts contracted and Engagements entered into, before the Adoption of this Constitution, shall be as valid against the United States under this Constitution, as under the Confederation.

This Constitution, and the Laws of the United States which shall be made in Pursuance thereof; and all Treaties made, or which shall be made, under the Authority of the United States, shall be the supreme Law of the Land; and the Judges in every State shall be bound thereby, any Thing in the Constitution or Laws of any State to the Contrary notwithstanding.

The Senators and Representatives before mentioned, and the Members of the several State Legislatures, and all executive and judicial Officers, both of the United States and of the several States, shall be bound by Oath or Affirmation to support this Constitution; but no religious Test shall ever be required as a qualification to any Office or public Trust under the United States.

Article VII

The Ratification of the Conventions of nine States shall be sufficient for the Establishment of this Constitution between the States so ratifying the same.

Done in Convention by the Unanimous Consent of the States present the Seventeenth Day of September in the Year of our Lord one thousand seven hundred and Eighty seven, and of the Independence of the United States of America the Twelfth. In Witness whereof We have hereunto subscribed our Names.

Articles in Addition to, and Amendment of, the Constitution of the United States of America, Proposed by Congress, and Ratified by the Legislatures of the Several States, Pursuant to the Fifth Article of the Original Constitution.

Amendment I [10]

Congress shall make no law respecting an establishment of religion, or prohibiting the free exercise thereof; or abridging the freedom of speech, or of the press; or the right of the people peaceably to assemble, and to petition the Government for a redress of grievances.

Amendment II

A well regulated Militia, being necessary to the security of a free State, the right of the people to keep and bear Arms shall not be infringed.

Amendment III

No Soldier shall, in time of peace, be quartered in any house, without the consent of the Owner, nor in time of war, but in a manner to be prescribed by law.

Amendment IV

The right of the people to be secure in their persons, houses, papers, and effects, against unreasonable searches and seizures, shall not be violated, and no Warrants shall issue, but upon probable cause, supported by Oath or affirmation, and particularly describing the place to be searched, and the persons or things to be seized.

Amendment V

No person shall be held to answer for a capital or otherwise infamous crime, unless on a presentment or indictment of a Grand Jury, except in cases arising in the land or naval forces, or in the Militia, when in actual service in time of War or public danger; nor shall any person be subject for the same offence to be twice put in jeopardy of life or limb; nor shall be compelled in any criminal case to be a witness against himself, nor be deprived of life, liberty, or property, without due process of law;

[10] *The first ten amendments were passed by Congress September 25, 1789. They were ratified by three-fourths of the states December 15, 1791.*

nor shall private property be taken for public use, without just compensation.

Amendment VI

In all criminal prosecutions, the accused shall enjoy the right to a speedy and public trial, by an impartial jury of the State and district wherein the crime shall have been committed, which district shall have been previously ascertained by law, and to be informed of the nature and cause of the accusation; to be confronted with the witnesses against him; to have compulsory process for obtaining witnesses in his favor, and to have the Assistance of Counsel for his defence.

Amendment VII

In suits at common law, where the value in controversy shall exceed twenty dollars, the right of trial by jury shall be preserved, and no fact tried by a jury, shall be otherwise reexamined in any Court of the United States, than according to the rules of the common law.

Amendment VIII

Excessive bail shall not be required, nor excessive fines imposed, nor cruel and unusual punishments inflicted.

Amendment IX

The enumeration in the Constitution, of certain rights, shall not be construed to deny or disparage others retained by the people.

Amendment X

The powers not delegated to the United States by the Constitution, nor prohibited by it to the States, are reserved to the States respectively, or to the people.

Amendment XI (1798) [11]

The Judicial power of the United States shall not be construed to extend to any suit in law or equity, commenced or prosecuted against one of the United States by Citizens of another State, or by Citizens or Subjects of any Foreign State.

Amendment XII (1804)

The Electors shall meet in their respective States and vote by ballot for President and Vice-President, one of whom, at least, shall not be an inhabitant of the same State with themselves; they shall name in their ballots the person voted for as President, and in distinct ballots the person voted for as Vice-President, and they shall make distinct lists of all persons voted for as President, and of all persons voted for as Vice-President, and of the number of votes for each, which lists they shall sign and certify, and transmit sealed to the seat of the government of the United States, directed to the President of the Senate;—The President of the Senate shall, in the presence of the Senate and House of Representatives, open all the certificates and the votes shall then be counted;—The person having the greatest number of votes for President, shall be the President, if such number be a majority of the whole number of Electors appointed; and if no person have such majority, then from the persons having the highest numbers not exceeding three on the list of those voted for as President, the House of Representatives shall choose immediately, by ballot, the President. But in choosing the President, the votes shall be taken by states, the representation from each state having one vote; a quorum for this purpose shall consist of a member or members from two-thirds of the states, and a majority of all the states shall be necessary to a choice. [And if the House of Representatives shall not choose a President whenever the right of choice shall devolve upon them, before the fourth day of March next following, then the Vice-President shall act as President, as in the case of the death or other constitutional disability of the President.] [12]—The person

---

[11] *Date of ratification.*

[12] *Superseded by the Twentieth Amendment.*

having the greatest number of votes as Vice-President, shall be the Vice-President, if such number be a majority of the whole number of Electors appointed, and if no person have a majority, then from the two highest numbers on the list, the Senate shall choose the Vice-President; a quorum for the purpose shall consist of two-thirds of the whole number of Senators, and a majority of the whole number shall be necessary to a choice. But no person constitutionally ineligible to the office of President shall be eligible to that of Vice-President of the United States.

Amendment XIII (1865)

Section 1. Neither slavery nor involuntary servitude, except as a punishment for crime whereof the party shall have been duly convicted, shall exist within the United States, or any place subject to their jurisdiction.

Section 2. Congress shall have power to enforce this article by appropriate legislation.

Amendment XIV (1868)

Section 1. All persons born or naturalized in the United States, and subject to the jurisdiction thereof, are citizens of the United States and of the State wherein they reside. No State shall make or enforce any law which shall abridge the privileges or immunities of citizens of the United States; nor shall any State deprive any person of life, liberty, or property, without due process of law; nor deny to any person within its jurisdiction the equal protection of the laws.

Section 2. Representatives shall be apportioned among the several States according to their respective numbers, counting the whole number of persons in each State, excluding Indians not taxed. But when the right to vote at any election for the choice of electors for President and Vice-President of the United States, Representatives in Congress, the Executive and Judicial officers of a State, or the members of the Legislature thereof, is denied to any of the male inhabitants of such State, being twenty-one years of age, and citizens of the United States, or in any way abridged, except for participation in rebellion, or other crime, the basis of representation therein shall be reduced in the proportion which the number of such male citizens shall bear to the whole number of male citizens twenty-one years of age in such State.

Section 3. No person shall be a Senator or Representative in Congress, or elector of President and Vice-President, or hold any office, civil or military, under the United States, or under any State, who, having previously taken an oath, as a member of Congress, or as an officer of the United States, or as a member of any State legislature, or as an executive or judicial officer of any State, to support the Constitution of the United States, shall have engaged in insurrection or rebellion against the same, or given aid or comfort to the enemies thereof. But Congress may by a vote of two-thirds of each House, remove such disability.

Section 4. The validity of the public debt of the United States, authorized by law, including debts incurred for payment of pensions and bounties for services in suppressing insurrection or rebellion, shall not be questioned. But neither the United States nor any State shall assume or pay any debt or obligation incurred in aid of insurrection or rebellion against the United States, or any claim for the loss or emancipation of any slave; but all such debts, obligations, and claims shall be held illegal and void.

Section 5. The Congress shall have the power to enforce, by appropriate legislation, the provisions of this article.

Amendment XV (1870)

Section 1. The right of citizens of the United States to vote shall not be denied or abridged by the United States or by any

State on account of race, color, or previous condition of servitude—

Section 2. The Congress shall have power to enforce this article by appropriate legislation.

Amendment XVI (1913)

The Congress shall have power to lay and collect taxes on incomes, from whatever source derived, without apportionment among the several States, and without regard to any census or enumeration.

Amendment XVII (1913)

The Senate of the United States shall be composed of two Senators from each State, elected by the people thereof, for six years; and each Senator shall have one vote. The electors in each State shall have the qualifications requisite for electors of the most numerous branch of the State legislatures.

When vacancies happen in the representation of any State in the Senate, the executive authority of such State shall issue writs of election to fill such vacancies: *Provided,* That the legislature of any State may empower the executive thereof to make temporary appointments until the people fill the vacancies by election as the legislature may direct.

This amendment shall not be so construed as to affect the election or term of any Senator chosen before it becomes valid as part of the Constitution.

Amendment XVIII (1919) [13]

Section 1. After one year from the ratification of this article the manufacture, sale, or transportation of intoxicating liquors within, the importation thereof into, or the exportation thereof from the United States and all territory subject to the jurisdiction thereof for beverage purposes is hereby prohibited.

Section 2. The Congress and the several States shall have concurrent power to enforce this article by appropriate legislation.

[13] *Repealed by the Twenty-first Amendment.*

Section 3. This article shall be inoperative unless it shall have been ratified as an amendment to the Constitution by the legislatures of the several States, as provided in the Constitution, within seven years from the date of the submission hereof to the States by the Congress.

Amendment XIX (1920)

The right of citizens of the United States to vote shall not be denied or abridged by the United States or by any State on account of sex.

Congress shall have power to enforce this article by appropriate legislation.

Amendment XX (1933)

Section 1. The terms of the President and Vice-President shall end at noon on the 20th day of January, and the terms of Senators and Representatives at noon on the 3d day of January, of the years in which such terms would have ended if this article had not been ratified; and the terms of their successors shall then begin.

Section 2. The Congress shall assemble at least once in every year, and such meeting shall begin at noon on the 3d day of January, unless they shall by law appoint a different day.

Section 3. If, at the time fixed for the beginning of the term of the President, the President elect shall have died, the Vice-President elect shall become President. If a President shall not have been chosen before the time fixed for the beginning of his term, or if the President elect shall have failed to qualify, then the Vice-President elect shall act as President until a President shall have qualified; and the Congress may by law provide for the case wherein neither a President elect nor a Vice-President elect shall have qualified, declaring who shall then act as President, or the manner in which one who is to act shall be selected, and such person shall act accordingly until a President or Vice-President shall have qualified.

Section 4. The Congress may by law

provide for the case of the death of any of the persons from whom the House of Representatives may choose a President whenever the right of choice shall have devolved upon them, and for the case of the death of any of the persons from whom the Senate may choose a Vice-President whenever the right of choice shall have devolved upon them.

Section 5. Sections 1 and 2 shall take effect on the 15th day of October following the ratification of this article.

Section 6. This article shall be inoperative unless it shall have been ratified as an amendment to the Constitution by the legislatures of three-fourths of the several States within seven years from the date of its submission.

Amendment XXI (1933)

Section 1. The eighteenth article of amendment to the Constitution of the United States is hereby repealed.

Section 2. The transportation or importation into any State, Territory, or possession of the United States for delivery or use therein of intoxicating liquors, in violation of the laws thereof, is hereby prohibited.

Section 3. This article shall be˘inoperative unless it shall have been ratified as an amendment to the Constitution by conventions in the several States, as provided in the Constitution, within seven years from the date of the submission hereof to the States by the Congress.

Amendment XXII (1951)

No person shall be elected to the office of the President more than twice, and no person who has held the office of President, or acted as President, for more than two years of a term to which some other person was elected President shall be elected to the office of the President more than once.

But this Article shall not apply to any person holding the office of President when this Article was proposed by the Congress, and shall not prevent any person who may be holding the office of President, or acting as President, during the term within which this Article becomes operative from holding the office of President or acting as President during the remainder of such term.

Amendment XXII (1961)

Section 1. The District constituting the seat of Government of the United States shall appoint in such manner as the Congress may direct:

A number of electors of President and Vice-President equal to the whole number of Senators and Representatives in Congress to which the District would be entitled if it were a State, but in no event more than the least populous State; they shall be in addition to those appointed by the States, but they shall be considered, for the purposes of the election of President and Vice-President, to be electors appointed by the State; and they shall meet in the District and perform such duties as provided by the twelfth article of amendment.

Section 2. The Congress shall have power to enforce this article by appropriate legislation.

Amendment XXIV (1964)

Section 1. The right of citizens of the United States to vote in any primary or other election for President or Vice-President, for electors for President or Vice-President, or for Senator or Representative in Congress, shall not be denied or abridged by the United States or any State by reason of failure to pay any poll tax or other tax.

Section 2. The Congress shall have power to enforce this article by appropriate legislation.

Amendment XXV (1967)

Section 1. In case of the removal of the President from office or of his death or resignation, the Vice-President shall become President.

Section 2. Whenever there is a vacancy in the office of the Vice-President, the President shall nominate a Vice-President who shall take office upon confirmation by a majority vote of both Houses of Congress.

Section 3. Whenever the President transmits to the President pro tempore of the Senate and the Speaker of the House of Representatives his written declaration that he is unable to discharge the powers and duties of his office, and until he transmits to them a written declaration to the contrary, such powers and duties shall be discharged by the Vice-President as Acting President.

Section 4. Whether the Vice-President and a majority of either the principal officers of the executive department or of such other body as Congress may by law provide, transmit to the President pro tempore of the Senate and the Speaker of the House of Representatives their written declaration that the President is unable to discharge the powers and duties of his office, the Vice-President shall immediately assume the powers and duties of the office as Acting President.

Thereafter, when the President transmits to the President pro tempore of the Senate and the Speaker of the House of Representatives his written declaration that no inability exists, he shall resume the powers and duties of his office unless the Vice-President and a majority of either the principal officers of the executive department or of such other body as Congress may by law provide, transmit within four days to the President pro tempore of the Senate and the Speaker of the House of Representatives their written declaration that the President is unable to discharge the powers and duties of his office. Thereupon Congress shall decide the issue, assembling within forty-eight hours for that purpose if not in session. If the Congress, within twenty-one days after receipt of the latter written declaration, or, if Congress is not in session, within twenty-one days after Congress is required to assemble, determines by two-thirds vote of both Houses that the President is unable to discharge the powers and duties of his office, the Vice-President shall continue to discharge the same as Acting President; otherwise, the President shall resume the powers and duties of his office.

Amendment XXVI (1971)

Section 1. The right of citizens of the United States, who are eighteen years of age or older, to vote shall not be denied or abridged by the United States or by any State on account of age.

Section 2. The Congress shall have power to enforce this article by appropriate legislation.

The following amendment was passed by Congress on March 22, 1972. As of November 1972 it had been approved by twenty-two states; thirty-eight are needed for ratification.

Amendment XXVII

Equality of rights under the law shall not be denied or abridged by the United States or by any state on account of sex.

index